TEACHING BUSINESS SUBJECTS

Third Edition

TEACHING
BUSINESS
SUBJECTS

LLOYD V. DOUGLAS

*Professor Emeritus and former head
of the Departments of Business and Business Education
University of Northern Iowa*

JAMES T. BLANFORD

*Professor of Accounting
University of Northern Iowa*

RUTH I. ANDERSON

*Professor of Business Education
North Texas State University*

PRENTICE-HALL, INC., Englewood Cliffs, N.J.

Library of Congress Cataloging in Publication Data

DOUGLAS, LLOYD VIRGIL,
  Teaching business subjects.

    Includes bibliographies.
    1. Business education. I. Blanford, James T.,
joint author. II. Anderson, Ruth I., joint author.
III. Title.
HF1106.D6 1973   650'.07   72-4728
ISBN 0-13-891457-5

10 9 8 7 6 5 4 3 2 1

Printed in the United States of America

PRENTICE-HALL INTERNATIONAL, INC., *London*
PRENTICE-HALL OF AUSTRALIA, PTY. LTD., *Sydney*
PRENTICE-HALL OF CANADA LTD., *Toronto*
PRENTICE-HALL OF INDIA PRIVATE LIMITED, *New Delhi*
PRENTICE-HALL OF JAPAN, INC., *Tokyo*

PREFACE

The reader will find this book is developed around three major and basic concepts of learning and teaching:

1. Learning is mostly an individual matter. Although certain general laws of adaptation, growth, conditioning, and learning are known, the many influencing factors present in the heritage and environment of each individual are so complex that each individual learner presents a different problem.

2. Hence, teaching combines an art and a science. Good teaching must be *based on* psychological principles known to be sound and must be *achieved through* techniques that are efficient and effective; to this extent it is a science. But the good teacher must be a true artist in *selecting and applying* these principles and techniques in accordance with the ever-changing needs of students, both as groups and as individuals.

3. New teaching techniques and new facts about learning are constantly being discovered and perfected. Modern teachers must be (and are) competent to intelligently choose from and add to this growing body of knowledge.

Thus, this book is not limited to presenting *a method* or *a best technique* for teaching various business subjects under specified conditions; it goes further than that. In the belief that teaching is both an art *and* a science, it also directs attention to many alternate and supplementary techniques, procedures, and devices which teachers may choose to use in appropriate situations.

The result of these basic concepts is a book that the authors are proud to present as a methods *text* for all business education students and as a handy reference or *handbook* for all business teachers and educators interested in ever-improving methods of teaching business subjects. It places carefully chosen emphasis on those known facts and established methods which the authors believe to be most helpful for all teaching of the various business subjects—a characteristic that will be greatly appreciated by the inexperienced teacher. Yet, it also encourages the future development and strengthening of the individual teacher as a true artist in the teaching profession by presenting numerous alternate and supplementary suggestions—and arranges it all under a readily understood plan of parts, chapters, and subheadings to form a most useful handbook for constant future reference.

An especially valuable feature of this book is the inclusion of special materials reviewing the learning process and its phases most important in teaching the skill subjects and the nonskill subjects. These materials provide welcome "bridges" between basic psychology and education courses and more advanced applications to the specific teaching situations in the business subjects.

Part Four, "Extending Learning Beyond the Classroom," brings into this single volume a treatment of that *professional extra* which so frequently is the difference between an ordinary business education program and one that achieves distinctly superior results. It is the belief of the authors that these three final chapters deal with three aspects of good education that are destined to become of ever-increasing importance.

An especially valuable group of projects and questions for discussion and case problems has been included for each chapter. These carefully selected questions and problems can readily form the basis for discussions that will both review and give greater meaning to the text material, as well as *extend* the learning to new related areas.

Finally, the authors wish to give credit to Dr. Harland E. Samson, Teacher-Educator in Distributive Education, formerly at the University of Northern Iowa and now at the University of Wisconsin, for contributing the original materials for the chapter "Cooperative Part-Time Business Education Programs."

L.V.D. / J.T.B. / R.I.A.

CONTENTS

7   Teaching Clerical Practice and Stenographic Practice   *216*

III. THE NONSKILL SUBJECTS   267

8   Teaching the Basic Business Subjects   *269*

I

introduction

The first four chapters of this book are intended to serve four major purposes:

1. To aid business teachers and prospective business teachers in "raising their sights" and broadening their professional horizons as they start this study of methods of improving their teaching

2. To provide a brief orientation to the entire field of business education and the emerging organizational environment in which the business teacher seems likely to work during the coming years

3. To provide a brief review of important psychological principles and educational procedures already studied by most business teachers and advanced students of education

4. To assist in making these same psychological principles *meaningful* to the business teacher and thus to establish an important foundation for future chapters and related studies

From Part One the reader should gain both general insight and understanding and specific professional knowledge.

experience *illegible*

1

THE BUSINESS TEACHER

A successful business teacher occupies an unusually favorable position in the teaching profession, since preparation automatically qualifies him for either of two careers—one in business or one in teaching. The experience he gains in either career usually strengthens his qualifications for both careers because his work, the dynamic, interesting, ever-changing subject matter—modern business, keeps him acquainted with his local business community and helps him to become a respected leader in it. In addition, his students are usually those extremely interested in their work and their future careers.

The modern business teacher is far removed from the too frequently painted picture of the stern pedagogue who devoted a great share of his time to being a drillmaster, a disciplinarian, and a penny-pinching character living in a twilight zone of citizenship. Occasionally one of the old school of relatively unprepared "commercial teachers" may have come close to fitting such a picture; such a teacher is comparatively rare today, however.

Instead, the successful business teacher of today is a happy, highly respected, and well-known leader in his school and community. Besides teaching his classroom work he is an active member of local social and civic clubs and organizations. He not only knows and visits in the homes of his students' parents but is similarly personally acquainted with the business people of his community. In the smaller and medium-sized towns of the nation, at least, he hears his name spoken in friendly greeting as he walks down the street.

Everywhere he is treated with respect. Frequently citizens and business people seek his advice.

Although he occupies a position of importance in his local school and community, his activities and personal acquaintances are not limited to this one locality. Through his memberships in professional and in business organizations he is an active member of many larger "communities" that are statewide and national in scope. Through his state business education association and state education association he gains professional friends throughout the state; he meets and talks with them at conventions each year. Similarly, through his membership in the NEA and in his own department of the NEA (the National Business Education Association) as well as in regional professional groups, he extends this pleasant and profitable experience to include the entire nation.

In brief, then, the successful business teacher of today has much to be happy about and much to look forward to throughout life. Let us now take a look at some of the many factors that help to give us a more complete picture of this career.

THE FORMER SETTING

Business education is a relative newcomer in the field of education. Like many of its predecessors, including even the field of science, in its infancy it was a "stepchild," not being completely accepted by the entire educational family and often quite uncertain of its own status. Thus, as has historically been true of various new areas of education, within the memory of many of us there often existed a connotation of unrespectability when the term *commercial education* was used in educational circles. In a very few localities this may still exist today, but it is the exception rather than the rule.

Perhaps, too, there was good reason for questioning the real values of "commercial education" in those earlier days. Admittedly the value of any study or group of studies pursued in schools is influenced by the ability, skill, and preparation of its teachers—and when a study is new to education it seems self-evident that really competent teachers for it must necessarily be scarce or nonexistent.

Thus, it was but natural that high school advisers of students frequently counseled their better students to study the more respectable, time-proven, "academic" or college-entrance subjects—leaving the commercial subjects quite largely for those pupils who for one reason or another were deemed unsuitable for any sizable amount of formal classroom education.

The result often tended to be a combination of relatively poorly prepared teachers holding classes that often were labeled the "dumping ground" of the school. The achievements in those classes often suffered when compared (loosely and unscientifically, perhaps!) with achievements attained in the more customary and standard academic classes with their more select group of students under the guidance of better-prepared teachers.

Actually, this setting has completely changed today—although some people, even in the education profession, still vividly recall the "dumping ground" era and can still hardly believe it already is a phase of history.

THE CHANGED SETTING

The setting in which the business teacher of today works is vastly improved over that of a quarter of a century ago. It probably was mostly in order to better overcome the impeding connotations attached to the term *commercial education,* and to permit the development of understandings and related implications more in accordance with existing conditions, that the use of the term *business education* came into common use. Commercial education is now officially considered to be an *obsolete* educational term.[1]

Details of the present-day *business education curriculums* appear in subsequent pages (see Chapter 2). It is recognized that this setting influences the picture of today's business teacher. It is sufficient at this time to state that business education no longer is limited to relatively narrow skills. Instead, it encompasses (*a*) information and abilities of personal and citizenship value to everyone, and also (*b*) relatively complete vocational education for each of several distinct career areas in our modern American business economy.

The business teacher of today carries the responsibility of assisting in the total education of all young people, *plus* responsibility for the career preparation of a more limited number of young people in one or more selected areas of work in the world of business.

AREAS OF SUBJECT SPECIALIZATION

The business teacher may either prepare to teach a rather wide variety of subjects or decide to choose one or more areas within business education in which to specialize. This is not an easy decision to make, since many factors must be considered. Perhaps of most importance in guiding the teacher's preparation is the question of the location, size, and type of school in which the teaching is to be done. For practical reasons, this frequently means the type of school in which the first teaching position is likely to be secured.

If the first position is likely to be in a one-business-teacher school, it is quite obvious that the teacher must be prepared to teach *all* business subjects commonly offered in such schools. In some states, such as those in the Midwest, these schools still exist. It should be noted, however, that the present trend is toward larger schools having more than one business teacher, each being somewhat specialized.

In general there are three main areas of subject specialization within the field of business education: (*a*) the secretarial and related office knowledges, abilities, and skills; (*b*) the accounting, bookkeeping, and related business management and office knowledges, abilities, and skills; and (*c*) the selling, retailing, merchandising, and related business management and store knowledges, abilities, and skills. Although the terms are not completely accurate, these frequently are referred to as the *secretarial*, the *accounting*, and the *distributive education* areas.

---

[1] Carter V. Good, *Dictionary of Education* (New York: McGraw-Hill Book Company, 1959), p. 112.

It is not to be inferred that all secondary business education is or should be grouped under these three classifications; such is not the case. For instance, certain phases of the above areas of preparation may be combined into a pattern of education designated as a *clerical curriculum*. Likewise the area known as *general,* or *basic, business education* is and should be of major importance in the high school; most of this, too, is derived from subject matter found in the three major areas of subject specialization.

Frequently the business teacher finds it desirable to be able to teach *all* business subjects offered in the school in which he secures his first teaching position. There is much to be said for the policy of making the undergraduate major in business education a relatively broad one, leaving a portion of the more highly specialized preparation for work on the graduate level. However, there is no one best answer to this problem for all students and for all situations; usually the student's college adviser is in a position to offer best advice on this point.

GENERAL AND LIBERAL ARTS PREPARATION

Like all teachers, the business teacher must be an educated person. It seems quite evident that the better informed one is about everything associated with life, the better his chances are of being an excellent and valuable teacher. Today nearly every degree-granting college specifically provides for this phase of the student's education, and it need not be discussed at length here. The business teacher should realize, however, that this *is* an important part of his preparation for becoming an outstanding teacher.

One should not make the mistake, however, of believing that abstract ability to reason and make judgments can always be successfully transferred to some other field of thinking once it has been successfully developed in one field of thinking. Sound reasoning must be based on knowledge and mastery of facts upon which to base the reasoning! One cannot afford to use too much of his college time in broad, liberal studies to the detriment of his knowledge of the field of study to which he proposes to devote the major portion of his career.

MINOR SUBJECT SPECIALIZATIONS

Most colleges, although not all, require degree students to have one or more "minor" areas of specialization or the equivalent. There probably is no one minor area that is *especially* to be recommended for all business teachers. The selection of the minor or minors *should* vary with such factors as

1. The interests, aptitudes, and abilities of the individual student
2. The area of major specialization of the student
3. The previous education and experience of the student
4. The probable demands of the schools in that section of the nation in which the student expects to teach
5. The student's plans for future graduate work

Here again the student's adviser is most likely to be in the best position to assist him in making his choice. However, there are three related ideas that the prospective business teacher might well consider in evaluating or selecting his minor preparation. First, there is a growing trend for the teacher with a major in business education to be called upon to teach very little, if anything, outside of his major area. This is true because the smaller schools that offer very little true vocational business education and that have need for only one part-time business teacher tend to prefer (and *should* prefer) teachers with majors in the more academic subjects; one with minor preparation in the field may be able to teach the business subjects in such schools. The significance of this statement will be better understood by the reader after completing the following chapter.

Second, somewhere there are schools and situations in which the business teacher who desires can *also* teach in the field of almost any "normal" minor. Regardless of what one's minor preparation may be, it is quite possible to find use for it in the teaching profession as a business teacher.

Third, the business education major should give due consideration to assuring himself of a good understanding of the field of economics. In some colleges and universities this may mean that a minor specialization in the field of economics is advisable; in others this becomes a part of the business education major.

The Minor in Business Education

Many business teachers have majors in other subject fields with only minor specialization and preparation in the field of business education. This often proves to be an excellent preparation for the teaching profession, and certainly it is to be especially encouraged for those teachers who expect to start their careers in the smaller high schools but who perhaps feel that eventually they would prefer to teach in some subject field other than business education.

Obviously most business education minors cannot be prepared to teach in all phases of business education. Thus, they usually find it advisable to confine their specialization mostly to one of the three main areas of subject specialization already mentioned as composing the field of business education. Again, the college adviser should be in the best position to assist in making this choice. It might be pointed out, however, that by far the largest student enrollment in any business subject is to be found in typewriting.

PROFESSIONAL PREPARATION

State certification requirements are usually basic in determining the amount and kind of special professional preparation a business teacher must have for entering the teaching profession. The student usually has but little choice in this.

However, it is worth noting that most of this preparation (commonly referred to as *education* and *psychology*) actually consists of learning how to understand, deal with, control, and lead other people. This is the basic study needed for success in the entire field of human relations—and is especially valuable for *all* who hold leadership positions, since any leadership position normally indirectly involves teaching or "guiding the learning" of others.

Contrary to commonly held ideas, *teaching* is no longer a simple process of "telling"— of "giving out information"— of "lecturing"— and of "making and checking assignments." Today, for the professionally successful teacher, it has become *more* a process of motivating, managing, and guiding and assisting the student *as he learns*. The teacher typically has many and varied mechanical and electronic instructional "tools" available as aids to learning. The master teacher plans in advance so that his students can make maximum use of these aids. He prepares appropriate audiovisual learning materials which he organizes in "learning centers" ready for his students to use. He then often works with individual students, and he holds informal discussions with small groups of students as they go about their learning. As a professional worker, he is at all times endeavoring to assist each individual student to *succeed* in his learning; he knows that "failing" a student is a poor substitute for helping him obtain an education!

All of this means that the business teacher today *needs* to include in his professional preparation (*a*) a thorough understanding of human psychology and human behavior, (*b*) an ability to operate, maintain, and demonstrate modern mechanical and electronic learning aids, (*c*) a thorough grounding in methods of applying psychological principles to the specific learning situations and problems to be found in the business courses he plans to teach, and (*d*) a suitable experience (student teaching) in integrating and applying all these professional knowledges and abilities in an actual teaching situation under competent supervision.

Thus, we can understand why the professional preparation of the business *teacher* also serves a unique function in at the same time *better* preparing that same individual for service and leadership in positions in the business world. It is small wonder that many large businesses, looking for young people with high managerial potential, frankly admit they especially like to find business teachers for such positions.

PERSONAL DEVELOPMENT

Some whose professional, general, and specialized subject-matter preparation in college seems to be about as perfect as possible turn out to be failures as teachers; others enjoy extremely successful careers. Likewise it may be said that many with relatively inferior college subject-matter preparation become extremely successful teachers. Why is this?

Almost invariably the key to a successful career lies in the individual as a person. This does not mean that proper subject matter and professional preparation is unimportant; on the contrary, it is distinctly important. Yet it is quite widely agreed that the individual as a person (or as a personality) has more influence on teaching success than has the individual as an educated product of the subject-matter classroom!

Certainly the business teacher is no exception to this. Owing to his customary work with his business community and thus with a more diverse group of adults and students, it probably is especially important for the business teacher to be ever alert to develop himself personally in every way possible.

EXTRACURRICULAR ACTIVITIES

Various group activities customarily referred to as *extracurricular* hold special significance for the business teacher. First, they provide him with one of his best and most practicable means of personal development while a student and also after graduation. Second, he will find they may be effectively used to assist in achieving the personal growth and development objectives that he desires for the youth whom he teaches.

The most successful business teacher today is likely to be one who has participated rather widely and intensively in college activities providing opportunities for group participation and leadership experience, and who sees to it that the students under his guidance also have adequate opportunity for a similar type of participation.

As a citizen and as a member of his community, the business teacher is likely to have opportunity to participate in community groups such as the Chamber of Commerce, the Junior Chamber of Commerce, the Business and Professional Women's Club, and service clubs such as Lions International, Rotary International, and Kiwanis. As a business teacher he will be called upon to give leadership and guidance as a sponsor for various organizations and groups of students.

Although most extracurricular activities sponsored by high schools provide important experience opportunities for students, the business teacher should perhaps have his attention especially directed to two national organizations for business students—FBLA (Future Business Leaders of America) and DECA (Distributive Education Clubs of America).

The Future Business Leaders of America is a youth organization sponsored by the business teachers of America and was originally developed through their national professional organization, the National Business Education Association. The NBEA is affiliated with the National Education Association and is the world's largest association of business teachers.

Today the high school and college divisions of FBLA are incorporated as Future Business Leaders of America–Phi Beta Lambda, Inc., and in 1971 approximately 110,000 student members regularly received its publication *Tomorrow's Business Leader*. More than five thousand local chapters have been organized throughout the nation, including Alaska, Hawaii, and Puerto Rico, with state chapters formed and annual state leadership conferences held in forty-five states. Delegates from state and local chapters attend an annual National Leadership Conference. It is a highly democratic type of organization with membership open to *all* business students in both public and parochial schools. Business teachers should become fully informed about it and its services for business students.[2]

2 For complete information consult NBEA publications or write to FBLA–PBL, Inc., 1201 Sixteenth Street, N.W., Washington, D.C.

The Distributive Education Clubs of America accept as members only those students enrolled in regularly approved programs in distributive education. These programs are organized under relatively high standards and are financially backed by federal vocational funds; they have the expert guidance of specially prepared career-oriented local coordinators and business teachers. State chapters have been organized and state leadership conferences are held in all states. Like FBLA–PBL, DECA also holds an annual National Leadership Conference, and its publication *The DECA Distributor* now goes to some 110,000 members.[3]

BUSINESS EXPERIENCE

Actual business experience for pay should be a part of the professional preparation of every business teacher. This is one of the principles adopted by the National Association for Business Teacher Education, and a number of state and city requirements for fully approved business teachers include it in some form.

The preferred business experience is that which is procured under the planned supervision of a regular business teacher training college or university; many of them now have such programs in effect as a recognized part of the professional preparation of business teachers.

However, there is much to be said in favor of such actual business experience as the business teacher may gain on the job either part time or full time prior to graduation, or during summer vacations after graduation. The important factor is that the business teacher who has had such actual business experience gains in know-how, in understanding of the requirements of the practical business world, in self-confidence, and in ability to win and hold the full confidence of his students.

It is to be preferred that business experience gained be in positions directly related to the subject area that is taught and that it include positions in different firms and involve both technical skills or knowledges and some degree of managerial or administrative responsibility.

THE BUSINESS TEACHER
IN THE SMALL HIGH SCHOOL

In some parts of the nation, as in the Midwest, some rather small high schools still exist. A high school that is considered "small" in the East, for instance, may well be considered "large" in some other areas. The national trend, however, is toward reorganizing small districts into larger ones. In Iowa, for example, in 1955 there were 819 separate high schools and the *median* enrollment for all was only about 85 students—which means that half of these high schools had *fewer* than 85 students! By 1964 reorganization of districts had reduced the number of high schools to 500 and had increased the

[3] For further information consult your state supervisor of distributive education or write to DECA, Inc., 1010 Vermont Avenue, N.W., Washington, D.C.

median enrollment to 120 students. By 1971 the number of districts had been further reduced to 435, and the median enrollment had increased to about 150 students.

One may wonder how the one business teacher usually found in such schools can possibly do well the task of teaching all the different business subjects that are or seemingly should be offered in the high school. However, frequently the work of that one business teacher is looked upon by the community as being a major contribution of its high school.

The standards of vocational proficiency reached by students in certain technical subjects may be relatively limited as compared with the achievements of students in those schools that are able to provide more specialized vocational curriculums. Yet these business subjects often provide the *only* readily marketable education that the smaller school has to offer its students—and thus become quite important for that school and community.

Also, it must be remembered that in the small high school the business teacher has a *much* better opportunity to become personally acquainted with individual students, their backgrounds, their abilities, their needs, and their hopes and ambitions. It must be remembered that usually it is the personal characteristics of the individual *as a person* that count most heavily in his future success. Frequently the business teacher in the small high school is able to prepare students who, though somewhat inferior in certain aspects of technical and skill development, have actually acquired a relatively superior type of personal development and ambition which enables them to compete successfully in the business world.

THE BUSINESS TEACHER
IN THE LARGE HIGH SCHOOL

As soon as a high school becomes sufficiently large to require the services of two business teachers instead of one, each teacher tends to specialize in some major area of the work. Thus in a two-business-teacher high school, one teacher is likely to teach mostly subjects such as typewriting, shorthand, and secretarial training, while the other one teaches subjects such as general business, bookkeeping, business law, or distributive education.

As the size of the staff increases, the scope of the subject offerings also tends to expand and the degree of specialization of each teacher to become more in evidence. Thus the business teacher in the large high school customarily becomes quite specialized in one or more subjects—bookkeeping, retailing, general business, typewriting, secretarial subjects, and so on (further details appear in Chapter 2).

Accordingly, one who plans for a professional career as a business teacher in a large high school, or in a high school of commerce in a metropolitan area, should give special consideration to the following factors in his career planning:

1. Sound undergraduate preparation including broad general education and also a broad base of business education on which to build special preparation later.

2. The necessity for a master's degree or equivalent graduate study, including additional preparation in the chosen specialized area of business education.

3. The need for realistic, actual (paid) business experience in preparation for the career desired. (Usually it is safe to estimate that this should be about one year of full-time business experience or its equivalent. Customarily greater importance is attached to such experience when it is obtained under competent college supervision.)

4. The frequent requirement that other teaching experience be gained prior to entering a more specialized position in the larger high school. (This requirement often has the effect of causing business teachers to start their careers in smaller one-business-teacher high schools.)

5. The desirability of taking advantage of every possible opportunity to develop personal leadership abilities.

In return for this special preparation, the position of business teacher in a large high school customarily offers superior rewards in terms of salary, security, and living conditions.

THE BUSINESS TEACHER
IN POST–HIGH SCHOOL WORK

For most of us the small high school offers a real opportunity for acquiring early experience in a setting where we can fully understand the many facets of education at work. Moreover it offers us much in the way of opportunity for personal development through assuming broader school and community responsibilities. For some business teachers it provides a most satisfying permanent career.

Yet for most business teachers the challenge and appeal of a career in a large high school in due time becomes even more attractive. Often the same can be said about the career opportunities offered by junior colleges, community colleges, four-year colleges, business colleges, and other forms of post–high school education.

Thus the business teacher should be fully aware of the many opportunities that will eventually unfold for him. Certainly he has an unusually wide selection of possible careers within the field of business education from which to choose. To this, of course, may be added an even wider variety of potential careers of comparable nature in the business world itself should later experience indicate the wisdom of making the change away from the teaching profession.

It must be recognized that success in most of these post–high school careers in the field of business education requires much special preparation. The master's degree customarily is the minimum educational requirement, and today we find many business teachers employed in high school and college positions who hold the doctor's degree.

The federal Vocational Education Act of 1963 specifically included "business and office" education *for the first time* among the federally recognized "vocational" fields. Because of the financial encouragement of this act and its subsequent amendments, this nation has since experienced a *very* rapid growth in the number of "area vocational schools" and community colleges. During 1970–71 new community colleges (or junior colleges) were organized at the rate of one every week! In all these new schools, which primarily serve post–high school and adult education, business education is of distinctly major importance. This has brought about a tremendous increase in the demand for well-qualified "vocational" business teachers at the post–high school and adult education levels.

ADULT AND EVENING CLASSES

Contrary to popular notions, education does not stop with the granting of a diploma or a college degree. In recognition of this, modern society is now providing many means of assisting individuals to obtain this needed "continuing" education. Evening classes, adult classes, forums, extension classes, and clinics of many varieties are to be found in abundance today throughout most parts of the nation.

The business teacher perhaps has greater opportunity to participate in these forms of education than has any other teacher. Even in the smallest communities evening classes, when offered, customarily include such subjects as typewriting, shorthand, and bookkeeping. Usually a demand exists for many other special courses for local citizens and business people and is dormant only because a qualified instructor is not available. The list of special adult and evening classes offered in large cities sometimes includes thirty or more separate subjects in the field of business education.

Often these special forms of additional education provide real opportunities attractive to the business teacher owing to factors such as these:

1. Substantial extra pay is usually received for the work involved.
2. Valuable experience is gained in working with adults.
3. The business teacher gains a better insight into the business education activities and needs of adults in his community.
4. The work and abilities of the business teacher become more widely known and respected among the parents and citizens of the community, with resulting high prestige for the business teacher and for business education.
5. In many cases the business teacher thereby has an opportunity to continue serving and improving the vocational abilities of his pupils who have graduated from school, resulting in greater pride in his work and in his product.
6. Not infrequently the contacts made with these adults in evening classes aid materially in the placement of students on suitable jobs in the future. (Such contacts have been known to assist the teacher, also, in securing summer or permanent employment in the business world!)

Whenever possible, the student preparing to become a business teacher should include in his program of studies appropriate preparation for organizing and teaching adult and evening classes. Frequently these classes require the use of special materials and methods adapted to shorter courses and to adult students.

ACQUIRING PROFESSIONAL STATURE

Teaching is today considered one of the world's important professions. As is true of other professions, within the teaching profession there exist various levels of professional attainment and various areas of professional work. Within each area of work, such as business education, an important part of the satisfaction derived by the professional worker is evidenced by his level of professional attainment, or his stature within the profession.

Acquiring a certificate as a business teacher actually constitutes admission into the teaching profession. In most states two or more types, or levels, of certification are available to business teachers. One type of certificate may be granted on the basis of the bachelor's degree with appropriate professional education, but a higher-level certificate may be granted on the basis of the master's degree or thirty semester hours of graduate credit, satisfactory teaching experience, or other considerations. It appears, then, that one route by which the business teacher may advance to a higher standing in his profession is through the securing of appropriate graduate credit. This method is recognized and used almost universally.

But of perhaps even greater importance to the teacher in terms of personal satisfaction, prestige, and promotions is the attainment of *professional stature* through participation and work within the teaching profession itself. It is assumed, of course, that basic to this is a "job well done" at all times in the classroom. But for true professional success it is equally important that the teacher join hands with others in the profession in constantly guarding and improving the work and standards of the profession.

Here in America it is proper and fitting that such professional associations be democratically formed on a completely voluntary basis, and that has become customary in all professions. Thus, here in the United States members of the teaching profession have voluntarily joined together into one national association known as the National Education Association (NEA); every teacher in the nation is eligible for membership in this professional association which has been in existence over a century and now numbers over a million members.

There are many, many opportunities for the business teacher to profit from and gain stature in his profession, and we can only briefly indicate a few of them here. For an average voluntary outlay of but a few dollars per month (far less than the common laborer often pays in union dues in order to work at his trade!), the business teacher may belong to his own local, state, regional, and national professional associations and be eligible to attend and participate in their many conferences and conventions, and have his own monthly, quarterly, and special professional magazines and bulletins currently on his desk. This is where he needs them and where he will *use* them.

Of special importance to business teachers is their own National Business Education Association. The NBEA has a full-time executive director and staff working in Washington, D.C., on behalf of business education throughout the nation. It provides many services to business teachers, including typewriting tests, monthly and quarterly and special professional magazines, regional representative assemblies, National Business Entrance Tests, and awards and certificates. It is also the headquarters for the national organization Future Business Leaders of America. Most state business education associations are affiliates of NBEA.

Business education students preparing to become business teachers should take advantage of the opportunity offered them by most of their professional associations to obtain student membership at reduced price. For instance, two years of student membership in the NBEA would, at low cost, provide a professional library of sixteen issues of the *Business Education Forum*, eight or more issues of the *National Business Education Quarterly*, and two issues of the *National Business Education Yearbook*. In addition there would be the satisfaction of a two-year history of professional membership plus opportunities of attending conventions and other professional meetings.

It should not be inferred that professional membership alone will result in recognized professional stature; such is not the case. However, if one will systematically read the professional literature that such memberships bring to him he will be assured of "keeping up" with his profession and thus of being in a good position to attain the desired stature. To this should be added attendance at conventions and meetings held by his professional associations, with active participation in discussions, programs, and forums whenever opportunity is presented.

Perhaps the following list of suggestions will be found helpful as a guide in better preparing for real achievement in the teaching profession as a business teacher:

1. Maintain your professional memberships, always; start early. This should include at least the NEA, NBEA, your state education association and state business education association, your local association if there is one, and the American Vocational Association (AVA) if you are to teach vocational aspects of business education.
   (*Note:* NBEA membership automatically includes state and regional association membership.)
2. Subscribe for one or two good professional business education monthly magazines in addition to your association literature.
3. Systematically read the literature that reaches you relative to your profession.
4. Attend *and participate* in the professional conferences, forums, and conventions that are available to you.
5. When you feel that you have achieved notably in your teaching efforts, or that you have an especially valuable idea for the teaching profession, share it with others in the profession by submitting it in written form for publication.
6. Acquire recent and appropriate business experience.
7. Continue working to meet requirements for any advance-level certification that may remain available to you; among other things, this normally includes graduate study.
8. Continue your *personal* development as an individual; this may well include participation in and acceptance of leadership responsibilities in your local community civic groups.

FUTURE CAREER POSSIBILITIES

No one is competent to completely and accurately predict the future. It is true that many excellent careers were available a generation ago that no longer exist. Rapid changes are to be expected during the next generation, and, of course, career opportunities will change. However, the well-prepared business education student would seem to have unusual assurance of excellent and dependable career opportunities of many varieties during his lifetime; he has basic preparation for two of the major fields of endeavor known to mankind, the education profession and the business world.

Moreover it should be recognized that our high schools even today are increasing in size rapidly; this means greater opportunities for more of the special curriculums such as those provided by business education. It likewise means relatively greater opportunities for business teachers to teach only their major area of specialization. And as the years go by the tendency definitely is for a greater percentage of youth to secure post–high school education, which already is directing attention to the coming need for more teachers with advanced preparation for teaching in these post–high school positions—a tendency that will continue to give the business teacher excellent opportunities for ever-expanding and growing careers in the teaching profession.

Finally, it must be remembered that our entire American economy is primarily a *business* economy. So long as we remain dedicated to the philosophy of democracy and freedom and respect for the individual we are going to maintain our American system of free competitive enterprise based on property rights and the profit motive; and that is the other major field of endeavor into which the business education teacher stands constantly ready to enter. Its opportunities likewise appear relatively unlimited.

PROJECTS AND QUESTIONS FOR DISCUSSION

1. Investigate and report on the size, organization, and services of the National Education Association.

2. Prepare a chart or an outline showing the regions, divisions, and services of the National Business Education Association.

3. Obtain the names and locations of the officers of your own state business education association, and report on the services of this association. Is it affiliated with NBEA? With AVA?

4. Investigate and report on the number and locations of FBLA and DECA chapters in your own state.

5. Prepare a display of current professional publications of special interest to business teachers.

6. Investigate and report on the services offered by your own State Department of Public Instruction for business education.

7. "A good business education teacher should have sufficient breadth of training to teach any business subject. For this reason all prospective business teachers should be required to be qualified to teach shorthand as well as basic business subjects."

Do you agree or disagree? What problems are connected with the points raised in the statement?

8. A state legislature recently passed a law requiring all students graduating from high school in that state to complete two units of foreign language, two units of history, three units of English, two units of science, and two units of mathematics. The typical high school requires sixteen units for graduation. Thus, the above law would permit students to have approximately five units of electives. Do you believe this law is a good one? Why or why not?

9. A teacher stated, "Why should I go to the trouble of starting a business club in my high school—I have all I can do now in preparing my lessons properly and teaching well the classes to which I am assigned. If I sponsor a business club for my students then surely my classroom teaching will suffer." Does this teacher have a valid argument?

10. Two teachers are discussing the relative merits of professional organizations for teachers versus the merits of the American Federation of Teachers which is affiliated with the American Federation of Labor. One teacher believes that teachers will obtain more benefits from a professional organization while the other favors the teachers' union. What are your points of view concerning the relative merits of the two types of organizations for teachers?

11. A superintendent of schools has stated: "I will never employ a beginning teacher; the poorest teaching is done during the first two years of teaching. A teacher really comes into his own after he has obtained several years experience." Do you believe this to be true? Why or why not?

CASE PROBLEMS

1. William Lloyd, a beginning business teacher, was employed for the coming year in Harlin High School. Prior to accepting the position he was informed by the superintendent of schools that he would be assigned to teach only business subjects. Lloyd was quite happy with this arrangement, as he did not wish to teach outside his major field even though he was theoretically qualified to do so because he had a minor in sociology.

When Lloyd reported to his school in the fall he found that (without his knowledge) he had been assigned to teach a class in social problems, a senior sociology course. He talked with the superintendent and reminded him of his statement during the employment interview that he would not be required to teach outside his major field. The superintendent regretted that he had to assign Lloyd to the social problems class, but scheduling difficulties made this necessary.

Lloyd feels he is being treated unfairly and his sense of justice tells him that he should resign in protest. Discuss the pros and cons of this situation.

2. John Samson, an undergraduate business education major in a state university, has just had a conference with his faculty adviser. The adviser has been concerned with John's grade-point average which is just above the minimum required by the college for graduation. John is a student with above-average ability, but his grades do not reflect his ability because of his interest and participation in extracurricular activities at the university. Time spent in these activities has been taken away from his studies.

John tells his adviser he is not too concerned about his grades because he feels it is important for a teacher to be able to get along well with people and his extracurricular activities are helping him greatly in this respect. "It is just as important," says John, "for a prospective teacher to have a solid social background as it is to have a solid academic background." Do you believe John is correct? What are the factors to consider in this case?

3. Harold Swanson is a student in a methods course concerned with specific methods of teaching business subjects. Harold feels quite bitter about the professional education courses he has had to take as a part of the requirements for graduation. He expresses the point of view in class that he would be much better off if he were permitted to take more specialized courses in business rather than the fifteen semester hours he has been required to take in educational psychology, introduction to education, and problems in education.

Although he does not say so there is the implication that he also includes the professional business education courses in this category. He feels these courses have been a waste of time and are too impractical. Is Harold right? What arguments could you give in support of his point of view? What arguments could you present in contradiction?

4. Mr. James Sloan is a beginning business teacher in the town of Van Horne, population four thousand. One day during the noon hour while lunching with a colleague he complains bitterly about the community and the townspeople in the community. Mr. Sloan's complaints center about the coolness of the townspeople toward the teachers in the school.

School has been in session about two months and not once have people in the community taken the trouble to invite him into their homes or even bothered to introduce themselves to him. Mr. Sloan feels that since he is a newcomer to the community it is proper etiquette for the townspeople to make the overtures toward making him feel a member of the community. He believes that it is not up to him to make any effort to become better acquainted.

Should he continue to wait or should he take the initiative in becoming acquainted? If he does take the initiative will he not be considered too forward? Perhaps he is right—the townspeople are cold and unfeeling and perhaps he should leave this community at his earliest opportunity. What do you think?

SUGGESTED READINGS

Birkholz, John R., "Teacher Preparation for the Community College," *The Balance Sheet,* October 1970, pp. 54–55, 69.

Blanford, James T., "Some Problems of Beginning Teachers," *Journal of Business Education,* January 1953.

Culver, Gordon F., "Today's Business Teachers: Directors of Learning," *The Balance Sheet,* May 1971, p. 339. Guest editorial.

Douglas, Lloyd V., *Business Education* (a volume of *The Library of Education*), The Center for Applied Research in Business Education, 1963, pp. 1–107.

Eisen, Irving, *Careers in Teaching and Education,* National B'nai B'rith Vocational Service Office, Washington, D.C., 1970, pp. 1–40.

Eyster, Elvin S., "Business Education and the Junior College," *Journal of Business Education,* April 1971, pp. 268–69. Editorial.

———, "The Role of Business Education Associations," *Journal of Business Education,* April 1969, pp. 270–71. Editorial.

Fuller, Marietta Cain, "Small Schools Can Initiate Vocational Business Programs, *Journal of Business Education,* December 1970, pp. 96–97.

Herndon, Frank M., "A Career in Teaching the Business Subjects," *Business Education Forum,* January 1964, p. 7.

Jelly, Herbert M., "Who Teaches Consumers?" *Business Education World,* January–February 1970, pp. 18–19.

Kessel, Robert M., "The Critical Requirements for Secondary School Business Teachers Based on an Analysis of Critical Incidents, "*DPE Journal*, September 1959. The 1958 DPE Research Award Study.

Lamb, Marion M., *Your First Year of Teaching*, Monograph No. 103, pp. 1–25. Cincinnati: South-Western Publishing Co., 1969.

Lowe, Ross E., "Interviewing for That First Teaching Position," *The Balance Sheet*, March 1971, pp. 244–46, 288.

Muse, Paul F., "Dare We Be Professional?" *Business Education Forum,* January 1964, p. 1.

Nolan, C. A., Carlos K. Hayden, and Dean R. Malsbary, *Principles and Problems in Business Education*, Part V, "The Business Teacher," pp. 589–628; Chap. 22, "The Business Teacher—His Work and Qualifications"; Chap. 23, "The Business Teacher—His Opportunities and Professional Activities." Cincinnati: South-Western Publishing Co., 1967.

Olson, Milton C., "Encouraging Professional Growth," *National Business Education Quarterly*, May 1962, pp. 54–59.

Pender, Albert, "Guidance in Business Education," *The Balance Sheet*, September 1970, pp. 7–11, 30.

Piland, William E., and William K. Ogelvie, "The Community College Business Teacher," *Journal of Business Education*, October 1969, pp. 16–17.

Smith, Gary R., "The Teacher as a Successful Salesman," *Business Education World*, September–October 1970, pp. 21–22.

Smith, Palsy C., and Ruth B. Woolschlager, "Prospective Business Teachers See Themselves as Others See Them," *The Balance Sheet*, March 1969, pp. 307–308, 336.

Thistlethwaite, Robert L., "To Beginning Teachers—Some Words of Council, Caution, and Encouragement," *Business Education Forum*, March 1963, p. 17.

———, "An Open Letter to a Beginning Teacher," *Business Education Forum,* February 1969, pp. 26–27.

Tonne, Herbert A., "Public Doubt about Education," *Journal of Business Education*, April 1971, pp. 270–71.

Wanous, S. J., "A Chronology of Business Education in the United States," *Business Education Forum*, XXIII, 1969, 36–44.

chapter

2

THE BUSINESS EDUCATION CURRICULUMS

The business teacher works mostly within the framework of an organized educational group, such as the high school. His objectives form a part of the objectives of the school itself. At the same time, he must achieve these objectives through a planned organization of his own area of work within the school. Frequently this planned organization of the work of business education in a school system is referred to as the *business education curriculum* or the *business education curriculums;*[1] it will vary from school to school, depending on the needs, objectives, facilities, and desires of the community being served. Since methods of instruction used by the business teacher will be materially influenced by (*a*) the objectives of the school and curriculum within which he teaches and by (*b*) that phase of the curriculum in which he is teaching at any given time, it is the purpose of this chapter to present some of the curriculum settings the business teacher is likely to encounter. The best curriculum is the one that has been intelligently planned to meet the needs of a specific school and community; no one curriculum is "best" for all schools. Yet intelligent planning must be based on knowledge of the experience of others. To succeed in his professional work as a teacher the business teacher must be

[1] The term *business education* is quite commonly used in preference to the term *business* (alone) to avoid confusion with the function of caring for the business transactions of the school itself. Thus a school may have a "business office" which is quite apart from the instructional department performing the function of "business education."

prepared to offer constructive advice and suggestions relative to the organizational plan within which he is to work.

THE GOALS OF SECONDARY EDUCATION

The field of work of the business teacher extends from the junior high school through the senior high school, the junior college, various types of adult and post–high school work, and college and university and post-college education. However, we are most concerned here with teaching students of the adolescent age; in general this encompasses grades seven through fourteen, commonly known as *secondary education*. The major portion of the work of the business teacher with which we are here concerned is to be found in grades nine through twelve in our American education system. Thus, it is appropriate that we briefly review the main objectives or goals of secondary education, of which business education forms a part.

A relatively brief yet practical and authoritative statement bearing on this question is to be found in the *Ten Imperative Needs of Youth,* as set forth by the National Association of Secondary School Principals in *Planning for American Youth.*[2] Actually, these ten "imperative needs" are a portion of this NASSP summary of *Education for All American Youth,*[3] a publication of the Educational Policies Commission of the NEA. The business teacher will do well to keep these ten imperative needs in mind as a background and framework within which to pursue his professional career.

TEN IMPERATIVE NEEDS
OF YOUTH OF SECONDARY SCHOOL AGE

1. All youth need to develop salable skills and those understandings and attitudes that make the worker an intelligent and productive participant in economic life. To this end, most youth need supervised work experience as well as education in the skills and knowledge of their occupations.

2. All youth need to develop and maintain good health and physical fitness.

3. All youth need to understand the rights and duties of the citizen of a democratic society, and to be diligent and competent in the performance of their obligations as members of the community and citizens of the state and nation.

4. All youth need to understand the significance of the family for the individual and society and the conditions conducive to successful family life.

5. All youth need to know how to purchase and use goods and services intelligently, understanding both the values received by the consumer and the economic consequences of their acts.

---

[2] *Planning for American Youth, An Educational Program for Youth of Secondary School Age* (Washington, D.C.: National Association of Secondary School Principals, 1944), p. 43.

[3] Educational Policies Commission, *Education for All American Youth* (Washington, D.C.: National Education Association, 1944).

6. All youth need to understand the methods of science, the influence of science on human life, and the main scientific facts concerning the nature of the world and of man.

7. All youth need opportunities to develop their capacities to appreciate beauty in literature, art, music, and nature.

8. All youth need to be able to use their leisure time well and to budget it wisely, balancing activities that yield satisfactions to the individual with those that are socially useful.

9. All youth need to develop respect for other persons, to grow in their insight into ethical values and principles, and to be able to live and work cooperatively with others.

10. All youth need to grow in their ability to think rationally, to express their thoughts clearly, and to read and listen with understanding.

Although many books and articles have been written in attempts to clearly explain the goals of secondary education, we believe that no better or clearer guide can be found for the business teacher than these ten "imperative needs" set forth by our Educational Policies Commission of the NEA and by the principals of our American secondary schools through their own NASSP. It is urged that they be studied carefully and thoughtfully for the purpose of helping to identify readily those phases of business education that may well contribute to some, several, or all of these needs of youth.

THE BROAD FIELD OF BUSINESS EDUCATION

Business education is but one of the many areas into which the entire secondary school program is divided in our efforts to plan suitable mediums through which to achieve our American educational goals. The final success of our entire secondary program must be measured in terms of accomplishment for each individual student, and we must never overlook the fact that usually every departmental area of the secondary school is actively contributing, in varying degrees, to the educational development of each individual student.

The business teacher who is concerned with the education of certain young people who profess a special interest in the business subjects must always realize that the entire school faculty is endeavoring to assist him, each in his own sphere of work—the speech teacher is employing his specialized ability to help improve the speech habits of the business student; the English teacher is doing the same for his English habits; the physical education teacher for his health habits; the social studies teacher for his citizenship habits; the science teacher for his understanding of "the influence of science on human life"; the music and art teachers for his appreciation of the beauties of his heritage; and so forth throughout the entire school faculty. Hence, instead of attempting to *himself* achieve for his students the entire gamut of educational goals, the successful business teacher concentrates major attention on those objectives that he is best prepared to assist the student to reach—although always being careful to do his best to assist and reinforce the work of his fellow teachers in their efforts to help this same student achieve other "imperative needs." Thus the major objectives of business education are most appropriately stated in terms of, and limited to, the special work of the business teacher.

Perhaps it should be pointed out, too, that likewise each of the other members of the school faculty must necessarily depend to some extent upon the business teacher for assistance in completing the education of students who may profess greatest interest in educational areas other than business education. Thus, the typewriting teacher may furnish the would-be author or journalist with a skill invaluable to his future career, and through various business classes the business teacher may well provide all youth with business knowledges, skills, and understandings invaluable to them as future homeowners, consumers, parents, and citizens exercising their voting responsibilities in our American free-enterprise economy.

Thus all business education endeavor may best be first broadly divided into two classes of goals or general objectives, namely, *vocational education* and nonvocational or *general education*.

Vocational business education has been defined as "a program of education which equips the student with the marketable skills, knowledges, and attitudes needed for initial employment and advancement in business occupations."[4] *General business education,* on the other hand, "provides the student with information and competencies which are needed by all, in managing personal business affairs and in using the services of the business world."[5] The goals in vocational business education include such areas as

1. Stenographic and secretarial work
2. Bookkeeping, accounting, and data-processing work
3. Clerical and general office work
4. Distributive education and store work
5. Business-management and ownership responsibilities

The goals in general business education include:

1. Consumer information, guidance, and education
2. Business understanding for management of personal business affairs
3. Business and economic understanding for intelligent citizenship
4. Common business skills for personal use

THE BASIC TWOFOLD CLASSIFICATION

It is important that the business teacher and the school administrator fully recognize the existence and importance of these two main classifications of business education, the *vocational* and the *general*. Too frequently there is a tendency to think of business education wholly in terms of its voca-

---

[4] *Definitions of Terms in Vocational and Practical Arts Education* (Washington, D.C.: American Vocational Association, 1954), p. 7.
[5] *Ibid.*

tional significance and goals, a viewpoint that limits the value of business education to only that portion of youth who evidence interest and/or aptitude for employment and potential careers in the world of business. Better methods of instruction might be adopted were it fully recognized that certain portions of the business education program in the secondary school are of vital significance in providing for the "imperative needs" of *all* youth aside from the need for vocational or occupational preparation.

Perhaps this concept of the twofold classification will become clearer if we take time for a look at some of the outstanding characteristics of each classification.

Characteristics of Vocational Business Education

1. It usually encompasses a series or sequence of related courses and subjects extending through one or more years of the secondary school and culminating at or near the time of graduation.
2. This series of courses or subjects usually constitutes a fairly well-defined separate pattern for each of the four main employment areas of business education, *i.e.,* the stenographic,[6] the bookkeeping, the clerical, and the distributive areas, although the pattern may vary somewhat from school to school. Each is often referred to as a *curriculum*.
3. It is usually provided for only a portion of youth of secondary school age, appropriately selected on the basis of such criteria as aptitude, interest, and ability.
4. Final measurement and grading of the student should be based heavily (and possibly totally) on the student's ability to meet employment standards of the business world.
5. Although by no means slighting more intangible mental understandings and abilities, instructional methods must be adapted to the extra task of also developing ability "to do" in terms of marketable skills and abilities and applied knowledges.

Characteristics of General Business Education

1. The various elements may usually be adequately learned through the medium of *individual* business subjects and courses.
2. Thus, there is usually no separate curriculum recognized as pertinent to the achievement of this objective of business education.
3. It is preferably arranged to provide for *all* youth of secondary age.
4. Final measurement and grading of the student may properly be based heavily (and possibly totally) on the extent to which the individual student has profited from the course or subject in accordance with his individual abilities and needs.

6 Since most high school graduates enter stenographic work, as distinguished from secretarial work, the term *secretarial* is best reserved to describe post–high school education in this area.

5. With the exception of the area of personal-use skill, instructional methods devote major attention to the development of understandings, attitudes, and knowledges as differentiated from marketable skills, abilities, and applied knowledges.

A comparison of these five major characteristics for each of the two classifications of business education purposes, or goals, seems to clearly indicate that the successful business teacher needs to know in which area his endeavors are being focused at any given time and adapt his instructional procedures and evaluations accordingly.

GENERAL OBJECTIVES OF BUSINESS EDUCATION

It is not enough that we get an overview of the nature of business education, such as that presented in the preceding portion of this chapter; we also need to look at it from another viewpoint, namely, that of the purposes it hopes to accomplish. It is true that a classification of the types of business education has inherent in it considerable connotation as to its purposes; yet educators find it also helps them to better guide their instructional activities if they carefully analyze and state the major purposes or objectives of the work they are doing.

In preparing a list of such objectives we must keep in mind that they are not intended to apply to only one subject or course but to the entire field of business education. Other statements of objectives, more specific in nature, are ordinarily prepared for each of the separate business subjects, courses, or programs.

The following list of eight general objectives for all business education may be used as a guide in evaluating the relative completeness of the business education offerings in any school system. Each is identified by an introductory descriptive word or phrase to assist the reader in remembering these eight objectives.

1. EXPLORATORY. To make available to *all students* opportunities to explore and learn about the world of business and the possible interests and potential careers it has to offer.

2. CONSUMER EDUCATION. To help develop in *all students* the ability to choose discriminatingly and to use wisely the goods and services that business has to offer.

3. OCCUPATIONAL INTELLIGENCE. To assist in developing an intelligent understanding on the part of *all students* of the various occupations to be found in the world of business.

4. ECONOMIC UNDERSTANDING. To develop in a practical way an understanding and an appreciation of the actual functioning of our economic system.

5. PERSONAL USE. To enable any student to acquire those business knowledges and skills that he may need for his personal use.

6. Vocational. To prepare students to enter and succeed in business occupations as beginners who expect to follow business as a career.

7. Semivocational. To prepare students to perform business activities common to many professional, industrial, agricultural, service, and homemaking careers.

8. College Preparatory. To prepare students for more effective study in the field of business beyond the secondary level.

It is to be recognized that some educators would question the wisdom of including "college preparatory" among the objectives of business education. Traditionally, business subjects have not been included in recommended college-preparatory courses; however, research evidence strongly indicates that this discrimination is unwarranted. Success in college is definitely not dependent upon any particular pattern of subject matter studied in the secondary school. Moreover, today's relatively large enrollments of college students in the fields of business, commerce, and business education indicate a distinct need for having many high school students include business subjects as a part of their college-preparatory work. Today the college or university is indeed rare that will not permit a reasonable number of business subjects to be included as acceptable college-preparatory work completed in high school.

"STANDARD" HIGH SCHOOL REQUIREMENTS

For many years America has tended to develop its high school offerings within a common "framework" of subject matter and official requirements. This is true even though the local school district is rather proud and a bit jealous of its right to determine its own offerings. The relative similarity of offerings has been the result of many influential factors, such as the presence of recognized professional leaders and the existence of numerous professional associations through which those interested in educational matters may democratically arrive at decisions for which there is a felt need. Some of these associations have become recognized accrediting agencies, and their decisions have an influence comparable to that of a law. In addition, various state legislatures do at times pass laws that prescribe and delimit the offerings of public high schools. We will now briefly identify a few of the factors that help determine the common or "standard" framework for the business education curriculum.

However, we are now considering what *has been* true for many years—and what *still is* true in perhaps 90 percent of the nation's high schools. But many of the controlling factors are *changing rapidly* today. The beginning teacher must realize that the school in which he obtains his first position will not necessarily fit into this customary framework! (*Note:* Reasons for these changes, and many of the resulting changes that are taking place, will be presented later in this chapter.)

One standard that is recognized nationwide is that high school graduation requires of the student the successful completion of sixteen Carnegie units of education. A Carnegie unit is represented by one full-time subject pursued throughout the entire school year of nine months. Thus if the student carries four subjects each year he will earn four units each year or the total of sixteen required for graduation by the end of four years in high school.

It is not unusual for a given high school to specify the content, or subject matter, of which a sizable portion of these units *must* be composed in the case of each individual student. These contents, or subjects, are often referred to as *constants* or *required subjects*. Thus in a high school having a typical subject curriculum[7] it is relatively common to find the requirement of three or four units of English, three or four of social studies, one or two of mathematics, and one or two of science. Obviously this uses from eight to twelve of the sixteen units, leaving only four to eight of the units available for all other studies. Such requirements may, of course, severely restrict the amount and kind of business education that may be offered in those schools.

In practice, these required subjects would be distributed in a specified manner over the four years of high school. Thus we might find the *required* units to be as follows:

9th grade	10th grade	11th grade	12th grade
English	English	English	Social Studies
Social Studies	Social Studies		
Mathematics	Science		

Only eight units are specifically required in the above illustration, leaving eight for "electives" to be distributed one in each of the first two years and three in each of the last two years; frequently fewer than eight units remain as electives.

It must be remembered that these eight "elective" units must now be made to serve the needs of the student for *all* other subjects, including homemaking, industrial arts, business education, foreign language, art, music, agriculture, and many others that might be mentioned! Obviously the number of units students may justifiably use for business education is likely to be considerably less than eight; perhaps a *maximum* of four or five units would be about right for most high schools. This will vary considerably with the needs of the students and the community and the size of the high school.

It should be observed that *most* of the elective work will come during the last two years of high school. This is especially favorable to vocational education, since it should be completed as near as possible to the time at which it will be put into use.

THE SMALL HIGH SCHOOL

As mentioned in Chapter I, a high school considered small in some parts of the nation would be considered large in other parts. In the more densely populated urban sections a high school enrolling but five hundred to

---

[7] Similar situations would exist in schools using fused, correlated, broadfields, core, and experience curriculums, although a different terminology would be in use.

six hundred students might be considered small, whereas in the sparsely populated rural states in the plains of the Midwest some high schools might have less than one hundred students enrolled. In some of these states only from one-fourth to one-third of the high schools will have more than one hundred students; enrollments of less than forty may still be found.[8]

It seems obvious that the very small high school must limit its offerings to relatively unspecialized areas of instruction that may seem appropriate for all or nearly all its students. This means that students in those schools will have little if any choice of preparation in the areas of vocational education; in fact, true vocational education does not exist in any form in many of these high schools. When the student body and the teaching staff are so small that all (or nearly all) students *must* study whatever subjects are offered, the problem of program planning becomes an important one for the school administrator; he must choose carefully and wisely the few subjects to be offered.

Therefore, it may be unwise (and practically impossible) to include business education courses that will permit students to obtain vocational preparation for the stenographic or the clerical or the distributive or the bookkeeping field. It is doubtful that complete vocational preparation can be justifiably offered in any one of these areas of business education, since to do so may easily force *all* high school students to prepare for this one field of employment. Certainly it would be unwise, for instance, to construct a high school program that would, in effect, require all students to study shorthand!

On the other hand, to meet the "imperative needs" of its students as well as possible such a school might feel justified in including general business, typewriting, and consumer education in its program; these courses or subjects contain information and objectives that *should* be a part of the high school education of *all* youth. Thus for the very small school we might have this situation:

MINIMUM BASIC BUSINESS EDUCATION PROGRAM
(GENERAL EDUCATION)

General Business (one or two semesters in 9th or 10th grade)
Typewriting (one or two semesters, any grade desired)
Consumer Education (one or two semesters in 11th or 12th grade)

These three business subjects can hardly be said to constitute a business education curriculum; rather, they constitute a basic offering in the field of business education of a type that every high school youth may well include in his general education. Probably these three subjects (or subjects of comparable materials offered under other names) should be a starting point of minimum business education to be included in the program of every American high school.

---

[8] Rapidly increasing population coupled with a current desire to improve administrative efficiency of school districts is causing the size of all high schools to rise rather rapidly, however.

Vocational Curriculums in the Small High Schools?

As already indicated, it is questionable whether the small high schools can and should attempt true vocational education; the exact answer must depend on the individual school situation—its size and purposes, and the needs of the community and young people it serves. However, there are innumerable reasons why such schools do wish to do "the best they can" to provide vocational preparation for their students, and as a result we typically do find them offering some type of education best classified as vocational. (In many cases the *name* of the subject or course offering would imply a vocational objective, but checking into the local objectives and procedures used would indicate an uncertainty in the minds of the teachers and the school administrators which probably results in hazy, fluctuating, multiple-purpose objectives. This situation is not likely to result in effective teaching and learning.)

We must remember, though, that in America the local school district has final control over the offerings of its own school. Thus the business teacher, although cognizant of the difficulties of attempting vocational business education in the small school, should not take it upon himself to try to dictate the policies of the school. Rather, if some form of vocational business education is desired, he should strive to use his very best judgment in recommending that which will best serve the needs of his pupils and of his community. This should be based on the best *factual* information obtainable, both as to the accepted or recommended curriculum practices and as to the needs of his community and pupils.[9]

Obviously the choice must be one or more of the main employment areas of business; these are customarily referred to as the *stenographic,* the *clerical,* the *bookkeeping,* and the *distributive education* fields or curriculums. Space in this chapter does not permit discussion of the relative values of each for the small high school, and the reasons therefor. It may be pointed out, however, that the two areas in which the *largest numbers* of high school graduates constantly find employment throughout the nation are general office work (clerical, filing, typewriting, and simple record keeping) and store work (selling, wrapping, delivering, stock work, and similar beginning duties). Both boys and girls are employed in each and both find careers in each.

BUSINESS EDUCATION IN A MEDIUM-SIZE CITY

Although local community and school history, needs, philosophy, administration, and other influencing conditions will cause some variations among communities, it will be worth our time to briefly review the exact situation relative to business education offerings in at least one public high school in a city of medium size. Such a school provides opportunity for a

---

[9] It is not within the province of this book to discuss methods of obtaining such facts, but it should be noted that many colleges offer excellent graduate work in business education and are prepared to assist business teachers in answering such questions. Appropriate research either has found or can find most of the needed answers.

reasonably diverse and complete offering in the various areas of business education. It would customarily maintain a relatively stable and relatively well qualified staff of teachers and administrators, and thus it might be expected to more nearly approach a program of studies that would be educationally justifiable in terms of the needs of its students and its community. In all probability its administrators and its business teachers would be rather well informed about the local business needs and opportunities.

For illustrative purposes we will look at the 1971–72 business education offerings in an actual Midwest high school in a community of about thirty thousand population having the customary diversified businesses.[10] The community maintains a three-year senior high school and two three-year junior high schools; it is proud of its reputation for excellence in its educational system. Located in this same community is a state university serving ten thousand students; it maintains a complete kindergarten through grade twelve "laboratory" school system which also functions as the public school system for that portion of the city immediately surrounding the university campus. "Downtown" merchants and the city have turned the business section of its main street into a beautiful, winding "Parkade," with linden trees and flowers, and these merchants continue to enjoy excellent business despite an important and totally enclosed and air-conditioned shopping center within the city limits less than a mile away housing some fifty retail businesses.

A much larger city[11] adjoins the community, making a total metropolitan area of 110,000 population, all lying within the same county. Within this metropolitan area also is an excellent business college and the campus of a large, partially state-supported "area school," and of course a considerable number of large industrial plants. The area school, the Hawkeye Institute of Technology, serves post–high school and "adult" students; this includes any dropouts and many students who are handicapped or disadvantaged.

For the 1971–72 school year, this three-year senior high school served approximately fifteen hundred students and employed eight business teachers. The two junior high schools, serving about fifteen hundred students between them, each employed one business teacher. (The university "Laboratory" high school also employed two business teachers.)

Graduation from this high school requires eight semesters of physical education and thirty credits[12] in *academic* subjects.[13] These academic credits *must* include the following:

Science.............	2 semesters	Speech................	1 semester
Mathematics.........	2 semesters	Social Studies..........	8 semesters
English.............	5 semesters	Elective Subjects......	12 semesters

Certain courses are required of all students and are normally taken in the following sequence:

10 Cedar Falls Community Schools, Cedar Falls, Iowa.
11 Waterloo, Iowa.
12 A *credit* is one-half of a Carnegie unit and is one semester of study.
13 All subjects carrying full credit are considered *academic* subjects.

9th grade

English 9 (2 credits)
Fundamentals of Speech (1 credit)
American History and Government I (2 credits)
General Science (2 credits)
General Mathematics or Algebra I (2 credits)
Physical Education (2/5 credit)

10th grade

English 10 (1 credit)
American History and Government (2 credits)
Physical Education and Health (2/5 credit)

11th grade

English (1 credit)
World History, or History of Western Man, or Asian History (2 credits)
Physical Education (2/5 credit)

12th grade

English (1 credit)
Economics or Political Science (1 credit)
Sociology or Psychology II (1 credit)
Physical Education (2/5 credit)

All students are required to carry a *minimum* of four academic subjects or the equivalent each semester in the senior high school. This results in a minimum of twenty-four credits in senior high school (tenth, eleventh, and twelfth grades), of which only nine normally are required courses—thus leaving fifteen *elective* credits. All business education courses are considered elective. (*Note:* Some students are permitted to carry five academic subjects at times; should this be done in each of the three years of senior high school, it would add six more elective credits, for a total of twenty-one semesters of elective credit.)

However, the business teacher must remember that each student is faced with the need for carefully choosing from among *many* elective courses. Usually this is no simple task. This particular high school offers 123 separate elective courses, carrying a total of 192 semesters of credit, from which the student must choose his normal twelve to fifteen elective credits. He is assisted in making his decisions by a director of pupil services assisted by four senior high school and five junior high school counselors. Besides business education, it must be remembered that other electives include the *many* courses available in subjects such as English and literature, Latin, Spanish, German, French, home economics, industrial arts, mathematics, music, sciences, social studies, and speech.

In this high school the business education offerings, including the career (vocational) areas of distributive education and office education, total around 35 semesters of credit; this forms only a small part of the 192 semesters of credit *available* as electives. Exhibit 2.1 gives details about these business education offerings. All students planning their programs for the 1971–72 school year received this information in a handbook given to each of them.[14]

Merely as *guidelines* to assist students in decision making as they plan their

---

[14] *Educational Planning Handbook,* Cedar Falls Community Schools, Cedar Falls, Iowa. (Revised edition, January 1971.)

Exhibit 2.1

BUSINESS EDUCATION

Subject	Grade	Credits	Prerequisite
General Business	9	2	None
Typing I	9–10 11–12	1	None
Typing II	10–11 12	1	Typing I
Typing III	10–11 12	1	Typing II
Salesmanship	10–11 12	1	None
Business Organization	11–12	1	None
Bookkeeping I	10–11 12	2	None Instructor's approval
Bookkeeping II	11–12	2	*B* in Bookkeeping I & instructor's approval
Record Keeping	10–11 12	2	None Instr. Appr.
Office Practice	12	2	Typing Skills
Shorthand	11–12	2	Typing Skills
Business Law	10–11 12	1	None
Note-taking	10–11 12	1	None

CAREER EDUCATION

Distributive Education	12	4	Salesmanship & Business Organization
Office Education			
Clerical Practice	12	6	Typing Skills Instr. Appr.
Secretarial Practice	12	6	Typing & Shorthand & instructor's Approval

programs, the *Educational Planning Handbook*[15] has the following suggestions (among many others) to offer:[16]

FOR STUDENTS CHOOSING TO PREPARE FOR COLLEGE

Mathematics	(2–3 years)	9th–12th
Science	(2–3 years)	9th–12th
Psychology	(1 semester)	11th–12th
Typing	(1 or 2 semesters)	9th–12th
Notetaking	(1 semester)	10th–12th
Foreign Language	(2 or 4 years)	9th–12th

BUSINESS—SALES FIELD

General Business	(1 year)	9th
Bookkeeping I	(1 year)	10th–12th
Bookkeeping II	(1 year)	11th–12th
Business Org.	(1 semester)	11th–12th
Salesmanship	(1 semester)	10th–12th
Speech Elective	(1 semester)	10th–12th
Psychology I	(1 semester)	10th–12th
Economics	(1 semester)	12th
Distributive Education	(4 credits)	12th

BUSINESS—SECRETARIAL

General Business	(1 year)	9th
Typing I, II, & III	(3 semesters)	9th–12th
Bookkeeping I	(1 year)	10th–12th
Bookkeeping II	(1 year)	11th–12th
Shorthand	(1 year)	11th
Office Education	(6 credits)	12th

BUSINESS—TYPIST AND CLERICAL

General Business	(1 year)	9th
Typing I and II	(1 year)	10th–11th
Bookkeeping I	(1 year)	10th–12th
Bookkeeping II	(1 year)	10th–12th
Office Practice	(1 year)	12th
Office Education	(6 credits)	12th

It must be remembered that the preceding are *general guidelines* only, but they are the result of careful cooperative thinking on the part of the counselors and the business education faculty members. These people have knowledge of the special content and objectives of the various courses and of the special strengths of those who are currently teaching the courses. They also have knowledge of both actual and potential job openings and employment op-

---

[15] *Ibid.*
[16] These suggestions are designed to prepare a student for most college general education requirements regardless of his prospective major.

portunities in the local community and throughout the nation. Students preparing for college are advised to choose their college early and are provided with names and addresses of the twenty-eight four-year colleges and universities, the twenty-four community and junior colleges, and the sixteen area schools with their thirty attendance centers that are in the state of Iowa.

The listing of business education courses and guidelines (Exhibit 2.1) is presented here *not* as a "model curriculum" suitable for general adoption by various high schools but, rather, as an illustration of offerings that have been developed by one specific school system through intelligent overall planning to best meet the needs of a specific community within its currently available financial resources. As previously indicated, however, this community has a reputation of providing excellent schools.

A word of warning! Up to now, at least, education has been strongly influenced by tradition. Perhaps many schools will retain traditional curriculums and practices for some time. *However*—by 1970–71 education had found itself in deep trouble! Taxpayers were rebelling at the increasing costs of education. Students were rebelling at traditional learning procedures and at traditional subject matter which they felt had little relevance to their current and future interests and needs. Hundreds of private enterprise firms were entering the field of education and selling their services to school boards—and providing considerable evidence of achieving superior results in education at a lower cost while profiting financially themselves! The word *accountability* became a watchword for education—accountability as applied to costs and also as applied to educational achievements.

As a result, business educators throughout the nation are *rapidly* developing new techniques and new procedures. Much subject matter considered nonessential is being deleted. Attention is now being focused *truly* on the individual needs of each student as contrasted with the former group instruction "sink-or-swim" policy so frequently found. In a few schools the business education subject matter and learning procedure is *individually prescribed* in detail for each business student![17] In preparing a new handbook for the guidance of its business teachers and school administrators, one state department of public instruction[18] has requested those writing the material to refrain from using "course" as much as possible! In brief, traditional "courses" and "class schedules" are giving way to "individual learning centers," and the individual business teacher is finding himself serving *more* students with *greater* attention to the individual needs of each one and with *improved* educational achievement—and often in *less* time!

These newer techniques and procedures will be discussed in more detail in other chapters, and especially in Chapter 4, "Teaching Techniques Applied to the Learning Process." For the most part, however, these newer techniques and procedures will still be directed at achieving the same educational goals and objectives represented by the illustrative courses and curriculums presented in this chapter.

[17] This procedure was started, for instance, in the 1970–71 school year at the University High School, University of Northern Iowa, Cedar Falls.
[18] State of Iowa.

THE IDEAL BUSINESS EDUCATION CURRICULUM

An "ideal" business education curriculum will probably never exist. But every school should attempt to approach it as nearly as conditions will permit. It is suggested that the business education faculty of every school system give thoughtful professional consideration to the following characteristics which are believed to be essential for any "ideal" business education curriculum.

1. It should be comprehensive and varied in its offerings of choices for those preparing for employment and careers in business.
2. It should include opportunity for all students to gain an understanding of the business world and the consumer world, thus facilitating intelligent consumer usage of the services and products of business.
3. It should provide opportunity for all students to learn those skills and business abilities that they can use effectively in their personal lives.
4. It should be built on a foundation of economic and work attitudes and understandings interwoven into the elementary and junior high school programs.
5. It should be organized so it will permit each student to progress at his own rate until he achieves valuable personal goals and also so interest and challenge him that he will maximize his opportunities and abilities.
6. It should be so organized as to reasonably assure the achievement of potentially salable skills and abilities by the student at several points as he progresses in his school career; each new or improved skill or ability should *further* increase his job potential. Such a curriculum will provide a salable skill for the dropout, when needed, and yet help to prevent or reduce the incidence of dropouts.
7. It should be closely interwoven into the total guidance program of the school.
8. It should provide appropriate continuing (adult) education for upgrading and retraining all who can profit therefrom.
9. It should be constantly reviewed, adjusted, and improved by administrators and teachers to assure that it continues to be appropriate for the specific community, student body, and social and economic needs being served.
10. In its vocational aspects, it should give due attention to *both* preparation for the beginning job *and* preparation for advancement in a career.
11. It should maximize the amount of attention given to the development of desirable personal qualities, traits, and attitudes in each individual student.
12. It should use only such physical facilities and equipment as will (*a*) meet the standards of modern business and (*b*) assist in building pride on the part of the student in his own achievement and his preparation for a career.[19]

Even though agreement may be reached on the many characteristics of an ideal business education curriculum, numerous difficulties are encountered in attempting to implement these ideas. Each school system and its business education faculty must find solutions for its own problems. In the following

[19] These essential characteristics form a part of a state handbook for business education published by the Iowa State Department of Public Instruction in 1972.

chapters of this book, however, will be found many ideas and suggestions which should help in implementing such a curriculum.

With this background of understanding of the characteristics of the business teacher of today (Chapter 1) and of the characteristics and functions of the curriculums and programs of study with which he must work (Chapter 2), we are now ready to direct our attention to the actual process of teaching. Teaching has the purpose of complementing and aiding the learning process. Thus we are now ready to deal with the learning process, and Chapter 3 will take us directly into that as the business teacher finds it. This will be followed by a study of the basic teaching techniques commonly used by the business teacher.

PROJECTS AND QUESTIONS FOR DISCUSSION

1. Investigate and report on any business education handbook or suggestions that may be distributed by your own State Department of Public Instruction.
2. Procure and report on the business education curriculums in one or more small, medium, and large high schools in your state.
3. Prepare appropriate bulletin boards to illustrate each of the five vocational education goals or areas outlined in this chapter.
4. Hold a panel discussion about the suitability of business subjects as a part of preparation for college.
5. Report on assigned or selected readings suggested at the end of this chapter.
6. Can you defend this statement: "Shorthand should not be taught in any school unless there is an opportunity in the community for the graduates to use this skill"?
7. Your superintendent wishes to require all students in your high school to take typewriting. Would you deter him or encourage him? Why?
8. Develop the minimum program of business education you would recommend for a high school located in a rural area with an enrollment of two hundred students. Defend your recommendations.
9. Do you believe that business education can contribute to the general education of students in the secondary school? In what way? Do you believe that it should?
10. Evaluate the business education offerings presented in this chapter as an illustration of a medium-size high school. Do you question any of it? If so, why do you suppose it has been adopted by this school? Would you make any changes? If so, why?
11. It has been said that the secondary school should not train students vocationally. This type of training can be done more efficiently and economically on the job. Can you agree with this idea? Why or why not?
12. The "personal-use" objective is quite important in the minds of some business educators as an integral part of the present-day business education curriculum. What do you believe?
13. Should the preparation of business education students in the secondary school consist of preparing more for the distributive occupations than for the secretarial or general business? Defend your arguments.

CASE PROBLEMS

1. Mr. Charles Coleman is a business teacher who has been teaching in the secondary schools for ten years. He is a superior teacher and has always been highly conscientious about his teaching. At present he is very discouraged about the future of business education in the secondary school. He believes that automation is going to play such an important role in the future that there will be little need for business teachers. He is convinced that bookkeeping, shorthand, and typewriting will all be eliminated and that machines will perform the work formerly done by people with these skills. He is considering leaving the teaching profession and seeking other types of employment that will have a more secure future. What advice do you have for Mr. Coleman?

2. Miss Jane Connoley is an enthusiastic and excellent business education teacher. Her main interest is in teaching shorthand, typewriting, and secretarial practice. Although she recognizes that general business and consumer education (among others) are classified as business education subjects, nevertheless she is convinced that the only valid objective for teaching business subjects in the secondary schools is for vocational use. Consequently she has stated publicly that unless a business subject can be justified on purely vocational grounds that subject has no place in the business curriculum. She refuses to recognize that general business or consumer education can be taught for other than vocational goals.

Miss Connoley is quite influential with the superintendent of schools and has convinced him she is right. She is advocating that the business curriculum should consist of two years of typewriting, two years of bookkeeping, and one year of secretarial practice. Would you attempt to thwart Miss Connoley? If so, what arguments would you use? Can you support your arguments by facts rather than opinion or logic?

3. You are a business teacher in Manson High School. You have been teaching bookkeeping, typewriting, and general business in this school for several years. A new superintendent has been employed for the present school year. Shortly after the beginning of the second semester he calls you into his office and tells you that he plans to recommend to the board of education that the subject of bookkeeping be dropped from the business education curriculum. He is convinced that the subject of bookkeeping has little effect in the training of bookkeepers and if the subject does not have this value then he cannot see any need for retaining it in the curriculum.

However, he states that he has an open mind and is willing to listen to your reasons for retention of the course, and if you can convince him, he will not make the recommendation to the board. What would you do?

4. Max Sherrill is a business teacher in Columbus, a small city of eight thousand population, which is a trading center for several counties. His superintendent has just returned from a professional meeting at which he spent a large amount of time talking with the state director of vocational education. This director has interested the superintendent in the advantages of a cooperative distributive education program for Columbus High School. The superintendent has asked Sherrill to investigate the possibilities of such a program for the high school and report back to him in approximately two weeks. What steps would you recommend for Max to take in completing this assignment?

5. Miss Sheldon is an excellent secretarial teacher in the Rutland High School. However, she is finding that for some reason her secretarial graduates of this high school are not as good as were the ones where she formerly taught. Yet Rutland seems to be a normal community with average-type people and families. The school offers two years of typewriting and two years of shorthand, both starting in the junior year. The first year of each

is also open to seniors. The courses are open to all juniors and seniors who care to take them. Miss Sheldon feels sure she is working as conscientiously as she ever did and actually feels that she is trying very hard to do a topflight job of teaching these subjects. What do you feel may well be some of the causes of her lack of success at this high school?

SUGGESTED READINGS

Bottoms, Gene, and George L. O'Kelley, "Vocational Education as a Developmental Process," *American Vocational Journal,* March 1971, pp. 21–24.

Brady, Mary Margaret, "Research in Curriculum," *Ohio Business Teacher,* April 1969, pp. 50–53.

Byrnside, O. J., Jr., "Principles for Evaluation of Business and Office Education," *NBEA Yearbook,* No. 7, 1969, pp. 3–13.

Conant, James B., "Recommendations for Improving Public Secondary Schools," in *The American High School Today.* New York: McGraw-Hill Book Company, 1959.

Courtney, Paul L., "Wholesaling: Insatiable Consumer of Trained Skills," *American Vocational Journal,* February 1971, pp. 60–61.

Dalton, Joan, "A Business Curriculum That Is Relevant," *The Balance Sheet,* November 1970, pp. 100–101.

Douglas, Lloyd V., *Business Education* (a volume of *The Library of Education*), The Center for Applied Research in Business Education, 1963, pp. 1–4, 21–45.

———, ed., *The Business Education Program in the Expanding Secondary School,* NBEA, 1957. *Note:* also a bulletin of the NASSP.

———, *et al.,* "Curriculum Study of Subject Matter Elements in Bookkeeping, Accounting, and Related Office Education," *National Business Education Quarterly,* December 1968, pp. 21–37.

———, "Some Controversial Issues in Business Education," *Business Education Forum,* May 1969, p. 4.

———, "Today's Educational Tragedy," *Balance Sheet,* May 1961, pp. 389–91.

Educational Policies Commission, *The Central Purpose of American Education,* National Education Association, 1201 Sixteenth Street, N.W., Washington, D.C., 1962.

Eiken, Shirley A., "New Systems Needed in Business Education," *Business Education Forum,* May 1969, pp. 5–7.

Faidley, Ray A., "Equal Emphasis for General Business Subjects," *Journal of Business Education,* March 1971, pp. 246–47.

Garrison, Lloyd L., "New Emphases in Curriculum Making," *Journal of Business Education,* November 1970, pp. 73–74.

Goldstein, Harold, "America's Manpower Needs for the Seventies," *American Vocational Journal,* April 1971, pp. 18–25.

Kell, Venetta B., and Josephine Sawaia, "Evaluation of Secondary Programs," *NBEA Yearbook,* No. 7, 1969, pp. 71–84.

McDonald, Loretta Ann, "Curricula Offerings in Business Education in Schools for the Deaf," *The Balance Sheet,* October 1970, pp. 62–63, 78.

Miller, Aaron J., and Angelo C. Gillie, *A Suggested Guide for Post-Secondary Vocational and Technical Education,* The Center for Vocational and Technical Education, The Ohio State University, Columbus, September 1970, 45 pp.

Mott, Dennes L., "The Changing Role of Business Education," *The Balance Sheet,* September 1970, pp. 26–27.

NBEA Yearbook, No. 8, 1970, *The Emerging Content and Structure of Business Education,* 322 pp.

Nolan, C. A., Carlos K. Hayden, and Dean R. Malsbary, *Principles and Problems in Business Education*, Chap. 3, "The Curriculum Today," pp. 66–96. Cincinnati: South-Western Publishing Co., 1967.

Policies Commission for Business and Economic Education, "Business Education for the College Bound Student," *Business Education Forum*, May 1964, pp. 21–22.

———, "This We Believe about Business Education in the United States," *The Balance Sheet*, April 1971, pp. 310–11.

Rhodes, James A., *Alternative to a Decadent Society*. Indianapolis: Howard W. Sanns & Co., Inc., 1969, 108 pp.

Roman, John C., *The Business Curriculum*, Monograph 100, rev. ed. Cincinnati: South-Western Publishing Co., 1966.

State of Iowa, Department of Public Instruction, Grimes Office Building, Des Moines, *Opportunities in Iowa's Area Schools, 1970–71*, 67 pp.

Talagon, Dean P., "Comprehensive Occupational Education: K through Life," *Business Education World*, January–February 1970, pp. 18–19.

Tonne, Herbert A., *et al.*, *Guidelines in Business Education*, State University of New York, Albany, 1969, 59 pp.

Woolschlager, Ruth B., *Responsibilities of the Business Education Department Chairman*, Monograph 120. Cincinnati: South-Western Publishing Co., 1969.

chapter

3

THE BUSINESS TEACHER LOOKS
AT THE LEARNING PROCESS

Learning is a continuous and a very personal process. Every individual is in the process of learning at all times—at school, in the home, at the store, in the daily work at the factory—in all economic, social, religious, and other activities in which the individual may engage. Teaching is partially a viewpoint toward learning. Teaching encompasses all factors in the learning process and attempts to guide and control those factors to provide a learning situation giving maximum effectiveness and efficiency. Teaching is the art of applying scientifically determined facts about learning, often referred to as *educational psychology,* in order to assist the learner in his learning.

Basically the individual is a creature of emotions whose responses to stimuli (including environment and motives) are largely the result of conditioning of his natural inherited powers, abilities, and tendencies. Thus the best teacher must be one who is thoroughly familiar with the field of educational psychology and the learning process, and who has adequate maturity of judgment and control (*a*) to interpret intelligently the present developmental status of the student, and (*b*) to be a true artist in providing for the student the appropriate learning situation.

The present chapter is a review of major aspects of educational psychology and of the learning process as they apply to the work of the business teacher.

Is it true that "if the learner hasn't learned the teacher hasn't taught"? How do I know when I'm doing the right thing? How do I know which of many factors is of most importance? What do I do when things go wrong?

Questions such as the above are almost sure to be in the minds of all business teachers; in fact, they frequently enter the mind of every business teacher who is worth his pay! There definitely is no one simple answer to such questions. The best answer is always going to be one based on (*a*) a complete knowledge and understanding of the individual student or students involved (*b*) by a teacher who is well versed in educational psychology and factors influencing learning and (*c*) prepared in pertinent subject matter or skills and (*d*) who has sufficient maturity of judgment and control to arrive at and carry through wise decisions.

Probably the most complicated single thing known to man is the human being. Over the years we have learned much about ourselves and "what makes us tick"; yet we still have much to learn and probably never will be able to reduce that learning to an all-inclusive body of definite statements as may be done in some of the more exact sciences. New knowledge about the human being as an individual and as a learner is being brought to light every year through continued research. This is why the successful teacher continues throughout his teaching career to subscribe to and to read and study the literature of his profession. And that also is why it is wise for us at this time to briefly review some of the major factors in the teaching-learning process on which educators quite generally agree.

LEARNING AS INDIVIDUAL GROWTH

When the business teacher faces a class, he must realize that he actually has before him as many individual learning situations as there are students in the class. Each was born into this world endowed with a central nervous system capable of automatically producing various muscular responses throughout the body in answer to various internally produced and exteriorly received stimuli. These responses, however, both verbal and otherwise, were largely of a random nature.

As the teacher faces the class, though, he now has before him individuals whose responses have been conditioned over perhaps from fourteen to twenty or more years. Owing to home environments, outside associates, sickness, successes, frustrations, previous formal learning situations—and innumerable other conditioning factors—there are bound to be wide differences in the development or learning status of the various students in every class. Although all students in typical business classes have now attained a high-order level of response, probably even including problem-solving ability, each has attained it through a different maze of influences. Thus, owing to previous conditioning, each can be depended upon to have different learning responses to each teaching situation.

In addition, it must be realized that each individual student also possesses native ability and characteristics different from those of each of the others; this refers primarily to inherited physical qualities and characteristics. One phase of this (but one phase only) may be measured in an individual in terms of intelligence quotient or in terms of mental age. Other phases may be measured in terms of various aptitudes, in terms of physiological growth, in terms of reaction time, or in terms of such measurements as number ability, or perceptual speed, or spatial-relations-recognition ability.

The business teacher is cautioned against the pitfall of oversimplification of his concept of learning and of teaching. A class, for instance, may consist entirely of girls and lead the inexperienced teacher to conclude that he has a "homogeneously grouped" class which will simplify his teaching procedures. Or it may be a class of "high-IQ" students, or of "below-normal" students, or of students carefully selected for high aptitudes and interests in a given subject such as shorthand, or of students all coming from apparently similar home backgrounds. The teacher should never make the mistake of believing that, therefor, a given teaching procedure or technique will apply equally well to every student in the class! Such is not the case—and for very good reasons.

In summary, then, in every business class the task of the teacher is to teach individual students. (And to teach means to give assistance to the student in his learning—not to "pour" or otherwise transfer the teacher's learning into the student!) Learning is an individual matter. Thus the good business teacher makes his efforts student centered as opposed to subject-matter centered or class centered.

MOTIVATION

In general it is true that we learn well only that which we want to learn well. Or, stated in other words, if one wants sufficiently strongly to learn something he is very likely to do so. Yes—he is even likely to do so in spite of the impediment of a poor teacher!

In the education profession we refer to this desire to learn, or to do something, as *motivation*. It is something that must always be present for efficient and effective learning. It is the drive that causes students to soar to real heights in learning. And it is one of the very major functions of the good business teacher, or of any teacher, to see that each individual student goes about his learning possessing the highest possible motivation.

Again it should be realized that motivation is an individual matter. That which motivates Mary to work until she has achieved a dictation speed of 140 words per minute in shorthand may be of no interest whatsoever to Tom. And that which motivates Richard to spend many interesting hours at the library and interviewing people downtown to prepare a report for his class on the subject of insurance may have no effect whatsoever on Marvin, who finds he would rather play hooky that day and go fishing. Yet, if he wanted to, Tom might develop higher shorthand speed than Mary, and Marvin might well outdo Richard in learning about insurance!

And so it goes throughout all learning—and throughout life. And the business teacher asks, "How can I possibly have the understanding and the time to provide the best motivation for each of the many individuals in my classes?"

To be honest, the answer probably is "You can't." At least you probably never can have the understanding and the time to be 100 percent effective in having the work of each student become the result of the highest possible motivation of which the student is capable. But as a skilled teacher you can, in various ways, assist each student in materially raising his motivation—his desire to succeed well in the learning process or problem with which he is faced.

Kind of Motivation

Broadly speaking, all motivation may be classed as either real or artificial. Where a real motivation appears to be lacking on the part of the student, it is the teacher's role to discover and provide learning situations that will develop or engender a real motivation on the part of each student. To some extent, owing to the individual differences existing among the students, this becomes a trial-and-error procedure. Yet the skillful teacher avoids an undue waste of learning time by artificially motivating the class constantly and by various means while permitting time for individual students to develop real interest and motivation.

The offering of prizes or pins or certificates to typewriting or shorthand students is illustrative of one type of artificial motivation. Desire for and pride in personal recognition and approval by one's associates is a common characteristic of all of us. This may almost be looked upon as an "inborn trait"; it is not something that we consciously reason out for ourselves and thereafter adopt as a characteristic because we reason that it is a good thing! Mother Nature has taken care of this for us and endowed us with this "built-in" response as a result of the functioning of the autonomic division of our central nervous system. Only through a conditioning process can we change it.

Artificial motivation, such as the use of pins and certificates, should be recognized for what it is—a means toward an end and not the ultimate goal. It is more desirable when the student feels an inward burning desire to achieve this same degree of skill (as in typewriting or shorthand) because he knows and feels that this skill is something that makes him, as an individual, happy and satisfied with himself; that will make him proud of himself throughout life as an individual possessing an ability that others do not have; that will make him feel more secure in his ability to earn his way through life successfully. Yet, if the possibility of earning a certificate or pin will help motivate him to at least "make a start," is it not worth considering?

This should not be construed as advocating indiscriminate use of pins and certificates as the best artificial motivation. The teacher should be an "artist" in skillfully selecting the best from the countless types of somewhat artificial motivation that may be available and in selecting that which seems to best suit his teaching personality, his teaching situation, and his students. Yet we must realize that such motivation does appeal to our deep-seated desire for recognition and, therefore, does tend to help increase our efforts.

For instance, the authors have observed (and happily participated in!) occasions at which adult professional and business men and women of a community have been called forward in meetings such as a service-club banquet to have bestowed upon them appropriate pins in recognition of such relatively minor achievements as perfect attendance for one year or continuous membership for ten, fifteen, or twenty years. And these people gave silent testimony to the pleasure it gave them by constantly wearing the pins thereafter! Moreover, they customarily made an even greater effort to continue to maintain and improve the records they had set.

Thus the business teacher should not belittle so-called artificial motivation. Make use of it. Choose intelligently, however. Recognition for achievements may also be given in many other ways, such as through posting the names of those students making "greatest improvement"; posting especially fine work; publishing in school and local papers the names of those achieving any of countless types of success; arranging for individual students to display their various abilities before local community groups, or through radio or television programs; posting or publishing pictures of students engaged in giving top-ranking sales talks, taking dictation, transcribing from dictaphones, or giving reports in any business class; publicly announcing the names of those elected to membership in student groups, such as the Future Business Leaders of America; and rewarding students in literally thousands of other ways which the alert business teacher is capable of devising.

Praise and Encouragement

Far too often does the teacher attempt to motivate through criticism, punishment, or grades. Far too seldom does the teacher motivate through deserved praise and encouragement.

It is true that both "reward" and "punishment" are recognized as potential means of motivating learning. Moreover, criticism is essential. However, the human being is known to respond better and to secure greater motivation from praise than from punishment. The skillful business teacher makes certain that he judiciously gives praise when it is deserved and that he typically makes his criticism constructive and encouraging. He reserves punishment and a destructive type of criticism for very, very few cases and then only when it is decided upon as a last resort after thorough, deliberate consideration of the individual toward whom it is to be directed. Administering it before other students usually results in more damage than good.

It has been claimed that the most powerful single drive in human nature is the desire to gain recognition. This might also be described as the desire to be appreciated. At times it takes the form of desire to be loved, to "belong," to be heard, to be seen, and various other modifications. This should constantly be recognized by the teacher in all business classes. The drive is always present in each student.

Moreover, should a given student fail to obtain this desired recognition in a desirable or approved manner, he will tend to be driven to obtain it in some other manner. This usually accounts for the boisterousness, the "paper wads," the shuffling of feet, the loud whispers, the interference with others, and the innumerable other petty annoyances sometimes encountered by teachers and referred to as *discipline situations*. One of the best means of avoiding such situations, and of motivating desired learning at the same time, is to be sure each individual student receives deserved praise and encouragement.

Thus, it may be that a bookkeeping student arrives at an incorrect net profit for his set of books or for a problem. Perhaps he has incorrectly classified a debit entry as an asset when it should have been considered an expense.

Some teachers might comment to him somewhat as follows: "Dick, you are careless. You've been warned that you must be accurate at all times. Apparently you haven't followed instructions, so it's your own fault. You deserve the *F* you'll get on this—and you'll now have to do it over besides."

It may be that Dick needs criticism on some of these points. Yet it is hardly possible that he has done everything wrong! Wasn't there anything in all of his work that deserved a word of encouraging recognition or praise? A more skillful teacher might have commented more like this: "I'm sorry, Dick, but your final net profit is wrong; you've prepared this more neatly and in better form than you sometimes do, and it's too bad to let some error creep in and cheat you. I presume you've checked your arithmetic already. Do you suppose you've made an error in judgment in analyzing some transaction? Would you like to look this over again and see if you can find it so I can give you full credit for your work? It really appears to be quite well done otherwise."

Comments more like the second one let Dick know that you are "on his side"; that you, as a teacher, stand ready and eager to give him credit and recognition when deserved; that you do recognize something good and worthwhile in his efforts; and that you have at least some degree of confidence in his ability to "come through." Yet at the same time there is the critical attitude toward his arithmetic and toward the use of judgment in analyzing transactions —but given in a constructive and friendly manner.

It requires only a moment of reflection to understand that the first type of comment to Dick, which fails completely to give him any recognition for whatever he may have done indicating improvement for him, can only help make Dick feel "rebellious" and perhaps turn to other means of gaining attention and recognition—helping to make of him a so-called discipline problem. And on the other hand, the second type of comment gave him opportunity to feel that his efforts were appreciated and that he was on the road to deserved recognition; it would be much more likely to encourage and motivate him to continued and improved learning.

ATTENTION, INTEREST, AND DESIRE

Recently a student in a salesmanship class was observed presenting a demonstration or practice sales talk before his classmates. He apparently had learned his principles of good salesmanship well and had prepared his demonstration sales talk carefully, for in it he demonstrated clearly the importance of first gaining favorable attention, of then using that attention to develop a real interest, and, finally, of encouraging and developing that interest until it became a desire—in that case a desire on the part of his prospect to purchase the item that was for sale.

In a way this student condensed into a twenty-minute class demonstration an excellent illustration of the entire process through which the business teacher must take his students in motivating and achieving real learning. First, of course, it is necessary to secure favorable attention of the students. Usually this is not too difficult to do. It is somewhat more difficult, however, to develop a real interest even though the teacher may have the attention of the students.

The real evidence of a top-ranking teacher comes, however, when he can get that interest to develop into a real desire for learning! Let us consider briefly what happened in this demonstration sales talk.

The student-salesman saw to it that he immediately got favorable attention. In the first place this applied to himself; he appeared neat and well groomed, pleasant, and confident. At the same time he was polite and thoughtful in dealing with his prospect. And in the second place he assured attention (at least) to his merchandise by casually placing it conspicuously on the table before his prospect. The fact that it was still covered by a beautiful display case which was closed merely aided in arousing curiosity and assuring continued attention while the student-salesman had an opportunity to "get under way" in his prepared sales talk. (Every time a teacher enters a classroom to face a class he encounters this same challenging situation; if he is well prepared, he will in some manner be duplicating this sales situation. And the good teacher is well prepared every time he enters the classroom!)

As the student-salesman proceeded then to develop interest he was careful to constantly keep before himself his prospect's viewpoint. It was obvious that the information he was giving was all directed toward the interests of his prospect. He encouraged his prospect to talk, to answer questions, and to ask questions. Moreover, he had his prospect actively participating by taking the merchandise (in this case a power drill) in his own hands, examining it, and then "trying it out" on a piece of wood which the salesman had ready for that purpose! Is it any wonder that the attention of the prospect was gradually changed into a real interest in the drill and, finally, to a desire to possess it? (Similarly, the teacher develops real interest on the part of his students by constantly keeping before himself his students' viewpoint, by encouraging them to ask and to answer questions, and by having them actively engaged in the many activities, both physical and mental, that are associated with learning. It is through this same method that the teacher develops a real desire to learn!)

In brief, then, to promote real learning it is necessary first to get the attention of the students and then to hold it and at the same time to develop interest; when his interest in the subject matter at hand can be sufficiently expanded and becomes a real part of the student's activities and thinking, the chances are good that he will also develop a desire to learn about it. The teacher who achieves this outcome consistently and repeatedly is in fact a "master teacher."

Attention-Killers

Psychology teaches us (as does experience) that it is relatively easy to get attention. All it takes is a bright light, a moving object, a bright color, a loud noise, something new or unusual, something attractive, a pleasant odor, or any of many, many other stimuli. The skillful teacher quickly becomes adept at getting attention.

However, holding attention may be more difficult. It must be remembered that any of these same multitudinous stimuli can just as easily steal the attention away from the teacher. This happens whenever there is some unusual noise or other sound either inside or outside the classroom; whenever a class is interrupted by the entrance of a tardy student; whenever "unruly" students attract attention to themselves; or whenever a student is called out of class.

What can the teacher do about this? How can the teacher prevent "attention-killers" from interrupting and interfering with the learning process of his students? In general, there are two things that the master teacher does: He plans to eliminate as many of them as possible and he keeps alert to counteract the others.

Every business teacher certainly should be businesslike in conducting all his business classes. This may seem to be a trite statement, yet it is the very heart of the success of many business teachers. If a class is conducted in businesslike manner—from the very moment the class is scheduled to start until the moment when it is dismissed—the number of attention-killers in that class will automatically be drastically reduced. In general, this means making maximum use of every second of class time. It means "starting" promptly—and making that a habit that becomes automatic with the students. It means entering the classroom with a well-laid plan of procedure each day. It means advance planning to see that roll call and other clerical duties are taken care of automatically and efficiently; that needed equipment and supplies are in place and in working order; that the classroom is "in order," properly heated, properly lighted, properly ventilated, and relatively free from outside distractions; and that advance cooperation of the administration has been arranged to cut to a minimum undesirable interruptions over which the teacher can have no control.

Yet, in spite of advance planning to be businesslike in all ways, unwanted interferences must be expected. This is where the master teacher demonstrates that he is a true "artist" in applying his knowledge of human psychology. He must then quickly but artfully use good judgment in counteracting the unwanted influence of such attention-killers. He must manage to motivate his students (perhaps almost unrealized by them) to redirect their attention to the problem of learning that currently is before the class. In doing this, he may of course choose from innumerable procedures potentially available. He may refer to some chart or other visual aid in resuming the discussion or explanation or summarization or other step in the learning process that was under way at the time of the interruption; he may make use of the chalkboard for this purpose; he may ask some student to continue the discussion, or explanation, or summarization, or to consider a pertinent question or problem posed by the teacher; or he may use other procedures seemingly well suited to the occasion, his students, and his own personal preferences.

It should be noted, however, that the master teacher does not simply exhort his students to "now forget" about the interruption! This would probably merely tend to continue to fix the attention on the interruption. Instead, through actively redirecting the attention to the desired topic, the master teacher has helped his students "forget" the interruption—and without even realizing they are doing so.

Fatigue and Boredom

It is quite possible, however, that interruptions and even "attention-killers" may be turned into real advantages by the master teacher. Thus the teacher should not permit himself to become overly concerned about them. Just as the alert salesman is prepared to accept objections and then to move immediately forward toward an advantage, so, also, should the alert teacher be prepared to accept interruptions and then to make use of them. After all, we all know that at times we become "fatigued" and sometimes "bored"—and that at such times almost any kind of a "pause" or "interruption" can enable us to then pursue our objective with renewed vigor and interest.

In some classwork, such as that in beginning typewriting or early shorthand writing, the fatigue that quickly sets in is largely physical. Muscles are clumsily performing new tasks and fatigue quickly until they become accustomed to these new activities. It is then that the business teacher should apply counteracting principles learned in his educational psychology. For instance, he may recall that in controlled experiments, the ergograph has clearly shown the adverse effects on both quantity and quality of output resulting from fatigue. (No wonder the beginning typewriting student tires, slows down, and makes errors if he tries hard for more than a minute or so at a time!) And he may also recall that less "work" time with appropriately spaced periods of complete physical relaxation will result in an actual increase in output—and of a better quality. (Small wonder, then, that even the very thought of facing a "double-period" typewriting class may cause the beginning typewriting student to "give up" and start saving himself from the beginning of the class period!)

In classwork involving the learning of new skills (something the business teacher often faces) constant care must be taken to permit the students (perhaps without fully realizing it) to sit back and relax and physically rest. Sometimes the best means of doing this is to have them relax physically while they watch the teacher as he explains or demonstrates something new to them. Certainly, though, it is necessary that they rest and counteract developing physical fatigue.

It is to be remembered that this matter of fatigue applies especially to the beginning stages of learning a skill. In due time it may be desirable to so develop the skill that the advent of physical fatigue is delayed for rather long periods. As muscles become more skillful at new tasks this ability will gradually develop.

Perhaps of even greater importance than actual physical fatigue is the matter of a general mental feeling of fatigue, often bordering on or becoming boredom. This is common to all life situations and is present in all classroom work, in both skill courses and nonskill courses. Thus it is quite possible that it may be in any class—bookkeeping, general business, typewriting, salesmanship, consumer education, shorthand, retailing, business law, or others—that the business teacher detects the presence of a "feeling of fatigue" (or is it boredom?).

What should he do about it? Give them a rest? In a way, the answer is yes. However, that which may best be a "rest" for his students is then likely to be merely a "change." In brief, the real cure for boredom is motivation. It is probable that the particular technique of learning in use in class at the moment needs to be changed. Are the students getting bored or "fatigued" from listening to too much talking by the teacher? Perhaps from listening to a long and uninspired report by a fellow student? Perhaps from sitting idly by while the teacher goes through a long explanation, or argument, or chastisement, primarily for the benefit of some one student? Perhaps from an unnecessary repetition of something they already know and understand? Or perhaps merely because the teacher has used the same old technique day after day in that class?

It is especially true that at times such as these almost any "interruption"— even an ordinarily undesirable "attention-killer"—may actually be used to advantage by the teacher!

A recent article in a professional education magazine, written by a nationally known business educator, advocated "change for the sake of change!" There was much merit in this man's advice. He would forestall feelings of fatigue, developing feelings of boredom, and general tendencies toward lack of interest, through a widespread use of the principle of "change." It is well to apply this idea constantly to motivation and teaching techniques. It may also be profitably applied to other factors, such as the teacher's clothing and appearance and the physical arrangements within the classroom.

Perhaps a word of caution is well, however. The master teacher discovers procedures and techniques that he is sure achieve high motivation and achievements when he consistently uses them. He is entirely justified in making repeated use of these procedures and techniques—subject, undoubtedly, to the occasional need for variations.

KNOWLEDGE OF RESULTS

Many business teachers are accused of having a strong preference for teaching skill subjects, such as typewriting and shorthand, and of having a dislike for teaching the sociobusiness subjects, such as general business and business law. Perhaps this is true. If so, at least one reason arises from the fact that both students and teacher get satisfaction from being able to actually see and measure the progress that is being made. If progress is not being made, this also is readily discernible and that tends to spur each to greater effort— again likely to be followed by satisfying results.

This illustrates another well-established psychological truth. A learner achieves more when he can know "how he is doing" than he does when kept in the dark as to the results of his efforts. Keeping the student well informed about the results of his efforts is an important psychological means of motivation. It should be noted, moreover, that this is a highly individualized factor in motivation and thus aids the student in realizing and in feeling that the learning going on in the classroom is a very personal thing for him.

At the same time, and probably as a result of its motivational value, knowledge of how he is doing materially retards the feeling of fatigue. Thus a double value accrues from keeping the student well informed about the results of his learning endeavors.

The business teacher has many opportunities for conveying this knowledge to the student. In typewriting, frequent timed writings checked by the students themselves accomplish the purpose admirably. Over longer periods of time this may be reinforced through individual progress charts—also kept by the students themselves. In various cooperative part-time programs students similarly are likely to know very well how they are doing, since they are on the job and actually producing. In secretarial classes they may have the self-measurement of mailable letters transcribed. In bookkeeping, success or failure in correctly analyzing, recording, and summarizing business transactions is again quite evident to the student—often at the time he prepares his trial balance or work sheet, and certainly when he "checks" his final results.

The master business teacher sees to it that each individual student in each class is kept fully aware of the extent to which he is progressing in the learning process itself, as just illustrated. It can also be done by direct comments (preferably deserved praise) by the teacher, by appropriate problems and exercises, and by reasonably frequent tests and "checks" of various kinds.

Although tests and examinations (evaluations) graded by the teacher have an important place in education, it should be noted that in many ways the student may be enabled to make this evaluation of his own progress for himself. Another excellent example of this technique is to be found in certain "study guides" (often used in business law, for instance) in which case it takes but a minute or two in class for the teacher to have each student check his own understandings and thereby to spot immediately any errors or inadequacies in his own learning. This can be used effectively in real motivation of individual students.

WHOLE VERSUS PART LEARNING

Imagine for a moment, if you can, a student who has never seen or heard about a typewriter but who has been advised to learn how to typewrite. He has no knowledge of what this is, of what the machine can do, of how large or small it may be, or of the purpose of the machine. He therefore procures for himself a special tutor—an expert typist who, as it happens, has had no preparation as a teacher.

Wishing to be very thorough in his new role as a teacher (for which he is not qualified), this tutor decides to begin with a detailed study of the typewriter itself. He also decides to make it "simple" and to break the learning down into small segments. Accordingly, he completely dismantles a typewriter and proceeds to present to his student only one part at a time! First, he happens to select the bell; he takes it to the pupil and proceeds to teach all he can think of about the typewriter bell. The student examines it and handles it and takes careful notes on the tutor's lecture, and that night diligently studies for hours trying to memorize all he has been told.

And so the learning process (if it could be called that!) might proceed for many, many days. What a horrible waste of time and effort!

Yet this might well exemplify teaching by a *part method,* or from the "simple to the complex." It would lack, however, one extremely important requisite of effective learning, namely, learning by the *whole method*—or learning through gaining some understanding of the "complete meaning" or the "ultimate goal" toward which the learner is striving. How much simpler and how much more effective it would have been for the tutor to sit down at a typewriter and demonstrate the complete process of typewriting! Then—and only then—would the student be ready to effectively attack the problem of learning the simple things and progressing to the more complex. Without some understanding of the whole process and the relation of its parts to each other the learner is confused, can have no clear goal toward which to work, finds himself constantly rebelling inwardly—and is likely soon to give up.

Today all master teachers make use of this principle of teaching parts in proper relation to the whole to which they belong. That is why nearly all bookkeeping today begins with a study of the final bookkeeping reports and the bookkeeping equation. That is why typewriting and shorthand students no longer spend long hours practicing the writing of single unrelated words or letters. That is why many typewriting teachers now have students writing complete sentences during the first day in class.

Each business subject offers its own peculiar need for having the student first gain some knowledge of "where he is going" and "what it is all about." Without this early understanding of the "whole," motivation soon deteriorates and learning is seriously impeded.

RIVALRY AND COMPETITION

Almost everyone loves to compete. When rivalry or competition is present we put forth more effort and enjoy doing so; at the same time the feeling of fatigue is seldom noticed. We are motivated more highly by the anticipation of "winning" and of receiving recognition as a member of our group. Competition is a device frequently used effectively by most teachers.

The factor of rivalry is present in many teaching techniques commonly used by business teachers. No student in a typewriting or shorthand class can be striving to attain a record of a given number of words per minute without being aware that a spirit of competition and rivalry exists. He at all times is, in a sense, competing with other members of his class. Of even more importance from the viewpoint of "student-centered" teaching, he is always trying to improve his own record.

On occasion, the alert business teacher may create a situation that makes a game of this rivalry. On other occasions, he may make use of this form of motivation by selecting his better students to represent the class in assembly demonstrations or talks, or to make similar appearances before the Parent–Teacher Association or business and professional groups of the community, or to be announced through the columns of the paper as honor-roll students in business education. At times he may emphasize this same factor through various forms of bulletin-board charts and displays.

Two warnings should be heeded relative to the use of competition and rivalry. *The competition for high achievement records should not focus too much effort and attention on only the few students who are attaining the best records.* This formerly was quite customary during the era of commercial contests. Too often the teacher was made to feel that his promotion in the profession, and sometimes even his job, depended upon winning contests. This caused him to confine his efforts largely to his "team" members and, accordingly, to give little assistance to the great majority of his students. *Care must be taken not to embarrass or discourage some students.* This can readily happen, for instance, when certain students continue to remain near the bottom of the class in spite of their best efforts—and this is a common occurrence. If, in addition, this fact is prominently displayed before everyone in a bulletin-board chart, these students may suffer severe psychological damage, become badly frustrated, and even be caused to develop inferiority complexes and very undesirable personalities. (On the other hand, progress charts showing results of "self-competition" can change this into a desirable influence; such charts may be constructed in terms of gain in words per minute or in terms of points of improvement shown.) It should be remembered that occasionally a very superior student also becomes embarrassed when his superiority is flaunted before his classmates by his teacher.

GOALS AND SUBGOALS

Throughout life most of us have goals that we wish to attain and toward which we strive. Our motivation and our efforts are greater when we are aware of such goals. As we approach the attainment of each of these goals we experience increased interest and motivation, have a pleasant feeling of satisfaction, and seldom feel fatigued even though we are increasing our efforts. Once we have attained a given goal we are likely to feel satisfied and confident, and to look for "new worlds to conquer."

Thus in each subject or class it is important that each student have an understanding of the goal (or goals) toward which he is striving in that course. True, this also should fit into the pattern that makes up his longer-term goal or goals for himself and his life. In a way this becomes a part of the "whole" pattern (Gestalt) composing the individual's personality and purpose in life.

Psychologically, however, it is even more important to the learner that the teacher arrange the course or subject so that it also contains many subgoals all along the way. If the student can have a definite subgoal before him that he may reasonably expect to reach each month, or each week, or each day, and toward which he is knowingly striving each day, he can reap over and over again the many motivational advantages of approaching the achievement of his goal.

We find modern textbooks divided into many chapters and sections, each providing a definite subgoal toward which the student may work. In addition the wise business teacher provides each student with a constantly changing pattern of daily "goals" made reasonably achievable in terms of the capacities and developing abilities of each student. Thus the immediate subgoal may be that of learning to identify the common forms of insurance policies, to correctly solve a specific problem, to discover how the seventeenth section of the Statute of Frauds applies to our ordinary business transactions, or to add five correct words per minute to our average typewriting speed.

Make liberal use of the principle of providing the learner with many goals and subgoals that are attainable for him.

SKILL DEVELOPMENT

Many people, including some teachers, make the mistake of considering learning to be entirely a mental process. Actually all learning is accompanied by and influenced by physiological factors both within and outside the individual who is learning. In some types of learning, known as *skill development,* the physical responses of the individual become much more important. This is true, for instance, in learning to typewrite, or to take dictation in shorthand, or to transcribe from the dictaphone, or to skate, or to ride a bicycle, or to play basketball, or to walk upright and with poise, or to speak before an audience, or to receive callers with poise and charm either in person at the office or over the telephone.

Similarly, many people, including some teachers, make the mistake of considering the learning of skills to be entirely a physical thing. Nothing could be further from the truth.

From the viewpoint of the learner, the learning of a skill is a much more complicated and difficult process than is the mere acquiring of knowledge and understanding. Learning a skill usually includes the necessity of acquiring knowledge and understanding, but there is also the necessity, usually, of much effort and time devoted to purposeful and controlled practice. Behind all this practice usually lies the necessity of fitting together many, many previously learned complex knowledges and understandings into what appears to be a simple skill that can be performed almost automatically! It is quite true that once a high skill is attained in something, the act can be performed automatically; in fact, it must be performed automatically without any "interference" from the higher brain centers.

Perhaps an example will aid in understanding this. A teacher once had in class a girl who was unusually expert in taking dictation on the Stenotype. She was often hired to record discussions and proceedings at conventions and important board meetings. She had the reputation of never missing a word in her recording. Yet, while she was recording, she habitually read a book or a magazine at the same time! She had developed her skill so highly that it was completely automatized; her fingers reacted instantly when the sound of the voice reached her ears. She had actually found that her records were more accurate when she deliberately kept her mind off her work.

Similarly we sometimes see a demonstration by an expert typist in which he (or she) copies with 100 percent accuracy from a printed page at an extremely high rate, far over one hundred words per minute, while at the same time carrying on a conversation and perhaps computing difficult arithmetic problems mentally. Here again is a skill so highly developed that it has been automatized. Yet, in both of these examples, the learning process while the skill was being developed had necessarily been difficult and had originally required a high order of mental concentration and a very real mental effort to gain the necessary knowledge and understanding.

Let us once more consider an example. The fingers of a secretary may fairly fly as she types a beautiful letter from her shorthand notes. As you watch, though, you are aware that this apparently simple physical skill actually is the culmination of years of study of many separate things and that now she is skillfully combining a very complex set of factors and previous learnings. First, she had to learn to typewrite. She probably learned to do this through and from the printed word. Later (preferably), she had to learn a complete new "sound language," shorthand. Not only did she have to learn it, but she also had to learn how to write it—and with accuracy, perfection, and high speed. Still later, she then had to "relearn" her typewriting; instead of using the printed page as the stimulus to cause her fingers to type accurately, she had to learn to change to the stimulus of her shorthand notes. And these notes constitute a "sound" language; they do not spell out the words as they must be typed. Her eyes now see shorthand characters that represent words, sounds, and phrases, but with many, many of the "silent" letters completely omitted! Nevertheless, from this incomplete stimulus she must now have her fingers correctly spell out every word. And in addition—her mind must be ever alert to insert all needed punctuation, to correct any bad English or poor sentence structure, and even to make sure that the dictator has used correct terminology.

These examples help demonstrate two concepts important for the skill teacher. First is the realization that so-called skill development also has in it an important basis of mental learning, of knowledges and understandings. Thus, this portion of the developmental process is influenced by all the factors and motivations that influence any other type of learning.

Second is the further realization that the development of an expert skill carries the learner beyond the purely mental process and into a status of automation or semiautomation controlled by direct response of the appropriate muscles to the stimulus received. (Psychologists tell us that "short-circuit" responses have been set up which operate without having the stimulus pass through the higher brain center on its way to the responding muscles.) Although this portion of the developmental process may be influenced to some degree by ordinary motivating factors, it is much more dependent upon intense drill.

PROBLEM SOLVING

Today's educational philosophy strongly emphasizes the desirability of producing a graduate of our schools who is capable of solving life's problems as he meets them. The final evaluation of the success of an education lies largely in the ability the graduate has to apply his learning in the solving of the problems he will meet. This same philosophy applies to the learning acquired through any given subject or course.

The master teacher, therefore, provides ample and appropriate opportunity for his students to practice applying their learnings to problem solving. At the same time this medium provides them with opportunity to check the results of their learnings, an important factor in motivation. Every course and every bit of learning may be applied in some fashion to the problem-solving situation. The bookkeeping student faces problem solving constantly. The business law student practices and checks himself through the use of appropriate legal case problems. The general business student and the consumer education student spend much time discussing the problem situations. Every business class provides opportunity for problem solving in some form.

In any subject, however, it is important that the solving of any particular problem be delayed until the learner is ready for that problem. The beginning bookkeeping student is obviously not yet ready to solve problems involving controlling accounts and subsidiary ledgers, nor is the beginning student in business law yet ready to solve cases dealing with real estate mortgages or decedents' estates. In general, real problem solving should constitute a relatively minor portion of the work in the early stages of any learning but become a more major function of the work in the more advanced stages of learning. No definite line of demarcation can be drawn.

In skill subjects it often is especially important to delay certain types of problem solving until the learner is ready; attempting solutions before the learner is ready causes a great waste of time and inefficient learning. It would be foolish in elementary typewriting to introduce centering and various styles of letters before the student has even developed reasonable ability to type sentences on the keyboard; such a beginning student might get the practice of setting up but one letter during a period of time in which an advanced student might get the practice of setting up a large number of letters.

INDIVIDUAL DIFFERENCES

We started this review of the learning process with a reminder that all learning should be looked upon as individual growth and that it is each separate student as an individual, and not simply "a class," that the teacher is assisting through a learning process. We have now briefly reviewed some of the major factors entering into a successful teaching-learning process and have given some thought to how they specifically apply to the professional work of a business teacher. Although other factors might be mentioned, probably the ones reviewed are of major importance. It now is appropriate that we finish this review by returning to our original concept that all learning is an individual matter. (*Note:* At this point it is suggested that the reader review the viewpoint expressed at the beginning of this chapter and also the materials under the heading of "Learning as Individual Growth" [p. 41].)

Professional educational literature frequently refers to "providing for individual differences." The pressing problem is that of how to provide suitable learning materials and situations to meet the many varying needs of all the individuals in a class and to get it all done in the limited time available to the teacher.

Obviously there is no one solution. Just as obviously, no teacher can expect to do a 100 percent perfect job of it. Yet the master teacher is always doing this to an appreciable degree in every class.

In typewriting, for example, are to be found techniques in which the teacher has control of the entire class, as a class, and yet at the same time is automatically adjusting the learning to the individual needs of each student. The "call-the-throw" drills, for instance, are so arranged as to permit each student to select almost automatically his own best practice rate under timed conditions! Again, in shorthand the teacher may dictate the material at several different speeds, permitting each student to transcribe it whenever he is satisfied that he has been able to successfully get it recorded in his shorthand notebook.

Of special significance in caring for the problem of individual differences in subjects such as shorthand and transcription are the recent developments in the use of tapes and records for individual, student practice. Today schools are rapidly becoming equipped with "laboratories" or practice rooms where such equipment is made available for student practice at learning levels needed by individual students. At times dictation records may be taken home by the student for home practice with the aid of a record player. An increasing number of schools are being provided with multichannel listening stations served by various types of electronic equipment which provides the necessary controlled dictation. (See Chapter 7 for further details.)

In group discussions the alert teacher is constantly allowing for individual differences in his class as he leads his students in expressing themselves, in asking and answering questions, and in attempting explanations. In addition, the alert teacher is constantly providing individual students with specialized activities, projects, assignments, and suggestions for preparations outside of class that are chosen because they especially fit the needs of the individual student.

Yes—treating the learning process as an individual matter and making appropriate provisions for the needs of differing individuals keeps the teacher busy. It also requires the successful teacher to be a true professional artist. But the satisfactions accruing to the teacher who does this are perhaps unmatched in any other profession.

PROJECTS AND QUESTIONS FOR DISCUSSION

1. Interview the sales manager or marketing manager of some large business or industrial firm and inquire about any means he may use for motivating salesmen to increase their sales.

2. Inquire of the secretary or president of some local chapter of an organization such as the Lions Club or Rotary Club whether or not it makes use of any kinds of "awards" for its members; if so, why are the awards used?

3. Check the various factors in the learning process described in this chapter with those presented in the text(s) used in your course in educational psychology; report on any additional factors or elements that you find.

4. Interview the personnel director of some large business; inquire about the individual differences they find among applicants for various office positions.

5. We often hear the statement, "We teach as we have been taught." Do you believe there is any truth in this point of view? Why or why not?

6. Discuss the pros and cons of the following two statements:
   "Man in his fundamental nature is everywhere and at all times the same; the apparent differences are of far less importance than the underlying similarities."
   "Individual differences, all kinds of differences, are vast and measurable. In educational planning these differences are far more important than are the uniformities."

7. Discuss the statement, "The use of grades is an excellent type of motivation device."

8. Would you say that fear of criticism or fear of punishment would be a stronger motivation for students than praise and encouragement?

9. Should a teacher attempt to gain the attention of his classes through use of such personal techniques as flashy dress, unusual mannerisms, slangy talk, or some other personal element that sets him apart from the usual?

10. When a teacher observes his students showing fatigue or boredom, should he do something to divert them even though the diversion is not a part of the learning process?

11. What are the techniques involved in solving problems? Should these techniques be used in teaching high school business classes?

12. A teacher has stated, "I never answer questions of students if it is possible for them to find the answers themselves." Do you believe this to be a good procedure?

13. What are the different ways in which people learn? How can these be applied to the teaching of business subjects in the secondary school?

CASE PROBLEMS

1. It is a Friday afternoon in late April. Miss Arthur, a beginning business teacher, is teaching a class in second-semester typewriting during the last period of the day. It is raining rather steadily outside.

All during the period Miss Arthur has noticed a lethargy on the part of the students. They don't seem to care whether they type well or not. Here and there several students are causing a slight disturbance. During a timed writing Miss Arthur noticed that several of the students stopped to talk briefly even though taking a timed test.

Miss Arthur is becoming somewhat irritated with the seeming indifferent attitude on the part of the class in general. There is still twenty-five minutes remaining in the period and Miss Arthur plans to introduce a new typing problem—manuscript typing with footnotes.

Would you suggest that Miss Arthur is doing something wrong? Normally this class has been very cooperative and there has existed a fine student-instructor relationship. If Miss Arthur were to ask your advice on what she could do to correct the present situation, what might you tell her?

2. You are observing a class in beginning typewriting. You notice that the teacher who has just presented a problem in tabulation to her students is using what you believe to be improper techniques. She gave very few directions to the students on how to proceed in the tabulation problem and now while the students are struggling with the solution the teacher is doing very little if anything to help those students who are having difficulty. In fact, you just noticed that the teacher observed one of the students doing something wrong but did not stop and correct him—she just walked right past him.

What, if anything, is wrong with this teacher? Is she lazy? Doesn't she know the answers herself? Give your evaluation of this procedure.

3. Two teachers in Sandusky High School are discussing the case of one of their colleagues, a Mr. Bright, who is a business teacher in the high school. It seems that many of the faculty of the school believe that Mr. Bright is an ill-prepared and ineffective teacher. He never appears to be in front of his classes teaching them—it always seems that students are conducting his classes. One or two students have reported that all they ever seem to do is to sit around and talk. However, there seems to be a high interest in Mr. Bright's classes. The classes never seem to have any direction but wander about and often do not even appear to be discussing the subject matter of the course (although in all fairness most often the topics that are being discussed are related to the subject matter).

The epithet "progressive" has been attached to Mr. Bright, and several of the other teachers in the school feel that he should be fired at the end of the school year. What course of action do you suggest should be taken? Should Mr. Bright be shown the "error" of his ways? How would you determine whether he was ineffective or not?

SUGGESTED READINGS

Allen, Dwight W., and Kevin A. Ryan, *Microteaching*, Chap. 2, "The Component Skills Approach," pp. 10–32. Cambridge: Addison-Wesley Publishing Co., Inc., 1969.

Barbour, Edna, "Evaluation of Business Teachers by Students—PRO," *National Business Education Quarterly*, May 1966, pp. 34–38.

Christensen, G. Jay, "Atmosphere for Learning a Skill: Chaos or Creativity?," *Business Education Forum*, April 1964, p. 23.

Claxton, James W., "Five Patterns of Individualized Instruction," *Business Education World*, May–June 1971, pp. 16–17.

Crawford, T. James, "At the Start of a New Decade," *The Balance Sheet*, January 1970, p. 195. Editorial.

Del Turco, Lorraine, "Handling All Levels of Ability in the Classroom," *Business Education World*, February 1964, pp. 21–23.

Everard, Kenneth, "Our Mess in Marks," *Journal of Business Education*, November 1971, p. 48–49. Editorial.

Hansen, Ethel D., "A Comparison of the Teaching Behaviors of Creative and Less Creative Basic Business Teachers," *Journal of Business Education*, February 1970, p. 208.

Lebeda, Agnes, "Teach and Talk about Business," *Business Education Forum*, March 1964, p. 5.

Lloyd, Alan C., "Recent, Current, Coming Innovations in Business Education," *The Business Teacher*, March–April 1969, pp. 10–11.

Mesarak, Grace H., "The Theory of Guided Permissiveness," *Business Education Forum*, March 1970, pp. 22–23.

Miller, George E., "A Computer Assisted Experiment on the Problem of Learning and Problem Solving under the Condition of Goal Direction," *Business Education Forum*, October 1970, p. 42.

Musselman, Vernon A., "Meeting Individual Differences," *Business Education Forum*, October 1964, p. 24.

NBEA, "The National Business Entrance Tests," *NBEA Yearbook*, No. 5, 1967, pp. 311–15.

Olson, Milton C., "Education of Tomorrow's Business Teachers," *Journal of Business Education*, February 1970, pp. 182–83.

Petrello, George J., "Implications of the Profit System for Business Education," *Business Education Review*, Fall 1970, pp. 9–15.

Robek, Mary F., "Cause and Cure of Business Teacher Obsolescence," *Business Education Forum*, February 1964, p. 16.

Rosenberg, R. Robert, "Ask Yourself: How Do I Rate as a Teacher?," *Business Education World*, February 1964, pp. 24–25.

Shell, Walter, "Developing Good Classroom Control," *Journal of Business Education*, December 1970, pp. 115–16.

————, "Planning for Effective Teaching—Part I," *Journal of Business Education*, November 1970, pp. 67–68.

Tonne, Herbert A., "Changing Concepts in Teacher Education," *Journal of Business Education*, February 1970, pp. 184–85.

Wood, Merle W., and Jane C. Burhoe, "Guidance and the Business Student," *The Balance Sheet*, February 1971, pp. 211–13.

4

TEACHING TECHNIQUES
APPLIED TO
THE LEARNING PROCESS

In Chapter 3 is found a discussion of some of the major aspects of the learning process. It is necessary for all teachers to understand thoroughly the fundamentals of the learning process and then to apply these fundamentals in teaching by using sound teaching techniques. Too often teachers overemphasize the importance of techniques of teaching without thoroughly understanding the basic elements of learning. The good teacher first understands the reasons and means by which students learn and then uses appropriate techniques to accomplish the desired ends. Many of the elements discussed in Chapter 4 will be discussed more fully in later chapters as they apply to specific subject matter in business education. In this chapter it is sufficient to point out some of the major techniques used by teachers in applying the fundamentals of the learning process, which are applicable to all business subjects.

TEACHING TECHNIQUES WILL VARY

It must be recognized, however, that different learning situations exist, and therefore techniques that are sound and important for one school may not apply to another school. For instance, teaching in a school that has excellent electronic individual learning aids and a policy of individually prescribed programs of learning may require *completely different teaching tech-*

niques from those used in a more traditional school with a fixed schedule of classes for specifically identified subject-matter courses.

While it is anticipated that in the immediate future most schools will continue to function along relatively traditional lines, it seems likely that during the decade of the seventies changes will appear rapidly. As already mentioned (Chapter 3), some schools have adopted a policy of individually prescribed study programs; many more have adopted various types of facilities and learning mediums especially adapted to individualized learning. It seems probable that such changes will continue and at an accelerated rate. Teaching techniques will change accordingly.

Yet fundamentals of the learning process will remain unchanged as we constantly seek new "techniques" for making learning more efficient and more effective. The successful business teacher will keep well informed about these developing techniques and will constantly evaluate them in terms of their effectiveness as aids to the learning process—keeping ever in mind that he is "accountable" for producing the best possible results for each learner as an individual and doing so while economizing both in time and in costs.

A MODERN LEARNING CENTER

Most students and teachers are quite familiar with the traditional classroom and schedule of classes; they have grown up with them. The traditional classroom is a relatively formal arrangement where groups of students gather with a teacher. The teacher is "in control" and is expected to direct the activities of a "captive" audience, with all students in the group tending to think and learn somewhat as a unit. The student must spend his day conforming to a "set" class schedule. This class schedule is definitely subject-matter oriented. The activities within the classroom are also subject-matter oriented, with the teacher directing the learning activities through such mediums as the lecture, questions and answers, demonstrations, reports, laboratory experiments, class drills, panels, and class discussions. The teacher personally evaluates the learning of each individual student, and usually according to preconceived standards resulting in a "grade" ranging from A at the top down to F (for failure) at the bottom.

But let us now also take a brief look at a hypothetical business education department in a high school which has seen fit to adopt many innovative techniques far removed from the traditional ones. For some time it has used "flexible" class schedules based on "modules" of eighteen minutes. A new class schedule is prepared each week through the use of an electronic computer, and it varies from week to week. At times this permits large groups of students to be brought together to witness an important demonstration, or a film, or a demonstration-lecture prepared by the teacher and presented by video tape. At other times students may meet for small group discussions only, or they may be working at the *learning center* (sometimes referred to as *resource center* or *learning laboratory*) as individuals.

Most students have individually prescribed programs of study. This means that the student, assisted by counselors and teachers, has arrived at certain conclusions about what he, as an individual, most needs to be learning at this particular time of life. He has helped select "units" or "packets" or "areas" of learning materials which he and his teachers or his counselors agree appear to be best for him to study. He has "set his goals."

It should be noted that in many cases the selected "packets" or learning units may consist of only *parts* of some traditional course or courses—thus eliminating the necessity of spending time studying for and attending classes where it appears that the learning taking place will not be especially relevant to the needs and interests of this student.

When the student is studying business, he will spend *most* of his time in the learning center in that department. Here he will proceed with his learning individually, spending much time working in an individual booth or carrel which is well equipped with learning aids such as a headset for listening to various recordings, projectors and monitoring devices for viewing filmstrips, slides, pictures, films and video tapes, and such other learning aids as may be needed. Should he have need for some learning aid not in his booth he knows where it can be used in some other booth. Typewriters and other office machines are readily available for his use.

At all times this learning center (or laboratory) has specially trained assistants (some known as librarians) available to help the student locate desired material or to assist him should he encounter a technical difficulty in operating equipment. The center has been well stocked with *various* kinds of visual, audio, and audiovisual learning material which can be quickly located for use; in many cases different packets of material (or tapes, etc.) cover the *same* subject, thus permitting the student to choose the particular learning medium he prefers to use or, at times, permitting him to further reinforce some apparently unsatisfactory learning by using an alternative medium.

The learning center is carpeted and relatively soundproof, and although each student is free to come and go at his own work or to stop and discuss it at any time with an assistant or another student—or with a teacher—the overall impression is one of quiet, purposeful work. One corner of the large center has a "lounge," equipped with tables and comfortable chairs, in which small groups of students meet with teachers from time to time for further discussion.

The posted weekly computerized schedule shows which business teachers will be in the learning center each hour of the day. Since most of the learning is taking place here, the business teachers have fewer scheduled group "classes" to meet and thus are free to spend several hours each day in the learning center helping individual students—or, at times, holding small group discussions with them. Usually two business teachers are available in the center throughout the day, and the center is open for student use all day. (It is also used in the evening for "adult" students who have chosen to learn certain business subjects and procedures by this individual study method.)

Periodically each student has a conference with his teacher, and at this time the student and the teacher cooperatively evaluate his progress. A form of evaluation is also constantly taking place through the small group discussion meetings, where each student has some opportunity to compare himself with others doing essentially the same type of work. At the end of the semester any final required grading is the outcome of cooperative thinking on the part of both student and teacher. At all times during evaluations, emphasis is placed on *helping* the student achieve his selected goals; everything possible is being done to help avoid a final evaluation of failure. Should a student need more time to master some phase of learning, such time can usually be made available to him.

Although certain skill classes, including typewriting and shorthand, do continue to hold regular group class meetings, while in class each student uses a set of headphones most of the time and has individual electronic controls at his desk. At times instructions are given by the teacher through the use of a microphone, with students receiving the instructions through the headsets. At *many* times the students in the classroom are working on several *different* drills or assignments or problems, each having been instructed to "tune in" on a specified channel according to his needs at the moment—after which he receives recorded instructions for his procedure.

Certainly this brief hypothetical picture of a school using modern learning facilities and innovations necessarily leaves many questions unanswered; however, it should be sufficient to make it quite obvious that the business teacher working in this school will be required to develop many *different* teaching techniques as contrasted with the teacher working in a more traditional school. For instance, he must become a skilled technician and operator and consumer of modern electronic equipment and must be able to either produce or intelligently select appropriate learning materials for use with the equipment. Moreover, his teaching techniques will be much less those of a dictator and much more those of a true democratic educational leader.

THE BUSINESS TEACHER AS A PERSON

Before we can discuss some of the more effective techniques used by successful business teachers, we first should consider some of the personal characteristics teachers must have in order to use these techniques effectively.

It is not sufficient for today's business teacher to be a possessor of knowledge alone. He must be able to develop an environment in his classroom that is conducive to making students desire to learn. It does not take one with great ability to use proven and tested teaching techniques in the classroom. Unless the teacher has the proper personality and character traits to use the techniques effectively, they will be of little help to him in developing the learning process in his students. Let us consider, then, what some of these personal traits are that must be present before technical devices can be used to the best advantage.

The Effective Business Teacher Is Dynamic

The business teacher who is vigorous, stimulating, dramatic, and exciting will be the one who is most successful in the classroom. His classes will move swiftly and surely and be free from boredom and monotony. Much of this dynamic atmosphere found in the classroom will stem from the actions of the teacher himself. His personal enthusiasm and interest should be such that it will be absorbed and projected by the students in the class. The teacher should have a flair for the dramatic even to the extent of being somewhat of a "ham" actor. Care should be taken, of course, not to be flashy or superficial or obtain the reputation of being a "screwball"—but the teacher who senses the drama in a particular situation and then uses this to advantage in instruction will be compensated for his actions in having a stimulating and interesting class.

Other simple yet important elements in developing a dynamic climate are the use of gesture, voice, and general mien. Use of expression in speaking, gesturing to emphasize a point—even the use of facial expression—are all necessary. The small yet important item of the clothing of the teacher has a bearing upon the classroom atmosphere. Variety and even color (in good taste) in clothing can often do much to overcome drabness in surroundings.

Today's business teacher is an adventurer who is always willing to project his thinking beyond what is known—not afraid of being unusual—and is curious and willing to experiment; these are the characteristics of the dynamic teacher.

The Effective Business Teacher Is Scholarly

The outstanding business teacher has a thorough knowledge of the subject matter he is teaching plus a breadth of knowledge covering many areas of human understanding. He has the ability to interrelate and use this knowledge for effective teaching and living. These are all an integral part of his scholarly achievement. His knowledge of his field and his knowledge of humanity will help him to develop a confidence that will be invaluable to him in the class-room. Students admire and respect scholarly attributes and will respond to teachers with these characteristics. Care must be taken, however, not to flaunt knowledge to the point of being obnoxious. A respect for knowledge coupled with a humble attitude toward its proper uses will aid in making a teacher liked, admired, and respected by students, colleagues, and members of a community.

The Effective Business Teacher Is Realistic

By being realistic the effective business teacher will seldom overestimate his own abilities nor will he misjudge the capabilities of his students. He will realize the limitations that society places on man and the burdens that man places upon society. He will be aware of the inequalities of life, but he will never subjugate his thinking to accept unjust inequalities. He will respect the limitations of the learning process and will use teaching methods that are based on the abilities of his students to acquire knowledge and to develop the qualities of an educated person.

He will realize that teaching can be both an enjoyable and yet a frustrating experience; that often the standards teachers set for themselves with respect to the degree of achievement of their students are higher than their (the teachers') ability to achieve. Because of this the effective teacher will acknowledge the need for relaxing activities so that he can meet his daily tasks without undue strain and concern. He will accept failure and disappointments with the knowledge that upon these things successes are often built.

The Effective Business Teacher Is Democratic

The democratic process is highly important to the effective business teacher. He believes in the inherent right of the individual, and he sees and knows the inherent goodness within youth and endeavors to direct the ideas, thoughts, and knowledges of these young people into useful and productive channels. He will understand that we cannot be responsible for our students but that they must learn from themselves; thus he will eliminate from his thinking the paternalism and authoritarianism that is so often found in teachers.

The atmosphere of his classroom will be democratic in that the ideas and opinions of his students are considered of importance even though they may vary from his own. He will respect the views of others and zealously guard their right to believe as they do. He will constantly seek the truth and will attempt to develop this concept in the minds of his students. Bigotry and prejudice will have no place in his thoughts, and he will express his faith in the democratic process and subscribe wholeheartedly to the American system of government.

THE TEACHER AS A TECHNICIAN

One of the first elements conducive to learning is the physical and mental atmosphere of the classroom. To a large extent the teacher is responsible for these important items, and although many teachers feel these are relatively unimportant as compared with other factors in teaching, inferior physical and mental atmosphere of the classroom can actually retard learning and cause teaching problems that are difficult to solve. Knowledge of and proper utilization of such factors as physical arrangement, lighting, equipment and supplies, student-teacher relationships, record keeping, and classroom organization may make the difference between a superior and an inferior teacher.

Physical Arrangements

The physical arrangement of the classroom should be a matter of concern and requires much study on the part of the teacher. Such factors as proper lighting, heating, ventilation, and room for both students and teacher to move about must be considered. It is not necessary for the teacher to be an expert in the physical properties of light and heat; the use of good common sense is sufficient. Anyone should be able to tell when a room is properly lighted or when desks and tables should be moved around to take advantage of available light. Comfort should be the best guide for heat and ventilation. Raising a window to adjust heating and ventilation to sensible proportions is a matter of good judgment. The aid of the school janitor might be sought for suggestions of maximum utilization of existing heating and ventilation facilities. It is obvious that students cannot perform their best work in overheated, underventilated, and poorly lighted surroundings. It will not always be possible in many schools to develop these facilities to an ideal, but at least the teacher should be aware of the best physical arrangement for learners and adapt existing conditions in the classroom to as near the ideal as possible.

Experiments with various room arrangements will often lead to the solutions of problems that the teacher may at first believe to be insoluble. One teacher in a typewriting class was plagued by students throwing wastepaper at the wastebasket with a resulting messy appearance where the thrown paper missed the mark. She solved her problem by the simple expedient of moving the wastebasket to a more convenient position for the students to use. Another teacher who had difficulty moving about his typewriting room because of crowded conditions solved his problem by arranging the tables of the class in the form of a square, and by so doing gave approximately 25 percent more space in which to move about and observe the students as they typed.

The problem of the physical arrangement of the classroom will become more important. Each teacher will be called on to use his ingenuity to solve these problems so that learning can take place in the best of physical conditions.

Classroom Organization

The organization of the classroom with respect to seating of students, distributing and collecting instructional supplies and papers, and taking attendance and issuing student permits are also important factors for the teacher to consider. Again common sense should be the guide. It will be well for the teacher to determine the practice in the school concerning these matters and then adapt his procedures to this practice. Although there is no set rule with respect to the best method for seating students in class, frequently a simple alphabetic arrangement will prove to be the most feasible. This method will often separate the "buddies" and the "lovebirds" and will thus eliminate at the beginning any minor problem that may arise because of the overfriendliness of certain students. Also, an alphabetic arrangement will facilitate handing out papers and taking roll, and in the early days of the class will facilitate learning students' names.

The teacher should learn the names of students as quickly as possible— usually within a day or two—and should follow the custom of the school with respect to calling students by name. In most schools addressing students by their first names is customary; usually the shortened version of the first name, such as Jim, Bill, Sue, or whatever the student prefers, is best. The more formal Mr. and Miss and the use of the last name only is often considered too cold and unfeeling.

The teacher should devise a good and fast method for dispensing graded papers, handing in papers, and passing out supplies. Sloppiness and carelessness in these matters can be distracting to both students and teacher and can cause petty annoyances which are not found in the best-organized classes. Care must be taken that classes are not overorganized to the point of highly formalized procedures and not underorganized to the extent of having time-consuming and improper procedures. A little care and preplanning on the part of the teacher can eliminate many minor difficulties which could grow to major ones.

Human Relationships (Discipline)

The problem of discipline is one that many teachers, both experienced and inexperienced, dread. Actually this problem is not the major one that many teachers feel it is. However, the mental anguish that can be caused by disciplinary problems tends to lead teachers to overemphasize both its importance and its magnitude. Some school administrators have helped to overemphasize this problem because too many principals and superintendents have tended to measure the ability of a teacher by the manner in which he controls his students rather than by the teacher's ability to teach. Superintendents have stated that more teachers fail because of a discipline problem with students than for any other reason. It is doubtful that this is true, because too few administrators actually get time to observe the teacher in action. They merely see the results of a discipline difficulty and thus assess the teacher's ability by this factor alone.

If the truth were actually known, difficulties of teachers with recalcitrant students, in all probability, are a minor part of the typical teacher's problems. In many cases young teachers have difficulty controlling students because of a predetermined fear that all students in the secondary school are a group of rowdies waiting for a chance to eject the teacher from the classroom. Of course, such is not the case.

In any event the management and control of students is one of the requirements of good teaching in order to maintain the proper atmosphere for learning in the classroom. It is difficult for the teacher to teach or for students to learn in a classroom in which an air of suspense is always present. The teacher cannot be at his effective best if he feels that he must be ever watchful for student disturbances. The students cannot be at their effective best if disturbances and distractions are always breaking out to disrupt their thinking.

What, then, is the solution for maintaining good disciplinary relationships in class? There is no one answer to this problem. Some teachers may say "Be tough from the very beginning—let them know who is boss." Another will say "Don't stand for any nonsense." Still another pet phrase is "Be friendly but firm." All these expressions may have some merit, but the truth is that each teacher must assess his own personality and the situation in which he is teaching and must then use the procedures that are best suited both to himself and to the situation.

The foregoing statement will not satisfy the teacher who is looking for a nice, neat answer to the problem of disciplinary control. It is unfortunate, but there is no nice, neat answer. The differences found in people are so pronounced that it is impossible to give one pat answer for every problem.

Several basic principles of human behavior, however, may give some key to the avoidance or elimination of conflicts between students and teacher. If teachers will only put out of their minds the thought that disciplinary problems are inevitable and treat their students with courtesy and respect as they would treat an adult, then the majority of the disciplinary situations will never appear. All teachers, regardless of their ability, are faced with the problem child at some time or another. The main thing to remember is that 99 percent of secondary school youngsters are well behaved and cause no difficulty. The other 1 percent can usually be controlled with patience, understanding, and common sense.

Although there is no one solution to problems arising from disciplinary breakdowns, the following list of suggestions may be considered possible procedures to minimize difficulties of this nature. It should be remembered that this list is not a final solution to problems but merely suggests procedures that may prove useful.

1. Study the seating of the students. Determine, if possible, any trouble spots that may result from students sitting near each other who are "buddies" or "sweethearts." Rearrange the seating of students (as inconspicuously as possible) to eliminate possible trouble spots.

2. Learn the names of your students as quickly as possible and call on students whose attention may tend to waver. Do not use this procedure to embarrass a student, however.

3. Be businesslike in the classroom. Know what you intend to do in each class and get to the task as quickly as possible. An informal businesslike attitude is best.

4. Avoid all suggestions of criticism, anger, or irritation before the students. Be careful not to lose your temper. However, if you do become angry, make every effort to hide your feelings.

5. By your actions let the students know that you are interested in them as human beings as well as students in a class.

6. Stop little disciplinary difficulties before they get out of hand and become major problems.

7. Do not become sarcastic or belittle your students.

8. Do not threaten or harangue individuals or the group.

9. When discussing a disciplinary problem with an individual or the group, be as impersonal as possible. Do not permit favoritism to show in your actions and do not require apologies.

10. When not certain what course of action to take in a disciplinary situation, don't do anything. It is much better to back away from a problem and attack it later than to take too hasty action without careful thought.

11. Handle your own disciplinary problems insofar as possible. However, do not permit a problem to become more complex before you seek aid from others.

12. In the long run the following factors on your part will eliminate many difficulties:

    a. Respect for your students as individuals.
    b. Courtesy.
    c. Your scholarship and preparedness.
    d. Your sense of humor.
    e. Tolerance and understanding.
    f. Fairness.
    g. Enthusiasm.

SPECIALIZED INSTRUCTIONAL EQUIPMENT

No teacher can be successful in his profession today without rather complete knowledge of the vast array of modern electronic and other equipment available as aids to efficient and effective learning, together with the newer instructional materials designed for use with such equipment. And each year brings new and improved ideas! It all adds up to a most interesting and exciting development, but one that is very demanding in terms of time and effort on the part of the individual teacher interested in teaching as a professional career. It is not the purpose of this textbook to explore technical details of various types of equipment; that is a continuous task which all professional workers must face.

Technical skill and know-how, however, must enter into the preparation of the business teacher who is to make use of specialized equipment in the classroom. Teaching larger classes while at the same time giving greater attention to *individual* student problems and to achieving more learning in shorter time all add up to a positive need for knowing how to make use of this equipment.

For many years now the more skillful business teachers have been experts in the use of film and filmstrip projectors, opaque projectors, and simple record players. More recently they have discovered the value of the overhead projector—and especially when its use is combined with the use of an aid such as the Thermofax copy machine for quickly preparing transparencies. And today the use of the tape recorder is becoming almost standard practice in many phases of office and secretarial education.

At present far too few business teachers are making use of the possibility of having students receive instructional materials through the use of headsets. This medium has the triple advantage of (a) concentrating the student's attention on his work through eliminating outside distracting sounds; (b) permitting various students or groups of students to each be working on his own needed materials and at his own needed speed; and (c) having all these various activities going on in one room at the same time but without each interfering with the other! Frequently it has the added advantage of permitting individual students to study and practice effectively without the need for direct aid from the teacher.

The source of information received through the headphones may be either a single tape or a single record; either one or many students may be receiving the sound simultaneously through "gangs" of headsets. Through the use of two or more record players or tape recorders the variety of simultaneously presented instructional materials may be multiplied manyfold—and all may be done in one apparently quiet room with each student hearing only *his own* instructional material! The equipment may be relatively simple or it may be of a more sophisticated type comparable to the well-known foreign-language "laboratories." In the more modern secretarial and typewriting electronic laboratories each student has at his desk his own selector and volume control, which permit him to "tune in" on the particular channel needed for practice at the moment and to individually adjust the volume to his own needs.

Similarly, modern equipment now permits the business teacher to positively control the content and speed of materials being presented visually; such equipment is an adaptation of tachistoscopic training which has long been in use in reading-improvement programs. Ready-prepared film is available for use with such equipment in teaching shorthand, typewriting, transcription, filing, arithmetic, machine calculation, business English, and other phases of business education.

Just as the modern surgeon must constantly add new technical skills as modern science comes to his aid, so too must the modern business teacher constantly improve and expand his ability as a technician in order to make effective use of the applications of modern science to needs of the teaching profession. Frequently, too, he finds it advantageous to prepare his own tapes, records, or film for use with this modern specialized equipment.

PROGRAMMED INSTRUCTIONAL MATERIALS

In all education it is the individual student who really counts—not the subject matter or the teacher. Too many teachers have had to learn this the hard way and have become relative failures in their careers. But we are learning. We now realize that any student really learns *best* when he can do so at his own pace. When learning as one of a group, the "fast" learner often becomes bored with the slow pace, often creates disturbances as a result, and may even lose interest in his studies. Similarly, the "slow" learner often becomes discouraged when he cannot keep up with the class, often rebels, and tends to drop out of school. Recognition of this failure on the part of education has recently brought about an "individualizing" of the learning process.

Among the many techniques now available for individualizing learning is the use of "programmed" instructional materials. Essentially, this means the use of material especially prepared to enable a student to study and learn largely "on his own"—at his own pace and with little or no additional help from his teacher. The idea is a good one, and when properly used and accompanied by appropriate discussions and evaluations, it can sometimes accomplish amazingly fine results.

The preparation of good programmed material is a slow and rather tedious process and requires considerable technical knowledge. For some time most of the material so prepared was for use in so-called teaching machines, which were widely publicized and are still popular. While at times certain types of machines prove to be valuable aids, it is quite possible to prepare and use programmed instructional materials without the "teaching machines." Today commercially prepared programmed textbooks and units of instruction are available for use in the teaching of most business subjects.

Among the more elaborate developments in the programmed instruction is a complete computer-controlled presentation—including the automatic control and use of such equipment as film projectors, slide projectors, tape recorders, video-tape projectors, and other equipment as may be needed—all interwoven and automatically presented in proper sequence with appropriate voice and other explanations! Once carefully programmed, such a presentation may be used over and over again, either with individual students or with multiple groups of students.

The necessity of teaching *more* students *efficiently* and with economy in the use of teacher time makes programmed instructional materials well worthy of consideration.

PLANNING

The planning of instruction is a highly important aspect of the teacher's work. The superior teacher not only will plan carefully for each day but will plan far in advance for an entire semester or for a year's entire program of instruction. In those schools where instructional materials and procedures have been heavily programmed and automated, much time has already been used making both daily and long-range plans far in advance; but even in such situations it is always necessary to (1) fully plan from day to day for the proper *use* of the materials and equipment, and to (2) constantly plan and make revisions in the materials and procedures to meet changing situations and to insure proper improvements. In other schools, operating under the more traditional classroom procedures, much of the total planning must be done each year by the individual teacher. The following suggestions for planning apply especially to the more traditional classroom procedures, which most business teachers will probably continue to encounter during this decade.

In the past, lesson planning by teachers took the form of very detailed and formal plans. Each day's lesson was stated in the form of objectives, aims, procedures, and so forth, which necessitated a great deal of laborious thought and work on the part of the teacher. Obviously this type of planning, though it had the advantage of making the teacher think through each day's lesson carefully, nonetheless had many limitations. In spite of the work and time required to prepare such plans, they usually were so detailed and restrictive that they actually had little value. If the work in the classroom were a set pattern that the teacher could forecast, these types of plans would be useful. However, the better teachers have found that learning will best take place when the activity of the classroom is patterned after current situations or stimulated by the interests of the students. The teacher who holds himself within the confines of a detailed lesson plan will not be an effective teacher because he will not be able to use current class situations as a point of departure for teaching. The superior teacher has found that a loosely constructed, flexible lesson plan, but one carefully thought through, is much more effective and applicable to the typical class.

The modern concept of lesson planning, then, is somewhat more liberal and less restrictive than the old-type formal plans. The importance of planning remains as great as before. However, the modern trend of planning permits more flexibility and adaptability on the part of the teacher to meet various learning problems as they are confronted in the class.

The well-prepared teacher is usually a confident teacher and one who commands respect from his students. The time spent in planning and preparing for the class by necessity requires much of the teacher's time. However, this time can be shortened considerably through a few days of concentrated effort.

Three main stages of planning in teaching are used today by superior teachers. The first is the long-range stage in which plans are laid for a particular course for a semester or a year. The second stage is planning for a shorter period of time, usually for a chapter or a unit of work composed of shorter chapters. The third stage is the day-to-day planning for each of the individual lessons that may have been assigned.

Long-Range Planning

A long-range plan for instruction is usually the first step in the teacher's preparation for a course. This type of plan is often in outline form and is the basis for future unit or day-to-day planning. The broad topics to be covered, or the units, are listed with an estimated time to be spent on each. The instructional materials that supplement the textbook are also listed, with notations of those on hand in the teacher's files and those that must be obtained. The audiovisual aids to be used are planned along with their approximate dates of use. If these materials must be procured, then the name and address of the supplier should be listed. Other resources or instructional materials that may be used should also be listed. Finally, the examinations to be used should be listed together with the approximate date for each.

Although at first glance it would appear that preparing such a long-range plan would be a time-consuming task, it should be remembered that the teacher will only have to do it once during the semester and that the time taken to prepare more detailed plans for units and day-to-day lessons will be cut accordingly.

In preparing basic textbooks and instructional materials for classroom use, authors and publishers have already planned carefully and have attempted to meet the needs of large numbers of schools and teachers. In general, each basic textbook published attempts to present, in a meaningful sequence, the subject matter and learning materials believed to be "right" for a certain course or courses. Competing texts often give opportunity to select the one that the individual teacher or the school believes best meets the local needs. Quite commonly the teacher is expected to provide supplementary materials, or to omit some portions of the book, or to use his prerogative of changing the sequence in which chapters or units are to be presented. Some present-day texts are even designed to *require* the teacher to make advance decisions and select only relevant portions of the text. Most teachers take advantage of this planning already done by others, and by examining several basic textbooks, find that it is not difficult to provide needed long-range planning.

The beginning teacher, however, is warned that the authors of many texts have sound psychological reasons for presenting learning materials in certain sequences and patterns and that serious problems may be encountered should an inexperienced teacher make changes in such a plan.

Although the overall long-range plan certainly need not be in detail, and may consist essentially of a broad outline, it quite naturally will be made up of a number of divisions or "units." These divisions will form a natural basis for then preparing a more detailed plan for each of the units.

Unit Planning

The planning of instruction for a unit of work (or for several related chapters in a basic textbook) is much more detailed than is the long-range plan. In the unit plan the major objectives (preferably stated in behavioral terms) should be listed to clarify them in the teacher's mind. A detailed outline is needed of topics to be covered in the unit, instructional materials to be used, student and teacher references, suggested student activities and projects, suggested applicable teaching techniques, and tentative examination or evaluation instrument. Care should be taken in preparing the unit plan, for it is from this plan that daily lesson plans will be developed.

An illustration follows of a guide now being used in the state of Illinois for teaching a unit on "Using Consumer Credit Wisely." The School Code of Illinois (Section 27–12; 1) requires instruction in consumer education in the public schools in grades eight through twelve and indicates certain minimum topics or units to be included. This led to a project whereby over fifty high school and university educators, business representatives, and other interested citizens cooperated with the Curriculum Services of the Office of the Superintendent of Public Instruction in preparing a set of guidelines for teaching consumer education.[1] The illustrative unit is one of the following twelve prepared at that time and may be looked upon as a total long-range plan:

General Principles of Consumer Purchasing
Budgeting or Money Management
Using Consumer Credit Wisely
Buying Goods
Buying Services
Purchasing and Maintaining Automotive Products and Services
Using Leisure Time, Money, and Energy
Renting or Owning a Home
Making Use of Insurance
Savings and Investments
Consumer Taxes
Consumer Rights and Responsibilities

The following statement pertinent to these twelve units, or topics, indicates the general nature of all of them: "Each topic is presented through a statement of rationale, a list of objectives stated in behavioral form, a suggested content outline, suggested student activities, and a few specific resources applicable to the topic. Additional resource materials for each topic are listed in the final section of this publication."[2]

[1] *Guidelines for Consumer Education,* Office of the Superintendent of Public Instruction, Springfield, Ill., June 1968, 89 pp.
[2] *Op. cit.,* p. 5.

AN ILLUSTRATIVE PLAN FOR A UNIT OF INSTRUCTION

Using Consumer Credit Wisely

Credit makes possible the acquiring of goods and services, and paying for them, while the goods are being used. Since this is an established fact in our economy, young people need to learn how to use credit wisely in order to avoid the financial entanglements which can result from over-use or misuse of credit.

When young people find it necessary to borrow money to continue their education, the cost of credit may be far offset by the earning potential in the career of their choice.

The American consumer is a credit consumer. He uses his credit cards, signs installment contracts and borrows money. He promises to pay for many of his goods and services at a later date. These promises may have pitfalls.

OBJECTIVES

To help students:

- —recognize the significant function of consumer credit in our economy
- —appreciate the values as well as the obligations involved in the use of credit
- —know that credit costs money and understand the expenses involved in providing this service
- —become acquainted with the sources for all types of consumer credit
- —understand laws concerned with consumer credit
- —learn how to use credit wisely.

OUTLINE OF CONTENT

1. What is Consumer Credit?
   Advantages and disadvantages
2. Kinds of Consumer Credit
   Purchase credit
   Service credit
   Cash credit
3. Forms of Credit Agreements
   Installment credit agreements
   Contract—description of items purchased, cash price, credit price, down payment, etc.
   Chattel mortgage
   Security
   Co-signers
   Revolving Charge Accounts
   Variety of names
   Add and subtract feature
   Service charge
4. Establishing Credit
   Credit rating—character, capacity, capital
   Credit bureaus

5. Using Consumer Credit Wisely
   Using the right kind of credit for the purpose
   Shopping for credit
   Taking no more debt than can be safely carried
   Paying debts promptly
6. Cost of Using Credit
   Dollar cost of credit
   Percentage cost of credit
   Reduction of purchasing power
7. Borrowing Money
   Kinds of cash loans
       Character loan
       Co-signer loan
       Collateral loan
   Places to borrow—only licensed lenders
       Banks
       Consumer finance companies
       Credit unions
       Life insurance companies
8. Consumer Credit Laws
   Small Loan Law of Illinois
   Consumer Fraud Act of 1961
       1967 amendments
   Retail Installment Sales Act of 1967
   Truth-in-Lending legislation

SUGGESTED ACTIVITIES

What kind of credit is used by the families represented in the class? This information may be obtained through an oral or written poll. Tabulate the results. Use the information as a basis for learning.

From problems in textbooks or actual consumer problems find out the dollar cost and per cent cost in each case.

Explain and discuss these credit terms: promissory note, conditional sales contract, default, garnishment, wage assignment, installment, principal, balance, co-signer,

Collect evidences of consumer credit: charge-plate, promissory note, installment contract, advertisements of consumer-lending agencies, brochure on the "budget" plan of a discount store, etc. These credit forms may be used as a bulletin board display, to clarify explanations, or bring realism to theory.

Ask students to visit different retail establishments, for example, a credit jeweler, a department store, an automobile dealer, a motorcycle dealer, a furniture store, a mail-order outlet and obtain all facts on the purchase of an item on an installment plan. Report on these to the class.

Provide for a role-playing lesson in which the members of a family are over-extended credit-wise. Show how they plan to work themselves out of this financial problem.

Ask four students to take an identical problem on borrowing money to four different lending agencies: bank, consumer finance company, credit union, life insurance company. Compare the percentage of credit costs. Does each agency have a particular advantage not considering the lending rate?

What is Illinois law—SB 977? Why was it passed?

What retail stores do not extend credit to consumers? Why not?

Discuss what can be done when excess of debt becomes a family problem.

SPECIFIC RESOURCES

Following are listed some suggested materials for background information on Using Consumer Credit Wisely. See also the extensive listing of materials in the last section of this publication.[3] [*Note:* Twelve references that follow are omitted here.]

Perhaps it is pertinent to also point out that, in keeping with modern instructional techniques in use in many schools, business teachers in Illinois have cooperated in preparing and publishing programmed instructional materials for teaching each of these units.[4]

Daily Lesson Plans

The daily lesson plan is based on the planning developed for the unit. For the experienced teacher it can usually be prepared on three-by-five cards which merely serve as a reminder of the planning for the day—a list of questions for discussion, drills to be used, or other elements pertinent to the lesson. No formal planning sheet is necessary. At times it may even take the form of brief notes. It is merely a reminder for the teacher of elements to be taught that day as a part of the master (unit) plan.

However, it is *extremely important* that there be daily lesson planning and that it be psychologically sound as well as logical. For the relatively inexperienced teacher and, especially, the apprentice student-teacher, good planning habits are best learned when some type of formal lesson plan is used. There appears to be no one best form. It should merely be so arranged as to *encourage* a well-planned lesson. There probably are four major factors to which the expert teacher constantly (and perhaps semiautomatically) gives attention as he prepares and teaches a lesson:

1. The content, topics, subject matter or "learnings" for the day, and the related sequences in which they are to be presented
2. The various procedures and activities *of the teacher* as he conducts the class and carries through the sequences planned
3. The activities and participations *of the students* as the class period proceeds—for an idle student learns but little
4. An *evaluation* of the success of the plan (How well did it work? Should it be changed before it is used again in the future?)

It is recommended that the beginning teacher adopt a two-, three-, or four-column "form" (as may be preferred) to use in preparing daily lesson plans,

---

[3] *Op. cit.*, pp. 15–18.

[4] *Consumer Education Programmed Learning Instruction in*——, Alpha Phi Chapter of Delta Pi Epsilon, Northern Illinois University, DeKalb, 1970. Permission to reproduce can be obtained.

Exhibit 4.1 THE DAILY LESSON PLAN

First, there are certain "constants" which must ALWAYS be cared for—heat, ventilation, light, proper seating, roll call, etc. But the MAIN items to be "worried about" in advance are essentially the "variables" from day to day. *Three* of them are always with you: (*a*) that which is being learned—subject matter or content, objectives, attitudes, knowledges, skills, etc., (*b*) the teacher—as a guiding, directing, motivating force constantly controlling the situation, and (*c*) the students—who *cannot* remain passive and disinterested if they are learning, but who should at all times be engaged in appropriate motivated ACTIVITY of SOME kind. At any one moment the teacher should have *planned control* of all three variables. Hence—What types of notations should go in each of a three-column lesson plan? (*Note:* This is merely a listing; not a lesson plan!)

1 *Topics and/or Learnings to Be Taught (Briefly!)*	2 *Teaching Procedures and Teacher Activities*	3 *Student Activities and Participations*	4 *Evaluation for Future*
Reminders of: (*In order!*) Major topics or subtopics Skills to be learned Attitudes to develop References to be used: in class in assignments A chart to be shown or prepared A film to be shown A pertinent assignment (reference) Concepts to master Problems to solve More content to be taught	Rather specific brief "guides"—*in the order they are to be used*—to help the teacher be sure to "get going" correctly on each item in lesson Might include: Questions to assure discussions Explain—using blackboard Drill—using chart, or flashcards, or chalkboard, or certain pages in text Demonstrate—as carriage throw Topic for a buzz session Call for a certain report Checking skill techniques Develop a point through questioning, how to get started	Might include: Listening—attentively Taking notes Asking and answering questions Individual recitations—while group listens Group discussions Panel reports and/or discussions Committee reports Individual reports Practicing on skills Problem solving Watching, watching and listening	

and mimeograph or duplicate a big supply (paper is relatively cheap!). These sheets may be punched for a ring notebook and thus provide a convenient reference while conducting the class. Use sheets liberally and avoid attempting to get too much on one page for quick, convenient reference. The form in Exhibit 4.1 is illustrative of one that may be used for this purpose.

As a further guide to preparing daily lessons and lesson plans, Exhibit 4.1 reproduces more detailed directions which have been used for completing a lesson plan form such as the one shown in Exhibit 4.2.

**Exhibit 4.2   A CONVENIENT FORM FOR PREPARING
THE DAILY LESSON PLAN**

$\bigcirc$ $\qquad\qquad$ $\bigcirc$ $\qquad\qquad$ $\bigcirc$

When to
LESSON PLAN. Subject: _____ Unit: _____ be used: _____ No.: ___
(Note: Course and unit objectives, contents, time allotments, etc., must first be fully decided. Daily lesson plans must conform to unit and course plans. Related physical conditions must be checked daily.)

Special materials needed:

Special learnings planned:

Topics and/or learnings to be taught	Teacher procedures and activities	Student activities and participations	Evaluation of the plan

Team Teaching

Consideration of modern techniques available as a part of good instructional planning would hardly be complete today without mention of team teaching. This modern and increasingly popular practice, simply stated, is based on the idea that two or more "heads" and two or more teachers are better than one!

Team teaching takes many forms, but it means that two or more teachers work together in *preparing* and in *teaching* various subjects, courses, and lessons. It is based on a pooling of ideas and a pooling of talents, abilities, and interests. Sometimes two teachers may be working together in a classroom; this may provide better individual assistance or may permit more students to be present in the class. At times several different classes or sections of a given class may be brought together to benefit from the special work of one master teacher. At other times the regular teacher of a course may bring to his students the benefit of hearing from some other teacher who possesses expert knowledge or ability in some unit of study. At all times the "team" of teachers works together in formulating the plans for the entire course and for the various units within the course(s) involved, dividing the work among themselves in accordance with their individual interests, abilities, and preparation. Thus, to a large extent, it is a further application to the teaching profession of the principle of specialization in work. Yet, at the same time, it encourages and attains greater cooperation and mutual assistance among the teacher-specialists. The result: both the teachers and the students profit!

Advisory Committees

An advisory committee ordinarily consists of a group of local business people and other local leaders who are interested in good local education. The committee is formed by the school to assist, in a purely advisory capacity, in making many decisions, including those dealing with needed courses and equipment, content of courses, and certain desirable procedures to use in the learning process. (See Chapter 13 for further details about such committees.)

Since these committees are composed of lay people, and not professional educators, they should not be asked to take responsibility for final professional decisions. However, because of their experience, recognized leadership ability, and present involvement in the real workaday world and their natural high interest in good education, their suggestions become invaluable in all educational planning.

Of all teachers in a school system, probably the business teachers most need and will profit from the help of appropriate advisory committees. Business is the very heart of the community; it is heavily responsible for the very existence of the community. And of course it is this with which the business teacher is dealing constantly! The more effective and successful business teachers everywhere today are profiting by the use of advisory committees. By heeding the advice of carefully chosen business people who have consented to act as such a committee, the business teacher can be much more certain that his students will be learning approved and practical business procedures and will be using in school the same types of machines and equipment they will eventually encounter as employees in the business world.

Members of such advisory committees often become "friends of the school" and as such are glad to help promote needed improvements in education. Business people are among the first to recognize any inadequacy, for instance, resulting from the use of outmoded equipment and facilities in a business education department. Frequently these same carefully selected business leaders of the community can effectively secure needed financing and needed decisions, whereas the voice of one lone teacher might go unheeded!

To summarize, there is no substitute for the development of confidence in teaching by being well prepared. It is much better to be overprepared than to be underprepared. A few hours of hard work at the beginning of the school year will do much to minimize the burden on the teacher of planning and preparing lessons, and the results from careful planning will also eliminate disorganized teaching. A well-prepared teacher is a confident teacher and one whom students respect. Respect from students will eliminate disciplinary problems and will often stimulate students, because well-planned lessons are usually interesting ones.

EVALUATION AND GRADING

One of the most difficult problems of teachers is that of evaluation of student ability and assigning of grades. In recent years there has been much dissatisfaction among educators with the systems of evaluation and the subsequent assignment of grades in the public schools. Many attempts have been made to improve present practices. Notably, the use of the parent-teacher conference has worked out quite well as a means of informing parents about their child's achievement as well as the development of his personality and character traits. However, this type of evaluation or grading has not yet been introduced successfully in many schools.

Some of the questions teachers always ask themselves and others concerning this problem are these:

1. On what basis should grades be given—subject-matter knowledge, attitude, improvement, social development, or what other basis?
2. Should students be compared with respect to their grades?
3. Should grades be used as a motivating device? Should a student who earns a high grade be graded lower if his conduct is poor?
4. Should students ever be failed?
5. Is the competition brought on among students to get high grades a good thing?
6. Should grades be based upon test results alone or should such factors as interest, class participation, or industriousness have a bearing?
7. How do you assign a grade to such subjective measurements as attitude, participation, or industriousness?
8. Should everything (every assignment) that a student completes be graded?

These and many other questions are often raised by teachers in their quest for a solution to the problems of evaluation and grading.

If you are looking for answers to these questions, you must look elsewhere than in this book. There is no answer other than the opinion held by each individual. One teacher may believe, for example, that no student should ever fail. The reasons advanced may be that our evaluative devices, at best, are not perfect and thus who are we to say who should fail? Also, perhaps the fact that a student has a poor knowledge of the subject matter of a course is not the student's fault, but the fault of poor teaching. A further argument may be that failing a student does not accomplish anything other than make the student feel inferior. Is it fair, the argument may be stated, to compare a student of limited intellectual capacity with one of superior capacity? It isn't his fault that he is "dumb." A final argument may be that there are more important things than subject-matter knowledge and that although a student may not have the essential knowledges of a subject, nonetheless he is learning how to cooperate with a group; perhaps the fact that he is in school and keeping out of mischief is sufficient reason to pass him so that he will remain in school.

On the other hand, it may be argued that if we do not fail a student who is weak in the subject matter of a course we may be doing him a disfavor. When he does get out of school he will have to face the reality of not having the same ability as others. What is wrong, the argument may go, with a student being failed in a course if he doesn't meet the standards set for the course? Are we not detracting from the students who do pass if we fail none? School should be similar to life—in life there are failures that must be overcome, why then should we protect students from knowledge of this fact? Are we not performing a disservice to employers of students if the employer is erroneously permitted to believe a student is capable in a given subject? The purpose of school is to help students learn. If a student does not learn, then he should be failed. And, finally, by passing everyone is there not a danger of destroying the respect and confidence of the public in our schools?

Both of the arguments in the foregoing paragraphs are strong ones. The frustrating thing to teachers is that neither point of view can be either proved or disproved other than by personal opinion. The point is that grading and evaluation is a major problem with many teachers and one that does not lend itself to an easy solution.

It is not the purpose in this book to suggest answers to all the problems arising because of evaluation and grading. Rather, the purpose is to suggest ways that teachers may solve their own problems more easily. Each teacher should formulate his own philosophy as to the purposes of evaluation and grading and then apply the proper technical procedures to fulfill this philosophy.

In later chapters of this book some of the specific techniques of evaluation and grading will be discussed as they apply to specific subject-matter courses in business education. In this chapter some of the more general procedures will be presented as they apply to most business education courses. No attempt will be made to go into the philosophical bases of evaluation and grading. The subject will be treated in terms of the practical approach with which the problems are confronted by the typical secondary school business teacher.

These facts about evaluation and grading are known:

1. Grades must be given in secondary schools today.
2. There must be some bases for determining these grades.

First let us examine various bases that might be used by a teacher in assigning a student's grade. The most common are:

1. Examinations
2. Class recitation
3. Student projects

Examinations

Various types of examinations are available to the business teacher for the measuring of a student's ability. Although the types of exams for use in measuring ability in the skill subjects are quite different in form from those used in the nonskill business subjects, they may still be classified under the following categories:

1. Objective examinations (true-false, multiple choice, matching, and so forth)
2. Essay examinations (subjective)
3. Problem examinations
4. Performance examinations

The so-called objective examinations, which are quite commonly found in use in business classes today, have many advantages. The greatest advantage is their ease in scoring, and this is important to the busy teacher of today with large enrollments in the class. Another advantage is elimination of the element of subjectivity. In other words, an answer to a question is either correct or incorrect, and the teacher does not have to make a subjective evaluation of the correctness of an answer as he must do in an essay-type exam. However, the characteristic of objectivity given to this exam does not always hold up under close scrutiny (except in the case of a fully standardized test) because the factor of subjectivity does enter into the picture in the sense that the teacher selects the item about which the question is asked, and by so doing he makes a subjective decision that this item is of sufficient importance to be worth determining whether the student knows the correct answer. However, the supposed objectivity or subjectivity of this type of examination is not of major importance. The important thing is that this type of examination is widely used in courses of the nonskill area of business, and in certain instances it can be effectively used in the skill areas. It is best used, of course, to measure the extent of knowledge of a student in the subject matter of a course.

This type of examination also has some disadvantages. Students may guess at an answer easily, the exam is difficult and time-consuming to prepare, and it does not always measure a student's ability to think or apply his knowledge.

Many objective tests provided by the publishers of the various textbooks are made available for teachers to use in almost all business courses. For the most part these examinations have been carefully prepared and are probably as good as, if not better than, those prepared by the teacher. However, the better teacher should try his hand at preparing his own examinations, for in many instances a published examination may not fit the content of a course.

Types of Objective-Test Questions

The best objective-type tests have included in them several different forms of questions. The most commonly used types are:

1. True-false
2. Multiple choice
3. Completion or single answer
4. Matching or master list

A true-false type of question is best used to determine whether students have acquired a misconception about an idea, to determine a single fact that is important for a student to know, or to determine whether a student knows the difference between two related but different concepts, such as socialism and government regulation. In the preparation of a true-false question several principles should be kept in mind:

1. Use questions that are either totally true or totally false.
2. Avoid the use of trick questions. This most often occurs in the development of a false statement.
3. Avoid the use of words such as *always* and *never*.
4. Avoid the use of the exact wording found in a textbook. .
5. Avoid the use of long questions that are highly involved.
6. Be careful of the placement of the questions on the exam so that the answers do not follow a specific pattern.

Although true-false questions have been criticized because students find it easy to guess, this can be minimized somewhat by requiring students to write a brief sentence on their reasons for answering a question either true or false. Partial credit may be given for an incorrect answer if the logic used in answering incorrectly is sound. For example, one point might be given for a correct answer to the question and one point for the reason given. Another method advocated by some educators to discourage guessing is to subtract from the right answers the number of wrong answers. In this method a double penalty is given for an incorrect answer and only a single penalty for a question not answered.

Multiple-choice questions can best be used to determine knowledge of cause-and-effect relationships, ability to make comparisons, and ability to differentiate among several possible correct procedures. Principles to keep in mind while constructing a multiple-choice question are:

1. The question should have four or five possible answers.
2. The correct answer should be completely correct. In other words, there should be no danger of two possible answers being too closely related.
3. Long involved answers should be eliminated.
4. It is sometimes good to include several correct answers in one question with one being indicated as the *best* answer.
5. The question should be stated positively rather than negatively.

The single-answer or completion-type question is one of the most difficult types of objective questions for students to answer and is one from which the element of guessing is eliminated. It can best be used for determining single facts or for replacing a question that asks for a definition. For example, instead of developing a question such as "Define insurance," the question might be stated in this way: "The sharing of economic risks is known as ———— ."

In developing single-answer or completion questions, the following points should be kept in mind:

1. Each answer should call for a single—but important—idea that can be stated as one word, a number, a phrase, or a short sentence.
2. Allowance should be made for expressing the same idea in several different ways.

3. Questions with so many blanks that it is difficult to follow the sense of the question should be avoided.
4. Indefinite questions of such nature that almost any word would apply to the missing blank should be avoided.

The use of matching or master-list questions has the advantage that it can be applied to almost any type of subject matter and retain the advantages of any of the other types of questions described. Particular care should be taken in the construction of these types of questions. Factors that should be considered are:

1. Directions should be explicit and clear.
2. Arrangement of the items in the basic list should be at random, such as alphabetic, numerical, or chronological.
3. More items should be in the basic list than in the secondary list.
4. Not more than fifteen items, nor less than five items, should be included in the secondary list.
5. Directions should state whether items in the basic list can be used more than once.

Essay-Type Questions

The essay-type question is one that can be used to advantage in evaluating the progress of students in business education courses. The essay question will have more application to measurement of information learned in the nonskill courses than to the skill courses because this type of question lends itself more readily to the measurement of subject-matter knowledge.

Some of the advantages given for the essay-type question are:

1. Students are required to think before answering the question.
2. Guessing is discouraged.
3. The ability to communicate is emphasized.
4. The questions are comparatively easy to prepare.

Some of the disadvantages are:

1. The essay question is difficult to grade objectively.
2. It takes much longer for the teacher to check.
3. Teachers are unsure as to whether to evaluate the ability to express ideas as well as the content of the answer.
4. Students' handwriting may be poor and thus difficult to read.
5. Only a small body of knowledge can be examined.

Although the disadvantages listed for using essay-type examination questions should be carefully considered, nonetheless occasional use of this type of question is important in the educational function. The argument that the use of essay questions in an examination is time-consuming for a teacher is a strong one. However, if the questions are carefully prepared, this argument loses much of its weight. The value gained through requiring students to use written expression involving analytical ability is an important one.

In preparing essay-type questions the teacher should consider carefully the type of information desired. If a specific answer is required, the question should be stated in a specific manner. Be careful in preparing the question to avoid one that can be answered in generalities. In answering a question that is too general, a student having limited knowledge can bluff. It is this type of essay question that is difficult to grade.

Broadly speaking, essay questions can be categorized into the following types:

1. *Recall of information*
   "Name four types of risk that everyone has, and suggest a type of insurance that could be used to cover each risk."

2. *Comparison of information*
   "Compare the advantages to a businessman who owns a grocery store of requiring customers to pay cash rather than extending credit to them."

3. *Cause-and-effect relationships*
   "Explain and give reasons why a good credit rating will be of benefit to an individual."

4. *Definition or explanation*
   "Explain how mass production increases the standard of living of the people."

5. *Evaluation*
   "Which is more serious to the average family whose income is from salary—loss of property or loss of income? Illustrate your answer by giving an example."

6. *Discussion—for or against*
   "Discuss the advantages and disadvantages of owning your own home instead of renting your home."

7. *Problem solving*
   "Joe Smith is planning to buy a new car. His old car is four years old and has been driven 30,000 miles. He has been offered a trade on a new car with automatic transmission for $3,100, receiving an allowance of $1,700 on his old car. Cars similar to his old car are selling in used-car lots for $1,300. His old car cost $2,500 new. Joe must finance the purchase of the new car and his payments would be $67.67 per month for 24 months.
   What should Joe do? Give your reasons."

One of the greatest problems in using essay-type questions is that of grading them objectively. The best procedure for a teacher to follow is to set up the answer to the question in terms of a series of points that should be developed by the testee. Each of these points should be weighted, and the final answer given by the student should be compared with the teacher's key. The teacher will have to make a decision (subjective) as to how well the student's answer brings out all of the points desired by the teacher. It is the authors' opinion that the ability to communicate his ideas to the teacher in the written paper should also be a factor in the grade received. However, this may or may not be a factor. It is whatever the teacher desires.

Problem Tests

Problem tests can be used most effectively in a course such as bookkeeping or in the skill subjects of typewriting and shorthand. In this type of test a question is developed around a problem situation and the student is expected to arrive at the correct answer. This type of test is one of the most objective kinds because there is only one correct answer. Either the student works the problem correctly or he does not. There is no need for a subjective evaluation. An example of this type of question for a bookkeeping examination is given below.

John Smith owns a grocery store. He purchases merchandise costing $500 and is entitled to a cash discount of 2 percent. What are the entries on the books of Mr. Smith if he pays cash for the merchandise?

Obviously, in this type of question there is only one correct answer. However, the teacher may be confronted with the question of whether or not he should give partial credit for an answer that is partially correct. In the preceding question, for example, what if the student got the account titles correct but made an error in arithmetic? Should partial credit be given? Conversely, if the arithmetic is correct but the account titles are misplaced, what then?

There is still a further difficulty in using this type of examination question. In working a long problem a student will often make a mistake early, which in turn will cause several other errors. The teacher is then faced with a decision—is the problem right or wrong? Should an error made early in a problem be followed through and further errors that are caused by this early mistake not be counted?

Other questions often asked by teachers are: Should an examination of this type have the element of speed in it? Who is the better student—the one who works slowly but accurately, or the one who works swiftly but slightly inaccurately? Teachers will often hear the complaint from students, "I didn't get finished (working the exam), but the problems I did solve were correct. If you would only have given me more time I would have gotten them all finished and correct." This is a difficult problem to solve. For example: Suppose that the teacher gives an examination consisting of four problems of equal weight—each problem is worth a maximum of 25 points and they total 100. One student works two problems correctly during an hour's examination period for a total of 50 points. Another student works all four problems but has errors on each one that cut his score down to 20 points per problem for a total of 80 points. Which is the better student? Probably it is the student who earned the 80 points. At least the teacher is sure that he has some knowledge of all the areas over which the test was developed, whereas for the student who didn't get finished the teacher can only speculate. However, these problems give the teacher cause for reflection in the evaluation of students.

The time element must frequently be considered in evaluating a problem examination. Ability to think and respond rapidly as well as accurately may be important. To eliminate the difficulty of tracing errors in long problems, it usually is best to develop a series of short-problem questions, all unrelated to one another. This plan avoids the dependence of one part of a question on another and at the same time broadens the examination to cover more areas of information.

Performance Tests

When evaluating the learning of a student, teachers should always keep in mind that the real purpose of education, in the long run, is to help the student improve on "what he does"—to help him "perform better," "think more rationally," "act more rationally." That is, the real question should be, "Will his learnings actually *function* for him in real-life situations?"

Obviously it is not easy to measure or evaluate that which will take place in the future! Yet at times it may be possible to do so reasonably accurately, and certainly any teacher who is a true professional will be endeavoring to measure outcomes of his students' learnings in terms of their ability to *function* for them in pertinent real-life situations. True education is much more than memorization, or ability to reproduce facts, or ability to "verbalize" *about* something; it involves changes and improvements in one's *performance*.

Unquestionably performance tests are a "must" in all programs of vocational education. The program is useless if the student cannot *do* that which he came to learn to do! Although less evident, perhaps the *need* for comparable performance tests is just as great in other areas of education; however, they may be much more difficult to prepare.

Incidentally, if a student is to be *evaluated* by measuring his ability to perform (performance tests), it is only fair to him—as well as being good educational procedure—to have the *objectives* of his course or learning program stated for him in terms of the performance that is desired—his "goal." This is why thousands of teachers have been spending many, many hours learning how to write valid "behavioral" objectives and rewriting the objectives for their courses and unit plans and lesson plans *in terms of* ability to show specified performance (or behavior) under specified circumstances.

While many educators question the value and effectiveness of performance tests and behavioral objectives in measuring certain types of desired learnings, such as the development of attitudes and understandings, business teachers have long recognized their adaptability and usefulness in subjects such as typewriting and shorthand—where a student is examined on his ability to type a letter, type straight copy, transcribe from dictation, or set up a tabulated problem either with or without the element of time entering in. Such performance tests are relatively easy to prepare and easy to score. Either a student can perform or he cannot!

As an aid to business teachers wishing to use performance tests, our professional associations and researchers are constantly striving to build up systematized sets of performance "criteria" that may be used for this purpose. Often the criteria are made applicable to a 'cluster" of jobs in the business world. Some publishers of instructional material for business education are now developing performance criteria for use with the instructional material in making evaluations of students.

Because of the relative ease in developing and grading this type of examination, there is danger of using it too much. Timed writings in typewriting are an excellent example of the overuse and abuse of this type of test. Too many teachers use at least one, sometimes two, and even three timed tests daily, recording the student's achievement on each. Performance tests of this nature should probably be given only once each week at the most.

However, it should be made clear that the present discussion refers to *testing*. There are many occasions when the typewriting teacher properly uses short timed writings, perhaps of a repetitive nature, as a drill technique for increasing speed or for other reasons; such timed writings are not in the nature of tests, and when used as learning devices, of course, no grades are recorded. This point will be discussed further in a later chapter of this book.

Although tests are an important instrument in the hands of the teacher as a means of evaluating student ability, the wise teacher will use test results carefully and with a certain amount of skepticism. Test results by themselves will not provide an accurate measure of a student's ability or worth, such as ability to think and solve problems while not under the pressure of an examination. His sense of responsibility in completing assignments, reciting in class, and completing student projects certainly is another value worth measuring.

Since any teacher can cite examples of students who were poor students in a subject as reflected by their scores on examinations, but yet were successful workers as adults, the teacher should remain humble about this method of evaluation. Use tests wisely to examine not only the ability of students but the effectiveness of teaching. After the results have been obtained, consider the other factors that may help determine the ability of students to achieve; only by putting all these factors together can the teacher be partially sure that she has evaluated a student's ability correctly.

Class Recitation and Participation

The measurement of class recitation or participation in discussion as a means of evaluating student achievement is necessary. However, the use of such evaluation has its limitations in that the evaluation must be purely subjective. Because of this factor teachers have not generally placed much emphasis upon classroom participation by students as a measurement device.

It is true, however, that some students can communicate better orally than by written examinations. The ability to think constructively and to express ideas effectively is one that should be developed. Care should be taken not to confuse intelligent recitation with loquaciousness. Some students will have the ability of eloquence yet not say much. The teacher must also be skilled in the ability to so lead discussion that all students will be encouraged to participate. In large classes this is difficult, but it can be done by using the technique of small-group discussion.

As has been mentioned, the greatest drawback in the measurement of class participation is the inability of the teacher to point to some specific and objective measure of achievement. However, this difficulty should not deter the teacher from attempting some type of measurement. At the conclusion of a class the teacher could make some type of code mark in the grade book relative to the participation of the students. This does not mean that a grade would be given every day. Only those people who had made a worthwhile contribution to the class discussion would be checked.

Although using this technique means that the teacher must recall evidences of participation and that there may be some danger of forgetting, nevertheless it is inadvisable to check participation at the actual time. To do so is disconcerting to the students and also makes it necessary for the teacher to withdraw his attention from the class momentarily while some kind of mark is being made. The obviousness of the teacher grading participation at the time of the act will detract and will perhaps even discourage students from contributing for fear of contributing something that may be considered inadequate.

Student Projects

Student projects such as practice sets in bookkeeping, special reports, notebooks, and displays present another means of evaluating student achievement. The bases upon which these projects may be graded will necessarily vary from time to time and from teacher to teacher. The more obvious and important bases are extensiveness of the project, care with which it was developed, originality, and importance of the subject matter to the class.

METHODOLOGY

Although the specific methodology that should be used by business teachers will be discussed in detail in later chapters as it pertains to specific business subjects, it is proper here to mention briefly some of the more general pertinent ideas.

It should be pointed out that there is no one best method or procedure. The method to be used by a teacher will depend upon many things:

1. The objective to be attained
2. The number of students to be taught and their stage of advancement
3. The character or the content of subject matter used
4. The nature and availability of the resources, such as reading materials, visual aids, and laboratory equipment
5. The place in the course, whether at the beginning, in the middle, or at the end
6. The ability of the teacher to use various methods

The wise teacher will consider all the factors listed and will adapt his methodology to specific situations.

The more common methods proper for use in teaching business in the secondary school are discussion, problem solving, demonstrations, drill, and question-and-answer. Drill, problem solving, and demonstration will be best suited for the skill type of courses such as typewriting, shorthand, and secretarial practice. The discussion method, question-and-answer (recitation), and problem solving will be best suited for the nonskill subjects such as bookkeeping, general business, and business law.

An important point to remember in teaching business subjects in the secondary school is to use a method that is student centered. Learning will be most effective if the methodology used places its greatest emphasis upon the activities and actions of the students rather than those of the teacher. The skillful business teacher will guide and direct the learning of his students while remaining in the background and not being the dominant person in the room.

Thus it would follow that there is little if any place in the secondary school for the lecture method or for excessive illustration, demonstration, or explanation by the teacher. A common fault of many beginning teachers is that they talk too much. Questions too often are so stated that they either call for only a yes or a no answer or are answered by the teacher himself. Typing classes have been taught in which the problem method was being used and yet the teacher would not permit the students to solve their own problems; he solved them himself.

A method may often be used by a teacher without the teacher fully understanding the implications or reasons back of the method. *Group dynamics* is a term describing a highly specialized type of discussion technique. In recent years it has received a great deal of attention and "glamour" as a progressive method. Yet this type of procedure can be used only by the teacher who has studied its various ramifications and fully understands its operations. Inexperienced or unwise teachers have attempted to use this type of teaching with sad results.

The superior teacher will assess his own capabilities and will use the method that suits him best as well as that which suits his students best. He will study and plan carefully the methods he will use in a particular situation and will quickly shift or change his procedure if he finds that it is not working. In these ways teaching methodology can be utilized to its greatest effectiveness.

PROJECTS AND QUESTIONS FOR DISCUSSION

1. Investigate and report on the EDL Skill Builder and its possible use in teaching business subjects.
2. Prepare a bulletin-board display showing and explaining the use of headsets and multiple-channel electronic equipment in teaching typewriting or shorthand.
3. Read and report on some article describing the use of team teaching in some business subject.
4. Choose some unit in a business subject you will be teaching, prepare a brief outline of its contents, and then prepare a detailed lesson plan for teaching one day or more of the unit.
5. Have a committee of class members investigate and report on teaching machines and programmed instructional materials. Try to obtain and bring to class actual programmed texts or units of instruction.
6. Do you consider it permissible for a student to call a teacher by his first name outside of school hours? What should the attitude of a teacher be toward his students—friendly or reserved?
7. Is it ever desirable to use the device of lowering a grade in a class as punishment for a serious disciplinary act? Explain.

8. What action would you take if you found that one of your students was cheating on an examination?

9. May an objective-type examination actually measure a student's ability in the subject matter of a course, or is there too much opportunity for guessing?

10. Do you believe it is better to grade your students on their ability or on their improvement? If you believe improvement is best, then who is the better typing student—one who improves in a six-week period from sixty words per minute on a five-minute writing to sixty-five or the student who improves from twenty words per minute to forty?

11. Is it necessary to spend much time planning lessons in typewriting when each lesson is planned for you by the organization of the textbook into daily lessons?

12. Is it ever a good idea to use the lecture method in a high school business class? Why or why not?

13. Do you believe that students should ever be permitted to assist you in planning the activities of a class in general business?

14. Should the element of time ever be introduced into an examination in bookkeeping? If it is, is this fair to the slow student who is very accurate?

15. Would you suggest that it would be a permissible procedure to teach a typewriting class and a bookkeeping class simultaneously in adjacent rooms?

16. Have a committee of students investigate and report on how to write behavioral objectives and prepare performance tests. The committee might report in the form of a panel presentation, to be followed by class questions and discussion.

17. Have a report on and discussion of a modern learning center for business students. This might be preceded by the viewing of a film showing such a center or by a visit to such a center in operation in some nearby school.

18. With the use of video-tape equipment, have students practice various teaching techniques presented in this chapter, perhaps using miniaturized (micro) teaching situations.

CASE PROBLEMS

1. The superintendent of Midvale High School is a firm believer in strong disciplinary control of students in the high school. He has cautioned his teachers time and time again not to permit any rowdyism in their classes. You are the teacher of a typewriting class and the following incident takes place. One of the students (a rather large boy), while taking a timed writing, becomes angry because of the errors he has been making. He tears his paper out of the machine with a large noise before the end of the writing, swears out loud, and then looks at you with a defiant look as if to say "Well, what are you going to do about it!" You have had minor disturbances from this lad several times before and have talked with him, but it has not done any good. What will you do this time?

2. You are the business teacher in a small high school. Every afternoon the room in which you teach your classes becomes very warm from the heat flowing through the radiators. The reason this situation occurs is that your room is nearest the heating system and in order for some of the rooms on the upper floors to be properly heated the furnace must be operated at full steam. There are no valves on the radiators with which you can turn them off. The janitor becomes irritated if you open the windows because he considers it a waste of heat. It becomes so warm most of the time in the afternoon that the students have a difficult time remaining alert or even awake. Is there any solution to this dilemma?

3. After she had given her class an examination, one of Miss Bauer's students complained

that copies of the test had been circulated among certain students prior to the exam. The student was certain he would have ranked higher on the test as compared with the other students if the test had not been out. What should Miss Bauer do?

4. At the end of the semester Mr. Johnson was amazed and chagrined to find that 60 percent of his students in general business had failed the final examination. Prior to this time he had given about a dozen short tests and had the students turn in much homework. On all this work the class had been an "average group." What should he do?

5. Mr. Able, in his freshman class in general business, found that a sizable segment of the class acted genuinely bored with the course. He tried hard to make the class stimulating, but he occasionally had to lecture because the class had thirty-eight students. He found that discussion was difficult in a class of this size. What might be the cause of the boredom? What might Mr. Able do?

SUGGESTED READINGS

Advisory Committees, Organization and Use, Bulletin No. 7–470, State of Illinois Board of Vocational Education and Rehabilitation, Springfield, 10 pp.

"Audio Learning Laboratories," *Business Education World*, March 1964, pp. 19–22.

Banerdt, Jack, "Planning for Multiple Outlets," *Journal of Business Education*, February 1964, pp. 187–88.

Bowden, Geraldine, "What Is a Student-Centered Business Laboratory?," *The Balance Sheet*, December 1970–January 1971, pp. 152–53.

Brown, Richard D., "Teaching for Consumer Conscience in Business Education," *American Vocational Journal*, May 1971, pp. 22–23.

Byers, Edward E., "Writing Performance Objectives: The Test of Professional Integrity," *Business Education World*, September–October 1970, pp. 18–19.

Croft Educational Services, Inc., "The What, Why, and How of Behavioral Objectives," a Professional Report in Croft Teachers' Professional Development Service, May 1971.

David, Donald H., "Evaluation of Facilities for Business and Office Education," *NBEA Yearbook*, No. 7, 1969, pp. 172–79.

Edwards, R. K., "At Lansing Community College: Audiovisual-Tutorial Instruction in Business," *Junior College Journal*, XXXIX, May 1969, 56.

Focus on Individualized Instruction. See the *Business Education Forum*, May 1971, for a group of twelve articles including flexible and modular scheduling, multimedia typewriting, and programmed shorthand.

Guidelines for Consumer Education, Office of the Superintendent of Public Instruction, State of Illinois, Springfield, 1968, 89 pp.

Lanham, Frank W., and Catheryn P. Weber, "NOBELS Action Verbs and Synonyms" (Part I of a report), *Journal of Business Education*, LV, No. 7, April 1970, 284–90.

Liguori, Mary, "Dictation Laboratories on the New Frontier," *Business Education World*, March 1964, p. 8.

McMahon, Gordon, "The Growing Importance of Occupational Competency Testing," *American Vocational Journal*, May 1971, p. 46.

Nixdorf, Marion E., "A Study to Determine the Effects of Using the Skill-Builder Controlled Reader in the Teaching of Beginning Shorthand," *National Business Education Quarterly*, October 1963, p. 38.

Opportunities in Iowa's Area Schools, 1970–71, State of Iowa, Department of Public Instruction, Des Moines, 67 pp.

Perkins, Edward A., *et al.*, "Anthology on Individualized Instruction," *Business Education World*, LI, No. 4, March-April 1971, 2–5.

Stenner, Jack, "Accountability by Public Demand," *American Vocational Journal*, February 1971, pp. 33–37.

Swanson, Edwin A., "Self-Instructional Equipment and Material," *NBEA Yearbook*, No. 7, 1969, pp. 148–60.

This, Leslie E., "What Is Simulation?" *American Vocational Journal*, September 1970, pp. 20–22.

Thompson, Scott D., "Beyond Modular Scheduling," *Phi Delta Kappan*, LII, No. 8, April 1971, pp. 484–87.

Tonne, Herbert A., "The Magerian Fallacy," *Journal of Business Education*, November 1970, pp. 50–51.

Wallace, William A., "A Philosopher Looks at Teaching Machines," *Catholic Business Education Review*, Winter 1963, pp. 13–23.

Ward, Ruth B., "Use of the Projector for Motivating, Teaching, and Grading," *Business Education World*, March 1964, pp. 13–14.

II

the skill subjects

Business educators agree that there are many important differences in methodology between the teaching of skill subjects and the teaching of nonskill subjects. Skills involve the development of muscular control and coordination in addition to the mental phases of understandings and attitudes. Part II of this text deals with the methodology of teaching the skill subjects in business, while Part III deals with the nonskill subjects.

The business teacher must learn to purposefully choose teaching techniques and procedures best calculated to attain the goals desired. Moreover, he must learn to judiciously divide teaching time among such techniques in accordance with the major purposes as compared with the many supplementary or minor purposes to be served.

Teachers of such business subjects as typing, shorthand, and clerical and secretarial office practice find that the major portion of the class time must be spent in skill development. This does not mean, however, that other learnings are ignored. The learnings that make possible the application of basic skills to business problems must be taught or these skills are of limited value. It is also necessary in the skills areas to understand the psychological principles and procedures most useful in the development of skills and abilities—those activities involved in "doing" as opposed to "understandings" only.

Similarly, the omission of a subject from consideration in Part II does not mean it contains no "skill development." Rather, it indicates that to best serve his students and the goals of those courses, it is believed the business teacher should look upon those subjects as requiring relatively less attention to skill development and more attention to understandings, problem solving, and similar outcomes.

In a methods text that deals with the entire field of business education, it is impossible to include a discussion of all future technological developments that may affect the teaching of skill subjects. Therefore, the discussion in the next three chapters is directed primarily to those techniques and procedures especially valuable in developing the skills essential for those persons planning to seek employment as clerical and stenographic workers.

5

TEACHING TYPEWRITING

Today more high school students are enrolled in typewriting than in any other business subject. In addition, thousands of young people are receiving instruction in typewriting at the junior high school level, and recently interest has been shown in the possibility of teaching typewriting to elementary school pupils. In 1970 it was estimated that over two million students were enrolled in typewriting. Typewriting is being identified more and more as general education, with the result that the majority of the persons now enrolled in the course are interested solely in developing typing skill for personal use. One of the major problems facing school administrators is that of finding some way to make typing instruction available to all those students desiring it. In many areas, a shortage of equipment and funds is necessitating the introduction of new procedures in typing instruction. Some administrators are attempting to solve these problems by using team teaching in large classes ranging in size from 75 to 125 or more. In other schools modular scheduling and closed-circuit television are being used to make typing available to a larger portion of the student body. Short, intensive typing courses are frequently offered in the summer school curriculum for persons wishing to develop personal-use skill. Many authorities believe typing has become such a common tool of communication that enrollments in the subject will continue to climb.

The first typewriter was patented in 1868 by Christopher Shoals, a printer and editor, and Carlos Glidden, an attorney. However, these two men did not have sufficient capital to perfect the machine. At this point James Densmore, a Pennsylvania oil man, agreed to finance the project; in 1873 he was successful in persuading E. Remington & Sons to begin manufacture of the Type-Writer. Today there are many different typewriters on the market, including standard, portable, and electric machines.[1] The young person planning to enter the business world may find himself seriously handicapped if he cannot type. Certainly he will find that the person who is a good typist has a skill that will help him gain entrance into the business office. In this chapter are discussed those techniques and devices that are generally recognized as being effective procedures in the teaching of typewriting.

THE TYPEWRITING ROOM

The typewriting room should usually be located near the shorthand and office practice rooms, away from outside noise and distractions. Because of the space required for typewriting tables or desks, the typing room should ordinarily be one and one-half times the size of a regular classroom. Preferably the room should be deeper than it is wide and should accommodate a maximum of thirty-five to forty students. Twenty-five to thirty square feet should be allowed for each typewriter. The ceiling should be of acoustical material to partially absorb the noise of the machines. The room should be so located that it is possible to take advantage of all natural light available.

The equipment in the typing room will vary from school to school. Most typing rooms are equipped with individual tables or desks which should be so arranged that the teacher has easy access to each student for demonstration purposes and individual assistance. It is recommended that the tables or desks be adjustable and free from vibration. A table twenty-two inches wide and thirty-six inches long will give the student space for his typing material and text. L-shaped tables are also excellent, but they require more floor space than other types of desks. If the tables or desks are adjustable, the teacher will need to see that the students adjust them to the correct height each day. Because adjustable desks are more expensive than other types, some schools prefer to purchase desks of various heights. In this case most of the desks will need to be twenty-eight to thirty inches in height, with only a few ranging from twenty-six to twenty-seven inches. Desks for some makes of electric typewriters need to be slightly lower than the desks for manual machines. The desk is the correct height for the student if his arms slope at approximately a thirty-degree angle, the same slope as the keyboard. Schools that use the typing room for other classes often purchase drophead desks. These desks are satisfactory for the other classes meeing in the typing room, but they are not suitable for the typing class because the typewriters are much too low to develop correct typing techniques. Typewriters are frequently bolted to the table or desk tops as a safety precaution. When this is done, the students seldom have sufficient

---

[1] A "simplified" typewriter keyboard was developed by August Dvorak and W. L. Dealey in 1932. According to Dvorak and Dealey, on the universal keyboard the left hand does 56 percent of all the stroking, while on their scientific keyboard the left hand does only 46 percent of the stroking. However, the Dvorak keyboard has not been widely accepted.

working space, since they cannot move the machines aside. If the room is also used for transcription, this is a serious problem.

Teachers do not agree about the advisability of using adjustable chairs in the typing room. All too often these chairs are not easily adjusted, and no attempt is made to change the height once the chairs are installed. Many teachers believe it is better to take care of any adjustments needed through the use of adjustable tables or desks. The chairs should not be fastened to the floor.

Much has been written regarding the advisability of using electric versus manual typewriters in the classroom. If a school has more than one typing room, then the room in which personal-use or first-year typing is taught is frequently equipped with one make of manual typewriter, with lettered keyboards and preferably elite type, since this is the size of type used by most businesses today. In the past, few persons taking typing for personal use purchased electric typewriters. Hence it was logical to provide instruction for such persons on manual machines. Today, however, the number of persons purchasing electric typewriters for their own use is increasing. The advanced typing classroom is usually equipped with electric machines, often of several different makes. In planning the layout of a typing room, electrical outlets should be provided at each typing station.

The teacher in the small school system having only one typing room must decide whether the room should be equipped with several makes of manual typewriters and perhaps several electrics or whether the equipment should be limited to only one make of machine. Obviously it is easier to teach beginning students to type in a room equipped with only one kind of typewriter, and it is generally agreed that if students become skillful in the operation of one make of typewriter, they have little difficulty transferring that skill to another make of machine. The prime consideration in the small high school is whether to equip the room with both manual and electric machines. It was recently reported that three-fourths of the typewriters purchased by business organizations were electric. Therefore, even in the small high school, students should have an opportunity to develop skill on electric typewriters as well as on manual machines.

Other equipment needed in the classroom will include a demonstration stand and typewriter for the teacher, copyholders, an interval timer, a stopwatch, dictionaries, storage cabinets and files, and wastebaskets. A teacher's desk is optional. The teacher who is working with his students as he should be will have little need for one. If the room is equipped with such a desk, it should be located in the back of the room.

TYPEWRITER MAINTENANCE

The typing teacher should keep an inventory of the typewriters for which he is responsible. He should also maintain a record of service costs for each machine, as this information can be helpful in determining those machines that should be traded in and in making decisions regarding the kind of typewriters to purchase. Ordinarily, when a typewriter needs repair, a serviceman should be called. However, the typing teacher can usually handle minor repairs such as the following:

1. If a student reports that the ribbon is not printing, check the setting of the ribbon indicator and the multiple-copy control lever.
2. If keys are sticking, the problem may be erasure dust in the machine. In that case, use a segment pick to dislodge the dust between the type bars.
3. If the ribbon fails to reverse, depress the reverse lever by hand.
4. If the paper slips in the machine, clean the platen and rollers with denatured alcohol.
5. If the tab setting does not hold, the tabulator set may be sprung. For a temporary solution, set the tab one space to the left or the right of the desired setting.
6. If the carriage sticks, check to see whether an eraser or other object may be blocking the carriage rails.
7. If the carriage or the keys lock on an electric machine, turn off the motor for a few minutes. Occasionally this will release the machine.

The most common typewriter maintenance problem is that of machines clogged with erasure dust. The teacher should insist that students move the carriage before erasing. Typewriters should be dusted and cleaned regularly and, when possible, covered at the close of the school day.

OBJECTIVES IN TYPEWRITING

Students who enroll in typewriting today do so either because they are interested in using typing as a vocational tool or because they wish to master this skill for their personal use. At present increased attention is being given to the personal-use objective in the curriculum, and many junior high schools are now offering one semester of typing for personal use in the seventh, eighth, or ninth grades. At one time business educators expressed considerable concern about these dual objectives; they believed it was impossible to teach students with different objectives in the same class. Today most authorities agree that there should be no difficulty in teaching a class of students having both personal and vocational objectives and that the content in the first course should be much the same regardless of the students' objectives. One of the dangers of setting up special personal-use courses is that of lowered standards for such classes. Teachers should remember that even though a person may have learned to operate a typewriter, he is not likely to use it to any great extent unless he has developed considerable skill in its operation. Consequently, while some persons may be able to develop a satisfactory personal-use skill in a one-semester course, many other persons will probably need a full year of typing to acquire a usable typing skill. In advanced typing, the course content naturally is focused on the development of vocational typing skill and the typing of office-production jobs. A person with a personal-use objective does not need these advanced skills and knowledges. If he does choose to enroll in the advanced typing course, he should be expected to meet the same standards and master the same subject matter as those taking the course for vocational purposes.

THE PSYCHOLOGY OF TYPEWRITING

Every typing teacher needs a thorough understanding of the basic principles upon which typing skill is built. These fundamental principles of skill learning have been developed over the years by Bryan, Harter, Book, and many others. All authorities in the teaching of typewriting agree that typing skill is a constantly changing phenomenon. When a student first attempts to type, his motions are diffused, awkward, and wasteful. As he gradually develops skill, his motions become fluent and sure, and waste movements are eliminated. The principles that follow represent a composite of the thinking of typing authorities regarding the psychology of learning.

Typewriting is a skill that is controlled more by the mind than by the hands. When a student is first learning to type, he is slow in his responses, not because he cannot move his fingers quickly enough, but because the mental stimulus required to activate the correct finger has not yet been established. With correct, purposeful practice, these stimuli which bring about the correct responses and typing sequences become so firmly established that the typist no longer struggles to recall which key is controlled by each finger but reacts automatically to the letters that he sees in the copy.

Typing skill can best be learned when the student is highly motivated. The student who is enrolled in typing because he wants to be able to type his own assignments or because he wants to have some means of earning a livelihood is ordinarily highly motivated. He will direct his full attention to mastering the keyboard and to building speed and accuracy in typing. The student who elects typing because he believes it is an easy course or because someone else has insisted that he learn to type is frequently poorly motivated and will not put forth the intensity of effort required for rapid skill development.

The development of typing skill is often accompanied by excessive fatigue. The student may concentrate with such intensity upon the locations of the keys and the manipulation of the parts of the typewriter that he is tense and nervous. He is afraid he will strike the wrong keys. Consequently he pushes the keys hesitantly rather than hitting them quickly with a firm stroke. The teacher should study each student in the class carefully to determine which students are working too hard and which students are not putting forth enough effort to make maximum progress. Students who complain of tired muscles and strain in their hands and arms are working too intensely with incorrect techniques. The teacher should help the student learn how to apply maximum effort without becoming emotionally upset or unduly fatigued.

The development of skill requires the elimination of waste motions and poor techniques. Too many teachers seem to believe that their function in the classroom is to build speed and accuracy in typewriting. That is certainly one function of the teacher, but speed and accuracy must be built upon correct techniques. The student should be given enough practice on the right kind of materials to enable him to gain confidence in his skill through the development of proper techniques.

Students should be given the opportunity to progress at their own learning rates at all times. In typewriting some students are able to master the keyboard in two weeks, some in three weeks, and some require a far longer period of time. Drill material should allow the learner to progress according to his ability. It should be remembered that some students are still typing on the letter-association level when other students in the class have progressed to the syllable and word-association level. Students should be encouraged to progress as rapidly as possible. However, they should never be pushed for speed and accuracy development at the sacrifice of correct techniques.

Since individuals do differ in their learning rates, one of the responsibilities of the teacher is to provide a learning situation in which each student has the type of practice that is best for him. Requiring all students to type the text material the same number of times, maintaining too rigid a classroom routine, requiring too much group activity, and giving too little attention to individual learners will interfere with the progress of some members in the class. Typing is a course that is readily adaptable to meeting individual differences of the students, and the teacher should see that these differences are properly met.

Practice on any single phase of the learning process should be given in a natural rather than an artificial situation. For instance, teaching the parts of the machine before they are actually used in typing results in little learning. Whenever a machine part is taught, it should be used immediately in the typing practice.

The repetition necessary to acquire typing skill should be discontinued as soon as it ceases to be effective. To get the most from any practice, the student must keep his mind focused on what he is doing. When his mind is no longer fixed on his practice or begins to wander, the typing practice soon loses its effectiveness. For instance, the expert rhythm drill can be an exceedingly effective warm-up at the beginning of the period. However, the drill should be discontinued and some other warm-up substituted when students no longer concentrate upon the purposes of the drill but begin to let their hands and wrists "bounce" as they type.

Opportunity should always be provided for relearning in a successive practice period what has been forgotten since the preceding practice period. In the early learning stages in typewriting, the warm-up practice should be immediately followed by the relearning process. The warm-up is designed to limber up the muscles used in typing. The relearning practice is designed to recall the letter locations learned from the previous periods. Some teachers are so eager to present the entire keyboard rapidly that they do not allow sufficient time for relearning of letters presented earlier. As a consequence, the students become discouraged or develop poor stroking techniques due to uncertainty regarding letter locations.

Practice of a skill is often ineffective when the learner is discouraged with the results of his practice. Teachers should realize that not every student needs to be typing the same drills at the same time. When a teacher sees that a student is discouraged in his efforts to complete a particular drill or exercise, he should suggest that the student try some other exercise which he may be able to type better than the one on which he is working. It is quite possible that repeated failure on the exercise has set up a "mental block" which the student cannot overcome. Once he has successfully completed the new exercise, he may return to the one on which he was working previously and be able to complete it without further difficulty.

Practice of a skill does not necessarily lead to perfection. Practice is not effective unless the learner is concentrating upon the work, knows the purpose of the drill, and is able to evaluate his own progress. Students should never be asked to type a drill unless they know what the practice is supposed to accomplish. All too often students in the typing classroom are not developing better typing skill when they practice the drills in the text because they are not concentrating upon their work. Students should be taught "how" to practice and the purpose of each practice period. Only correct practice can lead to perfection.

One phase of a skill should not be built at the sacrifice of another. In the past many teachers have become so dazzled by "high-speed" drills that they have pushed their students for high typing rates, ignoring the detrimental effects such drills may have had upon accuracy. Students need both speed and accuracy in typing. In addition they need the control necessary to apply these raw skills to typing problems and production jobs. Today's typing teacher must provide for the development of skill in all three of these areas.

Short learning periods are more effective in developing skill than longer ones. Whether a period is of "short" or "long" duration depends upon the stage of learning in typing. When the student is learning the keyboard locations, a fifteen-minute period will seem extremely long to him; but later in typing applied problems this period will seem very short. The elements of both interest and fatigue must be considered in determining the length of the practice period that will be most effective.

The learner should be working toward a goal that will be reasonably easy for him to attain. As soon as he reaches this goal, a new goal should be set up which will provide him with the incentive to continue working to increase his skill. The teacher should always avoid setting unreasonable standards, and he should adjust the assignments to the abilities of the individual students. A student will quickly become discouraged if he is constantly given goals that he is unable to attain. When the goals are within his reach, progress is apt to be steady; and he becomes convinced that he can reach the standard expected of him. Once he nears his objective, he may begin to lose interest or to practice carelessly unless a new goal is set. When the learner constantly has a definite series of goals to be attained, his interest is maintained at a high level and the practice patterns remain effective.

Plateaus in typing are not necessarily a sign that no learning is taking place. Nearly every typing student sooner or later reaches a plateau in his skill development. He may seem to be unable to build further skill. He may be having difficulty reducing the number of typing errors on his timed writings. Such plateaus are not unusual. The learner may have built his typing speed very rapidly at the beginning. He then needs a period of time to "fixate" the skill at that level before he can proceed to a higher level. A student may be making too many errors because he is afraid he is going to make errors; he may be practicing on the wrong kinds of material; he may be practicing using incorrect techniques; or he may simply need additional drill and practice before he can reach a higher level of accuracy. While a student may see little signs of progress when he is on a learning plateau, if he is doing the right kind of practice on the right kinds of material, then skill is actually being developed each day which will make it possible for him to eventually move on to a higher level of typing skill.

The development of a skill proceeds at a slower rate as higher levels of skill are attained. Most students are able to reach a typing rate of thirty to thirty-five words a minute quite easily and quickly. The student should understand, however, that he should not expect to continue to build his skill at the same rate. A longer period is required to build a typing speed from sixty to seventy words a minute than is required to increase one's speed from thirty to forty words a minute. In the same way, a longer period of time is required to attain a typing skill of ninety to a hundred words a minute than was required to move from sixty to seventy words a minute. If students are made to understand that the higher levels of skill do require more time and more intensive practice than the lower levels, they are less apt to become discouraged with their progress.

Most learners can increase their skill with correct practice. Students often claim that they cannot increase their skill because they have reached their maximum potential. In reality few persons ever attain the maximum typing skill of which they are capable. Even very rapid, accurate typists will admit that with intensive practice, using drill material selected to meet their individual needs, they could increase their typing skill. The expert typist who is typing one hundred words a minute may not find it feasible, however, because a great deal of time and intensive effort will be necessary to increase skill at these high levels. Probably the average typing student does not begin to attain the level of skill of which he is capable.

LENGTH OF THE TYPEWRITING COURSE

The number of semesters of typing offered in the high schools in the different states varies widely. Some schools offer two years of typing, some offer three semesters, and many offer only one year. Recently, with the emphasis upon an academic curriculum in the high school, many schools have transferred the typing program to the junior high school.

Many high schools that offer primarily an academic curriculum feel that they can only justify one year of typing. Other schools with strong vocational programs include two years of typing in the curriculum. In Pennsylvania it has been found that basic typing skill, applications, and knowledges can be developed during the first year and that a vocational skill in production typewriting can be developed in the third semester. In Virginia three semesters of typewriting are offered in the vocational program, followed by a one-semester course in clerical practice and vocational office training.

The year in which typing is offered will depend somewhat upon the overall curriculum. In a school offering two years of shorthand, students are usually encouraged to enroll in beginning typing in their tenth year. If only one year of shorthand is offered, the students usually defer typing until the eleventh year so that part of the time in second-year typing may be devoted to transcription.

TYPING IN THE JUNIOR HIGH SCHOOL

Personal-use typewriting courses are becoming increasingly popular on the junior high school and even on the elementary school level. The course may be either one or two semesters in length, with the major objectives being the development of sufficient typing skill to enable a person to use the typewriter in personal-use situations. Most textbooks that are especially prepared for personal-use typing classes on the junior high school level are designed for only one semester. The class should meet daily forty to fifty minutes; in schools using modular scheduling, the class may meet four days a week, with provision for a laboratory session the fifth day.

The major emphasis in a one-semester course should be upon the development of a basic typewriting skill, since the extent to which most students use typing later depends upon the degree of skill they possess. While the development of basic skill does require typing from the printed copy in the text, it should be remembered that few personal-use typists will be engaged in this type of activity later. Therefore, considerable attention should be given to teaching composition at the typewriter.

Some junior high school typing teachers do not set minimum typing rates students must meet to pass the course. However, in a one-semester course, the average students should be able to type at least thirty gross words a minute for three minutes with not more than three errors; in a two-semester course, most students should be able to type forty words a minute for five minutes with not more than five errors.

Peterson recommends the following course content for personal-use typing courses:

One-Semester Course

1. A high degree of emphasis in basic skill development. This skill should be developed to the highest possible degree, preferably to a minimum of thirty gross words per minute for three minutes with a three error tolerance.
2. A high degree of skill in the touch operation of typewriter service mechanisms to facilitate continuity in typewriting, especially the tabulator key for simple tabulation.
3. A high degree of skill in composing at the typewriter. Most personal typewriting students will use the typwriter as a writing instrument rather than as a copying instrument.
4. A few exercises in one common business letter style. Research reveals the typing of personal business letters to be a frequent typewriting personal-use activity.

5. An exercise or two in the typing of envelopes.
6. Several exercises in correct erasing techniques. Champion typists make errors and erase.
7. Several exercises in typing on ruled lines.
8. A few exercises in simple centering. The student should comprehend centering principles so as to arrange materials attractively.
9. An exercise in the use of carbon paper.
10. An exercise in typing a manuscript.

Two-Semester Course

1. The development of a typewriting skill of forty gross words per minute for three minutes with an error limit of three.
2. The development of a major skill in composing at the typewriter. This would include the ability to compose personal and business letters, themes, and to fill in application blanks. The ability to compose directly at the typewriter is comparatively difficult for the average student. A designed, simple-to-the-complex instructional procedure should be followed.
3. The development of a high skill on the touch operation of machine service mechanisms to facilitate basic typewriting and application skills.
4. The application of correct English usage, with stress on spelling, punctuation, syllabication, and so forth.
5. A high degree of skill in erasing, crowding and spreading, and alignment.
6. A few exercises on a commonly used business letter style.
7. A few exercises in the typing of envelopes.
8. A few exercises in simple centering.
9. A few exercises in simple tabulation.
10. An exercise in the use of carbon paper.
11. The development of an acquaintanceship skill with numbers and special characters. Numbers are found in ever-increasing quantity in modern communication.
12. A practical application skill in typing manuscripts.[2]

Many times persons who have completed personal-use typing courses in junior high school later decide to enroll in typing on the secondary level. An articulation problem immediately arises. All too often these students are automatically placed in the first semester of typewriting. Such a practice cannot be justified. The student who has had previous typing instruction should be given a straight-copy test in speed and accuracy. If he is able to meet the standards required at the end of the first semester of high school typing, he should be enrolled in the second semester. It is also possible that he may have sufficient typing skill to be placed in an advanced typing course.

[2] John C. Peterson, "Developments and Recommendations for Personal Typewriting Courses," *The College of Education Record,* The University of North Dakota, January 1960, pp. 58–59.

INTRODUCING THE KEYBOARD

A number of different approaches have been recommended for introducing the students to the keyboard. However, to date no research indicates conclusively that one approach is any more effective than another. The approaches most often used in the high school and college typing texts today are the homerow approach, the vertical approach, the skip-around or word-pattern approach, and the whole-keyboard approach.

Homerow Approach

Teachers using the homerow approach first teach the locations of the fingers on the homerow and then present extensive drills using these keys. Since the homerow is the base from which all typing reaches are made, this is an easy way to introduce the keyboard. However, only one vowel is included in the homerow locations, which means that much of the drill material consists of nonsense typing rather than word or phrase typing.

Vertical Approach

In texts following the vertical plan, all keys struck by one finger are presented at one time. For example, the reaches to *j, u, m, n, h,* and *y* are presented as a group. Usually the next group of reaches presented is the group controlled by the *f* finger—*f, g, v, b, r,* and *t.* Since *j* and *f* are the two strongest fingers, these reaches are taught first. Then the reaches for the *k* and *d* fingers are located, for the *l* and *s* fingers, and for the *;* and *a* fingers. This approach, like the homerow approach, usually results in the use of considerable nonsense-drill material.

Skip-Around or Word-Pattern Approach

Most texts using the skip-around or word-pattern approach present those key locations first that are needed to prepare meaningful copy. In some instances special effort is made during the first two or three days to concentrate on reaches controlled by the stronger fingers of the left and right hands. Almost no nonsense-drill material is found in texts using the skip-around approach. Attention is directed to mastering key locations through the typing of short, simple words in which the letters may appear at the beginning, in the middle, or at the end of the words. Often particular emphasis is given to words containing doubled letters, as these are the easiest letter combinations for the beginning typist and help him master these reaches quickly. Because they give him a feeling of confidence, he tends to strike the keys with a sharp, staccato touch.

Whole-Keyboard Approach

Teachers using the whole-keyboard approach present the entire alphabetic keyboard during the first day of typing. Although the entire keyboard is presented the first day, presentation is not the same as mastery, and additional drill must be provided on succeeding days to enable the students to learn the key locations.

Regardless of the approach used in presenting the keyboard, most authorities today agree that the student should carefully observe the location of the new key and make the reach several times, watching as his finger moves to the new location. This procedure gives him confidence that he is making the correct reach to the new location and enables him to get the feel of the reach even before the key is struck. After the student has observed his finger make this reach a number of times, he should be ready to practice the drill material in the text, keeping his eyes focused on the copy.

A survey of the typing texts now on the market reveals that authors today present the alphabetic keyboard locations in one to two weeks, with most texts requiring approximately seven days to complete these locations. Thus the letters are all presented in a relatively short period so that the student may quickly master them. Authors believe that students should master the alphabetic keyboard as soon as possible and should strike the keys rapidly from the very first day. This is possible if the drill material in the early lessons in the text is based solely on simple words, phrases, and short sentences. Key locations may be learned quickly through carefully constructed drills.

Teachers should remember that not all students learn at the same rate. Some students may master the keyboard locations rapidly while others appear to be very slow in learning them. The difficulty experienced by some students in learning to type may well be caused by forcing them to attempt new key locations before they have mastered the locations presented previously.

After the alphabetic keys have been introduced, most texts allow for a consolidation period during which the students are expected to improve their typing techniques, to thoroughly master the alphabetic key locations, and to increase their typing skill. Immediately following this period, figures and special characters are introduced. Teachers should be extremely careful not to introduce these keys too rapidly. In the past students have frequently failed to learn these locations because they were presented in too short a span of time. Many authorities believe that not more than two figures should be presented in any one lesson and that the teaching of the symbols located on these keys should be deferred until later in the course. For example, it is their contention that if the student is taught the $ together with the 4, he will always have to think of the location of the 4 before he is able to remember the location of the $. Thus, instead of teaching the student to make the reach in this manner—fr4$ or f4$f, the student is taught to reach directly to the figures—f4f, and later when the symbols are introduced—f$f. Such characters as @, #, ¢, &, and * are used so infrequently that there is actually no reason to introduce these symbols until much later in the course. All too often these symbols are introduced early but used so infrequently in the typing lessons that their locations are never mastered. Students would probably learn to type figures with much more confidence than they do now if they completely mastered the figures before the symbols were introduced.

THE FIRST DAY'S LESSON IN TYPEWRITING

The teaching approach used the first day of typewriting is of the utmost importance. Most students who enroll in typewriting are strongly motivated by the desire to type. They should, therefore, be permitted to type as much as possible the first day of class. Careful preparation on the part of the teacher is necessary. The margins of the typewriters should be preset, with the line spacer set for single spacing, and the paper inserted. If an advanced class meets in the room prior to the beginning class, the teacher may ask these students to set the margins and insert the paper. By following these procedures, the teacher can immediately demonstrate the correct stroking of the first key location, after which the student will look at the new key location on the keyboard, watch his finger make the reach several times, and then finally watch the movement of his finger as he strikes the key. He is then ready to focus on the drills in the text which should be dictated by the teacher. The student's first typing of textbook drills should be paced at approximately ten words a minute. Much of the material typed during the first two weeks should be paced at this rate, either by the teacher or by records or tapes.

The first-day procedures should be kept as simple as possible. Using the approach just described, only stroking and key locations must be demonstrated. No machine parts are mentioned until they must be used. Emphasis is on correct stroking of the new key locations. Talking by the teacher should be kept to a minimum. No nonsense material is typed except when practicing a new key location. By the end of the first day students should be typing short phrases. As a result, they leave the class with a feeling of accomplishment, eager to return the next day.

During the second and third days slightly more emphasis should be given to proper paper insertion, posture, and setting margins. During the first week the students should be given a standard procedure to follow in checking machine adjustments each day before starting to type, such as margins at 25 and 75; single spacing; paper guide at 0.

TEACHING MACHINE PARTS

In discussing the psychology of teaching typing, it was pointed out that the parts of the machine should be taught when they are to be used in typing. Beginning teachers sometimes make the mistake of presenting twelve or fifteen machine parts the first day the students are in class, even though the students are not interested in machine parts and will be using only a few of them that period. The cylinder knobs should not be presented until the students need to insert paper into the machine. The paper release should not be mentioned until paper is to be removed from the typewriter. The margin release should not be taught until the students need to use this key. On the other hand, when students need to use special parts of the machine, they should know where they are located and their purpose. Many students complete two years of typewriting without understanding the use of the various scales on the typewriter or knowing the difference between the line-space disengaging lever and the variable line spacer.

DEVELOPING CORRECT TECHNIQUES IN TYPEWRITING

Whether the student becomes an expert typist depends in large measure upon the techniques that he develops during the first six to eight weeks he is in the typing class. The teacher who attempts to build speed and accuracy in his class without proper attention to technique will soon find that he is attempting the impossible. Fast and accurate typing depends upon correct typing techniques. During the first few weeks the primary concern of both the teacher and the student should be to develop correct techniques and then build typing skill upon those techniques.

It has been stated by many speed typists that the difference between the amateur and the champion is largely one of waste motion. The expert typist has learned how to type with the least possible waste motion. His movements are rapid and accurate because they are efficient. The novice is still struggling with the manipulation of the machine. He has not yet learned how to reduce his motions to the minimum, and consequently many of his motions are wasteful and inefficient. Certainly the teacher should not expect the student to perform in the same manner as the expert when he first begins to type. He should, however, try to help that student eliminate useless motions and learn the typing patterns of the experts as soon as possible. To do this, emphasis during the early stages of typing should be placed almost entirely on correct techniques.

Stroking

When practicing the drills on new keyboard letter locations, correct stroking patterns are far more important than accurate copy. The teacher should demonstrate to the students as a group the correct stroking techniques. Following the demonstration the teacher may have the students type the drill with him, again emphasizing correct stroking. After the drill has been typed once or twice in this manner, the students may type the drill at their own individual rates, with the teacher observing each person to be sure he is using a quick, fast stroke. It is now generally recognized that one way to develop correct stroking is through building rapid stroking patterns. Students who hit the keys hesitantly tend to push the keys. Students who are taught to strike the keys quickly usually strike and release the key in the proper manner. Although little attention should be given to the accuracy of the copy, the teacher can determine from looking at the students' practice work those students having serious stroking problems. Skips in the copy and blurred letters are an indication that a student is not stroking the keys correctly and needs individual help.

Eyes Fixed on the Copy

The student who begins to look back and forth from the text to the keyboard or the copy that he is typing is setting up a handicap to the building of fast and accurate typing skills later in the course. Many teachers have found that students who are told to watch their fingers make the reaches to new letter locations before any drills are typed have the confidence they need later to type the drills in the text without looking back and forth from the copy to the keys. Other teachers have found it helpful to place drills on the board and have the students type the copy from the board. The use of such equipment as the EDL Speed Builder Control Reader in teaching key locations forces students to focus on the copy. Years ago it was thought that using blank keyboards would automatically force students to keep their eyes on the copy, but experience has proved this to be a poor teaching device. Those students who want to look at their keyboards will do so regardless. Today typing authorities agree it is far better to have lettered keyboards in the classroom. The importance of keeping "eyes on copy" cannot be overemphasized. Many times one of the major differences between the good typist and the poor typist is one of concentration on the copy.

Correct Reading Habits

Many students develop incorrect typing techniques because they have never learned how to read copy correctly while typing. Their typing errors may be traced to this problem. Most students attempt to read too far ahead of the word that they are typing. Research has shown that slow and careful reading should be required in typing. Students should not attempt to read too far ahead, as this results in constant eye regressions and typing errors. To some extent, however, looking back in the line is normal. It has been found that typewriting requires about 3.6 times more fixations and regressions than ordinary reading and that the eye span in ordinary reading is 3.4 times as long as in typing. The amount of the word absorbed at one time appears to be dependent on the speed of the typist. The eye span of the champion typist will include .67 to .70 of a word at one glance while the ordinary typist absorbs only .32 of a word at one glance.[3]

A few students develop incorrect techniques because they have not learned to concentrate on the copy. The slightest distraction causes them to lose their place, to look up, and to break their stroking rhythm. Failure to concentrate on what is being typed often causes serious typing errors in production typing. The problem is, of course, tied in closely with failure to keep their eyes on the copy.

Machine Manipulations

For years typing teachers seemed to believe that correct typing techniques applied solely to correct stroking. Today it is recognized that many persons

---

[3] Donald C. Fuller, *Reading Factors in Typewriting* (Doctoral dissertation, Pennsylvania State College, published by Oklahoma A. & M. College, 1945).

who have correct stroking patterns will never become expert typists because they are unable to manipulate the parts of the machine with dexterity. These machine parts require special drill because in most instances, even though they are used frequently, they are not employed as often as are the letters of the alphabet. Most typing texts now include special drills on the use of the back-space key, the margin release, the tabulator set and clear keys, the tabulator key or bar, the shift key and shift lock, and the space bar. The stroking of these keys is not the same as the stroking of the alphabetic keys, and because they are not used as frequently, all too often students do not learn to use them by touch. Special attention to the development of skill in the use of the manipulative parts of the machine will do much to build increased speed and accuracy in typing.

If teachers gave more attention to correct technique in first-semester typing and less to grading, undoubtedly students would also consider typing technique of greater importance than they now do. To stress the importance of technique, some typing teachers use technique-error charts to rate the students on their typing techniques and to call to their attention those areas in which they need improvement. The teacher may also have the student rate himself and then compare the two ratings. Remedial drills are then selected to correct those techniques that need improvement.

Technique charts are not as widely used as formerly because many teachers feel that they are too time-consuming for the benefits derived from their use. While the experienced teacher may not need a chart to help him analyze tech-nique errors, the beginning teacher may find such a chart helpful in analyzing the typing techniques of his students. All too many beginning teachers fail to observe incorrect techniques until after these techniques have become firmly established patterns. The charts also serve to impress upon the students the importance of technique in the development of typing skill.

APPROACHES TO THE TEACHING OF TYPEWRITING

Basically most typing teachers follow either the *block* or *unit* plan or the *cycle* plan in teaching typewriting, depending upon the approach of the particular textbook they are using. Since the two approaches are highly disimilar, the typing teacher should understand each.

In the block or unit plan, each block or unit emphasizes one particular typing skill. For example, the presentation of the alphabetic keyboard would be the first unit. The next might be a skill-building unit, followed by the unit on figures and special characters. Other units commonly included in textbooks following this plan are units on business letters, memorandums, centering, manuscripts, tabulation, and business forms. In each unit an at-tempt is made to build a high level of skill on the particular application being stressed.

In the cycle plan, the students usually type a different kind of material each day. The first day they may type short business letters; the next day, themes; the third day, tabulation problems; the fourth day, business memoran-dums; and the fifth day, business forms or perhaps a series of problems incorporating the types of material practiced the preceding four days. The cycle presentation is followed throughout the text, with the problems gradually increasing in difficulty.

Regardless of the approach used, the typing teacher should be concerned with developing the highest degree of skill possible in the time available. Experiments have indicated that one of the best procedures for achieving this goal is through frequent repetition. When the typist must continually type new material, he is likely to type hesitantly with unsure movements detrimental to the building of typing skill. On the other hand, the repetition of material tends to develop smooth, fast, efficient typing movements.

Unfortunately typing teachers often believe they are using acceptable methodology when they demonstrate the correct procedures for typing a specific application and then instruct the students to type the applications in the lesson. They may add that should a student complete the problems before the end of the period, he should repeat them. Such procedures are extremely wasteful and build little skill. The students are seldom strongly motivated by these instructions. They see no reason to work rapidly, since should they finish the problems before the period ends, they will only have to retype them. As a result, they type slowly, frequently starting over. Their typing rates either do not increase or may actually decrease. The teacher is then faced with the necessity of spending several days in skill-building drills.

The best repetition practice is that which is teacher directed. This kind of repetition helps motivate the students and provides a constant check on their progress throughout the class period. In this situation, the teacher presents the new learning technique in the current day's lesson. He demonstrates the technique and then has the students perform the technique with him, step by step. Following this, the students are given a series of short drills on the new technique. Each drill is performed under timed conditions. After each drill, the teacher asks the students to evaluate their work, calling attention to specific points to be checked to determine whether they have performed the technique correctly. Finally the students are given a number of applications in which the new techniques are applied. Here again the students type each application within a specified time period, and at the end of this period, evaluate their typing of that application. Three features of teacher-directed approach to typing are essential: first, that the new techniques be demonstrated and the students then have an opportunity to perform the technique step by step; second, that all further applications be typed under timed conditions; and third, that each application be evaluated before the next application is attempted. As the students type each application, the teacher moves above the room, checking the preceding problem to determine whether the students are typing the applications correctly. Using these procedures, there is little reason to spend time grading typing papers each day. Since each application is immediately evaluated, errors are corrected as they occur. The teacher immediately locates the cause of errors and assists the student individually, or should a number of students type the application incorrectly, he may repeat the demonstration. A typing production test should be given at the end of the unit, and only these papers need be graded.

Two major reasons exist for timing all applications. First, the students tend to work more rapidly with greater motivation when the applications are timed. Second, the students are typing a greater portion of the typing period, since they are instructed to repeat an application should they finish before time is called.

The same type of teacher-directed activity may be applied to typing drills. Short periods of repetition on high-speed drills under these conditions are highly beneficial in developing typing skill. Studies show that students who are given short periods of high-speed drill each class period progress more rapidly than those trained by traditional methods. Such students type more rapidly on straight copy, make fewer errors, and have higher production rates. The repetition permits the attainment of high speeds. The learner who has developed a high level of competency on the copy through repetition is able to type much more rapidly and smoothly than he would otherwise. By eliminating hesitating, inefficient movements, the student is able to perform better on all typing jobs.

In the past many teachers have deferred production work until the second year of typing. The students were taught basic typing applications during the first year, but seldom were they motivated to produce these applications rapidly. The purpose of most first-year typing courses has been to provide the students with the applications that they will need for their personal use. Since many first-year students do not have vocational objectives, teachers have felt that production work should be deferred until the second year. This approach overlooks the importance of being able to produce copy rapidly. Unless the typing student with a personal-use objective is able to perform typing jobs efficiently and quickly, he may actually use his typing skill very little. The teacher-directed approach to typing recognizes this truism. Since nearly all applications are typed under timed conditions, the student is actually introduced to production typing when the first applied typing job is presented. This first application in most typing classes is *centering,* which is introduced no later than the middle of the first semester and frequently much earlier.

Exhibit 5.1 illustrates a teacher-directed lesson in tabulation, using production typing techniques. Note that after the teacher has demonstrated each step involved in three- and four-column tabulation, the demonstration is repeated with the students performing each step with the teacher. If any of the students still do not understand the procedure, the demonstration is again repeated step by step with the students. Finally the students are given two-minute timings on each of the five applications. At the end of each timing, the teacher carefully checks with the students to be sure they have typed the application correctly. For instance, in application 1 the teacher might use the following check points:

1. Single spacing
2. Pica type: left margin, 26; tab 1, 38; tab 2, 50
3. Elite type: left margin, 36; tab 1, 48; tab 2, 60

It should be noted that simplicity is essential to build production rates on typewriting applications when they are first introduced in the text. In this lesson in which three- and four-column tabulation is presented, the student does not center the tabulation applications. He has already developed skill in centering. Therefore the only problem in these applications is tabulation. The typing activity is kept to a minimum through the use of extremely short drills. In tabulation low production rates are not ordinarily due to low typing rates but to inefficient, disorganized procedures in clearing and setting the

Exhibit 5.1   A TEACHER-DIRECTED LESSON IN THREE- AND FOUR-COLUMN TABULATION

Directions for Centering Tabulated Columns:

1. Move margins to the far left and right.
2. Clear tab stops.
3. Set paper guide 2 spaces left of 0.
4. Center carriage (pica, 40; elite, 50).
5. Backspace once for each two letters or spaces in the longest line in each column. If a column has an odd number of spaces, carry the extra space to the next column.
6. Backspace once for each two spaces between columns. (For example, assuming two space columns with six spaces each, backspace three spaces for each space column for a total of six spaces.)
7. Set the left margin.
8. Forward space once for each letter and space in the longest line in the first column plus the number of spaces between column one and column two. Set tab 1. Follow this procedure until all tabs are set.

Tabulation Applications

Type each application as many times as you can in two minutes. After typing each application, make sure you have arranged the material properly and corrected all errors. Type applications on one sheet; single space each application and double space between the applications.

Application 1 : Six spaces between columns.

pink	purple	black
yellow	green	blue

Application 2 : Eight spaces between columns.

flour	coffee	sugar
cotton	corn	soy beans

Application 3 : Four spaces between columns.

Alaska	Texas	California	Nevada
New Mexico	Montana	Colorado	Arizona

Application 4 : Six spaces between columns.

iron	copper	silver	gold
zinc	brass	steel	lead

Application 5 : Four spaces between columns.

pear	strawberry	peach	plum
apple	orange	banana	grapefruit

tab stops and the margin. Thus this is the area in which students need practice in tabulation, not in the typing activity involved.

The next lesson in this tabulation unit adds to the applications only a main heading with each problem. The third lesson adds the centering of a heading over a column. The fourth lesson drills on centering the column under a heading. The fifth lesson is a progress check on tabulation—a thirty-minute production period with very simple problems at the beginning of the test and increasing in difficulty throughout until all aspects of tabulation taught during the preceding four days are incorporated in the test. Since the first problems in the progress check are extremely simple, every student should be able to complete at least the first three without any difficulty. Because of the intensive teacher-directed approach used to teach tabulation, few students will be unable to set up the problems correctly. The major difference in the students' work will be in the number of problems completed.

MULTIMEDIA IN TYPEWRITING

Many special teaching aids are available today that are designed to help students build speed and accuracy to high levels. The tachistoscope can be used to encourage more rapid response to visual stimuli. This instrument provides for control of exposure time as well as area exposed. Through the use of filmstrips, the Controlled Reader automatically presents material at a predetermined, continuous, rhythmic pace measured in lines a minute. It may be used either to force speed or to drive for more accurate typing responses.

Recorded lessons on tapes and records free the teacher so that he may work individually with students needing assistance. These text recordings provide minute-by-minute instruction for the lesson in the students' text. Tapes designed for special speed and accuracy drills are also available. Rhythm records are another means of providing for group-paced typing and direct dictation. The tapes and records, when combined with the visual stimulus of the drills in the text, provide the students with multiple-sense learning opportunities.

Transparencies are especially helpful in reinforcing correct typing techniques. Transparencies may be used to illustrate keyboard locations, correct hand and finger positions, and other basic typing techniques. They may also be used to present illustrations *not* included in the text. They are excellent for improving proofreading habits and for analyzing student typing problems in applied typing jobs.

While typing has been offered by means of both open- and closed-circuit television, it now appears that its most effective use is within the classroom, utilizing portable cameras and monitoring equipment. With closed-circuit television, demonstrations may be seen equally well by all students. Video-tape equipment is especially valuable in analyzing students' typing techniques. Video tapes make it possible for the student to observe his own typing on the screen, to analyze his typing techniques, and to determine with the aid of the teacher how these techniques should be improved.

Another recent device designed to improve typing technique is the *diatype*.

The diatype is a motor-driven typewriting platen used to diagnose typing difficulties. The regular platen is replaced by the diatype which pulls the typing paper through the typewriter at a constant rate, thereby producing diagonal rather than the usual vertical lines of typing. These diagonal lines show the time lapses between the stroking of letters as well as hesitations in typing. Analysis of the diagonal lines makes possible the diagnosis of each student's stroking patterns.

SPEED AND ACCURACY IN TYPEWRITING

Speed and accuracy in typewriting are basic to the development of a vocational skill. The typist must possess both qualities. He will not be successful if he is a fast but inaccurate typist, nor will he be successful if he is an accurate but slow typist. The typing teacher must provide for the building of both these skills in his classroom.

There has been much discussion in the past as to whether speed should be built before accuracy, accuracy before speed, or whether the two skills should be built concurrently. Years ago teachers believed that accuracy should precede speed, and they required their students to type perfect copies of all drills and typing problems. Later typing authorities began to question this technique and advocated building speed first, then dropping back for control at regular intervals. Thus a student typing thirty words a minute might strive to reach forty words a minute in a speed drive. After he had reached forty words on speed-building drives, he was instructed to drop back to approximately thirty-five words a minute, typing for control. Once his control level had been established he might push his speed to forty-five words a minute, and so on. Many teachers used this plan of building speed and accuracy in their typing classes. Recently typing authorities have been advocating a middle-of-the-road course, building accuracy with speed. Teachers following this procedure place initial emphasis upon correct techniques. The technique approach enables students to develop the neuromuscular control essential for high speed. Once the pattern is developed and controlled, it is relatively easy to attain a high degree of accuracy at high speed. This emphasis on building accuracy with speed is based on the principle that the beginning typing student should be started at a fast pace so that he will develop correct stroking patterns and that a high degree of typing skill can then be developed fairly easily. Some authorities state that students should be typing at a minimum rate of ten words a minute after the fifth lesson and that after the early lessons most drills should be directed at a minimum rate of fifteen to twenty words a minute. Through repetitive one-half minute timings, it is possible to build the stroking rate of about 75 percent of the typing students to twenty to twenty-five words a minute on easy drill material.

A student should never be told to type as fast as he can regardless of errors. Such a procedure results in incorrect techniques and often completely destroys the student's ability to type with control even when this is his objective. The student will find when he attempts to type as fast as he can without considering errors that his fingers "become thumbs." He will clash the keys and have light and dark letters in his typing, irregular spacing, and other typing errors that are signs of poor technique.

Obviously the typing student must feel secure to type accurately. The importance of such security is illustrated by the number of errors students often make when typing figures and symbols and by their habit of looking at the top-row keys throughout the entire typing course. Poor posture also contributes to errors, as does inattention. Often errors are the result of "woolgathering" rather than lack of typing skill. Unless the student gives his full attention to typing correctly and shows a desire to type accurately, his practice will result in little change of typing patterns. Finally, the emphasis on accuracy must continue throughout the course. If a student is permitted to drive only for speed for extended periods without any regard for accuracy, he may soon be unable to type accurately, even when he attempts to do so. With the automated equipment now being used in business offices, which requires perfect input, accurate typing is more important than ever before.

Typing speed may best be developed through the use of easy copy in the early stages of learning. After the students have had an opportunity to type the material through once, they should be given short, repetitive timings on this same copy. Each student sets a goal for himself, and the timings force him to make a concentrated effort to reach this goal. Repeating the practice under timed conditions enables the students to build their speed rapidly. At first the timings may be only one-half to one minute in length and may be repeated as many as four or five times. Gradually as the students build their typing speed, copy of average difficulty is used and the length of the timings is increased from one to five minutes.

The importance of short, timed drills in building speed and accuracy cannot be overemphasized. When the learner is continually required to type new material, he types jerkily with unsure movements detrimental to the building of typing skill. The repetition of material is necessary to develop smooth, fast, efficient typing movements. Repetition on short timings must be teacher directed, with each student having a specific goal. Students will not necessarily have the same objectives on these timed drills. One student may be trying to reduce his errors on each repetition. Another student may be trying to increase his typing rate. Without such established goals, repetition can be boring and even detrimental to student progress.

While there is no better way to force speed to higher levels than through the repetition of easy copy, improved techniques will also contribute to the building of typing rates. If the student will learn to do each typing operation a little more skillfully than he has been doing it in the past, he will be able to increase his typing speed. If he can learn to throw the carriage a little faster, to return to the keys and start typing a little quicker, to decrease the time required to type capitals, to locate the backspace keys and the margin release, and to develop more rhythmic stroking, he will find that his typing speed will increase even though he may not have increased his stroking rate. The decrease in waste motions and the elimination of hesitation will automatically enable the student to obtain a higher typing rate.

In the early stages of developing typing skill, students should be encouraged to type with metronomic rhythm. Metronomic pacing helps students overcome hesitations and forces them to increase their stroking rates as the rate of the pacing gradually increases. Only as the students gain skill will they be able to type with continuity. In the latter case, the students still type rhythmically but so control their stroking that they will type easy reaches more rapidly than difficult reaches. It is possible that many students attempt to type with continuity before they have the skill required for this level. Textbook authors have encouraged students to type on the "word" level when, in actuality, very few persons are ever able to reach this level of skill. It is possible to type forty to fifty words a minute on the stroke level with metronomic rhythm. A typist who is inaccurate should be encouraged to practice typing on the stroke level.

Beginning typists sometimes think they will never be able to type thirty words a minute—that seems so much faster than twenty words a minute. If the teacher will demonstrate typing at twenty, thirty, and forty words a minute, the class will see that these rates are actually very slow, that the difference is largely one of rhythm, not of stroking the keys rapidly. To reach these levels the student does not need to be able to type fast—but he does need to type with continuity and rhythm, basic factors in building high typing speeds later.

Typing students need to understand that, as their typing rate increases, the length of time required to build to new speed levels will also increase. For example, on the average thirty-five hours of practice time would be required to build one's speed from thirty to forty words a minute; while approximately sixty hours of practice would be required to move from forty to fifty words a minute.

DRILLS IN TYPEWRITING

Much of the students' time in typewriting is devoted to typing drills. These drills may be classified in many different ways, but their basic purpose is to build typing speed and accuracy. The particular classification that the teacher uses is unimportant. However, it is imperative that both the teacher and the students understand what each drill in the text is supposed to accomplish. Drills that the students type are often totally ineffective because the students do not know the objective of the drill or how it is supposed to change or strengthen their present typing patterns. In many typing texts, the labels attached to the drills in no way indicate the nature or purpose of the drill. Usually this is carefully explained in the teacher's manual, but unless the manual is read and the purpose is interpreted to the students, the drill may not result in the desired learning.

Some of the more common classifications of typing drills are warm-up drills, letter-location drills, technique drills, accuracy drills, speed drills, and rhythm drills. Many of the drills in these various classifications overlap or may be used for different purposes, depending upon the directions accompanying the drill.

Warm-Up Drills

The chief purpose of the warm-up drill is to loosen or "flex" finger muscles used in typing. Secondary purposes include concentration on skill building, review of some part of or all of the keyboard, setting the pace for the period, and getting the students to begin work even before the bell rings. Warm-up drills seldom accomplish any of these purposes unless they are paced by the teacher or by tapes.

The warm-up exercise may consist of a single line embracing all the letter reaches on the keyboard. One the other hand, it may consist of two or three lines, each one having a different purpose. In this case one line may consist of the expert rhythm drill, the second line may be designed as an accuracy drill, and the third line may be designed to build fluency and speed at the beginning of the period.

A one-minute warm-up on the expert rhythm drill is an excellent way to flex the finger muscles and strengthen the fingers if correct technique is used in typing the drill. However, if the students use a "punch" stroke coming from the hand, arm, or shoulder, or permit their hands and wrists to "bounce," the drill may actually have a detrimental effect on their typing skill. This one-minute warm-up might be followed by one minute of drill material requiring close concentration, such as (*a*) typing the alphabet forward and backward, (*b*) typing an alphabetic sentence, (*c*) typing sentences using numbers and symbols, (*d*) typing numbers from 1 to 100, and (*e*) typing numbers with symbols such as $1, $2, 1¢, 2¢, 1%, and 2%. The third part of the warm-up might consist of a thirty-second or one-minute speed sentence. This part of the warm-up should result in fluent, fast typing and should set the pace for the rest of the period.

Technique Drills

When a technique drill is used, the student should be told the particular technique that is being emphasized and should not be expected to concentrate on several different techniques at once. For example, a margin-release drill should not be combined with a drill on the backspace key or the tabulator key. The purpose of technique drills may be to improve the manipulation of some part of the machine, to improve the student's typing rhythm, to keep his eyes on the copy, to keep the hands low, to improve the stroking of certain fingers on either hand, or to improve the student's technique in reaching from one bank of keys to another. The student should always be told the purpose of the drill before he is asked to practice it. (See Exhibit 5.2.)

Speed Drills

Probably more time is spent in most typing classes on speed and accuracy drills than on all other types of drills combined. Therefore it is most important that the teacher be familiar with the various types of speed drills he may use and the purposes of each. (See Exhibit 5.3.)

BALANCED-HAND WORDS AND SENTENCES. Since the letters in the words alternate between the two hands, this copy can be typed faster than any other kind of material.

TWELVE-SECOND TO ONE-MINUTE REPETITIVE WRITINGS; ALSO DRILLS BUILDING FROM ONE-HALF TO THREE-MINUTES.

Exhibit 5.2   ILLUSTRATIONS OF TECHNIQUE DRILLS

Carriage Throw

Set the margin stops at 10 and 75 and a tabulator stop at 45. Then practice the carriage return drill below until you can return the carriage quickly and begin typing with no break in your typing rhythm.

	She does not
try to learn.	She does not
try to learn.	

Margin Release

Have the students set their margins for a 60-space line. Then ask them to type line-for-line material in the text using a 70-space line. The students will be forced to use the margin release at the end of each line.

Backspace Key

Ask the students to type a paragraph in which they must backspace and underscore several short words in the paragraph. Drill on the backspace key may also be given through an exercise in typing uneven column tabulations such as the ones shown below.

721	776	110	921	4,592
1,493	29	1,092	623	3,731
565	583	3,318	545	76
8,109	4,712	766	11,001	890

Shift-key Drills

Have the students type material containing many proper nouns. Another procedure that will force the students to concentrate on the proper use of the shift key is to give them fifteen-second timings on sentences in which the number of words capitalized increases in each sentence. The students are to try to type each sentence at the same rate as the first sentence.

Many young boys do not know the value of a dollar today.
Many young Boys do not know the value of a dollar Today.
Many young Boys do Not know the Value of a dollar Today.
Many young Boys do Not Know the Value of a Dollar Today.
Many Young Boys do Not Know the Value of a Dollar Today.

Tabulator-Key Drills

Tabulator key drills should be designed to fit the typing level of the class. A beginning class should be given a simple drill in which the students are required to type only short words. Later they may be given a drill in which words and figures are combined. An advanced class may be given a drill composed entirely of columns of figures in which the length of the figures in each column is the same; eventually the drill may be increased in difficulty until the columns include figures of varying lengths, which will require the students to backspace or space forward from the point at which the machine stops when the tabulator key is depressed. If the stroke count is given for these drills, the students may be given thirty-second and one-minute timings on them.

Exhibit 5.2   ILLUSTRATIONS OF TECHNIQUE DRILLS (Cont.)

		Words		Strokes
now	too	for	war	16
you	any	the	are	32
got	say	all	can	48
him	far	men	lie	64

		Words and Figures		Strokes
use	421	one	123	16
too	897	now	989	32
has	603	not	766	48
her	510	dog	405	64

		Figures		Strokes
2233	9988	5566	2277	20
2345	9876	2389	4454	40
6789	9753	4567	7645	60
8901	8642	1023	9889	80

Type the foregoing drill, dropping the first number in each column of the second and fourth lines of figures (spacing forward from the tabulator set).

Type the foregoing drill, adding a 5 before each column in the second line and a 6 before each column in the fourth line (backspacing from the tabulator set).

Eyes on the Copy

Any material that is unusually difficult may be used to force students to keep their eyes on the copy. Materials containing extremely long words or unfamiliar or foreign terms will accomplish this purpose. Concentration drills may also be used to force students to watch the copy.

Stroking Drills

Almost any copy may be used to improve the students' stroking. The material should not be unusually difficult, however, or some of the students will not be able to maintain an even stroking rate. The teacher may call the strokes and may type with the students to get them to type evenly. Once they are typing rhythmically with good stroking, he may then have them continue this practice individually at their own rates.

Left-Hand and Right-Hand Words and Words Drilling on Particular Fingers

These drills are ordinarily designed to develop additional strength and power in the fingers.

Reaches from the Third to the First Bank of Keys; Reaches from the First to the Third Bank

These drills may be designed to increase the accuracy of the typist, but many times they will serve equally well to improve the students' technique in reaching from the first to the third or from the third to the first bank of keys. When attention is focused on such drills, it is often possible to eliminate waste motions and thereby increase the speed with which these reaches are made.

Exhibit 5.3 ILLUSTRATION OF A SPEED DRIVE

Power Drive

You will be timed for one-half minute on the sentence below. Type the sentence as may times as you can at your control rate.

	Rate Indicator		*Words*
I am sure the little girl is playing on the porch.			10
: 1 : 2 : 3 : 4 : 5 : 6 : 7 : 8 : 9 : 10 :			

Directions

Determine your score on the rate indicator as follows: Figure the total number of words typed in 30 seconds; multiply by 2. Now, using your final score on the rate indicator, locate your speed (or the speed nearest your rate) in the right-hand columns of the Power Drive. It also indicates the number of times the sentence must be typed in one-half minute. Note that this information is given under the letters *A*, *B*, and *C* above the figure columns. When you have typed a sentence the required number of times without error, you have passed the timing and should proceed to the next sentence. Your objective is to pass as many of these timings as possible.

Circle the appropriate rate figure in the right-hand column whenever you pass a timing.

	A	B	C
Number of Times You Complete the Line	2	3	4
	Your Speed in Words a Minute.		

		A	B	C
1.	The sparrows are flying north this week.	32		
2.	Spring is the very best time of the year.	33	49	
3.	April showers bring May flowers and colds.	34	50	
4.	We all feel like singing when spring comes.	34	51	
5.	We will have a watermelon party next August.	35	53	
6.	A beautiful lawn requires constant attention.	36	54	
7.	Our local band concerts always begin in April.	37	55	74
8.	His coach will begin spring training next week.	38	56	75
9.	The yellow daffodils are in bloom all over town.	38	58	77
10.	The youngsters are playing ball in the city park.	39	59	78
11.	If you want shade, you should plant a Chinese elm.	40	60	80
12.	I would like to sit in the sun all day on my patio.	41	61	82
13.	Bob would like to take swimming lessons this summer.	42	62	83
14.	They should wait until Easter vacation to go fishing.	42	64	85
15.	When the spring rains come, the grass will turn green.	43	65	86
16.	Peg and Ann have season tickets to the summer musicals.	44	66	88
17.	Polly will have to get up early to see the sun rise now.	45	67	90
18.	We believe it will be warm enough to go on a picnic soon.	46	68	91
19.	Nowhere else are the skies so blue or the clouds so white.	46	70	93
20.	If you like a hot, dry climate, you will enjoy living here.	47	71	94

GOAL WRITINGS. The copy is marked in five- or ten-word intervals. The student selects a speed goal five to ten words beyond his present typing rate. When he is able to reach this goal, he increases his goal another five to ten words. In some cases, as soon as the student reaches his first goal for one minute, he tries to build that speed to two minutes and finally three minutes before he goes on to a new speed goal.

CALL-THE-THROW DRILL.   The student selects a sentence slightly beyond his present typing rate. His objective is to finish typing the sentence before the carriage throw is called. If he is unable to complete the sentence, the next time he tries to type more strokes than he did the first time and continues in this manner until he is able to complete the sentence in the time allowed.

Sometimes the student is told to keep moving on to the next sentence each time the carriage throw is called as long as he is able to finish the sentence. When he is unable to complete a sentence, he remains on that sentence until he completes it before the carriage throw is called.

RHYTHM DRILLS.   The teacher sets the tempo for the class and gradually keeps increasing it until the rhythm of the class breaks. This type of rhythm drill is especially good for a beginning typing class. Later it may not be particularly helpful, since the speed range is so great that only a part of the class benefits from the drill. Records and tapes are often used to force students to develop smooth typing rhythm. Tapes or records in which the rate of pacing gradually increases are also excellent for building speed. Students type with the record or the teacher, maintaining the same rhythm and pushing for increases in speed. Records or tapes in which the students are instructed to type to music serve much the same purposes. These materials may highly motivate the students, but ordinarily they should not be used for more than five or ten minutes of any one class period.

REPETITIVE THREE-THREE-THREE PLAN.   Actually this is a special type of preview practice. The student practices in groups of three specific words and phrases which appear in the material to be typed. For instance, if he is previewing a letter, he may type this phrase: on on on the the the date date date on the date on the date on the date.

Accuracy Drills

Teachers now know that telling a student to type more accurately does not produce accurate typing. The student would certainly type more accurately if he could. He has no desire to make errors. His trouble is that he does not know what to do to reduce his errors. It is the function of the teacher to teach him what drills he should use to develop accurate typing, not simply to tell him to relax and type more accurately. It is true that usually relaxation and accurate typing go together. But the teacher must set a relaxed atmosphere for learning so the students will be able to type with the desired degree of accuracy. Excessive interruptions during the practice period, an unusual amount of noise outside the classroom, and too much criticism on the part of the teacher during the period—all create tension. Setting goals that the students cannot attain leads to discouragement and increases errors. All these factors the teacher can and should control. Once the unnecessary tensions have been removed from the classroom situation, the teacher may then introduce the accuracy drills that the students need to improve their typing skill.

ALPHABET DRILLS—WORDS, SENTENCES, AND PARAGRAPHS.   Alphabet drills may focus attention on one letter of the alphabet that causes the student trouble, or they may include all the letters of the alphabet for the purpose of increasing student mastery of the keyboard locations. A student making the same typing error consistently should be assigned a drill on words emphasizing the particular reach giving him difficulty. The alphabet sentences and paragraphs are excellent practice material for the entire class. Being slightly more difficult than most contextual material, they force the student to type a little slower than usual and help him find his control level of typing.

EXTREMELY DIFFICULT MATERIAL.   For those students who are typing much too rapidly to be accurate and who seem unable to distinguish between speed-spurt typing and control typing, exercises based on extremely difficult material are often helpful. To type the material, the student must slow down.

CALL-THE-THROW DRILL FOR CONTROL.   Call-the-throw drills may be used for the development of either speed or accuracy. Both the teacher and the student must understand the objective for which the drill is being used. The drills may be used in a number of ways. Occasionally the teacher may tell the student to select a sentence that represents his control level of typing, type it through once, wait for the carriage throw which will be called by the teacher, and then repeat the sentence. The drill may be continued in this manner for thirty seconds or one minute. At other times the teacher, after telling the student to select a sentence as before, may have the student type through the sentence, throw the carriage when the throw is called, and then go on to the next sentence. He will continue moving on to the next sentence as long as he is able to type it without an error and complete the sentence. At any time that he makes an error he will repeat the sentence until he types it accurately. If he does not complete the sentence, he will repeat it until he is able to finish it before the carriage throw is called.

REPETITION OF 30-SECOND TO 1-MINUTE DRILLS ON SENTENCES AND PARAGRAPHS WITH A LIMITED NUMBER OF ERRORS PERMITTED.   In some of these drills the student progresses to the next paragraph as soon as he completes the preceding paragraph without an error. In other cases he selects a goal that he will try to reach in the one-half minute. As soon as he is able to type to that point in the paragraph without an error, he increases his rate objective five words a minute. When he reaches this goal, he increases his rate another five words a minute. In this case an attempt is made to build speed and accuracy concurrently. These 30-second to 1-minute repetitions should not be continued until the students become exhausted and their errors begin to increase. Some teachers keep a chart on the board showing the number of students completing each timing without an error. When the number begins to decrease, they immediately go on to some other typing activity.

Still another way in which straight-copy paragraphs may be used to increase accuracy is to start with one-half minute timings and increase them by one-half minute each time. The student's objective is to type without an error for a longer period each day than he had been able to type previously. For instance, a student who typed for one and one-half minutes on Monday without an error would start Tuesday with the one-half-minute drill and try to build the length of time during which he types without an error to two minutes. If a student is unable to type some of the paragraphs without an error after repeated tries, the teacher may suggest that he go on to the next paragraph. Continued failure on the same material may set up blocks that the student cannot overcome regardless of the effort he puts forth. Some teachers allow one error on each timing.

DRILLS ON DIFFICULT REACHES. Many students hesitate or make errors whenever they encounter difficult reaches in the copy. For example, the reach from *e* to *x* often causes trouble. Many of the reaches from the third to the first or from the first to the third bank of keys are troublesome. Words and sentences drilling on these reaches will develop accuracy in typing them.

ONE-HAND WORDS. Obviously one-hand words are much more difficult to type than balanced-hand words. Most typing texts today contain a number of drills on one-hand words to build both speed and accuracy in typing these letter combinations.

DOUBLE-LETTER WORDS. Although double-letter words represent one of the easier stroking drills for the beginning typist, they represent one of the most difficult for the advanced typist. Frequently the doubled letter upsets his typing rhythm and causes him to omit one of the letters or to crowd the letters too closely together. A double-letter word is a slow word to type and therefore needs special drill.

ADJACENT-FINGER DRILLS. Occasionally some typing students confuse the location of letters controlled by adjacent fingers. This is particularly true of the reaches to *o* and *i, r* and *t, n* and *m,* and *v* and *b.* When a student is consistently having difficulty with one of these reaches, ne should be assigned an adjacent-finger drill on the letters causing the trouble.

OPPOSITE FINGERS, SAME REACH. A letter-location error similar to the adjacent-finger error is that caused by confusing the keys controlled by the same fingers on the left and right hands. Probably the reach most often confused here is *e* and *i.*

UNISON TYPING IN CLASS. One of the most important functions of the typing teacher is to help his students know the difference between typing for speed and typing for control. Many students are tense when they type because they always type at their top rate of speed. They have not learned when to type for speed and when to type for control. Unless the student learns how and when to type for control, he cannot hope to become an accurate typist. If a class seems to have difficulty relaxing after a speed drive or is not dropping back to the control level at the proper times, the teacher may occasionally find it helpful to do a unison-typing drill with the class. The drill should be paced at a rate at which everyone in the class can type easily, without any strain. Occasionally a drill such as this, just before beginning a timed writing, will help the students find their control level so that they will not start typing at too fast a speed.

CONCENTRATION DRILLS. Concentration drills are actually a special type of accuracy drill. Many students make typing errors because they are not concentrating upon their typing. Telling the student to concentrate on the copy may only further distract him. He may then worry lest he is not concentrating. He may also be distracted by someone who is typing next to him. Students often say that they are disturbed because their neighbor types faster than they do. In some instances if the student is only slightly faster, it may spur the slower typist on to greater efforts. But if the range is too great between the two, it may very well make it difficult for him to concentrate on his work. The student may be so concerned about some faulty technique in his typing that he cannot concentrate on anything else. A typist who has used the first finger on the backspace key for ten years will have difficulty concentrating on anything else if he decides to break the habit. It may have a very detrimental effect upon his overall typing skill. Listening intently for a weak bell may make it impossible to pay proper attention to the copy. Making too much effort to complete a certain amount of typing within a given period or trying to finish a job without making an error may distract the typist and make it difficult for him to concentrate on his work.

Every student should be urged to keep his eyes fixed on the copy. If he has developed a rhythmic, continuous pattern of stroking, he will find it relatively easy to focus on the copy, since he will have little trouble with clashing keys. If he is having difficulty in typing for control, the suggestion that he concentrate upon the meaning of the material being typed may be helpful. Any condition that causes unnecessary tension is apt to interfere with the typist's powers of concentration. Frequently teachers themselves are responsible for such problems through setting goals that are unattainable, demanding perfect copies, or hovering over the students as they type. All these practices should be avoided.

The ingenious typing teacher will find that many different types of drills may be used to increase the student's concentration while typing. For example, the teacher may time the students as they type a paragraph to see how long they can type without looking up from the copy. Difficult contextual material is excellent for building concentration and also serves to establish correct reading habits for typing.

TEACHING FIGURES AND SYMBOLS

At one time teachers did not consider it necessary for typing students to develop skill in the typing of numbers and symbols. Today with high-speed computers playing an increasingly important role in the business world, it is imperative that typists be able to type numbers and symbols rapidly and accurately. More and more information is being coded into figures rather than words, from seven-digit telephone numbers to zip codes. The use of punched cards and magnetic tapes emphasizes the importance of accuracy in the typing of figures. An error in the typing of a figure on a punched card or a magnetic tape does not represent one error, but a multiplicity of errors, since the error is repeated each time the card or the tape is processed. The typing teacher should have a definite procedure for building skill on the top row of keys. The following methods represent tested ways to build such skill.

1. Do not introduce the top row of keys until the student has first mastered the alphabetic reaches. Many typing texts defer the teaching of this row for at least two weeks after the alphabet keyboard has been presented. By this time the students should be typing fifteen to twenty words a minute for one minute.

2. Present the figures in a manner that will result in good stroking techniques. If the student is having to concentrate too much upon the location of the key, he may type it with a hesitant, push stroke rather than with the quick, sharp stroke that he uses on the alphabet keys. Some such pattern as this might be followed to get the students to use the correct stroking while learning these reaches:

    1   1   111 2 22 222 12 21 121 212 112 221 7 77 777 17 71
  171 717 771 117 27 72 227 722 272 727 271 721 ·217

3. Do not have the students type the intervening keys between the homerow and the figures. The student may practice in this manner once or twice before making the reach from the homerow to the top row. But continuing this type of practice results in hesitation when the student needs to make a direct reach from the homerow to the top row, as he will in typing contextual material. For example, the teacher might use a drill such as this to present the top row:

    f fr4 f4 44 444 k ki8 k8 88 888 48 84 848 448 488 884

4. Do not present too many figures and symbols in one period. Not more than two figures or symbols should be presented in any one period. All too often these keys are presented but are not thoroughly taught. Sufficient time should be allowed for thorough mastery of each key immediately after it is presented.

5. Dictate some of the number drills. This procedure helps the students think of the numbers as a group rather than as individual digits.

6. After the top row has been introduced, provide some practice in typing these figures and symbols every day. Sometimes the teacher assumes that once the top row has been taught, no further special drill is needed except at irregular intervals throughout the course. Actually special drill is needed on this row every day if it is no more than one or two minutes during the warm-up period.

7. Use many different types of drills to build skill on the top row. For example, here are some of the variations that may be used:

    a. Typing from 1 to 100.

    b. Typing by 2s, 3s, 4s, or 5s.

    c. Drills using the various symbols, such as $1, $2, $3, $4; 2%, 3%, 4%, 5%; 5c, 6c, 7c, 8c, 9c. (Review only one or two symbols each day.)

    d. Drills in which the last figure becomes the first figure in the next combination: 12, 23, 34, 45, 56, 67, 78, 89, 90.

    e. Drills using opposite fingers: 20, 39, 48, 57, 12, 93, 84, 75.

    f. Dictation of sentences containing numbers:

The room was 18′ × 22′.
His telephone number is 382-5786.
The book costs $1, but she reduced the price to 89 cents.

g. Speed drills on typing groups of figures. (The figures should be stroke counted so that the students can compute their typing rate. With practice on such drills, the students should be able to type them at 25 to 40 percent of their straight-copy rate. In the exercise below the last two digits in each row of figures indicate the number of groups of five strokes each that the student has typed. Thus in the first line the student has typed the equivalent of twelve words):

7201 8902 6403 8904 5605 6906 4407 5508 6609 7710 3411 5412
7613 4314 8715 4016 3217 4818 9819 5720 3421 5622 8723 3424
1234 7890 6712 8934 5606 4818 9327 4813 3590 9067 5832 1136

8. When typing copy containing nothing but figures, teach the students to move to the top row. This is sometimes called the *pipe-organ method* of typing numbers. The fourth finger of the left hand is placed on 2, the third finger on 3, the second finger on 4, and the first finger controls 5 and 6. If the typewriter has a "1" key on the top row, then the fourth finger would be placed on the 1, the third finger on 2, the second finger on 3, and the fourth finger would control 4 and 5. Students are usually taught to keep the right hand on the home keys because they will have to be in this position to strike a 1 and to reach the comma, which will be required in typing numbers of more than three digits. Most students can type figures much faster when they move their left hand to the top-row location. However, they should not be permitted to type all drills in this position, since much copy contains both figures and words.

9. Include drills containing both figures and words.
   a. The warm-up drills on figures might be: 1 and 2 and 3 and 4 and 5, and so on.
   b. Another device is to have the students type for one minute a sentence of average difficulty and compute their typing rate. Then the students take a number of thirty-second drills on a sentence containing figures and symbols, the objective being to reach the same typing rate as they attained on the first sentence.

ANALYSIS OF TYPEWRITING ERRORS

At one time most typewriting teachers believed in a detailed analysis of typewriting errors which were recorded on error-analysis charts. These charts might show the errors each student made most frequently, but they did not show why the student made the errors. Also some teachers began to suspect that too much time was being devoted to such analysis to the detriment of their classroom teaching. A few teachers today still keep error-analysis charts or have their students keep them. However, it has been found that such charts are of most value during the first semester of typewriting after the key locations have been presented. At that point they will show errors that students may be making consistently, and remedial drills may be assigned to correct these errors. The keys most commonly struck in error are *m* for *n, r* for *t, t* for *r, o* for *i, n* for *m, s* for *d, r* for *e, e* for *i,* and *a* for *s.* In the more advanced stages of learning, studies of students' errors have shown that at this stage there is little pattern in the errors. The students do not consistently make the same errors, and authorities are inclined to believe that the typing errors of advanced typists are chance errors dependent sometimes on the nature of the copy, sometimes on the physical condition of the student, sometimes on noise and other distractions making concentration difficult. Obviously it is impossible to assign remedial drills for such chance errors.

Today, rather than use error-analysis charts most teachers study the drill papers of each student, note any errors occurring consistently, and make notations on the paper suggesting the proper drills for each person. If certain errors occur in many of the papers, the teacher may then select some remedial drills to be practiced by the class as a group under her direction. Errors in technique that result in slow, faulty motions in the operation of the typewriter must be observed by the teacher during the class period. Many such errors cannot be found through an analysis of the paper alone. Errors should not be analyzed when the purpose of the practice is to force the students' typing speed to new levels. When the student is typing at his control rate and is not forcing for speed, however, errors may be analyzed effectively.

The beginning teacher needs to be alert to the common causes of typing errors. He should watch for these errors in his classes and know how to correct them. Most typing errors are due to the following causes:

1. Incorrect techniques in stroking and machine manipulation
   a. Faulty key stroking
   b. Fingers not held close to the keys
   c. Irregular typing rhythm
   d. Excessive arm and wrist motion
   e. Improper use of the shift key
   f. Faulty carriage return
   g. Incorrect stroking of the space bar
   h. Failure to operate machine parts by touch
2. Incorrect procedures in reading the copy
   a. Reading ahead of the word being typed
   b. Failure to keep eyes focused on the copy
   c. Looking up at the end of each line
   d. Looking to see what has been typed or if an error has been made
   e. Poor spelling which interferes with typing the copy correctly
3. Errors in typing knowledges
   a. Incorrect syllabication
   b. Incorrect application of typing usage rules
   c. Wrong form in typing problems

Blurred letters, skips in spacing, and too light or too heavy letters indicate that the student is using incorrect stroking techniques. Blurred letters are the result of pushing the keys instead of hitting them. The student should be shown how to strike the keys with a strong finger motion and to release the key immediately.

Students who jam the keys often do so because they are not certain of the reach to the proper letter. Instead of striking the key in the center, they strike between two keys, thus depressing both of these keys together. Jammed keys may also be the result of irregular, unrhythmic stroking. Crowding of letters is also a sign of irregular stroking and weak fingers. Rhythm drills, finger-manipulation drills, and drills on alphabet letters or on lines of two-, three-, four-, and five-letter words are often helpful.

Errors in which students confuse adjacent keys, strike the wrong vowels, or strike a key controlled by the same finger but on the opposite hand are frequently caused by uncertainty regarding the location of the letter. The students need further drills on these letters and should think each letter as it is typed. Transposition of letters may also be due to uncertainty about the letter location. Transpositions made by advanced students are probably the result of reading too far ahead in the copy. The student needs to type at a slower rate or on the letter level, keeping his eyes on the word that he is typing until this error has been corrected.

Some students make frequent errors because they let their fingers "fly" away from the homerow keys and thus lose their homerow position. These students should be taught the importance of well-curved fingers held close to the home keys. At the same time the importance of quiet hands and arms should be emphasized. Excessive motions not only cause errors but may inter-fere with the development of typing speed.

Many students pile letters at the end of the line of typing. This is the result of speeding up in an effort to crowd in extra strokes before the margin locks. The students should listen for the bell and should type somewhat slower with even stroking. When necessary, they should syllabicate rather than try to crowd the letters before the machine locks.

The omission and the addition of letters are common typing errors. The omission of letters may be caused by too light stroking, with the result that the key makes no imprint on the page, or by reading too far ahead. The students should practice even, rhythmic stroking on the letter level. The addition of letters may also be caused by reading too far ahead of the point at which the student is typing. It may also be due to poor concentration, with the result that the student types some familiar sequence on the root word which is not part of the sequence in the copy—for example, *importance* instead of *important,* or *perfection* instead of *perfecting.* Here again the students need to concentrate on the copy, making a definite effort to keep their eyes focused on the syllable or the word they are typing. Other errors due to poor concentration are caused by looking up at the end of each line of typing, looking at the typed copy after an error has been made, or being distracted by the bells on other typewriters. A person who is a poor speller may misspell words that are correct in the copy because he is not concentrating closely enough on the letters and words he is typing.

In two surveys of typing errors it was found that over 20 percent of the total errors made by students were due to incorrect use of the nonletter keys—errors in machine manipulation. A common error in this classification is raised or lowered capitals caused by failure to depress the shift key far enough or failure to hold the shift key long enough. Many students have irregular left-hand margins, the result of incorrect techniques in returning the carriage. Failure to space between words or extra spacing between words may result from poor control of the space bar. Lingering on the space bar may cause the machine to skip, or resting the thumb on the space bar may result in the omission of spaces between words. Another common error caused by faulty machine manipulation is unevenly tabulated columns. In this case the student has failed to hold the tabulator key or bar until the carriage stopped moving.

Excessive pushing for speed, incorrect posture at the typewriter, tenseness and lack of confidence, long fingernails, and fatigue may also contribute to inaccurate typing.

Because so many typing errors seem to be hit-and-miss errors, it is sometimes difficult to determine what type of drill will be most effective in increasing the students' accuracy. If these errors seem to be the result of poor concentration, then concentration drills may be used. The reason for the error is not always apparent, however. The teacher needs to realize that the letter that was struck incorrectly may be of no importance at all. For instance, it has been found that many typing errors occur because a student sees a difficult typing combination approaching. He tenses and makes an error in some simple word, but then types the difficult word correctly. The reverse can also happen. The student may manage to type the difficult word accurately but immediately thereafter make an error in an easy typing combination, not because he cannot type that word, but because his rhythm has been broken by the difficult typing combination. Many typing authorities recommend that a student be given directions similar to the following when he is typing to improve his accuracy. Suppose the student is practicing paragraph material. He types through the paragraph once, preferably previewing the paragraph before typing it. Then he checks for errors. When he finds an error, he should type the word once or twice slowly and then somewhat more rapidly. Then he should type the word in its normal setting, typing one or two words that appear before and after the word in which he made the error. Thus if some other word caused him to make the error, he will be practicing that word also.

PROOFREADING

Proofreading is a skill that should be taught. When the student tells his teacher that he did read his work carefully but simply did not see any errors, he is probably telling the truth. The eye tends to see what the student knows should be in the typed copy, not what has been typed. Then, too, proofreading is often hastily done, which results in many of the errors being overlooked. Because students feel that time spent proofreading is time that could be devoted to producing typed copy, they rush through the job much too quickly.

As offices install automated equipment, more and more typewriters will produce punched paper tape as well as the typed copy. Errors captured on this common language medium are repeated each time they are handled automatically by other machines. Consequently, high-level proofreading ability is essential. Students need to realize that while proofreading is time-consuming and costly, the error that is overlooked on the punched tape or card is usually much more costly.

Teachers have probably contributed many times to the careless manner in which their students proofread their work. Teachers have frequently been guilty of spending long hours grading typing problems and production work, marking every error that the students have overlooked. Thus the students never fully accept the responsibility of locating their own errors. On problem typing or production work, a better procedure might be to check the problem until an error is found. Then if the teacher would simply mark the problem unacceptable and return it to the student, the student would still be responsible for locating the error or errors that he had overlooked. The teacher should save many hours by not continuing to grade papers that are already unacceptable, and the student would have to proofread his work carefully to make sure he did find all the errors he had previously missed. If the teacher requires all problem and production typing containing errors to be retyed correctly, the students soon learn to take time to check their work carefully before removing it from the machine.

Lloyd points out that one reason students fail to find their errors is that they are penalized when they do.[4] He suggests that a better basis for grading would be to set a minimum number of errors allowed on a designated quantity of work or to grade the students on their improvement in proofreading. In other words, he would reward students for finding their errors rather than penalize them for locating errors. In proofreading, typographical errors are the easiest to detect and include all errors due to stroking incorrect keys or poor machine manipulation. Content errors are the most difficult to locate because they include incorrect dates, amounts of money, and other errors in the context.

Methods of Proofreading

Because proofreading is such an essential part of the typist's work, many procedures have been developed and used successfully by typing teachers in helping the student to improve his proofreading habits.

PROOFREADING BY THE PAPER-BAIL METHOD. By turning the cylinder until the paper bail is just below each line of writing, the copy may be checked carefully before it is removed from the machine.

PROOFREADING BY ANOTHER TYPIST. At times students may proofread each other's typing papers. Frequently a person who has not typed the material will catch errors the typist has overlooked.

PROOFREADING BY TWO STUDENTS. When students are typing complicated tabulations and reports, there is no reason why one student should not read the copy aloud to another student to check for errors. In business it is common practice to require that all tabulated reports be proofread by two persons working in this manner. The student who has typed the copy should read from the original while the other student checks the typed copy. The person reading the original material should read at an even pace, indicating the spelling of unusual proper names and terms, punctuation marks, paragraphing,

---

[4] Alan C. Lloyd, "Let's Make Proofreading Affirmative," *Business Education World*, March 1950, pp. 335–37.

capitals, possessives, and hyphenation. He should stop reading immediately if an error is found, so that the correction needed may be noted. The student proofreading the typed copy should read slowly, both for accuracy and for meaning. He should indicate any errors in the margin and should stop the reader at once if he has questions about the copy. No changes should be made without double-checking with the original.

Teach the students how to look for typographical, content, and technical errors.

Check for typing errors.

Check the placement of the material on the page.

Check the accuracy of figures in addresses, dates, amounts of money, and so on.

Check the dates in the copy.

Check the spelling of names in the copy. Be sure names are spelled the same throughout the material.

Check the division of words in the right-hand margin.

Check the punctuation within the copy.

Check for errors in grammar.

Check the spelling of cities, states, and other proper nouns.

Check for errors in typing form.

Check letters for any special lines such as carbon-copy notations, enclosures, and the like.

Particular care should be taken to check for errors often overlooked, such as errors in headings and subheadings, near the beginning or end of lines or near the bottom of the page, additions or omissions, footnotes, transpositions, proper nouns, and number combinations.

All copy should be proofread for arrangement and format, for meaning, and for typing errors. On very important typing jobs, students should be taught to proofread the material at least twice. Because of the importance of proofreading, the teacher needs to constantly remind the students to check all work carefully. Frequent proofreading exercises in which students are to detect errors in applied typing jobs help to develop error consciousness.

Students may be given letters to proofread in which the errors become increasingly difficult to locate. For instance, the first letter may contain only typographical errors. The next letter may contain typographical errors and errors in word division. The third letter may have some spelling and grammatical errors. Errors in content should be added last, since they represent the most difficult type of errors for most students to find. If students are given material containing too many different types of errors when proofreading is first emphasized, they will miss many of the errors. When the material being proofread gradually increases in complexity, they will have become sufficiently skilled in proofreading to find most of the errors without difficulty. Timing the students on these exercises helps to create interest in proofreading.

Many students have never learned to proofread for any kind of errors except typographical mistakes. The foregoing drills and instructions will make the students aware of the importance of checking the content of the copy carefully. They will soon realize that errors in content are usually far more serious than most typing errors.

RELATED KNOWLEDGES IN TYPEWRITING

At one time typing was strictly classified as a skill subject. Many persons who do not fully appreciate the content of the course still consider typing merely a skill. Typing is basically the development of a skill, but the development of that skill without the related knowledges used in applied typing jobs would be parallel to teaching shorthand without transcription. The student might be able to type accurately and rapidly, but he would not be able to apply that raw skill to an applied typing job. Students often have the idea that typing is only a skill and do not give enough attention to the knowledges they are supposed to master as they proceed through the course. As a consequence, although they may be fast, accurate typists on straight copy, they are not able to produce a satisfactory quantity or quality of work on typing production units.

The typing teacher should place enough emphasis on the importance of typing knowledges to make sure that the students are learning the knowledges that appear in each lesson. One way in which he can do this is to give a five- or ten-minute objective test on these knowledges every two weeks during the first semester. These short, objective tests will enable the teacher to determine whether the students do know the information that has been presented and will make it possible for him to cover much more material than would be covered through the use of typing exercises. It is not recommended that such tests be used extensively, as most of the time in the classroom should be spent in typing; but using short, objective tests occasionally to check the students' mastery of the informational phases of typing will impress upon the students the importance of this part of the work. Examples of such tests are given in Exhibits 5.4 and 5.5.

Exhibit 5.4   ENGLISH AND TYPING USAGE TEST

Check in the proper column whether the sentence is typed according to correct English and typing usage. If the sentence is typed incorrectly, underscore the error.

	Right	Wrong
1. The desk is five feet long and three feet wide.	___	___
2. He noted that 65% of the residents favored the bond issue.	___	___
3. Only 14 men and 12 women attended the meeting.	___	___
4. Jack left for New York on the 6:15 plane.	___	___
5. The secretary bought twenty-five 6-cent stamps.	___	___
6. The electric bill last month was $25.00.	___	___
7. Jill writes her "e's" exactly like "i's".	___	___
8. Frank asked, "Have you read the article, 'Dawn Must Come'?"	___	___
9. This notebook cost twenty-five cents.	___	___
10. I bought 15 sheets of bond paper for 25c.	___	___
11. Helen is 15 years old; Craig is nine.	___	___
12. The man lives at 1491 Twenty-Eighth Street.	___	___
13. My neighbors have a twenty-foot television antenna.	___	___
14. Please look up insurance policy No. 5, 023, 029	___	___
15. I paid $35000 for my new home.	___	___

Exhibit 5.5 CENTERING TEXT

Complete the following statements:

1. For a 60-space line, pica type, the left margin should be set at ____ and the right margin at ____.
2. For pica type, the centering point is ____; for elite type, it is ____.
3. There are ____ horizontal spaces in a 6-inch line, pica type.
4. There are ____ horizontal spaces in a 6-inch line, elite type.
5. A standard-size sheet of typing paper is ____ inches by ____ inches.
6. A standard sheet of paper has ____ horizontal pica spaces.
7. A standard sheet of paper has ____ horizontal elite spaces.
8. For a 60-space line, elite type, the left margin should be set at ____ and the right margin at ____.
9. A pica type machine has ____ line spaces to the vertical inch.
10. An elite type machine has ____ line spaces to the vertical inch.
11. To center the heading *The Declaration of Independence*, depress the backspacer ____ times.
12. A pica type machine has ____ spaces to the horizontal inch.
13. An elite type machine has ____ spaces to the horizontal inch.
14. An exercise contains five lines of typing, double spacing, plus a one-line heading. To center on a half sheet of paper, you would type the heading on line ____.
15. You are to center a problem with twelve lines of typing and a two-line heading, double spaced, on a full sheet of paper. You would start typing on line ____.

COMPOSITION AT THE MACHINE

Typing authorities are becoming increasingly aware of the importance of teaching students to compose at the typewriter. Special emphasis should be given to this skill for two reasons. First, composition at the machine, starting with simple words and building to phrases, sentences, and paragraphs, may help the students learn to type on the word level, since they are thinking not of strokes but of words. Second, students take typing for personal use and probably do much of their typing while they are composing at the machine. It should not be necessary for them to write everything they wish to type in longhand before they type it, yet many students follow this time-consuming practice because they have never been taught to compose at the typewriter. Students should be able to sit down and compose letters, rough drafts, and reports at their machines.

Because many typing experts believe that composition at the machine does help students type on the word level, they recommend that simple exercises be introduced during the second or third week of the course. Others feel that this type of practice should be delayed until the students have thoroughly mastered the keyboard and do not introduce composition at the machine until the middle of the first semester. Regardless of the exact time at which this practice is introduced, most persons agree that it is a skill that must be taught. The following steps represent a simple approach to building this skill.

Dictation to the Machine

It has been found that more persons are "visually minded" than "auditory minded." Up to this time the students have always had a visual image of the copy that they were to type. Learning to type from dictation may be used as a preparatory step to introducing composition at the typewriter.

Dictation of questions that may be answered in only one or two words.
   What is your first name?
   What is your last name?
   In what town do you live?

Dictation of questions that may be answered in short phrases.
   What musical instrument do you like best?
   What are your favorite hobbies?
   What is your home address?

Dictation of familiar expressions which the students must complete.
   An apple a day . . .
   A bird in the hand . . .
   Don't cross your bridges . . .

Questions that must be answered by complete sentences.

Topics about which the students are to compose a paragraph. The teacher may give the class two or three topics and let them choose the one on which they prefer to write.

Rowe suggests that composition at the typewriter can be built to even higher levels through advanced composition projects. He recommends synopsis composition in which the student is asked to read several paragraphs and then condense the material into a few sentences. He also recommends having students compose letters at the machine, type notes to their classmates, and fill in application blanks.

Typing teachers need to realize that very few persons are able to compose final drafts at the typewriter. If the student is asked to compose a memo, a business letter, or a theme, he should be given the key facts and then be permitted to jot down a brief outline. Using the outline, he would then type a rough draft of the material he is composing directly at the typewriter. He then edits this first draft carefully, after which he types the final copy. This is a realistic approach to advanced composition problems and one that is seldom used.

ERASING

Authorities do not agree upon the best time for introducing erasing. Many teachers like to defer the teaching of erasing as long as possible, contending that if students are allowed to erase they will soon clog their machines with erasure dust. Other teachers point out that deferring the teaching of erasing is not the answer—the students will erase whether they have been taught to do so or not. They believe the problem is not in erasing but in failure to teach the students how to erase properly early in the course.

There is little reason to teach erasing before applied typing exercises are introduced. When such units as business letters are presented, however, it is difficult to make the students appreciate the importance of accurate, neat work and careful proofreading if they are not required to correct all errors. On the other hand, the students should not be required to correct all material that they type, since this would result in a serious loss of time which could otherwise be devoted to typing practice. In most typing texts applied typing exercises are introduced soon after all the keyboard locations have been taught. If students are expected to produce accurate, acceptable material, then erasing must be taught early in the course.

Erasing should be carefully taught, not left to chance. Students should know the difference between hard and soft erasers and when to use each. They should be able to make effective use of eraser shields of all kinds. They should be given practice in erasing, crowding, and spreading until they are able to correct their errors neatly and quickly. The students should be given a number of these drills frequently and timed on them. Each student should try to decrease the time he required to make the different types of corrections, with final emphasis always being placed on neat erasures.

The importance of learning to erase neatly and quickly can also be emphasized by occasionally administering timed writings in which students are required to correct all their errors.

The typing teacher should recognize that correction devices may often be used profitably to save time. He should instruct the students in the proper use of correction fluids and correction papers and tapes. These devices are widely used by office workers, and students with vocational objectives should be given practice in their use.

PRODUCTION TYPEWRITING

Although much has been written during the past few years about production work in typewriting, many persons confuse the terms *problem typing* and *production typewriting*. Problem typing refers to the application of typewriting knowledges and skills to a problem situation. A teacher may present the principles of tabulation to a typing class and then require the students to type a number of tabulation problems. In a true production situation the student types a number of problems in a given period of time so that his production rate may be computed. Included in the production time are all those activities involved in completing the job, from the time the task is assigned until it is finished. Not only actually typing the problems but also reading and following the directions, planning the layout, handling materials, preparing carbons, and proofreading and correcting errors are all part of the total job on which the production rate is computed.

Typing teachers now realize that it is important to build typing skills to production levels—that it is a necessity for vocational students and desirable even for personal-use typing students. The objective in production typewriting is to combine basic typing techniques and skillful machine manipulation with the fundamentals of applied typing in such a way as to master the techniques necessary to perform at a high level of skill. Production-level typing can be developed only if the student has acquired dexterity in the manipulation of his machine, has built his typing skill on sound basic typing techniques, and has learned the fundamentals of applied typing.

Most students with low straight-copy rates are unable to do production typing with any degree of success. Research has shown that a positive relationship does exist between straight-copy speed and production rates, though it may vary somewhat with the complexity of the work involved. Because of this, straight-copy rates alone will not adequately indicate the typist's production capacity. However, since straight-copy skill is an important part of applied typing jobs, it follows that the higher the straight-copy rate, the greater the potential for transfer to production work. Research has also shown that straight-copy skill can be increased on production jobs, particularly if the teacher-directed approach is used as described on pages 111 to 114. On the other hand, a person who is highly inaccurate on straight-copy timings may type production work with much greater accuracy, while a highly accurate typist on straight copy may prove to be inaccurate on production work. Of course, part of this difference may be due to differences in proofreading skills.

To build production rate it is important to provide practice on each part of the problem that will, without practice, lower the student's production rate. Frequently overlooked is the need to provide practice in the nontyping functions as well. Planning the layout of a particular problem, making the proper machine adjustments, preparing a carbon pack, and proofreading often require more of the student's time than does typing the problem, yet seldom do teachers include drills on such nontyping functions in their classes. Since low production rates are frequently due to an inability to plan work and to handle materials efficiently, short problems should be used during the introductory phase of production work. Short problems will provide practice in the nontyping functions while requiring relatively little class time for the typing activity.

Production rates reported in production-typewriting studies have been low. A production rate of twenty-five words a minute on typing production tests from one to two hours long covering various kinds of typing activities is exceptional even for the very rapid straight-copy typists.[5] Naturally, on a ten-minute production test consisting entirely of short business letters, the students' production rates would come much closer to approaching their straight-copy rates than on longer tests covering more complicated material. Most production tests should be at least thirty minutes in length. Recent classroom

[5] Production rate in these studies was computed only on mailable typewritten material. Material containing errors should not be included in figuring production rate.

studies have shown that much more emphasis needs to be given to production work in the areas of tabulation and mixed types of production problems.

Those teachers who believe that production typing is the final stage in the development of vocational typing skill emphasize that production work does not involve new learnings but rather the building of further typing power in applying the learnings that have been taught previously. For example, the teacher may give the students several letter-production jobs. The students have already been taught the various letter styles and the typing of carbons, envelopes, and so forth. Now the student is expected to coordinate all these knowledges and skills into a letter-production situation similar to one he may encounter in an office. He is given a number of letters to type in a certain period of time. He is expected to follow all instructions accompanying the letters, to type carbons and envelopes just as he would in an office, and to proofread every letter, being sure it is mailable before he submits it to the teacher.

The students should be given definite goals. The teacher may require the completion of a specified number of mailable letters for a grade of *A, B,* or *C.* Or he may set up his standards in words a minute. On every production job the students should be timed and should know exactly what standards they are expected to meet. Otherwise much of the value of such production jobs is lost. Students who have been typing sixty words a minute sometimes find they are unable to average more than twenty words a minute on letter-production work. For the first time they begin to realize that speed and accuracy on straight-copy typing is not enough and that they must be able to transfer these skills to production jobs if they are to meet the requirements of an office.

Production jobs may be set up on all types of applied typing work—centering problems, tabulation exercises, stencils and master sheets, envelopes, letters with fill-ins, form letters, and so on. The most advanced types of production jobs that may be given to the students are those consisting of many different typing applications with specific directions for each. The production job may extend over an entire week. This type of job measures many skills that the typist should have: ability to follow directions, ability to handle materials efficiently, ability to type various kinds of problems, ability to produce under pressure for several consecutive periods, ability to proofread accurately, and ability to produce an acceptable quantity and quality of work.

STANDARDS IN TYPEWRITING

Although measurement and evaluation in typewriting is not an easy task, it is the responsibility of the typing teacher to determine those factors that he will include in evaluation and to acquaint the students with the minimum standards they will be expected to attain. The beginning typing teacher will find a wide disparity in the standards reported in the professional literature. In 1962 an analysis of typing standards in twenty-one states, counties, and cities having business education supervisors revealed that only slightly over half had minimum standards, and in those that did, the standards varied widely. The only conclusion drawn from the survey was that minimum standards were extremely low.

Standards may vary not only from school to school but also according to the objectives of the students. In the past many teachers have insisted that the standards for junior high school typing or personal-use typing should be lower than those required in the first year of the senior high school typing program. Recent surveys indicate that these assumptions are fallacious.[6] In a West Coast city tests given over a three-year period to two thousand students in thirteen junior high schools revealed that, at the end of a year of typing instruction, junior high school students averaged from forty to forty-two gross words a minute with seven errors on a five-minute test. Senior high school students averaged forty-two to forty-four words a minute with five to six errors on the tests administered at the end of each year of the three-year period. These results reveal that the standards for personal-use typing in junior high school can be almost identical with standards for the first year of typing in the senior high school.

In Los Angeles junior high schools four factors are considered in the evaluation of typing students: (a) basic techniques, (b) selected problems, (c) timed production tests, and (d) timed writings on straight-copy material. Basic techniques are checked by using a technique sheet. Selected problems are graded only after the student has had some practice in typing similar problems. The timed production tests administered on typing problems provide an evaluation of the students' typing ability in terms of speed, accuracy, and knowledge of correct form. The timed production tests include such problems as typing personal and business letters, addressing envelopes, and typing tabulations and manuscripts. The timed writings in the first semester are three to five minutes in length, while in the second semester only five-minute tests are used. The tests are graded on the basis of gross words a minute, with not more than one error a minute permitted. No separate grade is given for accuracy, and students must meet the end-of-semester standards shown in Exhibit 5.6 on at least three timings.

Exhibit 5.6 END-OF-SEMESTER STANDARDS ON TIMED WRITINGS
LOS ANGELES JUNIOR HIGH SCHOOLS

Personal Typing 1 (3–5 minute tests)	Grade	Personal Typing 2 (5 minute tests)
37 or more	A	45 or more
30–36	B	40–44
20–29	C	33–39
15–19	D	25–32

Source: *Instructional Guide for Typewriting in Junior and Senior High School,* Los Angeles City Schools, Division of Instructional Services, Publication No. SC–607, 1964, p. 35.

[6] Alan C. Lloyd, "The Changing Pattern of Typewriting Courses," *Business Education Forum,* November 1961, pp. 16–18.

Standards for vocational typing courses also vary widely, and studies have shown that office-entrance standards are frequently not in agreement with school achievement standards. Naturally straight-copy standards are easier to determine accurately than are production typing standards, yet even here there are many problems. Some teachers grade on net words a minute and some on gross words a minute. Some teachers allow only a certain number of errors on timed writings; others increase the number of errors as the student increases the number of words typed. Some teachers require their students to correct all their errors on timed writings. Some use new-matter copy for all tests; others use practiced material; and still others use a combination of the two.

Straight-Copy Standards

The trend today on straight-copy timed writings is to grade the student on gross words a minute in beginning typing. In the vocational typing course, the grading scale is often based on net words a minute to emphasize the importance of accuracy. Gross words in beginning typing will give a much more accurate picture of the rate at which a student is typing than will net words a minute. Suppose a student types one thousand strokes in five minutes with ten errors. That student has typed forty gross words a minute with ten errors and twenty net words a minute. Looking only at the twenty net words a minute, the teacher may conclude that the student is not typing fast enough when the problem may be that he is typing far too fast. If he would type with greater control, his typing rate computed on the basis of net words a minute would rise rapidly. It can be seen that net words a minute tends to distort the picture of what the beginning typist is capable of doing. Also the penalty for errors is much greater for the slow typist than for the fast typist. Gross words represents the fastest method of computing typing rates for both students and teachers.

Though teachers may not agree upon the standards that should be required in each semester of typing, they do agree that the student should be given certain goals throughout the semester. The grading scale for speed and accuracy shown in Exhibit 5.7 gives the student speed and accuracy goals for each six-week period. Although the student may not reach these exact standards each six weeks, the standards do give him a yardstick by which to measure his progress. Only one grade is given for speed and for accuracy.

The standards for grading typing students in the Los Angeles senior high schools include the same four elements considered in grading typing students in the junior high school typing program—basic techniques, selected problems, timed production tests, and timed writings on straight-copy material. In the first semester of typing, the final mark is primarily on the student's performance of basic techniques and on timed writings on straight-copy material. In the second semester of typing, the final grade is based equally on all four factors. In the second year the typing of problems and of timed production tests are weighed much more heavily than the other two factors in determining the student's final grade. The scale used for timed writings is shown in Exhibit 5.8. No separate grade is given for accuracy, but any timed writing containing more than five errors is not considered for grading purposes. Students must type at least three five-minute timings that meet the minimum speed and accuracy standard.

Exhibit 5.7 AVERAGE OF SPEED AND ACCURACY CHART

Gross speed per minute written in												Number of errors and grades							
5-minute test			10-minute test									Number of Errors							
Type 1			Type 2			Type 3			Type 4			0	1	2	3	4	5	6	7
25	30	33	35	40	45	48	51	54	57	60	63	A	A	A	B	B	C	C	D
24	29	32	34	39	44	47	50	53	56	59	62	A	A	B	B	C	C	D	D
23	28	31	33	38	43	46	49	52	55	58	61	A	A	B	B	C	C	D	D
22	27	30	32	37	42	45	48	51	54	57	60	A	A	B	B	C	C	D	D
21	26	29	31	36	41	44	47	50	53	56	59	A	A	B	B	C	C	D	D
20	25	28	30	35	40	43	46	49	52	55	58	B	B	B	C	C	D	D	E
19	24	27	29	34	39	42	45	48	51	54	57	B	B	B	C	C	D	D	E
18	23	26	28	33	38	41	44	47	50	53	56	B	B	B	C	C	D	D	E
17	22	25	27	32	37	40	43	46	49	52	55	B	B	C	C	D	D	E	F
16	21	24	26	31	36	39	42	45	48	51	54	B	B	C	C	D	D	E	F
15	20	23	25	30	35	38	41	44	47	50	53	B	B	C	C	D	D	E	F
14	19	22	24	29	34	37	40	43	46	49	52	C	C	C	D	D	E	F	F
13	18	21	23	28	33	36	39	42	45	48	51	C	C	C	D	D	E	F	F
12	17	20	22	27	32	35	38	41	44	47	50	C	C	C	D	D	E	F	F
1st 6 weeks	2nd 6 weeks	3rd 6 weeks	1st 6 weeks	2nd 6 weeks	3rd 6 weeks	1st 6 weeks	2nd 6 weeks	3rd 6 weeks	1st 6 weeks	2nd 6 weeks	3rd 6 weeks	STANDARD OF PROMOTION IN SPEED AND ACCURACY							

STANDARD OF PROMOTION IN
SPEED AND ACCURACY
Typewriting 1, minimum speed 20, and maximum errors 5
Typewriting 2, minimum speed 32, and maximum errors 5
Typewriting 3, minimum speed 41, and maximum errors 5
Typewriting 4, minimum speed 50, and maximum errors 5

Definition

The term "error," used in the above chart, signifies a deviation from a perfect typewritten copy as listed in the *International Typewriting Contest Rules.* Some modification of these rules may be necessary when modern types of timed writings are used and the copy is typed line for line as given in the original.

To Find Average Words per Minute

Determine the total number of strokes, divide by 5 to find the number of "average words," and then divide by the number of minutes.

To Find the Composite Speed and Accuracy Grade on the Chart Locate

1. Correct typing course
2. Correct column for current grading period
3. Gross speed per minute
4. 5-Minute writing—*double the number of errors* to determine the grade for all semesters of typing *except Typewriting 1*

Exhibit 5.7   AVERAGE OF SPEED AND ACCURACY CHART (Cont.)

5. Correct grade will be found at the point where the line giving the gross speed per minute intersects the column containing the number of errors in the test.

Example:

Typing 1, 3rd six weeks, 25 average words, 1 error is a grade of "B"
Typing 2, 1st six weeks, 25 average words, 1 error is a grade of "C"

Source: Adapted from the Speed and Accuracy Typewriting Chart of the Dallas Independent School District, 1971.

Exhibit 5.8   END-OF-SEMESTER STANDARDS ON TIMED WRITINGS LOS ANGELES SENIOR HIGH SCHOOLS

Typewriting 1	Grade	Typewriting 2
40 or more	A	50 or more
35–39	B	45–49
25–34	C	35–44
20–24	D	30–34
Typewriting 3	Grade	Typewriting 4
60 or more	A	65 or more
55–59	B	60–64
45–54	C	50–59
40–44	D	45–49

Source: *Instructional Guide for Typewriting in Junior and Senior High School*, Los Angeles City Schools, Division of Instructional Services, Publication No. SC–607, 1964, pp. 35–36.

Most teachers probably attach entirely too much importance to straight-copy timed writings in second-year typing. The emphasis at this point should be upon production standards on simulated office typing jobs. Little is to be gained by continuing to give frequent straight-copy tests. Such a practice wastes time that should be devoted to developing skill on production jobs, and notwithstanding the time devoted to typing straight copy, surveys reveal relatively little increase in student typing rates in advanced typewriting.

Production Standards

The importance of evaluating students' production performance and of setting up realistic standards has been repeatedly stressed during the past decade. Many typing teachers hesitate to set up minimum production performance standards, since such standards are much more difficult to determine than are the standards for straight-copy typing rates. It has previously been emphasized that skill in typing straight copy is an essential factor in production work; however, because basic typing rate is only one factor in production typing, it is possible for a slow but accurate typist to transfer a higher percentage of his stroking rate to production work than will the student who is fast but inaccurate. On the other hand, the person who is inaccurate on straight-copy tests will not necessarily be inaccurate on production work. In the latter case, when the student is aware that the work must be mailable, he may type much more accurately than he ever typed on timed writings.

Production work involves many more skills than does straight-copy typing. Production jobs may require such activities as handling carbon packs, typing business forms, typing business envelopes, making decisions regarding form and style, erasing and correcting errors, proofreading, following directions precisely, and even verifying information. Few business firms have developed production standards on various kinds of typing jobs. Even in the firms that have set up such standards, it is recognized that these standards can only be applied to the specific jobs on which they are based. Any suggested production standards must necessarily be approximate. For example, whether a typist can type business letters at one-half to two-thirds of his basic typing rate will depend upon the length of the letters, the difficulty of the material being typed, the amount of tabulated information, and the time needed for verifying the content. The number of envelopes that a typist can complete in an hour will depend upon the number of lines in each address and the familiarity of the typist with the names and addresses. Some rough drafts are relatively easy to type, while others are in such poor condition that the copy is difficult to decipher. Manuscripts with many footnotes will necessarily require more time to complete than manuscripts with only a few footnotes. Tabulation problems vary so greatly in difficulty that it is hazardous to even suggest what should be expected in the way of production without having the particular problems to be typed specified.

The teacher should keep the foregoing problems in mind when applying the standards suggested below to various types of typing production jobs:

Letters with carbons and envelopes	1/2 to 2/3 the basic typing rate (8 to 10 average-length letters an hour)[7]
Envelope addressing	50 percent of basic rate or minimum of 2 envelopes a minute (120 to 150 an hour)
Rough drafts	40 to 60 percent of basic typing rate
Manuscripts with footnotes	40 to 50 percent of basic typing rate
Manuscripts without footnotes	60 to 75 percent of basic typing rate
Tabulations	25 to 50 percent of basic typing rate
Stencils	4 single-spaced stencils an hour
Transcription from voice-recording machines	25 words a minute
Form letters with envelopes (medium length)	10 to 12 an hour

[7] This standard is the equivalent of a production rate of twenty-five to thirty-five words a minute based on medium-length letters averaging 150 words.

It can be seen that many of the standards suggested are highly arbitrary. For instance, a student with a net typing rate of 50 words a minute would have to type seven mailable letters an hour (averaging 125 words in length, with 50 words for the inside address, closing lines, carbon copy, and envelope) to attain a mailable letter production rate of 25 words a minute, approximately one-half his basic typing rate. A student with a stroking rate of 60 words a minute would have to complete eleven letters in an hour to reach one-half of his basic rate. It is improbable that many students could type ten or eleven mailable letters in an hour.

Production standards may be based upon two types of tests. The simplest production test is one in which all the problems involve the same kind of typing activity, such as the typing of business letters or the typing of tabulation problems. This kind of production test should be administered at the end of each unit to determine the degree of proficiency students have attained on that particular unit. The most difficult production test is that which includes a wide variety of typing activities—business letters, business forms, tabulation, manuscripts, rough drafts, and the like. The student may be asked to use his own judgment in setting up the problems and may be expected to total columns of figures on business forms or to verify the accuracy of totals given. Obviously on this type of production test the teacher can anticipate relatively low production rates because a great portion of the student's time will be devoted to nontyping activities. This kind of production test is best administered toward the end of the typing program immediately before job placement.

The business teacher should consider developing a series of production tests to be administered at the end of each unit of work. If the teacher will keep a record of the results attained on these tests, he will be able to set up realistic standards once the tests have been administered a number of times. If he wishes to change the tests, he must be careful to keep each problem the same length and the same degree of difficulty. Several short problems are better than a few long ones because students need to develop skill in the nontyping activities that cause low production rates.

Although production standards may be difficult to determine, teachers should attempt to develop such standards. Students need these goals to stimulate their interest and effort in production typing. The manuals accompanying the typing texts frequently offer suggestions regarding the standards that should be required in office-production jobs. In the past too much emphasis has undoubtedly been placed on straight-copy standards to the detriment of production typing. The present trend toward increasing the emphasis on production standards is a recognition of the need to decrease the gap between the school and the office by making the classroom standards more realistic.

TEACHING ELECTRIC TYPEWRITING

With the increasing popularity of the electric typewriter in the business office today, most high schools have purchased some electric machines. Some schools with vocational office-training programs have equipped entire rooms with electric machines. Most typing teachers in small high schools, though, report that their electric typewriters are installed in the same room as their manual machines. In this situation the problem is one of teaching the students to transfer from manual machines to electrics and from electrics to manuals so that all students will have an opportunity to operate both types.

At one time teachers hesitated to attempt to instruct students on both manual and electric machines in the same class. Today most teachers agree that the teaching procedures for electrics and manuals are so similar that this situation can be handled without difficulty. The students who learn to type on electric machines must have special instructions in setting their margins, adjusting the impression indicator, turning the motor switch on and off, returning the carriage, and stroking. The stroking technique represents the major difference in the operation of the manual and the electric typewriters. Although the students on the electric machines will be using a "tapping" stroke rather than a sharp "staccato" stroke, once the teacher has demonstrated the correct stroking techniques for both manual and electric typewriters, the students may be given the same drills for developing correct stroking regardless of the machine on which they are typing. The class may then be taught as a group and need not be divided into two sections. For the most part, the instructions will be the same for both groups.[8]

The First Lessons on the Electric Typewriter

Because stroking does represent the major difference between manual and electric typewriting, it should receive special attention during the first typing periods. One manufacturer of electric typewriters recommends drills such as the following to teach students to "tap" the keys rapidly from the beginning:

With motors off, ask the students to tap rapidly the homerow keys in this manner: *f* 1 2 3 4 5 6. The students tap *f* six times. Then *j, d, k, s, l, a,* and *;* are practiced the same way.

With motors on, have the students type this drill:

ffffffjjjjjjddddddkkkkkkffffffjjjjjj

To teach the correct stroking of the space bar, have the students repeat the foregoing exercise, spacing between each group of letters:

ffffff jjjjjj dddddd kkkkkk

To teach the students new letter locations, use a similar type of drill. With motors off, have the students feel the reach to *r,* watching as they make the reach. After the students have practiced tapping the keys with the motors off, they practice the same drill with the motors on. This insures rapid stroking of new locations from the beginning:

frrrrrrf frrrrrrf juuuuuuj juuuuuuj

---

8 Schools equipped with the new *Selectrics* will not need drills on the carriage return because only the "element" moves across the page. The element, which makes the key impressions on the paper, does not allow raised capitals, jammed keys, or overlap of typed letters even though the student may not be typing rhythmically. The student will, however, need special drills on the various ways in which the element can be moved rapidly to the desired position.

Next write short words on the board. Dictate the word and type with the class. Then combine these short words into easy phrases. At first dictate slowly, gradually speeding up the dictation:

> if it is in, to do so, he fed the hen, it is her red hen, it is too hot, it is not too soon

Time the students on these short phrases, starting with thirty-second timings and gradually decreasing to ten seconds. The students' objective is to type the phrase as many times during the ten-second timings as they typed originally on the thirty-second writings.

Changing Electric Operators to Manual

Students who have learned to type on electric machines have little difficulty transferring to manual typewriters. Here again, special attention must be given to the difference in stroking on the two types of machines. The students should be told frequently to "strike the keys," with the teacher demonstrating the correct technique. Special attention should also be given to the carriage return and to the shift key. At first the students will forget that they must now throw the carriage manually. Some of the students may have "raised" capitals, since they are accustomed to touching the shift key lightly rather than depressing and holding the shift key. Drills on stroking technique, carriage return, and the shift key will enable the electric operators to acquire skill on the manual machines quickly and easily.

Changing Manual Operators to Electric Typewriters

The problem in transferring students from manual machines to electric is, of course, the exact opposite of transferring electric operators to manuals. Since the students are used to striking the keys, they will tend to continue to do so when they first transfer to electric typewriters. Therefore it is important that the early drills be focused on "tapping" the keys. The same drills that were used for students who first learned to type on electric machines will work equally well here.

Students frequently think that because they are transferring from manual typewriters to electrics, they should immediately be able to type much faster than they were typing previously. Developing high speed should not be their major consideration when they first transfer to the electric typewriter. Correct techniques should come first. During the first two or three periods on the electric machines the students will usually be inaccurate in their typing. Some of them will tend to let their fingers rest too heavily on the keys, thereby activating those keys. The teacher should primarily emphasize correct techniques. This will enable the students to type rapidly and accurately on the electric machines much sooner than they will if their initial emphasis is on speed. Most teachers tell their students to type at somewhat less than their normal rate when they first transfer to the electric typewriter. Students who follow these instructions have greater control of the machine and will have more confidence in their ability to transfer without difficulty. The teacher should give the students a period of time to adjust to the electric typewriter before grading the problems they type on the electric machines.

PROJECTS AND QUESTIONS FOR DISCUSSION

1. Mrs. Hammond is teaching a beginning typing class. Despite her efforts to teach the students good proofreading techniques, they still overlook errors in their timed writings and in their typing problems. What suggestions could you make to Mrs. Hammond that might result in better proofreading habits on the part of her students?

2. This is your first year to teach typing. You believe that students should have some homework assignments in typing just as they do in any other subject. These assignments may require students to read the text material before class or to type certain problems for additional practice. Some of the students complain to the principal about these assignments, saying they do not have access to typewriters. You know that over half the students have typewriters at home and that the others could do the homework when there is no class in the typing room. The principal is hesitant to say you cannot make homework assignments, but he is not sure they are necessary. What explanation should you make to your principal?

3. Examine the typing room in your school. Make a list of the items pertaining to physical facilities that you believe could be improved.

4. Go to the library and examine some books on behavioral psychology. Make a summary of any principles found in these books that have an application to the psychology of developing a skill. Indicate any that would have value in the teaching of typewriting.

5. Miss Jackson, a new typing teacher in your school, says the best way to teach first-year typing is to let students proceed at their own rate. She feels that timed drills make the students nervous and interfere with the quality of their work. Do you agree with her statements? If you disagree, indicate your reasons.

6. Examine several typewriting textbooks available for use in the secondary school. What differences do you find between these and your college typewriting book? What differences are there among the supplementary materials?

7. Miss Wilson is always behind in her paper grading. She says she believes in grading every paper her typing students hand in. Would you follow this procedure? Why or why not?

8. Mrs. Hunter teaches five classes of beginning and advanced typewriting. She is very conscientious about discussing new typing problems with the students, but she never demonstrates any of the proper typing techniques the students should follow. She says if the students study the directions in the text, it is unnecessary to demonstrate these techniques.

   You have never seen Mrs. Hunter type anything and suspect her skills are rusty. If this is the case, would it be better for Mrs. Hunter to follow her present procedure or should she attempt to give demonstrations in spite of her lack of skill?

9. Read as many summaries of typewriting research studies completed within the last ten years as you can find in your school library. Then prepare a list of what you consider to be the most outstanding research findings related to the teaching of typewriting.

10. Miss Harris wishes to introduce erasing at the end of the twelfth week of the first semester of typing just before the first unit on business letters. Her department chairman insists that first-year typing students should not be permitted to erase because the erasure dust clogs the machines. Who is right, Miss Harris or her department chairman? Why?

11. You want a demonstration stand and typewriter in your classroom. Your principal says that the room is already crowded and that he does not believe the typewriter would be used enough to justify the expense involved. How would you answer his objections?

12. In your beginning typing class you find that a number of students are erasing and correcting their errors, although you have not yet introduced erasing and they know they are supposed to circle all errors. You are especially upset when you find this is also happening on timed writings. What would you do?

13. You are being transferred to a new high school in the fall. You ask your principal if the beginning typewriting room can be equipped with one make of machine. The principal says he feels that because there are three office equipment businesses in town, each handling a different make of typewriter, he must order an equal number of machines from each of these business firms. What would you do?

14. Your students in advanced typing are very inaccurate. What drills would you use to improve their accuracy?

15. Explain the probable difficulty in each of the following situations:
    a. The student's electric typewriter does not imprint on the page when the student is typing.
    b. The copy on the page appears dirty, although the student has just cleaned the type and put a new ribbon on the machine.
    c. The o's fall out when the student is typing a stencil.
    d. The student keeps getting streaks on his carbon copies.

16. A large business firm in your city recently changed the requirements for beginning typists from sixty words a minute with not more than one error a minute to fifty words a minute with not more than one error every two minutes. Why do you suppose the firm decided to adopt the new standards?

17. Miss Jones says that she does not believe it is necessary for students to learn the numbers and symbols on the typewriter keyboard by touch. She says very few people ever do master the numbers and symbols anyway, and if a student should later obtain a typing job involving this kind of typing, he could soon learn the numbers and symbols on the job. Do you agree with Miss Jones? Why or why not?

18. Miss Black instructs her beginning typing students not to type outside of the regular typing class period for the first three weeks of the course. Why do you suppose Miss Black asks her students to wait three weeks before typing outside of class? What should she do if she discovers some students have ignored her instructions?

19. You are chairman of a committee to select a new typing text for next year. One of the committee members believes that no book should be considered that does not have tapes to accompany it. One of the other members says that typing tapes are just "frills" and that a conscientious typing teacher can obtain just as good results without the tapes as he can with them.

    Look for articles or summaries of research studies relating to the use of typing tapes. On the basis of the information you find, write a paper indicating whether typing tapes are useful and, if so, how the tapes should be used for most effective results.

20. You have a student enrolled in first-year typing who has been absent for six weeks because of a very serious illness. When you tell your principal that you believe the student should drop typing because he will never be able to make up all the work he has missed, the principal tells you the student is a senior and it is your job to see that he passes the course. What could you do for a student in this situation?

21. Miss Larsen says she prefers to teach typing to any other subject—that it requires no advance preparation. "After all," she tells you, "all you have to do is have the students type a lesson a day." How would you feel about this statement?

22. The principal has recently decided that typewriting must be made available to more of the high school students. He calls you in to tell you that he is going to knock out a wall between two classrooms and set up a typing room with a hundred typewriters.

You object to the plan, saying you do not believe it is possible to do a good job of teaching typing to so many students. The principal asks you to do some reading in this area and write a report indicating the results other schools have obtained with large typing classes. Prepare the report.

23. Mr. Andrews complains that his typing students are too tense when they take timed writings and consequently make far too many errors. He says he keeps telling them to relax, but it doesn't seem to do any good. What suggestions could you make to Mr. Andrews that might help him with this problem?

CASE PROBLEMS

1. This is your first year of teaching typewriting. One day in your advanced typing class you discover that one of the students is using the *s* finger on the *c* key. You point out to the student that this is incorrect fingering and ask him to work on correcting this habit. The student does try; but since he has used the incorrect fingering throughout the first course, he does not have much success and says his efforts to change at this point are interfering with the development of his typing skill. What should you do?

2. Miss Wilson has decided to change her grading system in typing this year. At the beginning of the year, Miss Wilson gave her advanced typing students a couple of timed writings and announced that each person would be graded on his timed writings on the basis of his individual improvement. Each student would have to show an increase of thirty words a minute for an *A*, twenty words a minute for a *B*, and ten words a minute for a *C*. One of the students in the class typed sixty-five words a minute on the timed writings at the beginning of the course. She feels it is unfair to require her to type ninety-five words a minute for an *A* on timed writings when some of the students typed thirty-five words a minute on the initial timings and only have to type sixty-five words a minute for an *A* at the end of the course. What do you think of Miss Wilson's grading procedures?

3. Johnny Larson is enrolled in beginning typing. His father has a typewriter at home, and Johnny has been typing by the hunt-and-peck method for several years. In fact, he can type between thirty-five and forty words a minute using his hunt-and-peck system.

You have tried to help Johnny and have suggested repeatedly that he slow down and develop correct techniques. Johnny, however, sees no reason to use the touch method when he can type faster than anyone else in the class with his system. As long as the teacher is standing right beside him, Johnny does try to use the touch system, but when the teacher is not watching him, he reverts immediately to hunting and pecking. What do you think the teacher should do about Johnny?

4. Miss Powell has told her advanced typing class that they must be able to type sixty words a minute by the end of the course or they will fail. Most of the students have made excellent progress. One student, Jimmy Jolson, has shown little improvement. By May the best Jimmy has been able to type on a timing is forty-five words a minute.

On the last day of the course Miss Powell gave two timed writings and instructed the students not to turn in their papers unless they were better than any of their previous timings. That night when Miss Powell started to check the timings, she discovered that Jimmy Jolson had turned in both papers. On one his rate was sixty words a minute with no errors, and on the second, sixty-four with one error.

Miss Powell knows that someone in the class must have typed the writings for Jimmy. In checking she finds that Mary Jane Olson, who sits across the aisle from Jimmy, usually types between sixty and sixty-five words a minute accurately. She is certain that Mary Jane gave Jimmy her writings, but she has no proof. What do you think Miss Powell should do?

5. You are teaching typing in a large city high school. You have tried for years to convince your principal that the advanced typing room should be equipped with electric typewriters. However, he says that although he has submitted your request to the business manager, the request is always denied on the grounds that there is not enough money available to purchase electric machines. He admits he does not believe this is true but suspects it is a policy of the superintendent or the school board.

Recently you have received many complaints from former students who are now employed in local business offices. They say they found it difficult to produce acceptable work on their first job because they were not used to electric typewriters. You are also beginning to have inquiries from local businesses, wanting to know why you are not training your students to type on up-to-date equipment. What should you do?

6. This year is the first time that Mrs. Parker has taught second-year typing at Hilltop High School. By the end of the second week of the course she realizes that she is having some difficulty with the class. Basically the trouble appears due to the wide range of abilities in the class. Some of the students cannot type thirty words a minute. Others type sixty words a minute accurately. Many of the poorer typists are unable to complete even the simplest applied typing problems unless Mrs. Parker is working with them individually, telling them exactly what to do next. On the other hand, when Mrs. Parker selects simple problems for these students, the better typists are bored because the problems are not sufficiently challenging.

When Mrs. Parker asks the beginning typing teacher about the situation, the teacher says that it is a school policy not to fail any student in beginning typing. Consequently everyone who has taught second-year typing has had difficulty with the course. Mrs. Parker does not know whether she should devote most of her time trying to help the slow typists improve or whether she should select material that will interest the better typists and not worry about those who cannot do the work. What do you think Mrs. Parker should do with this class?

7. Mrs. Crawford is a conscientious typing teacher. She plans her lessons carefully, but she seldom grades many typing papers. She checks the timed writings that have no more than five errors and grades all production tests. However, she does not spend any time grading class work.

On the other hand, Miss Williams, another typing teacher in the same school, spends most of her time grading papers. She says she feels that the students expect to have their papers graded and that they will not do the work carefully unless she checks every paper they complete. Consequently, she has very little time left to plan her lessons. She says not much planning is necessary anyway, since all that is required is to cover a lesson a day. She thinks the instructions in the text are so simple that the text is practically self-teaching.

Would you agree with Mrs. Crawford or Miss Williams? In what ways do you think these teachers might change their teaching procedures?

8. This is Mrs. Carlson's first year of teaching at Northwest High School. Most of the students in her advanced typing class are very fast typists but highly inaccurate. Upon checking, she finds that the beginning typing teacher told the students to type as fast as they could. They were not to worry about their errors—they would take care of themselves.

Although Mrs. Carlson does not say so, she does not agree with this philosophy, since it is quite obvious that the errors have not taken care of themselves. She wonders whether the students will be able to do satisfactory work in production typing unless they reduce their errors. Should Mrs. Carlson give her advanced students typing drills before introducing production typing? Why or why not?

9. Thirty-seven students are enrolled in your beginning typing class, which is equipped with thirty-five typewriters. When you call this to the attention of your principal, he says you should not worry about it—there will always be at least two students absent every day.

You soon find, however, that students are frequently absent on Mondays and Fridays, but very seldom during the middle of the week. To compound your problem, the typewriters are several years old, and at least three or four are out of order all the time. Since the school is in a rural area, it is often two or three weeks before the typewriters are repaired. What would you do if you were teaching beginning typing under these conditions?

10. Miss Hale is a new typing teacher in a large high school. There are four other typing teachers. Before school started in the fall, Miss Hale asked the principal for a copy of the course outline for first- and second-year typing. The principal told her he did not believe in all that educational theory. He believes in permitting every teacher to teach his courses the way he wants to teach them.

During the first semester Miss Hale finds that this is exactly the situation. Some of the teachers cover a lesson a day in the text; others take two days for every lesson. Each business teacher sets up his own standards. Some of the typing teachers have relatively high standards, while others appear to have none at all. As a result, Miss Hale finds that some of her second-year typists have very limited typing skills, but others are excellent. She feels that the business teachers ought to work up course outlines and set standards that they would all agree to follow. When she asks the other teachers what they think of this idea, they make it clear that they have no intention of cooperating in such a project. Should Miss Hale make any further attempts to work on this problem, or should she teach her classes the best she can under the prevailing conditions?

SUGGESTED READINGS

Anderson, Ruth I., *et al.*, "Some Typing Authorities Speak," *Business Education Bulletin*, No. 2. Englewood Cliffs, N.J.: Prentice-Hall, Inc., 1960.

Business Education Forum, National Business Education Association, November issues (Typewriting Series), 1947–70.

Clem, Jane E., *Techniques of Teaching Typewriting*. New York: Gregg Publishing Division, McGraw-Hill Book Company, 1955.

Crawford, James B., *Production Typewriting*, Monograph 97. Cincinnati: South-Western Publishing Co., 1960.

Erickson, Lawrence W., "Changing Forces in Typewriting Instruction," *Business Education Forum*, November 1968, pp. 3–5.

Featheringham, Richard D., "Don't Overlook These Typing Drills," *Business Education World*, June 1969, pp. 17–20.

Fuller, Donald C., *Reading Factors in Typewriting*. Doctoral dissertation, Pennsylvania State College, published by Oklahoma A. and M., 1945.

Lamb, Marion M., *Your First Year of Teaching Typewriting*. Cincinnati: South-Western Publishing Co., 1947.

Lessenberry, D. D., *Methods of Teaching Typewriting*. Cincinnati: South-Western Publishing Co., 1949.

Lloyd, Alan C., "Building More Speed in Advanced Typewriting," *Business Teacher*, January–February 1969, pp. 8–9.

Methods of Teaching Typewriting, Eastern Business Teachers Association Yearbook, XXXVIII (1965).

Odell, William, and Esta Ross Stuart, *Principles and Techniques for Directing the Learning of Typewriting*. Boston: D. C. Heath & Company, 1945.

Peterson, John C., and John Staples, "Declare War on Undetected Typing Errors," *Business Education World*, March 1969, pp. 9–10, 22.

Production Typewriting, Monograph 117. Cincinnati: South-Western Publishing Co., 1969.

Rowe, John L., "How to Meet Changing Needs in Typewriting," *Business Education World*, September–November 1963.

Russon, Allien R., and S. J. Wanous, *Philosophy and Psychology of Teaching Typewriting*. Cincinnati: South-Western Publishing Co., 1960.

Stolurow, Lawrence M., "The Psychology of Skills—Parts I and II," *Delta Pi Epsilon Journal*, II (April 1959 and June 1959).

Tonne, Herbert A., Estelle L. Popham, and M. Herbert Freeman, *Methods of Teaching Business Subjects*, Chaps. 4–6. New York: Gregg Publishing Division, McGraw-Hill Book Company, 1957.

West, Leonard J., *Acquisition of Typewriting Skills*. New York: Pitman Publishing Corp., 1969.

chapter

6

SHORTHAND SYSTEMS

Although over a hundred different shorthand systems have been introduced in the United States, the only symbol system widely used today is Gregg. Pitman shorthand, a three-position shaded symbol system, is still taught in a few cities, such as New York, Chicago, and Philadelphia, but most persons learning a symbol system learn Gregg. In 1949, Gregg released *Gregg Shorthand Simplified,* a revision of the former Gregg anniversary edition; and in 1963, the *Gregg Diamond Jubilee Series.* Both the 1949 and the 1963 editions greatly reduced the number of brief forms, abbreviated words, and disjoined word beginnings and endings, resulting in a lighter memory load. However, there is little evidence to indicate that shorthand students have been able to master the system in less time or attain higher levels of skill with either of these two revisions. Some teachers feel that this is due to a lower caliber of student now studying shorthand rather than to the shorthand system itself and that without the modifications that have been made, the failure rate in shorthand would be even higher than it is now.

Whether decreasing the number of brief forms and disjoined word beginnings and endings and writing more of the shorthand vocabulary in full helps the student build his shorthand speed is debatable. Advocates of longer outlines point out that because more words are written in full according to sound, the student can write words confidently by sound. Opponents of longer outlines believe that many students often do not write shorthand by sound, but tend rather to memorize outlines. Then, when taking dictation, the students try to construct the outlines as they recall having seen them written in the text. Thus the longer the outline, the more memorization that is actually necessary and the more difficulty the student may have in building his shorthand speed.

ABBREVIATED LONGHAND SYSTEMS

Although abbreviated longhand systems are based on the longhand alphabet, most of these systems utilize a number of special symbols and characters to express certain combinations of sounds and joined and disjoined word beginnings and endings. The use of such symbols causes breaks and hesitations when notes are being written manually. In other longhand systems some of the basic alphabetic characters are so modified that they are difficult to distinguish later and can easily be confused with other letters. Ideally an abbreviated longhand system would have only slight modifications in the alphabet and would make no use of special symbols and characters.

Because the abbreviated longhand system does require the writing of longhand, it is obvious that it is impossible to obtain writing speeds comparable to those that can be attained with a symbol system. The early lessons in the longhand system may be easier to master than the early lessons in a symbol system because the students have been writing the alphabet for many years. If a person only plans to utilize the system for personal note-taking or for light dictation on the job, the abbreviated longhand system may be satisfactory. However, many people might question whether it would be suitable for sustained periods of high-speed dictation on the job. In some abbreviated longhand systems, if an individual completes the entire course, the memory load involved is surprisingly heavy. Only through extensive use of brief forms, abbreviated words, and numerous disjoined beginnings and endings can the abbreviated system develop the speeds that are needed on the job. On the other hand, for those persons simply wishing a shortened form for taking library or class notes, it would not be necessary to complete the entire course. Mastery of the basic principles might be sufficient for this purpose.

A longhand abbreviated system may be especially useful for adults who wish to learn some type of abbreviated writing system but who have only a limited time to devote to the subject and who are not interested in developing a high level of skill. It may also be useful for college-bound young people.

NOTEHAND

Notehand, introduced in 1960, is a highly modified version of Gregg shorthand and is designed to teach students in one semester to make meaningful notes. Unlike alphabetic note-taking systems, Notehand is based on Gregg Symbols, but only the alphabet and the basic principles are presented. It is recommended solely for nonvocational students who wish to learn a brief writing system for personal use or for academic students who plan to go on to college.

Because many of the brief forms and principles have been eliminated from

Notehand, the memory load is considerably lighter than it is in Gregg short-hand. Thus the theory and its application can be mastered in one semester. Notehand, however, must not be taught in the same manner as Gregg short-hand. In Gregg shorthand, the emphasis is upon the development of verbatim recording skill. In Notehand the objective is to develop skill in note-taking on lectures, in summarizing material, in composing, and in taking notes in any other personal-use situation where Notehand may be used advantageously. The course in Notehand includes not only instruction on shorthand symbols but also instruction on procedures for learning to take notes. While some homework assignments consist of copying Notehand plates, many assignments should require the summarizing in Notehand of articles, newscasts, television programs, speeches, lectures, and similar material. This type of homework assignment closely parallels the manner in which the student will later use Notehand in college or in his personal activities.

MACHINE SHORTHAND

Machine shorthand (Stenograph) was introduced over fifty years ago. The machine, which is manually operated, weighs four pounds, has twenty-three keys, and is noiseless in operation. High recording speeds are possible, since a syllable, word, or phrase may be recorded at one time. How-ever, because not all the alphabetic characters appear on the keyboard, various combinations must be used to represent the missing letters, with the result that some of the words on the tape bear little resemblance to the words they repre-sent.

At present employers appear to be somewhat hesitant about employing persons who know machine shorthand but do not know a symbol system. How-ever, they indicate that the individual is more important that the method. Studies reveal that machine shorthand is used most frequently in the legal field, in courts, and in government offices and that machine shorthand users receive higher initial salaries than manual shorthand writers.

Machine shorthand is ideal for court reporting, since it is less fatiguing than is the writing of manual shorthand. Because the letters are printed on the tape, anyone can transcribe the notes, which is not always true of notes written by manual shorthand writers. On the other hand, the individual using machine shorthand must ordinarily purchase his own machine. The use of a machine is not as flexible as the use of manual shorthand, which can be utilized anywhere at any time with only a pen and paper.

At present there does not appear to be any observable trend toward a great increase in popularity in machine shorthand.

SHORTHAND METHODS—MANUAL OR FUNCTIONAL

Today most shorthand teachers use either the functional or the manual (traditional) method or a combination of these two. Because the Gregg Division publishes two shorthand texts for the first semester—one designed for the use of manual teachers and the other for functional teachers —a brief discussion of the differences between the two methods is given here.

Manual (Traditional) Method

The manual method of teaching shorthand is characterized by the following features:

1. Use of rules
2. Use of word lists
3. Early introduction to writing
4. Use of penmanship drills
5. Vocabulary tests
6. Use of formal review
7. Use of an intensive reading and writing approach
8. Varied activities from the beginning

Functional Method

The features of the functional method of teaching shorthand, introduced by Louis A. Leslie in 1934, are these:

1. The reading approach
2. No rules taught
3. Use of the key in the back of the text
4. No word lists
5. No formal penmanship practice
6. No repetitive reading and writing practice
7. No papers corrected except for occasional tests
8. No tests except for administrative purposes
9. A simplified early learning situation (one activity introduced at a time)

It appears today that there are relatively few manual method or functional method teachers per se. A teacher will classify himself in one category or the other depending upon the particular textbook that he is using for the first semester of shorthand. But the only difference that may be caused in shorthand methodology through use of the functional text rather than the manual text is that the students with the functional books will have the key to which they can refer.

The first-year shorthand teacher who tends to rely heavily upon the teacher's handbook probably comes the closest to following either the functional or the manual method. This is generally advisable. After that, however, he will soon begin to make slight modifications. He will find that some suggestions may not work in his classes. He will start to select those suggestions that are most useful to him in his particular teaching situation and to reject others. He will introduce and try out some of his own ideas, striving each semester to improve his performance.

DAILY CLASSROOM PROCEDURES

Authorities are in general agreement that any time in the classroom not devoted to reading and writing shorthand is wasted. This is literally correct. The only way to build shorthand skill is through reading and writing shorthand. The inexperienced teacher might think that reading and writing shorthand for forty or fifty minutes five days a week would soon become monotonous and that he would lose the interest of his students. Building shorthand skill is like building any other skill—there must be correct repetitive practice, but it need not result in following a dull routine.

Shorthand teachers need to realize that not only the procedure used to begin the class but also the activity within the class period should be changed frequently. Beginning shorthand students soon tire of reading plate material. They will also become quickly fatigued if all the dictation practice is given at one time during the period. The teacher should plan his daily lesson in such a way that no one activity is continued for an undue length of time.

Throughout this chapter suggestions will be made for variations in the daily routine. These include a number of plans for speed building and the use of such mediums as transparencies, programmed materials, and tapes and records.

USE OF THE CHALKBOARD

Of all the visual aids available to the shorthand teacher, none is more helpful than the chalkboard when it is used effectively.

General Points on Chalkboard Presentations

The teacher should stand to one side so that his body does not obstruct the view of the class. He should, of course, talk to the class, not to the board, a common error of beginning teachers. The chalkboard presentation should move rapidly. For example, when planning the day's lesson, the teacher should determine which outlines he will use to illustrate the new theory principles and which outlines are to be previewed on the board before a letter is dictated. When the teacher has to search through the material for these words while he is at the board, he loses valuable time and the presentation soon begins to drag. When explaining new theory or spelling and reading outlines, the teacher's voice should express confidence. The teacher should call the students by name and should observe the class as they read from the board to determine which students are having difficulty with the presentation.

Presentation of Principles—Brief Forms

After the new principle has been explained clearly and accurately, the teacher should both spell and read the first word presented. Thereafter only the students should spell and read the words. This prevents the class from depending upon the teacher and enables the teacher to determine how well the class is responding. It also saves his voice for other classroom activities. The short-hand outlines should be spelled according to the sounds represented, such as "treatment, t-r-e-t-ment." When several sounds are expressed by the same stroke, each sound together with words illustrating the sound should be pre-sented individually, as *-nt* and *-nd*. If the *-nt* words are presented first and fol-lowed by the *-nd* words, the students can spell with confidence because they know which sound is represented in each group of words. Questions from the students should be answered quickly and concisely.

When presenting brief forms, the teacher should spell the strokes in each brief form and then pronounce the word it represents. However, the students should only pronounce the words.

Finally, the teacher's notes or lesson plan should not detract from the pre-sentation. Many teachers believe that small cards or even a shorthand note-book may be less distracting and easier to work with at the board than the textbook.

If the theory presentation is long, portions of the new theory should be presented throughout the period. The entire presentation should be reviewed before the end of the period.

Chalkboard Reading

According to the *Instructor's Handbook* accompanying the *Gregg Manual,* chalkboard reading should be rapid, repetitive, vigorous, and at random. During the first semester each outline should be spelled before being read, and any outlines causing difficulty should be respelled. Occasionally the teacher should ask individual students to read from the board.

Chalkboard Writing

The material on the chalkboard should be organized from left to right and should be within an area clearly visible to all students. The writing should have good proportion and should be dark enough so that the outlines are distinct even from the back of the room. The teacher should write the outlines fluently, as in this way he can demonstrate day after day the manner in which the students are to write in their notebooks. Should he write an outline in-correctly or with poor proportion, he should simply strike a line through it and rewrite the outline correctly. He should never "patch" or erase outlines on the board. All writing on the board should be done during the class period. The outlines may not be perfect, but the students have an entire text of artistically written shorthand plates. Only the teacher, however, can show the students how outlines are constructed and how they should be written. The demonstration of correct shorthand writing techniques is an important teacher function which must be performed during the class period.

TEACHING SHORTHAND THEORY

For many years authorities in the teaching of shorthand advocated that little attention be given to student mastery of shorthand principles. It was said that any shorthand outline was a correct outline as long as the student could transcribe it correctly. On the surface this explanation appears satisfactory, and teachers frequently paid little attention to their students' shorthand outlines. They were also told that tests on shorthand theory, such as word lists and brief form tests, would hinder the students in the development of their shorthand skill and would cause hesitation in writing because the students would be overly conscious of incorrect outlines and would not try to construct an outline if they did not know the proper form. It was stated that the reason teachers were unable to write shorthand fluently and rapidly was that they were too concerned about correct outlines which interfered with the development of high-level skill.

Today some shorthand authorities are beginning to challenge many of these statements. The shorthand teacher who has a thorough mastery of the shorthand system should be able to recall most shorthand outlines so automatically that there will be few hesitations in his writing. If he is unable to develop a high-level skill, it is far more likely due to insufficient mastery of the outlines than due to the insistence on writing correct outlines. Neither teacher nor students can record shorthand with fluency unless they can recall most of the outlines instantly.

It has been found that those students who learn to write accurate outlines from the beginning and who know their shorthand vocabulary are able to build their shorthand dictation speeds far more rapidly than those students who consistently write their own outlines. It has also been found that there is a positive relationship between accurate shorthand notes and transcription achievement. It is true that incorrect shorthand outlines may be transcribed correctly at times, but incorrect outlines do cause errors in transcription and decrease the student's transcription rate because of the need for frequent pauses to decipher the outlines. Thus accurate shorthand outlines are important both for speed development in shorthand and for rapid and accurate transcription. The student who does not know the correct shorthand outline but must construct his own outline usually hesitates, trying to decide what strokes to write. Frequently he writes the same word a number of different ways each time he encounters it in the dictation. Naturally this practice interferes with shorthand speed development. Likewise when the student tries to transcribe these incorrect outlines he may either misread them or hesitate frequently.

Incorrect outlines are often difficult for a student to transcribe if a period of time elapses between the dictation and the transcription. It does not seem logical that students should read one set of outlines in the text and be writing an entirely different set of outlines when taking dictation. Teachers often find, when they examine their students' shorthand notes, that the reason students are unable to read back the dictation is not so much due to the inability to write rapidly as to the number of outlines that have little resemblance to the forms in the text.

Research findings seem to support the procedures followed by those teachers who have insisted upon emphasizing the fundamental shorthand principles and who have continued to give vocabulary and brief form tests. Rather than being detrimental to learning, these procedures may be exceedingly helpful to the shorthand student. The learning load in shorthand is far less than that in many other courses, and the shorthand teacher may well find that insistence upon thorough mastery of shorthand theory will improve his students' ability to take dictation and to transcribe rapidly and accurately.

READING SHORTHAND PLATES

The student is introduced to shorthand reading when the first shorthand symbol is placed on the chalkboard. Beginning with the first period, as the students spell and pronounce the words, the emphasis is upon rapid reading. During those early periods, the reading of individual strokes is, for most students, the first step in learning to read shorthand. As the recognition of shorthand symbols becomes more rapid, the student's recognition unit should increase to words, phrases, and even eventually to thought units. The student who does not progress beyond the word-recognition level will never be a skilled stenographer, since his reading span will be so short that he will have difficulty in his attempt to transcribe for meaning rather than for isolated words. The transcription of meaningless sentences and phrases is often due to this basic weakness in shorthand reading. The final stage, then, in the development of reading skill is the ability to grasp thought units rapidly without looking back over the shorthand lines for the meaning.

What are the best ways to develop skill in meaningful reading of shorthand? Most teachers follow the practice of verbatim reading of the shorthand plates in which the students first learn to read shorthand by spelling out the shorthand characters letter by letter. To avoid the development of slow, meaningless reading habits, the teacher may ask the students to read each shorthand plate twice, trying to reduce the time required for the second reading. This procedure may also help students learn to recognize as word-wholes words occurring frequently throughout the shorthand plate. From this stage he progresses to the phrase and the thought level of reading. The dangers of word and symbol reading can be avoided by careful attention to the students' reading habits and by correct use of the shorthand key.

In the first few periods of shorthand, many teachers have the students read both individually and as a group. Group practice is particularly beneficial to the slower students, as they receive help from the others. Group reading should not be continued for too long a period, however, or the slow students will become dependent upon the rest of the class. Most of the period should be devoted to reading by individuals. The teacher should analyze the students' difficulties in reading so that he may make constructive suggestions to assist them in their daily preparation. Some students may have trouble learning word signs, while others may be unable to recognize phrases; still others may not easily differentiate the various shorthand characters and symbols.

When a student pauses or hesitates on a word, the teacher should prompt him quickly. This saves valuable class time, keeps the other students from becoming bored while the person reading is trying to decipher the outline, and helps the student retain the meaning of the sentnce that he is reading. In the beginning stages of reading, some teachers find it helpful to have the student spell as quickly as possible the outline causing the trouble. In this way the teacher can determine whether the student is simply unable to put the sounds together or whether he is misreading some of the shorthand strokes.

Later such a practice should be unnecessary. If, as one research study has shown, shorthand reading habits formed early tend to persist throughout the course, it is highly important that the student form correct reading habits from the beginning.

One way to encourage students to develop rapid reading rates in shorthand is to set up reading goals that the students are expected to meet throughout the course. Some authorities believe that students should be able to read shorthand plates at 150 words a minute by the end of the first semester. Others state that students should be able to read shorthand plates at two-thirds of their reading rate on printed material by the end of the year. Leslie has pointed out that requiring high reading rates is unnecessary, as students will never need these rates in transcribing their shorthand notes. Although Leslie is correct, it is also true that setting up reading-rate goals and timing the students on these reading rates in class provides excellent motivation. Since there appears to be a fairly close relationship between the ability to read shorthand rapidly and the ability to write shorthand, any procedure that will encourage students to develop rapid reading rates may be considered highly desirable.

INTRODUCTION OF WRITING

The point at which writing is introduced will depend primarily upon the teaching methodology being used. The teacher using the manual or traditional approach will introduce writing the first week of the course, frequently during the first period. The teacher using the functional approach will delay writing until after the eighteenth lesson, or for approximately one month. Some teachers vary the point at which writing is introduced, depending upon the ability of the students.

Writing may be introduced in a number of ways, but regardless of the manner of introduction, it is most important that the students write with fluency from the beginning. It is much easier to improve poorly written outlines through practice than it is to break students of the habit of drawing outlines. All the techniques for introducing writing described in this section provide for fluent writing from the beginning.

The teacher should insist that the students write with pens. At the lower writing speeds it may not appear to make much difference whether students write with pen or pencil, but when they begin to push for speed, the importance of using a pen quickly becomes apparent. As the tension increases with the strain of pushing for higher writing speeds, the natural tendency is to cramp the fingers tightly around the pencil and to bear down heavily on the paper. This cramped style of writing and unnecessary pressure is less likely to occur with a pen. Most persons find it possible to write for much longer periods of time without fatigue when using a pen. Later, when the students begin transcription, they will find pen-written notes easier on their eyes than penciled notes.

Regardless of the manner in which writing is introduced, easy material should be used. Some teachers go back to the first lesson in the text that contains easy letter material. Others prefer to use the current day's assignment.

Easy material encourages the students and convinces them that they will be able to master the art of writing shorthand skillfully.

1. Tracing Shorthand Outlines. The teacher may have the students turn to the shorthand plates that were assigned as reading practice for the day. The students are instructed to use a ballpoint pen with the point retracted to trace the outlines in the text as the teacher and the students read the plates together. The teacher will pace the reading at 60 to 80 words a minute. Because the students are simply tracing the material in the text, they will have no difficulty tracing the outlines at this rate of speed. Some teachers believe the class should be paced at rates of at least 80 to 100 words a minute. After the first letter has been practiced in this manner two or three times, the teacher will write a preview of words from the letter on the board and ask the students to practice writing the words in their notebooks. He will then dictate the letter several times at 60 words a minute. By the final dictation the students should be able to write the entire letter at 60 words a minute. As soon as the students begin to write their homework practice, the tracing is done over the homework notes rather than over the plates in the text. Some teachers have their students trace the outlines in the text whenever a shorthand plate is being read for any purpose. As the reading may be at 100 to 150 words a minute or faster, the students soon learn to trace the outlines in the text at high speeds.

2. Air Writing. Air writing is similar to the tracing technique but is slightly more difficult. Here the students are asked to write in the air or in their notebooks the shorthand plates as they are read in class. The teacher can again control the reading rate. In this case, since the students do not have the outlines before them, each letter needs to be thoroughly previewed before beginning the reading and the rate must necessarily be somewhat below the rate used when tracing the outlines. Here again, once the idea of air writing has been introduced, the students may be asked to air write whenever anyone reads back from his shorthand notes. The students should not be expected to air write all the material read in class, however, as it is most important that they see the correct outlines immediately before attempting to write them. They should be encouraged to practice air writing outside of class, for instance when listening to class lectures and television programs. Air writing is an excellent medium for teaching students "to think" in shorthand.

3. Short Spurts of Dictation. With this procedure the dictation is first given at fifty to sixty words a minute with frequent pauses. For example, the teacher may turn to one of the first letters in the text and have the students read the letter together. He will then write the letter on the board as one of the students reads it to him. The students will again read the letter, this time from the board, spelling any word that the teacher believes they may not be able to write without special drill. He may also ask them to write these words. He will then dictate at sixty words a minute for twenty seconds, pause ten seconds, dictate at sixty words a minute for another twenty seconds, pause

ten seconds, and dictate at sixty words a minute for a final twenty seconds. The second time he dictates this one minute of material, he again dictates at sixty words a minute but allows only a five-second pause between each twenty seconds of dictation. The third time he will dictate at sixty for thirty seconds, give a five-second pause, and then dictate for another thirty seconds. Finally he will dictate the entire minute at sixty words a minute without pausing.

In this manner the student learns to write outlines fluently and becomes accustomed to hearing one word while writing another, an important skill in recording shorthand dictation. The student who is not able to record the first part of a sentence while listening to the last part will later be confused when the dictation rate increases. Every shorthand student should learn to carry one group of words mentally while writing another group.

4. BROKEN-RECORD STYLE OF DICTATION. This plan of dictation is often helpful to the beginning student who needs repetition in order to automatize the shorthand outlines, but it should seldom be used with advanced classes.

> The teacher dictates each word in the sentence a number of times, then dictates the words in phrases, and finally dictates the complete sentence. The broken-record style of dictation is continued until the letter has been completed. The students are instructed to write each word or phrase as many times as they are able before the next word or phrase is dictated. For instance, suppose the first sentence read: Thank you, Mr. Smith, for your letter of January 10. The dictation might be given thus: Thank you Thank you Thank you Thank you Thank you Mr. Mr. Mr. Mr. Mr. Smith Smith Smith Smith Smith Thank you Mr. Smith for your for your for your for your for your letter letter letter letter letter Thank you, Mr. Smith, for your letter of of of of of of January January January January January 10. Thank you, Mr. Smith, for your letter of January 10.

The continuous dictation forces every student to write as rapidly as possible, yet the instructions allow for individual differences and keep all students writing all the time. The repetition enables the students to automatize common words quickly and does not seem to distract them when writing is being introduced. This procedure should be limited to not more than ten or fifteen minutes in any one period, as the high degree of effort and concentration involved will soon cause fatigue.

THE OVERHEAD PROJECTOR IN TEACHING SHORTHAND

If possible, the shorthand classroom should be equipped with an overhead projector. The use of the overhead projector enables the instructor to face the class while he is writing shorthand notes. As a result, the students are able to observe his hand movements as he writes. Shorthand outlines written on a transparency appear to be more realistic, and the transparencies can be made to more nearly resemble a page of a stenographic notebook than can the chalkboard. Finally, transparencies can be used for review later in the period or during another period, or they may be stored and used the next year. Notes on the chalkboard must be erased and rewritten each time they are needed.

Some of the ways in which transparencies may be used in teaching shorthand include the following:

1. Present new theory or review theory presented previously.
2. Review previously presented brief forms. New brief forms in the lesson may be added to the transparency.
3. Preview words to be dictated.
4. Preview words in the letters that are to be read and written in the homework assignment.
5. Preview words in the letters to be dictated.
6. Preview words to be used in conjunction with multiple-channel dictation tapes. If several overhead projectors are available, the transparencies for each dictation speed may be shown at the same time.
7. Present derivatives of words or brief forms.
8. Present drill on related phrases.
9. Present illustrations emphasizing correct proportions in shorthand writing.
10. Review spelling, punctuation, and typing usage rules.
11. Present letter that students are to punctuate correctly and transcribe.
12. Introduce transcription in thought units.
13. Introduce typed transcription. Since students' eyes are on the transparencies, there is less temptation to look back and forth from the text or shorthand notebook to the machine.
14. Teach placement of short and medium-length letters according to the amount of shorthand notes.
15. Provide speed drills in transcribing straight copy.
16. Provide speed drills in transcribing business letter copy.

It is not meant to suggest that the overhead projector should take the place of the chalkboard. Transparencies, however, do offer another teaching medium. Shorthand and transcription provide excellent subject matter for the preparation of transparencies which may be used and then stored for reuse at some future time.

HOMEWORK ASSIGNMENTS

Most teachers probably give less thought to the manner in which shorthand homework is assigned than they do to any other aspect of their shorthand teaching. It is so easy to tell the students to read the next day's lesson, or after writing has been introduced, to read and write the next day's lesson. The students know what the assignment will be each day, and those students who have more free time on weekends than they have during the week have been known to prepare a week's assignments in advance, dutifully turning in their assignments each day when due. Naturally they receive little benefit from such practice, but this is primarily the fault of the teacher, not the student.

Homework Instructions

The teacher who does not give his students specific instructions for completing homework and who does not provide for some variation in the homework assignments cannot expect the students to attach much importance to the manner in which they complete their homework. Their concern is largely that they have some written notes to turn in each day. Not only should there be some variations in the assignments but whenever a new element is introduced into the homework, specific directions should be given the students regarding the procedures to follow. For example the teacher might give the students the following instructions:

1. Always do your homework in a quiet place. Do not attempt to watch television or engage in conversation while you are studying your lesson.
2. Have a large, flat surface on which you can lay your textbook. You should not attempt to write shorthand notes on your lap.
3. When reading word lists, cover the key to the words with a card or paper. Spell the words aloud, if possible. If you cannot read a word, refer to the key. Do not spell brief forms and phrases. When you have finished, spell and read the word list a second time.
4. When reading shorthand plates, if your text has a key in the back, place your left index finger under the shorthand outline you are reading and the right index finger under the key to the outlines. Read the shorthand aloud, spelling each outline you cannot read. If after spelling the outline you still do not know the word, consult the key immediately. If you lose the thought of a sentence, reread the sentence. After you finish reading each letter, reread the letter, trying to reach the reading rate goal for the week. Circle outlines that continue to give you trouble so that you may give them special study.

   If your text does not have a key, copy the shorthand outlines you cannot read on a card and ask the teacher about these outlines when you go to class.
5. Always write shorthand with a pen. Read the first letter through. Then read the first phrase and write the phrase in your notebook. Dictate the material to yourself as you write. Do not write or copy isolated outlines but write in phrases and thought units. If you cannot read an outline, consult the key. If a word gives you exceptional difficulty, write the word several times immediately. Finally rewrite the letter a second time, self-dictating the material at a faster rate and preferably without consulting the text for the outlines.

   Instead of self-dictating the material a second time from the shorthand plates, the teacher may ask the students to self-dictate the material from the key in the text or to write the material from a recorded medium in the shorthand laboratory if one is available. Regardless of the technique used, the material should be written more rapidly and fluently the second time than was possible the first time.
6. Read the notes you have written from self-dictation to be sure they are legible and accurate.
7. Remember that your shorthand reading and writing practice is for your benefit, not the instructor's.

The teacher will note that the foregoing instructions for reading and writing the shorthand lesson require the student to think about what he is doing. Too many students today turn in pages of homework without this practice having resulted in any further development of their shorthand skill. They have merely copied the material while their minds were elsewhere. In effect the shorthand outlines went in one eye and out the other, with no learning taking place at all.

Homework Goals

At times the students may be given specific goals they should try to attain while doing their homework. If the teacher sets a reading goal for each week, then the number of words in the lesson divided by the reading rate goal will equal the time within which the students should be able to read the lesson. For example, if the lesson has 750 words and the reading rate goal for the week is 125 words a minute, then the students would have to read the lesson in six minutes to reach their goal. Similarly, goals may be set for self-dictation practice. When writing is first introduced, the self-dictation rate will necessarily be low, but by the end of the first year students should be self-dictating at 60 words a minute.

Variety in Homework

In addition to instructing the students in the correct procedures for doing their homework, the teacher needs to provide variety in the shorthand assignments. Basically the assignments will consist of reading and writing, but even slight changes will help to keep the students interested. During the week the students may be asked to do part of their writing practice in the shorthand laboratory if one is available. On weekends, however, the use of the laboratory is seldom feasible, but students may be able to check out shorthand records from the school library. The teacher may suggest that the students work in pairs and dictate to each other. In advanced classes the students may be asked to take dictation from newscasts, television shows, radio programs, or perhaps even sermons. Occasionally they may be told to write half a page of a newspaper or a page from a news periodical into shorthand. Or the teacher may give the students a printed take having a liberal shorthand preview, with instructions to practice the preview and then write the take in shorthand several times. If the teacher feels that the students are merely copying the shorthand plates in the text without reading or studying them, the use of such a printed take forces the students to think about what they are doing.

If typewriters are available, the teacher may have the students transcribe some of the letters in the day's lesson, either from the text or from their homework notes. At other times the teacher may ask the students to submit notes they have taken in other courses or notes written for personal use.

The teacher can emphasize the importance of doing homework correctly if he bases the students' reading rates on reading from their homework notes. Many students who can rapidly read the plates in the text write such poor notes in their homework that they are unable to read them the following day.

The use of assignments that encourage students to use their shorthand outside the shorthand class should be considered. Students often fail to attain a high-level skill in shorthand because they restrict its use to a forty-five- or fifty-minute period five days a week. Until the students actually begin to think in shorthand and use it in all their note-taking activities, they will seldom become expert shorthand recorders.

Amount of Homework Practice

The individual teacher must decide for himself how much homework he will require of his students. Years ago it was customary to require students to write a certain number of pages of homework each night. Such a plan does not allow for differences in the size of students' shorthand notes and may encourage poor penmanship practices. Students quickly learn that the larger they write the sooner they will finish their homework. The teacher should encourage his students to practice according to their individual needs. The best students in the class often do not need as much writing practice as the slower students. Usually the student who is unable to get the dictation in class the following day either is not spending sufficient time in practicing the shorthand plates at home or is not doing the homework in the prescribed manner. Many teachers ask their students to practice writing all the shorthand plates in the assignment at least once but not more than twice. An assignment usually consists of one lesson a day.

While the teacher must check the homework to see that it has been done, he does not need to correct or grade it. When the students first begin to write their homework, the teacher should check the papers for the correct proportion of outlines and for outlines that have been drawn rather than written fluently. At these times the homework should be returned to the students so that they may read any comments regarding their notes. Occasionally the teacher should check to see that the entire assignment is being written according to his instructions. Most of the time all that is necessary is a quick check to see that the homework is done each day.

PENMANSHIP PRACTICE

Most shorthand authorities today are of the opinion that penmanship drills are of limited value. They believe that with the right kind of dictation practice in the classroom and the right kind of homework practice at night most penmanship problems will soon disappear. Beginning teachers, however, should understand a number of points regarding penmanship.

First, their students' shorthand writing will usually look very much like their longhand writing. It will have the same distinctive characteristics. Furthermore, the students will usually carry over to their shorthand writing the same weaknesses that are found in their longhand writing. Students who write illegible longhand often write illegible shorthand. Students who write in longhand with a backhand slant or in a cramped style will write their shorthand in the same manner. When these characteristics interfere with a student's shorthand progress, it is often necessary to do remedial work with him in his longhand writing before any improvement will be seen in his shorthand writing. The wise teacher will not attempt to change the size or the slant of a student's shorthand notes as long as the student can write shorthand fluently and transcribe his notes accurately.

Second, the dictation practice in the classroom may at times cause penmanship problems for some students. Students whose shorthand writing speed is below that of most of the class must frequently make a great effort to get the dictation when the teacher increases the speed. A few students may find that the dictation is so far beyond their writing ability that the legibility of their shorthand breaks down completely. If much of the dictation practice in class is beyond their writing ability, they may eventually acquire sloppy, careless writing habits in an effort to get some outline written for every word dictated. Unless special attention is given to these students, they may soon form the habit of writing all their shorthand in this manner regardless of the dictation rate. These students should practice their homework carefully and make sure that every outline is legible. They should also exercise the same care when the dictation is given at low rates in class.

Third, pushing the entire class for the high speeds in dictation may result in illegible notes. It is true that if the students are to develop fast writing speeds, they must be pushed beyond their present shorthand writing ability. On the other hand, pushing too hard for high speeds may have a detrimental effect on the students' shorthand skill. When most of the period is spent in forcing the students' shorthand speed, it is a good practice to dictate some fairly easy material at a comparatively slow rate both at the beginning and at the end of the hour. This practice helps to insure that the students begin the period writing legible notes and that they drop back to a point at the end of the period where they are again writing clear, legible outlines. It also has an excellent psychological effect upon the students, as most of them will find that they are able to get all the dictation just before they leave the classroom.

DICTATION PRACTICE

Since it is impossible for the students to build their shorthand writing skill without proper dictation practice, the teacher should be especially careful to employ only those dictation procedures that will give the best results. The students should have clearly in mind the purposes of the dictation. Otherwise they will be unable to give proper attention to those points that the teacher wishes to emphasize. Teachers themselves sometimes do not fully appreciate the many purposes of and benefits to be derived from class dictation. Dictation may be given to teach the students to hear accurately; to improve their penmanship; to develop fluency and speed; to emphasize certain shorthand principles, brief forms, or phrasing; to build shorthand and English vocabulary; to provide practice in the construction of new outlines; and to provide material calling for the application of various rules of spelling and punctuation.

Many experienced teachers have found the following practices regarding dictation in the classroom helpful.

Time the dictation. The first few days that writing is introduced, only a small portion of the period will be devoted to writing, and the teacher may wish to defer timing the dictation until the second or third week. Other teachers may wish to start timing the dictation after the first two or three days. The class period when dictation is begun is not too important, but it is important that the dictation be timed soon after writing is introduced. The teacher cannot control the writing speed of the class unless he does time his dictation with a stopwatch or timer. When the teacher does not have a watch, the tendency is to dictate at a "sympathetic" rate. If a student in the first row is not getting the dictation, the natural inclination of the teacher is to dictate slower for him. Yet slowing down for this student may mean that the rest of the class receives little benefit from the dictation if they are all able to write at a much faster rate. Many teachers believe they can estimate their shorthand dictation speed, but experiments with experienced teachers have shown that in estimating the speed of the dictation, they miss the actual rate by ten to forty words a minute. Shorthand writing skill is built by a carefully controlled dictation speed, and this control is impossible without correct timing.

Dictate at a rate that will not permit students to draw their outlines. Dictation at thirty to forty words a minute results all too often in the drawing of outlines. Today most teachers recognize that, if necessary, when writing is first introduced it is better to sacrifice beauty of outlines than to endanger the students' ability to write shorthand fluently later.

Use easy material for speed building. Letters containing unusual proper names, technical terms, or long series are not suitable for speed building. The dictation material in the textbook has been edited to delete such problems and is therefore ideally suited for speed building.

Preview the dictation on the chalkboard. Before going to class, the shorthand teacher should pick out the words, brief forms, and phrases on which he feels his students may need special drill. Beginning teachers often ask how they can determine which words to include in the preview and how many should be included. The beginning teacher can usually remember those words or phrases that he found difficult when he was learning shorthand. The students in his classes will probably find many of these same words difficult for them.. The number of words to be included in the preview will of course depend upon the difficulty of the material to be dictated. In general, however, a preview of 7 to 10 percent of the material is ample.

The preview should be written on the board rapidly and fluently. The words not only should be spelled and read before the dictation is given but should be referred to whenever the teacher observes students looking for words on the board during dictation. Frequently the mistake is made of placing a preview on the board, reading it once or twice before dictating the letter, and then never referring to the preview again—the assumption being that no additional practice is needed. When students are still referring to the board for outlines during dictation, it is clear that the preview "has not taken" and that additional drill is needed.

Occasionally use a postview. Some teachers recommend the use of a postview. In this case the material is dictated before any outlines are placed on the board. Then the teacher places on the board those outlines that the students were unable to write fluently or could not recall. Authorities are not in agreement about the value of the postview, but some use of the procedure should prove helpful to the students before new-matter dictation tests are introduced.

Do not permit students to copy from the text while dictation is being given. Permitting the students to have their textbooks open and to refer to them when necessary may be a good teaching practice when writing is first introduced, but permitting the students to copy the shorthand from the text indefinitely without regard to the dictation is a poor teaching procedure. Students who become too dependent on the text will often write several sentences behind the teacher's dictation. They might as well be at home copying the shorthand plates. Furthermore, the student who becomes too dependent upon the text while taking dictation is certain to encounter serious difficulty when new-matter dictation is introduced.

Use short dictation spurts of one minute and build up to three minutes of sustained dictation as soon as possible. Gradually increase the period of sustained dictation to five minutes. Various types of speed building are discussed on pages 174 to 182.

Inform students of the dictation rate. The teacher should usually indicate the rate at which the next dictation will be given. At times when the dictation rate is announced afterward, the students find they have taken the dictation faster than they thought possible. Telling the student the rate of the dictation serves as an important motivating factor in the classroom.

It is important that the students understand the speed-building plan the teacher is using and that they know why the dictation is given at varying rates. Otherwise some of the students are apt to become discouraged when they are no longer able to record all the dictation.

Introduce some new-matter dictation the first semester, especially in schools where only one year of shorthand is offered. Most teachers find that where only one year of shorthand is offered, better results are obtained if new-matter dictation is introduced in the latter part of the first semester. This type of dictation can be introduced fairly early by composing material loaded with the words in the chalkboard preview. Teachers who are hesitant about composing their own material may prefer some of the graded materials available for use with the shorthand manual.

It is best to avoid talking about new-matter dictation in class. When new-matter dictation is introduced, it should consist only of words that students have written over and over again but that are rearranged in a new setting. If new-matter dictation is introduced during the first semester, the teacher may wish to delete any words that students have not previously encountered. Teachers who introduce new-matter dictation through the use of the chalkboard preview will find that these students will be able to write such dictation easily. The first-semester students should be told that though their dictation tests will not be on practiced material, they will not include any words that have not already been given in class. Thus there is no such thing as new-matter dictation. It merely consists of words already mastered, arranged in a new setting.

If new-matter dictation is introduced the first semester, do not use much new material in any one class period. A little new-matter dictation the first semester will go a long way. Usually one short letter, occasionally two, will be enough in any one class period.

Increase the amount of new-matter dictation for speed building during the second semester. Some authorities recommend the use of the text the second semester for homework practice only, with all dictation in class consisting of new material. Others believe that their students are able to attain higher speeds when they use the text material for speed building in class. Still others feel that a combination of these two procedures will give the best results. However, most teachers indicate that if they do use the text material for class dictation, they gradually increase the amount of new-matter dictation used for speed building throughout the semester.

Check your teaching procedures regularly to see how much class time is being devoted to reading and writing shorthand. Many teachers think they are spending the entire period in shorthand reading and writing. Actually they may lose several minutes at the beginning of the period, spend too much time having students read back their shorthand notes, or fail to make the best possible use of the time spent at the board, and as a consequence they have little time left for dictation and speed building. If someone were to time them with a stopwatch to see how many minutes in the period were spent reading and writing shorthand, they would be amazed to find how much class time they were losing each day. After the initial learning stages in the first semester, most of the class period should be devoted to dictation practice. The students can read the shorthand plates at home. They can even check their reading rates, but in most instances they cannot get a controlled dictation-practice situation at home. The teacher should therefore devote most of the period to giving the students the type of speed-building practice essential for fast shorthand writing.

Do not give dictation tests too frequently. Surveys show that most teachers give dictation tests once a week, beginning with the second semester. This is one-fifth of the available teaching time. Time spent testing does not build skill—it only tests to determine how much skill has already been attained. Dictation tests every two weeks should be sufficient to determine this. Rather than schedule a dictation test at specific intervals, the teacher may decide to give a test whenever most of the students in the class seem to have acquired sufficient skill to pass one. When tests are given too frequently, students become discouraged. Sufficient time must be allowed between tests to permit students to build additional skill.

Give dictation tests at ten-word-a-minute intervals rather than at twenty. Teachers who give dictation tests at ten-word-a-minute intervals find that their students progress with greater regularity and do not become discouraged as sometimes happens when they are attempting to build an increase of twenty words a minute.

Allow every student to proceed as far and as fast as he can. Teachers who permit their students to progress as rapidly and as far as they can seldom have any trouble with motivation or interest in their shorthand classes. This procedure means that each student is given an opportunity to work toward an individual goal. If a third of the class has passed a dictation test at sixty words a minute, a third at seventy, and a third at eighty, then the teacher will need to provide dictation tests at seventy, eighty, and ninety the next time a test is given. In other words, a test should be dictated to meet the needs of each student in the class. Under this plan many students will continue to work for higher speed levels even after they have attained the requirements for an *A* on shorthand dictation speed.

Require the students to pass at least two tests at each dictation rate before proceeding to the next rate. Some teachers require their students to pass three tests at each level. This plan helps prevent plateaus in shorthand progress. Every shorthand teacher knows that dictation tests vary in difficulty regardless of the standard word count.[1] Therefore, by requiring students to pass two or three tests at each rate, the teacher is sure that the student actually has the skill necessary to pass a test at that rate of speed before he goes on to the next level. When students are permitted to try the next speed as soon as they pass one test, they may have considerable difficulty passing the next speed level. Often the trouble is the result of going on to the next level before they have sufficient skill to do so.

Learn to dictate skillfully. The manner in which the teacher dictates will have a most important effect upon the ability of the students to get the dictation. The teacher should stand while dictating. Dictation should be given in a natural tone. Material dictated in a high, loud voice increases the tension in the class. If the students must strain to hear the dictation, they cannot give their full attention to their shorthand writing. The teacher needs to learn to enunciate distinctly and project her voice so that the dictation may be understood easily in all parts of the room.

The dictation material in most shorthand texts and teacher's manuals is marked in 20-standard-word intervals. Exhibit 6.1 gives the number of seconds to be allowed for the dictation of various standard word groups at shorthand speeds from 30 to 210 words a minute. For material that is to be used as a test at a given speed, probably the most satisfactory procedure is to divide the material into quarter minutes, using a diagonal bar to indicate the end of each quarter minute and the number of the minute to indicate each minute.

At first the beginning teacher may find it somewhat difficult to dictate smoothly and quietly from the printed page while timing the material and

---

[1] The *standard-word* method of counting dictation was devised by Louis A. Leslie in 1931. A word is considered to consist of 1.40 syllables rather than the actual word. The actual number of words in the material dictated may be either greater or smaller than the number of 1.40 syllable words.

Exhibit 6.1 CONVERSION TABLE FOR DICTATION SPEEDS

Words per Minute

	70	87.5	105	122.5	140	137.5	175	187.5	210	195.0	210	187.5	200
Groups of 35	70	87.5	105	122.5	140	137.5	175	187.5	210	195.0	210	187.5	200
Groups of 30	60	75.0	90	105.0	120	135.0	150	165.0	180	162.5	175	150.0	160
Groups of 25	50	62.5	75	87.5	100	112.5	125	137.5	150	130.0	140	112.5	120
Groups of 20	40	50.0	60	70.0	80	90.0	100	110.0	120	97.5	105		
Groups of 15	30	37.5	45	52.5	60	67.5	75	82.5	90				

Time Intervals in Seconds

30	24	20	17	15	13	12	11	10	9	8	8	7
60	48	40	34	30	26	24	22	20	18	17	16	15
30	12	60	51	45	40	36	33	30	27	25	24	22
60	36	20	08	60	53	48	44	40	37	34	32	30
	60	40	25	15	06	60	55	50	46	42	40	37
		60	42	30	20	12	06	60	55	51	48	45
			60	45	33	24	17	10	04	60	56	52
				60	47	36	28	20	14	08	04	60
					60	48	39	30	23	17	12	07
						60	50	40	32	25	20	15
							60	50	41	34	28	22
								60	51	42	36	30
									60	51	44	37
										60	52	45
											60	52
												60

Example: To dictate at 70 words a minute material counted in groups of 20, place your finger on the line that reads "Groups of 20." Run your finger along that line until you reach 70. Drop down to the first figure below the rule, which is 17. To dictate at 70 words a minute material counted in groups of 20 standard words, dictate each group in 17 seconds. The figures below 17 indicate the point on the watch where the second hand should be at the end of each group of 20 words. These time indications have been carried through the first two minutes.

Source: Charles E. Zoubek, *Dictation for Transcription* (The Gregg Publishing Company, 1937), p. xi.

also observing the students. He may experience some difficulty in gauging a dictation rate or in changing from one dictation level to another. With practice, however, he will become proficient not only in dictating evenly with a stopwatch but in judging the speed at which he is dictating. Should the teacher fall a few words a minute behind in the dictation, he should make them up over a period of several word groups and not try to make them up in one group. If he finds he is dictating too rapidly, he should drop a few words over a period of several groups. In this manner the students are not bothered by noticeable speeding up or slowing down of the dictation. If the teacher finds he has fallen very much behind in the dictation, he should not try to make it up. As soon as he discovers that he is considerably behind the point that he should be, he should make every effort to dictate the remainder of the material evenly at the desired speed.

Teach the students to dictate. If students understand that each superscript represents twenty words, they will be able to time themselves on both reading and dictation rates.

Base the student's dictation grade in the course upon his final achievement at the end of the semester. The student's rate of progress throughout the semester is not nearly so important as the final outcome. The dictation rate that the student can take at the end of the semester is the important factor, not how many tests he took to reach that level. Such a procedure greatly encourages the student, for in most instances he has never before been enrolled in a course where his failures were not averaged with his successes.

SPEED BUILDING

No speed-building plan will be effective unless the students desire to increase their recording speed and are willing to put forth the effort required. The teacher can help to create this desire by setting the stage properly at the beginning of the period. If the first dictation given is at a rate that all the students can get, then the students are apt to have a positive attitude toward what they can accomplish. The dictation at the end of the class period should also be at a control rate, since this helps to offset the sprawled notes caused by pressuring for speed and allows the students to leave the classroom with a feeling of accomplishment.

Types of Material

Building speed in shorthand is not so much a matter of learning to write faster as it is of learning to think the outlines faster. Consequently in the first year of shorthand it is most important that the teacher use easy practice material which will enable the student to automatize high-frequency words and phrases. During the first semester, material that the class has practiced for homework is excellent for speed building. Later the teacher may wish to use a combination of homework material and easy new-matter dictation material.

Preview

Before dictating material for speed building, the material should ordinarily be previewed either on the chalkboard or on a transparency. Only a few words at a time should be previewed, though of course the preview will be more extensive in the early stages of speed building than it will be in advanced shorthand. Then the teacher should dictate the material the first time at a rate at which all or nearly all the class can get the dictation. As the students record the dictation, the teacher should observe their writing to determine those words that they may be writing incorrectly or those words that they are unable to write without referring to the preview or the text. Any words causing difficulty should be added to the preview and reviewed before the dictation is repeated. The teacher should remember that repetition does not necessarily build speed—that unless a student masters the words giving him difficulty before the dictation is repeated, he will be unable to build his writing skill to a higher speed.

Word-Carrying Ability

Under most speed-building plans, each time the material is repeated it should be dictated at a higher rate. Since the students have written this material previously and have had an opportunity to practice any words giving them difficulty, they should be able to write each repetition at an increasingly higher speed. It should be noted that if a student is forced to higher speed levels through planned dictation practice whereby speed is gradually increased through repetition, he will automatically develop word-carrying ability. There will be no need to use artificial drills to develop this skill. As the speed is pushed higher and higher, the student finds that he is no longer able to write the material as it is being dictated but must develop the ability to hear what is being dictated while at the same time writing what has been dictated previously.

Penmanship and Speed Building

The objectives of speed building should not be confused with other aspects of shorthand such as the mechanical details of penmanship or exactness in phrasing. Most students who are writing at the top limits of their shorthand speed will necessarily write sprawled outlines, outlines much larger than they would write at their control shorthand writing speed, in which the proportion of their characters may be far from ideal. Occasionally a teacher may encounter a student who writes smaller outlines as he pushes to a higher speed, but this is unusual. The teacher should not expect the students to write well-proportioned outlines when forcing their speeds to new levels but should follow up these forced speed efforts with dictation at a lower rate during which the students are instructed to write at their control level. Students should understand that when the dictation is given at 120 words a minute, they are to attempt to write at this speed; but when the dictation is reduced to 80 words a minute, they are to write at 80. They are not to write at 120 with long pauses while waiting for the next group of words to be dictated. This is a point that the teacher frequently does not make clear to the students.

Phrasing

Teachers should not impede the students' speed-building progress by insisting that all students phrase in the same manner. Not all students will or *should* phrase in the same manner. The slower students probably do well to record the dictation, and initially they will be thinking of each word separately as they record it in shorthand. The better students are much more apt to think in phrases and to write short phrases from the beginning of the course. These students should be encouraged to phrase. The others should develop phrasing ability as they build additional skill and are ready and able to benefit from phrasing. Even the experts will not use exactly the same phrases. Too much insistence upon early phrasing may actually interfere with the speed-building development of some of the students.

Reading back dictation

It is, of course, unnecssary to read back all the material that is dictated. Not more than one-fourth of the material should ever be read back. In reading back, it is important that the teacher match the students he selects to read with the rate of the dictation. For instance, in first-year shorthand, if Mary writes at the lowest rate in the class, she should be asked to read back a part of the material the first time it is dictated because this will be the slowest rate. If Jane is writing at the top rate in the class, she should read back when the dictation speed has been pushed to the maximum.

In repetitive dictation practice it is possible for the students to memorize the dictation, especially if they have practiced the material as a part of their homework. One way to be sure that the students are taking the dictation is to occasionally change a word here and there as the dictation is given. When the students read back the material, the teacher can immediately tell whether the students were taking the material as it was dictated or were recording it from memonry. Incidentally, this procedure is also helpful in developing the ability to construct new outlines under pressure of time.

Speed of Dictation

The rate at which the material should be dictated for speed building depends upon the speed-building plan being used and the range of speeds on which the students are working within the class. It is generally recognized that a student can write for at least a half minute at a speed twenty to forty words a minute faster than he can write for five minutes and that he can write for two minutes at a speed at least ten to twenty words a minute faster than he can write for five minutes. The type of material also affects the dictation rate. A student can, through repetitive practice, build his rate on practice material to approximately forty words a minute above his writing speed on new material. The length of the dictation must also be considered. Research indicates that there is approximately a twenty-word a minute difference between a three-minute dictation test and a five-minute take. In other words, if a student can pass an eighty-word-a-minute take for three minutes, he can probably only pass a sixty-word-a-minute take for five minutes.

In building shorthand speed, the dictation rate should be pushed to the limit of the students' recording ability. All students should get all the dictation some of the time, but all students should not get all the dictation all of the time. Speed-building dictation should start at a rate at which almost all the students can record the dictation and should gradually be increased until the best students in the class are having to make a real effort to get the dictation. In this way all the students benefit from the time devoted to dictation. If dictation is given at a rate at which all the class is able to record it all the time, it is clear that no speed building is taking place. Students are simply getting practice in taking dictation at a rate they have already established.

Number of Repetitions

Speed-building plans often indicate exactly how many times the material should be dictated. In actual practice, however, some flexibility is desirable. Some letters and takes are easier than others. Some material may have to be dictated three or four or more times. Certainly there is little point in dictating over and over material students can take at a very high rate after the first few dictations. On the other hand, most material does have to be dictated several times before students begin to achieve maximum speed levels. It should be noted too that occasionally a teacher will find a letter or a take that is not suitable for speed-building, material that even with a thorough preview and repeated efforts the students cannot record. In this case the teacher should discard the take or the letters and use some other dictation material if much benefit is to be gained from the time devoted to speed building.

Sustained Dictation

Time should be allowed before the end of the period for three to five minutes of sustained dictation on the speed-building material. Many teachers today use three-minute dictation tests and feel that it is unnecessary to include sustained dictation in the speed-building period for longer than three minutes. Since this is practiced material, however, if the teacher builds the sustained dictation to five minutes, the students will find it much less difficult to take new-matter dictation for three minutes and will have less tendency to break down during the third minute of the dictation test.

Varying the Speed-Building Lessons

Unfortunately, many teachers select one speed-building plan and use it day after day throughout the entire shorthand program. The students know exactly what to expect each day they attend class. As a result they soon become bored and uninterested in shorthand. While it is true that, especially in the one-year course, the teacher must spend a great deal of time in some type of speed-building activity if the students are to attain a level of skill that meets the requirements of business, the teacher can still find many ways to vary her classroom procedure. For example, a number of different speed-building plans can be used to provide variety and interest. Some of these plans are described below.

1. ONE-MINUTE SPEED-BUILDING PLAN. The principle of building short-hand speed through the use of one-minute dictation spurts has been accepted as a sound teaching procedure for many years. The improvement of shorthand speed in taking dictation comes from briefer pauses between outlines and within outlines. The briefer pauses result from a quicker mental response, not from greater manual speed or dexterity. Repetitive dictation of one-minute spurts helps to develop the quick mental response necessary for building short-hand speed. Using this procedure, it is possible to build the student's writing skill to a rate thirty to forty words a minute above his recording speed on new-matter material. After a number of letters have been practiced according to the one-minute repetitive speed-building plan, these letters can be used for three minutes of sustained dictation at ten to twenty words a minute below the highest speed at which the one-minute spurts were dictated. By the second semester of shorthand, the teacher should be able to increase the period of sustained dictation to five minutes.

Suppose the objective of the class is to record three minutes of new material at 80 words a minute. Most of the class is now able to write material for three minutes at 70 words a minute with not more than 5 percent error. In this situation the teacher might dictate the first letter practiced by the students in their homework at 70 words a minute for one minue. This rate will make it possible for everyone in the class to get the dictation easily and accurately. The letter might then be dictated a second time at 90 words a minute and a third time at 110 words a minute. After several letters have been practiced in this manner, three minutes of sustained dictation should be given at 90 to 100 words a minute. The exact rate at which letters are dictated should be determined by the ability of the class, but in any case the one-minute speed-building plan should be followed in forcing the class to new levels of short-hand writing skill.

2. PYRAMID PLAN. In the pyramid plan a take is broken into parts of various lengths and each part is then dictated at a certain speed. The objective of the pyramid plan is to increase the student's speed twenty words a minute on the take. In the illustration below it is assumed that the students are writing at sixty words a minute. The steps in the plan are as follows:

1. Place the entire preview for the five-minute take on the board.
2. Dictate the entire take at 60 words a minute.
3. Have the first part of the dictation read back.
4. Preview the first half minute of the take.
5. Dictate the first half minute at 100 words a minute.
6. Follow steps 4 and 5 for the second, third, and fourth half minutes.
7. Redictate this material in two minutes at 90 words a minute.
8. Have the last minute of the take read back.
9. Follow the procedure in steps 4 and 5, giving four more one-half minute takes.

10. Redictate these four one-half minute takes at 90 words a minute and have the first half of the dictation read back.
11. Redictate the entire take of 400 words at 80 words a minute for five minutes.
12. Have the last half of the dictation read back.
    Total time required: 30 minutes

Note that in the pyramid plan the dictation begins at the highest speed and is gradually decreased as the length of the dictation period is lengthened.

3. STAIR-STEP PLAN. The stair-step plan is designed to build both speed and endurance. In the following illustration it is assumed that the students are now able to write eighty words a minute.

1. Select four or five letters from 80 to 100 words in length.
2. Preview the first letter on the chalkboard.
3. Dictate the first letter at 80 words a minute. If all or most of the students get the dictation, go on to the next step. If not, repeat the letter at 80 wam or at a lower rate, if necessary.
4. Dictate the same letter at 90 words a minute and the second letter at 70 words a minute. Do not pause between the two letters. Review any outlines needed on the board and repeat the step until nearly all the students get both letters.
5. Dictate the first letter at 100 words a minute, the second at 90 words a minute, and the third at 80. Write unfamiliar outlines on the board. Repeat this step, if necessary.
6. Dictate the first letter at 110 wam, the second letter at 100 wam, the third letter at 90 wam, and the fourth letter at 80 wam. Add any words needed to the preview. Repeat the step, if necessary.
7. Dictate the first letter at 120 wam, the second letter at 110 wam, the third letter at 100 wam, the fourth letter at 90 wam, and the fifth letter at 80 wam. Review outlines. Repeat if necessary.
8. Dictate the first four letters without pauses at 90 wam. This should represent approximately three minutes of sustained dictation material. If a longer period is desired, the fifth letter should be included.[2]

4. PROGRESSIVE-WEEK PLAN. Under this plan one letter is used for speed building throughout the week. This same letter is dictated four times each class period, the first three times at increasing rates of speed with the fourth time being dictated at a lower rate for control. Each day the dictation starts twenty words a minute faster than the preceding day. Thus the students increase their writing rate on this one letter from forty to sixty words a minute within one week. The illustration below indicates the manner in which the plan operates:

Monday

a. Dictate letter at 40 wam
b. Dictate letter at 60 wam
c. Dictate letter at 80 wam
d. Dictate letter at 40 wam

---

[2] Robert L. Grubbs, "Rx for Effective Shorthand Teaching," *Business Education World* (New York: McGraw-Hill Book Company, 1960–61).

Tuesday

a. Dictate letter at 60 wam
b. Dictate letter at 80 wam
c. Dictate letter at 100 wam
d. Dictate letter at 60 wam

Wednesday

a. Dictate letter at 80 wam
b. Dictate letter at 100 wam
c. Dictate letter at 120 wam
d. Dictate letter at 80 wam

Exhibit 6.2 SPURT DICTATION

If you dictate in six seconds a line of	*Your dictation rate is*
25 strokes— 5 words	50 wam
30 strokes— 6 words	60 wam
35 strokes— 7 words	70 wam
40 strokes— 8 words	80 wam
45 strokes— 9 words	90 wam
50 strokes—10 words	100 wam
55 strokes—11 words	110 wam
60 strokes—12 words	120 wam
65 strokes—13 words	130 wam
70 strokes—14 words	140 wam

Letter for Spurt Dictation

Dear Sharon: As president of Big D	70
Chapter, it is a pleasure to welcome you	80
as a member of NSA, and particularly our	80
Chapter. We know you will find our programs beneficial	110
and that you will benefit much from your membership and active	120
participation in our professional organization. You will be	120
contacted by Jean Smith, Membership Chairman,	90
concerning initiation ceremonies. These	80
ceremonies are quite impressive and mean much	90
to this organization. Our regular meetings are held on	110
the third Thursday of each month at the Sheraton-Dallas	110
Hotel. Announcements of the meetings will be in your bulletin, "Big D	140
Hi-Lites," which you will receive a few days prior	100
to each meeting. Reservations should be made with Mary	110
Payne, RI 2-8171, Ext. 543, or you may sign a	90
standing reservations form which will be available	100
at the registration desks at the regular meetings.	100
Cost of the dinner is $4.50 per person total.	90
We are happy to have you as a member for	80
Big D Chapter, and look forward to our pleasant association.	120

Thursday

a. Dictate letter at 100 wam
b. Dictate letter at 120 wam
c. Dictate letter at 140 wam
d. Dictate letter at 100 wam

Friday

a. Dictate letter at 120 wam
b. Dictate letter at 140 wam
c. Dictate letter at 160 wam
d. Dictate letter at 100 or 120 wam

5. SPURT DICTATION. This type of material is excellent for "break-throughs" of plateaus in skill development. Instead of dictating in twenty-standard-word groups, it is suggested that the teacher dictate by the line, using a six-second dictation interval per line. Thus, dictating each line in six seconds, a line of twenty-five strokes or five words would be dictated at the rate of fifty words a minute, a line of thirty strokes or six words at sixty words a minute, and so on. Each additional five strokes increases the rate of dictation by ten words a minute, since six seconds is one-tenth of a minute. Exhibit 6.2 illustrates a letter arranged for spurt dictation.[3]

6. PROGRESSIVE DICTATION. In progressive dictation the dictation rate gradually increases throughout the letter. The material is arranged in the same way as the spurt-dictation material except that in this case the lines steadily increase in length. Each line is dictated in six seconds, and the student

Exhibit 6.3 PROGRESSIVE DICTATION

Dictate Each Line in Six Seconds	*Approximate Wam Per Line*
Dear Mr. Fuller: Since returning to the	80
States, I have investigated our expected	80
usage of lumber on our present contract.	80
We would like you to send us a quotation	80
on sizeable quantities of Portuguese Pine, all	90
cut to 6'6" long by 5-5/8" x 3/4" Dimensions:	90
with only 20% moisture content, Export Graded	90
(equivalent to No. 2 under U.S. standards). The lumber	110
should be bundled for fork lift handling, not to exceed	110
3500 # per bundle. Quotation should be F.O.B. Houston, Texas.	120
Because of the nature of the Portuguese material, this is the	120
only size we shall ask you to bid. In the event we are able	120
to negotiate a deal with you, we shall follow your suggestion to	130
have you ship an initial quantity of 25,000 to 30,000 board feet	130
of this lumber. It was a pleasure meeting you and Mr. Jackson, and we	140
shall look forward to hearing from you by return air mail. Very truly yours,	140

[3] *Ibid.*

is forced to write at ever-increasing speeds as the dictation progresses. Exhibit 6.3 illustrates a letter arranged for progressive dictation.[4]

SHORTHAND DICTATION EQUIPMENT

Many schools today have installed some type of dictation equipment in the shorthand classroom. These installations range from a single tape recorder to elaborate multiple-listening units. Some require special wiring and represent a considerable investment, while others are relatively inexpensive and simple in plan and operation.

The simplest equipment consists of a single tape recorder or record player which is used to supplement the teacher's dictation. The teacher may prepare his own tapes or records or may purchase commercial dictation materials. When only one recorder is available, all students must take dictation at the same rate of speed. The principal advantage of using tapes and records under these circumstances is that the teacher is free to observe the students and work with them individually. The equipment may also be available to students for practice when no classes are scheduled in the shorthand room.

Small schools have found that even with a limited budget it is possible to utilize dictation equipment through the use of jacks and earphones. A single tape recorder may be installed with attachments permitting up to six students with earphones to listen to dictation given at one speed while the teacher dictates at another speed to other members of the class. The tape recorder is the only costly item—the jacks and earphones are inexpensive. As money becomes available, additional tape recorders may be purchased. Each recorder added to the installation increases the number of dictation speeds that can be given to the students simultaneously. Thus if a room were equipped with four tape recorders with outlet boxes serving up to six students each, placed at intervals around the room or with the outlets at each desk, the students would be able to select for their practice from any one of four dictation speeds. For instance, the tapes on Recorder A might be at the rate of 60 to 80 words a minute; on Recorder B, from 70 to 90; on Recorder C, from 80 to 100; and on Recorder D, from 90 to 110. This arrangement can be set up wherever it is needed and is especially suitable for schools that cannot afford permanently installed listening units.

More and more schools are installing permanent-type shorthand dictation laboratories. Three basic dictation systems are available:

1. WIRED SYSTEM.   The control unit or console of the multiple-listening system may have several recorders or playback machines. The installation may use tapes, records, or a combination of equipment using both tapes and records. When dictating machines make up the console equipment, they may also be used for machine transcription. In most systems each student has on his desk a volume control, a channel selector, an outlet into which he plugs his earphones, and a teacher monitor outlet. Occasionally the teacher

[4] *Ibid.*

controls the channel to which the student listens; in this case the student does not have a channel selector. The number of channels usually varies from three to five, which will adequately accommodate the range of dictation speeds in most class situations. Each student selects the dictation speed that he wishes to practice by "listening in" on the proper channel.

2. WIRELESS SYSTEMS. In the wireless systems each student has a student receiver which is completely transistorized and battery operated. There are no electrical circuits between the console and the receiver. The transmitter acts as a shortwave radio. The signals are relayed to the student receivers by an antenna which resembles a narrow tape surrounding the walls of each room in which the equipment is to be used. Since the wireless systems are mobile, the classroom arrangement can be changed at any time without affecting the operation of the equipment.

3. DIAL-ACCESS SYSTEMS. In this system a central learning center transmits taped materials for the use of various departments of the school. The classrooms are equipped with student-listening stations and a wall-mounted dial-access control plate. The teacher or the students dial the program number desired and receive the recorded program through headsets. Obviously several numbers would have to be assigned to a shorthand class to meet the different dictation levels within the class.

Teaching with the Equipment

If the shorthand teacher uses the dictation lab equipment correctly, he may find that, although he is relieved of the monotony of much of the class dictation, he must spend more time in class preparation than was necessary before the equipment was installed. Since the students in the class may be working on three or four different channels, he must in effect plan three or four different lessons. He must select the correct tapes or records for each speed level and see that a preview is prepared for each group. If one group is having difficulty building speed and needs individual assistance, he must plan a special lesson for that group. He must check the equipment and the tapes before class to be sure that they are ready to use. If the class is going to be working on a special section of a tape, he must have the tape positioned to the proper starting point when the class begins. If any of the tape is to be skipped, he should know exactly at which point he is to skip forward so that no class time will be wasted while trying to locate the desired material.

During the class period the teacher must be able to operate the equipment efficiently without loss of class time and have other activities planned for the students whenever it is necessary to rewind or skip ahead on the tapes. He will, of course, need to watch the machines to see that the tapes are changed and rewound when necessary. While the students are taking dictation, the teacher should work with them individually. He should make sure that each student is working at speeds that will force his skill development to higher levels. He should assist individual students with outlines they are unable to write and with other writing problems. If some students are weak in vocabulary or theory, he may work with those students as a group while the rest of the class works from the machines. He is free to give special assistance to students who have been absent or who are having difficulty keeping up with the class. If two or three students are slower than the others in developing their dictation rate or if two or three show unusual ability, he may dictate to those students at rates meeting their individual needs. The teacher who properly utilizes shorthand dictation equipment should be able to achieve better results in less time, but to do this he must carefully select the dictation material he will use, make sure the material follows sound principles of skill development, and plan how he may most effectively use his own time during each class period.

On days when dictation tests are to be given, the teacher can save considerable class time by dictating each speed on a different tape which will be played back through a different channel. Thus students might be taking dictation tests at sixty, seventy, eighty, and ninety words a minute simultaneously. Allowing for a warm-up, not more than five minutes would be required to administer all four speeds.

The shorthand dictation equipment should not be used in any one class period for more than fifteen minutes at a time. Using the equipment the entire period soon kills student interest. Some teachers report that they have found fifteen minutes of dictation using tapes followed by ten to fifteen minutes of teacher-controlled class participation to be a sound plan for the forty-five- or fifty-minute class period. Alternating between individual listening and full class participation provides the variety necessary to sustain effort and interest.

In addition to using the dictation equipment during the regular shorthand class period, the teacher should investigate the possibility of using the equipment as a laboratory during periods in which no classes are scheduled in the room or before and after school hours. In some schools a special dictation laboratory is provided which is available to the students throughout the day in the business department or in the library or in the student resource center. Such a laboratory is ordinarily available in schools that have instituted modular scheduling. If the students have access to the laboratory outside of class, the teacher may have them write the assignment a second time from dictation, or he may prepare some shorthand learning tapes for the students' use during the first semester of shorthand. The tapes should be carefully cataloged and filed each day, as should the previews or transparencies that are to be used with them. The teacher should keep a record of the tapes used for laboratory practice so that the students will have different material each time they attend lab.

Tapes and Records

All the lessons in the *Gregg Manual* and some abbreviated longhand systems may be obtained on tape. Shorthand dictation records may be obtained from a number of companies. In addition, many dictation tapes and records are available for use after the lessons in the *Gregg Manual* have been completed. Most commercial tapes follow the same pattern of dictation through the entire series. Usually a preview is dictated; then the one-minute spiral speed-building plan is used to build speed on a shorthand take. In most shorthand laboratories different material is played through each channel.

Students working at sixty words a minute practice a different take from those working at seventy or eighty words a minute. It is possible, however, to purchase multichannel tapes that use the same material for three different channels. Thus all students are practicing the same shorthand take regardless of their dictation speeds, only one preview is necessary, and the teacher may work with the members of the class individually or as a unit. For example, on Channel A, the material may be recorded at sixty to eighty words a minute; on Channel B, at seventy to ninety words a minute; and on Channel C, at eighty to one hundred words a minute. While this dictation situation is ideal, only one-third as much new material is available to the teacher for the money invested.

Since commercial tapes tend to follow one pattern of speed building, students may soon lose interest if no other tapes are available. The shorthand teacher who is willing to devote some time and thought to the problem can produce valuable shorthand learning tapes and tapes to be used in the introductory phases of transcription. There is no reason to limit the use of tapes solely to the speed-building objective. For instance, students may be asked to read aloud shorthand plates while listening to the same materials on tapes. This plan forces the students to develop more rapid reading rates than they would otherwise. A letter may be reread in this manner, with the second reading being paced at a faster rate. Or if the reading goal for the week is one hundred words a minute and the letter contains seventy-five words, the students may be told when to start reading on the tape, and at the end of three-quarters of a minute, told they have read the letter at one hundred words a minute if they have completed reading within the time allotted.

In practicing the new theory in the lesson, the student may be instructed to spell and read each word with the tapes. The words in the theory may then be spelled and read again at a faster rate. Finally the students may be allotted a specified amount of time on the tape to spell and read the words by themselves.

When taking dictation, the students may be told occasionally, after completing a letter, to check their notes while the letter is read back on the tape. Too often tapes make no provision for allowing the students to evaluate their progress.

If teachers would develop shorthand learning tapes in which emphasis was on building skill in spelling and reading the words in the new theory, building speed in reading shorthand plates, and assisting the students to build fluency when writing is introduced, it is quite possible that the shorthand laboratory equipment would be as valuable in the first semester of shorthand as it is for speed building in the following semesters.

PROGRAMMED INSTRUCTION IN SHORTHAND

One of the more recent developments in the teaching of shorthand is the use of programmed materials. These materials provide for the varying abilities of the students by permitting each student to progress at his own rate. The shorthand theory and principles are presented in small learning units, or *frames*. Each frame requires some response from the student, such as constructing or writing an outline, choosing from several alternatives, or transcribing a word or phrase. The student then immediately checks to see whether his response was correct. If not, he reviews the preceding theory frame and tries again. He does not go on to the next frame until he has thoroughly mastered all those preceding it.

The programmed materials may be used for individualized class instruction, for homework assignments supplementing the classwork, for self-study programs for those individuals unable to attend regular shorthand classes, or even for paced group instruction. In the latter situation, however, when the teacher requires all students to complete one lesson before starting the next, the advantage to the students of proceeding at their own learning rate is obviously lost.

If students are permitted to proceed at their own rate on the programmed materials, each student should record at the beginning of every class period the frame on which he is working and the last frame he completed at the end of the period. This will enable the teacher to determine how many frames the student is completing during the class period, how many he is completing outside the regular class period, and at what point he is working in the text.

Student questions should be answered individually. As soon as a student completes a lesson, he takes it to the teacher and is given a word theory test on the lesson. The test should be checked immediately, and any errors should be discussed with the student. If the student makes more than the number of errors permitted, the teacher should assign remedial work on the lesson. After completing this work, the student should rewrite the test before proceeding to the next lesson.

If multiple-channel equipment is available, the teacher can record the theory tests on tapes. Then, when several students finish a lesson at the same time, they can take the test from the tapes, freeing the teacher to work individually with the other students.

TESTING IN SHORTHAND

As was mentioned earlier, time devoted to testing in shorthand is time that cannot be spent in building reading and writing skill. The testing program in shorthand should be limited in the amount of time required and should include only those types of tests that will result in maximum benefits for the time so used. One way to secure such benefits is to incorporate in all shorthand tests the elements of speed and timing. The following are the most commonly used tests in shorthand.

Brief Form Tests

Most teachers follow the practice of giving brief form tests throughout the first semester of shorthand. The test may consist of fifteen to twenty brief forms given at frequent intervals, or it may be a longer list given near the close of each grading period. A higher percentage of accuracy is often required on brief forms than on word list tests. Regardless of the length of test, as soon as writing has been introduced, the brief forms should be dictated. By the end of the semester the students should be able to record the brief forms at the rate of one every two seconds.

Word List Tests

Of all the types of tests used by teachers, word tests have probably been subject to more criticism than any other type. Yet teachers continue to use them. The word test usually consists of ten to twenty-five words or more selected at random from the lesson. The words are dictated to the students who are instructed to write the correct shorthand outline and, in some cases, after the words have been written in shorthand, to transcribe the words in longhand. Both the shorthand outline and the transcripts should be graded. Such tests emphasize the importance of accuracy in shorthand outline construction, and when given unannounced, motivate the students to prepare their daily lesson more carefully and with greater regularity than they might otherwise. By the end of the semester the students should be able to record words dictated at the rate of one every three seconds.

Longhand Transcription Tests

Longhand transcription tests designed to measure the students' reading skill are especially helpful to teachers using the reading approach. The student is told to transcribe for two to three minutes whatever plate material the teacher may select from the text. The material may be from the day's lesson or it may be chosen from any material that has been assigned during the week. The student is graded on the number of correct words he is able to transcribe in this length of time. Such tests are not generally continued long after writing has been introduced and the students are able to take shorthand dictation. In using longhand transcription tests, teachers should remember that many students do not write more than thirty to thirty-five words a minute in longhand, and consequently no mater how fast they may be able to read the shorthand plates, they will never be able to transcribe more than thirty to thirty-five words a minute in longhand.

Shorthand Dictation Tests

The shorthand dictation test is considered the best type of shorthand test that can be used, since it gives a true picture of the student's ability to record dictation. Such tests may be introduced as soon as the students are able to take practice dictation at sixty words a minute. Since these are progress tests rather than occupational proficiency tests, a 5 percent error allowance is ordinarily permitted. This error allowance includes both shorthand and non-shorthand errors.

Some teachers will prefer to give two grades to the transcript, one for transcription and one for English. The English grade would include errors in spelling, punctuation, paragraphing, and so forth. In the transcription grade any deviation from the dictated material would be considered an error.

SHORTHAND STANDARDS

Shorthand teachers will probably never agree upon the standards that should be required. They argue, and rightly so, that some allowance must be made for different school situations and student backgrounds. Teachers in schools offering two years of shorthand may feel that it is not necessary for them to "push" their students so rapidly as do teachers in schools offering only one year. A recent survey showed that the standards most often required by shorthand teachers were sixty words a minute at the end of the second semester, eighty words a minute at the end of the third semester, and one hundred words a minute at the end of the fourth semester. For most jobs that would be open to high school graduates, one hundred words a minute should be sufficient; however, a writing speed of eighty words a minute may be entirely adequate in some offices.

The teacher in the school offering only one year of shorthand has a difficult problem in arriving at satisfactory standards. He knows that sixty words a minute is not sufficient for most office jobs—that eighty words a minute represents the minimum level his students should write if they are to secure employment. And not only must his students be able to record dictation at eighty words a minute, but they must also be able to transcribe mailable letters. Many teachers say it is impossible to reach these standards in one year. Other teachers have accepted the challenge and are meeting these standards year after year. If students are not reaching the minimum standards in the one-year shorthand program (and evidence shows they frequently are not), perhaps the teacher should consider whether it is advisable to continue offering the subject. This decision should be based on a follow-up of the students to see whether they are attending a vocational center, a business school, or a college for additional training before entering office work.

In the first-semester shorthand, the grading plan may include shorthand reading rates, transcription of practiced material dictated at seventy to ninety words a minute and of new-matter material dictated at sixty to eighty words a minute, knowledge of spelling and English fundamentals, and scores on brief form and vocabulary tests. The ability to write accurate shorthand outlines on shorthand vocabulary and brief form tests and to transcribe accurately practiced or new-matter dictation should constitute a large part of the student's grade. Teachers who weigh these factors heavily contend that they are the best indicators of students' probable success in the second-semester shorthand course.

Because many components affect the standards that students may attain, it is not recommended that all schools use the same standards. The *minimum* standards given in Exhibit 6.4 illustrate those factors that may be included in the grading system in the first-year shorthand course and suggest how these may be incorporated into an overall grading plan.

Using Exhibit 6.4 as a basis for minimum passing grades, the teacher can determine the amount of additional skill he wishes to require for grades of *B* and *A*. For reading rates and longhand transcription rates, he will simply increase the number of words a minute required for each grade level. On the word list tests he may reduce the number of errors permitted for each grade

Exhibit 6.4 GRADING SCALE—FIRST YEAR SHORTHAND

First Semester

Factor	First Six Weeks	Second Six Weeks	Third Six Weeks
Reading rates	80 wam	110 wam	140 wam
Longhand transcription from text	12–16 wam	20–24 wam	—
Word list and brief form tests	50 words, 90% accuracy	50 words, 90% accuracy	50 words, 90% accuracy
Practiced dictation	—	One 3-minute test on practiced material at 50 wam, 95% accuracy	Two 3-minute tests on practiced material at 70 wam, 95% accuracy

Second Semester

Factor	First Six Weeks	Second Six Weeks	Third Six Weeks
Reading rates	140 wam	150 wam	150 wam
Word list and brief form tests	50 words dictated in 5 minutes; 100 brief forms, dictated in 4 minutes; 95% accuracy	50 words dictated in 5 minutes; 100 brief forms, dictated in 3 minutes; 95% accuracy	50 words dictated in 5 minutes; 100 brief forms dictated in $2\frac{1}{2}$ minutes; 95% accuracy
New-matter dictation*	Two 3-minute tests at 60, 95% accuracy	Two 3-minute tests at 70, 95% accuracy	Two 3-minute tests at 80, 95% accuracy
Transcription of mailable letters	—	—	Three short, mailable letters in 30 minutes

*Minimum standards are based on a grade of C. In schools where a D grade is given, the scale may be lowered ten words a minute, but with the understanding that the student will not continue shorthand the second semester.

level. If a person making four or five errors on a fifty-word theory test received a grade of *C,* then a person making two or three errors might be given a *B,* and a person making one or no errors would receive an *A.*

Assigning grades to dictation takes is somewhat more difficult. A teacher might use some such plan as the following:

Second Six Weeks

Take	Errors	Grade
50, three minutes, practiced material,	6–8	C
95% accuracy	3–5	B
	0–2	A
60, three minutes, practiced material,	7–9	C
95% accuracy	4–6	B
	0–3	A

Third Six Weeks

Take	Errors	Grade
70, three minutes, practiced material,	7–11	C
95% accuracy	4–6	B
	0–3	A

Fourth Six Weeks

Take	Errors	Grade
60, three minutes, new material,	7–9	C
95% accuracy	4–6	B
	0–3	A

Fifth Six Weeks

Take	Errors	Grade
70, three minutes, new material,	7–11	C
95% accuracy	4–6	B
	0–3	A

Sixth Six Weeks

Take	Errors	Grade
80, three minutes, new material,	8–12	C
95% accuracy	4–7	B
	0–3	A

The teacher must decide the weight to be given to each of the factors included in the grade. This weighting will seldom remain constant throughout the course but will ordinarily change from one grading period to the next. For instance, longhand transcription from the text and reading rates may be weighted heavily the first grading period. After six weeks, however, the emphasis may switch from longhand transcription of plate material to accurate shorthand vocabulary. During the second semester the weighting given dictation tests would normally be much greater than that given to reading rates. The emphasis given to the transcription of mailable letters must be determined primarily by the amount of time devoted to typed transcription and the kind of course offered—whether this is a terminal course or is to be followed by a second year of shorthand.

PRETRANSCRIPTION TRAINING

Pretranscription training should be introduced during the first semester of shorthand. This training should not be deferred until typed transcripts are required because such a procedure will seriously impede the progress of the students. Some shorthand teachers administer pretranscription tests to their shorthand students early in the course so that they can determine the kinds of remedial work that should be included in the first semester. For example, such a test may include a list of spelling words, some of which are misspelled; a number of sentences involving choices between words frequently confused; sentences that may or may not be correctly punctuated; sentences involving problems in style usage; and sentences containing punctuation problems. If the material is arranged in an objective test format, it can be graded quickly and the teacher will know immediately which students need remedial drills and in which areas. Other teachers include in the shorthand program assignments in English, spelling, and punctuation to be completed by all students.

Marginal reminders in the shorthand texts now emphasize the English problems found in the shorthand plates. As soon as marginal reminders are introduced in the text, the students should be instructed to encircle in their notes the punctuation as they copy it, to look at the reminder in the margin giving the reason for the punctuation, and to study any spelling words in the margin. When the students read in class, the teacher should require words listed in the margin to be spelled as they read and punctuation marks read and briefly explained. For example, the student should read, "Although our rates are most reasonable (comma, introductory clause), you will find our accommodations (a-c-c-o-m-m-o-d-a-t-i-o-n-s) excellent." Occasionally the teacher should give a short spelling test on the words in the marginal reminders and on other words in the lesson that may need special attention. Early emphasis on these problems frequently pays rich dividends when transcription is introduced the second semester.

TRANSCRIPTION

No matter how skillful the student may be in recording dictation, he is not properly fitted for work in an office unless he can transcribe his notes quickly and accurately. For many years teachers assumed that if a student could take dictation rapidly, knew how to type, and was well grounded in English, he would be a successful stenographer. Experience has shown that this is not the case. A student may possess skill in each of these three areas but still not be succesful in transcription. The coordination of these three skills into effective transcription patterns requires correct training and practice.

TRANSCRIPTION IN THE ONE-YEAR
SHORTHAND PROGRAM

While most authorities believe that typed transcription should be deferred at least until the second semester of shorthand, many teachers introduce typewritten transcription early in the course and report excellent results. Whether early introduction to transcription is desirable will depend upon a number of factors. If the students have completed at least one year of typewriting, if machines are available in the classroom, and if transcription is introduced in easy stages, the teacher may wish to consider introducing transcription early in a school having a one-year shorthand program. In post–high school institutions serious thought should be given to this possibility, as many students may elect only one semester, possibly two, and unless the course has included provision for typed transcription, they are not equipped to utilize their shorthand vocationally. Yet such students, who often have a major in some area unrelated to business, may later find that shorthand is the only subject they have had that will enable them to secure a job.

Teachers who introduce transcription early contend that the development of transcription skill over a long period of time not only leads to higher transcription skills but motivates the students to review carefully words frequently misspelled and rules governing punctuation, capitalization, and typing usage. It is their belief that students have little interest in reviewing these areas before their application in a transcription situation. They also point out that transcription practice can then be included in the homework early in the course, which helps to make the homework a more purposeful activity. They emphasize that early introduction to transcription permits the student to practice shorthand as it will be used on the job and may even enable some of the better students to secure summer employment. Finally, the early introduction of transcription may assist both the student and the teacher in deciding whether the student should continue with advanced shorthand.

If the teacher decides to introduce typed transcription early, then it is important that the amount of time devoted to such procedures be strictly limited in the early stages when new theory is still being presented and even later when much of the period should be devoted to speed building. Not more than five to seven minutes should usually be devoted to transcription drills during any one period of first-semester shorthand. The teacher must recognize that the students have, during the first semester of shorthand, a limited amount of recording skill and that undue emphasis upon typed transcription is likely to interfere with the time needed to develop that skill.

EARLY INTRODUCTION OF TRANSCRIPTION

The teacher wishing to introduce typed transcription the first semester will need to use those techniques that will develop fluency in transcription and lay the groundwork for intensive transcription practice during the second semester. To do this, he must introduce the students to transcription through a number of easy stages:

1. PLATE MATERIAL.   Shorthand plates that the students have been assigned to read and write previously for homework practice are excellent material for the first *few* days of transcription, since they can easily be read and the students can concentrate on good transcription techniques. During this period emphasis should be placed on reading in thought units, keeping the eyes on the shorthand notes, and typing smoothly as the shorthand notes are being read.

2. HOMEWORK NOTES.   Since the students have copied their homework notes from the plates in the shorthand text, the notes should be accurate and easily read. This is extremely important in the early stages of transcription practice because it helps to insure that the students will continue to use the transcription techniques emphasized in the first stage.

3. PRACTICED DICTATION MATERIAL.   Material that has previously been practiced by the student as a part of his homework may be dictated in class for transcription. Emphasis continues to be on correct transcription techniques.

4. DICTATED REVIEW PROBLEMS.   If writing is introduced early, the teacher may dictate sentences containing various types of English, spelling, and typing usage problems. Such drills should preferably be transcribed as a part of the homework; but if typewriters are not available outside of class, the drills should be short so they may be transcribed and checked within ten minutes.

5. SHORT BUSINESS LETTERS.   By this time the students should be able to transcribe new-matter dictation consisting of short, easy business letter material.

6. MEDIUM-LENGTH LETTERS.   Transcription of new-matter dictation consisting of medium-length letters is the final stage which should be attempted in most one-year shorthand programs.

Special drills to develop accurate and fluent transcription skill are discussed on pages 201 to 203.

In the one-year shorthand course it will be necessary for the teacher to move through these transcription stages very quickly. Some teachers prefer to omit the introductory stages so that more time can be devoted to transcription of the students' notes.

Introducing Transcription the Second Semester

Teachers in a one-year program who defer typed transcription until the second semester may follow one of a number of plans. They may choose to devote a specified number of periods to shorthand and a specified number to transcription throughout the semester. For example, they might use one of the following procedures:

Plan A				Plan B		
	Periods a Week				*Periods a Week*	
	Shorthand	*Transcription*			*Shorthand*	*Transcription*
Weeks 1–6	4	1	Weeks 1–8		2	3
Weeks 7–10	3	2	Weeks 9–15		3	2
Weeks 11–15	2	3				

The transcription periods may be distributed throughout the week in any manner the teacher desires. The shorthand and transcription periods may be alternated during the week, or the shorthand and the transcription periods may be blocked. Many people believe that best results are secured by the block plan whereby the first part of the week is devoted to shorthand skill development and the last part of the week to transcription.

A second plan for teaching transcription in a one-year shorthand program is illustrated in Exhibit 6.5. In this program the students' shorthand and typing skills are developed to the highest possible point before transcription is introduced. Then, during the last six-week period, transcription is introduced following a carefully planned program. Only two letter styles are used, and while students are taught the correct placement of long letters, emphasis is strictly upon the transcription of short and medium-length letters. Those teachers desiring more emphasis on transcription may obtain additional

Exhibit 6.5. A SIX-WEEK TRANSCRIPTION PROGRAM

Week 1

Period 1	Dictation and speed building
Period 2	Dictation and speed building
Period 3	Dictation and speed building
Period 4	Drill on transcription techniques, with emphasis on "eyes on copy" and "transcribing in thought units" (demonstrate)
	Notes read from a letter written for homework; punctuate it
	Letter placement and style discussed (block with open punctuation)
	Letter written for homework, which has been read in class, transcribed
	Short letter of new material dictated; students read it back and punctuate it
	Letter transcribed
Period 5	Introduce comma rules: comma after introductory clause; before coordinate conjunction
	Have students punctuate illustrations
	Dictate two or three short letters, including only the foregoing punctuation rules (block style with open punctuation)

Week 2

Period 1	Dictation and speed building
Period 2	Dictation and speed building
Period 3	Dictation and speed building
Period 4	Introduce comma rules: comma in a series; parenthetical expressions
	Dictate two medium-length letters, including applications of four punctuation rules
	Note: Call attention to differences in length of short and medium-length letters and placement on page.
	Introduce erasing
Period 5	Introduce comma rules: appositives; introductory phrases containing verbal forms
	Enclosure notations
	Dictate two or three medium-length letters, including only the rules that have thus far been presented

Week 3

Period 1   Dictation and speed building
Period 2   Dictation and speed building
Period 3   Dictation and speed building
Period 4   Introduce comma rules: restrictive and nonrestrictive clauses; review word-division rules
             Dictate one short and one medium-length letter for transcription (modified block, mixed punctuation)
Period 5   Distribute "spelling demons" to be studied
             Dictate short and medium-length letters for transcription

Week 4

Period 1   Dictation and speed building
Period 2   Dictation and speed building
Period 3   Introduce comma rules: comma showing omission of conjunction between adjectives
             Introduce carbon copies
             Dictate short and medium-length letters for transcription (modified block, mixed punctuation)
Period 4   Introduce comma rule: use of the semicolon
             Dictate short and medium-length letters for transcription
Period 5   Introduce postscripts
             Carbon copies
             Dictate short and medium-length letters for transcription

Week 5

Period 1   Dictation and speed building
Period 2   Dictation and speed building
Period 3   Brief review of capitalization rules
             Introduce envelopes
Period 4   Introduce attention line
             Dictate short and medium-length letters for transcription, with carbons and envelopes
Period 5   Introduce subject line
             Dictate short and medium-length letters for transcription, with carbons and envelopes
             Include carbon-copy notations

Week 6

Period 1   Dictation and speed building
Period 2   Dictation and speed building
Period 3   Review of rules of use of hyphen; compound words written as one word and those written as two words
Period 4   Review placement for long letters, second-page headings; dictate last paragraph of two-page letter for drill in typing second-page headings (do not dictate long letters or two-page letters for transcription)
Period 5   Production period: Dictate short and medium-length letters for transcription, including carbons and envelopes

time for transcription practice by decreasing the number of periods devoted to dictation and speed building. In some schools offering only one year of shorthand but two years of typing, additional transcription practice may be obtained in the second year of typing.

TRANSCRIPTION IN THE TWO-YEAR SHORTHAND PROGRAM

The second-year shorthand and transcription program should be carefully outlined before the fall semester begins. After the summer vacation, the students' shorthand skill might have become somewhat rusty—if so, the first month or six weeks of the second year might be devoted entirely to speed building in shorthand.

The teacher in a two-year program can not only build his students' dictation skills to much higher levels than can the teacher in a one-year program, but he can also plan a comprehensive transcription program that will incorporate all the transcription skills that the beginning stenographer will need on the job. Exhibit 6.6 presents a one-semester transcription program in advanced shorthand.

Exhibit 6.6 TRANSCRIPTION PROGRAM IN ADVANCED SHORTHAND

Week 1

    Drill on basic transcription techniques
    Students' typing and English skills and knowledges determined
    Typing and transcription rates on straight copy; compared with rates on letters

Weeks 2–5

    Comma rules—All letters dictated will be loaded with comma rule being studied that period.
    Week 2: Comma before coordinate conjunction
                Comma following introductory clause
    Week 3: Comma in series
                Comma to set off parenthetical expressions
    Week 4: Comma to set off appositives
                Comma to set off introductory phrase containing verbal form
    Week 5: Comma showing omission of *and* between adjectives
                Comma with nonrestrictive clauses
    Drill on "spelling demons" and word division
    Pure block-letter style, open punctuation
    Carbon copies and envelopes

Week 6

    Use of the semicolon; letters illustrating use of semicolon
    Drill on spelling words; remedial drill on English problems
    Enclosure notations

Week 7

    Use of the dash, apostrophe, and quotation marks
    Introduction of the attention line
    Large business envelopes
    Modified block-style letter, block paragraphs

Week 8

    Rules on the use of the hyphen
    Introduction of the subject line
    Compound words, words written as one word, words
    written as two words

Week 9

    Capitalization rules
    Carbon-copy notations

Weeks 10–11

    Drill on correct usage of figures
    Postscripts

Week 12

    Blind carbon copies, special notations (airmail, special delivery)
    Proper names frequently misspelled

Week 13

    Office memorandums
    Multiple carbons

Week 14

    Letters with tabulations

Weeks 15–16

    Simulated office-style dictation projects
    Composition of letters and telegrams
    Note: All letters transcribed must be mailable.

Three periods a week were used for transcription. Two of these periods were devoted to drill on transcription problems, dictation, and transcription. The third period was devoted to transcription production, with the students transcribing all period without interruption or assistance from the teacher. Teachers having two semesters of shorthand would of course be able to allot more time to each of the learnings included in this program and would have more time to continue to build the students' shorthand dictation speed to new levels.

By the end of the last semester of shorthand, all types of dictation situations should be included in the transcription program. Though the early transcription practice should be based on easy material containing few transcription problems, additional problems should be introduced gradually until the student is able to handle any transcription situation he may encounter in the business office. Students should be given practice in such varied procedures as the following.

1. TRANSCRIPTION OF LETTERS.   Students should know two or three of the letter styles most commonly used in the business world. Bulletin-board illustrations may be used to show unusual adaptations of basic letter styles.

2. ENCLOSURES.   Students often have the attitude that the omission of the enclosure notation is a minor error—that it can always be added to an otherwise mailable letter. However, the omission of the enclosure notation may result in the omission of the enclosure, thereby doubling the cost of the correspondence for both companies involved.

3. CARBON-COPY NOTATIONS.   Some companies include only the names of the persons receiving carbon copies, others include the addresses, and still others often use blind carbon-copy notations. Students should know how to handle each of these situations.

4. SPECIAL MAILING INSTRUCTIONS, SUCH AS AIRMAIL, SPECIAL DELIVERY, REGISTERED.   Most companies believe these notations should appear on the letter for later reference should there be any delay in the handling of important correspondence. Students should be taught where to type these notations.

5. POSTSCRIPTS.   Students are frequently confused by the proper arrangement of reference initials, enclosure notations, and postscripts. They should know, too, that postscripts should never be typed alone on a second sheet unless the sheet is stapled to the letterhead.

6. TWO-PAGE LETTERS.   Although some companies staple the sheets of letters that are more than one page and do not use a second-page heading, many companies require a formal heading on these sheets. Students should be familiar with one or two of the most common styles of headings for two-page letters.

7. MULTIPLE CARBONS.   In offices multiple carbons are commonplace. Transcription of multiple carbons serves to emphasize the importance of accuracy in transcription. The inaccurate transcriber will find that his transcribing rate drops rapidly when he must correct four or five copies each time he makes an error.

8. ENVELOPES.   After the initial stages of transcription, students should be required to type envelopes, both business and legal size.

9. LETTER PLACEMENT.   Students should learn how to adjust the placement of a letter on the page. If a letter is slightly longer than they had originally planned, they should know how to make adjustments in the closing lines, such as allowing only three spaces for the signature, placing the reference initials on the same line as the signature, or single-spacing before typing the enclosure notation. If the letter is shorter than anticipated, the closing lines may be spread out to make any adjustments needed.

10. MISCELLANEOUS DICTATION MATERIAL.   The course should provide for transcription of various types of dictation material, such as office memorandums, articles, business reports, and telegrams.

11. OFFICE-STYLE DICTATION. Many teachers like to give some office-style dictation because it does simulate the kind of dictation students may be given on the job. This type of dictation teaches students the importance of making legible corrections, changes, insertions, and deletions, and it provides some practice in judging the length of letters containing such changes. Students enjoy the variation from the usual dictation procedures, and a little office-style dictation may be useful in advanced shorthand or transcription. It is not an essential element of the course, however, and in the one-year shorthand program the time might better be utilized for basic skill development that would lead to the production of mailable transcripts. The shorthand teacher should remember that a little office-style dictation goes a long way. Likewise, transcription of cold notes does teach students the importance of legible outlines, but here again it is not an essential element of the transcription program.

Rate of Dictation

Dictation for transcription should always be given ten to twenty words a minute below the student's shorthand transcription rate. It should be remembered that on dictation tests, the student is ordinarily given an error allowance of 5 percent, but in transcription the student is expected to produce mailable copy. If he is to do so, material dictated for transcription must be dictated at a rate somewhat below his top shorthand recording speed. A student who can pass a shorthand dictation test at one hundred words a minute with 5 percent error cannot transcribe mailable letters dictated at the same rate. The dictation speed must be lowered to eighty or ninety words a minute.

The necessity for reducing the dictation rate for mailable transcription work makes it all the more important that typing and shorthand speeds be built to the highest possible level before mailable-letter transcription is introduced. Few teachers believe that material dictated for transcription should ever be dictated at less than sixty words a minute. Thus a student would need to be able to record shorthand at seventy or eighty words a minute before he would be ready to transcribe letter material dictated at sixty words a minute.

Correlation of Teaching with Material Dictated for Transcription

Just as it is almost impossible to dictate material that is too easy when students first start to write shorthand, it is almost impossible to dictate material that is too easy when machine transcription is introduced. The letters should be carefully checked in advance to be sure they contain no unusual English problems. Many teachers find that the students build their transcription skill more quickly if the letters are carefully selected and contain only one or two types of punctuation. One of the most serious weaknesses in transcription teaching is the attempt to test students on transcription problems that the teacher has not yet reviewed in the transcription class. If during the first week of transcription the teacher reviews two comma rules, such as the use of the comma in a series and the use of the comma following an introductory adverbial clause, then the letters dictated for transcription that week should contain no internal punctuation other than these two comma applications. Ordinarily, however, little effort is made to coordinate what has been taught with the material to be transcribed. Students are supposed to be able to solve complicated punctuation problems before they are reviewed in class.

Exhibit 6.7 shows how punctuation rules may be presented in an introductory lesson in transcription. After the rules have been presented on the board and discussed and the students have been asked to punctuate the letter illustrating the application of these two comma rules, the teacher should dictate the letters that the student is to transcribe. The letters should contain no punctuation other than the application of these two comma rules and the punctuation required at the end of each sentence. This procedure of coordinating what is taught in the transcription class with the material dictated for transcription represents an orderly, logical approach to the development

Exhibit 6.7 ILLUSTRATION OF AN INTRODUCTORY LESSON IN PUNCTUATION IN TRANSCRIPTION

Rule 1

Use a comma to separate the main clauses in a sentence when they are of equal importance and are joined by a coordinating conjunction—and, but, or, for, neither, nor, and so on.

Examples

The clerks type the routine reports, but the secretaries prepare the complicated presentations.
He buzzed his secretary several times, for he had an important letter to dictate.
Note: Do not use a comma to separate a compound predicate.
The secretary attended the meeting but did not take the minutes.

Rule 2

Use a comma to set off words in a series.

Examples

Always bring a shorthand notebook, pens, pencils, bond paper, and erasers to class.
The clerk prepared a requisition for typewriter ribbons, erasers, carbon paper, envelopes, and correction fluid.

Problem: Punctuate the following letter

Dear Dr. Hendrix:

The Department of Office Administration has an opening for a person who has a terminal degree. The teaching assignment is flexible although it would probably include business correspondence report writing office machines and business education methods courses.

I tried my best to get Mrs. Jackson but she chose to remain in Texas. I liked her very much and know that she would have made a fine contribution to our program.

I have included several notices of this opening for your bulletin boards which indicate the nature of the position the degree requirements teaching assignment and salary range. I should appreciate any assistance you can give me and hope that you will have just the person we are looking for.

Cordially yours

of a complicated skill. The usual procedure of dictating any letter in the book is neither logical nor profitable. It is true that at some previous time the students have studied the principles of English they need to apply in transcription. But transfer of training does not take place automatically. The students are so engrossed in the problem of integrating these separate skills that many of them will not be able to apply principles previously studied without additional review. Once certain rules of punctuation, capitalization, and typing usage have been reviewed, however, the student should be expected to apply them correctly in all his transcription practice.

Keep the transcription learning situation as simple as possible. At first, when emphasis is solely on the development of correct transcription techniques, make every effort to see that the material to be transcribed contains few transcription problems. Some teachers have the students transcribe in paragraph form the first few days so that they are not confronted with the problem of letter style. When the students can transcribe paragraph material with facility, they are then introduced to short business letters. After a few days practice, they may be required to correct all errors. Next they may be asked to make one carbon copy of each letter. By the end of a two-year program the students should be able to transcribe material containing fairly difficult vocabulary, long two-page letters, material with multiple carbons, office memorandums, business reports, different letter styles, and so on. This procedure is merely the application of the long-accepted principle of education—always go from the simple to the complex.

In a one-year course the teacher will find that to build transcription speed and accuracy, she will need to concentrate on just a few of these transcription problems. The students should be able to transcribe short, medium, and long letters, but little time should be devoted to transcription of long letters. There is no time for involved problems such as two-page letters and multiple carbons. The development of basic transcription skill should not be sacrificed for these advanced learnings. Even though the transcription time may be limited, the transcription teacher must emphasize letter placement, erasures, use of carbon paper, proofreading, spelling, word division, commonly confused words, and punctuation. By keeping the transcription learning situation simple, the students will be able to build their transcription rates to much higher levels than would otherwise be possible.

Build Transcription Speed with Accuracy

Transcription speed without accuracy is worthless. Accuracy without transcription speed may not be totally worthless, but it can be expensive and annoying. Although most teachers agree that accuracy in transcription is far more important than speed, they also agree that transcription speed is essential for success in most stenographic jobs today. Slow transcribers are not usually the most accurate transcribers. It has been found that students with the highest production rate have the highest percentage of mailable letters.

Transcription Drills

Although most of the time in transcription should be devoted to transcribing the students' own shorthand notes written from dictation, special transcription drills are especially valuable when transcription is introduced. They may also be used from time to time to increase transcription speed and accuracy. Some of the drills that may be used are described below:

1. Transcribing in thought units. The material to be transcribed is marked in thought units with dotted or colored lines, and the students are instructed to read and transcribe in thought units, keeping the carriage moving at all times.[5]

2. Comparison of typing and transcription rates. The first day in transcription, the students may be given a five-minute timing on some straight copy material to determine their typing rates. They may next be given a five-minute timing on the same material written in shorthand. The transcription rate on straight copy is then compared with the typing rate.

3. A drill emphasizing the importance of accurate typing. The teacher may use a straight-copy drill to compare the typing and transcription rates of the students when they are required to correct all their errors. The drill is then repeated, the objective being to reduce the time required to correct errors.

4. Comparison of typing and transcription rates on letter copy.

5. Transcription of the same letter from shorthand notes two or three times to increase the students' transcription rate.

6. Drill on typing from shorthand outlines written on the board selected from words and phrases appearing in the letter to be transcribed.

7. A preview of the difficult shorthand outlines in the letters to be dictated for transcription.

8. Dual-purpose sentence drills.
   a. Six weeks before introducing letter transcription, the students transcribe a sentence in shorthand from the text for one-half minute. They repeat the drill several times, their objective being to increase the number of times they transcribe the sentence within the time allowance.
   b. Two to four weeks before introducing letter transcription, the teacher dictates a sentence to the students which they record in shorthand. The students' objective is to increase the number of transcripts of the sentence in each one-half minute timing.
   c. When most of the students have increased their transcription rate, the teacher may change from a speed to an accuracy objective on the one-half-minute timings. The students should try to reduce their errors to not more than one error in a half minute.

9. Dual-purpose paragraph drills.
   a. The students transcribe a paragraph from a shorthand plate for one minute. They repeat the drill several times, their objective being to increase the amount of transcribed material on each timing.

---

[5] When transcription drills consist of paragraph material, if the students use a 50-space line, they can compute their transcription rate by multiplying the number of lines typed by ten and dividing by the number of minutes. Later in the semester the teacher may instruct the students to use a 60-space line and multiply the number of lines by twelve; or use a 70-space line and multiply by fourteen.

b. When students have increased the amount transcribed by at least one line of typing, they take another one-minute timing on the paragraph, this time typing for accuracy. The drill is continued until most of the students are making not more than one error a minute.

10. Transcription power drive. This drill is designed to improve both speed and accuracy in transcription. An illustration of a transcription power drive is given in Exhibit 6.8.

11. Eyes on copy. The students are timed to see how long they can transcribe a paragraph or a sentence drill, keeping their eyes on the copy.

12. Manipulation drills. The students transcribe a series of sentences requiring a sixty-space line, but with their machines set for a fifty-space line. They must use the margin release to complete each sentence but are to concentrate on doing so without looking up from their shorthand notes.

13. Pacing the transcription rate. The teacher dictates a letter which the students are to transcribe. He then dictates the same material again on tape two or three times, gradually increasing the rates, such as at twenty-five, thirty, and thirty-five words a minute. The students listen to the dictation on the tapes while transcribing the letter from their shorthand notes. The objective is to transcribe the letter each time as rapidly as the material is dictated on the tape. This procedure stresses fluency in transcription and emphasizes the importance of developing a rhythmic pattern in transcription.

Judging Letter Length from Shorthand Notes

Those students who have been taught judgment placement of letters in typewriting are already accustomed to estimating letter length. When the teacher dictates the first letter the students are to transcribe from their shorthand notes, however, the students must immediately determine the line length to use for proper placement. If the teacher has used a letter of approximately one hundred words, he may ask the students to observe the amount of space used to record the letter in their notebooks. He then tells them the number of words in the letter and indicates that this will ordinarily be the maximum space required to record a short letter, since the letter dictated contained one hundred words. All letters dictated during the week would then be short letters to enable the students to build their transcription speed without wasting time on machine adjustments.

In the same way, when medium-length letters are introduced, the teacher may dictate a letter of 150 to 175 words and have the students note the amount of space used in their notebooks. Then all letters for that week might be medium-length letters. The following weeks both short and medium-length letters would be included in each day's dictation.

This is a simple plan for teaching letter placement quickly. It does have the disadvantage of giving the students a maximum-length letter to transcribe when judgment placement is first introduced. The teacher who prefers extremely short letters at the beginning may omit the transcription of the one-hundred-word letter and follow it immediately with a series of very short letters which the students will transcribe.

Exhibit 6.8 TRANSCRIPTION POWER DRIVE

Directions

Type each sentence as many times as you can in one-half minute. Your teacher will call "throw" at the end of a half minute, and you should start transcribing the next sentence, trying to transcribe as many words on each succeeding sentence as you did on the first sentence.

	Number of times you complete line		
	2	3	4
	Your speed in words a minute		
1.	32	48	
2.	33	49	
3.	34	50	
4.	35	52	
5.	35	53	
6.	36	54	72
7.	37	55	74
8.	38	56	75
9.	38	58	77
10.	39	59	78
11.	40	60	80
12.	41	61	82
13.	42	62	83
14.	42	64	85
15.	53	65	86
16.	44	66	88
17.	45	67	90
18.	46	68	91
19.	46	70	93
20.	47	71	94

Source: Adapted from E. R. Stuart, V. V. Payne, and Ruth I. Anderson, *Complete College Typing* (Englewood Cliffs, N.J.: Prentice-Hall, Inc., 1959).

Check but do not Grade the First Letters Transcribed

The first letters the students transcribe should be checked to determine the type of remedial work necessary. These letters should never be graded. Grading too early in transcription will result in incorrect transcription techniques.

Grade all Letters on the Basis of Mailability

When letters are graded, they should be graded on the basis of mailability. More and more teachers are insisting that all letters transcribed must be mailable if the student is to receive any credit for his work. A few teachers give partial credit for letters that are unmailable but in which all errors are correctable. Even this is a questionable practice, since the student should learn to locate his errors before submitting the letters to the teacher. In an office the boss can seldom afford to spend his time proofreading for his stenographer or secretary. Most teachers would consider a letter mailable if they would be willing to sign it. For persons desiring a more specific definition, a letter to be mailable must be well balanced on the page, neatly typed, correct in style, correctly punctuated, typed without spelling or English errors, and accurate in meaning and fact. Occasionally students complain that the teacher is much more particular in judging whether a letter is mailable than any businessman will ever be. That should be true. Most businessmen do not know the fine points of punctuation and typing usage—that is not their concern. They expect their stenographers to know them. Furthermore, if a student should work for a businessman who is more concerned with rapid transcription than he is with correct English and typing usage, the employee will soon learn that he need not be so particular in transcribing his letters. It is much easier to lower standards on the job than it is to raise one's standards after completing his transcription course.

The type of transcription errors students make should be analyzed, and remedial work should be provided in these areas. Some transcription teachers like to keep transcription-error analysis charts for their students or ask the students to keep them. Although such charts will show a teacher the types of errors occurring most frequently, many teachers prefer a less-formal method of analysis. For instance, a teacher may simply jot down the types of errors that appear in a set of transcripts as he corrects them. He can then select his material and illustrations for class discussion and remedial work on the basis of this list. How the error analysis is made is relatively unimportant. The follow-up of the errors occurring most frequently is of prime importance.

English errors account for over 50 percent of most students' transcription errors; content errors, over 25 percent; typographical errors, 10 percent; and letter mechanics, under 10 percent. The most frequent English errors are errors in punctuation owing to the omission of commas, omission of apostrophes, incorrect use of the hyphen, incorrect compounding and division of words, and unnecessary punctuation. Students often fail to use commas to set off introductory adverbial clauses, appositives, parenthetical elements, and independent participial phrases.

If a teacher does not have a transcription text that provides drills in spelling, punctuation, capitalization, word choice, and typing usage, he should devise his own drills in these areas. Some teachers use five minutes at the beginning of the hour to dictate sentences emphasizing one of these areas and ask the students to transcribe them as a part of their homework. Other teachers use drills on tapes or transparencies. For example, the teacher may have prepared a transparency consisting of sentences which the students are to transcribe, inserting the proper punctuation, at the beginning of the class. Or the students may be instructed to follow the directions on the tapes playing through the multiple-listening units. The material for transcription from the tape may include various types of English and typing usage problems. The sentences, correctly typed and punctuated, can be shown on a second transparency or dictated on the tape after the drill has been typed by the students. Short drills of this nature may often be completed while the teacher is handling the administrative details of the class.

Build Skill in the Use of Transcription Materials

Although in most classrooms it is not possible to duplicate the quality of materials used in the business office, all too often insufficient attention is given to the provision of proper materials and to their use. In some instances students have never been required to make carbon copies, have never typed letters on letterheads, and have never prepared envelopes. As a result they are confused when they are confronted with these tasks in the business office. Today, there is little excuse for not providing these materials in transcription. Inexpensive letterhead pads are now available. If it is not possible to purchase these pads, letterheads may be duplicated on the school's duplicating machine. Local printers and business firms often have supplies of letterheads that are no longer being used. If envelopes cannot be purchased, paper may be cut to the correct size. Many businesses save their used carbon paper for the business teacher.

Students should know the various types of erasers and correction devices now on the market and should be familiar with the kinds of paper used for carbon copies, interoffice correspondence, and so on. This type of knowledge should be a part of the training of every student in the transcription class.

Teach the Students How to Use Their Stenographic Notebooks in Transcription

Students should be given specific instructions on ways to use their shorthand notebooks efficiently. The following suggestions should prove helpful to them:

1. Keep your notebooks in a definite place on your desk. Then you will be ready to take dictation at a moment's notice, assuming, of course, that you keep a pen and pencils with your notebooks at all times.
2. Keep a rubber band around the used portion of your notebook.
3. Place the date at the bottom of the first page of the day's dictation.
4. Draw a line through each letter as soon as you transcribe it.
5. When you are interrupted in transcribing a letter, mark your place with a colored pencil.

6. Leave a space at the beginning of every letter for special instructions, such as mailing directions and multiple carbons.

7. Use a code or a letter system for corrections or insertions in the dictation. Then write the correction or the insertion at the end of the page; mark both the dictation and the point at which it is to be inserted with the same letter.

8. Write out unfamiliar names in longhand.

9. Indicate beside each letter any items to be checked, such as amounts of money and dates. Indicate by an *X*, a check mark, or a wavy line.

10. Before transcribing, rewrite any incomplete sentences or ambiguous statements.

11. When the boss is interrupted during dictation, use the time to read your shorthand notes, improving outlines and inserting punctuation.

12. Indicate the end of each item in some way, such as by a wavy line.

13. Indicate rush items to be transcribed first with a colored pencil.

14. When it is necessary to take dictation on loose paper, fasten the notes in the proper place in the notebook for later reference.

15. Learn to turn pages in your notebook while taking rapid dictation.

16. File your notebooks; the name of the secretary, the dictator, and the inclusive dates of the dictation should appear on the cover.

STANDARDS AND GRADING IN TRANSCRIPTION

Because of the many variables involved in transcription, teachers have often found grading in this area difficult. It is simple enough to grade on the basis of mailability, but what procedures should be used to convert mailability into grades? Some teachers follow the plan advocated by Leslie and assign points to the letters according to length and accuracy in transcription:[6]

Number of Words in Letter	Points		
	Perfect	Mailable	Not Mailable or Correctable
Up to 125	2	1	0
126–250	4	2	0
251–375	6	3	0
376–500	8	4	0

The points each student has accumulated are totaled at the end of the week, and grades are assigned on the basis of a curve. This plan makes no suggestions for handling individual differences in dictation rates. All letters may be dictated at the same rate, although there may be a range of forty words a minute in the students' recording ability. The teacher must then decide at what point in the semester to increase the rate at which the letters are dictated. Under this plan the letters are usually dictated to accommodate the students at the lower levels of dictation ability. Even then, they may have difficulty transcribing their notes because the letters were dictated at their maximum shorthand recording rate, while the students with higher skills will be able

[6] Louis A. Leslie and Charles E. Zoubek, *Dictation for Mailable Transcripts* (New York: Gregg Division, McGraw-Hill Book Company, 1950), pp. vi–x.

to transcribe their notes easily because they were able to write legible notes with little effort.

Some teachers follow the plan of dictating several groups of letters—perhaps three at sixty, three at eighty, and three at one hundred. The students are told to transcribe the group that they believe they can transcribe mailably. More credit is given for mailable letters dictated at one hundred than for mailable letters dictated at sixty. The teacher may require that every student pass at least two letter transcription production tests dictated at sixty before attempting the next higher speed. This procedure helps to ensure steady progress for most students, but so much class time is consumed in dictating the letters that students often do not have sufficient time to transcribe. If each group of letters to be transcribed can be dictated at the desired speeds on tapes in a multiple-channel shorthand lab, this procedure can be highly satisfactory because the students simply turn to the channel through which letters dictated at their present speed requirements are being played.

Where a shorthand dictation lab is not available, the teacher may decide to dictate the letters for transcription at various rates to accommodate the ranges of abilities in his class. Here again, some letters will be too slow for the best students and others will be too fast for the slower students. Nothing is more frustrating to the student than having to attempt transcription of illegible or incomplete notes.

For those schools that do not have dictation labs, Driska recommends a procedure that attempts to meet the various recording speeds of students and at the same time recognizes the need to give more credit to students transcribing mailable letters dictated at higher rates of speed.[7] Under his plan approximately fifteen minutes is used for a warm-up and for the dictation of the letters to be transcribed, and thirty minutes is allowed for the transcription production period. Seven letters, all of which contain 100 words, are dictated each production period. The seven letters would be dictated according to the following plan:

Letter 1	60 wam
Letter 2	70 wam
Letter 3	80 wam
Letter 4	90 wam
Letter 5	80 wam
Letter 6	70 wam
Letter 7	60 wam

For a *C* grade a student would have to transcribe three mailable letters; for a *B* grade, four mailable letters; and for an *A* grade, five mailable letters. Thus no student could make a C who did not transcribe at least one letter at seventy words a minute, and no student could make an *A* who did not transcribe at least one letter at eighty words a minute.[8] This plan again

---

[7] Robert L. Driska, "Evaluating Mailable Transcripts," *Business Teacher,* January–February 1969, pp. 4–5.

[8] If fifty words are added to each letter for the inside address, closing lines, carbon copy, and envelope, the student transcribing three letters should have a transcription rate of fifteen words a minute; the student transcribing five letters, twenty-five words a minute.

emphasizes the fallacy of trying to measure transcription production in words a minute. The student transcribing three letters is actually transcribing at ten words a minute, while the student transcribing five letters is transcribing at a rate slightly less than seventeen words a minute. Yet in most offices a stenographer who could produce a mailable letter every ten minutes would be well qualified for her job, and a girl who could produce a letter every six minutes would probably be considered a speed demon.

Leslie's *Dictation for Mailable Transcripts* contains a table for those teachers who wish to compute the transcription rate of their students in words a minute. According to this table, the student who transcribes 300 words has transcribed at the rate of 10 words a minute. Each additional 30 words of transcription increases the rate 1 word a minute. Thus a student transcribing 330 words has a transcription rate of 11 words a minute; 360 words, 12 words a minute, and so on. These figures are based on a thirty-minute production period.

Grubbs suggests still another plan which he calls production count. As all teachers know, when a student's transcription rate is figured in words a minute, there is usually a wide gulf between his mailable transcription rate and his typing rate on straight copy. Grubbs suggests that rather than using mailable words a minute, teachers consider using a production count. Under this plan, the following allowances are made:

Date	5 words
Inside address	20 words
Closing lines	15 words
Each paper change	10 words
Each margin change	10 words
Carbons	10% of basic job count
Erasing	2% of basic job count and 1/2 average typing rate[9]

The basic job count (BJC) consists of the total words in the body of the letter plus the 40 words allowed for the dateline, inside address, and closing. Thus if a letter contained 125 words and a student's average typing rate was 60 words a minute, the total job allowance, expressed in words, for that particular letter would be 280 (125 + 5 + 20 + 15 = 165 BJC; 165 + 16 [carbons] + 2% of 165 × 30 = 280 Total Job Allowance). Grubbs states that with this plan the students' transcription rates are comparable to their typing rates.

PROJECTS AND QUESTIONS FOR DISCUSSION

1. Make a list of what you believe are some of the more common errors a student learning shorthand and transcription tends to make.
2. Obtain some old letters that have been written to a business firm. Mark the letters for dictation in twenty-standard-word groups.

[9] Robert L. Grubbs, "The Production Count as a Challenge," *Business Teacher,* January–February 1968, pp. 28–29.

3. Contact some office-equipment firms in your locality and compare the various types of shorthand laboratory equipment these firms sell. Study such factors as cost of equipment, cost of installation, frequency of mechanical breakdown, repair charges, type of recording used (tape or record), length of the recording, and ease of loading and unloading recordings. Study the advantages and disadvantages of each system.

4. Write a short paper in which you describe some of the research findings in the teaching of shorthand.

5. Miss Sorenson has taught shorthand for several years at Bayview High School. She follows the practice of presenting all new theory appearing in the next day's lesson on the chalkboard each day. Miss Jackson is a new shorthand teacher at Bayview this year. She insists that writing on the chalkboard is old-fashioned. She uses an overhead projector and writes the theory on transparencies. It is her contention that students can see her write the outlines much more clearly, and because she is looking at the class, she can quickly locate any student who does not understand the presentation. Would you agree with the procedures followed by Miss Sorenson or by Miss Jackson? Why?

6. Write a short paper in which you discuss those areas of shorthand methodology on which shorthand authorities do not agree.

7. In most high school situations, the students have inadequate working areas for good transcription practices. What solutions can you suggest for classrooms with limited desk facilities?

8. You have been appointed to a committee to develop a state course of study in shorthand. Your particular assignment is to develop and present to the committee a schedule of standards for grading in shorthand and transcription in a one-year shorthand program. Set up the schedule you would recommend to the committee.

9. The committee working on the development of a state course of study in shorthand has decided that the course should also include a schedule of standards for grading in those schools having a two-year program in shorthand and transcription. You have been asked to develop specific recommendations for a two-year program. Prepare the standards and grading schedule you will suggest to the committee.

10. Businessmen are still saying that business students cannot spell. Should you as a shorthand teacher attempt to teach spelling or should your work in this area be primarily remedial? What procedures would you follow to emphasize spelling in your shorthand classes?

11. This is your first year of teaching shorthand. You are assigned a beginning shorthand class and decide that it will be wise to find out during the first week any deficiencies your students may have in the areas of English, typing usage, and spelling. Prepare a pretranscription test that you may use for this purpose.

12. Miss Franks and Miss Blair are both teaching beginning shorthand. Only one year of shorthand is offered in this school. Miss Franks wants to introduce typed transcription by the end of the first six weeks. Miss Blair insists that this is too early and wants to defer typed transcription until the latter part of the second semester. Which procedure do you think would give best results?

13. One research study has reported that during the period that persons typed in the transcription process, they typed at only half their usual typing speed. What procedures would you follow in teaching transcription to encourage your students to type more rapidly during transcription? What other factors should be considered in developing higher transcription rates?

14. Prepare a list of supplementary shorthand and transcription materials that would be helpful to you and your shorthand students.

15. You have decided to introduce transcription at the beginning of the second semester of shorthand. At first you plan to use only a few minutes a day on transcription drills designed to develop correct transcription techniques. Prepare three drills that you might use for this purpose.

16. Using the high school textbook for the first semester of shorthand, work out a series of homework assignments that you would give your students during the first semester. Be specific. Be sure to vary the assignments from time to time. You may want to consider giving the students goals toward which to work when they are doing their homework.

17. Mrs. Bixby is a shorthand teacher at Hillcrest High School. She says that the students should never be tested on their shorthand vocabulary, that shorthand theory is not that important. After all, she points out, the ability to take dictation and transcribe is what should be measured in the shorthand course, not how the students write thieir shorthand notes. Miss Franklin, a new teacher just out of college, insists that shorthand vocabulary is most important—that unless the student can write accurate notes, he cannot build shorthand dictation skill rapidly or transcribe his notes accurately and fluently. With which of these teachers would you agree? Why?

18. You are teaching shorthand in Grapevine High School. Only one year of shorthand is offered, and no typewriters are available during the period that the class meets. You can see no justification for permitting students to complete a shorthand program without any training in typed transcription. Under these conditions, what would you do?

19. In your transcription class you do not allow credit for letters that are unmailable. Miss Hendricks also teaches transcription in your school, and she uses a point-deduction system according to the seriousness of the error. Thus students may have several errors in a letter and still receive a passing grade. Your students are complaining about your unfair grading practices. Miss Hendricks insists your grading system discourages the students and impedes their progress. Is she right? If Miss Hendricks will not change her grading methods, what should you do?

20. Mrs. Williams says it is foolish to insist that students continue to spell shorthand outlines from the board after the first three or four weeks of instruction, since they are able to read the words by then without spelling the outlines. How would you explain to Mrs. Williams the need for spelling outlines at least until all the theory has been introduced in the first-semester course?

CASE PROBLEMS

1. Miss Wilson, a teacher in Hilltop High School, has talked with her principal a number of times about the need for a shorthand dictation laboratory in the business department. He has, however, never seemed receptive to the idea. Today the principal called Miss Wilson into his office and said he had enough money in the budget for the next school year to include the purchase and installation of a shorthand dictation laboratory, but he was still not convinced that such equipment was a sound investment. He indicated that he had visited two or three schools having such installations and had noticed that the shorthand teachers were not even in the classroom. Furthermore, several research reports he had read stated that the achievement of shorthand students who had worked with a dictation laboratory situation was no better than the achievement of those students not having access to such facilities.

Therefore, before ordering any dictation equipment, the principal wants to be sure that the laboratory will be worthwhile. He asks Miss Wilson to write a report indicating how the dictation laboratory will be used in their school, stating specifically the advantages of such equipment to the students and the teachers.

What information should Miss Wilson include in the report?

2. You have just accepted a position teaching shorthand at Valley View High School which is located in a metropolitan area just fifteen miles from a city of 350,000 population. There are two other shorthand teachers in the business department. The school offers only one year of shorthand. In checking the course guide, you find no definite standards for you to follow. The other teachers say they try to have the students attain a dictation rate of sixty words a minute by the end of the year, though they admit that not all students reach this standard. The other teachers tell you that they spend most of the time the first semester reading shorthand plates in the text and that writing is not introduced until near the end of the semester. No provision is made to include any instruction in typed transcription in the course because frequently the typing room is not available when the shorthand classes meet.

You are appalled by the situation, especially in view of the tremendous demand for stenographers and secretaries in the nearby city, and feel that some action should be taken immediately to correct the situation. What recommendations, if any, would you make to the other teachers? What other steps do you think should be taken?

3. Miss Martin teaches in a high school where the curriculum is largely college preparatory. The only business course offered is one year of typing. She is surprised, therefore, when a group of five of the most promising students in the school approach her one morning before classes begin and ask to have a conference with her. They explain that they have been talking with a number of other students in the school, and they all want the opportunity to take shorthand next year when they are seniors. They believe the course will be helpful to them in a number of ways. They have a list of the names of students who have agreed to take the course if it is offered, although this will mean an extra heavy course load for each of these persons during their senior year.

The students want to know whether Miss Martin feels that they can learn enough shorthand in one year to be useful to them, how much skill they can expect to attain, whether this will be sufficient to help them secure summer employment or jobs while they are in college, and, finally, whether Miss Martin will be willing to teach the course and will support them in their request that shorthand be added to the curriculum next fall. How should Miss Martin answer their questions?

4. Mr. Hammer is teaching shorthand and typing in Wright High School. The business curriculum includes one year of shorthand and two years of typewriting. At the end of his first year of teaching at Wright High School, he is dissatisfied with his students' achievement in shorthand. He feels that he did teach them shorthand, but that because he felt he had no choice but to introduce typed transcription the second semester, many of the students were unable to take dictation at the end of the semester at more than sixty words a minute and others, although capable of typing mailable letters, could do so only at production rates that would not meet the needs of business. Many students were unable to type more than one mailable letter in an entire class period.

Therefore, Mr. Hammer has decided that next year he will devote most of the shorthand class period to building shorthand skills and that, while it may be necessary to introduce transcription and provide some time for drill in the shorthand period, most of the work in typed transcription will be completed in advanced typewriting. All the students who take shorthand also take two years of typewriting, so this will be no problem.

What suggestions could you make to Mr. Hammer that would be of assistance to him in developing this approach to transcription?

5. Mrs. Gallo has taught shorthand and transcription for a number of years. She has always insisted that her students make neat corrections and has spent considerable class time demonstrating the use of eraser shields and various kinds of erasers to make sure all corrections were neatly made. However, Mrs. Gallo has discovered that her students are "cheating" on her. She has found that almost the entire class has been using special corrective devices such as fluids and correction tapes to cover their errors instead of erasing them as they have been taught.

When Mrs. Gallo accuses the students of using these materials when transcribing, they readily admit they have been doing so but point out that this is the way it is done in the office. A number of the girls had jobs during the summer, and according to them, all the girls used these correction devices.

Mrs. Gallo is badly shaken. It appears that what she has been teaching about erasing is good but incomplete. Develop a teaching plan for teaching the use of correction devices other than the typing eraser.

6. Your principal has asked you to consider the advisability of offering an alphabet system of shorthand for students who are planning to attend college. Investigation shows that approximately 60 percent of the students graduating from your school do attend college while the other 40 percent go to work directly out of high school. There is a demand for stenographers in the community, and in the past you have frequently been unable to fill many of the positions available because you did not have enough qualified persons completing the stenographic program.

Do you believe an alphabet system should be introduced for the college-bound students? Do you think an alphabet system would make it possible for you to train more stenographers for the local business firms?

7. Last fall Miss Cox, head of the business department at Crowell High School, requested a new tape recorder and a complete set of shorthand dictation tapes for use in the shorthand program. At the beginning of the fall term Miss Cox met with all the shorthand teachers and presented a demonstration lesson showing how these tapes could be effectively used to supplement the classroom teacher. Now, however, she finds that instead of using the tapes to supplement their instruction, the shorthand teachers are depending upon the tapes to do their teaching for them. When she passes a shorthand classroom, she frequently notices that the teachers are sitting at their desks grading papers while the students are taking dictation from the tapes. She does not believe that this is the proper way to teach a shorthand class and is concerned about the situation.

If you were Miss Cox, what would you do?

8. Betty is an excellent shorthand student. She can record new-matter dictation at one hundred words a minute without an error. Her teacher thought she would be one of the most outstanding students. When transcription was introduced during the latter part of the second semester, however, it became immediately apparent that Betty was going to have serious difficulties. She had no trouble recording the dictation; she could read her notes fluently. But she could not type a mailable letter. She seemed to have no "English sense" at all. She would transcribe *too* for *two*, *advice* for *advise*, *accede* for *exceed*, *principal* for *principle*. Punctuation was inserted without any particular reason, and sentence fragments were not uncommon. In addition to all this, Betty could not spell.

Betty had excellent grades in shorthand before typed transcription was introduced. The teacher does not feel that it will be fair to Betty to fail her in the course. On the other hand, it is quite impossible in the few remaining weeks to teach Betty all the English she needs to know, and Betty certainly is not going to be qualified for a stenographic position of any kind. Since only one year of shorthand is offered and Betty is a senior, there is little possibility of giving Betty much help with her English. What do you think Betty's teacher should do?

SUGGESTED READINGS

Anderson, Ruth I., "Utilizing Shorthand Research in the Classroom," *National Business Education Quarterly*, March 1968, pp. 46–54.

———, "The Teaching of Shorthand in the 1960's," *Changing Methods of Teaching Business Subjects, National Business Education Yearbook*, 1972.

————, "How Important Are Gregg Outlines?," *Business Education Forum*, October 1969, pp. 12–14.

————, "A Six-Weeks Transcription Program," *Business Education Forum*, March 1969, pp. 16–17.

Business Education Forum, National Business Education Association, October 1947–70. Shorthand issues.

Condon, Arnold, and Victor Van Hook, "How Can Shorthand Be Introduced More Effectively?," *Business Education Forum*, October 1964, pp. 10, 22.

————, *et al.*, *The Selection and Use of Multiple-Channel Equipment in the Teaching of Shorthand*, Monograph 121, Cincinnati: South-Western Publishing Co., 1969.

Driska, Robert S., "Teaching Transcription in a One-Year Shorthand Program," *Business Education World*, December 1969, pp. 31–32.

————, "Evaluating Mailable Transcripts," *Business Teacher*, January–February 1969, pp. 4–5.

Dry, Samuel W., and Nellie E. Dry, *Teaching Gregg Shorthand and Transcription*. Portland, Me.: J. Weston Walch, 1962.

Freeman, M. Herbert, and George A. Wagoner, "The Pros and the Cons for the Abbreviated Longhand Systems," *Business Education World*, October 1960, pp. 18–21.

Gibbons, Helen E., "Evaluation in First-Year Shorthand," *Business Education Forum*, January 1969, pp. 18–19.

Grubbs, Robert L., "Rx for Effective Shorthand Teaching," *Business Education World*. New York: Gregg Publishing Division, McGraw-Hill Book Company, 1960–61 Reprinted.

————, "The Production Count as a Challenge," *Business Teacher*, January–February 1968, pp. 28–29.

Haggblade, Berle, "Does Shorthand Accuracy Affect Achievement?," *Business Education Forum*, April 1969, pp. 19–20.

Hosler, Russell J., "The Open Lab for Shorthand Instruction," *Business Education World*, May 1968, pp. 6–7, 28.

Jester, Don, *The Shorthand Transcription Process and Its Teaching Implications*, Monograph 108. Cincinnati: South-Western Publishing Co., 1963.

————, "A New Approach to Theory Testing in Shorthand," *Business Education Forum*, March 1968, pp. 18–20.

Lamb, Marion, *Your First Year of Teaching Shorthand and Transcription*. Cincinnati: South-Western Publishing Co., 1961.

Leslie, Louis A., *Methods of Teaching Gregg Shorthand*. New York: Gregg Publishing Division, McGraw-Hill Book Company, 1953.

————, *Methods of Teaching Transcription*. New York: Gregg Publishing Division, McGraw-Hill Book Company, 1949.

Liles, Parker, "Issues in Teaching Shorthand," *The Balance Sheet*, October 1963, pp. 52–57.

Mitchell, William, "Learning Dividends in Shorthand Homework," *Journal of Business Education*, October 1968, pp. 15–16.

Newhouse, Howard L., "Shorthand Teaching Success," *Business Teacher*, September 1963–April 1964.

Pullis, Joe M., "Contrasting Beliefs Related to Shorthand Teaching Methodology," *Journal of Business Education,* December 1967, pp. 100–102.

————, "Methods of Teaching Shorthand: A Research Analysis," *The Balance Sheet*, September 1970, pp. 16–18, 41.

Rowe, John L., "The Four Arts of Shorthand Teaching," *Business Education World*, November 1959–February 1960.

Russon, Allien R., *Methods of Teaching Shorthand*, Monograph 119. Cincinnati: South-Western Publishing Co., 1968.

Stewart, Jane, "On These Things We Agree in the Teaching of Shorthand and Transcription," *Business Education Forum*, October 1964, pp. 7–9.

Strony, Madeline S., and Howard Newhouse, "Fifteen Stimulants for Teaching Gregg Shorthand," *Business Teacher*, May–June 1961, p. 13.

Taylor, Helen W., and Elsie D. Palmer, "Development and Evaluation of Programmed Materials and Multiple-Channel Dictation Tapes in Beginning Shorthand," *National Business Education Quarterly*, March 1964, pp. 28–38.

Tonne, Herbert A., Estelle L. Popham, and M. Herbert Freeman, *Methods of Teaching Vocational Business Subjects* (3rd ed.), Chaps. 9–15, New York: The Gregg Publishing Company, 1965.

Zoubek, Charles E., "Ten Commandments for Teaching Shorthand," *Business Education World*, October 1969, pp. 11–12.

chapter

7

TEACHING CLERICAL PRACTICE AND STENOGRAPHIC PRACTICE

Perhaps no course in the high school curriculum has changed more in the past five to ten years than has the course in office practice. Not only is the course designated by numerous titles, but the plans under which it is offered vary so widely that it is often difficult to determine the nature of the course without a description or an outline. From school to school the content differs widely, the objectives are frequently not the same, and the equipment and supplies available to the students and teachers range from classrooms having only a few typewriters to those simulating offices. It is small wonder, then, that with these variations in objectives and course content confusion often exists regarding the office practice course and the manner in which it should be taught.

This period has seen the introduction of hundreds of cooperative office education programs as well as office simulation and laboratory programs of various types. Teaching methodology in these programs often differs widely from the usual course in office or clerical practice which is closely tied to a textbook.

In this chapter office practice will be presented under a number of different course titles so that a clear distinction may be made between course content, level of course offering, and basic differences in procedures followed in teaching each type of course.

TYPES OF OFFICE PRACTICE COURSES

Office Practice

Office practice, as the name implies, is an attempt to bridge the gap between the school and the office. It provides for the fusion of separate skills and the teaching of additional skills and knowledges before the student enters the business world. The course is usually designed for prospective stenographers, bookkeepers, and general office workers. In some large school systems, the course is designated as *office practice—stenographic* and *office practice—book-keeping.* While all students may meet in the same class, it is understood that the units in the course will be adapted in line with the student's career objective. Because of the nature of the course content, a knowledge of shorthand or bookkeeping is often a prerequisite; and persons who have not completed these courses may not enroll. For many years this was the only type of office practice course found in most high schools, and it is still widely offered today. The course fulfills a real need, since it gives students an opportunity to develop new skills in such areas as filing and office machines and at the same time provides practice in doing office jobs such as they will be expected to perform in the business office. Where some students have previously taken shorthand and others bookkeeping, the units of work must be adapted to meet the needs of these students. Thus all students will complete some of the units, but at times students will be working independently on different projects.

This type of office practice course does have a serious limitation in those schools where bookkeeping or shorthand are prerequisites, since only those students who have previously studied these courses may enroll. Many students in high school who do not wish to take shorthand or bookkeeping may be interested in and have the ability to do general office or clerical work, yet their needs are not considered. Some schools permit students to enroll in a course that they call *office practice,* the only prerequisite being previous instruction in typewriting. Technically speaking, such a course is a clerical practice course. Again, this points out the difficulty of making any generalizations about office practice and its content, since this is largely determined by each individual school.

Clerical Practice

The course entitled *clerical practice* or *clerical office practice* was introduced into the high school curriculum to meet the needs of those students who wanted to prepare for office work but who lacked the interests or the capacities required for stenography and bookkeeping. Teachers who have had experience teaching the course have found that it is especially valuable for students of average or somewhat less-than-average ability. Because many of the general clerical duties performed in the office are routine, clerical work usually does not appeal to the superior student. The course is designed to prepare students for immediate initial employment and to provide students with the business background and skills that will enable them to secure promotions as they gain further experience in office work. In most schools students desiring to enroll in clerical practice must have completed at least one year of typewriting. Shorthand should never be a prerequisite. Bookkeeping or record keeping may or may not be required, depending upon the content of the clerical practice course.

In large metropolitan centers a special course in clerical training may be offered for those students experiencing learning difficulties. Such students are often poor readers, are uninterested in school, and will not remain there unless they are enrolled in some course where they can see an immediate application of the learning. These students ordinarily need remedial work in many areas. Such work is incorporated into business situations or jobs where its usefulness is apparent. The instruction is on an individual basis. Each student is taken at the point at which he enters the course, and an attempt is made to challenge him with simple, routine tasks that he can handle successfully. While school authorities hope that courses such as clerical training will help keep these boys and girls in school, it is recognized that some will still leave before graduation. However, any basic business skills or understandings that they may have acquired before dropping out may mean the difference between securing a job and being unemployed. Therefore the course is considered extremely valuable for those enrolled.

Clerical training is totally dissimilar to clerical office practice or clerical practice which is intended for students with much greater learning potential.

Stenographic Office Practice

A third type of office practice course is the course designated as *stenographic office practice, secretarial office practice,* or *secretarial practice.* Although the term *secretarial practice* is frequently used on the high school level, this designation is misleading. Actually the course should be called *stenographic practice* or *stenographic office practice.* Since it is designed for stenographic majors, shorthand and typewriting are prerequisites. The course is primarily intended to develop further accuracy in transcription. Units in other areas, such as filing and duplicating, may or may not be included, depending upon the individual school situation and the objectives of the course. In some schools stenographic practice is in reality the second year of shorthand. In other schools where only one year of shorthand is offered, one semester of second-year typewriting is devoted to stenographic practice for those students who have completed one year of shorthand. In still other schools stenographic practice is the "finishing" course for the students who have completed two years of shorthand, and the subject matter usualy includes such units as personality development, grooming, receptionist duties, and office etiquette.

Secretarial office practice or secretarial practice usually includes the elements found in stenographic office practice plus thorough training in such top-level secretarial duties as the composition of letters, preparation of minutes and business reports, handling business callers, and making travel arrangements. Obviously many of these duties would only be performed by a highly trained and experienced secretary. Therefore, the term should be restricted to courses offered on the college level. To provide clear-cut distinction between the high school and the college-level course, the trend in colleges today is to refer to the course as *executive secretaryship* or some similar title.

OFFICE MACHINES

Another course occasionally found in large city schools is entitled *office machines*. In this course the students are taught to operate such machines as the full-keyboard adding machine, the ten-key adding machine, the key-driven calculator, and bookkeeping and posting machines. The instruction given in this course is entirely dependent upon the machines available in the school. Combination textbooks and workbooks for such office machines as the key-driven calculator, the rotary calculator, the ten-key adding-listing machine, and the full-keyboard adding-listing machine may be secured from publishing companies specializing in business education materials.

CLERICAL PRACTICE

Clerical practice is designed for those students whose high school programs have not included shorthand. The skills and knowledges taught in this course are varied and range from the development of dexterity in handling routine office jobs to higher-level operations such as machine transcription and filing. Many persons believe that clerical practice is designed only for the low-ability student. Actually, a clerical-practice course that is properly organized and taught will be beneficial to any student who enrolls in it, provided the student has the mental and manual ability required to complete the units of work successfully.

According to the United States census, a much higher percentage of men workers are classified as clerks than are women workers. Therefore the course should be so designed that it will appeal to both boys and girls. Since shorthand is not a prerequisite, there is no reason why the course should not be attractive to high school boys planning to enter business.

AUTOMATION AND THE CLERICAL WORKER

Recently much has been published about the effect of automation on office workers. Some writers have indicated that the continuing practice of training clerical workers in large numbers cannot be justified now that so many offices are using automated machine operations. However, these writers fail to realize that for many years the schools have not been able to train enough specialized clerical workers. The schools train only a small percentage of those entering nonspecialized types of clerical work. Although it is true that automation creates many new jobs on the technical and highly skilled levels, it is doubtful that automation has seriously affected such specialized clerical workers as stenographers, bookkeepers, and typists. Automation is rapidly taking over routine, repetitive jobs, but not those clerical jobs requiring training and skill. Furthermore, automation cannot be satisfactorily applied to nonrepetitive tasks. Because of the cost involved, it is obvious that information used only once should be handled according to traditional procedures. Thus, while automation is being utilized for the performance of repetitive duties, many clerical jobs will not be automatized in the immediate future.

At present instruction on key-punch machines, collators, tabulators, and other data-processing equipment is limited primarily to technical and vocational high schools, business schools, and colleges. The teacher in the small high school that cannot afford the cost of leasing or purchasing this equipment should note that typewriting skill is needed in the operation of many electronic communication systems. A skilled typist can often be trained as a key-punch operator in a short period of time, and some companies train their own operators. Every teacher of clerical practice should, however, attempt to give his students an understanding of the principles of automated data processing. Students should have some knowledge of tabulated and electronic data-processing systems found in offices today. They should be introduced to the basic terminology of data processing, the language systems that the machines are able to understand, and the mediums used by those machines—punched cards, punched tapes, magnetic tapes, and forms printed with magnetic ink. The clerical practice teacher should include in the course illustrations of the various types of business forms and reports that can be prepared with automated data-processing equipment. Of primary importance to these students is the understanding of the processes involved and the systems to which these processes can be applied, not the actual operation of the machines themselves. Clerical students should realize that the offices in which many of them will be working will be automated to a large extent.

As rapidly as technology is changing today, no text can accurately predict the many ways in which the duties of office workers will be affected by automation in the future. But based on the predictions of the Department of Labor, it does appear that the demand for office workers is going to continue regardless of automation. It should be noted, however, that in at least one research study office executives did anticipate a reduction in the number of persons performing general office activities. This further emphasizes the importance of specific office skills.

Every responsible business teacher should be alert to changes in office techniques and procedures resulting from new applications of automation to office work.

DUTIES PERFORMED BY CLERICAL WORKERS

A number of studies have been made in the past few years to determine the qualifications and duties of beginning office workers. A survey made in Connecticut revealed that the beginning office worker was immediately expected to be a producer; no training program was provided. She was a high school graduate, had taken no training beyond high school, and did not plan to continue her training. She had studied business subjects in high school and felt that nothing she had been taught should have been omitted or learned on the job, but if she were to repeat high school, she would take more business courses. She felt that the typing and clerical office practice courses were of the greatest value on the job.

The three top-ranking tasks of these beginning workers were filling in or completing blank forms, filing correspondence and records, and typing letters and reports from rough drafts.

The three top-ranking skills, knowledges, and understandings dominant in all job families were writing numbers legibly, spelling correctly, and doing basic arithmetic.

The office machines used by the greatest number of beginning office workers were the ten-key adding machine, the photocopying machine, the full-keyboard adding machine, and the typewriter. The ten-key adding machine was the one machine used by workers in more office-work job families than any other one machine. Billing machines were used by a limited number of workers for a great part of the day.

The beginning workers felt that the personal qualities most important to success were accuracy in work and a sense of responsibility. Other important factors were regularity of attendance, dependability, neatness of work, being well organized, and ability to work well with a supervisor.

It was concluded that beginning office workers need skills and knowledges in the areas of typing, bank services, filing, computations, customer accounting, telephone usage, business language, and writing and typing for readability.

A study completed in 1962 in Fargo, North Dakota, of 106 high school graduates employed in office work revealed that the positions most frequently held by these persons were file clerk, receptionist, secretary, bookkeeper, switchboard operator, stenographer, and mail-department worker. Typing and filing were the skills the respondents had found most helpful to them. The duties performed daily by the greatest number of graduates were answering the telephone, filing, and typing letters.

Berry, in studying the role of office practice instruction in the training for general office assignments, concluded that office practice instruction should include the following, with such modifications as might be necessary to meet the local employment needs:

1. Acquaintance level of training in oral communications
2. Acquaintance, not a skill, level of learning in the area of filing activities
3. Acquaintance or skill level of training in machine transcribing activities, depending on local needs
4. Skill training in typing with more emphasis on accuracy
5. Acquaintance with key-punch machine operation and operation of related machines
6. Acquaintance with general clerical practices and procedures
7. Concentration on human relations and personal development throughout the course
8. Familiarity with employment procedures
9. Familiarity with principles, practices, and procedures of the modern business office, with a basic knowledge of data processing methods and environment

Areas in which Berry determined that less emphasis was needed in the office practice course were calculating machine instruction, with the possible exception of the ten-key listing machine; duplicating skills; and handling of mail.

OBJECTIVES OF THE COURSE

Clerical practice, like many office practice courses in which emphasis is placed upon the integration of office skills, attempts to bridge the gap between the classroom and the office. Although the objectives of the course will naturally vary from school to school, most clerical courses are based on the following objectives:

1. To improve and coordinate the office skills learned in other courses
2. To imporve, when necessary, previously acquired skills in the fundamental processes such as handwriting, English, spelling, and arithmetic
3. To understand the organization and flow of work of the business office
4. To gain an understanding of the techniques for work simplification in the office
5. To become acquainted with the principles and procedures of data processing, the equipment, and the systems to which it can be applied
6. To become familiar with those reference books frequently used in the business office
7. To become familiar with the latest office equipment, machines, and supplies
8. To become familiar with commonly used filing systems and to develop skill in filing and finding business papers
9. To develop skill in the typing of business papers and forms
10. To develop employable skill in machine transcription
11. To develop proofreading skill
12. To develop skill in the use of machines commonly found in the business office
13. To develop skill in the use of duplicating equipment
14. To develop skill in mailing routines and techniques
15. To develop skill in the composition of business communications
16. To develop skill in correct telephone techniques
17. To develop in students a sense of responsibility for the completion of office jobs without close supervision
18. To develop those personal traits and work habits needed in the business office
19. To acquaint students with proper techniques in applying for a job

PREREQUISITES OF THE COURSE

Since many of the units in clerical practice involve the integration of previously acquired skills, the course should be offered in the twelfth year in high school. The course may be either one or two semesters in length. Some schools offer a year course in clerical practice, while in some large schools a one-semester course is offered for clerical students and a one-semester course for stenographic students. Other schools include a one-semester course in advanced typewriting or clerical typewriting and one semester in clerical practice.

Students are frequently selected for clerical practice because the number wishing to enroll so far exceeds the facilities available. Although selection of students is certainly to be recommended, it is unfortunate that the schools are unable to provide training for many students who are interested in clerical work and who could be trained to be proficient clerical workers.

One of the most common prerequisites for enrollment in clerical practice is typewriting. It is true that some clerical jobs do not require typing skill, but an analysis of the duties most often performed by clerical workers indicates that many of these duties do require typing skill. It should also be remembered that many of the nonskilled clerical duties are gradually disappearing as more and more business offices become automated. Certainly clerical workers who type will have much greater job and promotional opportunities than those who do not.

UNITS TO BE INCLUDED
IN CLERICAL OFFICE PRACTICE

Because the length of the clerical office practice course and the objectives vary in different schools, it is difficult to set up a list of the units that should be included. Therefore, it is recommended that the units in the course outline be selected on the basis of the duties most often performed by clerical workers in the area, together with consideration of the course objectives.

The units listed below are typical of those found in most clerical practice courses; however, a teacher may wish to present these units in an order entirely different from that in which they are presented here. No attempt has been made to include all possible subtopics a teacher might include in each unit.

Some teachers might wish to combine many of these units. For example, the machines unit could include, in addition to adding and calculating machines, machine transcription, clerical typewriting, and duplicating. Another teacher might wish to combine the adding and calculating machines unit with record keeping, since these two areas can easily be integrated with proper planning. The units shown here should merely be considered as suggestive of those topics that most clerical practice courses might be expected to include:

Unit I. Office Organization and Routine
Job relationships
Operational charts and flow of work
Office routines
Desk organization; motion-mindedness
Tools and supplies

Unit II. The Personality of the Clerical Worker
Clerical aptitude tests and personality tests
Personal appearance—dress, hair, makeup, cleanliness, neatness, health, voice, posture
Personality—initiative, courtesy (manners), enthusiasm, sincerity, sense of humor, voice and speech, cooperativeness, tact, social aptitude, office etiquette
Mental skills—learning to follow directions, learning from previous mistakes, using initiative to solve a problem, open-mindedness to new ideas, suggestions, or criticisms

Responsibility—promptness, trustworthiness, loyalty, ambition, persistence, dependability

Character; business ethics

Attitude toward the job—promptness and regularity in attendance, pride in one's work, production of a day's work in a day

Unit III. Reference Books

Types of reference books
Handbooks for the office and for business
Dictionaries
Thesaurus
Atlases
Special dictionaries
Almanacs
Books of quotations
Handbooks on grammar and English usage
Typing style manuals
Special business references
Business periodicals
Special indexes
Reference book problems

Unit IV. Clerical Typewriting

Skill on electric typewriters
Statistical typewriting
Addressing envelopes
Preparation and typing of direct-process masters and stencils
Rough draft and manuscript typing
Preparation and typing of business forms and papers
Letter production techniques
Typing from direct dictation
Composing at the machine
Typing multiple carbons

Unit V. Duplicating

Stencil duplicating
Direct-process duplicating
Multilithing (if equipment available)
Photocopy and other processes

Unit VI. Machine Transcription

Unit VII. Filing

Alphabetic
Numeric
Other filing systems
Filing equipment and supplies
Filing procedures such as sorting, cross-referencing, charge-out, follow-up
Preparation of file labels, folders, and guides
Retention and transfer of papers

Unit VIII. Office Machines

Adding machines—ten-key and full-keyboard
Calculators

Unit IX. Record Keeping
  Petty cash
  Payrolls
  Verifying bills, invoices, and statements
  Bank deposits, reconciling bank statements

Unit X. Communications
  Telephone
    Placing and receiving business calls
    Telephone techniques and manners
    Operating the switchboard
    Types of telephone services and charges
    Telephone problems
  Telegraph services
    Types of telegraph services
    Mediums for sending telegrams
    Comparative costs of telegraph and telephone services
  Mail
    Handling incoming and outgoing mail
    Interoffice and intracompany mail
    Composing routine letters and messages
    Selecting and typing form letters and fill-ins

Unit XI. Automation in the Office
  Principles of automation
  Procedures followed in utilizing automated data-processing techniques
  Terminology of automation
  Common language used by automated data-processing equipment
  Systems to which data processing may be applied

Unit XII. Seeking Employment
  Personal interview and follow-up
  Application letters and data sheets
  Application blanks

Occasionally schools that have very limited equipment feel that they do not have the facilities required to offer clerical practice. In a survey in which data were collected from 239 companies regarding training demanded of beginning office workers on ten different types of office machines, it was found that businessmen did not require training or experience in office machines except for the typewriter. Large companies were more likely to use copying, duplicating, electronic accounting machines, and EDP equipment than were small companies; and large companies more frequently had in-service training programs, though often such programs were conducted on an informal basis. The investigators concluded that rather than purchase expensive office equipment, schools should rent the equipment for their school laboratories. Elaborate and expensive equipment is not essential to the teaching of office practice. Such equipment may rapidly become obsolete. If the policies of the school do not permit the rental of equipment, it is possible to provide students with valuable experience in an office practice course without the use of any office machines except typewriters. For instance, in the units outlined above, only Unit VI and Unit VIII specifically require special office machines—dictating-transcribing machines, adding machines, and calculators. These units could be omitted. Unit V involves duplicating machines, but these are frequently available in the school offices. Even if they may not be used by the class, the important skill for the clerical worker is planning the layout of the copy and typing the stencils and masters. Unit XI on automation could involve data-processing equipment if it were available. If it is not, students still need an introduction to the concepts of automation in the office and its applications to office work.

LAYOUT OF OFFICE PRACTICE LABORATORY

Since the prime objective of office practice is to train students to the point of occupational competency, the training laboratory should resemble an office as much as possible. The selection of office furniture and equipment will, of course, depend upon the nature and content of the office practice course. The arrangement of the room should simulate a business office environment. Similar machines should be grouped together. Desks should be placed so that the students and the teacher have easy access to all work stations. Exhibit 7.1 illustrates a satisfactory room arrangement for an office practice laboratory with twenty to twenty-five work stations.

Exhibit 7.1 OFFICE PRACTICE LABORATORY 20–25 PUPIL STATIONS

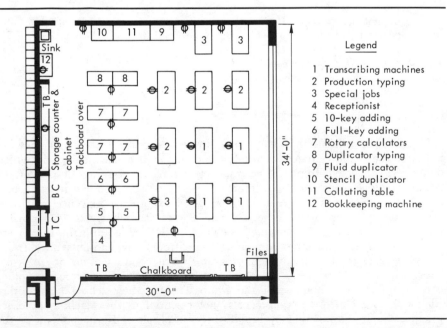

Source: *Teaching Guide for Vocational Office Training*, Part III, Business Education Service, Division of Vocational Education, State Department of Education, Richmond, Va., XLV, No. 10 (1963), 12.

EQUIPMENT AND SUPPLIES

A recent survey of the office machines equipment in high schools in the United States indicated that most schools having an enrollment of 450 to 1,100 students had the following equipment:

An average of 61.38 typewriters
An equal number of pica and elite typewriters
Two manual typewriters for every electric typewriter
Two key-driven calculators
Two rotary calculators
Six ten-key machines
One full keyboard machine
One fluid, one stencil, and/or one offset duplicator
One Thermofax copier and one other type of copier
Three dictating-transcribing machines
Nine pieces of data-processing equipment: five key punches, one sorter, one interpreter, one collator, and one accounting machine

Although the equipment and supplies needed to teach clerical practice will depend upon the course content, the teacher should be sure that he will have the minimum materials needed to teach the course effectively. The following equipment and supplies should be found in most clerical practice rooms if the training is to be realistic:

Typewriters of various makes—manual and electric, pica and elite type
One long-carriage typewriter (desirable but optional)
Miniature filing outfits or practice sets
Filing cabinets
Printing calculators
Rotary calculators
Electronic calculators
Ten-key adding and listing machines
Full-keyboard adding and listing machines
Stencil duplicating machines
Direct-process duplicating machines
Mimeoscope
Styli
Dictating and transcribing machines
Paper cutter
Practice telephones
Copyholders
Letter opener
Dictionary and other reference books
Stapler and staple removers
Tape recorder and tapes
Record player with records
Wall clock

Overhead projector

Letter trays

Wastepaper baskets

Small office supplies such as paper clips, pins, scotch tape, package labels, paste, rubber, and shears

Other specialized equipment might include photocopiers, billing machines, bookkeeping machines, mailing equipment, and data-processing equipment. If possible, the furniture should include adjustable typewriting desks and adjustable posture chairs.

Teachers sometimes find it difficult to decide which office machines should be included in the clerical practice course. Obviously teachers would be ill advised to select expensive, complicated machines, machines whose operation is extremely simple and can be learned quickly, machines that will soon become obsolete, or machines that are highly specialized and should usually be learned on the job. Any equipment selected should be similar to the machines found in local business offices and should teach basic operating techniques. Low-cost, hand-operated models can be used to teach basic techniques, but teachers agree that the unit in office machines should include some electric models. In the business office the students are much more likely to encounter the fully automatic models of the rotary calculator than the semiautomatic or manual models. If one type of adding machine is to be purchased, the ten-key adding machine should be selected in preference to the full keyboard. Because of the frequency with which both the ten-key adding-listing machine and the calculator are found in the business office, instruction on both of these types of machines should be considered an essential part of the office machines unit. Transcribing machines should also be included in the course. If at all possible, there should be a typewriter for each student. If the business department has no duplicating equipment, the time devoted to typing stencils and masters for spirit duplicators should be limited, as many firms are replacing such equipment with offset duplicating equipment.

The equipment should have a reputation for dependability and low-cost maintenance service which is readily available. Most teachers prefer machines for which instructional materials can be obtained.

ILLUSTRATION OF A STATE AND A CITY PROGRAM IN CLERICAL AND OFFICE PRACTICE

In Pennsylvania the course title *office practice* is used to designate the course designed for nonstenographic students. The Pennsylvania *Business Education Manual* recommends a one-year course with approximately half of the time devoted to instruction on office machines and the other half to subject areas such as arithmetic review, business forms, communications, filing, reference materials, personality development and job applications.

The objectives of the office practice course are:

1. To contribute to development of appreciations, ideals, and socially desirable attitudes and work habits which are necessary for success in an office situation.
2. To maintain and further develop knowledges and skills that have already been learned.

3. To help bridge the gap between formal instruction offered in school and the responsibilities of an initial job in the business world.
4. To offer experience in as practical a situation as possible in the performance of routine office jobs.
5. To develop the ability of judging the marketability of one's own work and to make the necessary adjustments or corrections.
6. To build both speed and accuracy in work performed in the business office.
7. To set forth desirable standards of office appearance.
8. To develop proper attitudes toward promotional possibilities, as well as the realization of additional responsibilities.
9. To give pupils experience in applying for a position.
10. To acquire additional competencies such as knowing how to operate the more commonly used office machines.
11. To learn to take care of equipment and supplies.

The content of the course is to be determined by considering the kind of instruction offered in other business subjects, by surveying the needs of business offices and stores, and by following up graduates of the course.

The manual suggests that one of two procedures be used in teaching the course: (*a*) alternating units taught by the rotation and battery plans throughout the year, or (*b*) teaching the first semester using the battery plan and the second semester using the rotation plan. A time schedule is included for teachers employing the alternate battery rotation plan:

Time Schedule

Number of Weeks	Teaching Plan	Topic
2	Battery	Personality Development and Use of Reference Materials
3	Rotation	Office Machines
2	Battery	Business Forms
3	Rotation	Office Machines
2	Battery	Communications
3	Rotation	Office Machines
4	Battery	Filing
3	Rotation	Office Machines
2	Battery	Applying for a Job
3	Rotation	Office Machines
6	Battery	Arithmetic Review
3	Rotation	Office Machines

The *Office Procedures Manual* for the Fort Worth Public Schools outlines the following program in Clerical Practice:

COURSE CONTENT FOR OFFICE PRACTICE

Weeks	Units of Instruction
1	Careers in Business
1	Personality Development
4	Filing

Weeks	Units of Instruction

$1^1/_2$ Communications
    Telephone
    Telegrams, Cablegrams, and Radiograms
    Interoffice Communications
    Mail and Messenger Service
$^1/_2$ Handling Office Callers
1   Keeping Financial Records
    Banking
    Cash Payments
    Payroll
    Credits and Collections

The following units taught on rotation require five 4-week periods:

4   Office Typewriting
4   Machine Transcription
4   *Duplicating (preparing and reproducing copy)
4   Adding machines
4   Calculating Machines

3   **Applying for and Holding a Job
    Letter of Application
    Data Sheet
    The Interview
    Follow-up Letter
    Application Forms
3   Business Correspondence
    Composing business letters
    Business English and Spelling
    Office Reference Books
    Secretarial Shortcuts and Techniques
1   Reserve Periods
    Interspersed throughout the year to allow for interruptions and to cover additional topics such as:
    Introduction to Data Processing
    Business Organization
    Business Information
    Small Office Supplies and Equipment
    Stock and Inventory Procedures

* In this unit the assignments should include additional and higher-level learning.
** This unit is interposed during March or April to give students time to apply for actual employment before graduation.

BASIC TEACHING PLANS

There are today at least four basic plans for teaching office, clerical, and stenographic practice. These may be briefly summarized as follows:

1. THE BATTERY PLAN.   In the battery plan, sufficient machines, equipment, and supplies are available to enable all students to work on the same unit at one time. The battery plan makes more economical use of the teacher's time in the classroom than do most other methods. Since all students are working

on the same unit, the teacher can give instruction on a class basis rather than on an individual or a small group basis. It is also possible that students may progress more rapidly because class time is utilized effectively. Very few schools are able to teach the course by the battery plan, however, as it necessitates a considerable investment in machines and other equipment. A few technical high schools in some of the large cities do offer Comptometer and calculating machines courses under the battery plan.

2. THE ROTATION PLAN. The rotation plan provides for individual or small group instruction on each unit. The class is divided into small groups with each group working on a different unit. Therefore, the teacher must instruct each group individually. When the students in one group complete the work on that particular unit, they rotate to the next unit of work. This system calls for very careful advance planning to insure that the groups are set up according to a workable rotation plan. Because so many different types of learning activities are taking place at once, job instruction sheets are frequently used to save time. A job instruction sheet is illustrated in Exhibit 7.2.

Under the rotation plan, office and machine training may be offered with a relatively low investment in equipment. The rotation plan is also more economical than the battery plan in that all equipment is constantly in use throughout the course. Since instruction is given on an individual or a small group basis, the plan allows for greater flexibility in providing for individual differences. However, many teachers find that the rotation plan does not result in the development of a high degree of skill on any one machine or unit, and much more teaching skill is required to handle the classroom situation because of the number of different activities taking place at one time. Frequently the teacher finds it impossible to give instruction to all those students who need help with their problems, and he must resort to such methods as requesting the more capable students to work with those who need assistance. From the teacher's point of view this procedure may be satisfactory, but it is questionable whether the plan is beneficial to the superior student. The rotation plan is undoubtedly the most widely used method of teaching specialized units in clerical practice today.

Beginning teachers sometimes encounter difficulty in setting up rotation plans for their clerical or office practice course. The steps involved in developing a rotation plan are as follows:

1. Determine the number of instructional periods possible for each student. Multiply the number of pieces of any one kind of equipment by the number of students assigned to each piece of equipment. The resulting figure is then multiplied by the number of rotation periods. The total rotation periods divided by the number of students will give the number of rotation periods for each student for each unit.

2. Total the periods for each unit and make any adjustment necessary for ease of operating the rotation schedule.

3. Keep related activities in the same block of instruction. For instance, typing production jobs on business forms, papers and letters, and duplicating all involve the use of the typewriter. If typewriters are not available for all students, then better results may be obtained by combining all activities involving typewriting in one block.

Exhibit 7.2 JOB INSTRUCTION SHEET: CARD PUNCHING OPERATION

Equipment: IBM 26 Printing Card Punch (program drum has card with entire field of 12
punches)
Materials: IBM cards, IBM Keyboard Exercises for IBM Card Punching Machines, IBM
Reference Manual for 24 Card Punch—26 Printing Card Punch
Directions: First read pages 5-11 and 13 in the IBM Reference Manual. Then make two
cards for each line in Lesson 1. (The two cards can be put together for checking
purposes.)

Steps	*Key Points*
1. Plug in machine.	1. Fan the cards before stacking and placing in hopper.
2. Stack cards at side of machine.	
3. Place cards in hopper on right of machine; turn on main-line switch.	2. Cards are placed in hopper face forward, 9s down, and are fed front card first.
4. Depress release key.	
5. Depress feed key *twice*.	3. The release key is depressed to make sure the star wheels are at one on the program drum.
6. Turn on automatic switches and print cards.	
7. Place first three fingers of right hand on "home keys" 4, 5, 6.	4. The cards are punched at the first station at the right. When the second card is fed to the machine, the first card is "registered" into position for punching.
8. Depress keys in line one.	
9. At the end of the line, reach up with middle finger to depress dash-skip key.	
10. When you are ready to punch the next-to-last card in the lesson, turn the automatic switches off.	5. Finger "one" controls 1, 4, 7. Finger "two" controls 2, 5, 8. Finger "three" controls 0, 3, 6, and 9.
11. Punch the last two cards.	6. Do not space between groups of numbers.
12. Depress the release and register keys alternately to remove cards.	7. After the card is punched, it automatically stacks in card stacker at left.
13. Turn print key off.	
14. Turn main line switch off.	8. Automatic switches should be turned off when you are ready to punch the next-to-last card so no blank cards will be stacked in the stacker.
15. Remove cards from stacker. Remove cards from hopper. Unplug machine.	

Source: *Business Education in the Secondary School,* Bulletin D–3 (Illinois Curriculum Program,
1963), p. 137.

Illustrations of rotation schedules are shown in Exhibits 7.3, 7.4 and 7.5.

A master plan should be prepared indicating the rotation periods, the
students assigned to each period, and the activities that they will be performing. The plan should be prepared as soon as the teacher knows the equipment available and the number of students per class, the instructional units
to be included, and the length of the course. Then there is no confusion later
when the students rotate from one instructional block to the next. With the
schedule prepared for the entire semester, students can readily see the im-

Exhibit 7.3 ROTATION PLAN

24 Pupils Divided into Six Groups	Six Three-Week Periods on Rotation Plan					
	1st pd	2nd pd	3rd pd	4th pd	5th pd	6th pd
Group A (4 pupils)	M	D	A	T	K	R
Group B	R	M	D	A	T	K
Group C	K	R	M	D	A	T
Group D	T	K	R	M	D	A
Group E	A	T	K	R	M	D
Group F	D	A	T	K	R	M

M—Manual Typewriters   T—Transcribing Machines
R—Rotary Calculators   A—Adding-Listing Machines
K—Key-Driven Calculators   D—Duplicating Equipment

Source: *Office Practice for Business Education Departments in Pennsylvania Public Schools*, Bulletin 274, Commonwealth of Pennsylvania, Department of Business Instruction, Harrisburg, 1956, p. 7.

Exhibit 7.4 DEVELOPING THE ROTATION SCHEDULE

Step 1

Six units—5 calculators, 5 ten-key adding machines, 5 transcribing machines, 3 electric typewriters, 5 filing sets, 5 practice sets in record keeping, 1 stencil duplicator, 1 spirit duplicator

Estimated number of students—30
Periods available for rotation (two-semester course)—120

Note: In this course 160 periods are available for instruction. Twenty periods a semester have been reserved for class discussion of units in personality development, telephone manners, office etiquette, grooming, films and filmstrips, demonstrations, speakers, and field trips.

Equipment	Students Assigned Simultaneously	Total Students Assigned
5 calculators	1	5
5 ten-key adding machines	1	5
5 transcribing machines	1	5
3 electric typewriters	1	3
5 filing sets	1	5
5 record-keeping practice sets	1	5
1 stencil duplicator	1	1
1 spirit duplicator	1	1
		30

Exhibit 7.4   (cont.)

Step 2

Pieces of one kind of equipment × students assigned simultaneously × number of rotation periods = total rotation periods ÷ by number of students = rotation periods for each student on each unit

Calculators	5 × 1 × 120 = 600 ÷ 30 = 20
Ten-key adding machines	5 × 1 × 120 = 600 ÷ 30 = 20
Transcribing machines	5 × 1 × 120 = 600 ÷ 30 = 20
Electric typewriters	3 × 1 × 120 = 360 ÷ 30 = 12
Filing sets	5 × 1 × 120 = 600 ÷ 30 = 20
Record-keeping sets	5 × 1 × 120 = 600 ÷ 30 = 20
Stencil duplicator	1 × 1 × 120 = 120 ÷ 30 = 4
Spirit duplicator	1 × 1 × 120 = 120 ÷ 30 = 4

Step 3

Total periods—make any necessary adjustments at this time.

Unit	Total Periods
Calculators	20
Ten-key adding machines	20
Transcribing machines	20
Electric typewriters	12
Filing sets	20
Record-keeping sets	20
Stencil duplicator	4
Spirit duplicator	4

Step 4

Arrange the units into related instructional blocks.

Instructional Block	Periods
A. Calculators	20
B. Ten-key adding machines	20
C. Transcribing machines	20
D. Filing sets	20
E. Record-keeping sets	20
F. Electric typewriters ⎫	
F. Stencil duplicator ⎬	20
F. Spirit duplicator ⎭	

Step 5

Prepare a rotation schedule showing the number of each instructional block and the students assigned to the instructional block. Each student is assigned a number and can determine by looking at the schedule the unit to which he is assigned each week. The first two weeks and the last two weeks of each semester are not included in the rotation plan as these are the periods that will be devoted to special group activities and class discussions.

Exhibit 7.4 (cont.)

Instructional Block	First Semester			Second Semester		
Weeks:	3–6	7–10	11–14	3–6	7–10	11–14
Calculators	A 1–5	B 6–10	C 11–15	D 16–20	E 21–25	F 26–30
Ten-key adding machines	B 6–10	C 11–15	D 16–20	E 21–25	F 26–30	A 1–5
Transcribing machines	C 11–15	D 16–20	E 21–25	F 26–30	A 1–5	B 6–10
Record-keeping sets	D 16–20	E 21–25	F 26–30	A 1–5	B 6–10	C 11–15
Filing sets	E 21–25	F 26–30	A 1–5	B 6–10	C 11–15	D 16–20
Electric typewriters ⎫ Stencil duplicator ⎬ Spirit duplicator ⎭	F 26–30	A 1–5	B 6–10	C 11–15	D 16–20	E 21–25

Note: Electric typewriting, stencil duplicating, and spirit duplicating will be included in the same unit.

The letters refer to the instructional unit; the numbers following, to the students assigned to that unit. Thus during weeks 3–6 in the first semester, students 1, 2, 3, 4, and 5 are assigned to instructional unit A, calculators, etc.

portance of keeping up to date with their work. In such a system, it is obviously impossible to permit a student to remain on any one instructional block beyond the designated period, as the equipment will be needed by the next student assigned to it.

3. COMBINATION BATTERY AND ROTATION PLAN. Because most clerical practice rooms are not equipped with sufficient machines to permit all students to be instructed in a specialized unit at the same time, in many schools the combination battery and rotation plan is used whereby those units that do not require special equipment are taught on the battery plan, while those utilizing office machines are taught on the rotation plan. Units frequently taught by the battery plan include office organization, personality development, reference books, filing, business communications, and job applications. Those usually taught by the rotation plan include office machines, clerical typing, duplicating, and machine transcription.

4. MODEL OFFICE PLAN. In schools using this plan the clerical practice room simulates a business office. The furniture, equipment, and machines are arranged according to departments, permitting the flow of work to proceed through these various departments or areas in the same manner in which work flows through an actual business office. The model office usually has a receptionist, is equipped with a telephone, and includes such departments as filing, duplication, typing, and billing, records, or bookkeeping. Students are rotated through each department in the model office. If properly equipped and arranged, the simulated model office has the advantage of duplicating an office atmosphere and office working conditions. The job assignments that the students complete are designed to integrate previously acquired knowledges and skills and are similar to those they will encounter on the job. However,

Exhibit 7.5

Example No. 1 MASTER ROTATION SCHEDULE — 100 hrs.   5 Rotation Intervals
(15 Students)   20 Hours Each

Intervals	Student Numbers and Rotation Sequence by Intervals				
1	1- 2- 3	13-14-15	13-14-15	4- 5- 6	7- 8- 9
2	4- 5- 6	1- 2- 3	1- 2- 3	7- 8- 9	10-11-12
3	7- 8- 9	4- 5- 6	4- 5- 6	10-11-12	13-14-15
4	10-11-12	7- 8- 9	7- 8- 9	13-14-15	1- 2- 3
5	13-14-15	10-11-12	10-11-12	1- 2- 3	4- 5- 6

INSTRUCTIONAL UNITS

Adding machine (1) 10-key, 10 hrs. (2) Full-key, 10 hrs.	Duplication (1) Stencil, 15 hrs. (2) Spirit, 5 hrs.	Rotary calculator 20 hrs.	Transcribing machine 20 hrs.	Typewriting problems 20 hrs.
A	B	C	D	E

Example No. 2   MASTER ROTATION SCHEDULE — 120 hrs.   6 ROTATION INTERVALS
(12 Students)   20 Hours Each

Intervals	Student Numbers and Rotation Sequence					
1	1- 2	3- 4	5- 6	7- 8	9-10	11-12
2	11-12	1- 2	3- 4	5- 6	7- 8	9-10
3	9-10	11-12	1- 2	3- 4	5- 6	7- 8
4	7- 8	9-10	11-12	1- 2	3- 4	5- 6
5	5- 6	7- 8	9-10	11-12	1- 2	3- 4
6	3- 4	5- 6	7- 8	9-10	11-12	1- 2

INSTRUCTIONAL UNITS

Adding machine (1) 10-key, 10 hrs. (2) Full-key, 10 hrs.	Duplication (1) Stencil, 15 hrs. (2) Spirit, 5 hrs.	Rotary calculator 20 hrs.	Transcribing machine 20 hrs.	Typewriting problems 20 hrs.	Posting machine 20 hrs.
A	B	C	D	E	F

Source: *Teaching Guide for Vocational Office Training*, Part III, Business Education Service, Division of Vocational Education, State Department of Education, Richmond, Va., XLV, No. 10 (1963), 14–15.

since in most instances students must be given basic training in such units as filing, office machines, duplicating, and machine transcription, it is clear that the model office plan cannot duplicate office conditions in all respects.

Teachers who use the integrated or model office plan point out that this teaching procedure emphasizes the importance of production of work that meets office standards, provides an opportunity for students to work cooperatively in completing job assignments, and makes it possible to teach students to apply good work habits in the production of these jobs.

The model office plan frequently creates many instructional problems. It is difficult to determine just how long students will take to complete the various activities assigned to them. Some jobs that involve very little learning may take a disproportionate amount of the class time which should be spent on jobs that would be more meaningful to the students. In some situations the work may consist of jobs that are to be used either by the school or by the community, resulting in the quality of the work being stressed at the expense of correct techniques. When the model office is used for this kind of work, it is sometimes difficult to provide for the lower-ability students. Everyone wants his work done by the most capable persons. Consequently, the students who least need extra practice in the production of office jobs are often the persons who must devote the most time to such work. No matter how carefully the teacher plans the work, the integrated or model office plan still represents an artificial situation. Office conditions may be simulated, but they can seldom be duplicated.

SPECIFIC TEACHING SUGGESTIONS

No course is more challenging to the business teacher than is clerical, secretarial, or office practice. Not only is the content of the course widely varied, but much of the instruction must be highly individualized to meet the needs of each student in the class. Since as many as four or five types of learning activities may be taking place at one time, it is important that the teacher develop as many time-saving instructional devices as possible. The following teaching suggestions are designed to make most effective use of the students' and the teacher's time.

A. *Course Organization*

1. Have both the classroom and the work well organized. If possible, have the entire course outlined before the beginning of the semester. Make adjustments in the outline as they become necessary. Always be sure all supplies and equipment are available when they are needed. Much valuable class time is lost when the work has not been carefully planned in advance.

2. Have the students assist in administrative details such as they will be required -to handle in an office. Assign students to such tasks as distributing and collecting materials, keeping attendance records, preparing requisitions for supplies, filing finished assignments, and serving as timekeeper, payroll clerk, office manager, or receptionist.

3. Have specific jobs that the students are to complete for each unit. The students should know exactly what they are to do, how it is to be done, and when it is to be completed.

4. Do not require all students to complete all the units in the course. Many authorities believe that students who show unusual skills in some areas should be allowed to specialize in these areas. Though all students should be expected to complete a certain minimum number of units, extra credit should be given to those students who complete additional units. However, these units should include additional learnings and should not represent simply

more practice at the same level of difficulty as the basic units all students must complete.

5. Use job instruction sheets in those units where they are practical. Many of the jobs in clerical practice can be taught through the use of job instruction sheets. These sheets free the teacher to move about the class and work with any individual needing his help. No time is lost starting work at the beginning of the period. The job instruction sheet is particularly valuable in office-learning activities. It should identify the machine or the unit to which it applies, the texts or manuals students are to use, and the supplies needed. In addition, it should indicate the jobs or assignments to be completed,

Exhibit 7.6   JOB ASSIGNMENT SHEET

Area B—Rotary Calculators

Texts :   Classwork—Office Machines Course
Homework—Clerical Office Practice

Instructions

1. Read each homework and classwork assignment with the job area, the textbook job number, and/or page number. Be sure your name and the date appear on your work.
2. Write your classwork answers in pencil on a sheet of theme paper and hand in the completed work at the end of each class period.
3. Write your homework in ink on the workbook pages indicated. If no workbook pages are listed, use theme paper. Hand in only complete, neat, and accurate copy.

Classwork Assignments	*Homework Assignments*
Station 1—Friden	
Job 26—p. 65, 1–10, 21–30	Read "Rotary Calculators," pages 134, 135,
Job 27—p. 67, 1–10	and write a brief summary of your reading.
Job 33—p. 83, 1–5	Complete Clerical Exercise 1 on page 136.
Job 25—p. 63, 1–10	Draw a complete form. Indicate whether the
Job 34—p. 85, 1–10	final column answers are plus or minus.
Station 2—Marchant	
Job 28—p. 69, 1–3, 6–10	Complete Clerical Exercise 3 on pages 137–138.
Job 29—p. 72, 1–10	Draw a complete form showing quantity,
Job 30—p. 73, 1–8	description, unit price, and extension for each
Job 34—p. 86, 1–10	section of the problem.
Job 23—p. 59, 31–36	
Section 3—Monroe	
Job 26—p. 66, 1–10, 21–30	Complete Clerical Exercise 4 on page 138.
Job 27—p. 67, 11–20	Draw a complete chart showing department,
Job 32—p. 80, 16–23	amount of sales, number of customers, and
Job 34—p. 86, 11–20	average sales per customer.
Job 29—p. 71, 1–6	

Source : *The Teaching of Office Practice, Grade 12, A Suggested Instructional Guide*, Secondary Department, Division of Curriculum and Instruction, Milwaukee Public Schools, 1966.

together with a step-by-step breakdown of the procedures to be followed. It may also call attention to special points needing emphasis and list review questions at the end. The job sheets may be typed and duplicated by the students in the duplicating unit and filed for use as needed.

6. Demonstrate the operation of each of the office machines. The teacher should be careful to follow the same step-by-step presentation given in the job instruction sheets.

7. Rotate the members of the class through the various units. In most clerical and office practice courses limitations of equipment and supplies make such a procedure necessary. (See Exhibit 7.6.)

8. Use information sheets or handouts to supplement the text. These sheets may cover a wide range of topics, such as grooming, work habits, personality traits, office equipment and supplies, trends in filing and records retention, telephone manners, recent developments in telephone and telegraph services and equipment, office etiquette, and tips to the job applicant. Masters or stencils may be prepared in the duplicating unit. An illustration of an information sheet is shown in Exhibit 7.7.

9. Keep assignments flexible to allow for outside rush jobs, but avoid interruptions unless the jobs will contribute to the students' learning.

10. Give the students actual clerical jobs to perform when such work is available and meets the needs of the class. For instance, the jobs in the duplicating unit should consist of the preparation of materials that may be used in the class. Other projects may include the duplicating of programs for school functions, business forms, and stationery for the letter-production units.

11. Integrate the classwork with the program of the business club, whenever possible. For instance, the preparation of a student directory or a business club yearbook can provide practice in sorting, filing, typing, and duplicating. The writing and typing of a letter requesting a speaker to talk to the business club on a topic such as grooming or office etiquette may be closely related to classwork. The students not only gain practice in composing and typing letters but also have an opportunity to demonstrate rules of good etiquette by seeing that the speaker has a host or hostess who meets him, accompanies him to the meeting room, makes a proper introduction, and sees that a thank-you letter is written and mailed promptly after the meeting.

12. Solve class problems and questions through committees. For instance, if students are not taking proper care of the equipment in the room, assign a committee to determine the value of the machines and other equipment and report back to the class.

13. On the inside of each student's Completed Work Folder, keep a cumulative record of his grades or points on each unit. Then the information is readily available when needed.

14. Ask the students for an evaluation of the course during the final week of the semester. Naturally these evaluations should not be signed.

B. *Bulletin Boards and Visual Aids*

1. Assign committees to prepare posters, charts, and other bulletin-board displays on the various units included in the course.

2. Reserve one section of the bulletin board for your own displays.

3. Store bulletin-board displays in fourteen-by-twenty-six-inch envelopes, with a label on the outside describing the contents and the units with which they are to be used.

Exhibit 7.7 AN INFORMATION SHEET

Rules for Office Etiquette

Office etiquette is based upon good manners. Eleanor Roosevelt once said that "good manners are always important in all contacts in life, but they must spring from real kindness of spirit or they will not ring true." Manners are the heart of courteous behavior. The ideal behavior consists of knowing the proper thing to do and doing it courteously.

1. Phrase your statements tactfully. Many office visitors and telephone callers have been deeply offended because a receptionist was tactless.
2. Give the other person your full attention when he is talking to you.
3. Greet all office visitors promptly. Never ignore an office visitor.
4. Learn to remember names. Everyone likes to be called by name.
5. Announce a caller to your boss before taking the caller in to see him.
6. Give callers with appointments priority over persons without appointments.
7. In making introductions, men are usually introduced to women.
8. In acknowledging an introduction, men always shake hands.
9. Observe the rules of good telephone etiquette. Identify yourself and the company or the person for whom you work.
10. If your boss receives a personal call while you are in his office taking dictation, leave quietly and return when the call is finished. If it is a business call, you need not leave unless the call is an extended one.
11. Be as considerate of all other employees in your office as you are of your boss and other office visitors.
12. Keep your desk neat and clean.
13. Maintain a good working atmosphere.
14. Learn to be on time.
15. Keep your private life separate from your business life.
16. Observe company regulations.
17. Avoid accepting gifts from salesmen or other office visitors.
18. Never indulge in office politics or gossip in or out of the office.
19. Address your boss and other superiors with the proper title of respect.
20. Be courteous in the use of "please" and "thank you."
21. Maintain an impersonal attitude in business matters.

---

4. Prepare bulletin-board exhibits that illustrate current developments in the business office. Such exhibits might include illustrations of filing supplies and equipment, business machines, and the like.

5. Make transparencies of office forms, case problems, and other materials useful in teaching various units.

6. Use films or filmstrips when they can add to or reinforce class discussions. Since such a wealth of visual aids is available, they should be previewed and carefully selected.

C. *Field Trips*

1. Visit a modern, up-to-date office where students may have an opportunity to see the latest office equipment and data-processing installations and to observe the types of jobs performed by office workers. The teacher should

have made the field trip in advance so he may give the students a preview of the equipment and activities they are to observe. The field trip should be followed later by class discussion. Each class member may write a thank-you note to the firm, or the teacher may announce that the best letter will be signed by all the students and mailed to the company.

2. Have students write a report on some efficient, up-to-date office they have visited.

3. If time is limited, select two or three of the best reports on visits to business offices and ask the students to present these orally in class.

4. Ask each student to interview a beginning office worker. In this assignment the student should compose a letter requesting an interview and prepare an interview sheet listing the questions he intends to ask. Then the student should write or present an oral report concerning "The Beginning Office Worker, His Responsibilities, Duties, and Problems."

5. Reverse the Career Day and let local businessmen visit your school to see your equipment, procedures, etc. This is also good for public relations.

6. If you have a club in your department, further the idea of community service by having the members of the club perform clerical services for citizens in senior homes or in nursing homes. They may offer to write letters, address Christmas cards, do typing, etc.

7. Plan a field trip to the United States Post Office to observe the procedures used and to acquaint the student with the quantity of mail that is handled each day. Ask a postal employee to discuss new mail services—delivery the same day between business firms within a city, consulting service to businesses, etc.

D. *Work Habits and Personality Development*

1. Have the students prepare a manual of the instructions given them during the orientation period. While such a manual may be prepared for each student before the course begins, there is considerable merit in requiring students to organize their own.

2. Emphasize the importance of regular attendance and promptness through some type of check-in or sign-in procedure. Library cards and pockets may be stapled to the bulletin board to be used for this purpose. Each student is then responsible for signing in at the beginning of the period and signing out whenever he leaves the room. Require students to make up any time lost through absence or tardiness.

3. Give the students practice in developing skill in proofreading. They should have acquired this skill in typewriting, but regardless of any previous training, too much emphasis cannot be placed on checking one's work carefully in clerical practice.

4. Have students follow both oral and written instructions. The first time instructions are given orally it may be necessary to repeat them, but thereafter such instructions should be given only once.

5. Make students responsible for cleaning their typewriters and changing ribbons. It should not be necessary to remind them to perform these tasks.

6. Demonstrate proper desk arrangement and other work simplification techniques.

7. Teach students to analyze the job and determine how to do it with the minimum of time and effort. Students should learn to organize their work

Exhibit 7.8 FOLDING AND INSERTING LETTERS IN ENVELOPES
(According to principles of motion and time study)

Steps	*Procedures*
1. Materials	1. No. 6 envelopes.
	2. No. 10 envelopes.
	3. Window envelopes.
	4. Letters for envelopes.
	5. Sponge.
2. Working conditions	1. Work on a clear desk.
	2. Lay letters face up on flat surface in front of you. Riffle the sheets so they will not lie directly over each other.
3. Folding letters for No. 6 envelopes	1. Grasp lower edge of paper with left hand and bring it to $1/4$ inch of upper edge of paper.
	2. With right hand crease paper, moving from left to right.
	3. With the right hand fold the right edge about one-third the width of the paper and crease, using the right hand.
	4. With the left hand fold the left edge over slightly less than one-third the width of the paper. Crease with the left hand.
4. Inserting letters in No. 6 envelopes	1. Place envelope to left of the letters, face down with flaps to right.
	2. Grasp envelope with left hand and insert the letter with the right hand.
	3. Insert the folded edge first, with the top of the letterhead at the left end of the envelope.
	4. Stack envelopes toward upper left in pile with left hand. Leave flaps open, address down.
	5. Expose gummed portion of flap and apply sponge with right hand.
	6. Take right hand and press gummed area. Slide envelope down with left hand. Repeat.
5. Folding letters for No. 10 envelopes	1. Lay letters face up on flat surface in front of you. Riffle the sheets so they will not lie directly over one another.
	2. Fold the bottom edge of the letter with the left hand to within one-third of the distance from the top edge. Use right hand to crease fold, creasing from left to right.
	3. Bring top edge down with left hand to approximately $1/4$ inch of first fold. Crease with right hand, from left to right.
	4. Place letter vertically to right side with fold to right.
	5. Take face-down envelope in left hand.

6. Folding letters for window envelopes

    6. Insert letter with right hand, inserting the folded edge (last fold) first.

    7. Seal as directed previously.

    1. Lay letters face up on flat surface in front of you.

    2. Take bottom edge of paper in left hand and fold up to point below inside address (approximately within one-third of distance from top of the paper).

    3. Crease with right hand, from left to right.

    4. With left hand turn the letter face down.

    5. With left hand fold top third back to expose the inside address.

    6. Crease with the right hand, from left to right.

    7. Place letters to right side with fold to right.

7. Inserting letters in window envelopes

    1. Vertically place envelopes face down to left of letters, with flaps open toward right.

    2. Hold envelopes with left hand.

    3. Turn all letters over with right hand. Be sure letters have been turned so that inside address is facing the desk.

    4. Insert the letter with the right hand. Be sure letter is inserted so that inside address shows through window of envelope.

---

and to arrange their materials according to the principles of motion and time study. An illustration of teaching the folding of letters and their insertion in business envelopes according to motion and time study principles is given in Exhibit 7.8.

8. Display outstanding papers on the bulletin board. Try to find some area in which each student excels.

9. Teach the students the value of the equipment and supplies with which they are working.

10. Require students to repeat jobs that are not usable or mailable. Students need to understand that in the office all work must be of an acceptable quality, even when it means working overtime to correct a mistake.

11. Throughout the semester have the students develop a manual that will be useful to them on the job.

12. Teach students to evaluate their own work. Have them complete and sign an evaluation form indicating that they have proofread and corrected the work. The sheet should be attached to the completed material.

13. Have the students rate themselves on a personality rating scale, both at the beginning and at the end of the semester. The teacher may also rate the students and compare the two ratings.

14. Each week post on the bulletin board an actual case situation describing a problem that has arisen in the office. Award bonus points to the student submitting the best solution to the problem. (See Exhibit 7.9.)

Exhibit 7.9 OFFICE CASE PROBLEMS

Case of the Week

Several years ago you moved to Texas to accept a position as secretary to Mr. Hill, president of the Hill Packaging Company. You knew no one in Texas, and Mr. and Mrs. Hill promptly "adopted" you. Mrs. Hill frequently asks you to dinner, and the Hills have treated you as one of the family. Consequently, you are in a quandary when Mrs. Hill comes by the office and leaves their son, Jimmy, age 11, with you while she goes shopping. This now occurs at least once a week. Jimmy is spoiled and difficult to control, and you can accomplish nothing while he is around. What should you do about this situation?

*   *   *

You graduate from college in June and immediately secure a job as secretary with the American Manufacturing Corporation. Miss Miles, supervisor of the office services division, is placed in charge of your "indoctrination." After you have been working a couple of weeks, you begin to realize that Miss Miles believes you were hired to replace her. She apparently feels insecure because she attended a business college for only one year, while you are a college graduate with a major in secretarial administration. Miss Miles criticizes your work constantly and goes out of her way to make life unpleasant for you. You are given all the difficult jobs in the office and are kept so busy you have to work late every evening and cannot even take a coffee break. You believe Miss Miles is hoping you will quit. You are tempted to do so but know that with her attitude, Miss Miles will never give you a satisfactory recommendation. What would you do?

*   *   *

Miss Hammond, who is responsible for materials in the files, frequently has a problem with one of the junior executives, Mr. Baldwin, who insists on keeping files in his desk long past the date on which he has promised to return them. He seems to think any material he takes from the files is his own personal property. When Miss Hammond objects, he points out that it is much more convenient for him to keep any files he is using in his desk drawer.

One day Mr. Allen, another junior executive, requests the file that Mr. Baldwin checked out over two weeks ago. When Miss Hammond asks Mr. Baldwin for the file, explaining that Mr. Allen needs it, Mr. Baldwin says he is not through with it and refuses to return it. What should Miss Hammond do?

*   *   *

You have an assistant in the office who is a whiz in typing and shorthand. You have so much work to do you wonder how you ever managed without her. However, occasionally when she is tired she is careless and makes errors. When you call her attention to these errors, she becomes upset, always cries, and is unable to do much the rest of the day. You find this characteristic very upsetting, and it always has a bad effect on the other office workers. They like the girl and act as though you have been unreasonable about mentioning the errors. However, you do not think it wise to ignore them. The girl is a valuable worker but seems unable to control her emotions. What would you do?

E. *Grooming and Office Etiquette*

1. Have a representative of a charm school or a person who has taught a charm course give the class pointers on poise, charm, manners, dress, cosmetics, posture, etc.
2. Have a fashion coordinator discuss with the class fashions for the beginning office worker, with emphasis upon their budget restrictions.
3. Have the students observe the dress of people working in offices in the area. If a career day is planned where students will be visiting area offices, assign dress as one of the things they should observe.
4. Develop handouts on office etiquette, protocol at meetings, acknowledgment of introductions, etc.
5. Toward the end of the semester have the students come to class dressed as they would dress in the office.

F. *Basic Fundamentals*

1. Use pretests at the beginning of those units in which the students have had some previous instruction to determine areas needing particular emphasis. Be sure to check the needs of individual students in such areas as basic math, grammar, spelling, punctuation, and typing usages.
2. Give a weekly ten-word spelling test on commonly misspelled words.
3. Provide special drills for the improvement of the fundamentals whenever necessary. Obviously there is not time in the clerical practice course to reteach the fundamentals. However, since much of the clerical work in the business office does involve handwriting, spelling, and simple computations, it is important that each student master these fundamentals.

G. *Reference Materials and Library Assignments*

1. Keep an up-to-date resource file of reference material such as articles and pamphlets related to office work that may be helpful to the students.
2. If possible, have the students subscribe to a secretarial magazine—and read it.
3. Have the students do some research in connection with office reference books. Let them study these books and select the ones they would prefer to have on their own secretarial desks. Have them tell why they selected certain books.
4. After students are familiar with various reference books used by the secretary or office worker, make outside assignments using these sources. Make sure the assignments are realistic. These references should include a standard secretarial handbook, the city directory, the crisscross directory, the zip code directory, and telephone directories.

H. *Telephone Techniques*

1. Have each student complete a check sheet on his present telephone techniques.
2. Give the students practice in the correct use of a business telephone. Every classroom should have a practice telephone. Teletraining equipment and accompanying materials may often be obtained from the telephone company.
3. Discuss the recording of telephone messages.
4. Obtain up-to-date brochures from the telephone company.
5. Provide for student practice on the switchboard, if one is available.

6. Have a representative from the telephone company discuss the latest developments and telephone devices.

I. *Typewriting*

1. Give the students practice in typing multiple carbons.
2. Have the students type some difficult statistical projects.
3. When desirable, use practice sets for the clerical typing unit.
4. Give the facts to be included in a letter or memo and have the students compose the message.
5. Have the students prepare a typing unit on the subject of data processing.
6. In some situations, clerical students may type correspondence and other materials for faculty members. This program requires careful supervision by the instructor, since students should only be assigned work that is related to the instructional units in clerical practice. They should not be expected to do an excessive amount of straight-copy typing, and they should never be asked to grade papers.

J. *Filing*

1. Use a practice set in filing whenever possible.
2. Have students file their work each day in two folders, Work in Process and Work Completed. Also have them prepare folders for, and file, handouts and information sheets copied in the duplicating unit.
3. Collect a file of actual business letters for filing practice.
4. If practice sets are not available, have these sets prepared in class during the duplicating unit. This will give experience in assembling and checking.
5. Have each student keep his own tickler file of due dates on assigned problems in all their courses.
6. Integrate data processing on an acquaintanceship level by showing how automation has affected filing and retrieval of records.

K. *Office Machines and Duplicating Equipment*

1. Prepare job instruction sheets and job assignment sheets for all machine units.
2. Invite a representative of one or more office machine companies to demonstrate new machines and explain techniques in using them.
3. Get a roster from the school secretary and have the students make a directory by duplicating the name, address, and telephone number of each student. The directories may be sold and the funds used for the purchase of small supplies and office applicances not furnished by the school.
4. Type and duplicate programs for school assemblies or for business club meetings. Prepare a yearbook for the business club.
5. Demonstrate typing and correcting a stencil and a master. Let the students practice in a group, with each one typing a paragraph on one stencil or master. When the stencil or master is run, compare the quality of duplication of each student's paragraph.
6. Have students prepare a master of a record sheet to be used during the year for recording jobs as they are completed.
7. Have students select two outstanding articles on office work from their library readings and prepare a one-page summary of them. Then have them type a

stencil and a master of these summaries and run enough copies for each member of the class.

L. *Employment Information*

1. Have the students clip an ad from the paper for a job for which they wish to apply. Then teach them to write an appropriate application letter. Emphasize related follow-up letters.
2. Give students practice in filling out application blanks. Have two or three businessmen select from these forms those of students they would like to interview and arrange for these students to be interviewed before all members of the class. The interview should be followed with a discussion of the strong and the weak points in the interview.
3. Determine the type of tests given to applicants in the area.
   Give the students practice on similar tests.
4. Have the students maintain a data sheet, adding new skills and experiences as they are gained. Have the students file a copy of this data sheet, together with a picture, in the school's files.

M. *Miscellaneous Suggestions*

1. Remember that clerical practice should be an activity course. Lectures and even class discussion should be kept to a minimum. Much factual information can be presented through the use of study guides or information sheets. Students should understand that they are expected to study these sheets and that they will be tested on them.
2. Give "blue slips" or demerit slips when necessary; also award "pink slips" for work of unusual merit.
3. Teach students some of the finer points about quality office work—type cleaners, eraser shields, and the like.
4. Acquaint students with the latest office supplies.
5. Occasionally invite former students now employed in office positions to speak to the class. Encourage them to bring examples of the types of jobs they do.
6. Collect files of various clerical jobs performed in local business offices. Note any special terminology used in these businesses.
7. Set up a Question Box and a Suggestion Box for the students' use. Give bonus points for usable suggestions.
8. Have the students undertake one class project during the semester—a class newspaper, a student directory, a Career Day project, etc.
9. Inform students of the current cost of a business letter so they can appreciate what an unmailable letter costs the company.
10. Illustrate the use of colored spirit masters by making tests in different colors.
11. Have the students prepare a list of the office supplies they would need the first day of work in a new office.
12. Have one student a week at the "receptionist's desk." Have this student prepare an autobiographical sketch with a picture, and post it in a special corner of the bulletin board.
13. Let one student in each group serve as a supervisor within each rotation unit. As the students rotate to a new unit of study, appoint a different student in each group to act as supervisor. By the end of the rotation periods, each student will have had the opportunity to serve in this position.

STENOGRAPHIC OR SECRETARIAL PRACTICE

Stenographic or secretarial office practice is designed for those students who have completed one or two years of instruction in shorthand and typewriting. The basic objective is to give the students training in those activities that they will be required to perform as stenographers in a business office. The specific objectives vary widely from school to school. Many of the objectives listed for clerical practice would apply equally well to the stenographic practice course. Like the clerical practice course, stenographic office practice attempts to integrate previously acquired knowledges and skills and to apply them in practical office situations. Considerable attention is usually given to the development of good work habits, attitudes, and personality. A major portion of the time is often devoted to building transcription skill. In an effort to simulate office conditions, some dictation may be given in "office style" toward the end of the course so that the students will be accustomed to the manner in which they will be given dictation on the job.

It is difficult to draw a line between the course content offered in the different types of office practice courses. A comparison of high school textbooks in clerical and stenographic office practice reveals that some of the units included in clerical practice that are omitted in stenographic office practice are handwriting, clerical typewriting, clerical arithmetic, adding and calculating machines, cash records and forms, and payroll activities. The stenographic office practice text may include these units not found in the clerical practice text: receptionist duties; dictation and transcription; secretarial equipment and supplies; letter writing; composition and typing of minutes, manuscripts, and business reports; business reference sources; travel and itineraries; employer's financial and personal records; and banking transactions. Many of the units are identical in both texts, and others are closely related.

OBJECTIVES OF STENOGRAPHIC PRACTICE

Many of the objectives of the stenographic practice course will be similar to those given for the clerical practice course. In addition, however, emphasis will be placed on the development of further skill in transcription and the application of that skill to practical stenographic problems. The *Office Procedures Manual* for the Fort Worth Public Schools lists the following general objectives for stenographic practice:

1. To help the students develop individual concern in the areas of responsibility, discrimination, personal effectiveness, and correct business attitudes
2. To assist students to develop dictation, transcription, and other skills which will make them more effective secretaries
3. To aid the student in better understanding the necessity of a well-planned day, of dressing appropriately, of arriving promptly, of performing "household duties," of being resourceful, of exhibiting initiative, and of being versatile

The manual describes the course in this manner:

> Stenographic practice is a two-semester course; one-half credit is given each semester. The primary purpose is to provide time for additional practice in taking shorthand dictation, to refine shorthand skills, and to practice transcribing mailable copy.
>
> The course will be taught in the larger schools in conjunction with the advanced shorthand class. Since more and more students will be taking beginning and advanced typing in Grades 9, 10, and 11, it will be necessary to offer stenographic practice to provide time for shorthand transcription especially. In the smaller schools, where students enroll for only one year of shorthand instruction, this should be taken in the junior year and stenographic practice elected in the senior year. In this case, a great amount of class time will be spent on additional dictation and transcription, and a lesser amount of time on stenographic duties as such. The two courses will vary in nature, depending on the needs of the students. In some schools, students will already possess a knowledge of such skills as filing and machines, especially if they are concurrently taking the VOE laboratory plan. In these classes it will be the responsibility of the teacher to adapt the course according to individual needs. It may well be that some students in the class will need the additional practice in one phase of stenographic practice and some in other phases.

UNITS IN STENOGRAPHIC PRACTICE

It has already been pointed out that many units taught in clerical practice are also included in stenographic practice. Most teachers, however, devote considerable time to improving their students' transcription skills. The units designed to meet the objectives in stenographic practice are outlined in the Fort Worth *Office Procedures Manual* as follows:

A. Careers as a Secretary
B. Personal Improvement
C. Grooming and Styling
D. Performing Necessary "Household" Duties
   1. Lighting
   2. Ventilation
   3. Sharpening pencils
   4. Filling pens
   5. Checking ash trays and matches
   6. Making coffee
E. Planning Day's Work
   1. Organizing personal desk
     a. How to use reminder system
     b. Calendar
     c. Typewriter
     d. Dictation materials
     e. Inventory supplies

2. Checking employer's calendar
3. Making notations of appointments
4. Confirming reservations or appointments
5. Placing needed files on employer's desk
6. Opening, sorting, and routing mail
7. Arranging mail in order of importance on employer's desk
8. Organizing personal work in order of importance

F. Performing Daily Routine Jobs

G. Taking Incoming Telephone Calls (Use teletrainer.)
1. Screen Calls
   a. Personal handling
   b. Employer's attention
   c. Delivery of messages promptly
   d. Telephone courtesy
   e. Employer's telephone policy
2. Rerouting or transferring to specific departments
3. Using judgment in placing and accepting personal calls

H. Placing Outgoing Telephone Calls
1. Calls for employer
2. Long-distance calls
3. Reservations or appointments

I. Coffee Breaks
1. Company policy
2. Relations with co-workers

J. Relationship with Others
1. Loyalty to company or employer
   a. Interest in advancement
   b. Participation in company activities
2. Chain of authority
3. Integrity
4. Cooperation with others
5. Social amenities

K. Office Receptioning

L. Business Correspondence
1. Dictated correspondence
2. Memorandums, messages, follow-up letters
3. Routine mail
4. Instructions on transcriber
5. Transmission of telegrams
6. Acknowledging flowers or considerations
7. Extending company sympathy letters

M. Maintenance of Accurate Files
1. Company filing (alphabetic, geographic, numeric, etc.)
2. Responsibility for locking files
3. Personal and general files

N. Business Meetings and Reports
1. Data for written or oral reports
2. Arranging final report
3. Minutes of company meetings
   a. Reserving meeting room

b. Contacting members
c. Preparing agenda
d. Having water and ash trays on hand

O. Financial and Personal Records

1. Employer's personal business records
2. Firm records
   a. Making checks and balancing checkbooks
   b. Making deposits
   c. Keeping record of donations and requests
3. Petty cash
4. Use of listing machines
   a. Ten-key adding
   b. Full-key adding

P. Duplicating Procedures

1. Operation of common types of duplicating and copying machines
2. Multiple carbons

Q. Travel Arrangements

1. Planning itinerary for employer
2. Preparing papers for business trip
3. Confirming hotel reservations and transportation schedule
4. Keeping employer informed of activities while out of town
5. Arranging for travel funds and expense account

R. Mail Service

1. Knowledge of postal regulations and services
2. Accuracy in addressing mail
3. Caution with attachments, enclosures, and special notations
4. Addressograph for large mailings
5. Folding machines
6. Familiarity with postage meter

S. Supervision of Other Workers

1. Tactful cooperative approach
2. Constructive criticism

T. Business Ethics

U. Reference Materials for Greater Job Efficiency

1. Secretarial books and booklets
2. Business newspapers
3. Business periodicals
4. Dictionary
5. City directory
6. Criss-cross directory
7. Hotel guide
8. Almanac

METHODS OF TEACHING STENOGRAPHIC
OR SECRETARIAL PRACTICE

The course in stenographic or secretarial practice is ordinarily taught the same number of periods a week as all other courses in the school. Usually it is one period in length, though in some schools a double period is allotted to it. The content of the course and the manner in which it is taught will depend largely upon the previous shorthand courses the students have completed. In those schools where one year of shorthand is required prior to enrollment in stenographic or secretarial practice, much of the time is devoted to further skill development in shorthand and transcription, with only a limited amount of time being devoted to such other activities as filing, duplicating, and office machines. The major objective of the course is to enable the students to produce mailable transcripts at an acceptable rate and at the same time provide for the inclusion of such knowledges and understandings as are involved in receptionist duties, grooming, office manners, business ethics, and correct telephone usage.

In schools that require students to have completed two years of shorthand prior to enrolling in stenographic or secretarial practice, the objective of the course is primarily that of utilizing skills previously acquired, teaching new skills and understandings, and integrating all of these into problem-solving situations similar to those a beginning office worker may encounter. In this situation some of the new learnings, skills, and understandings may be taught following the usual formal classroom procedures. In other units the students may be given specific jobs to perform, or they may be given cases to solve in which they will have to utilize many of the skills and knowledges they have already acquired. Some types of cases dealing with relationships in the office may be handled through class discussions, while other cases involving numerous activities requiring decision making and judgment will be completed by students working individually, in pairs, or in groups. Both of these procedures make use of the problem-solving approach in preparing students for the office.

SPECIFIC TEACHING SUGGESTIONS FOR STENOGRAPHIC PRACTICE

Many of the teaching suggestions given for clerical practice may be used equally effectively in stenographic practice. Other suggestions that may be helpful to the teacher include the following:

1. If possible, use the workbook that accompanies the text. It will provide business forms as well as excellent problem-solving assignments.
2. Avoid too much class discussion, recitation, and lecture presentation. On the high school level, stenographic practice should be primarily an activity course in which the students are given an opportunity to build skill in the production of office-type jobs.
3. Use case problems that have occurred in business offices as the basis of class discussion when teaching the importance of correct attitudes, judgment, cooperation, and other related qualities needed by office workers (a number of actual cases are given in Exhibit 7.9).
4. Try to obtain letterheads now out of date or on which printing errors have been made from local business firms and printers. This quality of paper makes it possible for the teacher to require neat erasures.
5. Do not correct all the students' transcripts. They should be taught to be responsible for locating their own errors. Check production tests carefully.

6. Keep two folders for each student, one containing work that has been completed and the other containing work in process. Students should be responsible for checking their papers in these folders and correcting all errors in their transcripts.

7. Give the students extensive practice in building transcription power. Emphasize the importance of both speed and accuracy in transcription.

8. Give the students definite goals. Time the students on their transcription production so that they may determine their rate of progress. Indicate either in words a minute or in number of letters what their transcription rate should be throughout the course.

9. Give the students some practice in taking office-style dictation and in transcribing such material.

10. Teach the students how to make the most effective use of their shorthand notebooks.

11. Teach the students good work habits, both in taking dictation and in transcribing.

12. Emphasize the importance of good tools with which to work in transcription—good quality paper and carbon, the right kind of typing erasers, erasing shields, and so on.

13. Stress the cost of wasted supplies caused by careless errors.

14. Occasionally interrupt students during the transcription period. Office workers are constantly being interrupted in their work and must learn to cope with such interruptions.

15. See that all students have an opportunity to build skill in transcription on electric typewriters.

16. Do not limit the dictation and transcription practice to business letters. Include practice in completing business forms, preparing business reports, typing minutes, and the like.

17. Have the students keep a list of their spelling errors and test them on these words occasionally.

18. Review important principles of grammar, punctuation, capitalization, and typing usage.

19. Provide some practice in the composition of letters and telegrams.

20. Teach the students to record all instructions in shorthand in their notebooks. Do not always provide written instructions or permit them to rely upon memory.

21. Occasionally dictate letters and other material to be mailed.

22. Review the correct techniques for inserting multiple carbon packs, chain feeding of envelopes, correcting bound manuscripts, and other specialized typing problems.

23. Assign one student a week to the "model secretarial desk." The student should be responsible for doing any stenographic or secretarial work that the instructor may assign to her. Insofar as possible, these jobs should consist of actual office work rather than simulated office activities.

24. During the latter part of the course, assign some dictation projects that will integrate many of the skills and knowledges that have been emphasized in the course. A carefully designed office-style dictation project will provide practice not only in transcription of office-style dictation but also in such skills as typing multiple carbons, making corrections, selecting correct titles in the

inside address and salutation, handling all kinds of letter problems (additions, deletions, postscripts, carbon-copy notations), composing letters and memos.

25. Occasionally collect the students' notes of material dictated during the class period and have them transcribe these notes several periods later. This procedure is an excellent way to impress upon the students the importance of writing accurate shorthand outlines.

THE VOCATIONAL OFFICE EDUCATION PROGRAM

The *vocational office education program* is designed to meet the needs of those students who have specific career objectives in office occupations.[1] The program was originally funded under the Vocational Education Act of 1963 and was further expanded under the amended act of 1968. Schools offering approved vocational office education programs may be reimbursed for 50 percent of their expenditures for furniture and equipment purchased for use in the program as well as for 50 percent of the teacher-coordinator's salary and travel expense.

The basic objective of the vocational office education program is no different from the objective of the clerical or stenographic office practice program—preparing students for office employment. Basic differences do exist, however, in the funding of the programs, in the time allotted to them, and in many instances in the teaching procedures utilized. Each state is free to develop the plan or plans that it will follow, as long as the overall state plan is in accordance with the provisions of the federal act and is approved by the United States Office of Education. This procedure gives each state considerable latitude in developing the plans it will utilize in its vocational office education programs, with the result that the programs offered in different schools throughout the country vary widely. Regardless of the vocational office program that a particular school utilizes, it should be remembered that the vocational office education program is a segment of the total business education program in the school. It is not and cannot be a separate entity. In many states, because the vocational office program is only funded for the twelfth year, the vocational office teacher must depend upon the other business teachers in the school to develop the basic skills students need for admission to the vocational program. What these prerequisites will be are largely determined by the student's career objectives. For example, if the student wishes to do general office work, he will usually be required to have had one year of typing before enrolling in the vocational office program. If he wishes to be a bookkeeper, he will usually need to have completed one year of typewriting and one year of bookkeeping. A girl interested in the stenographic area will be required to have completed a minimum of one year of typing and one year of shorthand. In such instances the success of the vocational office program will obviously be strongly dependent upon the quality of instruction the students have received in their typing, bookkeeping, and shorthand classes. In

[1] Some states designate this program as *cooperative office education*. However, since not all federally aided office programs include cooperative work experience, the broader term *vocational office education* is used in this discussion.

other words, the basic skills are ordinarily taught before the twelfth year and are frequently not a part of the vocational office program. The specific technical and related information needed by the student on the job is taught as a part of the vocational office program.

TEACHING PROGRAMS FOR VOCATIONAL OFFICE EDUCATION

As was mentioned earlier, the programs being used today in vocational office education vary widely. Some of the most commonly used techniques will be presented here, but it is recognized that variations of these basic plans may be found in many schools. Because similar terminology is often used to describe programs that differ in basic organization, the term used to describe each of the programs here will be carefully defined. Most vocational office programs today are operated under one of the following: (1) the cooperative plan, or (2) the intensive laboratory, block plan, model office or simulated office plan.

Cooperative Office Programs

In most cooperative office programs students spend one or two periods in the morning with the teacher-coordinator and work in the afternoon. The teacher visits the student on the job and talks with the student's supervisor. He coordinates the class instruction with the student's learning procedures in the office. Some units of work, such as grooming, office etiquette, business ethics, and applying for a job, will be needed by all students regardless of the duties they perform on the job. These units may be presented through group instruction. Other units must be taught on an individualized basis. Some units that can be taught to the students as a group must be taught on an individual basis because a few students may need instruction in these particular skills or job activities immediately after reporting to work, while other students may need to develop other skills. In many programs the students spend considerable time studying on an individual basis material that is directly related to their occupational goal. The course of study is based on the job requirements as determined by a job analysis made by the teacher-coordinator with the assistance of the employer. In developing the course of study, attention should be given not only to the job analysis of the training stations where the students will be working but also to any occupational clusters that may be noted. A student who is trained in a cluster of occupational skills in the area of office education will have a better opportunity for initial employment than the student who is skilled solely in the performance of a highly specialized task. The vocational office program is especially well suited to equip students with a cluster of job skills, so that they not only are highly specialized in one area but can adapt to employment changes when they occur. For example, the stenographer probably needs some training as a receptionist, while the receptionist or switchboard operator often needs to be competent in typing.

The cooperative plan gives students an opportunity to receive instruction in a realistic setting. The students can put into practice the knowledges and skills previously learned in the classroom, and at the same time they are acquiring additional skills and knowledges on the job. Thus students receive both general and specific office training.

In addition to the benefits the students receive from the program, the school is provided with valuable business contacts. The resulting feedback indicates the effectiveness of the classroom teaching and provides the teacher-coordinator with information regarding the procedures, systems, and equipment in use in local business offices.

While the cooperative office education program is found in hundreds of high schools today, it is seldom taught according to the plan that has been described here—although many teachers sincerely believe they are following these procedures. All too often the class sessions are taught in the same manner as any other clerical or office practice course. Although much may be learned during these class periods, the teacher who does not actually coordinate the class work with the activities the students perform on the job is not conducting a true cooperative office training program. He is teaching an office practice course in the morning, and the students are participating in a supervised work experience program in the afternoon. This may, however, be a better procedure than that sometimes encountered where most of the class time is devoted to individualized study of the policies, organization, and office procedures of the particular company for which each student is working. In this situation, a student may learn a great deal about a narrow specialization in the office of one company but may not acquire many of the new learnings that should have been incorporated in the course. In other words, a cooperative program, to be effective, requires a well-organized program which can, at the same time, be highly flexible. The classwork will include those units that all students should cover and will provide flexibility for scheduling individualized instruction in work that each students needs and which will be coordinated with his job activities.

Intensive Laboratory, Block Plan, Model or Simulated Office Plan

In the intensive laboratory, block plan, or model office plan, a two- or three-period block is used for group and individual instruction in office skills and related information. Ordinarily the student is first given a brief orientation to the model office and the procedures to be followed. He is then placed in a specific position in the company or assigned to a specific department. Departments frequently found in the model office program include sales, purchasing, accounting, records management, and secretarial services. There may also be a receptionist or a general manager. During the semester the student will rotate through the various departments. In some model office plans, the students possess a common core of skills and knowledges and are therefore expected to perform all the jobs encountered in the various departments. In other situations, where students have different occupational objectives, they perform only those jobs related to these objectives. For example, some of the students may have elected the bookkeeping sequence, while others may have elected the stenographic sequence. Obviously their previously acquired skills and knowledges would be vastly different and would not permit them to perform all the jobs that might be included in the simulated office program.

To be effective the model office program requires careful planning on the part of the teacher. He must know the career objectives of his students and then determine what should be accomplished through a simulated office operation. The office jobs to be performed must be prepared or selected, and any special materials needed must be prepared in advance. Some teachers use an office manual that simulates the manuals found in many business offices. Since the students will be working on many different jobs in different departments, all these jobs and accompanying materials must be ready at the beginning of the program. If a student supervisor is assigned to each department, the teacher may serve as the office manager. Otherwise, the teacher must supervise each department and will provide individual assistance or instruction as it is needed.

While the model office plan does provide a businesslike atmosphere in most schools, this simulation has certain limitations. At times there are areas of work in which the students have not had previous instruction. If the students have not had an office practice course before enrolling in the model office program, they must usually be given basic instruction in office machines, duplicating, filing, and machine transcription. At such times even when the instruction is on an individual or a small group basis, the office becomes a classroom. Until the students have acquired some basic skill in these areas, they cannot perform simulated office jobs. Unless the teacher is familiar with the work performed in offices in the vicinity, he may have difficulty in developing the office simulation.

Advocates of the model office point out that since this program is completely controlled by the business teacher, the students may obtain a wider variety of work experience than they will encounter if they are enrolled in a cooperative office program. In addition, the students can see the overall operation of an office and can develop an understanding of the relationships of individual departments within the company's organizational structure.

STATE AND CITY VOCATIONAL OFFICE EDUCATION PROGRAMS

In Ohio the business and office education program at the secondary level is divided into two parts. The *cooperative office education program* is offered during the twelfth grade and the *intensive office education program* during the eleventh and twelfth grades. The cooperative office education program brings together terminal students in different areas in business and office education.

The *intensive pre-employment* and/or *in-school secondary business and office education program* is a two-year program at the eleventh- and twelfth-grade levels and is designed for students who need depth training in skills and related areas of office occupations education and who cannot or are not yet ready to participate in a cooperative office education program. The intensive office education program consists of laboratory and related instruction designed to teach the skills basic for employment. The intensive laboratory enrolls only students having the same occupational objective. Students in this program have usually completed general business, business arithmetic, one year of typing, and one year of bookkeeping. The intensive office education program is divided into specialized areas—stenographic, clerk typist, general clerical, account clerk, and a special clerical services program. Students must complete a minimum of 1,080 clock hours of business and office education instruction in one of these specialized areas.

Each student in the intensive laboratory program attends a three-hour laboratory five days a week during the eleventh and twelfth grades in high school and is given concentrated instruction in the particular program he has elected. The clerical service program is a special program for handicapped persons and persons needing remedial instruction in addition to training in basic office occupation skills. The intensive laboratory program is operated on a systems approach by occupation, with six to eight teachers working with the students in one large room.

THE PHILADELPHIA COOPERATIVE OFFICE PLAN

In Philadelphia the cooperative office plan is one semester in length. Each job is filled by two students so that the students may work one week and be in school one week. During the fall semester, prior to their cooperative work experience, diagnostic tests are given to determine each student's ability in arithmetic, vocabulary, and grammar. Office skills such as typing, shorthand, transcription, and filing are also checked. During this semester further instruction is given in typing, shorthand, English, office practice, and information on job preparation and orientation.

Before assigning a student to his cooperative job station in the spring, the coordinator considers each student's previous scholastic record, attendance record, personality inventory, scores on aptitude tests, and level of office skills. He is then able to match the students with the jobs available. Each employer, however, interviews two students and selects his preference.

During the spring semester when the students are enrolled in the cooperative office program, instruction is given on both a group and an individual basis. Each student receives any special training needed for his particular job. The coordinator visits the students on the job regularly and maintains close contact with the employers. Following each visit, the coordinator holds an individual conference with the student, and the work that the student needs is planned for the coming week when he is back in school.

EVALUATION

Whether the course offered is office machines, office practice, or clerical practice, grades should be based on the achievement of specified objectives. If personal qualities and attitudes are to be considered in grading, then the margin of improvement should be considered. When evaluating rates of production, the teacher should consider office standards as well as the progress that the individual student has made. While all too often businesses have failed to set production standards for office work, the following are illustrative of the standards found in business offices in some metropolitan areas:

Copying	60–70 words a minute[2]
Addressing envelopes	2–3 a minute, depending on length of address
Four-line fill-ins	125–150 an hour
Stencils (8½×11) paragraph typing	3½–5 an hour
Transcription from records	125–240 lines an hour
Short form letters	12–14 an hour
Short form letters with carbons	10–14 an hour
Operating rotary calculator	Addition of 5 digits per column, 6 digits per item, 3 problems a minute
	Subtraction of 5-digit minuend, 5-digit subtrahend, 4 problems a minute
	Multiplication of 5-digit multiplicand by 5-digit multiplier, 4 problems a minute
	Division of 5-digit dividend by 5-digit divisor, 3 problems a minute

Many companies have still not adopted specific standards for measuring the performance of clerical workers. The critical shortage of clerical and office workers has forced businesses in many places to lower the standards set for hiring beginning office workers and has impeded efforts to establish standards for specific clerical jobs. Businessmen continue to report that clerical workers are deficient in spelling, English, typing, knowledge of office routines and basic business information, arithmetic, and shorthand skill. Teachers should consider these weaknesses in determining course content and in evaluating students in clerical and stenographic practice.

All too often standards appearing in business publications are not realistic. Because the nature of office practice, clerical practice, and stenographic practice varies from school to school, the teacher of this course must often develop his own production tests and determine the standards students will be required to meet. Standards will thus be dependent upon the importance of the particular unit, the time allotted to it, and the duties students will be expected to perform in the business offices where they will be employed. If the teacher is able to secure minimum employment standards from these companies, he may be able to utilize these standards in arriving at the minimum requirements for some of the units in the course.

Teachers follow widely different procedures in grading students in office practice. Many teachers use the point system. In this system each job to be completed is assigned a specified number of points. Students are required

---

2 In some cities where an acute shortage of clerical workers exists, fifty words a minute is considered an acceptable standard.

to complete a minimum number of points on each unit, and the jobs that must be completed are designated. Each job must be completed satisfactorily for the student to earn the points assigned to it. If the job is unsatisfactory, the teacher may require the student to repeat the job without credit, repeat the job for credit, or do another job, or she may deduct a number of points from those assigned the job. Individual grades are assigned on the basis of total accumulated points. For example, one thousand points might be required for an *A*, eight hundred for a *B*, six hundred for a *C*, and so on. This plan has the advantage of being definite and objective. However, the entire grading plan must be worked out before the beginning of the course.

Other teachers require the students to complete a certain number of jobs for a *C*, additional jobs for a *B*, and more advanced jobs for an *A*. Still others assign grades on the basis of the quality of the work. The problem of grading in office and clerical practice can be greatly simplified if all jobs are set up in advance and the students are told what they must do to meet the requirements of the course.

It is recommended that teachers consider the desirability of administering civil service examinations and the National Business Entrance Tests to their clerical and stenographic students during the final weeks of the course. Teachers using the National Business Entrance Tests can compare the performance of their students with that of other students throughout the country. In addition, students who pass the tests receive a certificate of proficiency which they may show to prospective employers when they are applying for an office position.

PROBLEMS AND CASES

1. What units do you believe should be included in both secretarial and clerical practice? What units are suitable only for clerical practice? What units should be offered only in secretarial practice?

2. Your principal, Mr. Hutton, wants you to teach a clerical practice course next year. You tell him you do not believe the school should try to offer a clerical practice course because the only equipment available is typewriters. Mr. Hutton says he would like to be able to purchase some office machines, but there just isn't any money for additional equipment at this time. He does tell you that you may plan to use the duplicating equipment in his office which includes a mimeograph, a spirit duplicator, and a copying machine. He also indicates that there is a little money which you may have for the purchase of workbooks and other supplies. Since Mr. Hutton insists that you teach the course next year, what units will you include? What supplies or workbooks would you need?

3. You are teaching a clerical practice course for the first time. Your principal seems to think that the main objective of the course is to give the students practice in completing typing and duplicating jobs for his office and for other members of the faculty. You are glad to have the students get some practice in these areas, but you feel the students also need to learn other skills such as filing and machine transcription. How would you handle this situation with your principal?

4. You are teaching an office practice course in which twenty girls and five boys are enrolled. The only prerequisite for the course is one year of typing. Some of the girls have had a year of shorthand, and all the boys have had a year of bookkeeping. You had planned

a course in which all students would complete every unit. However, the boys object to the unit on machine transcription, insisting that this is "girls' " work. Since this is the first time any boys have enrolled in the course, you simply had not anticipated this problem. What can you do to make the course more attractive to the five boys?

5. Some of your students in clerical practice can complete their assignments much more rapidly than other members of the group. You have tried to solve this problem by assigning additional problems to the students who finish early. These students are beginning to object to this practice. They contend that the extra problems are simply busy work to keep them occupied and that since they were able to finish the work correctly before the other members of the class, they certainly do not need additional practice problems. What is wrong with your present procedures and how should you correct them?

6. Last year was your first year of teaching. During the first few weeks, you discovered that your clerical practice class contained both students of low ability and students of average or even high ability. As a result you were constantly having difficulties with the class. The problems or projects that the low-ability students were able to complete were much too simple for the rest of the class. On the other hand, when you selected more difficult material, the low-ability students were unable to handle the work. At the end of the year, you ask the principal to restrict the enrollment in clerical practice to students of average ability or better. He replies that clerical practice is one course in which low-ability students should be able to experience some success and that he has no intention of depriving these boys and girls of the opportunity to get some vocational training. In fact, he points out that perhaps you were the one who failed in the course, not the students, and suggests that during the summer you give some thought to ways in which you can plan a course outline that will include instructional units that will be beneficial to any level student electing the course. What type of course outline would you develop?

7. You are teaching in a school that has been offering one year of bookkeeping, one year of shorthand, and one year of typing. The school has decided to add to the curriculum a one-year course in general business and a second-year course in typewriting. Since few of the girls attain vocational proficiency in the one-year shorthand course, you believe that it would be better to offer an additional semester of typing and one semester of secretarial practice. The principal, however, says such a plan would be impractical, as there would be no course for the nonshorthand students to take the second semester. He wonders whether in the second year of typing you cannot include some secretarial units for the girls who are interested in this area of work. What would you tell him? If you think it could be done, what units in secretarial practice would you include? How would you handle a typing class in which part of the students were doing typing jobs and part were completing secretarial units?

8. Because you wanted your secretarial students to have some actual office experience, you assigned each girl to one of the faculty members. At the beginning of the second semester, the faculty was sent a memo indicating that the girls were to be given dictation and that they were not to be used simply to type or grade papers. At the end of a month, you realize the program is not working as well as you had anticipated. Several of the girls complain that the only jobs they have been given are the typing of tests and instructional materials and that they are frequently asked to grade the papers, operate the duplicator, and run personal errands, none of which involves dictation or transcription. In checking the carbon copies of the letters that some of the other girls have typed for the teachers to whom they were assigned, you find gross errors. When you talk to the teachers, they laugh and say that they corrected the letters in pen and ink, that the girls were cute and pretty, and that they just couldn't ask them to do the letters a second time. What can you do to improve the structure of this program?

9. Recently, a local businessman was highly critical of Mr. Jackson, a business teacher in your department. He complained that none of his students could spell, that they knew

nothing about punctuation, and that they could not even add a column of figures accurately. He agreed that his students were good typists and that they could take dictation rapidly, but he felt it was the business teacher's responsibility to make sure students could perform neatly and accurately the duties assigned to office workers.

Mr. Jackson insists that his job is to teach the students to type and do shorthand and that the English teacher should teach the students to punctuate and the math teacher should teach them to add. He feels it is unfair for businessmen to blame the business teachers for deficiencies in these areas. Do you agree with Mr. Jackson? Why or why not? If you do not agree, what would you do to make sure your students were proficient in these areas?

10. The school in which you are teaching offers a course in clerical practice and a course in office practice. The only prerequisite for either course is one year of typing. Most of the basic units in the two courses are similar. However, since the lower-ability students are enrolled in clerical practice, they require longer to complete these units than do the students in office practice. Consequently office practice contains several additional units of work. You are teaching clerical practice, and your colleague, Miss Gordon, is teaching office practice. Miss Gordon insists that those units common to the two courses should be graded by the same standards. You are equally convinced that since you are teaching the lower-ability students, these students should not be expected to attain the same performance standards as the office practice students. How would you resolve this problem? What reasons would you give to support your solution?

11. Up to this time your office practice room has been equipped with electric typewriters, transcription machines, a spirit duplicator, and a mimeograph. Your principal tells you that you may order five adding-listing machines or calculators for next year but that he wants all five machines to be the same type and make because he has a limited budget for service charges. What machine would you select? Why?

12. Recently your division chairman attended a meeting in which the speaker stated that in his opinion electronic data-processing equipment would, within five years, make all clerical and office practice courses obsolete. It was his opinion that schools should be offering training in the operation of electronic data-processing equipment. He added that the only other business course that the public schools could justify including in the curriculum was typewriting—that in the future typewriters would be used to secure direct access to the information stored in computers. Now your chairman is debating whether he should drop office practice from the curriculum! What specific facts can you supply your chairman to support your view that office practice is important and should continue to be a part of the business curriculum?

13. Your principal has agreed that you may teach a class in clerical practice in the spring semester on an experimental basis. Since the course has never been offered before, the principal says he cannot approve the purchase of any textbooks until he is convinced that there is a need for the course and that it will fulfill a need of the students in the school. Thus you are faced with the problem of having to develop your own instructional materials and duplicate copies for the students.

> a. Prepare a job instruction sheet designed to introduce students to the electric typewriter.
>
> b. Prepare a job instruction sheet for students to follow their first day on machine transcription.
>
> c. Prepare an information sheet on "Good Grooming."
>
> d. Prepare an information sheet on "New Office Supplies and Small Office Appliances."

14. You have carefully prepared job instruction sheets for each unit included in your clerical practice course. The directions are detailed, and a step-by-step breakdown is given of the procedures students are to follow. You find that many of the students in the class are such poor readers that they cannot follow the directions and frequently do their work incorrectly. What changes or adjustments would you make in your teaching approach?

15. Miss Wilson, the other business teacher in your school, says that there is no justification for ever failing a student in clerical practice. Do you agree? Why or why not?

16. You have been teaching an office practice course in your school. Your principal tells you he is going to make application for funds under the Vocational Act of 1963 to support a cooperative vocational office program which will replace your present office practice course. Since the school is located in a metropolitan area, you agree that the students should be receiving this type of training. Under the new program, as coordinator you will have twenty students in class and will work with them for one hour each morning. In the afternoon you will supervise the students on the job. How will the instruction you give the students during the one-hour period in the morning differ from the instruction in the office practice course you are now teaching?

17. Your school hopes to receive funds for vocational office education under the provisions of the Vocational Education Act of 1963. The school is located in a rural community with a population of three hundred. Your principal favors setting up a cooperative vocational office program. Since there are very few businesses in the community and many of these are too small to provide the students with good job training stations, you believe the school should offer a block or intensive laboratory program. Write a report to your principal indicating why this approach should be used in your school. Describe fully how a block or intensive laboratory program will differ from the cooperative-type program he is considering.

18. You have twenty-five students enrolled in clerical training, all of whom have completed general business and one year of typewriting. The equipment in the clerical practice room includes five miniature filing sets (alphabetic, geographic, subject, and numeric), four electric typewriters, a mimeograph, a spirit duplicator, three ten-key adding-listing machines, three full-keyboard calculators, three transcribing machines, ten manual typewriters, and a large filing cabinet.

    a. Set up the rotation schedule you would use to teach a one-semester clerical practice course under these conditions.

    b. Indicate the materials you would use to teach each unit.

    c. Indicate the job assignments you would require the students to complete in each unit.

19. You are the cooperative office education teacher in your school. Most of the students in your program come from low-income families and may be described as economically and socially deprived. You know that many of the students in your classes have serious difficulties with English and mathematics, and therefore you are not surprised when employers begin to complain about the quality of their work on the job. The situation has become so serious that it appears it will be impossible to secure training stations for next year's cooperative education students. What do you think should be done to solve these problems? What recommendations would you make to your principal, if any?

20. Helen Young is enrolled in your clerical practice course. During the second week you discover that she has not had the prerequisite of beginning typing but is now enrolled in the course. As many of the topics involve typing activities, you are afraid Helen will have difficulty with the course. When you discuss the matter with the principal, he explains that Helen, up to this fall, had been taking an academic program. During the summer her father had been killed in an automobile accident, and not only is it going to be impossible for

Helen to attend college because of the family's financial situation, but the girl must find work as soon as she finishes high school to help support her younger brothers and sisters. Because of these problems, the principal flatly refuses to consider your request that Helen drop the subject. He feels that Helen will need the course to help her secure employment upon graduation. How can you help Helen?

SUGGESTED READINGS

Archer, Fred C., "A Formula for Enriched Training," *Business Teacher*, November–December 1967, pp. 14–15.

———, "Practical Tips for Better Office Practice," *Business Teacher*. New York: Gregg Publishing Division, McGraw-Hill Book Company, 1961. Special Reprint.

———, "Selecting a Model Office Plan," *Business Teacher*, March–April 1968, pp. 26–27.

———, *The Clerical Training Program in the Large High School*. New York: Gregg Publishing Division, McGraw-Hill Book Company, 1961. Special service brochure.

Barger, Virginia, "Office Simulation: An Effective Technique," *The Balance Sheet*, February 1970, pp. 259–61.

Berry, Doris, "The Role of Office Practice Instruction in the Training for General Office Assignments," *Delta Pi Epsilon Journal*, February 1965, pp. 35–52.

Business and Office Occupations Handbook, Curriculum Bulletin No. 506, Fort Worth Public Schools, Fort Worth, Texas, 1969.

Business Education Forum, National Business Education Association, February 1947–71 Clerical Practice Issues.

Cook, Fred C., and Eleanor Maliche, "Office Machines Used in Business," *Delta Pi Epsilon Journal*, May 1966, pp. 1–15.

———, and Francis Brown, "Status of Office Machines Equipment in American Secondary Schools," *The Balance Sheet*, May 1967, pp. 391–94.

Curtis, Etta May, "Through the New Media Approach to Office Practice, *Business Education Forum*, February 1969.

Harrison, Lois Y., "What Business Looks for in Clerical Workers," *Foundation for Business Education*, March 1967, pp. 16–18.

Hodges, Gail T., "Clerical Training for Special-Needs Students," *Business Education World*, December 1969, pp. 2–3.

Huffman, Harry, and Dale D. Gust, "Business Education for the Emergent Office," The Center for Vocational and Technical Education, The Ohio State University, Columbus. U.S. Department of Health, Education, and Welfare, Office Of Education, Bureau of Research, Project No. 8–0414, June 1970.

Iannizzi, Elizabeth, "[Preparing Office Clerical Workers] Through Experience in Making Decisions," *Business Education Forum*, February 1967, pp. 9–13.

Kilchenstein, Delores, "Planning a Rotation Unit," *Business Education Forum*, February 1968, pp. 11–14.

Malsbary, Dean R., "A Profile of Beginning Office Workers in the State of Connecticut," *The Balance Sheet*, May 1968, pp. 401–3.

Matsuyama, Janet, "A Model Secretarial Laboratory Initiated in a California Junior College," *Journal of Business Education*, February 1969, pp. 190–1.

Office Education, Division of Curriculum and Instruction, Milwaukee Public Schools, Milwaukee, Wisconsin, 1968.

Office Procedures Manual, Curriculum Bulletin No. 503, Fort Worth Public Schools, Fort Worth, Texas, 1969.

Paddock, Harriet L., "Personnel Needs for High-Level Secretarial Positions," *Delta Pi Epsilon Journal*, February 1969, pp. 17–22.

Rollason, Peggy Norton, "That Extra Plus in Secretarial Training," *Business Teacher*, May–June 1969, pp. 12–13, 28.

Straub, Lura Lynn, and E. Dana Gibson, "Office Practice Equipment," *American Business Education Yearbook*, National Business Education Association, 1963.

Teaching Guide for Vocational Office Training, Part III, Business Education Service, Division of Vocational Education, State Department of Education, Richmond, Virginia, 1963.

Teaching of Office Practice, Grade 12, Secondary Department, Division of Curriculum and Instruction, Milwaukee Public Schools, Milwaukee, Wisconsin, 1966.

Tonne, Herbert A., Estelle L. Popham, and H. Herbert Freeman, *Methods of Teaching Business Subjects*, Chap. 15. New York: Gregg Publishing Division, McGraw-Hill Book Company, 1965.

Wagoner, Kathleen P., "The Role of the Secretary in a Changing World: An Analysis of the Duties and Functions Performed by the Secretary," *Ball State Journal*, May 1968, pp. 3–9.

III

the nonskill subjects

As already indicated in the *Overview* to Part II, the subjects considered in Part III may often require special teaching techniques and procedures specially adapted to developing physical skills and abilities. Thus the teacher will at times continue, in these subjects, to use adaptations of many techniques and procedures already presented.

However, it is the belief of the authors that the subjects presented in Part III will *best* serve their educational purposes if the teacher considers them *primarily* to require teaching methodology of the nonskill-development type. Thus the teacher should learn judiciously to devote a major portion of his teaching efforts to those techniques and procedures calculated to best achieve the many understandings, attitudes, and other mental developments associated with these subjects.

It should be understood that often the objectives of a given course, a given school, and a given teacher will require and will justify the treatment of a course as being primarily skill development, whereas under other circumstances it might best be treated otherwise. Unless unusual factors intervene, though, the business teacher will do well to treat the skill-development factor as relatively minor in the teaching of the subjects presented in Part III.

In one sense this simplifies the teaching of these subjects, since the rather specialized psychology of skill development is absent or of less importance. Yet it raises another problem for the teacher: the natural interest and motivation that accompanies skill development will be absent or less noticeable, and thus the teacher must give special attention to the proper planning for adequate motivation.

8

TEACHING THE BASIC
BUSINESS SUBJECTS

An integral and important element of the secondary business education curriculum consists of those nonskill subjects referred to by business educators under various titles. These subjects have been designated within a broad framework as *basic business* education or *social business* education.

These courses are included in the business education curriculum not only because they provide the business student with knowledges, procedures, and understandings about the business world but, more importantly, because they have a general education objective—that is, their content is valuable for *any student* to master in his basic role as a responsible citizen in our economic society.

Courses falling into this category in the secondary business curriculum are generally identified by names such as these:

General business
Business law
Consumer business
Business mathematics
Business English
Economic geography
Business organization

The methodology and the teaching techniques best suited for the various courses in basic business education are quite similar, and those described in this chapter are applicable in some form or another to most of the courses listed above.

We will begin with a presentation and description of methodology for teaching the course *general business,* as this subject is one of those most frequently taught in the basic business category. Brief descriptions of problem areas in teaching will be identified for the other courses listed, but the methods student should keep in mind that the methods utilized for teaching general business are applicable to all basic business courses.

GENERAL BUSINESS

General business was formerly an exploratory course designed and taught for a select group—those students of limited ability who were quite likely to drop out of school before graduation. Consequently, the content of the course was elementary and superficial.

While it was claimed by business educators that the general business course was valuable for all students regardless of whether they were on a vocational or a college preparatory track, this claim did not hold true. Fortunately, in the late 1960s business educators realized that a *new* general business course should be developed, one that did substantiate the claim. The subject matter was upgraded, and an emphasis was placed upon economic understandings and business consumer practices.

The importance of these types of understandings has been greatly increased through the interest shown by state and federal authorities in developing government-sponsored organizations to give citizens both a better understanding of our economic system and helpful consumer protection information.

Objectives of General Business

The objectives of teaching general business in the high school can be summarized into four principal goals:

1. To develop in the student a knowledge of those business activities that affect everyone regardless of economic status.

Everyone is a participant in business activities in normal everyday life. It is the purpose of a course in general business to analyze these activities and to enable the student to understand, appreciate, and perform them in the best possible manner.

2. To develop in the student an ability to improve his competency as a consumer of business activities.

Everyone is a consumer of products of business. Through an improvement of consumer practices there should result an improvement of the activities of business enterprise and a consequent improvement of the welfare of the individual.

3. To develop in the student an understanding of the economic concepts under which our free enterprise system works.

In order for an individual to be well educated it is necessary for him to understand those basic economic principles that affect his economic well-being, both as an intelligent citizen and as a consumer.

4. To develop in the student certain attitudes and appreciations with respect to our free enterprise economy.

Too often in our schools, teachers have taken for granted certain benefits and advantages of our economic system and have failed to give students an opportunity to discover for themselves the many advantages that result from the economic system under which our country operates. This does not mean that students should be propagandized or indoctrinated. In a study of any economic system, an analysis should be made of shortcomings as well as superior features. Teachers sometimes have neglected the latter, taking them for granted, and have only pointed out the former with the resulting danger of developing cynical attitudes in students.

The Content of a General Business Course

Several excellent textbooks in general business are available for use by the business teacher. One thing common to most texts is the topics that are usually covered. Authors of the textbooks may give different treatment to the various topics or may present the material differently, but basically the units of subject matter are as follows:

SUBJECT-MATTER UNITS TYPICALLY TAUGHT IN A GENERAL BUSINESS COURSE

1. Relationship of the individual to the business world
2. Economic relationships and free enterprise
3. Money and banking services
4. The role of the consumer in business
5. The use of credit
6. Insurance and risk management
7. Savings and money management
8. Travel, communication, and transportation services
9. Consumer aids and protection
10. Government relationships to business
11. The free enterprise system
12. Economic citizenship in a free enterprise economy

Although at first glance the units of subject matter in the foregoing list may appear to be highly technical for study by a high school freshman or sophomore, the teacher must remember that the treatment of the several topics is not exhaustive and that the authors of the textbooks attempt to relate the units to the everyday business activities that a high school student may find himself experiencing. The objectives are to *familiarize* the student with and introduce him to the many and varied business activities that will have an important effect upon his life.

College Courses That Will Aid the Teacher in Teaching General Business

There are many college courses in which knowledges gained should be of invaluable aid in the teaching of general business in the high school. Such courses as introduction to business, accounting, economics, management, money and banking, marketing, consumer behavior, and finance are a few that should be especially valuable.

Careful preparation of notes taken in college courses in the areas mentioned above, combined with the saving of textbooks used in these courses as a basis for a permanent reference library, will be of great aid in teaching general business.

INSTRUCTIONAL MATERIALS

The Extent of Instructional Materials

The extent and the availability of instructional materials for the teaching of general business are almost limitless. Some modern textbooks are supplemented by workbooks, teacher's manuals, practice sets, and tests. These textbooks are kept up to date through frequent revisions and are well illustrated and extremely teachable.

Another vast source of instructional material lies in films, filmstrips, pamphlets, and graphic illustrations which are made available to teachers and students through trade associations and business firms. Many of these materials are either free or available at a nominal cost, so that the business teacher can build up an extensive library of supplementary instructional materials with little or no expense. These materials cover a wide range of topics but can be classified under the general heading of "economic appreciations." Consequently, teachers find these supplementary materials quite valuable for enriching the general business class.

The teacher should carefully sift the material thus obtained to eliminate that which might be prejudicial or biased. There is such a wealth of material that the teacher can pick and choose only that which has true educational value and thus eliminate material that attempts to distort facts. Bibliographies of free and inexpensive instructional materials are listed at the end of this chapter.

Methods of Using Instructional Materials

There are many methods by which the various instructional materials available for teaching general business may be used to the best advantage. The textbook, of course, should be used as the basic guide for the course. This does not necessarily mean that the textbook material must be followed by the teacher and students in exactly the same order presented by the author. The teacher should feel free to change the order of presentation as he sees fit. The interests and aptitudes of the students in the class should be the determining factors in this matter. No one unit of subject matter in general business is particularly dependent upon another. Thus, it is not necessary to master one unit before proceeding to another. There may be a logical presentation of subject matter as indicated by the authors of the text, and it may well be that the teacher should follow the order of presentation as the simplest means of organizing the course. However, the teacher should not feel it mandatory and should experiment with different orders of presentation if it would appear more desirable from the standpoint of appropriateness and expediency. The text, then, should be used as a guide for the course, but not necessarily a rigid one.

Although all the textbooks written for general business are rich in illustrative and textual material, the teacher will find it advisable to supplement the text with the many types of supplementary material mentioned above. These supplementary materials can be used in a variety of ways.

One highly desirable method is to enrich the teacher's method of presentation. It is stimulating to a class when the teacher brings in new areas of knowledge that are beyond the scope of the textbook. It not only helps to motivate and develop interest on the part of the students but also helps to develop a respect for the knowledge of the teacher. Students like to have pertinent materials brought into the class discussion for which they see an application of the textual matter.

The use of an opaque or overhead projector to illustrate visually pertinent and up-to-date material related to a topic being studied is very effective.

For example, preparing a transparency for use on the overhead projector of material such as illustrated in Exhibit 8.1 can be used effectively in teaching a unit on occupational information.

Another method of using supplementary instructional material is the development of a reference library for individual student and class projects, including displays of pamphlets and charts pertaining to the topic being studied. Reliance on the school library for sources of information for these types of activities is not wise, for often school libraries are woefully inadequate with regard to resource materials for business.

Supplementary instructional materials can also be used to motivate students who are unusually interested in a particular unit, as these students will have an opportunity to develop their interests further. This technique is also an excellent means of providing for individual differences in students.

The material should be made accessible to the student by having it placed in a filing cabinet appropriately filed by subject. If a filing cabinet is not available, it will be up to the teacher to use his ingenuity to provide some means of storing the material so that the students may have access to it. It may be desirable to have the class aid in collecting material, storing it, and filing it. This could be an extremely worthwhile class project. Care should be taken that the material is stored neatly and is properly replaced when it has

Exhibit 8.1

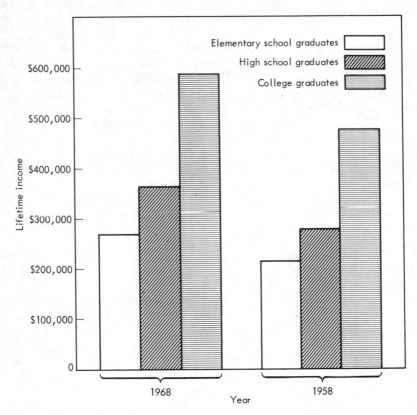

Lifetime Income

Lifetime income of $358,000 is the average estimated by Census Bureau for males 18 years of age in 1968. Level of education and likely future earnings are correlated. Completion of eight years of elementary school would point to lifetime income of $277,000 or 23% below the average. The detailed estimates by the Census Bureau indicate that four years of high school should add $94,000 to bring lifetime income to $371,000, four years of college should add another $213,000 for a lifetime income of $584,000, and graduate study of one or more years should add another $52,000 for lifetime income of $636,000.

For all men estimated lifetime income from age 25 to death increased from $243,000 in 1958 (in 1968 dollars) to $348,000 in 1968, or 43%. Estimated lifetime income of these men who completed 4 or more years of college was $580,000 in 1968—67% above the average; in 1958 this group's lifetime income was estimated to be 91% above the average. Estimated income from 25 years of age to death for high school graduates was 12% above average in 1958 but only 4% above in 1968 while those with only an elementary school education could look to an estimated lifetime income 24% below the average in 1968 whereas in 1958 it was only 18% below the average.

been used so as to avoid the appearance of a cluttered and disorderly class-room. Besides the learning of subject matter, this type of project has several other educational values, such as instruction in filing, neatness, and responsibility.

The Community as a Source of Instructional Material

A rich source of instructional material for the teacher of general business is the community in which the school is located. Business activities and the results of business activities can be found everywhere. The local grocery store, telephone exchange, bus depot, drugstore, grain elevator, and manufacturing concern are just a few of the many sources in a community to which the teacher may go to obtain supplementary materials for his class. No community is so small that business activity is nonexistent. Too often, teachers overlook the obvious business establishments in their local communities whereby knowledge obtained in the classroom can be seen in action. Look about you to see what is available and then use these sources to enrich your classes.

METHODS OF TEACHING GENERAL BUSINESS

Problems in Methodology

Before taking up specifically the various methods of teaching that pertain to general business, we should consider some of the problems that are involved in the methodology. If we can pinpoint these problems perhaps we will then be able to understand some of the difficulties involved in teaching this subject and should be able to appreciate better the need for some of the recommended methods.

First, it is fairly well established that business teachers in general prefer to teach the skill subjects such as shorthand, typewriting, and office practice rather than the so-called nonskill subjects into which category general business falls. The reasons for this preference are that business teachers are usually better prepared for teaching the skill subjects, the teaching methods are very specific, and the results of instruction are obvious. It can be easily ascertained by a teacher whether a student is improving in his typewriting or shorthand ability. However, in general business where not only subject-matter knowledge is acquired but also certain attitudes and appreciations are a desired outcome, it is difficult to measure the extent to which these latter disciplines are developed in the student. This situation can be frustrating to a teacher. Also, it is sometimes true that while teachers obtain sound subject-matter training in college courses that have application to the teaching of general business, they obtain little training in the methodology of teaching general business. When taking *skill* courses the prospective teacher can see approved methodology in action. When taking *nonskill* courses the prospective teacher does not get an opportunity to see methodology in action that will be appropriate for use in a secondary school classroom.

The type of methodology that can best be used in teaching general business, such as informal discussion, is seldom seen in the typical college class. The prospective teacher has little or no opportunity to observe this type of method because he is not a participant in a discussion but a listener—a "jotter-downer" of notes and too often a "parroter" of the instructor's lecture.

This latter difficulty points to a second problem often experienced by teachers of general business. The emphasis placed upon the mastery of subject-matter knowledge in college courses is often so impressed upon the prospective teacher's mind that he will insist upon the same level of and degree of attainment on the part of his high school students. There is probably no better way to destroy interest in a high school general business class than to insist upon detailed mastery of the subject matter. General business textbooks are full of detail. Too many teachers insist that their students master all this detail, which in actuality destroys the chances of achieving the major objectives of the course. There is no implication here that knowledge of subject matter is unimportant. It is important in its proper perspective. That perspective is *how the subject-matter knowledges may be used to understand the broader concepts to which they apply.*

A *concept* is a mental image or insight one has about an idea or a related group of ideas. The concept results from the knowledge one has about the idea and is reflected in his attitude and point of view toward the idea. Factual knowledge without application of this knowledge in the development of a concept is meaningless.

For example, a teacher of general business in teaching about automobile insurance might be quite satisfied if his students have learned about the various kinds of auto insurance available and the particular function each serves. However, this information is important only to the extent that the student develops a concept of the risks involved in owning property and, more important still, the concept of the sharing of economic risks.

To illustrate: Teacher A in presenting a topic on automobile insurance requires that his students memorize the various kinds of insurance available, such as liability, comprehensive, collision. A student can memorize these satisfactorily and can explain their function without having the slightest idea of the purpose of insurance. On the other hand, Teacher B (who is much wiser) will develop with his students the idea of the sharing of economic risk through the medium of insurance and will then determine what these various risks are. By this method of developing the concept of risk sharing he will develop mastery of subject matter in his students as a matter of course.

A third and final problem that causes some business teachers to prefer not to teach general business is that, relatively speaking, this subject is much more difficult to teach than the skill subjects because of the methodology involved. The general business teacher in presenting a lesson must primarily use a class-discussion technique, which involves a great deal more preparation than do the drill and problem techniques typically used in teaching a skill. A teacher can hide inferior ability in the teaching of a skill subject much more easily than can an inferior teacher of general business because of the very nature of the class. In a typewriting class, for example, the teacher can assign work for the students to perform in class individually and the teacher can remain passive with respect to the teaching function. In a general business class the teacher must always be active in performing the teaching function and cannot hide his inadequacies (indefinitely) through class-time assignment.

So much then for the problems in methodology encountered by the teacher of general business. Let us turn to some of the specific methods that can be used.

THE DISCUSSION

Many business educators believe that the *best* method of teaching general business in the secondary school is through the use of the discussion technique. Undoubtedly it is one of the best procedures for learning and teaching, because the learner not only has to acquire the subject matter of a course but also must be able to use it effectively in communicating ideas and facts to others.

Several different types of discussion techniques may be appropriate for use in the secondary school classroom. Some of the procedures are rather informal, whereas others are highly formal. Although some of the formal discussion techniques can be used effectively with high school students, it is probably true that the more informal techniques will be most successful.

Two main types of informal discussion are pertinent for use in the general business classroom. The first can be called simply *classroom discussion*. In this type of discussion the entire class participates in the topic being discussed, with the teacher guiding and directing the class. It is this factor of teacher direction and guidance that makes this type of discussion different from the other informal types. More will be said about this later.

A second method of informal discussion is the use of the *committee,* or *round table.* In this method, if it is used properly, a small group of students discusses a problem informally before a class in a conversational manner. The discussion is pointed up by the chairman of the committee; after the conclusion of the discussion by the committee the topic being discussed is referred to the students in class for contributions and questions.

To be effective the committee should get together several times prior to their scheduled meeting to organize their presentation so that a definite direction and purpose can be achieved. Too often the use of a committee merely results in four or five students giving four or five reports with the use of small group discussion becoming nonexistent.

In using the committee technique the teacher must assume the responsibility for working with each committee to see that the discussion objective is not lost. The teacher does not have to dominate by any means, but neither can he forgo all responsibility for the guidance of learning. Committee techniques will fail unless the teacher properly supervises the group.

CLASSROOM DISCUSSION

For a majority of teachers of general business, informal classroom discussion that is both teacher guided and teacher directed will be best. Many educators believe that discussion cannot be used effectively in large classes. It is the opinion and experience of the authors that the size of classes will not materially affect the degree of discussion. On the contrary, large classes may improve the quality of discussion.

The reasons put forth for the effectiveness of classroom discussion in small classes or groups only are that in this manner everyone will have an opportunity to participate and that in small groups the timid person may be willing to participate more often.

These reasons would perhaps be valid if it were considered necessary for everyone to participate every day in the discussion. If the discussion techniques are used the majority of the time in the classroom, then it is logical to assume that some time during the semester everyone will participate. It does not always hold that in a small group the retiring student will tend to talk more. The retiring person will not be any more willing to speak up in a small group than in a large group. He is the problem of the discussion leader (teacher), and if the proper procedures are used he will assume his share of the participation in the class.

The following elements should be considered for effective participation in the discussion method.

Setting for the Discussion

The physical setting for informal discussion is highly important if the discussion technique is to be used effectively. If the classroom has movable furniture, desks should be arranged so that the participants may see each other. The teacher should identify himself with the group so that the psychological barrier of a desk between the teacher and the students is removed. Adequate chalkboard space should be provided for use in listing discussion points or summarization of the discussion or illustration. Students participating should speak loud enough to be heard by everyone.

Another important factor in an effective discussion is the relationships among the students and the teacher. A friendly atmosphere must prevail, with everyone having the feeling that he has something worthwhile to report. Each contribution should be accepted as important. Courtesy, tolerance, and attentiveness should prevail. The discussion should not develop around the theme of argument, but of enlightenment.

Techniques of Informal Discussion

Several major techniques are basic with respect to teacher action in using the discussion methods. In the majority of cases in classroom discussion the teacher should act as discussion leader, starting, controlling, and pointing-up the group expression in such a way as to provide a common sense of achievement.

Considerable preparation should be made by the teacher before a topic is discussed in class. Judgment should be made as to the appropriateness and nature of the problem in question. Too many teachers fail in using the discussion techniques because of inadequate planning.

Successful discussion cannot start from scratch. Students cannot discuss intelligently without knowing something or at least having some conception about the topic being discussed—even though these conceptions are erroneous ones.

It is necessary, then, that prior to the discussion the teacher assign for reading the topic that will be discussed the next day. He should point out the particular areas of information that are important to the study. The teacher should then plan with considerable care the means by which he will get the discussion launched. It is easy to say merely "start discussing," but high school students do not react or always cooperate in this way. *The teacher must develop a way to start the discussion that will stimulate and challenge the student.* Discussions seldom arise from direct, specific, or factual questions. The teacher may think that he can start a discussion by asking the class to "discuss the functions of commercial banks." Very little if any discussion will be obtained through the use of this type of direct question because the question calls for a specific answer rather than the uses, values, and analysis of the activities of commercial banks.

In starting a discussion, comparative, analytical, judgment, or evaluative-type questions should be raised by the discussion leader or teacher. The following types of questions are illustrative:

1. Several financial authorities have stated that in the very near future we will be living in a "cashless" society—that because of the extensive use of computers by which a customer's purchase can be charged immediately and directly to his account at his bank there will be no need for cash to change hands. Computers will handle all these transactions. What do you think of this procedure and can you see any advantages or disadvantages, or both?

2. The two major economic systems in the world today are the free enterprise system and the communistic system. Do you believe it is possible for these two systems to operate in the same world without conflicting with each other?

3. Federal and state governments have passed many laws and regulations whose primary purpose is the protection of the consumer. Should there be a limit or some restriction on governmental action in this area? Do you believe there has been any infringement on an individual's freedom of choice?

The use of questions such as those listed above would result in the teacher obtaining answers similar to those received from a direct question approach. However, additional advantages would accrue. The students would be stimulated to think through the various problems involved and by so doing the various interrelationships would be developed. In addition, the students would be encouraged to participate in a discussion in which their various ideas would be heard and evaluated rather than merely "parroting" back some points listed in a textbook.

Many pitfalls may befall the discussion leader if he is not aware of them—such dangers as sidetracking or getting off the subject, monopoly of time by a few people, nonparticipation by members of the group, and lack of a feeling of accomplishment. This latter pitfall is probably the most dangerous one for both student and teacher because in the discussion method intellectual growth and maturity is difficult to envision.

Discussion pitfalls can be circumvented by good preparation prior to the discussion. Also, certain mechanical techniques may be employed to good advantage. Charts or forms developed for the discussion on the chalkboard or a flannel board can be used effectively. Typical outlines that may be used are:

Problem

Possible Solutions   *Recommended Solutions*

Issue

Reasons For   *Reasons Against*

Another technique that may be used to advantage is that of "buzz sessions" within the class. In this device the class is divided into small groups of four or five people, with each small group discussing the general topic and then reporting back through a spokesman the results of the discussion. In this way the benefits of small groups are achieved and class activity is varied.

To illustrate how classroom discussion technique might be used in a general business class, let us assume the following fictitious situation:

Situation

For the past several weeks a class in general business has been studying a unit on credit. The topic for the next several days which has been assigned is installment buying and borrowing money for making purchases. The teacher has asked the class to read the chapters in the textbook pertaining to this topic and be ready to discuss the material tomorrow in class.

Procedure

The teacher sets the stage for the discussion of the topic by developing the following case problem. This problem is duplicated and passed out to the class.

Charles Green is a sophomore in high school and is sixteen years old. He has obtained a driver's license and is a capable driver, but his father will seldom let him use the family car. Charles would like to have a car of his own and has found one in a used-car lot that can be purchased for $500. Charles has saved $150 which has been deposited in a building and loan savings association which pays interest at 5 percent. The owner of the used-car lot is willing to accept this $150 as a down payment on the car if Charles will pay off the balance at the rate of $21.50 a month for the next eighteen months. Charles gets an allowance from his parents of $5 a week for performing specified jobs at home.

Charles's father has no objection to his buying the car, but he refuses to assume any responsibility for it. He does insist that Charles buy liability insurance before he gives his consent.

What are some of the factors Charles should consider before buying this car? What are some of the problems he will have if he does buy it?

Points that should be raised from discussion

1. Of what quality is the car and what are the problems that may arise from maintenance costs?
2. How much interest will he have to pay?

3. How much will he lose by taking his savings out of the savings association?
4. What are the operating costs of the car?
5. Are there any nonquantitative factors that should be considered?

The development and use of short case problems such as that illustrated is an excellent means of stimulating thought and discussion on the part of students. Cases can be developed quite easily by the imaginative teacher, and they can be related to the experiences that can be understood by the students.

In the illustrated case an emphasis would not be placed upon such specific topics as the advantages or disadvantages of installment buying, or how to compute carrying charges. Actually these things are not important in an isolated state. A person may know or memorize the disadvantages of buying on credit, but if he actually desires something, typically, he will not weigh his desire in terms of whether to purchase or not to purchase. It is much more important that he discover how to solve his problem by thinking of all the difficulties that may be involved. This is what he will or should do as an adult, and if he will use these techniques as he will in solving the case problem, then the student has learned. He has not filled up his mind with abstract facts that will soon be forgotten, but he has seen how he must use these facts to help him solve his problems, which in the last analysis is the process of becoming educated.

Advantages of Informal Discussion

There are several advantages in the use of the discussion techniques in teaching. Some of the more important of these are:

1. Discussion requires both listening and speaking. Consequently it should provide information and stimulate thinking.
2. Discussion requires a student to learn that he must apply the subject matter of his studies, that he must become competent in using ideas in his thinking and in applying them in solving problems.
3. Discussion speeds up the intellectual activities of the student, for the group sets the pace which is often more rapid than that of most individuals.
4. Discussion stimulates the student to express his ideas and thus they become clearer to him, for as he talks he must arrange the ideas in logical sequence so they can be more easily followed.
5. Discussion provides opportunity for actual practice in learning and teaching how to solve problems.
6. Discussion often adds materially to a participant's stock of ideas.
7. Discussion provides opportunity to correct erroneous ideas and false information.
8. Discussion lends itself easily to the consideration of particular problems that confront students.
9. Discussion affords opportunity for testing, for the student discovers his own strength and weakness. These are revealed to him by the inadequacy of his conceptions, his lack of understanding, and his omissions and neglect of study.
10. Discussion stimulates original thinking as distinguished from imitative thinking.

Disadvantages of Informal Discussion

The discussion technique is by no means a panacea for all our ills in the teaching of general business. There are several disadvantages to the use of discussion; these should be pointed out. Specifically, some of the disadvantages are:

1. Certain limitations arise from the nature of groups generally—heterogeneousness with respect to abilities, intelligence, interest, and mental alertness.
2. It is slow and time-consuming.
3. It is limited to certain types of subject matter; it cannot be used to determine scientific fact.
4. Often a student is thinking more about what he intends to say when he has a chance to say it than about what others are saying.
5. It is unsuccessful unless those who participate have considerable knowledge that pertains to the questions to be discussed.
6. Sometimes certain traits and characteristics found in teachers negate their use of discussions.

In summary, the following factors are the important ones to consider with respect to the use of the informal discussion method in teaching general business in the secondary school.

1. *The group spirit of the class*—unless the class is willing to cooperate with the teacher in using this method as compared with the traditional question-answer technique, it will not be successful.
2. *The teacher's skill in dealing with certain types of individuals in the group*—
   a. The loquacious members who talk on every possible occasion
   b. The assertive and dogmatic member who talks without evidence
   c. The nonparticipating and shy member
   d. The antagonistic member who is angry with the teacher or with the members of the group
3. *Comprehension of the techniques employed in the discussion method*—too often teachers attempt to use discussion techniques while not fully comprehending the procedures involved. Both class and teacher morale will usually break under this condition with the result that both teacher and class will dislike the group approach.
4. *Qualities of the teacher*—the ability of the teacher, as leader of the informal discussion, to be sufficiently flexible mentally so that he can adapt or change method and procedure quickly and adjust immediately to the thinking of the group will be of paramount importance to the success of the group discussion method.

QUESTION-AND-ANSWER METHOD

The question-and-answer method has often been confused with classroom discussion. Many teachers have erroneously thought they were using discussion when using the question-and-answer method; actually there is little similarity between the two methods.

The question-and-answer is a telling method with the telling being mutual between the teacher and the student. The teacher raises a question and asks that either volunteers or a specific student give the answer. The answer is usually in the form of a factual description of the contents of textbook material. The teacher will often elaborate on the answer returned by a student before going on to the next question.

Question-and-answer requires factual background on the part of the learners. It appeals to learners who like to get specific, factual knowledge, and it appeals to their feeling of accomplishment when doing so. However, because of this factual element, the use of this method will contribute little to the obtaining of the objectives set out for a course in general business.

There are some advantages to the question-and-answer method, as it can be used effectively to spot individual weaknesses, difficulties, and interests, thus enabling the instructor to adapt his instruction to student background. Some valuable uses of the question-and-answer method might be:

1. Check reading assignments.
2. Secure and maintain attention or contact.
3. Explore student background.
4. Develop informational background.
5. Set the stage for discussion.
6. Involve nonresponsive students in class activity.
7. Reveal student difficulties, work habits, interests, and levels of development.
8. Develop factual basis for a principle or a generalization.
9. Review work covered.
10. Motivate students to read assignments.
11. Prepare for tests.

Many of the questions to be used in this technique may be written into the lesson plan. The questions should be well phrased, definite, and clear. It is usually more effective to state the question first before the entire group and then direct it to some specific individual. Such a practice tends to keep the group on the alert.

MISCELLANEOUS TECHNIQUES

Group and Individual Projects

Written and oral reports, notebooks, accumulations of information about various aspects in general business, and posters and displays are some of the projects that can be used effectively in teaching general business. These projects may be used on both an individual and a group basis. If at all possible the projects should not be specifically assigned by the teacher to the students but should come as suggestions from the students. Assigned projects lose their appeal to students because they are assigned.

Getting students to suggest or volunteer to work out a project will tax the motivational ability of the teacher to the utmost. However, the successful teacher is one who can accomplish this task without the students being aware that the idea did not stem from themselves.

Some student or students will be overeager in this respect, while others may have a disinterested attitude. The conscientious teacher will attempt to stimulate all his students to do something in this direction.

The students may be motivated to work out a project in several ways. If a topic that is currently being discussed in class appears to have special interest to the group, the teacher may ask the class (or individuals in the class) if they know of any means whereby the topic may be explored further. Through careful questioning the teacher should be able to get some student or group to suggest a specific project.

In one freshman and sophomore class a discussion was being carried on concerning the newer methods of packaging goods. A friendly argument developed as to whether people could tell the difference between a cake baked from a packaged mix and one baked by mixing all the ingredients by hand. The teacher suggested that the only way one could really tell was by comparison. Students in the class volunteered to bake a cake using both methods and bring both cakes to class to see whether the members of the class could actually determine the difference.

The foregoing example could be severely criticized as a "frill"; someone may object that a project of this type has no place in the general business class. However, the wise teacher can use this type of project to point out how demands by consumers on manufacturers for more convenient ways of packaging goods often result in higher prices. A discussion could be developed as to the pros and cons of this sort of thing, with resulting learning taking place in important economic concepts.

Sources of information for student projects can be developed by the students with the teacher's help. The teacher must stay in the background, however, and make suggestions only when they are asked for. The teacher's file of supplementary instructional materials will be quite valuable here, and he should be constantly building up the file for this purpose.

Field Trips

Tours and visits to business firms are another means of valuable instruction in the general business class. Classroom learning becomes more meaningful if students have the opportunity to see some of the concepts learned in class actually in operation. Plans for the field trip should be made by the students if at all possible—under careful supervision of the teacher. The trip should be planned well in advance, and the group should be oriented on what to look for at the place to be visited and also on what is to be accomplished. After the trip is concluded, a thorough discussion should be held concerning what has been seen and what has been learned. Specific techniques for conducting a field trip can be obtained from various publications available to the business teacher. It is important here only to point out that this type of technique can be a valuable supplement to the classroom instruction.

Field trips are often considerable trouble and take much planning on the part of the teacher, but the values received are often worth the trouble. Students often consider the field trip a lark and a means of having a good time. There is nothing wrong with having a good time on a field trip, but the idea should not be lost sight of that primarily the trip is an educational venture. It should be pointed out to the students that they are representatives of the school and that any improper behavior will reflect not only on themselves but on the school as well. Generally, students on a field trip will behave as the ladies and gentlemen they are, but occasionally one or two individuals will not conduct themselves properly. The teacher, if he knows his class well, will undoubtedly know those individuals who may cause problems and will take steps prior to going on the trip to eliminate any embarrassing situations.

The teacher should also make sure that the administration of the school and the other teachers are informed about the trip well in advance. It is often necessary for the students to miss other classes. Tact and courtesy should be used in making sure that other teachers in the school are in accord with the trip and that any disruption in the normal procedure in the school is met with the minimum of inconvenience to others.

Teachers in small schools are often located in rural areas where visiting opportunities are limited. However, many values can be obtained from visiting the local grocery store, filling station, garage, or mill, even though these establishments are not large. The student may be very familiar with the business establishment as a consumer, but visiting the business from the point of view of determining and learning how it operates will often open his eyes to many things he had not noticed before.

Audiovisual Aids

Audiovisual devices are commonly employed by many teachers of general business, and the technique is found to be quite valuable. Recordings, films, posters, and displays pertaining to business are available from many sources, and much of the material is extremely worthwhile. The teacher should have some knowledge of what the film contains so that he can judge its appropriateness for the class. Some films, for example, contain propaganda and advertising and have little in the way of concrete information. It is impossible to get away entirely from this sort of thing, but the teacher should watch and choose his films judiciously.

The teacher should also be careful to make sure that the visual aid is an educational device and not one of amusement. Excessive use of films tends to fit this latter pattern to the extent that the class is not aware of the important aspects of knowledge that can be obtained from observation.

Methodology in General

The capacity of the teacher to vary his procedure and to adapt his method to fit the abilities and attitudes of the class will be an important factor in his success or failure. The use of only one method to the exclusion of all others will be boring to both students and teacher. Certain units of subject matter will adapt themselves to the use of particular methods whether it be discussion, question-and-answer, project, or individual instruction. The effective teacher must be flexible enough to determine what method best suits the subject being taught and then use that method. In some instances this may involve changing methods even in the middle of a class period.

Another important consideration will be how the teacher presents his method. Enthusiasm, vitality, and dynamic action on the part of the teacher will determine whether a particular method will succeed. The dull, lifeless teacher will have little success regardless of how able he may be in the technicalities of method. The dynamic teacher through such things as gestures, voice, and enthusiasm will accomplish much in maintaining interest and enthusiasm on the part of his students. Motivation accordingly will be less difficult.

EVALUATION AND MEASUREMENT

One of the major problems of the general business teacher is the measurement and evaluation of the abilities of his students. This is a problem with all teachers regardless of ability or experience. It is probably a greater problem with superior teachers because they realize their limitations and inadequacies in this respect more than do the inferior teachers. It is not intended, at this point, to go into the specific details of developing measurement and evaluative devices. These techniques have been taken up in detail in Chapter 4. However, some problems in this area pertain specifically to the teaching of general business, and these should be examined here.

Teachers are faced with the practical problem of assigning letter or percentage grades with respect to student achievement. There are two main methods by which this may be done in the general business class. In the first method the teacher may observe student behavior during class discussions, in the performance of reports or projects, and in the results of class recitation. This type of evaluative technique is necessarily subject to the teacher's opinion as to the value of the student's activity. Although it is possible to assign letter or percentage grades through observation, teachers much prefer to have more tangible evidence of the value of the student's performance in class. This tangible evidence can only be obtained through the use of the second method of evaluation, the examination.

Developing examinations poses some particular problems for the teacher of general business, especially if he subscribes to the idea previously presented— that of teaching for concepts rather than for specific items of subject-matter knowledge. The type of evaluative device used will be different from the traditional type. This does not mean that the so-called objective type of examinations such as true-false, completion, multiple choice, or matching cannot be used. These types can indeed be used, but in the preparation of the questions care must be taken that the evaluation is of concepts rather than of specific items of subject matter.

Some illustrations of the types of questions that serve this particular objective are given below. These questions were developed by a group of business educators attending a workshop on economic education at New York University.

Evaluation by Written Tests—Although observation is an important means of evaluation, because of the limitations and subjectivity of observation as informal evaluation, this type of evaluation must be supplemented in other ways. Probably the most frequently used means of supplementing evaluation through observation is by written tests. The illustrations which follow are examples of different types of questions which may be constructed for the purpose of measuring achievement of the types of outcomes indicated. In other words, no illustrations of the commonly known true-false, multiple-choice, etc., test are given; rather those types are illustrated which may be used to measure more than mere facts and information, specifically attitudes, understandings, appreciations, and so on.

1. Evaluation of Abilities.

One of the abilities which should be and can be developed in basic business is the *ability to distinguish between statement of fact and statement of opinion*. The type of test questions illustrated here can help in the evaluation of this ability.

Directions

In the list below, some of the sentences are statements of opinion, and others are statements of fact. Indicate to which class you think each statement belongs by placing the proper letter in the space provided for it. Do not try to decide if each statement is true or false, but only whether it should be classified as a statement of *fact* or of *opinion*.

—— 1. Insurance may be obtained to provide protection against every type of economic loss.
—— 2. Big business leads to monopoly.
—— 3. High tariffs increase the prosperity of the country.
—— 4. The economic cost of war is extremely high.
—— 5. One who buys stock in a company is a part owner of that company.

Another ability that can be evaluated by test as an outcome of the giving of economic emphasis to the teaching of basic business education is the *ability to make wise choices*. The following type of test might give an indication of the extent of this outcome:

Mr. C. E. Lucas has been employed for the past twenty years by the Kollege Korner Kitchen as a waiter, cook, and cashier. His current earnings are $500 a month. He has saved $10,000. The average net earnings of the Kollege Korner Kitchen for the past ten years has been $14,500 per year. The management offers Mr. Lucas:

1. a promotion to general manager with a salary of $600 a month (the promotion will, of course, add to the duties and responsibilities of Mr. Lucas), and
2. an opportunity to buy the entire business including building, equipment, and the present inventory for $50,000.

After some investigation, Mr. Lucas finds that the local banker is willing to accept a mortgage on the property and to lend him the additional cash needed. The loan is to be repaid in monthly installments over a ten-year period. An interest rate of 7 per cent is to be the cost of the loan. He also finds that his brother-in-law, a capenter by trade, is willing to invest the additional $10,000 provided a general partnership agreement is duly executed. Under the partnership agreement, the duties and responsibilities and the profits or losses are to be shared equally.

1. Underline the choice you think best for Mr. Lucas.

    (a) To continue working for the Kollege Korner Kitchen as general manager

    (b) To purchase the business with bank financing

    (c) To form a partnership with his brother-in-law

2. On the following sheet expand on number 1.

    (a) Defend your choice

    (b) Reasons why each of the other two alternatives was not chosen

2. Evaluation of Understandings.

Evaluation of understandings is one of the most difficult processes of evaluation. Great care must be taken to be sure that the acquisition of mere information alone is not being measured. Test questions must be so constructed that the student's comprehension of the relation of facts (understandings) is evaluated. This does not mean, however, that students should not be taught basic facts. Information serves as a tool in the solving of problems as they arise and assists in providing understanding.

Questions such as the following may be of assistance in evaluating student understandings:

On the meaning of corporate stock:

1. XYZ Corporation sold $200,000 worth of stock, of which Mr. Wilson purchased ten shares for $100 each. Mr. Wilson therefore (a) becomes a creditor of the company; (b) is an owner of the company; (c) has loaned the company money; (d) is a customer of the company.

On the meaning of index figures:

2. The cost-of-living index figure for 1971 is, let us say, 137 (1960 = 100). In 1960 Mr. Adams earned $6,000 a year. In 1971 he earned, in the same job, $8,000 a year. Is Mr. Adams' real income greater or less than it was in 1960?

The essay question or the completion-of-sentence type of question also may be used to evaluate understanding, thus:

1. Explain how borrowing from a commercial bank, as distinguished from other sources of borrowing, increases the supply of money.

2. Complete the statement: "Inflation exists when ——."[1]

The foregoing examples are excellent illustrations of the types of evaluative devices that can be used in measuring the abilities of students in a general business class. Obviously, it will be difficult for the teacher to develop evaluative devices of his own of the type and nature illustrated. However, the time taken will be very worthwhile and the teacher will not be placed in the embarrassing position of teaching for the broad concept and then measuring students' ability by devising examinations that measure specifics. It is this type of teaching that is open to criticism—and in which students lose confidence.

Before leaving this section on evaluation and measurement, mention should be made of one type of evaluative device that is rarely used any more, specifically, the essay-type question. This type of question has great value for use in teaching general business, not only to determine the measurement of

---

[1] The material is taken from part of the workshop report and is titled "Evaluation of Outcomes." This workshop was held under the joint auspices of New York University and the Council on Economic Education.

concepts but to provide the student with practice in written communication. Teachers traditionally have complained about the inability of their students to write effectively and have placed the blame on the elementary school teacher or the teacher of English. Written expression is the responsibility of all teachers, not just of one particular group. The teacher of general business has just as much at stake in the development of this ability as any other teacher.

Of course, there are difficulties in using this type of examination question, such as the time involved in grading the papers and the lack of objectivity. However, both of the objections may be overcome. Better planning of the teacher's time to eliminate waste motions will permit time for grading essays. The argument of lack of objectivity is overruled to some extent by the fact that upon analysis, any examination question is subject to the teacher's wording and selection of the question.

ECONOMIC EDUCATION

Any discussion of the teaching of general business in the secondary school would not be complete without pinpointing one of the major problems which has confronted educators in general during the past thirty years. This has been the problem of "economic illiteracy" found in a large segment of the American public. Since the major Depression of the 1930s there have been many changes and developments in the economic structure of the United States and in the world, with a consequent conflict of many points of view.

These conflicting points of view in addition to the increasing complexities of our economic system have resulted in a problem for the American people in comprehending fully the economic phenomena that have a major influence upon their lives.

Both educational and lay organizations have attempted to overcome the economic illiteracy problem through various means. Required courses in economics are quite common on the high school level. However, too often these courses are highly theoretical and emphasize abstract concepts.

One organization that has been established to help overcome the lack of knowledge in basic economic concepts is the Joint Council on Economic Education. The council has sponsored workshops for teachers and has distributed educational materials for their use. Business educators have also been concerned with this problem, and much of the literature in their field has dealt with economic education. As far back as 1958 the *American Business Education Yearbook* was devoted entirely to the problems of educating the youth of America in economic concepts and principles.[2] Major efforts are continuing to be made by schools, governmental agencies, and independent organizations to help overcome this problem.

Many leaders in the field of business education firmly believe that economic concepts can be taught effectively in conjunction with a course in general business. The various units of subject matter as listed on page 271 have significant economic implications. The teacher of general business can do much

[2] *Educating Youth for Economic Competence,* The American Business Education Yearbook (1958).

in this course to develop attitudes, appreciations, and understandings of our economic system, using as a basis for this instruction the content of the general business course.

Elvin S. Eyster of Indiana University has set forth in a complete and concise manner the areas of economic concepts necessary for the general education of every person.

1. The essential characteristics and principles of the American business and labor system, what it is, how it operates, and the role it plays in the economic and occupational lives of all people.
2. An understanding of business practices and procedures, such as consumer credit, installment selling, guarantee of quality, and service agreements that enable consumers to utilize completely and to benefit fully from the economic goods and services offered by business.
3. Principles of management of personal business affairs enabling one to enjoy the highest possible standards of living compatible with his income.
4. The business of government (not the organization and operation of government), with special emphasis upon government business, such as the management and use of public lands, production of power, insurance against possible losses, lending of money, and subsidization of industries.
5. Basic economic principles, such as the operation of the law of supply and demand, real wages, prices, and marginal utility.[3]

If an emphasis is placed in the general business course on the development of economic understandings, prospective teachers should be aware of some inherent dangers to this approach.

Many of the concepts in the above list are controversial. Since students often reflect the attitudes of their parents it would be uncommon not to have conflicting ideas on the part of students enrolled in a general business class. This is as it should be because one of the strengths of our American heritage is based upon the freedom of belief with the free expression of these beliefs. *It is not the place of the business teacher to question the beliefs of his students but to enable the students to obtain factual information from which to develop their own points of view and beliefs.*

Inexperienced teachers will often shy away from controversial issues in the classroom or sometimes get into them without giving the problem proper forethought and preparation. The use of the so-called Socratic approach in which the teacher "questions" the point of view held by a student under the guise of "making him think" in order to justify his idea has often had unfortunate results. Students have been known to misjudge a teacher's point of view about a controversial issue merely because the teacher's idea appeared to be in conflict with their own.

The use of discussion techniques and procedures are excellent for use in the presentation and implementation of controversial issues. However, the teacher must insist that rational thinking based upon factual information, not emotional reaction, take place in the discussion. In this way, the teacher of

[3] *Ibid.,* p. 16.

general business can make a significant contribution to the education of our youth and to society in general.

OTHER BASIC BUSINESS SUBJECTS

Business Law

Business law in the secondary school is commonly taught in either the junior or the senior year. Although the subject matter is technical, by no means is it the purpose of instruction to make business law, in the secondary school at least, a technical, legal course. Some of the more commonly stated objectives for teaching business law are:

1. To familiarize students with basic principles of business law and their applications common to daily life as an aid in avoiding legal difficulties
2. To train students in the use of common legal documents
3. To develop in students an awareness of the organization of our local, state, and federal court system
4. To help students realize when they should consult competent legal authority in legal matters
5. To develop in students a respect for law and constituted authority

To achieve these objectives most business law textbooks are developed around the following items of content:

1. Nature and background of law
2. Contracts
3. Negotiable instruments
4. Agency
5. Sales
6. Bailments
7. Real property
8. Personal property
9. Suretyship and guaranty
10. Court structure

The foregoing list of topics of content appears to be an imposing one for high school students to study, or for that matter even for adults. The technical aspects of the subject matter impose one of the major problems of teaching business law. Too often business law courses are taught from the viewpoint of requiring strict mastery of subject-matter detail. The fallacies of teaching business law in this manner should be obvious.

A technical course in business law should be offered only to those individuals who intend to become practicing lawyers. Obviously, then, a course of this nature should not be offered to high school students. The legal language itself often is a deterrent to learning for high school boys and girls. Despite herculean efforts by the authors of secondary business law textbooks, the technical language cannot be entirely eliminated or minimized.

Subject-matter mastery of detail in business law can also lead to another problem. Students (especially high school students) might possibly develop an unwarranted confidence in their ability to interpret the law for themselves and for others. This is not only illegal but can be dangerous and can lead to much hardship and disillusionment because of failure to consult trained lawyers when the need arises.

Business educators generally subscribe to the principle that the subject matter of the business law course should not be mastered as other subject-matter courses but that the primary purpose is for students to obtain an appreciation of the principles by which present-day business law is formed. If this concept is accepted, then the methods by which business law is taught will be materially directed toward this end.

SOME SPECIFIC TECHNIQUES FOR TEACHING BUSINESS LAW. Although business law is a recitation-type course (as distinguished from a drill-type course), some specific techniques may be used by the teacher, other than the classroom discussion, to make the course both interesting and stimulating. These techniques are as follows:

1. Use of supplementary instructional materials
2. Use of community resources as an aid to instruction
3. Use of student experiences and their relationship to the principles found in business law

USE OF SUPPLEMENTARY INSTRUCTIONAL MATERIALS. Without question there is sufficient material in the typical business law textbook to keep both the teacher and the student busy without the use of outside supplementary materials. However, for an enriched course and to illustrate the universality and importance of business law problems, the teacher will find it highly valuable to make reference to sources other than the text. It is almost mandatory in the well-taught business law class to use supplementary instructional materials and resources because of the proximity of the textual material in business law to the ordinary day-to-day living of the student.

One of the richest sources of supplementary material is the daily newspaper. Practically any newspaper picked at random will have news stories concerning such items as contracts, sales, or some other element of concern to the business law class.

Much of the content of a business law course can be developed around case problems as a basis for discussion by the use of cases found in the newspapers and in magazine articles. These can certainly make the business law class more realistic and practical. In the foregoing illustrations, for example, very realistic discussions can be developed which will vividly bring out the principles of contracts, bailments, warranties, and torts.

Many other types of supplementary instructional materials are available to the teacher. Materials from trade associations, legal societies, and Better Business bureaus are just a few of these types of sources. Films, filmstrips, and bulletin-board materials for illustrative purposes are available for teaching the many concepts found in business law.

USE OF COMMUNITY RESOURCES.   The community in which the school is located is an excellent source of reference for teaching business law. Regardless of the size of the community there should be some resources available for any school. Individuals in the community such as attorneys, police officers, businessmen, and city officials can be of much help in making presentations to students. Discussions by these resource persons of the more common business law problems in which people become involved, the everyday principles of law with which the businessman comes in contact, and the legal principles involved in operating a municipal or a county government are all illustrations of the types of legal activities that can be explored.

The community is also an excellent source of information with respect to visitations to places where legal activities are carried on. The local court when a business trial is in session is quite valuable. In some communities the local bar associations have been following a practice of coming into the classroom and presenting a mock trial for the benefit of the students. Visitation to city council meetings to see local government in action, though of more interest to a government class, can still have many applications to business law. Such items as the awarding of contracts, or the legal implications of commercial zoning, are illustrative of the actions that may be observed.

Most communities are rich in resources for the business law class. It merely takes a discerning teacher to pick out those everyday activities that will be applicable.

USE OF STUDENT EXPERIENCES.   One of the most successful techniques that can be used in the teaching of business law is the adapting of the instruction to the maturity level and experiences of the students in the class. Many activities experienced by the typical junior or senior in high school have a definite application to business law.

Many of the students will either own or drive automobiles. The implications found in buying a car through financing, the responsibility to other people through insurance coverage, and the element of torts might be applicable.

Because of the nature of our present economic condition, many boys and girls of high school age are participating in business activities that formerly were not available to them. Examples such as employer-employee relationships, laws affecting both employers and employees, buying on credit, and borrowing money all have significance in business law. The responsibilities and legal requirements of minors and the difficulties that may be encountered by minors through ignorance of the law are other illustrative factors.

With these elements in mind the superior business law teacher will utilize the present experiences of students in developing the content of the business law class around these experiences. This type of instruction should not only motivate the class but have the valuable result of making the instruction meaningful and helpful to the students.

Although the use of discussion techniques will prove to be most successful in teaching business law and will be the most dominant method used, the teacher will find some other supplementary devices useful and enriching to the class. The content of business law lends itself readily to stimulating student reports on topics appropriate to the subject. Mock trials dramatized by students, exhibits of student projects, bulletin-board and room displays, and student debates can be most effective. By using a variety of devices and by using the many sources of supplementary materials around him, the *dynamic* teacher will be highly successful in teaching business law.

Consumer Business

Consumer business or *consumer education* is commonly taught in the modern secondary school by the business education teacher. Sometimes this course is taught by the home economics teacher, or it may be offered in the social science department under the title of *consumer economics*.

Consumer business may be classified as another course in the basic business area. The primary objective of the course is to provide general education values to high school students. For this reason, consumer education may be considered to have value for all high school students regardless of their educational or vocational futures.

In consumer business an attempt is made to bring together into one course much of the consumer information often taught in various courses in home economics, science, social science, and business education. The aims are to give students basic knowledges concerning available goods and services. No attempt is made to give specific information concerning the purchase of all commodities. Rather the course seeks to teach the consumer to choose discriminatingly in purchasing goods. The importance of such information comes from the fact that one's standard of living depends not only on the salary earned but upon the utilization of that salary and the values derived from the wise expenditure of income.

The common objectives typically listed for teaching consumer business are:

1. To develop in students a knowledge of basic economic principles with particular attention to the problems of consumption
2. To provide students with sufficient information to evaluate goods and services intelligently
3. To enable student consumers to make intelligent buying choices
4. To teach students the elements of personal financial affairs, including budgeting, saving, credit, insurance, and investment of funds
5. To provide students with the knowledge concerning the sources of aids for consumers and to develop the ability to choose wisely between true and false information
6. To instruct students concerning the part played by government and the contribution that government makes to the protection and advancement of consumer welfare

To meet these objectives, the typical consumer business textbook incorporates the following types of information:

1. Basic consumer problems
2. Aid for the consumer
3. Propaganda analysis
4. Advertising
5. Consumer cooperatives
6. Grades, standards, labels
7. Money and banking
8. Budgeting, credit, savings, investments
9. Insurance and social security
10. Education and advisory services for consumers
11. Housing
12. Taxes
13. Health services
14. Frauds
15. General buying principles
16. Current topics of interest to consumers

An analysis of the several topics of content reveals that much of consumer business is concerned with the personal financial problems of people. Appropriately enough, many high school students today have personal financial problems that can be readily fused into the content of the course. Because consumer business is typically offered in the senior or combined senior and junior years, the several topics of content are usually of much interest to these students because of their level of maturity.

METHODS AND PROBLEMS OF TEACHING CONSUMER BUSINESS. Because consumer business is also another "recitation"-type course, the subject matter lends itself most readily to the discussion method. It is another course in the business curriculum where student experiences can be used quite readily as a starting point for class discussion, since many of the students have experienced some contact with the topics of content.

There is a danger in teaching consumer business that an inexperienced teacher may inadvertently make the course a technical one, as a vast amount of technical information is available for consumers. The dangers in this type of approach should be most apparent, as nothing will kill interest more readily than concentration on technical detail.

The objective, then, in consumer business is to provide the student with the knowledges with which to make wise choices. Through the educational process it is hoped that he will use the tools that are provided him in making these wise choices. A student should not be compelled in the consumer business course to make detailed studies of the differences in values of one size can or another, or to make a chemical analysis of some type of cloth. Rather he should be given some basic principles of consumership plus sources of information which he may use in making his decisions. This, then, coupled with the ability to use his knowledge rationally, should prepare a well-trained consumer.

RESOURCES FOR TEACHING CONSUMER BUSINESS. There is a vast wealth of resources for teaching consumer business, of which the superior teacher will avail himself in teaching the course. Much of this material is free. Many businesses today realize that an informed consumer actually reduces their costs and increases their goodwill. A satisfied consumer is one of the best sources of advertising. Any good business educator's bibliography will provide many such sources of information. There are also commercial agencies such as the magazines *Consumers Guide* and *Consumers Union*. In these magazines space is given to the study and reporting of information for consumers. Pamphlets from the federal government and from local agencies such as Better Business bureaus are also highly valuable sources of information.

Much help can be obtained from the local business community. Businessmen in the community can be very helpful in providing students with information on both good and poor consumer practices that they have observed in their own customers. As has been stated in preceding paragraphs, American businessmen, contrary to the opinion held by some people, do not all subscribe to the principle of "let the buyer beware" and are desirous of having an informed consumer.

The consumer business course can be one of the most interesting classes taught in the business curriculum if the teacher will keep in mind the procedures mentioned above.

MISCELLANEOUS BASIC BUSINESS COURSES

In the preceding sections of this chapter the basic business courses most frequently taught in the secondary school were discussed. The business teacher may be called upon to teach several other courses that are borderline with respect to their being placed in the basic business category. Certain features about the content of these courses, however, justify their inclusion here.

A brief description of these courses is given below. Methods and techniques for teaching them will in many instances be similar to the methods already discussed with respect to the general business course. In other instances some of the methods discussed in relationship to the skill courses should be utilized. In any event, if the business teacher should find himself assigned to teach one or more of these courses, an inadequate knowledge of the content of the courses would probably be his major problem—not the methods whereby the course could be taught most effectively.

Business Mathematics

Business mathematics is a course quite commonly taught in large high schools as a part of the clerical curriculum. Sometimes it is offered in small high schools as a substitute for other mathematics courses. It may be either a one-semester or a two-semester course.

The content of the business mathematics course generally covers the following topics applicable to business and personal activities.

1. A review of the fundamental processes of arithmetic (including fractions and percentages)

2. The mathematics of financial record keeping and reporting (including payroll, record keeping, comparative analysis of business reports, graphs)
3. The mathematics of business finance (including interest—both in borrowing and in lending, investments in stocks and bonds)
4. The mathematics of personal finance (including insurance purchasing, taxation, etc.)

Normally the course is taught at the freshman or the sophomore level so that the skills and understandings learned can be applied to other business courses taken at a later time. An additional objective is to provide students with the mathematical knowledges and skills necessary for both vocational and personal use.

One might wonder about the need for a course in business mathematics because of the widespread use of calculating machines and electronic computers. It is for this very reason that such a course can be quite valuable. In today's business environment more and more use is being made of quantitative manipulation and analysis of data for the purpose of making decisions. While highly sophisticated machines are available for making calculations, it is necessary that the individual understand the basic mathematical concepts that are being applied. This can be accomplished effectively in a business mathematics course. In addition, almost every citizen uses some form of business mathematics in his normal everyday activities. For example, the passage of the Truth-in-Lending Act by the federal government has indicated that everyone should be aware of the true interest charges made on credit purchases. As consumers we are constantly being bombarded with numerical data from newspapers, television, radio, advertisements, and so forth. Everyone should have the ability to evaluate these data.

The business teacher may encounter or should be aware of several problems in teaching business mathematics: a wide range of abilities among the students enrolled in the course; weaknesses on the part of some students in the fundamental processes of arithmetic; and the fear that many students have with respect to anything that requires computational abilities. While these problems are not major, they can present difficulties to the teacher and require skill, patience and understanding to overcome them.

The methodology for teaching business mathematics is much like that for teaching bookkeeping—teacher explanation of a principle or a concept, illustrations of techniques for solving the problem, followed by students working problems. Usually much drill is involved, followed by short quizzes to determine the student's understanding. Most business mathematics textbooks have supplementary instructional materials available for use, such as study guides and workbooks.

In spite of the emphasis placed upon the student's ability to solve problems, there is still much opportunity to use discussion techniques in the business mathematics course. For example, an excellent discussion could be developed about the value of quantified data to the businessman in his making of decisions—such items as the accuracy of the data, the misinterpretation of the data, or the impersonality of the data. Much discussion could be developed about the various means of obtaining taxes—such as the sales tax as opposed to the income tax.

As was stated earlier, there are so many applications of business mathematics to our everyday activities that the list of discussion possibilities is unlimited. The main criteria for evaluating the effectveness of a business mathematics course will be those of developing not only mathematical skills but also the student's understanding of the basic concepts and applications involved in business computations.

BUSINESS ORGANIZATION AND MANAGEMENT

A course sometimes found in the secondary school at the fourth-year level is *business organization and management.* This course will probably be of most interest to boys and girls who hope to own or manage their own business after graduation. There may also be a secondary objective for students enrolled in this course, since by studying the principles behind the organization and management of a business enterprise, the students, who will eventually be working in a business, will have a better understanding and appreciation of business operation.

The units of content usually included in a course in business organization and management are:

1. Problems involved in organizing and starting a business
2. Production management
3. Distribution management
4. Personnel management
5. Governmental relationships with business

This course can be an excellent supplement to the basic business offerings in the secondary school and can be used most effectively to integrate the principles found in such courses as business law, bookkeeping, general business, and office and secretarial practice. It is doubtful that its inclusion in the secondary curriculum in any but the large high schools would be justified if it meant that one or more basic business courses would be excluded.

BUSINESS ENGLISH

Another course sometimes found in the curriculums of large high schools is *business English.* In this course an emphasis is placed upon a rapid review of grammar and sentence structure, with a major emphasis being placed upon the principles of business letter writing.

This course has value for all types of students in business, both in the secretarial and in the general business fields. Besides giving prospective stenographers a basic knowledge of grammar (as it may apply to business letters), it also provides them with a knowledge of the proper form and tone of business letters. For the clerical or bookkeeping student, business English can be helpful in providing understandings of report writing and the ability to express oneself clearly and concisely in terms of those documents typically found in business.

One problem with respect to business English is that in the typical high school a student will be enrolled in at least three years of English. A course in business English may duplicate to some extent the general English courses. If the terminology and form peculiar to business are stressed, however, it is doubtful that this overlapping will be particularly harmful.

ECONOMIC GEOGRAPHY

A course in *economic geography* is sometimes found in business curriculums; it is a type of course that can be very helpful for all students. The emphasis in this course is placed upon the natural and economic resources of the various countries of the world rather than upon their physical characteristics. It is difficult to distinguish between the two for economic purposes, however, because very often the physical and cultural characteristics to a large extent determine the economic factors. In any event, economic geography can be very useful in helping students to understand the political, cultural, and social characteristics of the various peoples of the world through the study of their economic forces.

PROJECTS AND QUESTIONS FOR DISCUSSION

1. Examine several textbooks for use in teaching general business. Compare their similarities and differences. Write a short paper on how the text material can be utilized to achieve the objectives of this course.
2. Examine the supplementary instructional materials included with general business textbooks (workbooks and study guides). Make a list of their advantages and disadvantages for use in instruction.
3. Examine, if obtainable, the teacher's manuals included with general business textbooks. Describe how useful these manuals would be to a teacher of a general business course.
4. Make a list of reasons for and against teaching topics of a controversial nature. What types of controversial topics do you think might develop in a general business course?
5. Develop a series of discussion questions that might be used effectively in starting and continuing a class discussion on some topic or topics in general business.
6. What are some specific techniques that you might suggest for teaching a unit on savings and investment in general business? Consider that the class you are teaching is composed of freshmen and sophomores.
7. Do you believe it is possible for freshmen or sophomores in high school to comprehend some of the major economic concepts that affect our business economy today? Is it important for them to understand certain economic principles that will affect them as adults? Can you cite any student experiences that illustrate the workings of certain economic phenomena?
8. Develop several case problems that might be used effectively in teaching a topic or topics in general business by use of discussion techniques.
9. Assume that a class in general business is composed of a highly mixed group of students with respect to abilities and interests. What suggestions do you have for maintaining interest and motivating these students?
10. Do you believe it is possible to improve attitudes and appreciations with respect to business activities in a general business class? How might you go about it?

CASE PROBLEMS

1. This is your first year of teaching and you have been assigned to teach, among other subjects, a course in general business. Near the end of the first semester you sense an attitude of boredom among your students, and as a result you find it difficult to get your students to discuss some of the topics being presented.

One day, during a particularly exasperating class session, you ask your students the reason for their attitude. At first no one responds, but eventually one student complains that the course material is not relevant to his world, that it is too "rinky-dink," and that it is "stuff" the students already know. At this point several other students also complain about the course material. What would you do about this situation?

2. You are teaching a course in business law and you find that many students are coming to you and asking for advice pertaining to legal matters in which they are involved. How would you advise these students? What steps would you take to encourage or discourage students in bringing these matters to you?

3. Because of a high degree of publicity given to consumer problems involving manufacturing firms, the students in your consumer economics class are developing a cynical attitude toward business and free enterprise. They believe that the consumer is being taken advantage of whenever he buys anything, and they are raising some rather disturbing questions in class about our economic system. Do you believe that you have any responsibility to change their attitude and if so how will you go about it?

SUGGESTED READINGS

Crabbe, Ernest H., Joseph S. DeBrum, and Peter G. Haines, *Methods of Teaching General Business*. Cincinnati: South-Western Publishing Co., 1968.

Daughtrey, A. S., *Methods of Basic Business and Economic Education*. Cincinnati: South-Western Publishing Co., 1965.

Price, Ray G., Vernon A. Musselman, J. Curtis Hall, and Edwin E. Weeks, Jr., *Teachers Source Book and Key for General Business for Everyday Living* (3rd ed.). New York: Gregg Publishing Division, McGraw-Hill Book Company, 1966.

Tonne, Herbert A., and Louis C. Nanassy, *Principles of Business Education*, Chap. 23. New York: Gregg Division, McGraw-Hill Book Company, 1970.

———, Estelle Popham, and M. Herbert Freeman, *Method of Teaching Business Subjects*, Chaps. 19, 20, and 21. New York: Gregg Publishing Division, McGraw-Hill Book Company, 1965.

Visual Aids for Business and Economic Education, Monograph No. 92, rev. ed. Cincinnati: South-Western Publishing Co., 1969.

Bibliographies of Free and Inexpensive Material for Use in Teaching Business Education Subjects

Bibliography of Free and Inexpensive Materials for Economic Education, Joint Council on Economic Education, 2 West 46th Street, New York 36.

Educational Aids For Schools and Colleges, National Association of Manufacturers, 2 East 48th Street, New York 17.

List of Free Materials Available to Professors and Students, The Wall Street Journal, The Educational Service Bureau, 44 Broad Street, New York 4.

chapter

9

TEACHING BOOKKEEPING

The teacher of bookkeeping represents one of the most significant aspects of the business education curriculum of the secondary schools. In terms of enrollment and number of courses offered, bookkeeping is second only to typewriting.

Historically, bookkeeping instruction began in the private business colleges and was introduced in the public schools in the early part of the nineteenth century. From its inception until the middle 1960s, the subject matter of the bookkeeping course varied little. The content was updated from time to time —particularly with relationship to new terminology and certain procedures that had become standardized, but essentially few major changes in content were made.

Beginning in the late 1960s new developments in the subject matter of bookkeeping textbooks were introduced which will have a major effect upon the instructional procedures and development of bookkeeping courses taught in the 1970s. These changes have been brought about primarily because of the widespread use, by both large and small businesses, of mechanical and electronic machines which can perform bookkeeping procedures more efficiently, accurately, and often more economically. The use by business firms of independent service organizations specializing in the supervision, and in some cases maintenance, of a firm's financial records has given an impetus to a change in emphasis in the content of bookkeeping courses.

Because of these developments it is not to be implied that the importance of teaching bookkeeping in the secondary schools will be less significant in the future. Business firms will continue to need employees trained in the clerical aspects of record keeping. In addition, an expanded bookkeeping course that includes some of the major characteristics of accounting (as well as record keeping), plus mechanical and electronic data-processing procedures, will provide the business employer with a much better informed and vocationally trained employee. This will be particularly true if a *systems approach* to the teaching of bookkeeping (explained later in this chapter) is utilized by the bookkeeping teacher.

As for the future, it is quite likely that during the next decade secondary school instruction in the broad subject matter that comprises the financial activities of a business will be organized as follows:

1. A course (one or two semesters) in record keeping taught as a part of the clerical curriculum, with emphasis upon the techniques of routine clerical record keeping activities
2. An upgraded one-year beginning bookkeeping course in which an accounting emphasis is given primarily to provide future employees with a basic understanding of both the internal and the external financial operations of a business
3. A one-year advanced bookkeeping-accounting course for those students who desire to gain more depth in the area of bookkeeping-accounting and who are either preparing for a college major in accounting or planning to obtain an initial position in a business as a bookkeeper-accountant

OBJECTIVES FOR TEACHING BOOKKEEPING

A search of the literature pertaining to the teaching of bookkeeping reveals many lists of specific objectives for teaching the course. A composite list of these objectives would include the following:

1. To develop in students the ability and desire to keep records for personal use
2. To develop in students the ability to interpret and analyze business papers and records in the capacity of consumers
3. To give students preliminary training for the advanced study of accounting
4. To develop in students traits of neatness, accuracy, and orderliness
5. To develop in students an understanding of some of the problems and characteristics of a business enterprise
6. To provide students with knowledges of record keeping necessary to carry on a small business
7. To train students to become bookkeepers

Essentially, bookkeeping objectives fall into two main categories:

1. The *vocational objective*—to train a student to become a bookkeeper
2. The *personal-use-general education objective*—to prepare a student to maintain his personal financial records and in addition to provide him with an economic understanding of the business world

These objectives are not mutually exclusive. That is, they can both be accomplished in a bookkeeping course, depending upon the emphasis given each by the bookkeeping teacher.

In any event, regardless of the objective or objectives to which the bookkeeping teacher subscribes, the importance of the teacher's carefully reflecting about the objectives he wishes to achieve cannot be emphasized too strongly. *What the teacher believes will have a definite effect upon how he teaches the course and what he will accomplish.*

In the opinion of the authors, the prime objective for teaching bookkeeping should be vocational basically. This does not mean that we should train a student to become initially employed as a bookkeeper. Rather we should provide him with those tools and knowledges necessary for him to become an employee who is well informed about the operation of a business. A mastery of bookkeeping fundamentals should provide him with these knowledges. Specifically, a study of the financial operations of a business will provide him with the following information:

1. Knowledge of the meaning and significance of ordinary common terms used in the business world today, and an ability to differentiate among them, such as

   a. Asset
   b. Liability
   c. Net worth
   d. Expense
   e. Income
   f. Gross profit
   g. Net profit
   h. Depreciation
   i. Bad debts
   j. Accruals

2. Familiarity with many different kinds of transactions common to the business world and to the people who deal with it, and an understanding of the significance of each, such as

   a. Cash expenditures
   b. Cash receipts
   c. Credit transactions
   d. Discounting notes
   e. Taking and giving discounts
   f. Exchange of assets
   g. Prepayment of expense
   h. Issuing notes
   i. Returns and allowances
   j. Payment of interest

3. Understanding of the advisability of performing certain functions and of following certain principles and procedures in order that any given investment may be adequately protected, such as

   a. Allowance for depreciation
   b. Proper valuation of inventories
   c. Adequate insurance
   d. Revenue vs. capital expenditures
   e. Protection of working capital
   f. Control of expenses
   g. Interpretation of financial statements
   h. Prompt collection of accounts
   i. Need for conservatism
   j. Accurate records

4. Recognition of those factors that, directly or indirectly, reduce profits, income, and net worth, such as

   a. Accrued expenses
   b. Bad debts
   c. Depreciation
   d. Obsolescence
   e. Inefficient labor
   f. Insufficient margins
   g. Seasonal fluctuation
   h. Competition
   i. Unusual losses
   j. Excessive inventory

5. Knowledge of the meaning and purpose of many record-keeping devices commonly in use, such as

a. Cash books
b. Purchases book
c. Sales book
d. General ledger
e. Subsidiary ledgers
f. Valuation accounts
g. Book inventories
h. Columnar records
i. Account classifications
j. Trial balance

6. Knowledge of various means of estimating the financial worth of a given investment or enterprise, such as

a. Examination of two or more balance sheets
b. Examination of two or more profit and loss statements
c. Interpretation of comparative statements
d. Percent of income earned on investment
e. Proportion of earnings left in the business

7. Development of an awareness of common types of "problems" facing a business executive, such as

a. The taking of inventory
b. Proper valuation of inventory
c. Selection of profitable items
d. Protection of cash
e. Securing of credit

8. Some knowledge of the possible uses of records, and some ability in their use, as a means of executive control of a going business, such as

a. Comparative volume of sales for periods
b. Ratio of net profits to sales
c. Current ratios
d. Turnover of accounts receivable
e. Use of credit records and ratings

9. Development of specific attitudes, concepts, and mental habits as applied to situations arising in business transactions, such as

a. The habit of analyzing business transactions and situations in terms of their effects upon the two main financial statements
b. The habit of systematic classification of business information
c. The habit of accurate and complete recording of business information
d. The correct concept of what constitutes profits
e. The concept that business success is fundamentally dependent upon service and efficiency

10. Knowledge of the basic concepts of modern data-processing procedures, such as

a. Manual devices for pegboard and keysort equipment
b. Mechanical equipment for bookkeeping and posting machines
c. Punched-card equipment for key punches, sorters, collators, and tabulators
d. Electronic computer systems

Obviously, technical competence in the knowledges listed above would not be expected of a high school student. However, close scrutiny will reveal that *familiarity* with and an understanding of the various items is not too much to expect of the vocationally trained employee.

In the subsequent pages of this textbook, the general and the specific teaching techniques presented will be based upon the vocational objectives for teaching bookkeeping in the secondary school.

BOOKKEEPING IN THE
SECONDARY SCHOOL CURRICULUM

Grade Placement and Types of Bookkeeping Courses
Offered in the Secondary Curriculum

Typically the bookkeeping courses offered in the secondary school are being offered in the sophomore-junior years of high school or in the junior-senior years. The latter pattern with a one-year course is the most common. An increasing number of schools are offering either a one-semester or a two-semester course is record keeping as a part of the clerical curriculum. A second-year or advanced course in bookkeeping-accounting is also becoming quite common in some of the large high schools, particularly where a specific vocational curriculum is offered.

While the junior year is the normal time for offering bookkeeping, the teacher should be prepared to find students enrolled in the course who are sophomores, juniors, and seniors. This lack of homogeneity in terms of maturity does create teaching problems which are difficult to overcome. This situation often requires the teacher to provide much individual or small group instruction.

Course Content

In general, the content of a first-year high school bookkeeping course is somewhat standardized, as can be seen by examining the several available textbooks. However, the format of presentation of the various topics covered in the course will vary considerably from one textbook to another.

Normally, the subject matter is presented by using a spiral or pyramid technique—going from the simple to the complex—covering the same basic principles several times, but each time adding more comprehensive and difficult material. The first cycle is very elementary, taking up the records maintained by a service type of business. After this cycle is completed, a second cycle is begun using a merchandising type of business with its accompanying adjustments for inventories. The third cycle brings in special problems such as payroll records, special journals, depreciation and accruals; and, finally, a fourth cycle includes partnership and corporation accounting. In the modern-day texts an additional section contains material about mechanical, electromechanical (punched-card) and electronic data-processing procedures. Bookkeeping seems to be the logical course in which to teach this information.

An outline of units that may be found in the typical bookkeeping textbook follows.

Units of Content

1st Cycle (Service Business)
1. Bookkeeping fundamentals
2. The use of accounts
3. Analyzing transactions

4. Journalizing
5. Posting
6. The trial balance and work sheet
7. Financial statements
8. Closing the books

2nd Cycle (Merchandising Business)
9. Purchases
10. Sales
11. Cash receipts and cash payments
12. Work sheet and adjustments

3rd Cycle (Special Problems)
13. Payrolls and taxes
14. Fixed assets and depreciation
15. Notes and interest
16. Accounts receivable and bad debts
17. Accrued and deferred items
18. Bookkeeping systems
19. Partnerships and corporations
20. Data-processing techniques

In several of the available bookkeeping textbooks, the procedures dealing with data-processing fundamentals are often described in a separate section, with perhaps two, three, or four chapters devoted to these topics. Instructional procedures in the techniques of manual, mechanical, punched-card, and computer data processing are usually found. It is quite common for these concepts to be taught in the bookkeeping course.

The course content for the second-year bookkeeping course is essentially an elaboration of the topics taught in the first-year course. More detailed attention is given to the various balance sheet and income statement items, with an emphasis given to internal control, cost accounting, and management decision-making based upon accounting data.

INSTRUCTIONAL MATERIALS AVAILABLE FOR TEACHING BOOKKEEPING

The instructional materials available for use by the bookkeeping teacher fall into two main categories—those provided by textbook publishers and those prepared by or obtained by the teacher from other sources. Materials available today from textbook publishers are excellent—probably as good or better than those for any other subject taught in the business education curriculum. Some of these materials are free to teachers and students upon adoption of a text.

Instructional materials available from sources other than textbook publishers are quite plentiful and are particularly valuable for illustrative purposes. The only restrictions in obtaining these materials are the teacher's time and effort in seeking out these materials from the various sources. It is debatable whether the teacher should spend much time preparing his own instructional materials —other than making transparencies—because of the many excellent materials already available.

Materials Available from Textbook Publishers

Materials available from textbook publishers fall into several different categories. Obviously, the prime material is the textbook itself. Several excellent textbooks on the market are extremely teachable and are kept up to date.

The selection of a textbook will depend upon several factors. Some states follow a policy of statewide adoption with respect to the use of a specific text. In other states, multiple adoption is practiced—that is, several books are placed on an approved list and the local school district or the teacher selection committee is given the option of selecting a particular text from several on the list. Bookkeeping textbook publishers generally follow a four- to five-year revision policy so that the material incorporated in the text will be kept current.

The importance of selecting a text carefully cannot be emphasized too strongly. In addition to the materials in the text itself, that is, the methods by which the subject matter is presented, the teacher should carefully examine the illustrative materials; the readability of the material; the kinds of problems, exercises, and cases; and, highly important, the vocabulary. Fortunately, the teacher cannot go too far wrong in the selection of a textbook because of the excellent books available.

Supplementary Published Instructional Materials

The most common types of supplementary instructional materials provided by the textbook publisher are:

1. Working papers for use by students in their solutions of the end-of-chapter exercises, cases, and problems
2. Study guides for use by students, in which questions are to be answered pertaining to the reading material in the text
3. Projects, which are essentially long comprehensive problems reviewing the various concepts developed in several preceding chapters
4. Practice sets, which are essentially long problems covering the business transactions of a firm over a period of several months
5. Self-contained units relating to the textbook but apart from it, which cover such special problems as payroll procedures and social security and income tax procedures
6. Teacher's manuals and solution keys to problems, which also include time schedules for teaching the various topics, lesson plans, and suggested teaching techniques
7. Overhead projection transparencies (or masters for preparing transparencies), which can be used to provide visual illustrations of specific topics

8. Printed examinations (usually provided free after the adoption of a text)
9. Miscellaneous materials, such as bulletin-board posters, achievement award certificates, and film strips

Examination of the materials provided by publishers should provide the teacher with significant information with respect to the adoption of a particular textbook.

In addition to the items listed above, the teacher can supplement these materials through various additional instructional aids:

1. The accumulation of corporation reports to stockholders in which the corporation's financial statements are listed
2. Bulletins from governmental agencies pertaining to federal and state regulations of accounting practices
3. Illustrative materials from brokerage firms pertaining to accounting reports
4. Materials from trade associations relating to corporate accounting data of specific types of manufacturers and service businesses
5. Journals published by public accounting firms

The availability of these kinds of supplementary materials is almost inexhausable, and with a little effort the teacher can get on a permanent mailing list to receive these materials, as they are generally furnished free of charge.

Certain types of instructional materials are essential for the teacher's use. The most important of these is the teacher's solutions manual. It is not always practical nor does the teacher always have the time to work out in advance the solutions to all problems and exercises that have been assigned. The teacher should be aware of the various concepts covered in an assigned problem or a project, and through careful perusal of the solutions manual he can often determine where student difficulty may arise. An excellent teaching device is to provide the student with some key element to the solution of a problem so that he can check himself to see if he is working toward the solution in the right direction.

Some teachers recommend that students be permitted to use the solutions manual so that they can check their own work. This procedure can be a useful learning device and can often save a teacher time; however, the teacher must have control over the use of the solutions manual and must develop some method of security.

Workbooks

Every bookkeeping textbook published today is accompanied by a workbook for students' use in working the questions and problems at the ends of the chapters. The use of these workbooks is optional with the instructor. There is some difference of opinion as to the value of workbooks in teaching. Some teachers believe that students will learn more of the principles of bookkeeping by not using workbooks because they must rule their own journals and ledgers and thus should have a better conception of keeping records. The majority of teachers do use workbooks, for they doubt that there is much gained educationally by making students rule their own paper. Necessarily, there is much "busy work" involved in working problems in bookkeeping, and if any short cut can be employed to cut down the amount of busy work it is commendable. The use of a workbook aids in cutting down this busy work and permits the student to spend the major portion of his time in solving problems rather than doing preliminary spade work in developing his own journals and ledgers. In the long run, the use of workbooks will be more economical in savings of both time and paper.

Practice Sets

Another type of instructional material useful in teaching bookkeeping is the practice set. A practice set involves the working of a long problem usually covering a one- or two-month time span of business transactions. The student is provided with a set of journals, ledgers, and working papers specifically designed for use in working the set. It has the twofold purpose of providing the student with practice in working a problem covering the entire bookkeeping cycle and of motivating the student by providing him with a complete set of books of account. Practice sets may be purchased with or without business papers. Without business papers the set is worked by using a series of printed descriptive transactions found either in the text or accompanying the set. The set with business papers is worked by the use of transactions determined from printed forms such as checks and invoices. Either type of practice set is valuable in instruction. The set with practice papers probably has greater motivational power, as the student works with simulated business papers typifying those found in a business. Thus the working of the set appears to be more realistic.

Overhead Transparencies

The use of overhead transparencies in the teaching of bookkeeping has become a basic tool. Few schools today are without an overhead projector, and the utilization of either a teacher-prepared transparency or one that has been commercially prepared is practically essential. Some overhead projectors have a roll of plastic film connected to them on which the teacher can write directly while talking to the class and at the same time can illustrate some difficult concept. The modern bookkeeping textbook is well illustrated; however, these illustrations are not always self-explanatory. The use of the chalkboard is a necessary device to further illustrate visually some specific topic or concept. In many cases, however, a chalkboard may be somewhat limited in size in a classroom, and in addition it is time-consuming for the teacher to use.

On the other hand, an overhead transparency can be utilized, for example, to visually project the solution to a problem or a project and thus save the teacher much time. Also, students can visually compare their solutions to an exercise with the correct solution and can spot procedural or conceptual errors quickly and easily. The degree of flexibility available to the teacher in the use of transparencies is unlimited. They can be used to illustrate accounting forms, accounting documents, the flow of bookkeeping procedures, and the development of bookkeeping concepts. In the opinion of the authors, the use of transparencies is mandatory to the successful teaching of modern-day book-keeping.

BASIC CONCEPTS OF TEACHING BOOKKEEPING

It is not practical in a general methods-of-teaching-business-subjects textbook to cover in detail all the specific teaching techniques applicable to a particular subject. Consequently, suggested solutions will be given only for those special techniques in teaching bookkeeping that seem to be the most significant and, from past experience, seem to cause teachers and students the most difficulty.

Several good and highly specialized books have been written for the book-keeping teacher, and they cover in much detail all of the instructional elements found in a bookkeeping course. It is strongly recommended that the teacher acquire these books as a major part of his professional library.

This section will examine some of the major concepts of teaching book-keeping—that is, some of the major decisions that a teacher must make before embarking on the course.

One of the most significant decisions that must be made by the teacher of bookkeeping is the degree of effort that will be placed upon the mechanical aspects of the course. The decision will have a material effect upon the methodology used by the teacher in presenting the subject matter.

Essentially, there are *two* major goals in the teaching of bookkeeping—the development in students of mechanical proficiency in keeping financial records and the development in students of an understanding of the uses of the information or data resulting from bookkeeping records. Inherent in this latter goal is the development in students of the ability to make use of bookkeeping data when making decisions about the various problems found in operating a business.

Both goals are important. It is necessary for a bookkeeping student to be able to master the mechanical aspects of keeping a set of books—this is the job of the bookkeeper. Equally important is the ability to understand the significance of bookkeeping data and to apply these data to the solutions of specific business problems. In other words, it is important to develop "thinking bookkeepers."

Obviously, the teaching methodology involved in achieving each goal is different. To teach mechanics involves the use of drill and memorization, the solving of mechanical problems on the part of the students, and a great deal of illustration and explanation on the part of the teacher.

To teach an understanding and application of bookkeeping data to the solutions of business problems involves the use of discussion, problem definition and solving (not mechanical problems but business-decision-type problems), and analytical judgments on the part of students.

It is possible to achieve both goals in a bookkeeping course by varying the methodology used and the techniques employed by the teacher. In the modern bookkeeping course it is important that both goals be achieved, and the successful teacher will find ways to vary his presentation to this end.

The Systems Approach to Teaching Bookkeeping

A significant basic concept of the teaching of bookkeeping can be referred to as the *systems approach*. This approach is not so much a method of presenting the subject matter as it is of emphasis placed upon the subject matter by the teacher. It is the authors' belief that a much clearer understanding of the subject can be achieved by students through this approach and, in addition, a more logical procedure can be utilized.

In the systems approach the financial record-keeping organization of a business is usually divided as follows:

1. A system for handling cash receipts and cash payments
2. A system for billing customers and maintaining records of accounts receivable
3. A system for handling purchase orders and maintaining records of accounts payable and inventories
4. An inventory system
5. A payroll system
6. A capital asset system
7. An internal control system
8. A general ledger system

All these systems are interrelated but in a sense are also isolated from each other in terms of the work performed by the bookkeeper. Normally, it is the responsibility of an independent auditor to accumulate all the data resulting from the records of the individual systems and to summarize these data into the financial reports. The basic concept the teacher should develop is that the day-to-day financial transactions of a business are *not* usually recorded in what is termed *in line*—that is, different kinds of business transactions are not recorded by the bookkeeper in the sequential order in which they are received. Rather, transactions of a similar nature are "batched"—that is, grouped together into the same kind and then processed as a unit.

For example, during certain hours of a day or days of a week, all invoices may be prepared, recorded, and mailed to customers, with the resulting updating of the accounts receivable file. At the another time all purchase orders may be processed, with the accounts payable file being updated. Cash receipts and cash payments may be recorded several times a day, with the various files affected being updated. Payroll is normally performed once a week or every two weeks or monthly. Inventories may be updated daily or handled in some other way compatible to the system devised by the business firm.

The typical bookkeeping textbook material is not organized using the systems approach, and it is probably not practical for it to be so organized. Problem transactions are normally presented to students in an in-line fashion so that the student can see a complete business cycle and be exposed to a variety of transactions. Nonetheless, a teacher can emphasize that transactions are actually recorded in a batch mode and thus give a more realistic emphasis to the course. An additional advantage of this approach is that it leads logically to a description of the various data-processing methods of maintaining records.

If a teacher wishes to modernize his bookkeeping course, this approach will help serve that purpose. The concept that bookkeeping records are maintained in *files* (accounts receivable file, accounts payable file, inventory file, etc.) and can be processed independently is actually how it is done in financial record keeping today.

It is true, however, that in the more sophisticated data-processing systems all these files can be integrated and processed in-line (as the transactions occur). Normally, only the large business firms have these comprehensive data-processing systems. Instructional techniques in the utilization of electronic data-processing procedures for financial record keeping will be covered in Chapter 10.

GENERAL METHODS OF TEACHING BOOKKEEPING

A variety of general methods are sound for use in teaching bookkeeping. Discussion, problem and project, and individual instruction are the most commonly used methods. No one method can be said to be the best nor should any one method be used entirely. The effective teacher will vary his method to suit the abilities of his students and the type of subject matter being studied. In teaching the analysis of financial statements the discussion method might prove to be the most beneficial, while in teaching the trial balance the problem method would be the most effective. In any event it is wise to adapt the method to fit the situation at hand; the good teacher will be able to sense when it is proper to change methods.

Discussion Method

The class discussion method can be used to great advantage in the teaching of bookkeeping, particularly in the teaching of understandings of the uses of bookkeeping data. A teacher can develop many problem situations, either actual or imaginary, and can present them to the class to illustrate the various situations when the records of a business are of value to the businessman. For example, the following is an illustration of a case problem that could be developed by a teacher as a basis for discussion in teaching an understanding of the application of bookkeeping data to a specific situation.

During the night of February 19 thieves broke into the Alexander Jewelry Store and stole some of the merchandise. The theft was discovered the next morning when Mr. Alexander, the owner of the store, arrived to open up. He immediately called the police, and since he was fully insured against any loss of this type also called his insurance agent.

Since many small items of jewelry were taken, it was not readily apparent how much the thieves had stolen. Both the police and the insurance agent suggested that an inventory be taken immediately. Mr. Alexander did this, and after several hours of counting he determined that the inventory of goods on hand after the theft amounted to $30,000 at cost price. However, since Mr. Alexander had purchased and sold merchandise since the last time he had taken an inventory (December 31 of the preceding year), he still was unable to determine exactly the amount of the theft.

What information will Mr. Alexander have to obtain from his records before he can find out how much was stolen?

Assuming that Mr. Alexander's records reflected the following data, can you determine the loss?

Sales, January 1 to February 19		$10,000
Purchases, January 1 to February 19		$15,000
Inventory, December 31 previous year		$40,000
Sales	$100,000	
Cost of goods sold	60,000	
Gross profit	$ 40,000	

The development of real or imaginary problem situations by the teacher as a basis for discussion can be an effective device. Using analogies from the teacher's own experience can also be valuable because it often gives an air of realism to the activities of the classroom. The bookkeeping teacher does not necessarily have to have had actual bookkeeping experience (although this experience is highly recommended) to use actual illustrations or analogies drawn from business firms. This information can be readily obtained merely by talking to businessmen about their problems in bookkeeping or by visiting places of business.

In addition, the modern bookkeeping textbooks include, along with the traditional type of problem, case problems of the type previously illustrated. These, along with teacher-developed cases, should provide a wealth of material for class discussion use.

Problem-and-Project Method

The bookkeeping course is highly adaptable to the problem-or-project method of teaching. The use of the short problems or the exercises that are found at the ends of chapters in the bookkeeping textbooks is almost mandatory for the successful learning of the theory and mechanics of bookkeeping. Longer problems or projects in the form of practice sets are also highly valuable. Personal projects such as determining the costs and profits of raising a farm animal for future sale or personal budgeting can be very stimulating. In some instances opportunity is provided for bookkeeping students to maintain school or class records. The teacher must always be aware of the availability of projects of these kinds and use them in his teaching as conditions warrant.

When using the problems at the ends of chapters as a teaching device, the teacher must be alert to see that this type of activity does not become dull and monotonous. Unavoidably, there is much "busy work" connected with the solving of problems, but through the careful selection and assignment of problems for students to work, unessential material can be kept to a minimum.

The teacher must keep certain techniques in mind in the assignment of problem material. Each problem assigned should be thoroughly discussed and illustrated so that students can determine their errors and thus make any corrections. As indicated earlier in this chapter, one of the best devices for the illustration of the solutions to problems is a transparency of the solution which can be shown on the overhead projector. These can be either copied from the teacher's key or· purchased from the publisher. It should not be necessary for the teacher to collect the problems and check them himself, but he should motivate the students to do this for themselves. Bookkeeping teachers often feel that they must collect all problem assignments if only for the purpose of checking on the student to see whether he has completed the assignment. The responsibility for completing assignments should be left to the student.

Some teachers often worry about students copying problem solutions from other students. Students very often copy as the result of the attitude and actions of the teacher. If the teacher insists upon 100 percent accuracy and criticizes the student who is inaccurate, then that teacher may well expect some of his students to copy work of others. If, on the other hand, the teacher expresses the attitude that errors in bookkeeping are a matter of course and that errors will be eliminated through understanding, then the problem of copying will be minimized. The teacher should encourage students to help each other in solving problems or, if difficulties develop, to come to him for aid.

Teachers must also be careful, using the problem technique, not to give so much aid to students that they do not have an opportunity to weigh judgments or make decisions for themselves. The inexperienced teacher, in order to be helpful, will often aid his students to the extent that solving the problem becomes a matter of the teacher's judgment rather than of the students'. Teachers will also find it advisable to work out the problems assigned themselves to predetermine where students will have difficulty and to avoid embarrassment if the teacher does not know the solution.

Individual Instruction

Teachers of bookkeeping will often find it necessary to give a large amount of individual instruction to members of the class because of the wide range of abilities that are commonly found in the bookkeeping class. This method can be used with special effectiveness in large classes. The procedure is to assign problems for the students to work in class. The teacher then goes about the room giving individual help where needed. When the teacher, as he moves about the class, observes a number of students having the same difficulty, time is taken out to make the relevant concept clear. After the concept has been taught, the class returns to working individually. More will be said in the latter part of this chapter concerning the various methods of allowing for individual differences in bookkeeping students.

METHODS OF TEACHING THE MAJOR INSTRUCTIONAL PROBLEMS IN BOOKKEEPING

As was stated earlier in this chapter, it is not practical in a general methods textbook to cover in detail methods of teaching all the various topics presented in a bookkeeping course. Consequently, this section will present some general suggestions pertaining to the major instructional problem areas encountered by bookkeeping teachers. The effective teacher, after gaining experience, will be able to develop his own specific techniques as a result of his own intelligent planning and ideas obtained from his professional reading.

The instructional problem areas encountered in the teaching of a first-year bookkeeping course can be broadly outlined as follows:

1. Introduction of basic bookkeeping concepts
   a. Purpose of bookkeeping system
   b. Language of accounting (bookkeeping)
   c. Introduction of accounting equation
2. Introduction of ledger accounts
   a. Purpose and form of ledger accounts
   b. Theory of debit and credit
   c. Special ledgers and control accounts
3. Introduction of journals
   a. Purpose of journals
   b. General journal
   c. Special journals
4. Introduction of working papers
   a. Purpose of working papers
   b. Adjustment of accounts
5. Introduction of financial statements
   a. Balance sheet
   b. Income statement
6. Introduction of closing process
   a. Purpose of closing process
   b. Procedure to be followed
7. Special bookkeeping problems
   a. Depreciation
   b. Inventories
   c. Bad debts
   d. Notes and interest
   e. Payroll procedures
   f. Problem solving

Introduction of Basic Bookkeeping Concepts

The starting point for bookkeeping instruction is very important and should be planned with great care. Getting the class off to a good start will do much to insure the students' future success in understanding the theory and mechanics of bookkeeping. The use of the discussion method can be valuable at the beginning to bring out the reasons for keeping accurate records for a business.

An effective method for developing the reasons for the bookkeeping function is to relate the study of bookkeeping to the study of the history of one's country. Historical events are recorded and analyzed in history books. The purpose of studying history is to learn about world events and traditions and development and the relationship of one's own country within that world. In addition, the study of history has significance to government leaders in charting future courses of action.

Similarly, a study of bookkeeping is a study of the recording and analysis of the financial history of a business. Like world or national history, study of financial history can aid a businessman in making financial decisions that will enable him to chart future courses of action.

To record the financial history of a business, a systematic method has been developed called *double-entry bookkeeping.* It is the various elements of this system that are to be learned by the student, and while at first glance it appears complicated, in actuality it is quite simple and logical. One of the greatest difficulties that students have in becoming familiar with the system is in learning the unique language of business. Accounting has been called the "language of business." Attempts have been made to standardize the terms used so that they will have the same meaning to all businessmen. Unfortunately, the language used in accounting can have different meanings when used in a nonaccounting sense, just as certain English words used by young people today can have an entirely different meaning to adults. This leads to lack of communication and understanding. Since terms used in accounting are unique, the teacher must make a determined effort to explain these terms and their variations carefully.

Almost all bookkeeping textbooks begin with a presentation of financial statements. This method has been proved over the years as having a sound psychological basis—the presentation of the end result of financial record keeping followed by the techniques for developing the end result. This procedure is known as the *balance sheet approach.* The most important element of this approach is known as the *basic accounting equation,* which is simply stated in the formula

$$\text{Assets} = \text{Equities}$$

The method of presentation and explanation utilized by the teacher in the development of this equation will determine the students' success in understanding the bookkeeping system. An understanding of the accounting equation will determine the students' ability to be able to

1. Comprehend the logic of double-entry bookkeeping
2. Analyze financial transactions
3. Record financial transactions properly
4. Understand the system that has been developed for maintaining financial records
5. Understand the differences between cash basis accounting and accrual basis accounting

The importance of student understanding of this basic equation cannot be overstated because every business transaction that a student will analyze and record in future problems assigned will affect the accuracy of the equation.

Another major requirement in the presentation of the accounting equation is a detailed explanation of the accounting terms used. The term *assets* can be simply explained as "any property of value used in a business." *Property* can be defined here as such physical items as cash, buildings, machines, supplies, and inventory.

The term *equities* can be simply explained as "the claims that various parties may have against the assets." It would be advisable at this point to repeat that while the purpose of bookkeeping is to maintain records of the physical assets used in a business and also of the equities in those assets, of greater significance is the recording of assets and equities in terms of their *dollar value*. Thus, the accounting equation can be further illustrated by the statement that "the dollar value of assets used in a business is always equal to the dollar value of the equities in those assets." We now have a simple mathematical equation

$$\$value \ of \ assets = \$value \ of \ equities$$

It is not unusual at this point for students to wonder "so what." What does this all mean? What it means is that every financial transaction affecting a business is analyzed in terms of the effect of the transaction on either the assets or the equities or both. After every business transaction the equation must always be in balance in terms of dollar amounts.

After the initial accounting equation is presented it will be necessary to expand it into its final form. The reason for this is that normally there are two types of *equities* in the *assets* of a business—creditor's equities and owner's equity. The common accounting term applied to creditor's equities is *liabilities* (note the difference in meaning here in a term as used in the accounting sense and in the nonaccounting sense). Liabilities represent the dollar value of claims against the assets used in a business. Thus the final form of the accounting equation is

$$Assets = Liabilities + Owner's \ equity$$
$$(\$value) \quad (\$value) \qquad (\$value)$$

The teacher should be cautioned again to proceed slowly during this initial presentation. It may well be that several class hours will be used in developing the foregoing theory. Do not be afraid of going over the equation again and again, using many different kinds of illustrations, and do not make the mistake of presenting unfamiliar terms to the students until they are ready for them. The elements of expenses and income should not be presented until later when the theory of debit and credit is explained.

One final word of caution before leaving this section. At the beginning of a bookkeeping course students often do not differentiate between the owners of a business and the business itself. Financial records are maintained for businesses rather than for those persons associated with the business. It is necessary that students understand this concept. A simple diagram such as the following may help to eliminate this confusion.

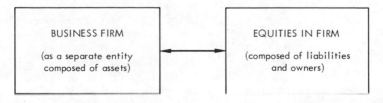

BUSINESS FIRM		EQUITIES IN FIRM
(as a separate entity composed of assets)	← →	(composed of liabilities and owners)

Introduction of Ledger Accounts

The bookkeeping device that has been utilized over the years to record business transactions is known as the *account*. It is a device peculiar to bookkeeping for use in recording changes in the type and value of assets used in a business and the type and value of equities in those assets. The simplest type of account is called the *T account* and is in the following form.

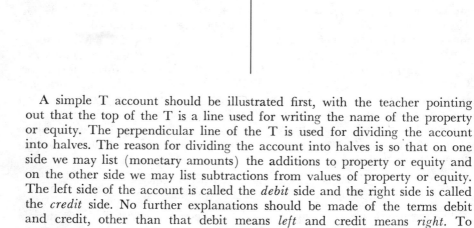

A simple T account should be illustrated first, with the teacher pointing out that the top of the T is a line used for writing the name of the property or equity. The perpendicular line of the T is used for dividing the account into halves. The reason for dividing the account into halves is so that on one side we may list (monetary amounts) the additions to property or equity and on the other side we may list subtractions from values of property or equity. The left side of the account is called the *debit* side and the right side is called the *credit* side. No further explanations should be made of the terms debit and credit, other than that debit means *left* and credit means *right*. To explain what accounts are credited for additions and debited for subtractions, and what accounts are debited for additions and credited for subtractions, reference can be made again to the bookkeeping equation, Assets = Liabilities +Owner's equity. Assets are on the left-hand side of the equation and thus should be debited for additions and credited for subtractions. Liabilities and Owner's equity are on the right-hand side or credit side of the equation and thus should be credited for additions and debited for subtractions.

There is no particular logic for this technique other than that custom has decreed that the procedure be followed, just as custom has decreed that we drive on the right-hand side of the road. Accordingly, students should be urged to memorize the theory of debit and credit. Any attempts to show a logical motive behind the theory of debit and credit will only confuse the students in most cases. The idea that debit means left and that credit means right is a very simple concept. By using the equation to recall which accounts should be debited for increases and which should be credited, the student should master the theory with little difficulty.

When the items of expense and income are presented, the bookkeeping equation can be used to good advantage. Income increases owner's equity and expense decreases owner's equity. The equation can be developed that Assets= Liabilities + Owner's equity + (Income − Expense). The fact that this equation appears complicated can be used to the teacher's advantage. Through the principle of transposition, Expense can be transposed to the left-hand side of the equation and thus eliminate the minus sign so as to make the equation appear like this:

$$\text{Assets} + \text{Expenses} = \text{Liabilities} + \text{Owner's equity} + \text{Income}$$
$$(\$\text{value}) + (\$\text{value}) = (\$\text{value}) + (\$\text{value}) + (\$\text{value})$$

It should be evident, then, that Expenses are debited for increases (because of being on the left-hand side of the equation) and Income is credited for increases (because of being on the right-hand side of the equation).

The theory of debit and credit is the foundation of double-entry bookkeeping as compared with single-entry bookkeeping. Every transaction is recorded in two parts in double-entry—a debit and a credit, with the debits always equaling the credits. In single-entry bookkeeping the theory of debit and credit is not followed; thus the information resulting from this type of bookkeeping is less complete than that resulting from double-entry bookkeeping. Single-entry bookkeeping provides information only for increases or decreases in assets without the corresponding increase or decrease in the equity. Accordingly, single-entry bookkeeping is not as desirable as double-entry because it provides inadequate information for the typical business.

While the foregoing explanation of the theory of debit and credit can be rationalized by the student through examination of the accounting equation, it may be easier for the student to memorize the following rules.

1. Assets are increased by debits; decreased by credits.
2. Liabilities are increased by credits; decreased by debits.
3. Owner's equity is increased by credits; decreased by debits.
   a. Expenses are increased by debits (resulting in decreases in owner's equity); decreased by credits (resulting in increases in owner's equity).
   b. Income is increased by credits (resulting in increases in owner's equity); decreased by debits (resulting in decreases in owner's equity).

The use of the simple "T" account does not provide sufficient bookkeeping information, although its use at the beginning of instruction is quite valuable to illustrate the recording process. The formal account form is normally set up in the following format.

CASH

Date	Explanation	Post Ref.	Debit	Date	Explanation	Post Ref.	Credit

A group of accounts of a similar nature is known as a *ledger*, with the name of the ledger indicating the types of accounts found therein. A *general ledger* contains all the asset and equity accounts. An *accounts receivable ledger* contains the detail about all the firm's customers. An *accounts payable ledger* contains the detail about all the firm's creditors. Ledger accounts may be in many different forms other than that illustrated above, depending upon the manual, machine, or electronic accounting system being used. Teachers should obtain illustrations of these various forms to show to students.

Introduction of Journals

The teacher should experience little difficulty in teaching the books of account, the general and special journals, and the general and subsidiary ledgers. The use of the general journal to record transactions prior to posting them to the various accounts can be justified on the basis of convenience. Journals would not necessarily have to be used in bookkeeping. However, it is often necessary for a businessman to refer to a transaction that occurred on a specific day of the month. This commonly occurs where there may be a difference of opinion between the owner of a business and a customer as to whether or not a bill has been paid. Students should be made to understand that the chronological recording of transactions can provide an easy means of reference for a businessman with respect to a given transaction; thus, transactions should be journalized in chronological order. The teacher can provide illustrations of the difficulty encountered in locating specific transactions when a general journal is not used.

The extra work involved in bookkeeping by the use of a general journal can be used as a means of introducing the special journals (sales, purchases, cash receipts, and cash payments). The use of these journals should be justified primarily on the basis of minimizing the work of posting. When transactions of a similar nature occur frequently enough in a business, it is most logical to place these similar transactions in a special journal so that the total may be posted in one amount. Illustrations by the teacher showing the extra work involved by not using special journals should appeal to students. Whenever new concepts are introduced in the bookkeeping course, they can usually be justified on the basis of either providing more complete information for the businessman or simplifying the record-keeping processes. Students should be made to understand the necessity for the large amount of detail work in keeping a set of books and that whenever it is possible to simplify this detail work, savings are realized both in money and in the work time of the bookkeeper.

The use of controlling accounts with the consequent use of the subsidiary ledgers is usually not presented in bookkeeping textbooks until the final chapters. By this time the concept of simplification should be fairly well developed in the students' minds with consequent little difficulty in comprehension. Difficulty is sometimes encountered concerning the posting to two ledgers, the general ledger and the subsidiary ledger. Students are sometimes confused by the procedure, feeling that double posting is taking place. It should be carefully pointed out that the use of subsidiary ledgers eliminates the use of a large number of accounts in the general ledger, thereby shortening the number of accounts that will be listed on the trial balance.

Many teachers feel that a great deal of time must be spent upon the mechanics of ruling accounts in the ledger, insisting upon neatness and exact procedure. The authors believe that this technique is inconsequential as compared with the more important principle of understanding the use of books of account. Accordingly, emphasis on the details of this nature should be kept to a minimum.

Introduction of Working Papers

Emphasis by teachers of bookkeeping on the work sheet as a device used by bookkeepers has been greatly out of proportion as compared with other important aspects of the course. Understanding of the work sheet is necessary, but it is often given disproportionate attention because it embodies many important concepts of bookkeeping. Teachers have used the work sheet for examination purposes because it represents a relatively easy problem to develop for examinations. Used out of context in this manner it is often placed in the students' minds as one of the highly important statements for a business. Consequently, there has been much memorizing of the form of the work sheet with little knowledge of the reasons for its use.

The work sheet, as its name implies, is merely a device used by bookkeepers for accumulating the information from the books of account for the purpose of performing the work necessary at the end of a fiscal period. It can be likened to an outline prepared by a student for use in writing a theme or to the notes used by a speaker in giving an address. In introducing the work sheet for the first time, the teacher could illustrate its value and use by asking students the following: "Let us suppose that I have made an assignment in which I have asked you to keep a record for one month of every receipt and expenditure of money. Let us assume that at the end of the month you had a notebook full of individual transactions listing each receipt and expenditure. I then asked you to type a report in which you would list your receipts under the headings of gifts, earned, and miscellaneous; and you would list your expenditures under the headings of entertainment, clothes, personal, car, and miscellaneous. This report is to be handed in and graded. How would you proceed in writing your report?"

Although the teacher might get a variety of answers as a result of this question, nonetheless through skillful directions he should obtain from the students the procedure that each student would first summarize on scrap paper the classifications of the various receipts and expenditures called for prior to the final typing of the report. The fallacy of attempting to type the report without making this "rough summarization" can easily be pointed out.

Illustrating, then, how this technique is comparable to the techniques of the bookkeeper using a work sheet for the preparation of his reports should fix in the students' minds the necessity and logic of this tool. The mechanics of classifying and adjusting accounts should then be more meaningful if established upon this broad base of understanding.

The first work sheet to be introduced in bookkeeping is the simple six-column type with no adjustments. The purpose of this work sheet is to determine the accuracy of posting through listing the trial balance and to classify the accounts into profit and loss statement accounts and balance sheet accounts for preparing statements. Little difficulty should be encountered in teaching the students the use of this device. Time should be taken to explain the steps to be followed if the trial balance does not balance, such as analyzing the difference to determine where the error might be located. Although many teachers make a fetish of accuracy, it should be pointed out that errors often result from maintaining a set of books. Students should be taught how to analyze errors to determine what steps should be taken to locate them. For example, in the trial balance errors may arise in transferring numbers from the account in the ledger to the work sheet. An error of this type may be located by dividing the difference of the trial balance by nine. If the difference is equally divisible by nine there is a good likelihood that this type of error has occurred. Another step to be taken is to divide the difference by two. After dividing by two, the bookkeeper can look to see whether any number in the trial balance is the same as this figure and is incorrectly placed in either the debit or the credit column. An error of this nature will double the difference in the trial balance. These are only a few of the checks a student may make to locate errors. Others should be brought to his attention. By this procedure greater understanding is developed.

A second difficulty that may be encountered in using the simple six-column worksheet is the classifying of accounts for statement purposes. The teacher should, at every opportunity, direct the attention of the student to the differences between the temporary and the permanent accounts. It may be advantageous to drill the students on the classification of accounts into the major classifications of Assets, Liabilities, Owner's equity, Expense, and Income. Students should also be well versed in classifying accounts into the subclassifications under these major headings. Only through a thorough knowledge of the various classifications into which accounts fall will students be able to prepare financial statements properly.

The work sheet with adjustments poses more difficult problems than does the simple six-column type. This device is usually not introduced into the course until the latter part when a merchandising type of business is being studied. The types of adjustments usually developed at this time are the adjustments for supplies, insurance, and merchandise inventory. The major concept to teach when presenting the adjusting entries is to help the students understand the need for them. Adjusting entries are necessary because of the principle of expediency. Some accounts are not kept up to date because it would be too much trouble for the bookkeeper to do so. Because there are certain accounts that are not kept up to date, adjusting entries are necessary to bring them up to date at the end of the fiscal period.

The teacher can use many different types of illustrations to show why it will be impractical to maintain certain accounts currently. For example, use the account, store supplies. It would appear rather silly for the check-out clerk in a grocery store to run back and inform the bookkeeper every time she used a paper bag to pack groceries for a customer. The best way, obviously, would be to count the paper bags on hand at the end of a fiscal period and subtract this number from the paper bags purchased. By making this computation the actual number of paper bags consumed could be easily determined. From this type of illustration it is an easy step to the need for adjustment entries. Similar illustrations can be developed for the prepaid insurance account, salaries, interest, and so forth.

The merchandise-inventory adjustment presents a somewhat similar problem. However, more careful consideration must be given to this entry. The beginning inventory is closed out because it is a part of the cost of goods sold. In a sense, at the close of a fiscal period, a business will not have any of the goods on hand that were on hand at the beginning of the period because theoretically the first goods on hand are the first sold. Thus, the beginning inventory is closed to the income-and-expense summary account, since this account is used to summarize cost and expenses and income. The ending inventory, on the other hand, is recorded as a debit to the inventory account because it is the correct amount of inventory at the present time. Since any goods on hand at the end of the fiscal period reduces the cost of goods sold, then the ending inventory should be credited to the income-and-expense summary account to offset the beginning inventory, which was debited to this account.

The teacher should teach this adjustment very carefully, making sure that the students understand the *why*. Again, the use of practical illustrations will be of great benefit.

Introduction of Financial Statements

The teaching of financial statements in elementary bookkeeping is not a difficult task. However, the emphasis placed upon these important documents by teachers varies. Teachers who place an undue emphasis upon the mechanics of bookkeeping often fail to pinpoint the financial statements as the end result of keeping books—without the financial statements, bookkeeping would be meaningless.

A large amount of time should be spent upon the income statement and balance sheet to show how these statements disclose the profit-making ability of the business and its financial condition. Mere preparation of statements is not sufficient—interpretation and understanding must also take place. The teacher should build a file of financial statements from various types of businesses and use these illustrative materials to show how stockholders, lending agencies, and prospective owners of a business can use these data for their various purposes.

Is net worth stated accurately? What are some of the evidences that indicate that a business should adjust its financial procedure? These are among the questions that should be discussed and answered. The forms of the various statements are relatively unimportant as compared with understanding their functions and what they reveal. It is the latter that should be emphasized in teaching bookkeeping.

Introduction of Closing Process

The work that must be performed at the close of a fiscal period is known as the *periodic summary*. Besides the work of taking a trial balance to test the equality of debits and credits, work must be performed that will bring certain accounts up to date (adjustments), and the financial statements must be prepared. The final work to be performed is the closing of those accounts that are temporary so as to clear the books for the succeeding fiscal period. The mechanical work of closing out the temporary or nominal accounts is relatively simple and should not cause the teacher much difficulty in helping students to understand *why*. If students do have difficulty in understanding why certain accounts are closed out at the end of a fiscal period, it is good evidence that students do not understand the nature and characteristics of temporary accounts and thus this concept should be retaught.

By the use of "T" accounts the teacher can illustrate that the cost and expense and income accounts are merely subdivisions of the Owner's equity account. Actually, there is no need to classify transactions into either income or expense, as these transactions can be entered directly into the proprietorship account. [Refer to the equation, Assets = Liabilities + Owner's equity + (Income − Expenses).] However, according to the principle of obtaining complete information about a business, certain transactions are classified as either expenses or income so that they may stand out more clearly as either increasing or decreasing proprietorship. The following diagram could be used:

Consequently, after the cost and expense and income accounts have served their purpose of providing information concerning these elements to the proprietor for a fiscal period, they are no longer needed and thus are closed out. The information provided is transferred to the proprietorship account through the closing-out process.

The mechanics of closing the temporary accounts is sometimes confusing to students because of the many steps involved. This procedure can be clarified to some extent by first showing how the temporary accounts can be closed directly into the proprietorship account and then giving a contrasting illustration that shows them being closed into the profit-and-loss summary, thence to the drawing account, and finally to the proprietorship account. The advantages and disadvantages of the latter method could be discussed as well as the advantages and disadvantages of the direct method. Through this type of activity, students will be able to understand the procedure better, as well as learn the mechanics.

Care must be taken not to confuse the students with the closing process and the ruling and balancing of the permanent accounts. This latter procedure has no connection with closing accounts but is followed for the purpose of setting out the balances of the permanent accounts at the start of the new fiscal period. Careless use of bookkeeping terminology often leads to confused students. Detailed explanations should be made of such terms as *ruling an account, balancing an account,* the *balance of an account,* and the *closing of an account.* Students may experience difficulty because of lack of understanding of these terms.

Special Bookkeeping Problems

Some special problems that often cause difficulty to bookkeeping students should be carefully considered by the teacher—such topics as payroll and tax procedures, accruals, interest determination, and allowances for depreciation and bad debts.

Payroll procedures and income tax have been given increasing emphasis in the past few years by authors of bookkeeping textbooks—and rightfully so. Payroll bookkeeping is a specialized field in itself and not much time can be devoted to it in the typical bookkeeping class. In any event, the teacher should be well versed in payroll taxes such as the social security taxes, old age benefits, and unemployment insurance. As there have been several changes in social security taxes in recent years, the teacher should inform himself of the most recent changes in the laws. An excellent device that may be followed (if available) is to visit a business firm that has a large number of employees so that students can see firsthand how payroll procedures are handled. If the teacher can obtain some practical experience in payroll accounting, his presentations of this point will also be materially improved. If a field trip is not feasible, resource persons can be invited to the class for discussion of payroll information. Such persons as businessmen, personnel managers, or field representatives for the district social security office would be valuable sources of information.

The teaching of income tax in the public schools has also been given increasing emphasis in the past few years. Typically, this instruction has been found in the bookkeeping class, which makes it necessary for the bookkeeping teacher to have up-to-date information about income tax procedure. The Bureau of Internal Revenue has developed an income tax unit which covers a period of approximately two weeks. This income tax teaching kit provided by the Bureau of Internal Revenue consists of teacher's manuals for a general course in income tax and a farm course. Each student is provided with a handbook for use in working both courses; the handbook includes income tax blanks. Also included are large income tax forms for purposes of visual instruction.

The policy of the Bureau of Internal Revenue of providing teaching materials for income tax instruction in high school has been very successful. Consequently, it is highly probable that there will be increases in emphasis on instruction in this area with the teacher of bookkeeping being given the responsibility of seeing that it is carried out.

Other special problems that will be encountered by the teacher of bookkeeping will be the teaching of accrual bookkeeping. Such concepts as allowances for bad debts and depreciation, accrued receivables, and accrued payables may sometimes be difficult to explain. One method may be to explain and illustrate carefully the differences between cash-basis bookkeeping and accrual basis. Federal income tax regulations may be used as another illustration. Personal illustrations such as a wage that is earned daily but not paid until the end of a week or a month can also be used. The idea of income being earned, or costs and expenses being owed, prior to their being paid, should be developed early in the course. When sales or purchases on credit are first taught it is not too early to discuss the principle of accrual bookkeeping. Early introduction of this concept will help to make it easier to teach when it is stressed more in the latter part of the bookkeeping course.

. At this point it should be pointed out to teachers to be aware of a common problem that students have with respect to solving bookkeeping problems. Regardless of the teacher's technical teaching competence, bookkeeping can best be learned through the students' activity in working problems—learning through analyzing their mistakes. However, in many instances students become frustrated in their problem-solving activity because of their inability to understand the language used in a problem transaction.

Authors of bookkeeping textbooks are sometimes inconsistent in the format and language used in developing a problem transaction. This leads to confusion on the part of students as to what has actually transpired in the transaction.

For example, a transaction might state that "Customers are to be billed for sales made during the week." Obviously, the student is supposed to debit accounts receivable and credit sales. In the same problem another transaction might state that "Brown purchased $100 worth of merchandise on account." The same entry should be made; however, because of the inconsistency used in wording the transaction, students become confused.

In an actual business environment there would be no question as to what the bookkeeper should do. In textbook problem transactions students might not be so sure. Thus, teachers should examine problem assignments carefully and point out to students any inconsistencies so that these frustrations can be minimized.

MISCELLANEOUS PROBLEMS IN TEACHING BOOKKEEPING

Several other problems in the teaching of bookkeeping must be faced by the teacher. While these are not all directly related to the methodology of teaching the content of the course, because of the nature of these problems they have a significant effect upon the methodology that will be used.

One problem is the wide range of student abilities typically found in a bookkeeping class. This problem is one of the most annoying and frustrating to the bookkeeping teacher because it is so difficult to cope with. In almost every class some students will be unable to comprehend fully the principles involved in bookkeeping and other students will have little or no difficulty in mastering the concepts of the course.

One solution for teaching the weaker students is individual instruction. This may be accomplished either in or outside of class, but in any event it is a poor solution because of the extra work thrust upon an already overburdened teacher. However, one must either use this type of teaching or else let the poorer students get along as best they can with the teacher giving individual help whenever possible. This is a real problem because understanding in bookkeeping is built upon certain fundamental knowledges. Unless these fundamentals are thoroughly understood at the beginning, a student is destined to have difficulty. It is not practical or fair for the teacher to hold back the majority of a class until everyone in the class is thoroughly versed in the fundamentals. Consequently, someone must be left behind.

In the case of better students there are several possible solutions to the problem. The most common "solution" heard mentioned by teachers is to provide the better students with extra work. This is often impractical because it is conceivable that the attitude of the better student might be, "The more I study the more work I have to do—so why study?" A much better technique to use in the case of the superior student would be to encourage him to work ahead in the course at his own speed. Do not attempt to keep this type of student with the rest of the class, but stimulate him to proceed as fast as he wishes. Another procedure is to ask the superior student to help the slower students. A student can often help another student much better than the teacher because of better understanding of difficulties. Still another procedure might be to give the superior student an advanced textbook, perhaps a college accounting text, which he might study. A personal project might be worked out. In any event, the superior student should be encouraged to work ahead. This should not be mandatory, of course, because then the working ahead might be interpreted as extra assignments. Any technique of this nature must be used with the student's approval or on a volunteer basis. Only then will it be successful.

One development that seems to hold much promise for a solution to the problem of handling individual differences in students is the use of programmed learning materials. On the college level, programmed learning materials for accounting have been used successfully. As yet few programmed learning materials have been developed for use in the teaching of bookkeeping. However, because of the nature of the subject matter found in bookkeeping, programmed learning could be used effectively. Some research has been carried out in this area and the results have been promising. It is not unlikely that future developments in the instruction of bookkeeping in the secondary school will find programmed learning materials being used extensively.

Another problem that often confronts bookkeeping teachers is a weakness on the part of students in the fundamental processes of arithmetic. Teachers will often find that some students have difficulty in addition, subtraction, division, and multiplication, all of which are so often used in bookkeeping. Teachers have to decide, when this condition is apparent, whether to take time out from the content of the bookkeeping course to give instruction in these fundamentals. There is no one solution to this problem. It will be up to the individual teacher to make his own decision on whether to teach arithmetic if students are having difficulty. Some of the bookkeeping textbooks provide exercises at the ends of chapters that are developed for the purpose of meeting this weakness of students. Some schools provide adding and calculating machines for their bookkeeping classes. It is recommended that whenever machines are available, they should be used by students—as certainly in most businesses they would be available. Interest tables can be provided for students for use in computing interest, and payroll or sales tax tables should be used.

Still another problem found in the teaching of bookkeeping is the paper work with which the teacher may become involved. To what extent should the problems worked by students be checked by the teacher? Should the assignments merely be given a check mark of completion or should they be thoroughly checked? If a teacher is teaching one or more classes in bookkeeping, this paper work can become a tremendous burden. The other extreme is to do no checking at all. This can be accomplished by thoroughly going over in class the problems that have been assigned, each student then checking his own paper. Any errors on the student's paper can be used as a basis for discussion or explanation by the teacher. This method will not ·determine whether a student has worked the assignment, but if the teacher has instilled the idea that success in bookkeeping to a large degree will be determined by the student's applying the principles of the course in the solving of problems, there should be little difficulty on this score. The teacher should be able to determine by observation those students who are not working the assignments; an individual talk to these students should help to motivate them to perform their homework. The job of the teacher is primarily to teach, not to check papers. Accordingly, paper checking should be kept to a minimum.

An administrative technique that appears to be particularly suited to instruction in bookkeeping is *modular scheduling*. Modules of various numbers and lengths of time can be organized so that students can concentrate on their bookkeeping assignments in the bookkeeping class depending upon the amount of time required for specific topics. It is reasonable to believe that bookkeeping instruction in the future will be organized in this manner.

VISUAL AIDS AND MOTIVATION DEVICES FOR TEACHING BOOKKEEPING

Many types of visual aids and motivation devices for the teaching of bookkeeping are very helpful to the teacher. Bookkeeping is a subject that requires the use of a large number of visual devices for thorough comprehension of the instructional material. The subject matter usually provides motivation in itself, but the course can be greatly enriched by the use of certain techniques that stimulate the student to greater interest in bookkeeping.

Visual Aids. An effective type of visual aid that can be used by the teacher is the chalkboard. Adequate chalkboard space is a must for working all problems that have been assigned, as these problems should be thoroughly illustrated and discussed. It is usually not sufficient merely to go over the problem assignments in class orally. The teacher will find it to his advantage to use the chalkboard to visually illustrate how the transactions are recorded, the form of financial statements, the development of work sheets, and any other problem involved in bookkeeping. Any explanation by the teacher of a bookkeeping procedure should be accompanied by visual illustration. The chalkboard will provide an excellent means for this.

The use of the overhead projector and transparencies supplements the use of the chalkboard effectively. In fact, the overhead projector can be more effective than the use of the chalkboard for illustrating the solutions to problems. As indicated earlier, most textbook publishing firms will sell, at a nominal cost to users of their textbook, transparencies that show the solutions to all the problems given in the text. The projection of these solutions on the screen will save the teacher a tremendous amount of time and will give the students an opportunity to check their work against the correct solution. Also, for those schools fortunate enough to have a copying machine the teacher can prepare his own transparencies with little trouble and cost.

Films and filmstrips are also available for instruction in bookkeeping. The films that are available are not particularly helpful with respect to methodology but are organized more on the basis of guidance. Several filmstrips available for instruction are correlated with specific textbooks. These filmstrips can be extremely valuable, especially in teaching the mechanical aspects of bookkeeping.

The bookkeeping teacher can develop many types of visual aids himself through the preparation of charts, diagrams, bulletin-board displays, and so on. The following are some of the techniques that the teacher may use in developing these materials.

SUGGESTIONS FOR TEACHER-MADE VISUAL AIDS IN BOOKKEEPING

Use color without fail!
Don't try to put too much on one chart or poster.
Use faint pencil guidelines (layout!) and then do it *freehand*.

1. Flash cards are easy.   (one side)   (other side)

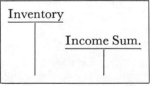

| An entire set is useful on closing and adjusting entries. | Inventory | Income Sum. | Entry to record the NEW Inventory |

Also, use a set having merely account names—for drill on account classification, recognition of debit or credit balance, in which statement used, whether closed or not, and the like.

2. A series of ledger accounts; use four-colored ball pen for colored lines. Might be: Cash Account with entries only; another showing it "forwarded"; another showing it balanced. Then an account like Sales or Purchases, showing it open, then forwarded, and finally CLOSED. Use accounts from the text.

3. Copy the first simple P & L Statement or Balance Sheet on a large chart from which to talk to the class! (Use color.)

In a P & L Statement (or Income Statement) you MIGHT write certain important items in RED—as the GROSS profit, the NET profit—or the word *Cost* in "Cost of Goods Sold."

4. A poster—just to hang in the room at the appropriate time or times—relating to any item:

> Steps in the bookkeeping cycle
> "Closing" the ledger
> "Adjusting" the ledger
> Showing DAYS responsible for any accrued item
> Showing, by lines or arrows, the "Posting" of a journal entry; of the totals of a special journal, and so on (section of original book and then the accounts concerned)
> The "discount period" in a note receivable discounted; a "personal" balance sheet—copied from text, perhaps

5. Print up the HEADINGS for all columns in a work sheet—on a cardboard strip that can be placed above the top of your chalkboard; perhaps show the BEGINNING of the vertical ruled lines, in colors. Then it is easy to CONTINUE these lines down the board—using colored chalk—and have a MUCH BETTER chalkboard work sheet. This might also be done profitably with special journals.

6. For CONTROLLING ACCOUNTS, show a special journal, totaled and ruled, and beside it a book marked SUBSIDIARY LEDGER (Accounts Receivable?) and another marked GENERAL LEDGER—with arrows or colored lines going from the TOTAL to the general ledger, and from the (bracketed) individual items to the subsidiary ledger. Make "ledgers" different colors!

Recommendations: A set of eight Speedball BLICKER pens costs very little. India ink comes in MANY colors. Use reasonably heavy cardboard or poster board; it CAN be had in color itself! (Use white MOSTLY though.) Clean the pen well after using; temporarily let it set in water when you are not using it. Use art-gum eraser for pencil marks and slight dirt. Learn a simple alphabet to use—printed.

Motivation Techniques

Although for many bookkeeping students the subject matter of bookkeeping is motivating in itself, nonetheless there are certain techniques that the teacher can use to advantage. Visitations to places of business to observe bookkeeping records has proved to be highly motivating. Prior to visiting places of business, the teacher should warn the students that the records they will see will in all likelihood be dissimilar to the records they have studied in their textbooks. There is a logical explanation to this in that bookkeeping procedures have certain fundamental processes that will be found in any bookkeeping system. However, different types of businesses will adapt the fundamental processes to their own peculiar problems, which results in dissimilar practices. The teacher can take advantage of this situation to ask the students to look for the application of the fundamental processes during the visitation. Another point that should be discussed prior to the visitation is that much bookkeepnig today is done on machines. Consequently, the records observed may not appear to be like any the student has studied. Actually it should be pointed out that the records will be similar in many respects but that machine records must be adapted in size and form to be used in a bookkeeping machine.

Visitations by the teacher to places of business to observe bookkeeping procedures will also be helpful to the teacher in enriching class presentation. The teacher's familiarity with actual bookkeeping procedure can be used in class discussion to illustrate how textbook procedures are comparable to actual business practice. Personal experiences of the teacher in actual bookkeeping, through either observation or work experience, can do much to stimulate class discussions. Students will feel that the subject matter has more life if the teacher can point out actual business problems that are applicable to the topic being studied.

Keeping records of personal projects engaged in by students will also prove of value to stimulate interest in bookkeeping. Farm students who are raising farm animals or produce for sale could have a type of project in which practice using adequate records of income and expenses would be of value. The keeping of records for class projects such as those sponsored by junior or senior classes to raise funds for some purpose can be used. Many other types of projects, either individual or group, could be used by the bookkeeping teacher to stimulate interest in bookkeeping. The teacher should be constantly on the lookout for projects and should weave these into the course whenever possible.

EVALUATION IN BOOKKEEPING

Several problems in evaluation are peculiar to bookkeeping; they revolve around the various bases for assigning grades to students for achievement. The most common bases for assigning grades are examinations, homework assignments, and practice sets or projects. Each of these bases is discussed in the succeeding paragraphs.

Examinations

Examinations for determining student achievement in bookkeeping can be placed into two categories, namely, published tests and teacher-prepared tests. Published tests, usually of an objective nature containing questions of the true-false, multiple-choice, and completion type, are very comprehensive. These tests are typically furnished by the publisher of the textbook free to teachers who are using the text. The questions in the test are correlated with the textbook material, and in some cases norms have been developed so that the teacher can compare the achievement of his students with others in terms of the norms. These examinations are quite easy to use, since the teacher does not have to prepare the examination and the tests are quite well developed.

Teacher-prepared examinations can be the objective type similar to the published tests or can be in the form of problems similar to those worked by the students as a result of assignments. It is in this latter category that some difficulties develop.

One of the main difficulties that occurs in the use of problem-type tests is in the grading. If one long problem is used for examination purposes, the teacher is faced with the difficulty of what to do if an error is made by the student in an early part of the test that will cause subsequent errors in the final answer. This difficulty may be eliminated through the procedure of counting off only once for an error that may affect later parts of the problem. Following this procedure will make it necessary for the teacher to follow each error through the problem, which obviously causes much careful analysis of each error and, consequently, takes a great deal of time.

Another problem in using this type of test is that of determining how much to count off for each error made. Some scheme must be developed whereby the test is divided into parts for grading, with a proportionate number of points being given to each part. Again the teacher is faced with the problem of determining the weight to be given to each part. For example, let us suppose that the examination is composed of a problem over the work sheet. The student is given a list of accounts with balances plus information for adjustments of account and with these data he is asked to complete the work sheet. One grading scheme that might be used would be to assign twenty points each to the columns containing the trial balance, the adjustment, profit and loss, and balance sheet, with an additional twenty bonus points given if the work sheet is completed in the time allowed without error. Perhaps two points could be taken off for each error in a column. Thus, if a student made one error his score would be seventy-eight. If he made no errors his score would be one hundred. However, errors made in the trial balance column should not be penalized again when they are carried over to the remaining columns.

Another problem encountered is the time element. Should students be given a problem that can be completed within the time limit by the poorest student? If so, then the best students are not being challenged. If not, then some students may say, "I only completed half of the problem, but what I did complete was 100 percent accurate. I am sure that I would have gotten the problem all right if I had had more time." Whether time should play a part in a problem examination is a decision that will have to be made by the individual teacher. It is the belief of the authors that time *should* play a part and that the best students are those who can work rapidly as well as accurately.

Many of the difficulties of scoring problem-type tests, as indicated above, can be eliminated by using short problems that test one concept or part of a larger problem. For example, an examination containing short problems such as illustrated below can be used effectively.

(10 points) John Short, an employee of the ABC Company, has been paid $4,500 in wages from the beginning of the year. His wages earned for the period October 3–17 are $250. His income tax withholding is $19.90. For what amount

will Short's paycheck for the period October 3–17 be made? (Use the current F.I.C.A. tax rate.)

One type of question that is not used frequently in determining achievement in bookkeeping is the essay type, the reasons being the lack of objectivity and the time required in grading. However, this type of question has great value, especially in determining if students can communicate their ideas to others. Occasional use of this type of question is highly recommended.

Homework Assignments

Another problem in evaluation is to decide to what extent homework assignments should be checked or graded. If the teacher examines every homework assignment carefully, an extremely large amount of time will necessarily have to be spent on the activity with less time available for planning. It is a question of values. Which is more important—preparation for instruction or checking the results of instruction? There is no easy answer to this question. However, if the teacher carefully goes over each assignment in class, discussing the difficulties that have arisen, then there should be little necessity for checking the homework assignments that are turned in. The teacher may wish to determine whether the students have completed the assignment, and this can be done rapidly. Perhaps an occasional spot-checking of the papers for accuracy can be made, but as a general procedure it is recommended that the completion of assignments should be a student responsibility and that the students be encouraged to get individual help from the teacher concerning the answers to assignments that are worked incorrectly.

Practice Sets

The grading of practice sets can be another onerous chore for the bookkeeping teacher unless some system is developed whereby this can be done with a minimum of time. Neatness and form of practice sets can be determined by a casual look through the sets, noting these particular characteristics. The age-old debate as to whether practice sets should be worked in pen or in pencil is unimportant. Those advocating the pen justify their stand by stating that the books of a business are kept in ink and thus the student of bookkeeping may as well keep his set of accounts in the same manner. Teachers holding this belief undoubtedly place a great emphasis on the *how*. On the other hand, those teachers who advocate pencil stress the *why*. These teachers assume that learning bookkeeping is a practice situation and that a student's assurance should not be marred by being required to use ink and thus being unable to erase a mistake. The latter approach seems to be the more practical. In any event, the choice of pen or of pencil is unimportant.

The accuracy of the practice set can be determined by the use of an open-set test over the practice set. The teacher can develop a series of questions which the student may answer by referring to his set. These questions typically can call for the totals of the columns in journals, balances of accounts, net profit, total of selling expenses, and the like. Thus, accuracy of the set can be determined as well as the student's familiarity with the set in knowing where to look for the answers.

PROJECTS AND QUESTIONS FOR DISCUSSION

1. Examine and compare two high school bookkeeping text books. Pay particular attention to the following points:
   a. Order of presentation of the various topics covered in the text
   b. Types of study material for students at the ends of chapters
   c. Illustrations
   d. Major differences in presentation of subject matter
   e. Supplementary materials available, such as teacher's key, workbooks, study guides, and tests
2. Develop a case problem or case problems for use in class discussion by a secondary school bookkeeping class. Adapt the cases to some specific topic covered in a secondary school textbook.
3. Prepare five short problem-type questions that would be suitable for an examination of a unit in bookkeeping.
4. Prepare a visual aid of some type to illustrate a particular topic in bookkeeping. Select a topic that you think students may have difficulty with and develop the visual aid in such a way that it will help in understanding.
5. Select a specific unit in bookkeeping and prepare a lesson plan for teaching the unit. Include with the plan any visual aids or motivating devices you would use in teaching the unit. Be specific and describe in detail all of the procedures you would follow in presenting the unit.
6. Obtain examples of bookkeeping forms such as ledger cards and journals that are used in a local business. Write a short paper about how these forms relate to the kinds illustrated in a bookkeeping textbook.
7. Prepare three transparencies that can be used to illustrate some particular concept in the teaching of bookkeeping.
8. Interview a bookkeeping teacher to obtain his views with respect to the major problems he has encountered in teaching bookkeeping. Present an oral report to your methods class concerning the results of your interview.
9. Demonstrate to the methods class how you would teach a specific topic in bookkeeping.
10. Prepare a short paper in which you summarize some of the significant and timely articles written for professional journals on the teaching of bookkeeping.

CASE PROBLEMS

1. The head of the business department has asked you to give him a detailed analysis of the techniques and procedures you plan to use for evaluating your bookkeeping classes. He would like to see examples of examinations you plan to give and any quizzes, homework assignments, projects, and other evaluative materials. In addition, he wants to know how you plan to weigh each item for assigning nine-week and semester grades.

Imagine that you consider his request unreasonable because you prefer to keep your evaluative procedures as flexible as possible and plan to develop these evaluative procedures according to the ability of your students as the semester goes along.

What arguments would you present to your department head to convince him that your plans were better than his (or *would* you disagree with him?)?

2. An article in your local newspaper reports that a bookkeeper has been able to embezzle several thousand dollars from a company because of the lack of internal control and the large amount of trust placed in him.

Your students have asked you to explain how a bookkeeper is able to embezzle funds, so you have taken time to discuss the various ways this may have been done. As the discussion progresses in the class, you sense that many of your students are amused by the embezzlement and that they have a feeling of admiration for the cleverness of the thief.

What steps would you take to emphasize the seriousness of the crime without preaching about morality? Is it your responsibility to develop in your students a sense of ethical values? Are you wrong even to explain how various bookkeeping thefts can take place?

3. As a teacher of bookkeeping as well as of typewriting and general business in Attica High School, Jim Simmons found himself swamped with grading papers. He had two sections of bookkeeping with a total of forty-five students, two sections of typewriting, and one section of general business. Because of this situation Jim decided not to require his bookkeeping students to hand in their problems that he had assigned. He told his classes that to learn bookkeeping it was necessary to work the problems, that he was going to place this responsibility upon them, and that he would not require papers to be handed in for grading. Each student was to correct his own paper from the solutions developed in class.

After several weeks Jim found that few of his students were working the problems and were waiting until class to complete them. Jim then decided to make the students hand in their papers again, but he told them he would not grade them but merely check them off as being completed. The students complained about this procedure because they felt that if they worked the problems the least the teacher could do would be to check them over for accuracy. Is there any solution to Jim's problem or is he destined to check many papers?

SUGGESTED READINGS

Boynton, Lewis D., *Methods of Teaching Bookkeeping-Accounting* (2nd ed.). Cincinnati: South-Western Publishing Co., 1970.

———, Paul A. Carlson, Hamden L. Forkner, and Robert M. Swanson, *Manual for 20th Century Bookkeeping and Accounting* (23rd ed.). Cincinnati: South-Western Publishing Co., 1967.

Freeman, M. Herbert, J. Marshall Hanna, and Gilbert Kahn, *Source Book and Key for Accounting 10/12*. New York: Gregg Publishing Division, McGraw-Hill Book Company, 1968.

Musselman, Vernon A., and Russell A. Johnston, *New Media in Teaching the Business Subjects, Business Education Yearbook*, Vol. III, Chap. 8, 1965.

Tonne, Herbert A., and Louis C. Nanassy, *Principles of Business Education* (4th ed.), Chap. 19. New York: Gregg Publishing Division, McGraw-Hill Book Company, 1970.

Williams, Jackie, Harry Huffman, and Sara Anderson, *Business Education: An Evaluative Inventory, National Business Education Yearbook*, Vol. VI, Chaps. 5, 6, and 7, 1968.

chapter

10

TEACHING DATA PROCESSING

Formalized teaching of electronic data processing in the secondary schools is becoming more and more widespread. More instructional materials for use in this field are becoming available, and more business teacher-trainees are being given an opportunity to enroll in college data-processing courses as a part of their subject-matter preparation. In the past a lack of knowledge of data-processing procedures by experienced teachers and the nonavailability of adequate instructional materials tended to discourage teaching in this area. Summer seminars held at various universities plus broadened course offerings have provided an impetus in eliminating this problem. The inclusion of data-processing procedures in various business textbooks at the secondary level has also forced teachers to learn about and cover these topics or risk having their students ask, Why not?

Two major practices are followed in teaching data processing in today's secondary school. The less common one consists of a separate data-processing curriculum which provides students with an opportunity to work with both unit record equipment and electronic computers. Normally, separate data-processing curriculums are found only in the large urban high schools or the vocational-technical schools. The objective of these programs is to train data-processing technicians, and the teachers are highly knowledgeable and skilled. These teachers have usually had either a great deal of data-processing experience or a strong background in college course work.

The more common method of providing data-processing knowledges in the

secondary schools consists of integrating the various topics in an already existing course such as bookkeeping or teaching them as a separate unit in a
bookkeeping course, in an office practice course, or in some other course in
which data-processing knowledges would be applicable.

In this latter practice, there is usually little or no opportunity for students
to have access to a computer. Consequently, the various data-processing topics
that are taught are presented in a somewhat theoretical manner. This does
not mean, however, that this kind of instruction cannot have a practical application. As students come in contact with the business world, a knowledge
of sophisticated data-processing techniques and procedures will be quite valuable to them even though their knowledge may be somewhat superficial. In
addition, since they will come in contact with computers as consumers in
business activities and as well-educated citizens, they should have some knowledge of how computers will affect their lives.

The teaching techniques and procedures discussed in this chapter will be
directed toward helping those teachers who will be teaching data processing
with little or no equipment available to them and who will be teaching data
processing as a separate unit in a course or integrating it in an already existing
course.

WHAT IS DATA PROCESSING?

Data can be defined simply as information. (The term *data* is
the plural of *datum* and correctly calls for a plural verb, e.g., "data *are*."
Through common usage, however, it is quite often used in the singular.)
Data processing, then, is the manipulating of data (information) in some manner so as to provide an organization with meaningful information from the data
that are generated as a result of the normal activities of the organization. For
example, a high school is an organization. Students attending the high school
generate data in the form of courses they take, grades they receive, and so
forth. These data must be manipulated in various ways to provide the high
school (organization) with the information it needs to report grades to students, provide a record of attendance, and provide a record of completion of
work by students for graduation.

In a broad sense, any time we manipulate data in any way we are processing them. Typing a letter, transcribing dictation, and summarizing notes
taken in class are all examples of data processing. However, as the term is
usually applied in today's language, it refers to the manipulation of data by
either electrical or electronic machines—the latter typically being computers.
The processing data, a continuous and usually repetitive operation, is known
as the *data-processing cycle,* commonly illustrated as in the following diagram:

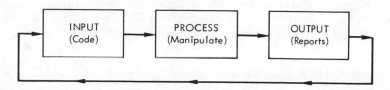

The various procedures for describing and teaching about the data-processing cycle are discussed later in the chapter.

OBJECTIVES FOR TEACHING DATA PROCESSING

The objectives for teaching data processing in the secondary school are as follows:

1. To develop in students the methods and procedures for processing data, with an emphasis being placed upon processing business data
2. To develop in students an understanding of the basic concepts of electronic computers and how they work
3. To provide students with a knowledge and understanding of common data-processing terminology
4. To provide students with an understanding of the use of computers in business applications
5. To provide students with the knowledge of how computers will affect the society in which they live

It will be unwise, in the secondary school, to attempt to develop depth in data-processing procedures, particularly as they relate to the electronic computer. The goal shoulld be *not* to try to develop computer programmers or systems analysts, but rather to provide students with knowledge of the basic functions. Consequently, teachers should not attempt to "lift the lid" of the computer to see how it works other than in a rather broad way. With the rapid changes in computer technology, any attempt by the teacher to make the course highly technical would result in chaos both for the student and for the teacher. However, the "broad concept approach" will be effective and appropriate for years to come.

TECHNIQUES FOR TEACHING DATA PROCESSING

The basic problem in teaching data processing is usually a lack of knowledge on the part of the teacher. However, this problem is being overcome through improved and expanded courses in teacher-training curriculums. In any event, the teacher must have some depth of knowledge in the field; and if the undergraduate or graduate background of the teacher is weak, he must in some manner improve himself. This may be done through formal course work, actual experience, self-study programs, or a combination of these. In the following pages, it is assumed that the teacher does have this depth in background or knowledge.

A good place to start instruction in data processing is through the systems approach. Every business or organization has some system for processing the data generated by its activity, which can be classified as:

1. A manual system
2. An electrical machine system

3. A unit record (punched-card) system
4. An electronic computer system

It does not necessarily follow that a business will use one of the foregoing systems to the exclusion of the others. It is quite possible that a business may process its data using all or a combination of the systems mentioned. For example, in one business with which the authors are familiar, an electric utility firm calculates and sends electric bills to its customers by means of a computer while the firm also calculates and bills its industrial consumers manually. The reason for this is that the industrial customers are few, and it is actually easier and less expensive to calculate these bills manually.

In any data-processing system the same basic functions are performed. These are:

Function	Example Using Manual Bookkeeping
1. Origination of data from source document	Preparation of sales ticket for customer
2. Classifying or coding data	Determining accounts to be debited or credited (account name may be coded by number)
3. Recording and re-recording	Entering the transaction in journal and posting in ledger
4. Manipulation (calculating, comparing, sorting)	Sorting sales tickets in alphabetical order, computing sales tax, etc.
5. Summarizing	Taking a trial balance
6. Storing	Filing accounts receivable records for later use
7. Communicating	Sending out statements to customer

Not all these functions will necessarily be performed in the data-processing cycle each time nor in the sequence as they are listed. Some functions may be performed several times and some may be omitted, depending upon the desired results from the data being processed.

BASIC CONCEPTS NECESSARY FOR STUDENT TO UNDERSTAND

There are certain basic concepts of data processing, including terminology, that all students should understand. The first of these might be the development and evolution of systems and the reasons behind them.

First, let us begin with manual systems. Probably the best method of illustrating these would be the procedures followed in a bookkeeping course. It should not be necessary for the teacher to spend much time on manual processing other than to point out the advantages and the disadvantages.

The advantages, of course, are that when there is a relatively small volume of data to be processed, it can be done more economically through manual methods and is somewhat flexible. The disadvantages are that it is time consuming and error prone. It is axiomatic but should be mentioned here that 99 percent of the errors in data processing are human errors. Today data-processing machines are highly reliable. In newspaper articles it will often be pointed out with glee that a computer made an error. Usually, it is not the computer that made the error, but a human being who performed some erroneous function in using the computer.

One reason for the large possibility of error in manual systems is the large number of transactions that must be transcribed from one place to another (e.g., in bookkeeping—the process of journalizing, posting to ledger, taking a trial balance of ledger, etc.). Each time data have to be manipulated manually, the possibility of error exists. Also, it is time-consuming.

The teacher will find it valuable in teaching about manual processing to point out at least one illustration of procedure to minimize the recording of the same data several times.

The most common method is the use of *one-write* systems in which data are recorded once on a special form and by use of carbon paper the same data can be posted and summarized on other forms. This system is generally referred to as a *pegboard* system and is commonly used in service types of businesses.

It would be valuable for the teacher to obtain sample forms utilized in this system and illustrate the procedures to his students. Normally, sample forms may be obtained by contacting the salesman who sells these types of systems to business firms.

MACHINE SYSTEMS

The next step upward which should be presented in the hierarchy of data-processing systems is processing data by means of electrical machines such as bookkeeping machines, posting machines, and calculators. Again, it should not be necessary to dwell at any length or go into a great amount of detail in the area other than to point out the reasons for a business evolving to machine processing.

The main reason, of course, is that as businesses grow larger, more data are generated. Thus, it is necessary to find faster ways to process these data. For example, one company which had been billing its customers using a manual procedure found that as the volume of sales grew, it was taking almost two weeks from the beginning of the month to send out bills. This resulted in an even greater increase in the amount of accounts receivable outstanding, with a resulting decrease in cash flow.

In addition, machine processing is more accurate, as most machines are set up with built-in controls so that the accuracy of the machine operator can be checked. Of course, machine processing is more costly and is only as fast as the speed of the operator, but still it is much better and more accurate than manual processing.

One element that the teacher, particularly the bookkeeping teacher, will need to demonstrate to students is the difference in the format of the business journals and ledger cards, and so forth. The basic bookkeeping procedures are the same as in manual bookkeeping, but the form of records is much different. The teacher should try to obtain sample copies of the business forms used in machine processing and then point out their differences and similarities.

PUNCHED-CARD (UNIT RECORD) PROCESSING

It is quite important that teachers of data processing take time to explore punched-card processing. It is true that the utilization of punched-card processing is declining somewhat because of the lessening difference between the cost of punched-card equipment and the cost of some of the smaller computers. However, the principles involved in punched-card processing are so similar to those of electronic computers that an introduction to them should make the basic concepts of computers much easier to understand.

The history of the development of the punched card can be read in almost any general textbook on data processing. The punched card as a method for processing large amounts of data was developed approximately a century ago and was first used in tabulating census data. At that time, it was found that after a census had been taken in the United States, the data from the census were not completely tabulated and processed until it was almost time to take another census ten years later. The development of punched-card processes eliminated this problem.

The basic idea behind punched-card processing is that once data have been captured and placed upon the card and verified as to their accuracy, the data can be used over and over again in various ways with a minimum of manual operations. This is done by specialized machines which are described later in this section.

The major concepts that should be taught about punched-card data processing follow.

THE PUNCHED CARD

The teacher should begin with a description and use of the eighty-column card. The most significant factors to develop are the use of the card on which to punch data from a source document; the punched-card coding structure for the numeric, alphabetic, and special characters; the concept of *fields* of data; and the concept of the card as a *record*. It is particularly important to develop the idea that punched-card processing is organized to fit the various data-processing procedures required in an organization as they pertain to the business systems. That is, there would be one punched-card system for processing payroll, .another for processing accounts receivable and billing, still another for inventory control, and so forth.

It is also important that the student fully understand the various terms used in relation to the punched card, particularly the hierarchy of data in the form of *characters* (numeric, alphabetic, and special); *fields* of data, which are composed of characters; *records,* which are composed of fields; and finally *files,* which are composed of records. This concept of file-record-field is basic. A punched card composed of fields of data is known as a record. A deck of cards pertaining to related records is known as a file. Files are usually referred to as either *master* files or *transaction* files. One of the most common data-processing procedures is known as the updating of a master file.

For example, to illustrate a master file updating procedure, let us assume that a business has one thousand credit customers. For each customer they have one punched card (record) in which is encoded:

Card Column	Data
1–4	Customer identification number
5–25	Customer's name
26–56	Customer's address
57–62	Balance owed on account
63–79	Blank
80	The digit 1 to identify the card as a master record

Thus, there would be one thousand cards of the type described above (one for each customer), and all these cards would be known as an accounts receivable master file.

This file would be stored in a filing cabinet in sequential order by customer number until such time as it would be updated—for example, at the end of a month.

During the month, some of the firm's customers would be buying additional merchandise and paying the balances owed on their accounts. Each of these kinds of transactions would result in a card being punched which would contain:

Card Column	Data
1– 4	Customer identification number
5–25	Customer's name
26–56	Customer's address
57–62	Amount of purchase or amount of payment
63–79	Blank
80	The digit 2 to identify the card as a purchase or a transaction; or the digit 3, as a payment-on-account transaction

These cards would be known as *transaction* cards and would be combined in a transaction card file.

To illustrate more in detail, a sampling of our two files might appear as follows:

Master Card File

Cust. No.	Name	Address	Old Bal.	Card Iden.
1011	Brown	City	$300	1
1022	Jones	City	500	1
1033	Smith	City	600	1
1044	Harris	City	900	1
1055	Cox	City	200	1
1066	Lee	City	400	1
1077	Parr	City	800	1

Transaction Card File

Cust. No.	Name	Address	Amt.	Card Iden.
1066	Lee	City	$400	2
1011	Brown	City	100	3
1077	Parr	City	800	3
1044	Harris	City	600	3
1011	Brown	City	200	2
1055	Cox	City	400	2
1066	Lee	City	100	2
1033	Smith	City	700	2
1022	Jones	City	200	3
1044	Harris	City	300	3
1033	Smith	City	600	3

Note that the transaction card file *is not* in sequential order.

The first step would be to put the transaction card file into the same sequential order (by customer number) as the master file. Then these two files would be merged into one file for processing as follows:

Merged File

Cust. No.	Name	Address	Amt.	Card Iden.
1011	Brown	City	$300	1
1011	Brown	City	100	3
1011	Brown	City	200	2
1022	Jones	City	500	1
1022	Jones	City	200	3
1033	Smith	City	600	1
1033	Smith	City	700	2
1033	Smith	City	600	3
1044	Harris	City	900	1
1044	Harris	City	600	3
1044	Harris	City	300	3
1055	Cox	City	200	1
1055	Cox	City	400	2
1066	Lee	City	400	1
1066	Lee	City	400	2
1066	Lee	City	100	2
1077	Parr	City	800	1
1077	Parr	City	800	3

The merged file would then be processed by specialized punched-card machine so as to—

1. Add all purchases transactions to the old balance.
2. Subtract all payment on account transactions from old balance.
3. Print a statement showing old balance, purchases, payments, and new balance to the customer.
4. Develop a new master card record with an updated balance for each customer to be used the following month when the file would be updated again.

The new master card file would appear as follows after updating:

Updated Master Card File

Cust. No.	Name	Address	New Bal.	Card Iden.
1011	Brown	City	$400	1
1022	Jones	City	300	1
1033	Smith	City	700	1
1044	Harris	City	000	1
1055	Cox	City	600	1
1066	Lee	City	900	1
1077	Parr	City	000	1

The method of processing data in the above illustration is known as *batch* processing—that is, data are not processed or files updated until such time as a sufficient amount of data are accumulated to make the effort worthwhile. One disadvantage of *batching* is that a data file is normally not up to date. The advantage is the economy involved in the use of personnel and machines.

The opposite of batch processing is *in-line* or *random* processing in which data transactions are processed as they occur. This type of processing keeps files current but normally requires highly sophisticated equipment. It is not practical to process data by means of punched cards in other than the *batch* mode.

PUNCHED-CARD EQUIPMENT

The basic punched-card equipment utilized in a card system should be described by the teacher along with the function or manipulative process the machines perform. Since it is unlikely that machines will be available for the students to see in operation, it will be necessary for the teacher to rely on pictures or other types of illustrations.

It is not advisable that the teacher go into much technical detail on how the machines work, but he should explain their functions. The basic machines discussed should be:

1. Key punch
2. Verifier
3. Sorter

Exhibit 10.1

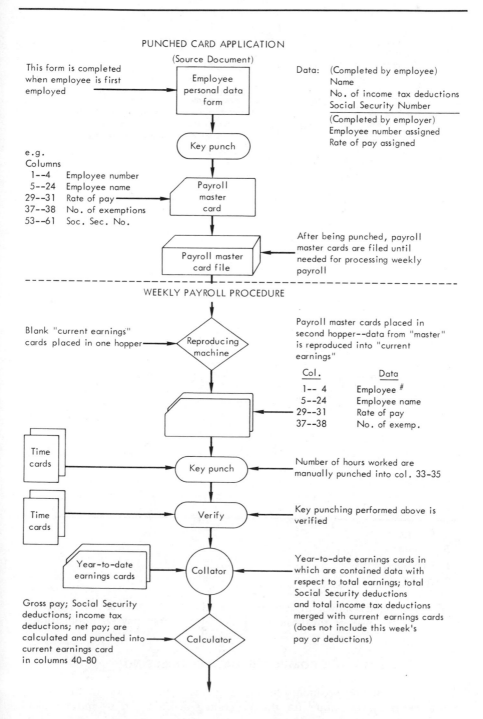

PUNCHED CARD APPLICATION
(Source Document)

This form is completed when employee is first employed

Employee personal data form

Data: (Completed by employee)
Name
No. of income tax deductions
Social Security Number
(Completed by employer)
Employee number assigned
Rate of pay assigned

Key punch

e.g.
Columns
1--4   Employee number
5--24   Employee name
29--31 Rate of pay
37--38 No. of exemptions
53--61 Soc. Sec. No.

Payroll master card

Payroll master card file

After being punched, payroll master cards are filed until needed for processing weekly payroll

WEEKLY PAYROLL PROCEDURE

Blank "current earnings" cards placed in one hopper

Reproducing machine

Payroll master cards placed in second hopper--data from "master" is reproduced into "current earnings"

Col.   Data
1-- 4   Employee #
5--24   Employee name
29--31 Rate of pay
37--38 No. of exemp.

Time cards

Key punch

Number of hours worked are manually punched into col. 33-35

Time cards

Verify

Key punching performed above is verified

Year-to-date earnings cards

Collator

Year-to-date earnings cards in which are contained data with respect to total earnings; total Social Security deductions and total income tax deductions merged with current earnings cards (does not include this week's pay or deductions)

Gross pay; Social Security deductions; income tax deductions; net pay; are calculated and punched into current earnings card in columns 40-80

Calculator

345

Exhibit 10.1 (cont.)

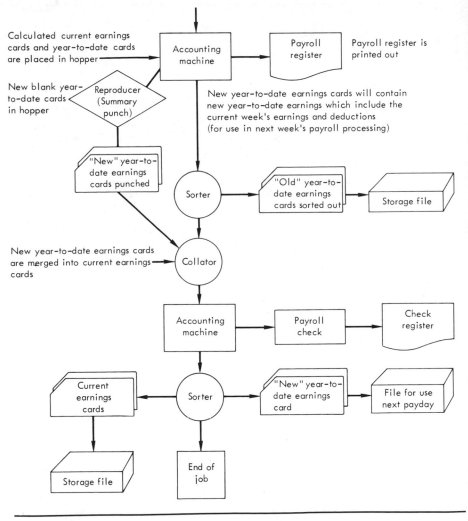

Calculated current earnings cards and year-to-date cards are placed in hopper

Accounting machine

Payroll register

Payroll register is printed out

New blank year-to-date cards in hopper

Reproducer (Summary punch)

New year-to-date earnings cards will contain new year-to-date earnings which include the current week's earnings and deductions (for use in next week's payroll processing)

"New" year-to-date earnings cards punched

Sorter

"Old" year-to-date earnings cards sorted out

Storage file

New year-to-date earnings cards are merged into current earnings cards

Collator

Accounting machine

Payroll check

Check register

Current earnings cards

Sorter

"New" year-to-date earnings card

File for use next payday

Storage file

End of job

4. Collator
5. Calculator
6. Reproducer
7. Accounting

The flow chart shown in Exhibit 10-1 may be helpful to the teacher in illustrating the uses of the basic machines in a simple payroll application.

ELECTRONIC COMPUTER DATA PROCESSING

Teaching secondary school students about the operation and use of the electronic computer for the processing of data can be quite difficult, particularly if there is little or no access to a computer by either the students or the teacher. However, it is possible to do this effectively if the teacher does not get involved in the technical characteristics of the computer and if he will limit himself to the teaching of two main elements:

1. The basic principles of a computer system
2. The way computers are used in the processing of business data

The key to the presentation of these two elements is to *keep it simple*. It is not necessary nor is it advisable to go into any large amount of detail concerning the technology of the computer. Little time should be spent on computer arithmetic or computer programming in other than a superficial way. Remember you are not training computer technicians or computer programmers, but rather you are presenting the basic concepts of processing data by means of a computer—or in a general way, how the computer works.

The Basic Principles of a Computer System

A computer system is composed of the following elements:

1. Computer equipment (hardware)
2. Personnel (systems analysts, programmers, machine operators)
3. Procedures to be followed in processing the data (flow charts—both systems and programming plus all documentation of the procedures)
4. Programs (computer instructions)
5. Software (forms, manufacturer-supplied routines, operating and programming publications)

Of all these elements, the *hardware* is commonly alluded to as the computer. In essence, however, the computer system can be simply diagrammed as follows:

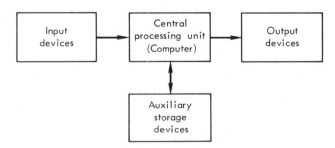

The main characteristics of any computer system should be discussed under the headings of:

1. Getting data into the central processing unit (Input)
2. Storing data in the central processing unit and auxiliary storage unit (Storage or Memory)

3. Processing data in central processing unit (Manipulation of Data)
4. Decision-making capability of the central processing unit (Computer Logic)
5. Automating the central processing unit (Stored Program)
6. Retrieval of processed data (Output)

Input Media and Devices

As computer data processing is becoming more sophisticated almost daily, it is extremely difficult for the teacher to keep abreast of all the technological changes that are taking place. Consequently, it is advisable for the secondary school teacher to stress only the basic methods of getting data into the computer system and to expand on the more sophisticated methods as he becomes more knowledgeable in these areas.

The basic methods of input should be discussed by means of the following:

Input Media	**Input Device**
Punched cards	Punched-card reader
Paper tape	Paper tape reader
Magnetic tape	Magnetic tape drive
Document (with optical font characters)	Optical scanner
Document (with magnetic ink characters)	Magnetic ink character reader
Telephone or telegraph signals	Data phone or teletype
Typewriter signals	Console typewriter

The teacher should be familiar with each of these devices and media and should use them whenever possible to provide illustrations and examples. The major factors to be stressed are

1. All the foregoing devices must be on-line (connected to the central processing unit).
2. Data must be coded in an appropriate form on the input media so that the computer can store the data for processing. (A simple explanation of the coding structure is important for students to understand and will be discussed later in this chapter.)

Storage

Computers are generally measured in terms of the amount of data that can be stored in the central processing unit. A computer referred to as having 20K capacity is one that has twenty thousand positions of storage. This means that in each of the twenty thousand positions one alphabetic character, one numeric digit, or one special character can be stored. In other words, a 20K computer could store twenty thousand digits—the symbol K standing for one thousand.

It is important that the student grasp this storage concept in order for him to understand how data are processed. First, storage should be explained under the heading of classifications of storage.

Classifications of Storage

1. Main storage	Storage in the central processing unit
2. Auxiliary storage	Storage on-line with, but outside, the central processing unit
3. External storage	Off-line storage and not connected to the central processing unit

Main storage in the central processing unit is where all the processing of data takes place. This is also where the program of instruction is stored.

Auxiliary storage is where data can be stored on-line and called into main storage for processing. No processing of data can be performed in auxiliary storage. However, auxiliary storage supplements the capacity of main storage and is available for processing whenever it is called for by the CPU.

External storage is referred to when data is stored on some form such as punched cards, magnetic tape, or paper tape and is filed away for use whenever it is needed.

In addition to a knowledge of the classifications of storage, particularly main and auxiliary storage, the student should be provided with some degree of knowledge about the kinds of storage media. For example, main storage is usually in the form of circular magnetic cores in an array or set of six cores, with each set being individually addressable.

$$0 \quad 0 \quad 0 \quad 0 \quad 0 \quad 0$$
Address

Thus, in the main memory of a 20K computer, there would be twenty thousand sets of cores (each set is known as a *byte*), with each set having an address. In each set, it is possible to store a numeric, an alphabetic, or a special character.

Auxiliary storage is usually in the form of magnetic disks—large metal phonograph-type records on which data are stored in the form of magnetic dots in the same format as the cores are arranged in main memory.

There are other kinds of storage media, but magnetic core storage and magnetic disk storage are the most common. It would be advisable for the teacher to discuss only these two kinds, as the major concepts of storage can be developed by means of these two illustrations—discussion of other types may only lead to confusion on the part of the students.

Processing Data

The processing of data in the central processing unit will require that the student have some knowledge of computer arithmetic. Many textbooks on computer data processing contain extensive material on computer arithmetic, but to understand how a computer processes data a student need know only the basic principles behind the binary (Base Two) numeric system and the concepts of binary coded decimal (BCD).

Internally, computers can represent only two states or conditions—*on* or *off*. In other words, a memory position can be either magnetized (on) or not magnetized (off). Thus, a computer can perform arithmetic in what is known as the binary number mode (Base Two) which has only two symbols, 0 and 1, as compared with our decimal system which has ten symbols, 0 through 9.

Binary	Decimal Equivalent
0	0
1	1
10	2
11	3
100	4
101	5
110	6
111	7
1000	8
1001	9

When a decimal number is fed into a computer, the computer automatically converts the number to its binary equivalent, performs any necessary arithmetic in binary, and when completed reconverts it to decimal for output.

For example, if we had two decimal numbers punched into a card, such as 6 and 3, and we would like the computer to add these two numbers to get the sum 9, the computer would convert:

$$\begin{array}{ll}
\text{Decimal 6 to Binary} & 110 \\
\text{Decimal 3 to Binary} & 11 \\
\hline
.\text{Sum} \quad 9 & 1001
\end{array}$$

Another system of arithmetic used in a computer is binary coded decimal (BCD). If we were to take an array of four cores and assign positional values to these cores as follows:

$$\begin{array}{cccc}
0 & 0 & 0 & 0 \\
8 & 4 & 2 & 1
\end{array} \quad \text{Positional Value}$$

we could represent any of the ten decimal digits in binary by various combinations of these cores (1 representing ON, 0 representing OFF).

Each core is known as a *Bit*—contraction for binary digit. Thus, if in an array of four bits, the 4 and 2 bits were ON, the decimal number 6 would be represented in binary coded decimal mode. If the 4, 2, and 1 bits were ON, then decimal 7 would be represented.

By adding two more bits to an array of four cores, it is then possible to represent all the alphabetic and special characters in one byte in addition to the numerics:

$$\begin{array}{cc}
00 & 0000 \\
\uparrow & \uparrow \\
\text{zone} & \text{digit} \\
\text{bits} & \text{bits}
\end{array}$$

The first two bits in the byte are the zone bits, and any combination of

1 (ON) or 0 (OFF) will correspond to the 12, 11, or 10 zones in the punched-card coding structure. For example:

110000	12 zone
100000	11 zone
010000	10 zone

Thus, the letter *A* would appear as 110001; the letter *J* would appear as 100001; and the letter *S* would appear as 010010.

The basic elements that a student should learn about BCD coding structure internally in a computer are that in each byte can be encoded one numeric, alphabetic, or special character; that it will take several bytes to compose a field of data; and that each byte has a specific address in memory. A student's name and age (John Doe, age 17) would take nine bytes and would have the following format:

| 100001 | 100110 | 111000 | 100101 | 110100 | 100110 | 110101 | 000001 | 000111 |
| J | O | H | N | D | O | E | 1 | 7 |

Processing of Data in the Central Processing Unit

Once data are stored in the CPU, they can be processed in many different ways. Arithmetic can be performed on the data; they can be moved from one place in memory to another; they can be sorted; they can be edited; they can be compared—in fact, any of the manipulations necessary in processing data can be performed.

It is not necessary that the student understand the technicalities of how the various manipulative techniques are performed. If the teacher wishes to go into more detail with respect to the various procedures of internal processing, no harm will be done unless the teacher gets so technical as to cause confusion and misunderstanding. The teacher may wish to provide some explanation as to the characteristics of *random* and *batch* processing or *serial* and *parallel* processing. This will be a matter of personal choice and will depend to some extent upon the caliber of the students in the class and the teacher's understanding of the internal processing of data in the CPU.

Decision-Making Ability of the Central Processing Unit

One of the most unique and powerful characteristics of the CPU is its ability to test a condition and thus branch from the main line of a program of instructions to some other place in the program. This characteristics is often referred to as the logic ability of the computer.

In essence, this logic is quite simply yes-or-no logic and is based upon the element of testing for the equality or inequality of a number. For example, let us assume that stored in the memory of a computer is an unknown number between 1 and 1 million. By asking the computer to compare the unknown number with the number 500,000 and testing to see if the unknown number is equal to or greater than 500,000, the answer will be either yes or no.

Thus, we have automatically eliminated 500,000 numbers in our search for the unknown. By a series of similar consecutive questions the unknown number will ultimately be determined in a matter of a few seconds.

Students can be taught the simplicity of this yes-no logic by comparing it with the light indicators on the dashboard of an automobile. For example, most autos today have a red light on the dash which comes on when the hand brake of the auto is set. Thus, an indicator light is on when the brake is set and off when it is released.

Similarly, in a computer there are internal indicators that will be *on* when two numbers are equal or unequal, and these indicators can be tested as to their state when comparisons are made. An illustration of this logic will be shown in the following section.

Automating the Central Processing Unit (Stored Program)

In spite of the many wonderful abilities attributed to the electronic computer, it can only and will only perform those things that it is told to do by means of the instructions given it by a human being. A computer program is a series of sequential instructions written by a programmer and when needed is stored in the CPU. When the computer is activated, it will start at the beginning of the program of instructions and process the data being inputed. After each data set has been processed, the computer will go back to the beginning of the program of instructions and process the next data set until all the data are processed.

A simple device to illustrate this procedure to students would be to refer back to the file-updating procedure illustrated on page 342 for punched-card processing. Let us take the merged file shown on page 343 and process these data by a computer using the illustration in Exhibit 10.2.

By placing the illustration shown in Exhibit 10.2 on the chalkboard, the teacher could have his students use the sample data file and actually go through the program steps. One main point to remember is that when data are read into an area or moved into another area, the data previously stored in these areas are destroyed and the new data replace them.

Unless a computer is available to students, it is debatable whether the teacher should attempt to teach students to do some programming in any of the many available programming languages. If the teacher is familiar with a language, he may find it worthwhile to show students what it looks like and describe the procedures that are followed to translate either a symbolic or a procedure-oriented language into machine language by means of a computer.

While programming is a highly developed skill, it is the authors' belief that in the very near future it will become less important as more and more software programming packages are developed for use by businesses, which will lessen the need for the writing of original programs. It will be more important for the teacher to spend some time teaching students to develop program flow charts from which programs are written. By the use of a few simple data-processing problems, the teacher can instill in students the logic behind computer programming and to some extent develop in students the skill of logical thinking.

Exhibit 10.2

Internal Memory of Central Processing Unit

Input Area	
Working-Storage Area	
Output Area	
Program of Instructions Stored Here	Unused Memory

Program of Instructions:

1. Read in data on first data card into input area.
2. Move data to working-storage area.
3. Read in data on next data card into input area.
4. Compare customer number in input area with customer number in working-storage area. If numbers are equal, go to Instruction 9; otherwise, continue to next instruction (5).
5. Move data in working-storage area to output area.
6. Print data in output area on output report.
7. Punch data in output area on new master card.
8. Go to Instruction 2.
9. Compare the card identification number in the input area with the number 2. If equal, add the amount in the input area to the old balance amount in the working-storage area; otherwise subtract the amount in the input area from the old balance amount in the working-storage area.
10. Go back to Instruction 3.

If the teacher does spend time on program flow charting, it will be wise to keep the problems relatively simple. The teacher can develop many problems that are of a type closely related to the students' experience.

For example, let us assume that in a large urban high school the principal wishes to have a list of the names and the total number of the boys who are scholastically eligible to play football. To be eligible, a boy must have a grade-point average of 1.5 or higher. There are four thousand students in the school, and for each student there is a punched card on which is coded the student's name, sex, and grade-point average.

The program flow chart logic for solving this problem on a computer might be as shown in Exhibit 10.3.

Students should be informed that there are as many ways to develop the logic in solving a problem by means of a computer as there are ways in which people think. Obviously, some ways are better than others; but if given the opportunity, students can become quite innovative and skillful in the art of logical thinking. In addition, students will often develop a better understanding of how the learning process takes place.

Exhibit 10.3

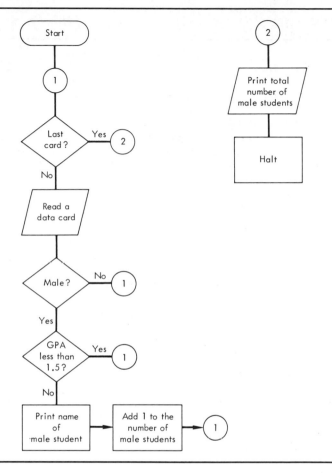

Retrieval of Processed Data (Output)

The last of the six major characteristics of a computer system that should be developed with students is the various ways by which processed data can be outputted from a computer. Like the methods of input of data, output media and devices are becoming more and more sophisticated. It would be wise for the teacher to illustrate the most common methods rather than go into some of the more sophisticated techniques.

The most common output media and devices are those listed below:

Output Media	Output Device
Paper reports	Line printer
Punched cards	Punched-card unit
Paper tape	Paper tape unit
Magnetic tape	Magnetic tape drive
Visual display	Cathode-ray tube terminal
Microfilm	Microfilm developer
Audio response	Audio response speaker
Typewritten message	Typewriter terminal

As with the input devices, all the foregoing must be on-line with the central processing unit.

Data-Processing Terms

One of the greatest difficulties encountered by persons learning about data processing is the unique language used to describe various components of a computer and the techniques involved in processing data. Many of the textbooks used in teaching data processing contain a glossary of terms that are commonly employed. Listed below are some of the basic terms which students should understand. This list is not all-inclusive but contains what the authors believe to be the most significant ones. The teacher may wish to add to, or delete from, this list. Definitions can be obtained from glossaries found in reference material.

Basic Data-processing Terms

ADDRESS
ALPHA
ALPHANUMERIC
ANALOG COMPUTER
AUXILIARY STORAGE
BATCH PROCESSING
BCD.
BINARY NUMBER SYSTEM
BIT
BLOCK DIAGRAM
BRANCHING
BYTE
CARD PUNCH
CARD READER
CATHODE-RAY TUBE (CRT)
CENTRAL PROCESSING UNIT
  (CPU)
CHARACTER
COBOL
COMPILER
CORES, MAGNETIC
CORE STORAGE
DATA
DATA PROCESSING
DIGITAL COMPUTER
EDIT
FIELD
FILE
FIXED WORD LENGTH
FLOW CHART
FORTRAN
HARDWARE
HOLLERITH CODE
INDICATOR
INFORMATION RETRIEVAL
INPUT

INSTRUCTION
INTERNAL STORAGE
KEY-PUNCH
LOOP
MAGNETIC DISK
MAGNETIC DRUM
MAGNETIC TAPE
MAIN STORAGE
MERGE
MICR
MICROSECOND
MILLISECOND
MNEMONIC
NANOSECOND
OFF-LINE
ON-LINE
OPTICAL SCANNER
OUTPUT
PAPER TAPE
PICOSECOND
PRINTER
PROGRAM
PROGRAMMER
RANDOM ACCESS STORAGE
REAL-TIME
RECORD
SOFTWARE
SYMBOLIC CODES
TABULATING EQUIPMENT
TIME-SHARING
UNIT RECORD EQUIPMENT
VARIABLE WORD-LENGTH
WORD
ZONE

Computer Applications

There are many different kinds of computer applications to the processing of data, and it is important that the teacher develop some of these in the data-processing classes. The majority of these applications involve some form of file maintenance, such as updating accounts receivable files and billing customers, updating inventory files, and updating payroll files. In presenting the various kinds of applications, it may be necessary for the teacher to review the procedures involved in batch processing, random processing, and real-time and on-line processing.

By an extensive review of the literature dealing with data processing, many .applications can be vividly illustrated. The following selected list of reference material will be of value to the teacher in this respect.

SELECTED LIST OF PUBLICATIONS FOR AID IN TEACHING DATA PROCESSING

Magazines

Bell Telephone Magazine, Room 417, American Telephone and Telegraph Company, 6195 Broadway, New York, N.Y. 10007. Sent free upon request.

Business Automation, Hitchcock Publishing Company, P.O. Box 3007, Hitchcock Building, Wheaton, Ill. Published biweekly. Sent free upon request.

Computer Decisions, Hayden Publishing Company, Inc., 850 Third Avenue, New York, N.Y. Published monthly. Sent free upon request.

Data Processing Magazine, 134 North Thirteenth Street, Philadelphia, Pa. 19017. Published monthly, subscription $8.50.

Data Processor, International Business Machines Corporation, 112 East Post Road, White Plains, N.Y. 10601. Sent free upon request.

Journal of Data Education, E. Dana Gibson, Executive Director, San Diego State College, San Diego, Calif. 92115. Subscriptions available to members of Society of Data Educators.

Books

Accounting 10/12, Part IV, Business Data Processing Fundamentals; Freeman, Hanna, Kahn; Gregg Division, McGraw-Hill Book Company, New York, N.Y., 1968.

Computer Concepts; Science Research Associates, Inc., 259 East Erie Street, Chicago, Ill. 60611, 1970.

Computer Data Processing; Gordon B. Davis; McGraw-Hill Book Company, New York, N.Y., 1969.

Introduction to Data Processing; Carl Feingold; William C. Brown Company, Dubuque, Iowa, 1971.

Modern Computer Concepts; Edward J. Laurie; South-Western Publishing Company, Cincinnati, Ohio, 1970.

Principles of Business Data Processing; Science Research Associates, Inc., 259 East Erie Street, Chicago, Ill. 60611, 1970.

PROJECTS AND QUESTIONS FOR DISCUSSION

1. Formulate three or four short data-processing problems (e.g., computing sales commissions) that could be assigned to students for developing program flow charts.
2. Talk to a businessman in your community to determine whether he has a data-processing problem. If so, write a short paper on how this problem could be processed on unit record equipment or on a computer.
3. If you are familiar with a programming language, write a short program that can be used to demonstrate and illustrate a computer program understandable to a high school class.
4. Prepare a series of transparencies that would be useful in teaching some concept of data processing.
5. Develop an objective-type examination that will test a high school student's knowledge of computer data processing.
6. Write a brief description of a file-updating procedure for a master inventory file, a master insurance policy file for an insurance company, or a master file for students currently enrolled in a college.
7. What procedures would you follow in keeping yourself up to date on data-processing procedures and techniques?
8. Demonstrate to the methods class how you would teach high school students the necessity for coding data in a data-processing system.
9. Prepare a visual aid that will illustrate how a program compiler works.
10. Examine several high school bookkeeping texts in which data-processing techniques and procedures are discussed. Make a list of those topics that you believe you would be unable to teach, based upon your present level of understanding. Describe how you might go about learning about these topics with which you are unfamiliar.

chapter

11

TEACHING
THE DISTRIBUTIVE SUBJECTS

As a natural result of our worldwide economic specialization and of today's large-scale methods of producing goods, the efforts and costs entering into the distribution of those goods to ultimate consumers is great. This means, accordingly, that the vocational opportunities also are great in the area of distribution and that there is much specialization within the field.

Techniques and procedures used in getting goods from the hands of the producer and into the hands of the consumer change rapidly. Under our American free, competitive, and profit-motivated economy, new and improved ideas are in demand and hence tend to appear rapidly. To a considerable degree the problem of teaching distributive subjects well for vocational objectives becomes a problem of keeping informed about current practices and techniques.

Yet throughout all teaching of distributive subjects runs a common and basic idea, namely, that we are dealing with the needs and likes and desires of people—of human beings. By profession, the teacher already has a superior understanding of the psychology that prompts people to act as they do. The teacher who is interested in distributive subjects is in a position to be of real service to students who contemplate entering this field vocationally.

The final process of teaching distributive subjects therefore may be said to have three main bases: (*a*) learning techniques, procedures, terminology, practices, and policies applicable to the area of distribution under consideration; (*b*) keeping informed about the current practices in the business world;

and (*c*) developing actual facility in the many required relationships with people. The first of these may be achieved largely through regular classroom procedures. The last two are usually best achieved through actual experience at appropriate work in the business world.

DISTRIBUTIVE OCCUPATIONS DEFINED

Changing times, new developments, and advanced thinking create needs for new terminology. New terminology frequently results in a temporary confusion in the minds of people accustomed to the limitations of terminology formerly used. Today the use of the term *distributive* still results in a degree of confusion in the minds of some people, since it is relatively new to the teaching profession.

In 1947 the United States Office of Education provided a pertinent definition, quite clear and helpful, as follows:

> Distributive occupations are defined as those followed by workers directly engaged in merchandising activities or in contact with buyers and sellers when (*a*) distributing to consumers, retailers, jobbers, wholesalers, and others the products of farm and industry, or (*b*) selling services, managing, operating, or conducting a retail, wholesale, or service business.[1]

In 1966 this same source provided the following definition:

> A distributive occupation means an occupation that is followed by proprietors, managers, or employees engaged primarily in marketing or merchandising of goods or services.[2]

It will be noticed that in limiting the distributive occupations to workers engaged in *merchandising activities* (or in contact with buyers and sellers), the above definitions remove from consideration those workers engaged in what may be termed the more manual and mechanical trades and occupations even though a necessary part of the distribution of goods; it obviously would not include such workers as engineers on trains, mechanics, traffic managers, and similar occupational classifications even though they might be directly associated with the physical distribution (transportation) of goods.

Those engaged in distributive occupations are therefore engaged in *merchandising* or are *in contact with buyers and sellers* while assisting in merchandising functions. This specifically does include those managing or operating a retail, wholesale, or service business. In terms of the total number of people employed, this is one of the largest occupational classifications in our nation. It employs both men and women and to a very high degree *is* our American

---

[1] *Vocational Education*, Bulletin No. 1, General Series No. 1 rev., Federal Security Agency, U.S. Office of Education (Washington, D.C.: Government Printing Office, 1947).

[2] *Administration of Vocational Education, Rules and Regulations, Vocational Education*, Bulletin No. 1, Department of Health, Education, and Welfare, U.S. Office of Education, (Washington, D.C.: Government Printing Office, 1966), p. 44.

business economy. Thus it offers a very real and practical opportunity for successful achievement of the objectives of vocational education.

DISTRIBUTIVE SUBJECTS

Names given to the subject matter taught and to the courses in which it is taught are extremely varied when we examine the entire field of education for the distributive occupations. Some subject matter and some courses are organized for and taught to regular full-time secondary students; others are intended for college students; still others are intended for employed workers and managers who can attend only a limited number of evening classes. Some courses are intended as basic introductions to the field, others as advanced courses for students already familiar with the field, and still others as short "refresher" courses in various highly specialized areas of the field. The variety of *course titles* used will depend, then, upon the individual school or community, its pertinent objectives, and the students it serves.

Here is a partial list of course titles that have been used at various times and places. Most of these have been relatively short courses intended for employed adults.

Receiving and Marking Goods	Store Organization
Stock Control	Store Location
Window Display	Retail Selling
Interior Display	Credits and Collections
Salesmanship	Fashion Selling
Shoe Salesmanship	Store Equipment
Store Arithmetic	Specialty Shop Management
Advertising	Store Services
Newspaper Advertising	Cashiering
Store Layout	Package Wrapping
Retailing	Display Signs
Store Management	Specialty Selling

It will be observed, however, that all these course titles are indicative of subject matter centering around the field of selling and retailing. With minor exceptions, this is the case.

When offered for regular full-time high school students, all the subject matter indicated by various specialized courses such as those just mentioned is frequently combined into one or two high school courses. These high school courses are given titles such as salesmanship, merchandising, retailing, retail selling, or distribution. This chapter deals with such courses.

DISTRIBUTIVE EDUCATION

The term *distributive education* is applied most accurately to a relatively complete program of vocational education for distributive occupations. It includes not only appropriate separate courses such as those already mentioned but also appropriate laboratory experiences through approved and educationally supervised on-the-job actual work experience. As needed to achieve local educational objectives, it may include preemployment vocational preparation, vocational education to upgrade those already employed full time, or vocational education appropriate for aiding adults in a guided preparation to change from other occupations into distributive occupations.

In the early history of this nation approximately three-fourths of the total economic effort was directed toward production, including manufacturing, with only about one-fourth of it devoted to the work of distribution. Today, however, well over half of our nation's economic efforts are devoted to the work of distribution. It is currently estimated, for instance, that approximately fifty-six cents out of every dollar the consumer spends goes for costs of distribution.

Over the years student enrollment statistics have indicated that the educational profession has been reticent about attacking this problem of improvement of the field of distribution. Yet it is quite widely recognized that better and more efficient workers result in better services at lower cost. Accordingly, in 1936 Congress passed the George–Deen Act providing for federal financial assistance to those states that adopted approved state plans for providing high-quality vocational education for distributive occupations. This was followed in 1947 by the George–Barden Act, in 1963 by the Vocational Education Act, and in 1968 by the Vocational Education Amendment, all of which greatly increased the possible available financial support for distributive education.

Perhaps largely as a result of the impetus given by these federal acts, *distributive education* today generally refers to a rather specific form of high-quality vocational education conducted under a plan set forth by the individual state and approved by the United States Office of Education. Although each state is free to devise and adopt a plan or plans best suited to its own educational needs, distributive education quite universally includes these common factors as offered to students in secondary education:

1. A regularly certified high school teacher who also meets special requirements of subject matter and of actual business experience qualifying him to coordinate the classroom work with the approved part-time on-the-job work program of the student
2. Appropriate designated classroom courses for the student trainees
3. A plan of regular part-time paid work experience for the student on approved types of work in selected work stations and under competent supervision
4. A relatively high degree of attention to the individual students in terms of selection, placement, instruction, and follow-up work

The relative importance of these popular and effective complete programs in distributive education (commonly referred to as *D.E.* programs) is now indicated by the fact that the United States Office of Education uses distributive education as one of a total of twenty-two subject-matter areas in collecting national and state statistical information about instructional programs.[3] The taxonomy of distributive education as presented in the United States Office of Education handbook *Standard Terminology for Curriculum and Instruction in Local and State School Systems* includes nearly one hundred different titles from which selections can be made in preparnig a course or offering in D.E. Moreover, as the result of a page-by-page examination of the *Dictionary of Occupational Titles,* this same taxonomy now identifies for education hundreds of job titles falling within the vocational and career objectives of distributive education.

The purpose of this chapter is not to present a complete treaties on distributive education, but to deal with instructional techniques and procedures in such *courses* as salesmanship and retailing—which may or may not be part of a more complete vocational program in distributive education. It should be clearly understood, however, that the addition of other factors necessary for an approved D.E. program does result in a higher quality and more complete type of vocational education for distributive occupations.

PURPOSE OF THE COURSE

Teachers with limited experience, especially, frequently tend to look upon "objectives" as some nice-sounding professional jargon used as a sort of window dressing. However, the longer one teaches and the more successful one becomes as a member of the teaching profession, the more one tends to realize the futility of attempting to teach a course without having clearly in mind the special knowledges, skills, attitudes, or other results that one plans to achieve through the medium of that particular course. Perhaps this applies especially to the teaching of some of the distributive subjects. Hence, one of the first requisites of planning to teach such a course is the necessity of deciding upon the basic purpose of the course.

Is the course primarily vocational? If so, then its main objective, in broad terms, is already established. Such, for instance, should be true of a course entitled retail selling.

On the other hand, a course title such as salesmanship (which may be perfectly appropriate as a course title and is often so used) carries far less specific implication relative to the true purpose of the course. It has been quite truthfully said that we all are salesmen throughout our lives. The tiny baby in the crib uses salesmanship in this broad meaning when it desires and secures attention for its own pleasure. Children at play constantly use salesmanship in attempting to get their small friends to join in the games and activities of their choice. Although used for somewhat different purposes, the waking hours of most adolescents are heavily loaded with salesmanship of the highest type directed toward some member or members of the opposite sex. It has been claimed that courtship is applied salesmanship practiced under the strongest kind of motivation!

[3] Edwin L. Nelson, "The Taxonomy of Distributive Education and Distributive Occupations," in *The Emerging Content and Structure of Business Education,* Yearbook No. 8, National Business Education Association, 1970, pp. 135–44.

To the extent that a course in salesmanship has as its purpose the understanding of basic principles and practices applicable to everyone throughout life, it really is a course in applied psychology. Possibly it might better be entitled personal salesmanship—or even applied personal psychology—if that is intended to be its *major purpose*. Thus we find schools in which salesmanship is used as a sort of "catchall" course in which students with varied interests and abilities and plans are found—a "convenience" course available to everyone in selecting a suitable current schedule. Under a skillful teacher it may be pointed out that such a course *may* gain a reputation of being one of the most valuable courses in the school. At the same time, it should be realized that such a course *very frequently* becomes the proverbial "dumping ground" for students who appear to be misfits in many courses with better-established content and objectives.

Most courses in salesmanship are considered business courses; they are also most frequently taught by business teachers. Certainly this would seem at least to imply that the learnings in the course are expected to pertain heavily to the use of salesmanship as a worker or employee in some business activity—to be quite largely vocational or prevocational. It is recommended that advisers and teachers adopt this viewpoint.

However, it must be recognized that a basic vocational or prevocational objective does not eliminate or negate the use and value of learnings for personal use, consumer information, economic understanding, or other purposes. Rather, it appears quite likely that the purposefulness and motivation provided by the vocational or prevocational viewpoint will actually provide a superior medium through which these other (but presumably minor) objectives may be reached.

As already indicated, it seems apparent that distributive subjects offered under the various titles other than that of salesmanship tend automatically to indicate the major purposes or objectives of such courses.

MEASURING ACHIEVEMENT

The proper measurement of achievement is always closely associated with and largely dependent upon the objectives of the course taught. In distributive subjects such as salesmanship, especially, the teacher must be alert to the dangers of focusing too much evaluative endeavor on some one phase of the course. Success in selling, like success in teaching, is based on principles that have been to at least some extent scientifically established; yet it quite largely is the "art" of applying these principles to specific situations that measures one's success in terms of ability to sell.

The teacher of most distributive subjects must realize he has two main factors to consider in measuring the achievement of his students: (*a*) the knowledge and understanding of principles, of needed terminology, of factual information, and of current business practices, and (*b*) the personal ability of the student to skillfully combine and apply these knowledges to specific practical situations in personally solving practical distributive problems involving only himself and involving desired action on the part of other people.

Illustrative of factual knowledges that might be found in a course such as retailing are terms like maintained markup, retail method of inventory, loss leaders, open-to-buy allowance, merchandising, regenerated cellulose, price line, audit-strip, stock control, resident buyer, Willmark Service System, and margin. No great difficulty is experienced by most teachers in evaluating the extent to which individual students have mastered the meaning of such terms and factual knowledges. It is possible to do this through the use of rather common testing devices.

But measuring the ability of each individual student to skillfully and artfully and accurately combine his personal abilities with his course learnings in solving practical problem situations is not so easily accomplished with valid conclusions. Certainly it cannot be done successfully through the medium of an objective-type written test! It usually can be best done through the medium of an actual work station or through the use of an appropriate make-believe situation or case problem.

It should be observed, also, that the time and effort needed to provide and carry through either an actual experience on a work station or an appropriate make-believe situation are far from negligible. In the distributive subjects such techniques are customarily used *primarily* as learning devices. Yet at the same time they do provide an almost automatic evaluation of the achievement of the individual student. For instance, in a class in salesmanship the student may present a sales demonstration before the class. In so doing his preparation for the demonstration and his actual presentation provide excellent learning methods. At the same time, the presentation provides the teacher with observable evidence of the extent to which the individual student has achieved his goals.

The remainder of this chapter will be concerned mostly with illustrations of specific techniques and devices that the teacher of various distributive subjects may employ in furthering the objectives of the course. These should be looked upon *primarily* as learning devices, procedures, and techniques. Yet each one often does provide the teacher with an excellent additional opportunity for specific evaluation of achievement of the individual student.

Additional information relative to these and other methods especially applicable to the teaching of distributive subjects will appear in Chapter 12, "Cooperative Part-Time Business Education Programs."

GROUP DISCUSSION

Teachers of the various distributive subjects usually make extensive use of group discussions as an important method of learning. They generally rate its effectiveness high. Undoubtedly they are correct in so doing.

It is to be recognized, however, that effective group discussion may take place in many different types of discussion situations, and necessarily must be preceded or accompanied by a very realistic motivation. The discussion may be an informal one, or it may be centered around the report of a committee, or around a debate, or around a panel or a symposium. Similarly it may have been motivated primarily by a preceding demonstration or sales kit, or by a field trip, or by a display or a case problem.

The successful teacher of distributive subjects is likely to fully realize that related discussions are important aspects of nearly every technique, device, or procedure he may be using in his course. Thus the specific suggestions that follow would also provide excellent motivating materials for group discussions.

As is true of all group discussions, in teaching these subjects the teacher must be constantly alert to quietly help keep the discussion oriented toward worthwhile goals. A final summarization is quite essential, accompanied by final conclusions whenever possible.

DEMONSTRATION

There are sound psychological reasons why a demonstration always tends to attract and hold the attention. In selling, it is necessary to attract and to hold the attention in order to develop interest and a real desire—all of which ordinarily precedes the closing of the sale. It is generally recognized today that such things as getting the attention, holding the attention, demonstrating, developing interest, and making the close are important and basic parts or steps in the entire process of selling. Thus the technique of using a demonstration as a part of the learning process in connection with classroom work is highly appropriate and proper. It not only possesses its own peculiar psychological values but at the same time tends to duplicate a part of the real-life situation encountered in most sales work; and *skill* in demonstrating can be attained only through a requisite amount of practice, either in the classroom or on the job.

Frequently a demonstration is but a part of a larger skit or sales talk (described next), but it also may be and frequently is used as a separate activity on the part of an individual student. In a true demonstration it is quite customary for the student to have rather full control of the situation, without encountering the additional difficulties occasioned by interruptions and questions and comments from others. This gives the student an opportunity to experience a greater degree of success in learning how to demonstrate than might be encountered were he to launch immediately into a complete sales "skit" in which he, at the same time, must be concerned with all steps in the "sales talk" while reacting to questions, objections, and comments of other parties.

Thus the skillful teacher frequently provides for demonstration practice (either before the class or otherwise) as a separate learning activity *prior to* setting up a demonstration situation embodying other problems and frequently looked upon by the student as a "test" situation.

A demonstration is especially suitable to a situation in which a tangible item, as opposed to an intangible idea, forms the basis of the demonstration—although it may be claimed that a step comparable to demonstration exists in every selling situation. And when something must be actually handled and shown and demonstrated it must be remembered that skillful handling of the tangible item is something that may well be learned separately and distinct from the entire selling process. The salesman of heavy-weight aluminum specialty items, for instance, is often instructed to spend several evenings at home alone *practicing* the unpacking, the setting out for display, and the repacking of his wares; were he to fail to develop skill in doing this his entire sales talk might well be ruined by a clumsy arrangement of utensils scattered about the room—not to mention his embarrassment should he later find it necessary to unpack and repack his cases because he failed to get everything in on his first attempt after completing his demonstration!

Nevertheless, there comes a time when it is necessary for the student to combine the physical demonstration with the mental process that accompanies the entire sales talk or sales skit. Though it is desirable to "practice" on certain skills separately, it perhaps is even more desirable to gain experience in exercising all of them at the same time!

THE SALES TALK

The sales talk is a technique whereby the student organizes into one meaningful whole (a talk) all the various factors or steps and procedures pertinent to the making of a specific sale. He may present it before the class or a committee of fellow students somewhat as one may present a very purposeful lecture. In this case he has complete control of the organization of the talk and can present his points and comments in a previously determined sequence believed to be best calculated to produce the results he desires. Or he may present it in a less formal manner with one or more fellow students participating in the role of the prospect, or customer, who presents questions and objections and other unrehearsed comments which influence the character and sequence of items in the talk. Perhaps this procedure might more properly be termed a *sales skit*.

In general, the sales talk includes the introductory greeting or securing of appropriate attention, the holding of the attention through explanations and demonstrations while an attempt is made to develop a real interest on the part of the "prospect" or customer, the developing of this interest into a desire and a willingness to purchase, and, finally, the closing of the sale followed by appropriate termination of the talk. It can readily be seen that the making of a sales talk presupposes at least some degree of understanding of all "steps" in the making of a sale together with the many psychological influences and reactions accompanying each. To ask the student to give a sales talk before he is ready is likely to result in much waste of time and effort; it is like being asked to practice something before one knows what it is!

A well-prepared sales talk often takes considerable time—time to prepare for it and time to give it. Many teachers make the mistake of using too much of the entire time available for classes in having individual students present such talks before the entire class; it often becomes impracticable to have each student in a class of normal size use the time of the entire class while he presents his talk. Moreover, after hearing the first few talks the class tends to lose interest.

As an alternative, skillful teachers frequently divide the class into small groups and have each individual talk presented before only a small group of fellow students. This group may then follow through with a discussion of the quality of the talk and may even "rate" (evaluate) the talk on the basis of some predetermined rating scale. The giving of the sales talk may well serve at least three major purposes:

1. It enables the student to actually practice on the information, principles, and ideas he has been learning while also reviewing and further learning them by intelligently combining all of them into one unified whole.
2. It aids in further clarifying and fixing in mind the learnings through discussion in a small group where each student can actively participate in the discussion.
3. It also serves as a basis for an evaluation of the individual student's achievement.

THE SALES SKIT

All demonstrations and sales talks are, in a sense, a form of dramatization. The sales skit goes a step further, however, and provides a setting in which the dramatization presumably is more realistic. It is ordinarily based on the use of at least two students, one being the salesman and the other being the prospect or prospective customer. It, of course, assumes advance preparation by the student-salesman to such an extent that he will hope to quite largely direct the course of the conversation. Considerably less preparation is assumed on the part of the student-prospect, although he, too, is expected to come prepared with some specific ideas pertinent to his acceptance of the endeavors of the student-salesman. However, the exact conversation and skit is *not* ordinarily rehearsed or talked over in advance. A part of the value to the student-salesman lies in his opportunity to try out his plan and his abilities and knowledges in a situation that to an extent simulates that to be found by the salesman in real life.

All the desirable factors to be found in an ordinary sales talk or demonstration are ordinarily present in the sales skit; in addition the presence of the student-prospect adds a challenge and the excitement of constantly being alert and ready to meet the unknown in the questions, objections, statements, comments, and various reactions of the student-prospect. It really tends to provide about the maximum in the way of truly putting the student-salesman "to the test"; he must be fully prepared in all ways in order to successfully cope with the situation in most instances.

In using sales skits the teacher must take appropriate advance steps to assure on the part of the prospect a seriousness of purpose; otherwise the natural tendency of exuberant youth is to bring into the skit unusual statements and situations calculated to cause laughter—and on occasion even calculated to embarrass the teacher! Most teachers can find suitable means of avoiding this. Some of the types of precautions sometimes taken by teachers follow:

1. Having the student-prospect thoroughly understand the true purpose he is serving
2. Selecting dependable students to take the part of the prospect

3. Adopting the policy of having each participant in the skit outline for the teacher in advance the specific items he hopes to include in his part of the skit and requiring that an appropriate endeavor be made to confine remarks to those points
4. Having the teacher act as prospect in the first skit or two in order to help establish the proper attitude, which the prospect is expected to maintain
5. Incorporating into any rating scale used for evaluating the sales talk or sales skit an appropriate evaluation, also, of the part played by the prospect

Of course, it is to be recognized that any impromptu or semi-impromptu skit may legitimately and unintentionally result in humorous or even somewhat embarrassing situations; the teacher who has developed a wholesome interest on the part of his students certainly need have little worry about this. If there is doubt in the mind of the teacher, however, precautions such as those suggested tend to be conducive to the development of a more stable and dependable classroom situation.

CASE STUDIES

A case study is actually a problem situation presented to provide a medium for problem solving based on prior learnings and as a motivation and basis for related class discussion. It becomes an important learning device through (*a*) requiring the student to call into use and to review and examine his prior learnings, (*b*) requiring the student to be selective in applying prior learnings to the solution of the problem at hand, (*c*) giving the student a situation or a problem that requires the use of judgment based on prior learnings, and (*d*) motivating further learning and the development of related abilities through group discussion.

A case study may be, or may be based on, a real situation or it may be entirely hypothetical; it really is immaterial which so long as it is presented to the class in a manner that makes it seem real. Often student-prepared cases are excellent and in addition provide an extra learning activity through the preparation of an appropriate case.

Due care should be taken to avoid using actual cases in which names or facts are familiar to students and others locally and may cause embarrassment or undesirable personal connotations. Providing the students with ample hypothetical cases frequently goes far in helping to eliminate the natural tendency of students to turn to actual local cases about which they have some information but which all too frequently involve personalities and touchy local subjects likely to produce some undesirable outcomes in the class.

However, at the same time the teacher should be alert to *use* local real case problems whenever opportunity arises and when it can be done in a manner that will not infringe on good taste or the personal rights of people involved. Certainly real cases within the knowledge of the students or associated with their own community have considerably more interest and meaningfulness to the students than do purely hypothetical cases. It is important, though, that such real cases be introduced in a manner amenable to suitable control of the discussion by the teacher.

SHOPPING TOURS AND SHOPPING REPORTS

As a means of adding meaningfulness and motivation and of learning through observation, there comes a time in most classes in the distributive subjects when students profit considerably from reporting on purposeful observations made right in their own communities. Occasionally this technique may be valuable as a part of the introduction to the course; however, it is often more valuable when used after students have completed appropriate major units of the course.

In a shopping report the student discusses his observations and evaluations of actual salespeople at work. The report may be written, or it may be given orally and as a basis of class discussion. Again, however, it is most important that the bounds of good taste be observed in respect to the use of names of specific people and businesses. If the evaluation is favorable, no real harm is likely to result from the use of actual names. On the other hand, since the character of the evaluation cannot be known in advance, it simply is "good taste" to omit names when giving the report.

The observations presented in a shopping report are customarily made on a shopping tour. For this purpose it is best if two students go together. It also is best if at least one of the students is an *actual* shopper or prospective purchaser in at least one situation. Similarly, however, it is also desirable that the students observe the salespeople at work with *other* prospective customers, in order that the students may be more free to observe details of the sales presentation. Most frequently, practical reasons limit the report of each student to the observation of but one actual sales presentation.

Before making a shopping tour a check sheet of points to observe should be prepared. These should be points that the students have already studied—unless the tour is being used as an introductory motivational device; in that case, the points should be those that are to be studied in the next few units taken up in classwork.

As with most other techniques commonly used in distributive courses, the shopping report provides excellent motivation and material for purposeful group discussion; full advantage should be taken of this opportunity in making overall plans for the course. It provides for the class a number of actual case studies.

POSTERS AND DISPLAYS

Everyone today realizes that appropriate displays and other types of visual presentations are an important part of selling and of many other phases of the work involved in the distributive occupations. Accordingly, students not only are learning about the subject matter of their course when they prepare appropriate posters and displays but also are becoming familiar with the main characteristics of a technique commonly used in the business world. At the same time such activities create interest, enthusiasm, and pride in their work, since they are calculated to bring the endeavors of the students to the attention of others. Attractive displays bring to the business student a personal pride and feeling of being appreciated somewhat comparable to that experienced by the skilled musician or the athlete who gains the applause of his audience.

In preparing displays and posters major attention should be given to these points:

1. Have a *single theme* for each display.
2. "Tell a story" and tell it simply.
3. Use color whenever possible.
4. Avoid "too much," with the resulting cluttered appearance.
5. Be sure the background is attractive.
6. Be sure that the final result produces something that is pleasing to the eye.
7. Provide a setting that is appropriately lighted.
8. Provide a new one frequently.

Local merchants and businesses are often excellent sources of suggestions and aids when preparing displays or posters. From time to time the local merchant must discard rather attractive displays in favor of a "change" or of newer displays better depicting the current status of his product or customer demand for it. Sometimes these displays have been provided by manufacturers at considerable cost. The time may come quickly for the local merchant when any specific display of this type no longer is of value to him; in most cases he is quite happy to pass it on to a business teacher for classroom use.

FIELD TRIPS AND SPEAKERS

Although field trips and speakers obviously are separate and distinct types of instructional activity, they are mentioned together here because, actually, often either may be used as a means of bringing the same information to the class; one is a visual method and the other an audio method.

The shopping tour may be considered a type of field trip, too, but it usually does not permit attention to such a wide variety of information as is customarily given consideration in what is termed a field trip.

In using either a field trip or a speaker, much of the effectiveness, as always, depends on the advance planning. Certainly students going on a field trip should know what they are to look for and observe and should be in some appropriate manner prepared to make rational observations; similarly, a visiting speaker should know what it is the teacher is currently interested in teaching to his class so that he will be better able to determine what information is most pertinent to that particular learning.

Field trips, and often speakers, may be used in studying distributive subjects such as these: store arrangement and layout, cashiering, store location, fashion merchandising, window and interior display, credits and collections, store records and merchandise control, customer services, receiving and marking goods, textiles, store organization, and distributive careers. To this list could be added many other ideas, the number and nature depending considerably on the specific distributive subject being taught.

CASE STUDIES OF LOCAL BUSINESSES

Since distribution is an area of endeavor so widely spread and so common that it is to be found represented in all communities, both large and small, the distributive subjects provide excellent opportunity for individual students to prepare case studies of local businesses. At times it may be best for two or more students, or for an entire class, to work on the same case study.

When properly approached such case studies also provide the teacher, the school, and education with one of the most effective means of public relations and of building goodwill. Usually everyone likes to receive the compliment of having others interested in his work. Also, we each usually like to give information that others may seek. Thus when a class in a secondary school decides it wishes to prepare a manual or scrapbook or history of a local business, it is indeed a most unusual business management that is not eager to cooperate fully! And after having given this cooperation, it also is an unusual business management that does not feel increased goodwill for that teacher, that school, and education in general.

Many, many different types of items might well be considered in writing up the case study of a local business. Certainly appropriate space would need to be devoted to the people who founded and manage it, to its early start and history, to the services it renders, to the goods it handles, and to the people it employs. But in addition such a study may well become the medium through which the students in the class gain illustrative and meaningful information about those particular phases of business the class is studying. Thus merchandising and customer-service policies may be included; the chief media of advertising and the main lines of merchandise handled may be described; pictures may be taken and details included about any new equipment or desirable store layout or arrangement; in fact, it is unlikely that any single item of information will be studied in class that cannot be illustrated in a case study or store manual or scrapbook devoted to some local business.

Case studies of local businesses, then, provide a most practical and meaningful method of learning in the distributive subjects. At the same time the accumulation of such materials in school, associated as it must be with many and constant pleasant school-community contacts, can result in tremendous values through good public relations.

OTHER INSTRUCTIONAL AIDS

A few suggestions have now been given pointing out some of the effective instructional methods especially well fitted for use in the various distributive subjects. However, this by no means exhausts the possibilities available to the alert teacher. Subjects such as salesmanship and retailing are both broad and flexible in content and thus provide opportunities for the use of almost any teaching technique or aid that is available to teachers.

Many films and filmstrips are available for the use of the teacher, most of them at little or no cost. Larger businesses in the field of distribution frequently have their own in-service training programs for which they have prepared special teaching aids; at times they will lend them to teachers for classroom use. In addition many businesses are quite anxious to make these and similar films available as a means of promoting goodwill. It is true that all such aids should be previewed and those rejected that may contain undesirable advertising, misleading statements, or too much material not of value to the particular class in which it is to be used. This still leaves many more desirable aids available than any one teacher needs or can effectively use.

In addition, many teacher education colleges and universities and many state departments of business and distributive education have prepared special films and filmstrips which are available on loan. The teacher can usually obtain some of them through the assistance of personnel in his own state department of public instruction.

COOPERATIVE PART-TIME PROGRAMS

Although not confined to the distributive subjects, it is well to remember that much of the most effective teaching of distributive subjects for vocational purposes comes about through the use of a good, well-supervised, cooperative part-time program. Many of the techniques already mentioned are most readily and effectively used when such a program is correlated with the classroom study; it also provides opportunity for additional instructional techniques which may be used in a planned and purposeful situation.

Since Chapter 12 is devoted entirely to a consideration of such programs, the reader is referred to that chapter for additional suggestions of effective methods of teaching the distributive subjects.

PROJECTS AND QUESTIONS FOR DISCUSSION

1. Obtain from the vocational division of your state department of public instruction a copy of the state plan for distributive education. Determine and report on the qualifications for (a) a teacher-coordinator and for (b) an approved program in distributive education.

2. Investigate available textbooks in salesmanship (or courses of study in salesmanship) and determine whether stated objectives appear to be primarily vocational or primarily of a personal-use nature.

3. Interview the personnel director or manager of a large retail store and determine whether or not any endeavor is made to help salespeople improve their salesmanship ability.

4. Have each member of the class keep a "shopping report" for a week for the purpose of discovering either the presence of or the lack of good salesmanship on the part of retail-store employees (identification of stores should be avoided).

5. What conclusions might one tentatively draw upon hearing that the distributive subjects are relatively neglected in many schools and that the consumer typically spends over half his money for costs of distribution? What other factors might enter in?

6. It is often pointed out that beginning pay in retail stores is relatively low. Do you think better education of youth in retailing and in the distributive subjects would tend to alter this situation any?

7. If you could arrange for but a very limited number of field trips for students in your retailing class, would you give preference to visiting a relatively large store or a relatively small one?

8. What special advantages can you see in having students prepare and give sales talks and sales skits? What possible problems or difficulties might you encounter as the teacher?

9. Why is it that so many schools offer courses (such as typewriting and shorthand) that prepare for office work while comparatively few offer courses that prepare for store work? Does this appear to be sound educational planning?

CASE PROBLEMS

1. Harry Jamison has been D.E. coordinator and teacher two years at the Wapsie Lake High School and seems to have had a successful program. His students take the distributive practices course and have their cooperative program during their senior year. Prior to that year many of them, but not all, have had general business, typewriting, and bookkeeping. Harry now asks his principal to start a course in salesmanship in the junior year in which all students planning to take the D.E. work will have to register; the course thus definitely would be basically for his D.E. students. But his principal objects and states that since salesmanship is something every person has to use all his life the course should be a purely elective one open to all students who wish to take it. He believes D.E. students should not be required to take it, since failure to do so might prevent some students from taking D.E. in the senior year should they decide to do so. What do you think should be done?

2. Joan Roberts teaches a class in salesmanship. As a means of adding interest and motivation to the class, she invited a successful local businessman to talk to her class on "How to Be Successful in Selling." His talk consisted mostly of a lecture on why theoretical "book learning" is useless in learning to sell and why the only way to learn how to sell is to "go get yourself a job and learn from experience." This has now created a skepticism on the part of her students toward their textbook and their classroom work. Discuss the situation.

3. In having his students present sales talks toward the end of his course in salesmanship, Floyd Walker instructed each to have a classmate act as the prospect or customer. He also asked that anyone acting as a prospect do his best to seriously represent a typical customer who at first is unconvinced and who asks many questions. One student, Harry Unzer, had access to materials and information from the local Ladies Lingerie Shoppe which his mother owns and operates. Accordingly, with his pal Wallace acting as the customer, Harry prepared a sales talk based on a nationally advertised line of fine lingerie. Both boys handled the situation well and with tact and good taste; however, other boys in class occasionally tried to insert improper humor and a few of the girls in class were obviously somewhat embarrassed, as was Mr. Walker. Discuss the entire situation.

4. The retailing class at Huron High School was about to start a unit on window display and as a part of their preparation for the unit the students were assigned in pairs to observe and be prepared to describe the window displays downtown. Each pair of students was

assigned to one side of a specific block of business houses. In reporting on one display, Jane and Virginia criticized it severely, since it obviously had not been changed for a long time; there were spider webs and dead flies in the window, and an open container of candy had melted from the sun and dust was on the candy. Unknown to them one of their classmates was closely related to the proprietor of this particular business and naturally felt embarrassed. Discuss the entire situation and suggest what you would do as the teacher (*a*) to avoid such a situation and (*b*) to handle it in case it should inadvertently arise.

SUGGESTED READINGS

"Standard Terminology Is Provided to Describe Curriculum Instruction," *American Vocational Journal*, May 1971, p. 62.

"Careers Unlimited," *DECA Distributor*, April 1971, pp. 8–11.

Crawford, Lucy C., "Basic Beliefs in Distributive Education," *American Vocational Journal*, March 1968, pp. 24–26.

Eggland, Stephen A., "Meaningful Methods for Distributive Education," *Business Education Forum*, March 1969, pp. 20–21.

Ferguson, Edward T., "A Challenge for the Distributive Education Program of the 70's," *The Balance Sheet*, January 1969, pp. 208–12.

Forr, William A., and Lester M. Yerkes, "Modulizing Distributive Education," *Business Education Forum*, May 1971, pp. 22–23.

Harris, E. Edward, "The Changing Levels of Distributive Occupations," *The Emerging Content and Structure of Business Education, NBEA Yearbook*, No. 8, 1970, Chap. 9, pp. 67–75.

Knouse, Reno S., "Innovations in Distributive Education—Planning to Teach," *Business Education Forum*, April 1967, pp. 5–6.

Logan, K. Otto, "Checker Training Is Rolling in Washington State," *American Vocational Journal*, May 1971, pp. 56–58. History of a mobile classroom.

Samson, Harlan E., "The Changing Nature of Distributive Occupations," *The Emerging Content and Structure of Business Education, NBEA Yearbook*, No. 8, 1970, pp. 60–66.

———, "The Teaching of Distributive Education," *Contributions of Research to Business Education, NBEA Yearbook*, No. 9, 1971, Chap. 9, pp. 78–86.

Tonne, Herbert A., and Louis C. Nanassy, "Education for Distributive Occupations," *Principles of Business Education*, Chap. 22, pp. 316–32. New York: Gregg Publishing Division, McGraw-Hill Book Company, 1970.

Trimpe, Adrian, "Distributive Education at the Post-Secondary Level," *Business Education Forum*, January 1969, pp. 26–28.

"What Is DECA?," *DECA Handbook*, 1970, pp. 3–4.

IV

extending learning beyond the classroom

No clear-cut line can be drawn separating good teaching "methodology" from the many other phases of good teaching. It is beyond the scope of a single text such as this to include everything of value in improving the work of a business teacher.

Yet there are some areas of the work of the business teacher so closely associated with and so greatly influencing his methodology that to ignore them would almost be to ignore a portion of common practice in methods of teaching business subjects. Part IV further broadens the teacher's concept of "methods of teaching" to include many of these important related concepts.

Much of the effectiveness of teaching in the area of vocational business education will depend on the available opportunity for effective practice or apprenticeship applications. The modern, educationally directed, cooperative part-time work-experience program is an important answer to this need. Every business teacher should know about such programs, since they materially alter teaching methods for advanced vocational students.

Likewise, although personal development, habits, traits, and attitudes are extremely important educational objectives, quite often extraclass activities provide superior mediums for teaching them. Thus the methods the business teacher uses in the classroom may be both supplemented and influenced by the presence of well-organized and expertly directed associated activities for the business student—such as a chapter of the Future Business Leaders of America.

In Part IV are presented a number of these modern concepts which are materially influencing both the achievements and the learning procedures of today's business students. The business teacher will do well to include them in his plans for improvement of methods of teaching.

12

COOPERATIVE PART-TIME
BUSINESS EDUCATION PROGRAMS

Work has always been at the center of man's total integration—social, emotional, cultural, and vocational.[1]

The growth in the use of and participation in cooperative training is a notable development in business education. Ever since cooperative part-time training for the distributive occupations was formally recognized by the George–Deen Act in 1936 more and more youth have found cooperative training the real answer to their vocational preparation, both in the distributive and in the office occupations. The educator and the businessman should be commended for their encouragement of such programs.

When business firms were small the employees learned the business directly from the employer. But even before 1900 concentrations of population developed department stores, multipurpose offices, and other large business establishments. Personal contact between owner and employee was lost, and the beginning clerical or sales worker had to learn his job through trial and error or under poorly qualified, poorly motivated fellow workers. Expansion of many related fields demanding office and distributive workers paralleled the growth of stores and offices. As the field of business grew in size and importance, the need for training in all business occupations became necessary.

---

[1] Milton Gold, *Working to Learn* (New York: Bureau of Publications, Teachers College, Columbia University, 1951).

To provide the student who was going into business occupations with occupational counseling and supervision while he was adjusting to real work situations, various work-study programs were inaugurated. These programs were immediately successful; they have grown in number as the demands for trained distributive and office workers have increased.

Today more and more educators realize the importance of planned work in the education of greater numbers of youth who enter adult employment upon leaving high school. Many of those youth who are going on to college also have real benefits to gain by training under a school-work program. The extent of this practical education is reflected in United States Office of Education statistics. The number of high-school students in work training programs, both federally reimbursed and the nonreimbursed, shows steady growth in our nation's high schools.

During the development of planned work programs in business education several different titles were used to indicate this type of training. The title that finally emerged and is now generally accepted in business education circles was *cooperative part-time training*.

WHAT IS COOPERATIVE BUSINESS EDUCATION?

Cooperative part-time training programs for students interested in office or distributive (retailing, selling, service, and wholesaling) occupations operate in many high schools, large and small, in the United States; and they provide a unique opportunity for the secondary pupil to begin his career in business.

Cooperative programs enrolling business students can be classified into four basic types.

1. Straight Office Education Program—so called because the related classes enroll only students in office occupations. These office occupations may be of a secretarial, clerical, or bookkeeping nature.
2. Straight Distributive Education Program—so called when all students are in retailing, wholesaling, outside selling, or service occupations. The related class is made up only of students in these occupations.
3. Business Education Occupations Program—a combination office and distributive program wherein related instruction is given to a class made up of both office and distributive students.
4. Diversified Occupations Program—so called because students are in office, distributive, trade, and industrial occupations.

The cooperative part-time program operates on what is known as the *alternation plan*. Usually students spend the morning in school and afternoons on the job. Some notably successful programs, often in the larger school systems, use a plan of alternating a week in the classroom with a week on the job. Students in programs obtaining state and federal reimbursement must meet the standard of fifteen hours minimum per week on the job. They generally have either two periods of related instruction in school for one year (called plan B in distributive education) or one period of instruction for one year plus meeting certain prerequisite courses (called plan C in distributive education). Some programs operate over a two-year period (called plan A in distributive education) in which students receive one period of related instruction during both the junior and the senior years. The related instruction hours may be taught by the coordinator, who knows firsthand the job-training needs and problems of the trainees, or by a teacher of a related subject. If circumstances permit, the teacher-coordinator role is preferred.

The heart of the cooperative program is the on-the-job training under the supervision of the coordinator, and the correlation of instruction in the related class with the job needs of the student. The chronological order of instructional units in the classroom is determined by the requirements of the student on his individual job. Much of the instruction is individual, since every student has different needs. His job duties, his firm, and his personal requirements are dissimilar from all others.

The uniqueness of cooperative part-time programs, therefore, presents the qualified teacher-coordinator with a need for methods and procedures not commonly used in classroom situations. The instruction is heavily individual, mostly vocational, and in every case specifically pointed to and developed around an occupational area.

WHAT ARE THE ADVANTAGES OF COOPERATIVE BUSINESS EDUCATION?

When any one program in a single field has had consistent enrollment increases since its beginning about 1935, we may justly say that it has enjoyed a phenomenal growth. Such is the story of cooperative part-time programs in distributive and office education.

What is the significance of the high school cooperative program? What advantages exist that make this such an attractive program for students, schools, and businesses? Here are some of the reasons:

For the Student

1. It furnishes practical training of the kind that makes the student more efficient and valuable to his employers.
2. It offers him a natural method of choosing an occupation. In doing so, vocational guidance opportunities are inherent. Moreover, the student is imbued with the desire to know the important everyday use of his school training.
3. The method that combines theory and practice has been found to be a sound, workable educational method.
4. It prolongs and makes meaningful the school life of many students who would otherwise not be receiving training toward an occupational goal.
5. It helps the student bridge the gap between the school and the business world.

For the School

1. It brings together the business community and the school community.
2. The school learns the problems of the business community and becomes better equipped to teach students how to cope with them.
3. Cooperative education has immense public relations value, since the business world meets and tests the products of the school. Many of the projects carried on in the program result in favorable publicity.

For the Business Community

1. It provides for the constant and systematic infusion of desirable beginners into office and distributive work.
2. The school training "upgrades" the level of all other workers in the business firm and attracts a better grade of employee.
3. The school aids in the initial training, helping the business firm reduce its training problems and expense.
4. It reduces cost by increasing the efficiency of the office or distributive worker.

Education at public expense can be justified only in terms of the contribution it makes to the general welfare of society. A program of cooperative education under public supervision and control can be justified only when it provides training that enables those engaged in the business field to give better, more economical, and more efficient service. The social and economic benefits that will accrue from an adequate program in distributive and office education will be shared by business workers, business firms, producers, and consumers.

TERMS USED IN COOPERATIVE DISTRIBUTIVE AND OFFICE EDUCATION

Certain terms used in the field of cooperative education should be defined and understood so that all teachers and others connected with business education will be able to communicate adequately as well as comprehend fully the professional literature in the field.

Cooperative education is a method of education that integrates learning experience in the school with work experience made available in some cooperating agency outside the school. This is all under the regular supervision of a school representative called a coordinator.

Coordinator is a person who holds a secondary teaching certificate plus special technical and professional requirements in the office, distributive, or trade field, as well as a certain amount of actual occupation experience in his particular field. He is directly charged with the planning of the program as well as with the selection, placement, training, and promotion of students connected with a cooperative part-time training program. A *teacher-coor-*

dinator is one who, in addition, teaches the related instruction class in school.

Related instruction is instruction provided under a vocationally competent instructor and is directly meaningful to the student enrolled in a cooperative program. This class is usually titled *distributive practices* in the distributive educational programs and *office practice* or *secretarial practice* in the office education programs.

Training station is a cooperating business that agrees to employ a student on a part-time basis and to provide this student with a variety of experiences and training necessary to develop occupational efficiency. The agreement is usually only for the period of a regular school year.

Sponsor is an employee appointed by the business firm to carry out the training and rotation of the student through a series of experiences. He supervises the training of the student, evaluates the student's progress periodically on forms provided by the school, and consults with the coordinator on the student's overall training. He may be called a *training supervisor*.

Student learner is a student who has elected to take part in the cooperative program. The student is usually a senior (some programs do start in the junior year) and has a sincere interest in a chosen business occupation. He is mature and employable, and he has the necessary aptitude for the job for which he will be training. The student learner either plans to enter the field upon graduation from high school or needs the occupational background in preparation for advanced study.

Advisory committee is a group of business people and others of the community who are interested in the welfare and advancement of the cooperative program within the school. They provide suggestions and advice to the school in matters concerning the cooperative program, especially in those phases directly involving business. They may also assist in the promotion, course determination, selection of instructors, and other matters pertaining to the adult program in the school.

Reimbursed program is a cooperative program that, by maintaining certain standards, receives state and federal moneys under provisions of the state and federal vocational legislation. The Vocational Education Act of 1963 and the Vocational Education Amendments of 1968 provide reimbursement to cooperative programs and also to preparatory programs meeting vocational standards. Standards involve coordinator and teacher requirements, student selection, employment schedules, course content, facilities and equipment, and other factors which help assure an educationally sound program.

THE NATURE OF LEARNING IN COOPERATIVE PART-TIME EDUCATION

One of the most important and difficult parts of the coordinator's job is the provision for school training directly helpful to each student trainee. Since the entire purpose of the cooperative program is to train youth, not just to find them employment, there is little excuse for operating a program unless it is prepared to offer the related instruction and coordination needed.

Importance of Coordination

Coordination is the integrating factor that unites all necessary elements of a cooperative program and directs them toward a common purpose. Coordination is essentially a combining activity which brings in and fits together the various parts needed to make a complete and functioning cooperative program. Without coordination a training program ceases to be cooperative and lacks the element that makes such training truly vocational.

A broad definition of coordination is "all activities carried on by the teacher-coordinator." These can be grouped as: (a) promotion, (b) organization and administration, (c) selection of trainees and training stations, (d) placement of trainees, and (e) instruction. Efforts in each of these areas must be blended together to produce a well-trained, fully qualified worker upon graduation. Lack of work in any one of the areas will seriously hamper the effectiveness of the program and the quality of the training. As we examine the nature of the learnings provided in cooperative training it must be remembered that for these learnings to be fully achieved they must be carefully coordinated with all other areas, especially on-the-job activities.

Categories of Learnings

The total learnings expected of a trainee can be classified into four areas: (a) general related learnings, (b) occupational group learnings, (c) specific job learnings, and (d) on-the-job learnings.

General related learnings are received in those subjects embracing problems common to all workers regardless of kind of work. This would include such topics as employer-employee relations, work habits and attitudes, human relations, employee benefits and protection, personal habits affecting work, government-business relationships, labor organization, and occupational planning.

Occupational group learnings would include auxiliary technical and non-technical information that is necessary to the individual for confidence, understanding, and job pride. It would not be necessary for the student to study this area at the time he is actually performing the skills on the job. In office occupations this would include such subjects as typewriting, bookkeeping, shorthand, filing, duplicating, and office machines. In distributive occupations this would include such subjects as store organization, color, line and design, speech, principles of display, store record keeping, and salesmanship.

Specific job learnings would include the technical information needed to perform skills and to make judgments. Office topics would include credit, office procedure, medical stenography, and dental-receptionist duties. The units for the distributive worker might include merchandise analysis, specific selling techniques, unit control, and salescheck systems.

On-the-job learnings include the technical information learned on the job, such as special machines, special business forms, policies and practices peculiar to a single business, and other skills or knowledges that can be learned on the job under the supervision of the student's sponsor or training supervisor.

Categories of learnings provided in post–high school cooperative programs are the same as in high school, although the content is designed to prepare the post–high school student for middle-level occupations.

Ways of Presenting Learnings

GENERAL RELATED LEARNINGS.   These are usually learned through group-instruction methods with full use of community resources such as committees, informal discussion, resource persons, field trips, and visual aids.

OCCUPATIONAL GROUP LEARNINGS.   The content in this area is handled through group work—with allowances for individual differences, of course. In the business education occupations program and the diversified occupations program, the class may be divided into broad fields of interest—office, distributive, or trades. Further breakdown may be made as the situation warrants.

SPECIFIC JOB LEARNINGS.   This material is usually handled in small groups or on an individual basis according to its nature in the particular case. It may be provided through individual study guides such as the Minnesota card system (also Ohio and Oklahoma) or through individual study manuals such as those of Texas, Missouri, and Alabama. Students may also make individual manuals or notebooks about their job or the merchandise handled. Generally a combination of these devices is necessary. The sponsor or training supervisor assists in this type of training.

ON-THE-JOB LEARNINGS.   Coordinator, student, and training supervisor work out a job breakdown, also called a *schedule of processes* or *plan of experiences.* The various sections of the breakdown are placed in a suitable sequence, and the trainee performs one duty after another as he is ready for them. In training stations where all tasks are performed at the outset of the training period, a sequence of study is planned.

In actual teaching practice the distinctions among areas of learning are not as fine as indicated here. A class period may be scheduled for related study, but the division of the class period among the different kinds of learnings is left to the discretion of the teacher. The teacher can correlate or integrate according to the dictates of his judgment.

Most students have the bulk of their general related learnings before reaching the senior year and their entrance to the cooperative program. Some of the occupational group learnings will be received in preemployment classes, but much will be received in the related class. Specific job learnings are entirely taken in the related instruction class. On-the-job learnings are received only at the student's training station.

Because of the flexibility and adaptability of teaching methods, most can be used in two or more of the learning areas. The committee, for example, can be used just as effectively in general related learnings as it can in occupational group learnings. To give some core of focus to the cooperative training methods, however, each method is listed under the learning area where it is most often used.

The methods explained here should not be construed as the only ones used or needed in cooperative training, but these are effective and common. The examples are given merely to show specific application. It is assumed that the teacher has a complete mastery of the methods needed in general classroom teaching.

Typical Curriculum Patterns in High School Cooperative Business Education Programs

In order that the reader may better visualize the curriculums, a sample curriculum pattern for each cooperative program is given. The patterns shown would be changed somewhat for the larger schools where more offerings could be made. The usual high school requirements and electives are not shown.

The business education occupations program is found in the smaller schools where the total number of students enrolled in cooperative training is not sufficiently large to warrant a separate class for each group. A curriculum pattern for this type of program would rest heavily on the school's current offerings. It is highly recommended that the pattern include general business, typewriting, bookkeeping, and occupations practice plus cooperative training.

Distributive Education Curriculum Pattern

9th grade General Business *10th grade* Typewriting	*11th grade* Bookkeeping Salesmanship ½ and Business Law ½ or Consumer Education ½ or Business Arithmetic ½	*12th grade* Distributive Practices (2 periods if plan B, 1 if plan C) Cooperative Training (on the job)

Office Education Curriculum Pattern (Secretarial)

9th grade General Business *10th grade* Typewriting	*11th grade* Bookkeeping Shorthand Office Machines	*12th grade* Secretarial Practice Cooperative Training (on the job)

Office Education Curriculum Pattern (Clerical)

9th grade General Business *10th grade* Typewriting	*11th grade* Bookkeeping Office Machines Business Law ½ and Consumer Education ½ or Business Arithmetic ½ or Business English ½	*12th grade* Clerical Practice Cooperative Training (on the job)

The pattern for a diversified occupations class must be built around the offerings of very small schools. This is best worked out under the guidance of state supervisors of the fields represented.

Sample Distributive Practices Instructional Schedule

The following is a sample outline of what a coordinator may plan to provide in the distributive practices class. The general related learnings would be the most variable, depending on what has been provided in other classes prior to the student's enrollment in the cooperative program in the senior year. This plan is based on a plan C distributive program. The plan B program, having two periods per day for the school year, would give approximately twice as much time for each type of learning. Plan A would also have about twice as much time for each learning, as it has one class period in both junior and senior years.

Area of Instruction	Number of Weeks (1 hour per day)
General Related Learnings	6
Occupational Group Learnings	20
Specific Job Learnings	10
	36
On-the-Job Learnings (15 hours per week minimum)	36

The coordinator would break down each of the learnings into a time schedule so he could draw up his units of study. The occupational group learnings might look like this.

Occupational Group Learnings Outline

Channels of Distribution	1 week
Basic Salesmanship (review)	4
Related Skills in Selling	2
Job Analysis	1
Store Operation	2
Store Organization	2
Merchandise Information	1
Problems in Selling	2
Advertising	1
Display	2
Fashion Merchandising	1
Buying	1
Total	20 weeks

The general related learnings would be drawn from those units not covered in previous classes (these units are listed later under "Techniques in Providing General Related Learnings"). The specific job learnings would vary considerably from student to student but would undoubtedly include a great deal of merchandise study as well as specific skills in advertising, display, merchandising, and buying. With this overall view let us now examine methods that might be used for each of these learnings.

Typical Curriculum Patterns in Post–High School Cooperative Business Education Programs

Post–high school cooperative programs in distributive and office occupations vary considerably. Frequently they may be more specialized than the high school programs and may offer a greater depth of education in the occupation under study. In modern area schools and the vocational-technical (non-college-transfer) divisions of community colleges, we find new courses and programs being introduced each year to provide currently needed job preparation for distributive and office occupations; some may be of only a few weeks duration, while others require one term, one semester, one year, or two years. Most of those extending over longer periods make use of cooperative part-time programs. Many of the degree (two-year) programs in these community colleges include subject matter and courses provided by the arts and sciences (college-transfer) division of the college. These latter programs usually contain sixty-four to sixty-eight semester hours of course offerings, frequently organized somewhat as follows:

First Year		Second Year	
Communication Skills	6	Occupational Analysis	3
Business Mathematics	3	Economics	3
Accounting	6	Field Experience	6–12
Psychology of Human Relations	3	Occupational Subjects (Marketing	
American Institutions	3	or Office Skills)	18–22
Business Law	3		
Occupational Subjects (Marketing			
or Office Skills)	10		

Field experiences may be arranged on an alternating schedule of half day in school and half day on the job as in the high school program or may be blocked into periods of twelve to eighteen weeks alternating with semesters of full-time attendance at the post–high school level.

TECHNIQUES IN PROVIDING GENERAL RELATED LEARNINGS

It has been pointed out that general related learnings are those common to all workers regardless of the field of work. Courses that usually present general related learnings would be general business, English, business arithmetic, salesmanship, bookkeeping, and, to a lesser degree, nearly all other required classes in the secondary school.

The methods used in providing general related learnings are those common to any group instruction involving the use of community resources, audiovisual aids, reference work, discussion, and lecture. A sample list of the units or topics providing general related learnings is given below.

These units are found in the courses mentioned above or, in some cases, are grouped together and offered in a class called *occupational relations*. The merits of a separate course have been argued pro and con, and certain values do accrue from having such a class. However, the integration of these topics into several courses taken by nearly all students is the current trend.

Units Containing General Related Learnings for the Cooperative Trainee

How Can I Find My Place in the World of Work?
How Can I Get the Job I Want?
How Can I Work Successfully with People with Whom I Come in Contact on a Job?
How Do Existing Labor Laws Affect Me?
How Will Labor Organizations Affect Me?
How Can I Advance in My Occupation?
How Can I Keep Healthy as a Worker?
How Can I Make Best Use of My Earnings?
How Can I Protect Myself and Others from Accidents and Injuries on the Job?
What Deductions Are Made from My Wages and Why Are They Made?[2]

The teacher-coordinator will continually check to see which of these learnings have been covered in other classes. Those not covered will have to be scheduled for the related class. Often a brief visit with a fellow teacher will result in a change in classes to accommodate some part of the general related learnings.

For example, a unit in English on "Occupations" would touch on several of the above topics. A unit in a social studies class on "Labor Unions," if approached from the effect on the individual worker, would satisfy at least two of the above units. The bookkeeping class is a natural for discussion on taxes, social security, and other information about payroll deductions. The physical education classes would cover good grooming and personal health habits.

If the general related learnings are not being covered in these classes, it is seldom because the teachers will not do it—it is usually because they are not aware that these units are desired by the coordinator for the students going into the cooperative program.

TECHNIQUES IN PROVIDING OCCUPATIONAL GROUP LEARNINGS

Occupational group learnings are taught in the distributive practices class for distributive trainees, in the clerical or secretarial practice class for office trainees, and in the occupations class for business or diversified programs. Half or more of the time in these classes is given to occupational group learnings, with the remainder of the time used for specific job instruction. It can be seen, then, that considerable attention should be given methods used in this type of instruction.

Instruction in this area of learning is built around units that apply to all students in an occupational field. In distributive practices all the students are

[2] *Units of Instruction for the Occupational Relations Course* (St. Paul, Minn.: Vocational Division, State Department of Education).

employed in some distributive occupation, and the learnings provided are those necessary for all workers in distribution. The methods used in occupational group learnings, however, are equally applicable to all occupational fields—distributive, office, and trades. Several methods used in occupational group learnings will be explained briefly, and examples will be given.

Individual Reports

The use of the individual report combines several worthwhile learning activities into one project. The student would carry out the following steps in preparing a typical report.

1. Define the problem on which the report is to be given.
2. Gather the information needed to satisfy the problem.
3. Draw together related facts and reach some conclusions.
4. Organize the report in a logical manner.
5. Present to the class the problem, findings, and conclusions.
6. Answer questions and defend conclusions.

For example, in a unit on store organization, questions may arise as to local practice on such things as leased departments, receiving and marking, or chain-store managership. A student could be asked to prepare a report on one of these questions and present his findings to the class. After getting the problem clearly in mind, the student may draw background information. When the necessary information has been acquired, a written report would be prepared and the findings presented orally to the class. Questions and discussion would naturally follow the report, thus providing the entire class with some understanding of the particular area that one student has studied.

A valuable part of the individual report is the experience the student gets from presenting his report to the class, answering questions, and defending his conclusions. This skill is very important to those in selling and office work where they meet with customers and clients. It is not necessary that every student in class prepare an individual report at the same time. Reports have more meaning when they are assigned as the result of a recognized need rather than just as a problem "drawn from a hat."

Resource Person

A resource person is usually defined as a person who has, through experience and/or training, acquired a fund of information that he is willing to share with others. The resource person may take the form of a guest speaker in the classroom, a member of a panel, or someone who meets with students conducting field interviews.

The resource person can best be used to provide information needed by students in an area in which the coordinator has little or no background. The person usually has a clear understanding of the topic and can draw from many local examples that are real and interesting to the students. The students, through questions that may be prepared ahead of time, can clarify views they already have on the topic. The resource person has also been used effectively in introducing new units or in climaxing a unit of instruction.

For the class to receive the utmost value from the resource person, the coordinator should be sure that the subject matter dovetails satisfactorily into the objectives and learning outcomes that he desires. When selecting an individual the coordinator should make sure that the person will present information in keeping with the philosophy of the community. Above all it should be kept in mind that the resource people should be used only if they can present additional information or clarify information already covered.

Case Study

The case-study method is the relating of some story, anecdote, or the like, usually in the third person, often used to add variety and human interest to a classroom situation. It probably has its greatest usages in illustrating a particular point or opening a new subject or unit.

When either a true or a hypothetical case is presented by the teacher, the students have alternative solutions from which to choose, and it is up to them to select the most appropriate one. A case is most effective if the student is asked what he would do if he were in the particular situation. It is recommended that the coordinator write the facts of the case on the blackboard before beginning the class period so that the student will be able to use them as a frame of reference.

In using this technique the instructor asks the students to put themselves into a pseudosituation and decide what they would do if confronted with a specific problem.

The case method often shows the teacher what knowledge the students lack and creates or instills in them the desire to continue with the subject until they have mastered it.

Field Interview

A field interview is an activity wherein a student contacts someone—employer, co-worker, customer, consumer, parent, government official, or any other predetermined person—in an informal situation for the purpose of securing authentic opinions and facts related to a problem that he is studying. It is ordinarily a question-and-answer process which can be altered to fit the circumstances.

The interview is much more important than the space that has been allotted to it in recent publications would indicate. Because virtually all distributive workers employ the method, and because a very definite skill is involved that is valuable in many life situations, it should have a prominent place among the learning activities of students in cooperative training. Through the field interview, the student will gain confidence in himself and in the community. When the interview is well executed, those who have been interviewed will acquire respect for the school and the program.

The planning of the field interview should be a cooperative activity between the teacher-coordinator and the individual, committee, or entire class. Arrangements should be made well in advance of the interview. Frequently the teacher will "scout" the persons to be interviewed. This may or may not be known by the students involved.

In teaching salesmanship, the field interview might well be used to study the sales practices of various types of stores or service enterprises, to examine company policy concerning particular merchandising situations, or to investigate customer reactions to sales procedures. In the retailing course, it might be applied to the study of store organization, store system, merchandising policies, or advertising procedures. In the area of occupational relations, it is appropriate to an investigation of the desirable traits of workers in the several fields of distribution, common deficiencies of personnel, human relations problems, and safety practices. The opportunities for using the field interview are many indeed.

Role Playing

Role playing is an unrehearsed, spontaneous dramatization stressing the role of the individual. The primary purpose of role playing is to have a student achieve successful technique for handling a given situation. Two or more students may reenact a problem situation that actually occurred or has been observed on the job. They may take their own roles or assume the role of someone else. Pseudosituations may also be created in which special problems are dramatized. The role-paying activity can be presented to the entire class or carried out as a group activity while other students are conducting sales practice or individual study.

The degree to which a role-playing situation is structured is a matter of choice depending upon your objectives. If you are using role playing to present information or facts, you may want a rather carefully controlled situation. If, on the other hand, your main purpose is to develop confidence, control, or skills in the student, a spontaneous portrayal may suit your needs.

The more important purposes of role playing are: to develop specific skills, to develop an appreciation of work standards, to present information and facts, to try out new techniques, to develop desirable attitudes, to point out common problems, to improve communication, to develop self-confidence, to correct undesirable attitudes and habits, to provide practice in adaptability, to motivate learning, to reduce emotional tension, and to evaluate progress and achievement.

Like most new learning devices, role playing must be introduced gradually with a great deal of tact and salesmanship. A full explanation of what is to be accomplished, along with coordinator participation, helps to make it a valuable device.

Demonstrations

Demonstrations take two basic forms: teacher demonstrations and student demonstrations. Appropriately used, the demonstration elicits high interest and attention, which other devices may not do. It can be used in nearly all cases where a skill, technique, or procedure is to be taught or practiced.

The teacher demonstration can be used to introduce a topic for discussion, to highlight a unit, or to create interest in an area that students may feel is unimportant. Through the medium of a demonstration the teacher can introduce a great deal of showmanship and can point out the need for finesse in a particular skill or technique. Naturally the teacher will want to make sure the demonstration is motion perfect before presenting it to the class.

Student demonstrations offer the students an opportunity to show what they have learned in class or on the job. They can be used equally well by students of both high and low ability, merely by controlling the complexity of what is to be demonstrated. The sales demonstration is the most common type in the distributive field. In this two students take part, one as a customer, the other as a salesperson. These points can be well demonstrated by this method:

Steps of the sale	Receptionist duties
Handling customer complaints	Operation of a machine
Taking telephone orders	Human relations problems
Demonstrating merchandise	Nonselling skills
Customer viewpoints	Job instruction
Telephone procedure	Service procedure

Certain props are sometimes necessary in order to present an effective demonstration. A well-equipped distributive or office classroom will usually have enough variety of equipment to provide everything except in the very special case. Where additional merchandise or equipment is needed, it can often be borrowed from a local business firm for a short time. With a little encouragement students can develop very workable props for demonstration purposes. The creative coordinator will not hesitate to use the demonstration method, for he recognizes that it can often be the final clincher to a good lesson.

Committee Work

The committee is a device wherein students are divided into small groups for the purpose of working out activities, topics, problems, or assignments instead of working on them individually or as a class. It allows more opportunities for the individual student to participate actively in the learning situation. Learning is greatest when the student gets response from others to his ideas and actions. Responses of a committee to a member's ideas will stimulate his thinking, help him to evaluate himself as a person, and see himself as others see him. During the course of committee work the student develops skills for effective group participation and individual expression.

In office education the committee could be used for topics such as business forms, reception procedures, recording procedures, and office practices. In distributive education the committee has been successful in nearly all the courses in the field—salesmanship, retailing, occupational relations, merchandise information, and display. How to treat the various kinds of customers— silent, talkative, hard of hearing, indefinite, shopper, and so forth—lends itself to committee study. Surveys of various kinds, such as shopping habits, window display, store practices, personnel policies, and consumer preferences, generally call for committee treatment if the projects are to be adequately covered. In the occupational relations field, certain aspects of labor legislation, labor organizations, employer-employee relations, social security, safety, health, and management of personal affairs are suitable to this method.

Shopping Reports

The shopping report is used to evaluate and record the activities of salespersons and their physical environment as observed in an actual buying situation. The report is a prepared form listing the information to be obtained, reactions to be noted, and points to be observed, with provisions for a graduated system of evaluation by the shopper. The form and content of the report may vary according to the purpose for which it is used and the particular points to be emphasized.

This method is generally used when the student is being shopped or where he is rating another salesperson. The shopping report can be incorporated as an activity in various types of units of instruction. As it involves a complete sales transaction, it is pertinent to almost all areas of training in retail selling, including customer relations, sales steps, merchandise handling, display, and preemployment units.

The shopping report develops the customer's point of view in the student. By introspection and subjective analysis the customer's reaction can be analyzed. He can better appreciate the value of cordiality, tolerance, and willingness to serve in his relationship with others. The report can also be used as a means of evaluating and measuring the student's progress in his learnings.

Field Trips

The field trip is "any kind of definitely organized trip with a primarily educational purpose, made by a group of pupils as a part of their regular school work."[3] It has no definite time duration and may include several incidental activities. Most generally it takes the form of a class visit to a business firm, industrial plant, office, or other institution, exposing the student to first-hand experiences in the everyday world of work and business.

In cooperative training where students are regularly working in business on a part-time basis, one might feel that field trips would have little value. Actually this is not true. The field trips add much to the experience of those already engaged in "live" contacts.

The field trip is a wonderful device to provide a preview of forthcoming work. It is a question provoker and a discussion stimulator. If used as a preview, however, it will naturally be limited to primary observation. When used as a means of instruction, the trip is probably operating at its best. In the distributive field it would allow the coordinator to teach specific retail techniques to a large class. This is especially appropriate where facilities such as window display, advertising makeup rooms, and ticket machines are not available in the classroom. The field trip can also be used to tie together phases

---

[3] Henry C. Atyeo, *The Excursion as a Teaching Technique* (New York: Teachers College, Columbia University, 1939), p. 27.

of a unit already studied—for example, pulling together all phases of store operation.

In the office occupations the field trip can be used to show the various ways offices are organized, special types of office machines, progression of work through an office, and many other important office learnings that can not be provided for in any other way.

Field Observation

The field observation is a learning activity in which the individual student procures firsthand information by intelligent observation of real-life situations outside the classroom. It frequently takes the form of an assignment in which one or more persons bring information of interest back to the group. On the other hand, it may be used by a particular student for individual study. In the distributive occupations field the learner gets his information by actually going into the store, warehouse, shopping center, or other place with the express purpose in mind of noting or observing certain previously determined items, practices, or situations. In the office field such observations may be somewhat more difficult, as many offices are not open to the public; nevertheless, this device can be used effectively.

Field observation differs from the field trip in that a group does not visit a single place at one time. Each student is on his own. Were it not that field observation did not entail a special excursion, it might be termed an *individual field trip*. In reality, when the field observation is modified it blends into the field trip or the field interview.

The field observation differs from the field interview in that personal contact with an interviewee may be entirely lacking. On the other hand, a few questions asked of a person in charge would not disqualify it as field observation.

TECHNIQUES IN PROVIDING SPECIFIC JOB LEARNINGS

One of the cardinal features of the cooperative part-time training program is the aid it offers in the adjustment of the student to the business world. "It bridges the gap between the school and the job" is a statement frequently used. Adjustments of students to their jobs involve individual problems, and thus we must work with these students as individuals. We should seek out the abilities and inabilities, habits and attitudes, that contribute to the success or the failure of each student. This section deals with the procedures and methods we can use to help individual students with their particular job problems and adjustments.

Individual Study Methods

Specific instructional needs of individual students should be determined from (a) occupational needs of the student and (b) personal needs of the individual. For example, the occupational needs of a trainee in a men's specialty store are definitely different from those of a trainee in a hardware store. The specialized knowledges for each job would be completely different. The personal needs will vary with the background of each student and could consist of a need for emotional adjustment as well as for instruction in some basic skill such as arithmetic, salesmanship, or speech. In evaluating the quality of an approved program, the criteria commonly recommended and used indicate that up to half of the related classroom time should be given to specific related instruction. Individual study then does have a major place in the instruction for cooperative trainees.

The use of a job study guide often provides motivation for the student worker in the classroom and on the job. Some of the reasons for this might be that the material is immediately applicable to the student's work; it frequently leads to favorable recognition by the employer; the student works relatively independently of the other students; the quantity and quality depends entirely on him; the student can see his progress; he knows where he is going and where he has been; and the on-the-job trainer can give specific help and encouragement in training the student.

The most widely used individual study guide today is probably an individual study manual that directs the student as he learns about his particular cooperative job, or work station. Many of these manuals are now available and are produced by various states and universities and publishers. The manual typically follows a pattern of outlining the area to be studied, referring the student to certain readings, and then assigning questions and activities to be completed by the student based on his particular work station. Many coordinators have found that manuals containing an information section, such as those produced by the University of Texas, are very easy to use effectively. With a "Texas manual," or one of that type, no other references are needed, and the student works with just one piece of material.

Coordinators in some states (Minnesota, Ohio, Oklahoma) have developed a "card system" as a study guide. With this type of guide, the content is provided on variously colored five-by-eight-inch cards, which include Information, Bibliography, Activity, and so forth. One set of cards is placed in the coordinator's file and a second set is arranged for student use. If a card from a trainee's set is lost, a copy of the missing card can conveniently be made from the coordinator's set. Cards are coded and can readily be obtained, and additional material can easily be added. However, reference material for study is not included with the set of cards.

Perhaps the strongest appeal in the use of job study guides is to good teaching practice. It is one place where the teacher-coordinator can give real proof to the claim that cooperative education provides a separate curriculum for each student. The job study guide is geared to the needs of each particular student in that it is written for one particular kind of work. It is flexible because only the parts needed by the student worker are selected for study. The student may draw from several guides if his position cuts across two or more occupational fields.

The actual procedure for using individual study guides will vary according to the type of guides used. Many coordinators set aside one or more class periods each week for individual study. The coordinator can work with individual students checking work, answering questions, assisting them in locating reference material, and explaining further assignments. Individual study can be used when a special need arises on the job for the student to learn a skill in order to move along on his learning program. Individual study is especially useful because it is flexible and can be used at any time without prior preparation. The alert coordinator will follow the professional writings to keep up to date on this phase of instruction.

Job Manuals, Merchandise Manuals, and Scrapbooks

What is a job manual? It is a manual containing the basic facts a learner should know about the business place in which he is working. It is, in effect, an orientation to the store policy, procedure, organization, and other fundamentals every good employee should know about his firm. Most manuals are merely outlined by the teacher, and the student is obligated to fill in the manual with information about his place of employment. Sample outlines of job manuals would be:

For a Distributive Occupation	**For an Office Occupation**
Facts about My Store	Facts about My Office
Store Rules and Policy	Office Rules and Policy
List of My Duties	List of My Duties
Store Layout	Office Layout
Sales Check System	Office Jobs Breakdown
Personnel Policies	Filing
Advertising-Display	Telephone
Customer Services	Typing
Credit Policies	(and others as needed)
Nonselling Duties	Receptionist Duties
Technical Terms	Handling Mail
Store Maintenance	Record-Keeping Procedure
My Store and My Community	Technical Terms
	Office Housekeeping
	My Office and My Community

What is a merchandise manual? It is a manual prepared by the student including whatever information a salesperson needs to know about his merchandise to sell it effectively. A merchandise manual is a logical means of directing the learner's efforts specifically to the knowledges needed to sell. It would include brand-name understanding, merchandise knowledge, how to display or demonstrate the merchandise, plus information needed to talk to customers in terms of their enjoyment or use of the product. A sample outline of a merchandise manual would be:

Introduction
What Your Customer Wants to Know
Qualities Customers Look For
How to Recognize Merchandise Factors
Steps in Making the Sale

Learning Your Products' Language
Summary of General Information
List of Information Sources

A similar manual is used in the office field; the student prepares a manual on material used in the office, such as paper, machines, or the products handled by the company.

What is a scrapbook? Typically a scrapbook is a collection of pertinent articles, advertisements, labels, reports, samples, and other items concerning a product, job, business organization, or other factors about an occupation. The scrapbook is a long-term project wherein the student gathers information that will help in his future development as a distributive worker or as an office worker. There appears to be no special outline for scrapbooks. The organization, layout, and content are left to the creativity of the student.

Additional Suggestions for Specific Instruction

Individual study guides and various student-prepared manuals are the two major means of providing specific instruction. Many other techniques can also be used. A few of these will be described briefly.

Demonstrations—planned demonstrations provide an opportunity to assign individual instruction.

Example: A person who has proved proficient in gift wrapping through class or on-the-job training may demonstrate dexterity to other members of the class who may not perform this skill as part of their work.

Displays in the classroom—

Example: A trainee who has learned how to display hardlines through specific instruction for his job may, as a part of his training, prepare a display for other members of the class to evaluate.

Preparation of reports to be presented to the class—the organization of a report may be used as specific instruction. This report may have valuable basic information useful to other members of the class.

The service of other teachers—other teachers may be asked to help with certain problems.

Example: The home economics teacher may be willing to talk with the students on textiles. The English teacher can assign students projects that will help them meet their occupational requirements. The science teacher may help students with technical information on merchandise qualities.

Student project—each student may be assigned a project. It should be one that will benefit the student in his specific situation.

Example: A student may develop a notebook-scrapbook combination of "tricks" that help him in his particular job. Typing tricks, magazine articles, lists of often-misspelled words, display techniques, personality suggestions, or lists of selling phrases are projects that would be worthwhile. To be educational these projects should apply to the person making the book.

Coordinator-student interviews—planned interviews at stated intervals will serve as a means of discussing individual problems, especially those of a personal nature.

Example: An interview could be held to discuss how the student could get the most out of a new experience to be undertaken on the job. It may also serve as a means of drawing together several pieces of study carried out on an individual basis.

PROCEDURE FOR PROVIDING ON-THE-JOB LEARNINGS

Instruction on the job is usually handled by a sponsor or a training supervisor appointed by the store or office management. Seldom does the teacher-coordinator do any great amount of actual instruction at the place of the student's employment, and then only if it is with the approval of the trainee's employer. The coordinator does have the responsibility, nevertheless, of making sure adequate training is given the student. The coordinator should be sure the sponsor understands his role in the cooperative program, and just what things he should be training the student to do. Only a close and well-planned program of instruction can make on-the-job experiences worthwhile.

When the coordinator places a student in a training station, it is the result of previous evaluation of the business, acceptance of the cooperative program by management, and understanding of the duties and obligations by all concerned. In small business firms the training supervisor may be the owner or manager. In larger firms a sponsor is usually appointed by management. In either case this person is the one that the coordinator will work with in the training and evaluation of the student.

At the beginning of the student's employment, the coordinator and the sponsor plan a series of job experiences that will lead to the ultimate goal of giving the student learner a complete and well-rounded background in a particular occupation. If possible, the student should be introduced to each phase of his job as he is ready for it. Some students will thus progress rapidly on a job while others will progress more slowly. A student in a small business firm may have to work in all phases of the business the first few days of employment; therefore, the sponsor and the coordinator will have to use considerable judgment as to which part of his work will receive classroom study first.

Several methods are used to insure the sponsor's being ready and able to give the instruction needed by the student. The amount of direction that the coordinator gives the sponsor will depend on that need, the cooperation of the training firm, and the ability of the student. The use of a sponsor handbook, advisory committee action, training profile, and sponsor meeting to facilitate training will be explained.

Sponsor Handbook

The coordinator will give a handbook to the sponsor as soon as a student has been assigned to the cooperating firm. One coordinator prepares a handbook for his sponsors by assembling the following materials into a manila folder:

Suggestions for Supervising the Student Employee
Employer's Confidential Rating Report for Cooperative Trainees
Trainee's Progress Report
Training Profile Sheets with Instructions
High School Publication on Cooperative Training
Complete Set of Forms Used in Selection of Cooperative Trainees
Summary Sheet on the Student the Sponsor Is to Train.

The coordinator and the sponsor discuss this material and plan the student's learning experiences in the store or office. One copy of this plan will be added to the folder. Such a handbook provides the sponsor with a reference to turn to during the training period for information on how to work with youth, how to fill out rating forms, and other questions that come up during the year. The coordinator may remind the sponsor from time to time to review some part of the contents for ideas on training the student.

Advisory Committee Action

The advisory committee is an integral part of the cooperative training program. It is a body appointed by the superintendent of schools to assist in smooth functioning of the cooperative program. The membership is usually made up of leaders in the business community and thus carries a great deal of weight with all businesses in the community. It deals with such things as student-trainee wages, evaluations, selection of training stations, instructional materials, placement procedures, and training assistance. From time to time during the school year it may find material or information that it feels should go to businesses training students. In such cases this material can be obtained or duplicated and sent to each sponsor and cooperating firm. The coordinator can then follow up such action and help the sponsor carry through on the advisory committee's suggestions.

Training Profile

The training profile is a listing of job duties, experiences, or procedures the trainee in an occupation must generally learn to become a proficient worker. Trainees are periodically asked to rate each item on the list in terms of how much training they have received. This list can then be used as a measure by the coordinator and the sponsor of what has been accomplished, and to what degree the student feels he has learned each of the items included in the profile. It provides the sponsor with a check sheet on his training efforts and gives the coordinator a picture of how the training is progressing in a certain business or situation.

Sponsor Meetings

Holding meetings of all sponsors to discuss job training is not currently a common practice in cooperative training. It is being used very effectively by some coordinators, however. Such a meeting at the beginning of the training period does provide the coordinator with the opportunity to orient the entire group of sponsors to the program and to answer the various questions they may have. Meetings during the school year can motivate sponsors to do a better job of training as well as inform them of new ideas in training and supervision.

Coordinator-Sponsor-Trainee Conferences

Whenever questions arise about on-the-job training, a three-way meeting should be arranged to discuss possible solutions. Most often only two-way discussions are conducted, coordinator-student, coordinator-sponsor, or student-sponsor, on problems that are of importance to all three. Naturally some cases will merit only two-way discussion, but the value of all three parties discussing progress, problems, weaknesses, and strengths cannot be overlooked.

IN CONCLUSION

The teacher-coordinator of a cooperative training program should not assume that the foregoing devices are the only ones to be used in presenting the learnings needed by cooperative students. These devices are presented only to give some idea of how they can be used to provide special instructional needs. The effective teacher will modify, adapt, combine, add to, and in many ways improve upon these devices to fit his own particular abilities and the needs and desires of the students.

In no case will any amount of special methods and devices take the place of adequate classroom preparation based on the students' needs and blended together with interesting and meaningful content. Sound classroom procedure should be the teacher-coordinator's first goal. The use of additional methods will then add meaning and depth to a worthwhile base.

PROJECTS AND QUESTIONS FOR DISCUSSION

1. Some educators have been known to object to cooperative part-time programs on the grounds that they "cannot justify excusing students from school in order that they may go to work." What answers might be given to this objection? Is the objection valid?

2. Occasionally educators have been known to object to having cooperative part-time students receive wages for the work they do on the grounds that it is an educational program for which the students receive school credit and that it is wrong for them to receive both pay and credit for their work. What answers might be given to this objection? Is the objection valid?

3. It has been claimed that students on cooperative part-time programs mature in citizenship more rapidly than do other students. It there any real basis for such a claim?

4. Why is it that some schools operate cooperative part-time programs without receiving state and federal financial aid?

5. Student learners in cooperative programs are constantly exposed to business practices at their training stations. Many of these practices do not conform to recommendations found in texts or trade periodicals. How should the teacher-coordinator handle resulting student inquires about "the correct practice"?

6. Learning activities used in cooperative education frequently involve interviews, observations, or collecting materials outside the school proper. What procedure should the teacher follow to assure that students carry out these learning activities in a tactful and businesslike manner?

7. How important, relatively, are the consumer-citizenship learnings of the student-trainee in a cooperative part-time program as compared with the learning that is of a vocational nature?

8. Proper selection of students for a vocational distributive or office program is essential. Prepare a list of things the teacher-coordinator might do to aid and facilitate the proper selection of students by the guidance staff.

9. Have a committee find out as much as possible about individual study manuals currently available for the use of student-trainees in distributive occupations. Are any of them in use in your state? Report the findings to the class.

10. Do the same for the office occupations, making use of a different committee.

CASE PROBLEMS

General:

1. The student has been at the training station about four and a half months, and according to the employer he is doing a good job. The coordinator has felt for several weeks that the student was not being exposed to new learnings with his present tasks. (This was confirmed by the student in conference.) What steps should the coordinator take to get the trainee back to a learning situation?

2. A coordinator who regularly visits every training station (and feels that everything is going well) receives a phone call wherein an employer of a P-T co-op student says "that trainee has been coming in late half the time for the last five weeks. Either get that trainee here on time or keep her in school!" What information would you want and what steps should be taken to appease this situation?

3. On the six-week report a sponsor rates a trainee *very poor* on personal grooming. Upon discussing this deficiency the coordinator finds that the trainee has a severe case of body odor and bad breath. It is so bad that it has caused considerable comment by fellow workers. The sponsor has tried several times to get the trainee to do something about the problem but without success. He wants you, as coordinator, to do something about it. What action would you take?

Office:

1. A P-T co-op trainee has completed the unit on mimeographing and seems to have done quite well. During a regular visit the coordinator finds that the employer is unhappy with the trainee's mimeograph work. A check reveals that the training station has the same type of machine used at school. What steps should be taken?

2. A trainee in carrying out her work must answer and use the telephone. The sponsor reports that although he has tried to teach her proper procedures she is still difficult to understand, because of her poor diction, but often she ignores set procedure for handling a telephone call. The result has been some confusion and misunderstanding both in this office and to those that have called. What can you as the coordinator do?

3. An employer states that unless the trainee "straightens out" he will have to let her go. The trainee is an *A* student in school and does an excellent job in the office practices class. On the job, however, she is flighty, prone to giggle, and in general not very responsible. List the steps the coordinator should take to correct this.

Distributive:

1. The employer of a student learner tells you the student has made excellent progress in the men's clothing department. The student has worked in the stock room, sold men's accessories, and put in displays. The employer now would like to have the student move into selling men's slacks, sports coats, and possibly suits in about three weeks. What learning activities would you assign the student to prepare him for these new activities?

2. The employer of a trainee reports that many of the trainee's high school friends stop at the store after school and talk with the trainee, sometimes for as long as forty-five minutes. The employer doesn't want to kick these students out but is concerned over the trainee's not waiting on "paying" customers during this time. He has mentioned this to the trainee, but the condition still exists. What action can the coordinator take?

3. Millard Cooper is the coordinator of a distributive education program for the Kingston High School. He has conducted an excellent program there for five years and has received strong backing from all businessmen associated with the program. In the spring of 1973 Mr. Cooper is contacted by a representative from a new shopping center that is planning to open in September 1973. The representative asked Mr. Cooper to provide twenty student learners for the various stores opening in the new center. Most of the stores are businesses new to the community. Mr. Cooper has tentatively placed all but eight of his twenty-four students for the 1972–1973 school year.

Mr. Cooper tells his advisory committee of the request. Five of the eight advisory members are against placing any students in the new shopping center; the other three are non-committal. Animosity of the established business community toward the new shopping center is quite evident. What action would you suggest Mr. Cooper take in this situation?

SUGGESTED READINGS

American Vocational Association, *The Advisory Committee and Vocational Education*, 1969, 45 pp.

———, *Vocational Technical Terminology*, 1971, 77 pp.

Edling, Jack W., "Individualized Instruction. The Way It Is—1970," *Audiovisual Instruction*, February 1970, pp. 13–16.

Haines, Peter G., and Ralph E. Mason, *Cooperative Occupational Education*. Danville, Ill.: Interstate Printers and Publishers, Inc., 1965, 525 pp.

Judd, Eunice, "An Ethical Dimension of Cooperative Office Education," *Business Education Forum*, May 1971, pp. 36–38.

Keller, Louise, "The Teaching and Coordination of Cooperative Office Education," *Contributions of Research to Business Education*, NBEA Yearbook, No. 9, 1971, pp. 114–30.

Kimbrell, Grady, and Ben S. Vineyard, *Succeeding in the World of Work*. Bloomington, Ill.: McKnight and McKnight Publishing Co., 1971, 484 pp.

Law, Gordon F., *Cooperative Education Handbook for Teacher-Coordinators*, American Technical Society, Chicago, 1970, 64 pp.

Meyer, Warren G., and Richard D. Ashmun, "Media in Distributive Education," *Audiovisual Instruction*, April 1970, pp. 33–36.

"1970 Youth: More Numerous, Better Educated, Job Oriented," *American Vocational Journal*, April 1971, p. 52.

Poland, Robert, "Block-Time Approach in Office Education," *The Emerging Content and Structure of Business Education, NBEA Yearbook* No. 8, 1970, pp. 263–69.

Raines, Pearl L., "Standards for Selecting Work Stations for Cooperative Part-Time Students," *Business Education Forum*, May 1964, pp. 34–36.

Roberts, Ray W., *Vocational and Practical Arts Education*, Chap. 9, "Business Education for Bookkeeping, Stenography, and Clerical Work," pp. 174–95 ; Chap. 10, "Vocational Distributive Education," pp. 196–219. New York: Harper & Row, Publishers, 1971.

Tonne, Herbert A., and Louis C. Nanassy, "Work Experience in Business Education," *Principles of Business Education*, Chap. 12, pp. 158–68. New York: Gregg Publishing Division, McGraw-Hill Book Company, 1970.

Unruh, Glenys G., "Can I Be Replaced by a Package?" *Educational Leadership*, May 1970, pp. 763–66.

Venn, Grant, *Man, Education and Work*, American Council on Education, Washington, D.C., 1964.

Wallace, Harold, "Block-Time Approach in Distributive Education," *The Emerging Content and Structure of Business Education, NBEA Yearbook*, No. 8, 1970, pp. 270–77.

Note: Annotated listings of current curriculum materials available from public education agencies in most states may be obtained from the Curriculum-Instructional Materials Program, Division of Vocational and Technical Education, U.S. Office of Education, Washington, D.C. 20202, under the following titles : *Curriculum Materials for Distributive Education, Curriculum Materials for Office Occupations*, and *Instructions for Ordering Curriculum Materials*.

13

ADULT PROGRAMS IN BUSINESS EDUCATION

Adult education in its many forms continues to grow and to gain in relative importance in the United States. Owing to the rapidly increasing percentage of our population classified as adult, as well as other factors, this trend can be expected to continue and perhaps to accelerate. Business education will continue to be a major factor in adult educational programs.

When teaching adults the business teacher must fit his instructional materials and his teaching methods to the felt needs and desires of his students; must adjust his psychology to recognize and make use of the experience and mature judgment of his students; and must constantly recognize that these adults *are there for a purpose*.

Great numbers of business teachers conduct adult classes each year; many of them even do so during their first year of teaching. It is the purpose of this chapter to provide for the beginning business teacher an orientation toward adult education that should enable him to approach more intelligently the responsibility of preparing for and teaching adult classes when called upon to do so.

This is not a complete treatise on adult education; that is a broad field! Rather, this chapter serves to direct attention to those factors that are of major importance to the business teacher who hopes to *successfully* prepare for and teach adult classes in the field of business education.

ADULT EDUCATION IN GENERAL

What Is It?

The term *adult education* is not an easy one to define in a meaningful manner; it is too broad. However, our question may well be answered by taking a look at some of the well-recognized characteristics of adult education. At the same time this listing of important characteristics can form the background on which one may base his preparation for teaching any adult class.

The basic characteristics common to all adult education (now frequently designated as *continuing* education) remain very much the same today as they have been for many years; they are well recognized. A quarter of a century ago the Department of Public Instruction in one state described adult education in these words:

1. It is general and vocational education on the adult level.
2. It has to do with voluntary learning acquired outside the conventional school program.
3. It includes those activities with an educative purpose carried on voluntarily by adults usually on a part-time basis, such as adult evening classes, forums, discussions, round-tables, and institutes.
4. It is self-education starting with an adult student where he is and taking him in the direction he wishes to go.
5. It involves purposeful learning on the adult level which tends to give a new zest to life.
6. It usually results in action on the part of the group that participates.
7. Its students are students by volition who participate in its courses so long as these courses give them what they desire.
8. Its students come to select from its offerings and are not told which courses they are required to take.[1]

Obviously, then, adult education means much more than simply classes held for students who are adults! It involves, also, the use of an additional professional psychology distinct and different from that customarily used in the classroom education of adolescents.

What Are Its Purposes?

Obviously, if adult education is to be designed to take the student "in the direction he wishes to go," the purposes of adult education are as broad and diversified as are the desires of the adults to be served. However, here are a few of the purposes more commonly served by adult education:

1. Occupational training or retraining—in one form or another this is applicable to any occupation or vocation.

---

[1] *Adult Education Handbook for Iowa Schools,* published by the state of Iowa, 1947, p. 5.

2. Pure enjoyment through broadening one's viewpoint and interests—music, art, literature, psychology, and sports are illustrative media.

3. Personal enlightenment regarding world affairs and social and political trends.

4. Increasing one's knowledge in specific fields or fulfilling some specifically felt deficiency—this may range all the way from learning how to read or write through learning how to typewrite, learning business law, learning accounting, learning a foreign language, or learning how to repair electric appliances in the home.

The purposes of adult education remain well summarized by George C. Mann, chief of the Bureau of Adult Education, California State Department of Education, in these two sentences:

> People generally are increasingly convinced that adult education must be designed to meet the interests of adults and the needs of society, which can be met by education and which are worthy of being met at public expense. There is firm agreement that adult education must offer a program which makes important contributions to those aspects of life which have long been held in high merit by the American people.[2]

Beginnings of Adult Education

The beginning business teacher, when first confronted with the problem of teaching an adult class, all too often looks upon it as something relatively new which is being added to his professional work and endeavors. This rather hazy concept should be corrected, for adult education has been recognized and practiced in the United States since early colonial days.

Originally these adult evening schools were private undertakings conducted for profit; thus the early history of adult education has much in common with the early history of business education. Such evening schools are known to have been in operation in New York State as early as 1661 and were in operation in Boston, Philadelphia, and Charleston, South Carolina, before 1750. These evening schools, institutes, and lyceums continued to grow in number and expand in functions so rapidly that by the early 1880s demand was rising that adult education be conducted at public expense.

As early as 1857 there were twenty-five evening schools in New York City conducted at public expense and operating classes five evenings a week. Probably the first state to pass a general legislative enactment providing for evening schools at public expense was Ohio, which passed such legislation in 1839. As early as 1823, however, public funds were appropriated by the state of Massachusetts for use in evening schools, and by 1869 the major cities in Massachusetts all had opened evening schools. Similarly we find that publicly supported evening schools were established in Pittsburgh and San Francisco in 1856, St. Louis in 1859, Chicago in 1862, and shortly afterward in the larger cities throughout the nation. By 1900 at least 165 major cities

---

[2] *Public School Adult Education,* a publication of the National Association of Public School Adult Educators, 1956, p. 1.

of the United States had established evening schools whose primary function was to meet the educational needs of adults.[3]

Modern Scope and Trends

There is no universally accepted classification of areas in which adult education is offered today. Courses of various types and contents have been developed in the various states and communities to meet desires and needs. However, to the extent that the states and the federal government have given financial aid there has tended to be some uniformity in the general curriculum form and practices.

Today many states prescribe courses that will meet with approval of the state department of public instruction. At least two states, New York and California, have classified the accepted fields of adult education in this manner:

Agriculture	Civic and Public Affairs
Americanization	Engineering and Technology
Arts and Crafts	Elementary
Business and Distribution	Parent and Family Life
Safety and Driver Education	General Academic
Industrial and Trade	Homemaking
Remedial	Health and Physical
Miscellaneous	Music

Thus the business teacher must realize that any contribution he may be able to make to adult education is but a relatively small part of the entire field of adult education throughout the nation. A large city school system may even include all these diversified branches of adult education in its one program. Yet, on the other hand, it sometimes happens that in a small community the *only* adult education offered is the evening classwork taught by the business teacher!

A greater uniformity of course offerings and instructional practices tends to be found in the vocational areas of adult education. This has been influenced by the greater availability of state and federal funds for vocational education, as evidenced by educational developments fostered by legislation such as the Smith–Hughes Act of 1917, the George–Deen Act of 1936, the George–Barden Act of 1946, the National Defense Education Act of 1958, the National Vocational Education Act of 1963, and the Vocational Education Amendments of 1968. Over half of the funds used in providing vocational education of all kinds comes from direct state and federal appropriations, and the general field of vocational education has always been one of the major areas of adult education.

Briefly stated, it appears that the three most important aims of adult education are (1) to prepare better for vocational competence and economic

---

[3] Further details relative to the current development of this field of education may be found in *Public Continuing and Adult Education Almanac,* starting in 1970 published annually by NAPCAE, an affiliate of the NEA.

efficiency, (2) to provide for the enrichment of life, and (3) to help adults become more aware of their civic and social responsibilities.

Today we are living in a rather complicated economic world. We are a part of a population that has a rapidly increasing percentage of adults. We are a part of a society that maintains a high standard of living and that strongly favors excellent educational opportunities for all. It seems relatively certain that adult education will continue to expand and probably in all its areas. Certainly the fact that we live in and largely exist by means of a "business economy" can only mean that the business teacher should be prepared to witness an increasing demand for adult education in the field of business and distributive education in the future.

APPLIED PSYCHOLOGY FOR ADULT BUSINESS EDUCATION

Younger business teachers frequently hesitate to accept evening classes or other classes intended for the education of adults. Undoubtedly this is partly because one just is not accustomed to the idea of older people turning to younger people for instruction and leadership in the classroom. Certainly this situation does not exist during the twelve years of elementary and secondary education in the nation's schools with which everyone is quite familiar. Similarly, in our homes we grow up accustomed to the idea that leadership and instruction come from those who are older, and not from "young" people. Thus the hesitancy on the part of younger business teachers is a normal one.

To some degree this hesitancy is also a logical and rational one; after all, it is *true* that these older and more experienced adults will know many things pertinent to the subject being studied that the younger business teacher will not know!

In spite of these facts, the younger business teacher who is competent, well prepared, and fully qualified for his profession need have no fear of conducting adult classes. This is not to say that preference should not be given to older and more experienced business teachers in taking responsibility for adult classes when they are available, for often they definitely are in position to conduct the classes more successfully. Yet even the younger teacher has in his favor the powerful factor of know-how in applying appropriate psychology to the learning situation!

Basic Adult Psychology

It seems almost trite to mention that adults belong to the same species in the animal kingdom as do adolescents; both are human beings and, as the saying goes, "Like father, like son!" Both have the same type of sensory apparatus, the same types of nervous systems, the same types of musculature, the same internal glands, and the same native capacities at birth. One should never forget that the various basic psychological factors affecting learning (such as those outlined in Chapter 3 of this text) are just as much in evidence in an adult class as in any other class.

Thus, as in any other educational situation, learning is a matter of *individual* growth; it takes place best when *motivation* is best; it wanes when attention or interest is lost, or when fatigue or boredom is present; and it thrives under the influence of knowledge of results, of rivalry and competition, and of attainable goals. Also, among the members of any adult class is likely to be found the usual wide range of individual differences in ability.

Yet, by virtue of the very fact that the class members are adults, (*a*) they bring to class an important background of experience not possessed by younger students and (*b*) they attend class only because—and when!—they *want* to and not because they are required to attend. These two important factors must be given heavy weight in planning for a successful adult class. They materially influence the methods used in *applying* the basic psychology of learning.

Build Courses Around Adult Needs and Interests

It is the individual adults to be served who determine the nature of an adult course that is to be successful. That is why communities with well-developed adult education programs make use of advisory councils or similar groups of adults; one of the duties of such a group is to help decide the nature of courses needed or desired by adults of the community. The advice *know your students* is especially applicable to adult classes, for only then can the teacher intelligently decide on the best content and procedures for any given adult class.

In determining the needs and interests of adults of the community, it is desirable to go somewhat into detail; otherwise there is risk that the *content* of the course planned by the instructor will be far from that which the interested adults may expect it to be. For instance, a group of housewives might make it known to school authorities that they would like to study family bookkeeping. In due time word reaches the business teacher that an adult class in bookkeeping is requested. The teacher would probably make a serious error should he therefore conclude that the regular text he uses in his high school double-entry bookkeeping could serve as his lesson plans for the course!

When adults voluntarily seek educational aid—and all adult education is entered into voluntarily—the motivation obviously is already present. Thus the teacher is immediately relieved of one of the most persistent and troublesome problems found in classes of young people. Although the motivation may be very strong in the case of these adults, it must also be recognized that it is *very specific*. The housewives, for example, strongly wished to learn better methods of helping to keep the family records. As a result, failure to offer a course that will satisfy the objective of that strong desire almost certainly will stifle and kill the enthusiasm and motivation that brings the housewives to class. The result: They simply quit coming to class!

Hence, perhaps the number one guide for the teacher of adults who desires to have a successful class is: Know your individual students, their needs, and their desires and then build your course around those needs and desires.

Maintain an Atmosphere of Informality

The formalized class with the instructor being the "center of attention" and perhaps the authoritarian has little place in adult education. Occasional exceptions do occur, mostly in the area of skill development, such as typewriting and shorthand classes. For the most part, though, the students should themselves be the center of attention. They should actively participate in discussion and in bringing new ideas to the class.

In developing this friendly, informal atmosphere, most adult teachers prefer to be on hand before it is time for the class to start in order to greet and get acquainted with individual class members. The informal conversations that develop enable the class to begin with a far different feeling from that which is customarily present when, as the class is about to start, the teacher walks in to his "station" in front of a hushed and "cold" class! In planning to develop this informal atmosphere, some adult teachers have been known to deliberately arrange to be putting the finishing touches to equipment and teaching aids just prior to class; this often permits getting one or more of the class members to assist, or getting them into conversation about the materials being prepared, thus starting active participation of the class in a normal and informal situation. Once the ice is broken, future class participation comes easily.

In keeping with this desire to encourage individual participation by class members, it is frequently desirable to have them grouped around a conference table where all are face to face. This encourages each to talk to the entire group and also to listen to what other members of the group may have to say. At the same time the resulting interchange of ideas among the class members relieves the instructor of the pressure of carrying the entire burden and permits him better to be the true *leader* that he should be; he can then devote thought to directing the discussions into most desirable channels, to seeing that each class member has appropriate opportunity to contribute, to raising pertinent questions, to offering needed periodic summaries, and to supervising many other factors that can contribute heavily toward a successful class.

Make Use of the Knowledge of Adult Students

The combined knowledge of the adult enrollees on most subjects is almost certain to exceed the knowledge of the teacher. Each adult enrollee is likely to have had experience giving him knowledge that is relatively unique and distinct from that gained by the other enrollees. And at the same time the instructor is almost certain to possess knowledge that none of the enrollees possess. In most adult classes maximum benefits will be derived from a pooling of the experiences, ideas, and knowledges of everyone there—with the instructor, of course, always playing the role of leader and skillfully directing the contributions and discussions toward the desired goal.

This again suggests the desirability of having most classes grouped around a conference table. This physical arrangement often materially aids the group in becoming acquainted and further encourages active individual participation, especially if a name card is prominently displayed in front of each enrollee so that all may see the name of each person at the table. The name should be in print sufficiently large to be easily read by all. If regular card holders are not available, the cardboard on which the name is printed can be bent to form its own support.

Make the Course Functional

Most adults have little desire to learn merely for the sake of learning; they are not inclined toward learning mere facts. Instead, they want information that they *feel* will *actually function* in their lives. Special attention is directed to the word *feel* in the preceding sentence. The actual content of a course that is "functional" may be essentially the same as that found in one that is nonfunctional; the difference lies largely in the way in which the material is presented and developed.

Thus if the housewives previously mentioned were informed at their first meeting that they would begin their study of bookkeeping by learning the names of typical assets and by learning what a balance sheet is and how it is constructed, they would probably fail to see any connection between the lesson and their own special needs—and might well tend to rebel at what to them seemed a waste of their time. On the other hand, the housewives might well feel that this same information was important and would immediately function in their lives if the first meeting of the class were to start off with a thorough discussion and identification of their record-keeping needs and problems; under the guidance of the instructor they might then well arrive at the conclusion that one of the first steps in deciding how to classify information and in learning how to properly differentiate between expenses and investments, or assets, would be to study assets and the balance sheet.

Actually there is nothing new in the idea of keeping the course functional; quite likely that is a good rule to follow in almost all classes, adult or otherwise. Yet failure to do so is not always as fatal to success in regular school work as it is in adult work, since younger people are less insistent that all their learning seem meaningful to them in terms of their own less well defined objectives—at times, at least, they will proceed with their learning merely because the teacher tells them to! Even regular classroom work results in more efficient learning, though, if it is made functional.

Another way of expressing this same idea is to say that the adult class should essentially be devoted to "learning to do" rather than to "learning about" something.

Use Visual Aids Liberally

Success in teaching adults demands alert, efficient, and meaningful teaching. Most teachers already recognize the great value of visual aids in effective and efficient teaching. Often teachers simply do not have the time to prepare all the special aids they would like to use in regular classroom situations; when each course meets daily and the teacher has four, five, six, or even more classes to teach daily there is not adequate preparation time for developing the needed aids. But in many situations the adult class meets only once or twice each week, and this relative infrequency of meetings makes it all the more imperative that each one be the best possible. This also tends to give the teacher greater opportunity to fully prepare for the next class meeting.

Though certain types of visual aids are more useful with certain types of adult classes, on the whole adult programs may be said to make great use of just about every possible type of aid. In addition to the available commercially prepared films, filmstrips, exhibits, pictures, charts, maps, replicas, and other aids, adult group instructors typically make much use of their own specially prepared charts, diagrams, chalkboard illustrations, flannel-board aids, and mimeographed or duplicated materials.

Perhaps there is little justification for finding more evidence of better preparation and better teaching in adult classes than in other classes; yet that seems to be the situation, and the business teacher who assumes adult education responsibilities should be aware of it. This probably is partially brought about by the motivation felt by the teacher in dealing with adult minds, and by his knowing that these students are there for a purpose and, moreover, knowing that they will not hesitate to drop out of class at any time when they fail to feel they are in some way profiting by attendance. Incidentally, they often do feel they are profiting when they find the class to be interesting —and they probably are right! And appropriate visual aids certainly do add considerably to gaining the participants' attention and interest.

Use a Variety of Teaching Techniques

Sameness in anything is likely to become monotonous and boring. This is especially true when your students are adults with ambition and a purpose. Some one teaching method or technique may be especially well adapted to a given subject or adult group; if so, then that technique should be given a major role in the conduct of the class. Nevertheless, this does not preclude the introduction of variations or of completely different techniques at times in order that new interest and renewed attention may be achieved and the chance of monotony diminished.

Moreover, even though one method seems best and is basically used most of the time, various techniques may be introduced within that method. The discussion, for instance, is quite widely recognized as being most effective for the purposes of most adult classes. Yet there are many ways of inaugurating and conducting a discussion. For example, the discussion may start with a symposium or with a presentation made by several class members who may hold different ideas or points of view. This may be followed by questions and comments from the rest of the class and, depending on the circumstances and size of the group, lead directly into an excellent discussion. A variation might be to start with a panel and an informal conversation before the group or, if preferred, with a more formal debate type of presentation. At times the discussion might well follow a lecture presented either by the instructor or, preferably, by some authority—or it might follow the viewing of a relevant film or other visual aid.

SPECIAL ADMINISTRATIVE CONSIDERATIONS

It is the responsibility and prerogative of the properly constituted educational authorities in any given community or school system to determine what adult courses, if any, shall be offered; also to determine the pertinent conditions under which the courses shall be offered and to select and employ the instructional staff. Such arrangements will usually be made by or through the local school board, or the superintendent of schools, or the director of adult education, or some teacher designated to assume this responsibility. Administrative considerations are not the immediate concern of the individual teacher.

Nevertheless, the individual teacher chosen to teach an adult class must complete his work within the governing administrative framework. Since the administration of adult education involves a number of rather special considerations, it is highly desirable that potential teachers of adult classes have some awareness of the more important ones; otherwise misunderstandings and irritations are likely to arise.

Meeting Financial Needs

Certainly the small fees usually paid by enrollees in adult classes do not cover the total costs involved. On an average, the fees paid account for less than 10 percent of the total costs of adult education in the nation. The teacher should understand, then, that some administrators first take the necessary steps to assure availability of adequate funds to cover costs.

Over the nation as a whole between one-fourth and one-third of the cost is being met through local taxes. Thus it may be that the local school board allocates funds for adult education; however, this is not always true. In many states direct aid is available from state funds for adult education. And in certain types of adult education additional funds are made available as a part of state and federal vocational aid and through Veterans Administration Educational Benefits. These last two, taken together, account for much more of the funds than do local taxes when the nation as a whole is considered.

The teacher interested in holding an adult class should consult with his principal or superintendent and should realize that the financing problem may be one that requires considerable thought and work on the part of some administrator.

Salary Paid to Instructor

The major financial cost of adult education is the salary paid the instructor; it accounts for approximately 70 percent of the total cost. However, the rate of salary paid varies extremely among the various cities and communities. In larger cities the median salary in 1954 was about $3.50 per hour, but today it will range from a low of $3.00 per hour to a high of $25.00 per hour.[4]

4 *Public Continuing and Adult Education Almanac,* 1970, NAPCAE, p. 39.

By 1964 the typical (median) salary had risen to $5.00 per hour, and by 1970 it was $6.00 per hour.·

Fees Charged Students

There is no common pattern of fees charged for adult education courses. Some courses are offered free of charge, others charge only a nominal fee, and still others depend on the fee for defraying all costs of the course. Some, for instance, might charge all the way from 10 cents to $1.50 per class meeting. Others might charge fees such as $3, $5, $10, $15, $25, and $50 for the entire course.

Length of the Course

The length of any specific adult education course will vary with its purpose and content, the season of the year in which it is offered, the availability of potential students, and other related local factors. Occasionally an adult group may be brought together for a discussion or a special lecture or demonstration that may be completed in one evening. Some courses run almost continuously, however, with students entering and leaving at various times. Thus one should have no preconceived idea that there are definite limits to the length of adult courses.

On the other hand, it is frequently true that the total time available for a course will be quite limited. In some communities and in some states many adults find they have more time to devote to furthering their education during about three months of the winter season. In such cases a teacher might be asked to offer a beginning shorthand class, for instance, but will find that instead of having the usual nine months in which to teach it he will have only about twelve weeks. Moreover, these adults will probably be able to attend class only one or possibly two evenings each week! Obviously this teacher has a difficult problem on his hands.

However, this apparent limitation on time is somewhat offset by the fact that adult evening classes customarily meet for a longer period of time each time they meet. Thus, in one state report it appears that two hours is the customary length of class meeting; ninety-four schools reported class meetings of two hours in length, while thirty-four reported class meetings of ninety minutes in length. Others varied considerably, but almost all reported meetings of from one hour up to three hours in length.

Records and Reports

Although the factors of grades and credit earned do not enter into most adult classes, the instructor nevertheless must give attention to certain records and reports. Usually attendance records are important. Often the financial aid to be received from sources other than enrollees will depend somewhat on the number of students in attendance at each meeting; this figure then becomes extremely important to the administrator charged with the responsibility of financing the course. And in many instances appropriate certificates are awarded to those enrollees who have maintained a designated attendance standard.

Even aside from these immediate practical reasons, rather complete records are needed to assist in numerous reports and studies that the administrator is likely to be called on to prepare in the future. Such information is quite likely to become important in guiding the future plans for adult education in that community.

Public Relations

To a very great extent today the success of any undertaking is measured by and dependent upon the opinion of the general public. No matter how good a program or an undertaking may be in the opinion of those who may be in the best position to evaluate it, if the public acquires and maintains the attitude or opinion that the program or undertaking is poor or bad or unworthy or unsuccessful—then it is doomed to eventual failure! Since adult education directly serves a relatively unorganized and heterogeneous section of the public who participate entirely voluntarily, good public relations becomes especially important for its success.

In brief, public relations consists of keeping the public informed. This is a simple yet basic concept of public relations. However, getting the public to intelligently absorb or acquire information frequently is even more difficult than having a class do so! In both situations perhaps the key word to success is *interest*. If he will but take advantage of it, the teacher, with his professional knowledge of human psychology, is in an especially favorable position to assure good public relations for his adult education program. Interesting and appropriate news items, announcements, pictures, and "doings" of the class definitely need to be released to the general public from time to time if the continued interest, backing, and financial support of the general public is expected in the future.

BUSINESS CLASSES FOR ADULTS

One cannot generalize about the specific business subjects that are offered or should be offered for adult classes. Rather, it must be recognized that the demands of the local community should determine which subjects to offer—and the resulting course titles may well be very different from those customarily found in high schools. Moreover, the curriculum available through any one school often shows constant changes in the courses especially organized to serve adults.

As the needs of adults to be served in the community are learned, through the expression of individuals and of business and of advisory committees, classes are opened and closed. Every course organized for adults should ordinarily be represented by a lay advisory committee actively serving at all times, so that all instruction will be guided by people who are best equipped to know the type of training that will meet real needs of the community.

Large School Systems

In many large city school systems we find special divisions or schools devoted entirely to adult education, or to adult and vocational education. Courses offered are extremely diverse in order to meet the needs of the home life, the economic life, and the sociocivic life of citizens of the community. Yet those courses that deal with or are closely related to various aspects of business continue to be of major significance in the total program offered.

The Emily Griffith Opportunity School, for example, is the adult and vocational division of the Denver Public Schools. It typically enrolls annually some forty thousand or more students in approximately 750 different classes taught by four hundred to five hundred full- and part-time instructors. When it was established in 1916, its courses were limited to typewriting, shorthand, bookkeeping, spelling, telegraphy, and subjects for foreigners. Today courses to meet *specific needs* in the area of typewriting, shorthand, and bookkeeping continue to be a major part of the offerings in business education.

But there are *many other* courses now in business education, including courses in filing, clerical practice, comptometry, accounting machines, posting machines, key punch operation, tabulating machines, transcription, voice-writing machines, duplicating machines, business writing, business speaking, selling, personnel, office supervision, business law, real estate, insurance, and data processing. In the area of distributive education alone, dozens of special adult classes are held annually. Typical course titles often are such as these:

Advertising	Purchasing Policies
Window Display	Supervisory Training
Interior Display	Customer Service
Layout	Retail Salesmanship
Cashiering	Textile Fibers
Package Wrapping	Markup and Pricing
Inventory Control	Sales Psychology

Small School Systems

In small school systems, where many business teachers start their professional careers and also teach their first adult classes, the community is less likely to have sufficient demand to support highly specialized courses. In such situations the course titles are much more likely to be somewhat similar to those offered in the regular high school classes; frequently the actual content, too, is quite similar. Even so, time limitations and the diverse interests, backgrounds, and needs of the students enrolled result in a content and procedure often quite different from that found in the high school classes bearing similar titles.

One of the difficulties encountered when offering an adult class in a smaller community is the natural tendency to accept into the course enrollees with widely differing objectives and backgrounds. This is done to assure a class enrollment of reasonable size. Yet each enrollee is likely to come with rather specific individual needs or desires in mind. The result is that instead of conducting one class, the instructor finds himself almost conducting a separate class for each individual! In some types of learning this may be done quite satisfactorily, but in others it causes difficulties.

An adult class in beginning typewriting, for instance, would likely attract a different group of enrollees than would one in advanced typewriting or in typewriting review. However, should it seem advisable to merely offer one course under the general title of typewriting, the instructor in all probability would find it necessary to plan his teaching to include some enrollees who had had no previous typewriting training along with others who might already have had a year or more of high school typewriting! Yet this is exactly what some smaller communities find is a desirable type of adult class. When possible, more satisfactory learning certainly is likely when beginning and more advanced students can be scheduled in separate classes.

Course Content and Instructional Materials

Frequently the contents of the course for adults and the instructional materials used must be specifically tailored or composed to meet the needs of the particular group of students enrolled. As already pointed out, time limitations alone often demand this. In addition, the wishes of the enrollees must be considered. Yet at other times, as when the course is one in beginning typewriting, it is quite possible to make use of regular commercially available text material.

Yet even in a subject such as beginning typewriting the instructor has available a relatively large selection of instructional materials and should use judgment in making his choice. Thus it may well be that for a beginning typewriting course consisting of no more than ten weekly two-hour classes it will be better judgment to select one of the briefer texts (frequently referred to as *personal-use typewriting* or by other names implying a shorter course) rather than to use a more complete text that proceeds at a slower and more thoroughgoing pace. Yet the experienced typewriting teacher can readily select from the longer regular texts those materials that will best serve the needs of the adult class; certainly, though, he will need to eliminate and reorganize much of the material in order that his adult group may feel that it has accomplished its purpose in the ten meetings scheduled.

In the attempt to teach beginning shorthand to adults in a limited number of class meetings, a serious mistake will have been made if the course ends with only a portion of the shorthand theory having been presented! This makes it an especially difficult task for the instructor to teach some types of symbol shorthand and frequently results in the use of some system in which the fundamentals may be mastered in a shorter length of time. It should be observed, however, that instructors can be found who claim real success with either type of shorthand; thus much still depends on the instructor and on his ability to properly organize and present his materials to the class.

Office machines and clerical practice illustrate other business courses that are commonly taught in adult classes and that require time devoted to drill. In these courses, however, it frequently is possible to actually have each student working continuously on his own chosen machine or special project and thus to actually achieve rather substantially in his learning. This is greatly aided by the use of job sheets and special projects. Recommendations previously given relative to introducing variations in procedures into the class still apply even though the classwork may be mostly drill.

In most nondrill business subjects taught in adult classes, it is usually desirable to choose only specific units or applications or areas of the subject. This then permits greatly needed group discussions within the available class and course time limits. Frequently, too, it is necessary for the instructor to pull together pertinent materials from many sources, to make liberal use of reproduced materials, and to prepare special teaching aids in order to successfully teach such adult courses.

Checklist of Procedures

Good teaching in adult business education includes the same principles, procedures, and practices that good teaching requires in the ordinary classroom. Yet, owing to each enrollee's experience and his adult situation, many practices become *especially* important in conducting almost any adult class in business. Not all the suggestions given in the following checklist are equally applicable to every adult course, but most of them are. Thus this list is presented to the business teacher as a guide and as a means of checking on the completeness and appropriateness of his preparation and procedures in teaching any adult class in business.

Advance Preparation

1. First determine whether there is a demand for the course proposed.
2. Identify the potential enrollees. Know their needs and desires.
3. See that necessary administrative questions are cleared with your administrator.
   a. How many weeks may be used for the course?
   b. Will a minimum enrollment be required?
   c. How many class meetings per week?
   d. How long should each class meeting last?
   e. What fee must enrollees pay?
   f. Must enrollees pay for supplies in addition to paying the fee?
   g. Will the cost be supplemented by local, state, or federal aid?
   h. How much will the instructor be paid?
   i. What records are required?
   j. Will regular school facilities be made available for use?
   k. Where, to whom, and when must enrollees pay their fees?
   l. Will certificates be awarded? If so, on what basis?
   m. Will special instructional materials be obtainable? How?
   n. Who will be responsible for proper publicity?
4. Confer with an appropriate advisory committee relative to the course.
5. Plan the course to meet exact needs of probable enrollees, but keep it flexible.
6. Aid in getting proper publicity released about the course.
7. As needed, see that sufficient texts and supplies are on hand or ordered sufficiently in advance of the first meeting.

8. Prepare needed charts, flannel boards, outlines, mimeographed materials, and other instructional aids.

9. Order needed films, filmstrips, records, free handouts, pictures, or other aids you will need but cannot make yourself.

10. See that needed equipment will be available and in good condition.

11. Arrange for any outside speakers or special discussion leaders you may need.

12. Secure additional special information you may need; much of this should usually come from your own community.

13. Plan in advance for the comfort of your enrollees in matters such as coffee breaks, smoking facilities, and having the room opened, heated, ventilated, and lighted.

14. Decide which major instructional techniques will best apply to the needs of your class most of the time; prepare to use them.

15. Provide yourself with suitable additional techniques for needed variety.

CLASSROOM PROCEDURES AND REMINDERS

1. Start on time—always!
2. Stop on time—always!
3. Be there in advance of your students; put each at ease as he arrives.
4. Have all instructional materials and equipment ready and convenient.
5. Be prepared to care for needed registrations at the first meeting.
6. Look your best.
7. Be businesslike.

PROJECTS AND QUESTIONS FOR DISCUSSION

1. Collect printed folders, newspaper announcements, and other published statements about adult courses offered in selected communities in your state and prepare an appropriate bulletin-board display.

2. Inquire of the state supervisor or teacher-educator for distributive education or office education in your state about the adult courses offered throughout the state; report to your class.

3. Investigate and report on the types of adult education offered in your state through technical institutes, area vocational schools, junior colleges, and similar types of post–high school education.

4. Check with the local chamber of commerce in your community or some other community and determine whether or not it has cooperated in promoting or organizing any adult classes during the past few years.

5. Interview one or more personnel managers in large businesses and determine what type of educational work they may have conducted during the past few years for employees of the business.

6. Would you say that the psychology the teacher of adults should use is predominantly a rather uniquely adult psychology or one that is essentially regular psychology of learning? Defend your choice.

7. Which would you say is more important to include in an adult course—that which the class members need or that which they desire? How would you justify your choice?

CASE PROBLEMS

1. Velma Higgins is teaching her first year at Planora Consolidated School. She teaches all the business education classes and has a relatively full schedule, including her fair share of extracurricular activities. When she accepted the position, nothing was said about teaching adult classes. In November her principal, Mr. Stephens, reminds her that "as is customary in Planora" she will be expected to teach an adult class in beginning typewriting on Wednesday evenings for ten weeks starting early in January. He says nothing about any additional pay. What should Velma do about it?

2. Jim Baughman is teaching an adult class in small business records. Twenty students are enrolled, most of them being young owners or managers of small local businesses. One of them, Tom Thorpe, graduated from a university with a major in accounting and has now taken over his father's business, the Thorpe Dairy; it maintains its own herd of dairy cows, processes milk, and sells directly to local customers. Tom is a friendly, congenial student, but he falls into the habit of doing too much of the talking—since no other class members seem to have any formal knowledge of accounting. He does not realize it, but other members of the class are tending to resent his continual suggestions. How can Jim Baughman best handle this situation?

3. Edith Horton is an experienced secretarial teacher in a large high school in Minneapolis, Minnesota. She has also had considerable secretarial experience. One evening the office manager of a large Minneapolis concern asks her whether she can arrange to hold a special series of late-afternoon classes for about fifteen of his younger secretaries. He is primarily interested in getting them to improve their transcriptions. He offers to furnish meeting facilities in his office rooms and to pay Miss Horton a rather substantial fee. She is interested in his proposition. What advice would you offer Edith?

4. While chatting informally at the weekly luncheon of his Lions Club, Bruce Campbell, a high school business teacher, is told by a fellow Lion that many young men of the town are entering local business careers but lack the know-how necessary for promotion and real success. Bruce feels that if this is true he may be able to help them some through special adult evening classes. Since the community is only of medium size, he believes it may be well to start with an evening course in business management. Accordingly, he draws up a tentative general outline for such a course and then goes to his principal and superintendent to get permission of offer such a course. They, too, like the idea but tell Bruce there are no local funds available to help defray costs and they feel it will be unwise to assess the total costs against the enrollees. Bruce now is undecided as to whether to drop the idea until financial aid can be secured in the future or to go ahead and offer his services free or practically so. What would seem best?

SUGGESTED READINGS

Adult Business Occupations Newsletter, published in May and December by Continuing Business Education, Department of Business Education, University of Northern Iowa, Cedar Falls.

Aker, George F., J. R. Kidd, and Robert M. Smith, *Handbook of Adult Education*. New York: The Macmillan Company, 1970.

Bakalis, Michael, ed., "Continuing Education," *Illinois Journal of Education*, LXII, No. 1, January 1971, 75 pp. Superintendent of Public Instruction, State Office Building Springfield.

Cardozier, V. R., "Individual Instruction in Adult Education," *Journal of Business Education*, May 1968, pp. 37–38.

Carter, Joseph B., "Learning Labs Spur Back to School Movement," *American Vocational Journal*, January 1971, pp. 32–34.

Dutton, Donnie, "Should the Clientele Be Involved in Program Planning?," *Adult Leadership*, December 1970, pp. 181–82.

Finch Robert E., "Continuing Education," *Business Education World*. See recent and current issues.

————, "Planning a Balanced Curriculum," *Business Education World*, September–October 1970, p. 30.

————, "Programmed Instruction for Adults," *Business Education World*, May–June 1970, p. 26.

————, "Teacher In-Service Education," *Business Education World*, May–June 1971, p. 29.

Fredrickson, Patricia A., "Shorthand in Small Community Adult Evening School," *Business Education World*, November 1967, pp. 27, 29.

Hansen, Glenn L., Aurelia Klink, and Barry L. Reece, "A Philosophy and a Plan for Adult Business Education," Part I, *Business Education Forum*, December 1970, pp. 3–4.

————, "A Philosophy and a Plan for Adult Business Education," Part II, *Business Education Forum*, January 1971, pp. 3–5.

Knowles, Malcolm S., "Androgogy: An Emerging Technology for Adult Education," Chap. 3 in *The Modern Practice of Adult Education: Androgogy versus Pedagogy*. New York: Association Press, 1970.

Larson, Curtis G., "The Adult Learner," *American Vocational Education*, XLV, No. 6 (1970), 67–68.

Miller, Malvern L., "Hard-Core Unemployed Can Be Trained," *Business Education Forum*, April 1971, pp. 13–15.

Paulus, Edward W., "Adult Business Education and the Community College," *Balance Sheet*, October 1968, pp. 68–69.

Pine, Gerald J., and Peter J. Horne, "Principles and Conditions for Learning in Adult Education," *Adult Leadership*, October 1969, pp. 108–10.

Shaw, Nathan C., ed., *Administration of Continuing Education*, National Association for Public School Adult Education, Washington, D.C., 1969, 436 pp.

Steeves, Roy W., "Relevancy and Reason in the Development of Adult Education Programs," *Adult Leadership*, February 1970, pp. 241–42.

Walsh, Lawrence A., "Motivating Adult Students," *DE Today*, June 1970, p. 5.

Yarborough, Ralph, "Lifetime Education: A Basic Human Right," *Adult Leadership*, December 1970, pp. 187–88.

14

BUSINESS STUDENT ORGANIZATIONS

Although formal classroom learning still constitutes the backbone of education and is still considered of major importance in acquiring an education, today's educators realize full well that learning is taking place at all times. Many of us are even quite sure that more often than not things learned outside the classroom, and in no way directly a part of formal education, make a more lasting impression and influence one's habits, ways of thinking, attitudes, and future life to a greater extent than do the more formal classroom learnings.

Accordingly, the modern school makes appropriate plans to assist in channeling nonclass, or extracurricular, activities of students into various desirable group activities. Participation usually is completely on a voluntary basis and is entered into primarily because the student enjoys doing so. This enjoyment may be derived from doing something that itself is enjoyable to the young person. It may also be derived from a naturally gregarious nature and from being a part of a group. Associated with both may be the enjoyment derived from social approval, either as a part of a recognized group or as an individual performer of merit.

The important factor is not that the school assist the students in finding enjoyment, but that it assist them in finding enjoyment through an activity that in itself is helping to develop them into more desirable and useful and satisfactory individuals and future citizens.

Today nearly everyone is familiar with some types of organized group—or so-called extracurricular—activities sponsored by our public secondary schools for the benefit of students. It would be both useless and difficult to attempt listing all of them; the more common ones range from activities such as athletics to activities such as music, Future Farmers of America, camera clubs, dramatics, student councils, teen-age dances, debate, pep organizations, secretarial clubs, Latin clubs, Future Business Leaders of America, Future Homemakers of America, Distributive Education Clubs of America, junior chambers of commerce, class organization, bridge and purely social clubs, and hundreds of other activities organized to meet special needs and interests. Serving especially the young people interested in the field of business are groups such as commercial clubs, secretarial clubs, junior chambers of commerce, junior sales clubs, retailing clubs, and, on the national level, the Future Business Leaders of America (FBLA), Distributive Educational Clubs of America (DECA), Office Education Association (OEA), Junior Achievements, Incorporated (JA), and others serving special interest groups of students.[1]

THE PSYCHOLOGY OF STUDENT ORGANIZATIONS

What urge is it that causes students by the thousands to voluntarily associate themselves with these various student groups—and often to spend many hours working for the good of the group with an energy and purpose which the classroom teacher all too often must sorrowfully admit is not apparent when it comes to studying for regular classroom assignments? The answer, of course, is a many-sided one. It will vary somewhat with individual students and among the various types of group activity. However, the teaching profession recognizes psychological drives that are at work. Many of these drives are quite familiar to the student of educational psychology; others are more closely associated with social psychology and the psychology of personality development.

It is true that the *skillful* teacher makes use of these same psychological drives in connection with his regular classroom work. Yet no teacher can achieve perfection in his profession or even approach it at all times. These voluntary student organizations provide a sort of "self-feeding" process by which the individual student frequently and almost automatically satisfies some of these drives which otherwise are becoming relatively starved. And when his activities in the organization are well directed through competent leadership, much supplementary learning of direct value is taking place. In fact, owing to the presence of strong motivational drives the learning may be unusually efficient and effective!

Desire to Excel

The desire to be recognized for our excellency is so strong in all of us that failure to excel in *some* way is almost sure to result in a frustrated individual

[1] An illustration of a special interest group would be the *Future Secretaries of America,* with chapters throughout the nation sponsored by the National Secretaries Association.

who is unhappy and dissatisfied with his place in life. Such individuals create serious problems for society, as well as for themselves and their immediate families. On the other hand, it matters little what medium affords an opportunity for the individual to excel so long as it is recognized and approved by others. If it can be approved by all of society, so much the better, but, failing in this, some individuals do not hesitate to attempt "excelling" even in unsavory activities so long as the approval of even a few can be obtained. Certainly this drive has much to do with recent juvenile gang activities.

When one considers the fact that our secondary schools typically require all students, regardless of abilities or interests, to spend half or more of their time and endeavor in the same common core of required subjects, it is not too difficult to understand that many students must almost necessarily find themselves unable to "excel" to an appreciable extent in the usual classroom activities. Of course, we must remember that this is not the *only* drive at work, and these same subjects may aid in satisfying other important drives for almost all students.

Extra voluntary activities, such as athletics in its various forms, frequently provide ideal opportunities for individual students to gain the feeling of importance and well-being that comes so largely from recognition of their excellence in some facet of life's activities. And this feeling of success, importance, and recognition is extremely vital to the development of a well-adjusted and desirable personality.

It is pertinent at this point to mention that psychologists quite generally agree that most lasting and most effective good results come from a recognition of excellence when that excellence can be associated with an area or activity that is to be one's lifework; a secondary choice would be an area that might become a hobby or a form of relaxation during one's lifetime. Since the world of business is going to provide the vocation or lifework for a very sizable portion of today's secondary students, it is a most serious mistake to deprive them of opportunity to voluntarily participate in extracurricular activities associated with this major interest in life.

Students interested in business most assuredly should also be encouraged to develop interests in other things, such as music, dramatics, and athletics. Yet it must be recognized that when they are *limited* to these other types of activities they also are being forced to *limit* their chances of special recognition to areas in which they actually are in competition with other students who have a major *interest* or ability in those areas! Thus failure to provide them *also* with suitable voluntary clubs or other organizations in their major field of interest certainly is stacking the cards *against* the business students in any endeavor to develop excellency in an activity associated with their chosen lifework.

Gregariousness and Belongingness

It is well known that man is a gregarious creature; he enjoys being with others rather than by himself. Owing to this natural trait it is almost inevitable that young people are going to voluntarily associate themselves with groups of one kind or another. That being the case, education much prefers that these voluntary groups be socially approved groups appropriately organized and directed for maximum natural benefits to the members.

Closely associated with this gregarious trait of mankind, and growing directly out of it, is the negative feeling of uneasiness and discontent when one does not "belong" to a group—when one has *failed* to be accepted by his fellow students as a recognized equal. This is often described as a desire for the satisfaction of a feeling of "belongingness." Thus again we find all secondary students naturally feeling more comfortable and satisfied with their lot in life if they can "belong" to one or more groups.

Again it is pertinent to point out that this feeling of belongingness also has its most beneficial and long-lasting effects when it can be associated with something that is to be a part of one's life activities. We find strong psychological reasons for providing business students with opportunity to belong to and participate in some voluntary activity associated with their chosen major interest of business, such as a business club or a chapter of Future Business Leaders of America or some other appropriate organization.

Self-Assertion

Though not always fully agreeing as to whether to label it an instinct or not, psychologists for many years have considered self-assertiveness to be one of the common characteristics of all mankind. Certainly the desire to assert oneself is a universally recognizable trait, and opportunities constantly appear for observing it in action among young children! And the urge or drive is one that remains with us throughout life.

Undoubtedly one major reason for the success of democracy is the great opportunity it gives its participants for freely asserting themselves. Each knows that his vote is as important as the vote of anyone else; that he is free to speak his mind and assert his views; that he may choose his own religious activities and beliefs and his own economic activities and way of life. Democracy provides us with maximum opportunity for self-assertion.

All too frequently the student feels he must somewhat restrain himself from complete self-assertion in the regular classroom; in fact, the rules, regulations, semiregimentation, and supervision customarily and necessarily associated with today's mass education at the secondary level very largely are admittedly restraints on the self-assertiveness of youth! Nor is the situation too much different in the normal home, for there, again, youth feels it is being restrained by adult authority.

But what a difference exists when the adolescent (or young adult) finds he is largely "on his own" in his own student organization! Here he expresses his views and "asserts" himself quite freely. He then feels that, just as in any adult democratic society, his opinions are important and his vote counts. Moreover, he then feels more like giving expression to his thoughts and feelings—and usually does so. He not only expresses them but not infrequently asserts them in words, gestures, and connotations so powerful that no doubt is left in the minds of his associates as to the point he is making!

Again it is appropriate to point out to the business teacher that the business students are at some disadvantage in selecting their extracurricular activities if they do not have available an appropriate student organization within their own sphere of special interest from which to choose; it is but natural that one feels less restrained in asserting his ideas—in asserting himself —when he is on the familiar ground of his own major area of interest and knowledge. And failure to find suitable opportunity for asserting himself in approved situations (such as approved student organizations) can readily lead to finding nondesirable outlets for this self-assertion urge.

Other Psychological Factors

It is to be recognized that many other psychological factors do enter as a part of the basis on which student organizations are built. Some groups may provide opportunities for pure enjoyment of the competitive urge, others may provide suitable settings for the urge to mingle with the opposite sex, still others may help satisfy the urge to gain special approval through excellence in vocational ability, and so on. It thus is quite appropriate to develop student voluntary groups that make use of and cater to various other additional psychological bases. As a whole, however, probably the most basic psychological reasons underlying successful student extracurricular or cocurricular organizations are the desire to excel, the tendency toward gregariousness, the desire for belongingness, and the urge toward self-assertion. It is important that the teacher who acts as sponsor for a student organization or activity be at least partially guided by these psychological factors at all times if he wishes to be successful in his job as sponsor.

Causes of Unsuccessful Activities

Not infrequently a given student activity, such as a chapter of the Future Business Leaders of America or a local business club, will be a comparative failure in one school while a similar organization in another and perhaps nearby school will have the reputation of being one of the most active and valuable organizations in its school. Why is this?

Frequently the cause is attributed to "lack of leadership." Probably that is right—in one sense or another. It may be more exact, however, to say it is due to misdirected or ill-advised or uninformed leadership, since in all probability the sponsor is actually trying. And usually careful analysis of the situation will indicate some situations or practices that directly thwart or are opposed to the free operation of basic psychological drives through participation as members of the organization.

The most frequent causes of lack of success in a student organization may be identified if the sponsor will but ask himself certain types of questions relative to the functioning of the organization. The following list may be used as a guide.

1. Who makes the decisions? Is it the sponsor or the members? Within a minimum framework of regulations the members should be free to make their own decisions in a democratic way. It is the sponsor's job to assist them in knowing *how* to do this successfully, but it should be the responsibility of the individual members to decide *what* is to be done. Authoritarianism on the part of the

sponsor, although necessary in upholding school regulation, is fatal when applied to decisions that should be the prerogative and the responsibility of the student members.

2. Is every member given something to do? Students belong to an organization because they feel the urge to be *doing* things—to have opportunity to "work with" others in an adult fashion and to gain approval of others for what they do. This does not mean that the sponsor must dole out duties; under skillful suggestions of the sponsor the members will themselves see the desirability of having actively participating members and will develop their own methods of providing desired activities for all.

3. Is the sponsor contagiously enthusiastic about the organization? This situation may not always be possible, yet its absence does tend to unwittingly detract from the importance of the activity in the minds of the students. What student is likely to voluntarily enter enthusiastically into something that does not seem to be recognized as important even by those who sponsor it?

4. Is the opinion and judgment of every member sought *and respected?* Only in that way can the real feeling of "belongingness" be fostered. Moreover, the student enters the organization partly to satisfy his urge to be considered important; when he feels that he is a respected and important part of the organization he has fulfilled his need for "belongingness." He also is then further encouraged to assert himself and to attempt to excel.

5. Are students in other organizations gaining more credit or public acclaim (publicity) than are members of your organization? If so, your organization by comparison is *felt* to be a failure, regardless of how well it may be functioning or how much good it may be doing.

6. Are businesslike procedures used comparable to similar situations in adult life? When members recognize the presence of slipshod methods they unwittingly lose respect for this immature situation; instead, they seek activities where they can feel they are being adult. True, many members will go right along with unbusinesslike procedures and actually give overt evidence of approval; subconsciously, though, they are likely to be building up a psychological distaste for the whole organization!

In addition, it is important that the organization and its activities have inherently worthwhile values; such values may be assumed to exist in almost any organization that would meet with the approval of the sponsor and the public school. These values will be further identified in the following section.

WORTHWHILE CONCOMITANT LEARNINGS

In the well-advised extracurricular student organization care is taken to see that members have every possible opportunity to develop desirable and improved habits, attitudes, skills, knowledges, and understandings. Failure to properly guard such aspects of their activities can easily result in actual damage to the personalities and futures of the individual student participants.

Opportunities for these important developmental learnings will vary with student organizations, but most such groups will find it worthwhile to give due attention to nearly all the following items:

DEVELOPMENT OF CORRECT TECHNIQUES, HABITS, SKILLS, AND ATTITUDES—

1. In keeping financial records
2. In recording minutes of meetings
3. In participating in and conducting discussions, programs, and various types of group meetings
4. In cooperating and working with others
5. In orally presenting viewpoints and arguments
6. In meeting and solving practical problems "on their own"
7. In assuming leadership responsibilities over others
8. In preparing and giving special reports and recommendations
9. In participating in social gatherings
10. In working within the framework of specified regulations
11. In arranging details of business transactions
12. In arranging details connected with program responsibilities
13. In carrying on membership or sales campaigns
14. In paying attention to and respecting opinions of others
15. In spending money
16. In using various communication media, including telephone, mail, and telegraph
17. In maintaining files
18. In learning the use of various appropriate types of equipment
19. In interpreting constitutions, by-laws, and other official documents and writings
20. In deciding upon membership in a local or national organization

OBJECTIONS TO STUDENT ORGANIZATIONS

On the whole there are few serious objections to good voluntary student organizations that meet with adult approval. Certain types of student extracurricular activities, such as music, athletics, and dramatics, are almost demanded by entire communities today. Thus objections usually do not involve anything inherently objectionable about the organization as such.

However, it is true that most public schools of today already do have a relatively large number of well-established student organizations. The objections one is likely to encounter are therefore not so much objections to an organization as they are objections to *another* organization. The business teacher who wishes to start a chapter of FBLA, for instance, is often told by his principal that the students already have so many organizations they have no time left for study; that they already have more organizations than the school can justify; or that they have many organizations now doing an excellent job and that the school does not wish to decrease the effectiveness of present organizations by encouraging students to spread their endeavors over additional ones.

The viewpoint of the principal, as indicated above, is quite understandable and has much logic. Yet it is not necessarily the final and best answer to the problem. We know that one of the faults of education that must be guarded against is its definite tendency to protect the *status quo* and its vested interests. It is a well-known fact that in many, many instances educational practices lag far behind those of society in general.

Moreover, in these years of rapidly expanding enrollments in our schools it is more than likely that an actual need is developing for *more* student organizations in order to maintain the former standards of opportunities for each student to actively participate. And with a larger student body it also seems logical that a greater variety of personal interests will be found among those students—again pointing toward the desirability of *new types* of student organizations catering to interests not now represented among existing organizations.

The business teacher desirous of forming a new student activity group in the area of business education should therefore not hesitate to seek approval; he may very well be aiding in the filling of a most important need in our expanding schools of today. Perhaps of even greater importance than the increased enrollments are the psychological reasons already mentioned indicating the need for business students to have opportunity to channel their extracurricular activities into organizations related to their chosen lifework.

One must recognize, though, that in the smaller schools an additional student organization often merely means one more organization for the *same* students to join; too few students and too many organizations can do real harm to the students! In such situations choices must often be made.

Occasionally objections are made to the costs involved in connection with student organizations. Certainly costs to the students—and thus to their parents —are important considerations. It is inadvisable to approve plans that are excessively costly. All too frequently the financial situation of some students dictates that they refrain from participating in activities that involve additional unnecessary expense. Perhaps it would be better if the costs of all approved activities could be paid by the general public rather than by the individual participants so that none would be deprived of opportunities to participate. Since this usually is impracticable, we must realize that it is equally unjust to deprive other students of opportunities at reasonable cost simply because a few cannot afford even the reasonable cost.

We should also recognize that business teachers themselves quite often raise an objection of a different type; sometimes they object to an organization on the grounds that it will require considerable extra time and effort on their part and they feel that they are already doing a full day's work or more and should not burden themselves further with the task of organizing and sponsoring an additional organization. Sometimes such objections are well founded.

If the teaching profession is going to approve and advocate the development of student organizations—as it does—then it follows that the development and sponsoring of such organizations is one part of the professional work of the teacher. This work then deserves equal consideration along with classroom and other work in determining the total work load of the teacher. This customarily is the practice in well-administered schools of today.

It might be mentioned in connection with this objection, though, that business teachers who do organize and sponsor successful student organizations (such as FBLA or DECA) everywhere are most enthusiastic about that part of their work. Many of them actually feel that they are doing more for their students through such activities than they are able to achieve for them in the formal classroom.

NATIONAL ORGANIZATIONS FOR BUSINESS STUDENTS

Four national organizations for students and young people interested in business deserve special mention—the Future Business Leaders of America, the Distributive Education Clubs of America, Office Education Association, and Junior Achievement, Incorporated. Business teachers should be familiar with all four of them.

In adult life we have no doubt about the merits of voluntarily associating together into a national organization those groups of people throughout the nation who have comparable interests and purposes. America seems to thrive on voluntary national organizations, and we deal with them in our daily lives. They include all types of human interests such as mutual insurance associations, religious and charitable associations, chambers of commerce, hundreds of national trade associations, and innumerable national professional associations. In the business world of today we are accustomed to national chains of stores, national advertising, and big-scale factory production for national distribution. National political parties and national TV programs and national labor unions and various other activities that are national in scope provide a daily diet of news for the American public. Thus we are being very unrealistic when we occasionally question the advisability of permitting American students to associate themselves together in national organizations.

No attempt will be made to enumerate all the potential advantages to be derived from being a part of a national organization. Obviously, the major advantages accrue from strength resulting from united numbers. It is only the sufficiently large and "strong" organizations that can afford the efficiency and effectiveness of a full-time executive director and his staff, of a paid editorial staff and an acceptable and recognized printed publication issued regularly, and of dozens of other highly desirable and effective aids and activities that such a national headquarters is capable of furnishing consistently.

Objections are often raised on two major points—both of which also exist in connection with our adult American national organizations: One is the objection that it raises costs, and the other is the objection that "outside" control or influence will be brought to bear. Perhaps both are more in the nature of "excuses" than of "objections." In terms of achievements and of learnings derived from a student organization per dollar spent, it may easily be much more expensive *not* to belong to a national group. Just as the more successful and professionally minded business teachers feel they *cannot afford not to belong* to their voluntary national professional associations, so also do many local student organizations feel that they cannot afford not to be a part of an available national association. At the same time it must be admitted that we cannot expect to receive values without paying for them.

As to "outside" controls and influences, the actual situation is quite the contrary—these American voluntary associations typically are democratic forms of organization and the basic power lies in the individual votes of the members throughout the nation! And experience in exercising this power as students in a national student organization can go far toward preparing them to do a much better job of exercising the same type of power later as adults.

Future Business Leaders of America

It may properly be said that FBLA was sponsored by the business teachers of the nation. This was done through their professional association, the National Business Education Association, which is one of the departments of the NEA. Besides the many thousand individual teachers holding NBEA membership, over two hundred colleges and universities engaged in the preparation of business teachers form one division of NBEA through institutional memberships; thus they, too, aid in sponsoring FBLA.

The first high school chapter of FBLA was chartered in 1942 at Johnson City, Tennessee, and the first college chapter was chartered that same year at the Iowa State Teachers College, Cedar Falls (now the University of Northern Iowa). Although a purely voluntary organization, by June 1971 over five thousand local chapters had been organized throughout the United States (including Hawaii and Alaska) and in Puerto Rico, Panama, and the Canal Zone. The newly expanded magazine *Tomorrow's Business Leader* was being sent monthly to approximately 110,000 members. Forty-five states had their own chapters and were holding annual conventions; many states also had district organizations, officers, and conventions. The first national FBLA convention was held in Chicago in 1952, and national conventions have been held annually since then. Over 2,000 representatives from local chapters, as well as state, regional, and national officers and their sponsors, attended the twentieth annual national convention held in Miami Beach, Florida, in the spring of 1971.

From the beginning, FBLA has included some chapters on college campuses. In time these chapters formed their own "college division" of FBLA under the name Phi Beta Lambda. Today PBL has its own separate national organization, and some twenty states have state chapters of PBL in addition to their FBLA (high school) state chapters. However, both FBLA and PBL continue under one "umbrella" parent organization and, although holding separate national "leadership conferences," these conventions are held cooperatively at the same time and in the same city.

Significantly, FBLA–PBL is a highly democratic youth group; it is open to *all* business students in both public and church-related schools and is nondiscriminatory in all ways. For instance, some chapters are located in schools with Spanish-speaking students and some in schools with black students; many, of course, have different races, languages, and religions integrated into the same chapter. As an organization, it is financially self-supporting—it is *not* supported by federal or other tax-based funds. It is *extracurricular* (not *cocurricular*) and is thus essentially a true "youth" organization run by the students themselves and is not a "part of" any one business class or program which necessarily must be under the direction of the teacher and the school. (However, each chapter does have a business teacher as an adviser.) Thus the activities of FBLA–PBL are aimed at benefiting each individual student member, regardless of his study program or business career interest.

The purposes of the Future Business Leaders of America are admirably stated in the national FBLA *Handbook* as follows:

1. Develop competent, aggressive business leadership.
2. Strengthen the confidence of young men and women in themselves and their work.
3. Create more interest and understanding in the intelligent choice of business occupations.
4. Encourage members in the development of individual projects and in establishing themselves in business.
5. Encourage members to improve the home and community.
6. Participate in worthy undertakings for the improvement of business and the community.
7. Develop character, train for useful citizenship, and foster patriotism.
8. Participate in cooperative effort.
9. Encourage and practice thrift.
10. Encourage improvement in scholarship and promote school loyalty.
11. Provide and encourage the development of organized recreational activities.
12. Improve and establish standards for entrance upon store and office occupations.[2]

The FBLA pledge taken by each member consists of the following simple statement: "I do solemnly promise to uphold the aims and responsibilities of Future Business Leaders of America, and as an active member I shall strive to develop the qualities necessary in becoming a Future Business Leader."

The Creed that has been adopted as a guiding philosophy for business students belonging to FBLA is indeed an excellent one; in fact, it might well be adopted as a guiding philosophy by every business teacher. It is reproduced in full below.

The organization is served by a full-time paid executive secretary and his associated staff with well-equipped permanent headquarters provided in the NBEA national headquarters in the NEA Building in Washington, D.C. It is here that *Tomorrow's Business Leader* is published and various services to local chapters and members originate, such as membership cards, official seals and plaques, official pins and emblems, official handbooks, and numerous suggestions and aids for organizing and successfully conducting a local chapter. Business teachers who are not already familiar with this organization through information received from their own professional association, NBEA, should

---

[2] *Future Business Leaders of America Handbook,* 3rd ed., National Business Education Association, NEA, Washington, D.C., 1963, p. 3.

request FBLA information from the headquarters office in Washington, D.C.[3] The current cost of a local charter is one dollar and the annual national fee (dues) for each student member is one dollar; annual national dues for members of Phi Beta Lambda, the college division, are set at two dollars.

CREED

Future Business Leaders of America

I believe that free education is the right of every young person in America.

I believe that the future of America depends upon mutual understanding and cooperation of business, industry, labor, the home, the church, the school, and by the peoples of our own and other lands. I agree to do my utmost to bring about better understanding and cooperation on the part of all of these groups.

I believe every young person should prepare himself for a useful occupation, and that he should carry on that occupation in a manner that will bring the greatest good to the greatest number.

I believe every young person should be actively interested in better social, political, community, and family life.

I believe every young person has a right to earn his living at a useful occupation and that this right should not be denied him because of race, color, or creed.

I believe every young person should take responsibility for carrying out assigned tasks in a manner that will reflect credit to himself, his associates, his school, and his community.

I believe in my own ability to work efficiently and to think clearly, and I pledge myself to use these abilities to make America a better place for everyone.

Among the competitive events encouraged by FBLA and customarily conducted on local, state, and national levels are the following:

1. Best chapter project
2. Most unique chapter project
3. Best chapter exhibit
4. Extemporaneous speaking contest
5. Public speaking contest
6. Selection of Miss FBLA and Mr. FBLA (high schools) and of Miss Future Business Executive and Mr. Future Business Executive (colleges)
7. Spelling team contest (high schools) and vocabulary team contest (colleges)
8. Outstanding chapter award (state and national levels)
9. Parliamentary law team contest
10. Selection of Miss Future Business Teacher and Mr. Future Business Teacher (colleges)

Various other events are sponsored from time to time by local and state chapters. One of the very interesting and valuable features of the national

---

[3] The address of the national executive secretary of FBLA or the national executive director of NBEA is 1201 Sixteenth Street, N.W., Washington, D.C.

convention is the National Delegate Assembly at which the delegates cast their ballots for national·officers according to a roll call of states in very much the same fashion that our great American political parties select their candidates for national offices.

Distributive Education Clubs of America

The recognized meaning of the term *distributive education* has already been presented (see Chapters 10 and 11). Distributive Education Clubs of America is a national organization open to all students enrolled in officially recognized distributive education programs. However, membership of the individual student in DECA must be achieved through his membership in his local D.E. Club.

High school distributive education programs were started in various parts of the nation in 1937 following the passage of the George–Deen Act. From the very first, local clubs were being formed for students enrolled in these programs. As early as 1940 these clubs had formed state associations in some states and were operating as local clubs in a state organization. The movement has been distinctly successful and has expanded rapidly. The twenty-fourth annual national convention of state distributive education clubs was held in the spring of 1971, the national organization having been initiated at Memphis, Tennessee, in 1947.

The youth organization of DECA is sponsored by DECA, ·Incorporated, originally formed in 1947. In 1970, at which time its articles of incorporation were amended and updated, DECA consisted of fifty-two officially designated state supervisors of distributive education and the American Vocational Association vice-president for distributive education; the supervisor of distributive education in each affiliated state or territory automatically becomes a member of this governing body, and AVA is now the official sponsor of DECA. DECA is managed by a board of directors consisting of thirteen members.

For many years the various activities of DECA have been well financed; at least partially responsible for this is the DECA Foundation, a nonprofit educational and charitable corporation chartered in 1960 for the purpose of receiving and dispensing funds in support of DECA. The DECA Foundation is managed by a board of trustees composed of the board of directors of DECA, Inc.

During the period 1954–56, a National Advisory Board was formed. This board consists of people from the world of business who lend support to the promotion of DECA and serve as a liaison for all financial matters connected with DECA development. Each business interest contributing five hundred dollars or more annually to DECA Foundation is asked to name an individual for membership on the National Advisory Board. Over the years members of this board have been influential in the establishment of numerous new developments in the DECA organization.

DECA differs from FBLA in a·number of ways. First, it accepts as members only those students enrolled in the officially approved ("reimbursible") vocational D.E. programs, whereas FBLA accepts *all* business students, both vocational and nonvocational, in all areas of business education, including both the office and the distributive occupations. Second, activities of the local DECA club are *cocurricular* (not *extracurricular*) and are thus considered an integral part of the D.E. program and classwork. Club meetings customarily, for instance, take place during regularly scheduled school time, and club activities for the most part are intended to help develop and strengthen the classroom and on-the-job learnings. Third, DECA is greatly dependent upon the guidance and advice of vocational and career-oriented personnel of the various state departments of public instruction, the United States Office of Education, the American Vocational Association, and representatives of the business world; whereas FBLA, while also making use of advisory personnel from business and from state departments of public instruction, remains more under the influence of professional personnel associated with the NEA and its business education department, the NBEA.

The Creed of the Distributive Education Clubs of America follows. It certainly sets forth an excellent philosophy for young people about to engage in careers in distribution.

THE DISTRIBUTOR'S CREED

I BELIEVE in the future which I am planning for myself in the field of distribution, and in the opportunities which my chosen vocation affords.

I BELIEVE that by rendering the highest measure of service to my customers, and by cooperating to the fullest extent with my fellow workers, I will be rewarded with a feeling of inward satisfaction as well as with material wealth.

I BELIEVE in the democratic philosophies of private enterprise and competition— that these philosophies allow for the fullest development of my abilities and the fullest use of individual initiative.

I BELIEVE that the ethics of conduct laid down by The Great Distributor of all good gifts should apply to my personal relationships in the field of business.

I BELIEVE that by doing my best in every way to live according to these high principles, I will be of most service both to myself and mankind.

The revised national constitution of DECA provides for five divisions: High School Division, Junior Collegiate Division, Collegiate Division, Alumni Division, and Professional Division. Membership in DECA has had a phenomenal increase over the years, and in 1970 its monthly magazine, *The DECA Distributor,* was sent to approximately 110,000 members. In 1953 the American Vocational Association provided space for the establishment of a national DECA headquarters at 1010 Vermont Avenue, N.W., in Washington, D.C., and the national headquarters still remains at that same address.[4]

The DECA *Official Handbook* gives rather complete information and provides much help for local chapters in preparing members for entering state, regional, and national contests. Many different types of contests are provided for the five divisions of DECA, but the following list is indicative of competitive

---

[4] Information about DECA can also be obtained from the Career Division of your state department of public instruction or from distributive education teacher-educators at many universities.

events commonly sponsored by DECA at various conventions and leadership conferences:

1. Best chapter display
2. Best sales talk
3. Best sales demonstration
4. Best advertising layout
5. Best merchandise manual
6. Best job application and interview
7. Public speaking contest
8. Essay contest
9. Best club activities manual
10. Best window display
11. Best state newspaper and newsletter

Since DECA members are students participating in distributive education programs, they all hold part-time positions in the business world. One of the very important and significant activities of each chapter customarily is an Employer Appreciation event, frequently a dinner, to which the students invite their employers as their guests.

Office Education Association (OEA)

The Vocational Education Act of 1963 for the first time specifically recognized "Business and Office Education" and made this phase of vocational education elegible to receive federal funds. Accordingly, the need was immediately felt for a cocurricular youth organization to serve these new reimbursable programs in a manner similar to that of DECA in distributive education programs.

Over the next few years the term *office education* gradually became accepted as an official designation of this new type of program which met the requirements for having portions of its costs reimbursed from federal funds. Thus the students in such programs became known as office education (or *OE*) students. In 1966, largely through the combined efforts of OE state supervisors in the departments of public instruction of Wisconsin, Iowa, and Kansas, the national Office Education Association was incorporated to serve the special needs of this youth group.

As the OEA is a relatively new youth organization, it must be looked upon as still being in its developmental stage. It has already become well established, however, and over two thousand high school and post–high school local chapter representatives and sponsors attended its Fifth Annual Leadership Conference (national convention) held at Indianapolis in the spring of 1971. It publishes a monthly *OEA Adviser's Bulletin* and a quarterly *OEA National Newsletter* which goes to all student members. Its own OEA jewelry, club items, sweaters, certificates, banners, and so forth, are available to members, and its national office stands ready to supply the official OEA Guide, Local Chapter Handbook, High School and Post Secondary Contest Manuals, Local Chapter Officers Handbook, and many other helpful items.

As evidence of OEA's progressive leadership, manuals for the 1972 national contests discontinued the older subject-matter-oriented tests in favor of evaluating contestants on the basis of total job competency. Since this is a youth organization composed only of members who are enrolled in approved vocational programs, it would seem to be an "enlightened" approach.

Since official estimates indicate a tremendous increase in the total number of office employees during the next few years, it seems reasonable to assume that the youth organization OEA will continue to expand rapidly both in its membership and in its sphere of influence. A new national headquarters office was established in Ohio during the summer of 1971.[5]

Junior Achievement, Incorporated

Next fall probably more than five thousand new corporations will start business—and all will be completely staffed, from workers up through management and including the president of the corporation, by American boys and girls between the ages of fifteen and twenty-one. All these young people will also be stockholders in these corporations. By the end of the school year all the corporations will have completed their business, balanced their books, settled their accounts, and closed their doors forever. And many thousands of American young people will have gained for the first time a clear understanding of and insight into our American economic system of free private enterprise and its interrelated problems of labor, management, and capital.

Occasionally a business teacher is heard to say that business will not cooperate and back good business education; certainly Junior Achievement, Inc., disproves such statements completely. Here is one of the nation's outstanding educational organizations for young business people and, instead of being sponsored by professional educators, it is completely promoted, sponsored, and backed financially through time, effort, and money contributed voluntarily by business and business people.

The movement was started in 1919 in Springfield, Massachusetts, by Horace A. Moses, then chairman of the Strathmore Paper Company. Cooperating closely with him during these early years was the president of the American Telephone and Telegraph Company, Theodore N. Vail, and Senator Murray A. Crane of Massachusetts. The movement was incorporated in 1926 and later, in 1942, organized on a national basis with headquarters in New York. During the school year JA will be serving some 110,000 young people through approximately 17,500 JA companies located in some four hundred communities throughout the United States, Canada, and some foreign countries. They will be served by 17,500 adult business advisers and will have available sixty-four national and hundreds of local scholarships.[6] It is a movement with which every business teacher should be acquainted.

---

5 Those interested in additional information about OEA can obtain it from the Career Division of their state department of public instruction, from distributive education teacher-educators at many universities, or from the national Office Education Association, 20 Leland Avenue, Columbus, Ohio, 43214.

6 Information about JA and assistance in getting new groups organized and conducted may be obtained by writing to Expansion Department, Junior Achievement, Inc., 51 West Fifty-first Street, New York, N.Y., 10019.

The company is organized through the assistance of local branches of Junior Achievement, Inc. It may be started when ten to fifteen boys and girls (usually juniors and seniors in high school) decide to manufacture and sell some product or business service and have the proper sponsors as arranged through Junior Achievement, Inc.

Each Junior Achiever must own one share of stock in the miniature company and may not own more than five, at fifty cents a share. These student owners must decide upon the exact product or service to be marketed, select a name for their company, decide upon the capital to be needed, and take all the necessary steps to incorporate, including the sale and issuance of real certificates of stock. Junior Achievers become the board of directors, decide all general policies, elect officers from among themselves, and delegate powers as they believe best. They also become the labor force in producing and selling their product or service. They usually work two hours during one evening at the business center which cooperating businesses provide for them at a nominal rental of two dollars per month.

Complete double-entry books are kept, wage and labor disputes are settled, additional stock is sold when needed, dividends are declared (if earned), equipment is purchased, raw materials and supplies are purchased and used, customers are found, sales programs are mapped out, bottlenecks and breakdowns are encountered and solved, competition is met, stockholders' reports are issued—in fact, everything that must be done by any comparable regular-sized corporation is done by this miniature corporation, and it all is done by these Junior Achievers themselves. The final act is the issuance of the liquidating dividend to cancel the outstanding stock.

The real purpose of Junior Achievement is to give youth a realistic but clear understanding of how American free enterprise works. In the process it is true that they become sold on our American economic system; even though, realistically, many of these miniature corporations fail to make a profit and about 10 percent of them actually fail before the year is ended. Evidence that the organization is accomplishing its purpose well is overwhelming.

Evidence of the widespread interest in Junior Achievement throughout the nation can be found in the following *partial* list of publications in which descriptions of Junior Achievement activities have appeared from time to time. In addition, metropolitan and local newspapers constantly carry items and pictures dealing with local, state, and national awards won by Junior Achievers.

The Business Education World	*Investment Dealer's Digest*
Dun's Review	*Catholic Digest*
Open Road	*Better Homes and Gardens*
American Paint Journal	*Bankers Monthly*
Pageant	*Railway Age*

Over the years the types of different products that have been manufactured and sold by these miniature student-operated companies have been legion, of course. Some idea of the variety of products may be gained from this illustrative listing.

Toys	Neckties
Aluminum products	Stain removers
Water softeners	Hand-decorated items
Candy	Charcoal grills
Leather goods	Insulated glasses and coasters
Wooden products	Personalized matches
Lamps	Memo pads
Plastic products	House signs
Jewelry	Various chemical products
Cookies	Newspaper and cookbook holders

Among the service fields in which Junior Achievement companies have operated are the following:

Advertising	Photography
Art and decoration	Printing
Banking	Publishing
Broadcasting	Sales
Business services	Silk screening
Entertainment	Stenography

Definite effort is made to have most of the products handmade so far as possible. Nearly as many girls as boys are Junior Achievers.

As an incentive to outstanding high school Junior Achievers who have above-average scholastic ability, Junior Achievement provides a broad college scholarship program. More than one hundred scholarships are available each year; most of them provide free tuition to specific colleges, although others are cash awards supplied by business in lieu of tuition and other expenses. The New York Stock Exchange, for instance, provides a trip to New York each year for the president and treasurer of the Junior Achievement company that prepares the best stockholder report.

Since Junior Achievement is business sponsored, the first important requisite for starting a JA company is a community sufficiently strong in business developments and business personnel to assure (1) adequate interest and financial backing by business, and (2) the necessary business personnel with know-how, ability, willingness, and time to provide approved sponsorship. Each Junior Achievement company must have three advisers: a business adviser for financial matters, accounting, and business practice; a production adviser for guidance in efficient production techniques; and a sales adviser for guidance in selling, promotion, advertising, public relations, and other marketing factors.

PROJECTS AND QUESTIONS FOR DISCUSSION

1. Obtain a list of all FBLA chapters in your state, together with the names of all current state FBLA officers. Prepare a map bulletin board showing the locations of these chapters. Also indicate any college chapters of Phi Beta Lambda.

2. Similarly investigate and prepare a bulletin board showing the DECA chapters and the OEA chapters in your state.

3. Arrange for a committee to visit some FBLA, DECA, or JA chapter, or several of them, and to report to class on the chapter activities.

4. Invite several sponsors or representatives of FBLA or DECA or OEA chapters to visit your campus for a special meeting to discuss their activities with your class and other business education students.

5. Set up a display of FBLA (or DECA or Ja or OEA) publications and other materials. (*Note:* Write to headquarters addresses given in this chapter and request appropriate free materials and a price list of other materials. Many excellent "career" folders are issued by FBLA at ten cents each.)

6. How does the learning that takes place through extracurricular or cocurricular activities compare with classroom learning as to quality and future value to the learner?

7. Should a business teacher be willing to sponsor an extracurricular activity in his own major area in addition to a full load of regular classwork?

8. Do most of today's college graduates who are prepared for careers as business teachers have appropriate preparation and know-how to act as sponsors and advisers for business student organizations? In what ways may they be weak in such preparation?

9. Discuss the values of each of these learnings which are presumed to be a part of the student's experience in most extracurricular activities. Are these learnings being properly achieved in most such organizations?

How to keep financial records
How to conduct a business meeting properly
How to work cooperatively with others
How to present oral arguments effectively
How to direct the work of others effectively
How to plan and conduct membership or sales campaigns
How to conduct various business transactions properly

10. If a business teacher is convinced his school and students should have a chapter of FBLA but his principal is opposed on the grounds that the school already has enough student activities, what should be done about it?

11. Show how the Distributor's Creed or the FBLA Creed might provide a valuable basic philosophy by which a business teacher might well be guided in his professional career.

12. Which do you feel are in better position to provide the most effective guidance and advice for a student organization—business teachers who are members of NBEA and NEA, educators within AVA, or business people?

CASE PROBLEMS

1. For a number of years the Blue Mound High School has had a local student organization known as the Commercial Club. Its membership has been restricted to students who have earned a grade of *B* or higher in shorthand. All members are girls. With expanding high school enrollments it has now seemed advisable to add other business subjects to the typewriting, bookkeeping, and shorthand already offered, and a second business teacher has been secured for that purpose. New courses now include general business, salesmanship, retailing, and clerical practice. In the near future the school plans to add a third business teacher and to start an approved cooperative program for both office and store occupations.

The second business teacher now feels that a chapter of FBLA is needed which will serve all business students, but of course the other business teacher objects strenuously to discontinuing her Commerical Club, which she says has been extremely successful.

She especially feels that "standards" are important and objects to the fact that FBLA admits all business students regardless of academic achievement. The principal points out that very soon a DECA club may be appropriate. What would seem to be the best solution to the problem?

2. Esther Jones is having difficulties as sponsor of the Springer High School chapter of FBLA. The chapter president, Ed Powers, quite properly believes in assuring democratic decisions made by the membership of the chapter and feels that the organization belongs to the student members and that they should be protected from having "pressure," as he calls it, brought on them to do things in ways that the sponsor feels would be better. Miss Jones has been trying to encourage her president to suggest that the various committees get their plans completed early and do their work in a more businesslike manner prior to the last available minute. Ed feels that this is the sponsor's idea and not the idea of the students, and hence refuses to do anything about it. Who is correct? What should be done about it?

3. At a state convention of one of the national business student organizations recently, a certain high school girl won a state competitive honor which entitled her to represent her state at the national convention. She very much wanted to enter the national competition and was encouraged by others to do so. However, the national convention met at a city some distance away, and because of rather nominal financial assistance toward her expenses provided by the state and national organizations, she simply was financially unable to make the trip. Sensing the girl's embarrassment, her teacher, who was sponsor for the local organization, arranged to drive her own car to the national convention and take the girl along without personal cost to the girl. Actually, though, this did result in an expenditure of about one hundred dollars by the teacher which she had not intended and which she could ill afford. Could the development of this situation reasonably have been avoided in advance? If so, how?

SUGGESTED READINGS

Bender, Ralph E., "YOUTH ORGANIZATIONS—A Significant Part of Vocational Education," *American Vocational Journal*, March 1964, p. 6. See other youth organization articles in this same issue.

Bernard, Louise, "The Dawning of a New Frontier," *Tomorrow's Business Leader*, May 1970, pp. 23–24.

Byrnside, O. J., *Today's Secretary*. See articles in 1970 and later issues.

Clanton, Richard D., "The Future Business Leaders of America," *National Business Education Quarterly*, May 1962, pp. 77–81.

Forkner, Hamden L., "A Call to Service—Proposed Plan for a National Organization of Youth," *Journal of Business Education*, November 1940, p. 30.

———, "How FBLA Got Its Start," *Business Education Forum*, May 1957, pp. 30–32.

———, "Why Your Students Should Belong to FBLA," *Business Education Forum*, November 1955, pp. 41–42.

Frueling, Rosemary, *Today's Secretary*. See articles in 1970 and later issues.

"Future Business Leaders of America," *NBEA Yearbook*, No. 5, 1967, pp. 318–35.

Hutchinson, Betty, "Future Business Leaders of America—A Preparation for Adult Living," *Economic Facts*, Spring 1970, p. 3.

McGorman, George B., "Project 70001: New Route for Cooperative DE," *American Vocational Journal*, April 1970, pp. 60–61.

Nottingham, Larry, "Extra-curricular Business—FBLA," *Journal of Business Education*, April 1971, p. 306.

Patton, Lucille W., "Collegiate DECA: Recruiting Source," *Journal of Business Education,* October 1970, pp. 19–20.

Simon, Joseph, "Is There an FBLA Chapter in Your School?," *Business Education Observer,* Winter 1970–71, pp. 27–28.

Steinberg, A., "Mini-business of Junior Achievement," *Reader's Digest,* May 1971, p. 19.

Thomas, Ralf J., "Youth Organizations," *NBEA Yearbook,* No. 7, 1969, pp. 189–94.

Tonne, Herbert A., and Louis C. Nanassy, *Principles of Business Education,* pp. 112–113, 329. New York: Gregg Publishing Division, McGraw-Hill Book Company, 1970.

"Wanted: Teachers of Free Enterprise," *Forbes Business and Finance,* July 1, 1963. Description of Junior Achievement work.

INDEX